This volume is a must read for anyone grappling with how we create, support and sustain truly inclusive and equitable communities, integrated by income and by race. The essays range from provocative to practical, explicating the complexity and tensions in existing approaches while proposing new frames and strategies. With racial equity as an explicit goal, they provide the best thinking on how to undo the existing spatial system of exclusion in the U.S.

— Katherine O'Regan
Professor of Public Policy and Planning,
Wagner Graduate School of Public Service at New York University
Former Assistant Secretary for Policy Development and Research,
U.S. Department of Housing and Urban Development

I have seen firsthand the transformative and catalytic impact of replacing concentrated, isolated public housing with healthy, vibrant, mixed-income housing. But housing is just the beginning. Creating healthy neighborhoods and healthy people must be the ultimate goal and outcome. This collection of the best thinking and best practices on planning and developing inclusive, equitable mixed-income communities comes at an important time. We get one chance in a generation to get it right.

— Ismael Guerrero
President and CEO of Mercy Housing

WHAT WORKS
to Promote Inclusive, Equitable Mixed-Income Communities

National Initiative on Mixed-Income Communities

Jack, Joseph and Morton Mandel School of Applied Social Sciences

Case Western Reserve University
and
Federal Reserve Bank of San Francisco

NATIONAL INITIATIVE ON MIXED-INCOME COMMUNITIES

Jack, Joseph and Morton Mandel School of Applied Social Sciences
Case Western Reserve University
11235 Bellflower Road
Cleveland, OH 44106

FEDERAL RESERVE BANK OF SAN FRANCISCO

101 Market Street
San Francisco, CA 94105

Editors
Mark L. Joseph
Amy T. Khare

Copyright © 2020. Federal Reserve Bank of San Francisco and National Initiative on Mixed-Income Communities, at the Jack, Joseph and Morton Mandel School of Applied Social Sciences, Case Western Reserve University.

This book may be reproduced in whole or in part provided that it is:

1. For noncommercial, personal, or educational purposes only (i.e., not for private gain) and

2. Appropriately credited to its author, the National Initiative on Mixed-Income Communities, at the Jack, Joseph and Morton Mandel School of Applied Social Sciences, Case Western Reserve University.

The views expressed herein do not necessarily reflect the views of the Federal Reserve Bank of San Francisco, the Federal Reserve System, the National Initiative on Mixed-Income Communities, the Jack, Joseph and Morton Mandel School of Applied Social Sciences, or Case Western Reserve University.

ISBN: 978-1-7358790-0-0

Library of Congress Control Number: 2020919314

Printed in the United States of America

We dedicate this volume of essays to all those inspired by the events of the summer of 2020 to initiate and sustain concrete action to ensure a future where inclusion and belonging reign, and racism and classism are vanquished in all their forms.

ADVISORY COMMITTEE

Richard Baron
McCormack Baron Salazar

Alan Berube
Brookings Institution

Paul Brophy
Brophy and Reilly, LLC

Alexandra Curley
AMC Research and Consulting

Xavier de Souza Briggs
New York University

Carol Galante
University of California, Berkeley

Salin Geevarghese
Mixed-Income Strategic Alliance
SGG Insight, LLC

Ingrid Gould Ellen
New York University

Willow Lung-Amam
University of Maryland

Bart Mitchell
The Community Builders, Inc.

Rolf Pendall
University of Illinois –
Urbana Champaign

Erika Poethig
Urban Institute

Esther Shin
Urban Strategies, Inc.

Doug Shoemaker
Mercy Housing California

Sarita Turner
Institute for Sustainable
Communities

TABLE OF CONTENTS

1 **Acknowledgments**

5 **Foreword**
Rip Rapson
The Kresge Foundation

Ian Galloway, Naomi Cytron, Laura Choi
Federal Reserve Bank of San Francisco

10 **Introduction**
Prioritizing Inclusion and Equity in the Next Generation of Mixed-Income Communities
Amy T. Khare
Mark L. Joseph
National Initiative on Mixed-Income Communities, Case Western Reserve University

1 WHAT IS THE CURRENT LANDSCAPE FOR MIXED-INCOME STRATEGIES?
Spatial Realities, Challenges and Opportunities

24 **Spatial Context: The Geography of Mixed-Income Neighborhoods**
Elizabeth Kneebone
Carolina Reid
Natalie Holmes
Terner Center for Housing Innovation, University of California, Berkeley

45 **Attainability and Stability of Mixed-Income Neighborhoods**
Elizabeth Luther, *Capital Impact Partners*
Noah Urban
Stephanie Quesnelle
Ayana Rubio
Data Driven Detroit

55 **Mixed-Income LIHTC Developments in Chicago: A First Look at Their Income Characteristics and Spillover Effects**
Raphael Bostic, *Federal Reserve Bank of Atlanta*
Andrew Jakabovics, *Enterprise Community Partners*
Richard Voith, *Econsult Solutions, Inc.*
Sean Zielenbach, *SZ Consulting*

2 WHAT POLICY INNOVATIONS DO WE NEED?
Innovations in Policy Strategies: National Strategies

87 **Reflections on the Role of the Federal Government in Promoting Greater Urban Equity and Inclusion**
Salin Geevarghese, *SGG Insight, LLC*

103 **HUD's Affirmatively Furthering Fair Housing Rule: A Contribution and Challenge to Equity Planning for Mixed-Income Communities**
Katherine O'Regan, *NYU Furman Center, New York University*
Ken Zimmerman, *NYU Furman Center, New York University*

Innovations in Policy Strategies: State and Regional Strategies

127 **California For All: How State Action Can Foster Inclusive Mixed-Income Communities**
Ben Metcalf, *Terner Center for Housing Innovation, University of California, Berkeley*

141   **Qualified Allocation Plans as an Instrument for Mixed-Income Placemaking**
Bryan P. Grady, *South Carolina State Housing Finance and Development Authority*
Carlie J. Boos, *Affordable Housing Alliance of Central Ohio*

158   **Embracing Odd Bedfellows in Odd Times: How to Sustain Financial and Political Support for Mixed-Income Communities**
Robin Snyderman, *BRicK Partners*
Antonio R. Riley, *Former HUD Regional Administrator for Region V*

Innovations in Policy Strategies: Local Strategies

171   **Promoting Mixed-Income Communities by Mitigating Displacement: Findings from 80 Large U.S. Cities**
Adèle Cassola, *Global Strategy Lab*

188   **Mixed-Income Housing in New York City: Achievements, Challenges and Lessons of an Enduring Mayoral Commitment**
Alex F. Schwartz, *The New School*
Sasha Tsenkova, *University of Calgary*

3   ADVANCING INNOVATIVE APPROACHES
Building Mixed-Income Communities through Community Land Trusts

212   **Community Land Trusts: Combining Scale and Community Control to Advance Mixed-Income Neighborhoods**
Emily Thaden, *Grounded Solutions Network*
Tony Pickett, *Grounded Solutions Network*

233   **Multi-Sectoral Partnerships for Social and Affordable Housing: The Community Land Trust Portfolio Model**
Penny Gurstein, *University of British Columbia*

Inclusion and Equity through Inclusionary Housing

248 **Beyond Counting Units: Maximizing the Social Outcomes of Inclusionary Housing**
Amy T. Khare
Emily K. Miller
Mark L. Joseph
National Initiative on Mixed-Income Communities,
Case Western Reserve University
Shomon Shamsuddin, *Tufts University*

269 **High-Opportunity Partner Engagement: Creating Low-Income Housing Options Near Good Schools**
Peter Kye
Megan Haberle
Poverty & Race Research Action Council
Laura Abernathy
Scott Kline
National Housing Trust

287 **The MTO Fund: Harnessing the Market to Promote Opportunity and Inclusion**
Hans Buder, *Moving to Opportunity Fund*

4 WHO HAS A SAY AND WHO BENEFITS?
Activating Community Change: Voice, Power and Influence

310 **Community Building and Neighborhood Associations: Strategies for Greater Mixed-Income Inclusion in Seattle's HOPE VI Neighborhoods**
Stephanie Van Dyke, *Seattle Housing Authority*
Ellen Kissman, *Consultant*

331   **Weinland Park, Columbus, Ohio: Building Community as a Neighborhood Transitions to Mixed-Income**
Kip Holley, *The Ohio State University, Kirwan Institute for the Study of Race and Ethnicity*
Matthew Martin, *The Columbus Foundation*
Stephen Sterrett, *Weinland Park Collaborative*

355   **The Role of Community Benefits Agreements in Increasing Equity and Inclusion**
Ralph Rosado, *Rosado & Associates and Metropolitan Center at Florida International University*

Confronting Exclusion through Changing the Narrative

369   **How Do Fish See Water? Building Public Will to Advance Inclusive Communities**
Tiffany A. Manuel, *TheCaseMade*

393   **Changing the Narrative and Playbook on Racially Concentrated Areas of Poverty**
Edward G. Goetz
Anthony Damiano
Rashad A. Williams
Center for Urban and Regional Affairs, University of Minnesota

415   **Addressing Resistance to Mixed-Income Communities through Empathetic Planning Techniques**
Aly Andrews, *Project Management Advisors, Inc.*
Sydney VanKuren, *Farr Associates*

Who Benefits? Focus on Special Populations

439   **Black Feminist-Centered Community Organizing as a Framework for Developing Inclusive Mixed-Income Communities: Nicetown CDC's Village Network and Outreach Initiatives in Philadelphia**
Akira Drake Rodriguez, *University of Pennsylvania*
Majeedah Rashid, *Nicetown CDC*

460 **Untapped Assets: Developing a Strategy to Empower Black Fathers in Mixed-Income Communities**
Clinton Boyd, Jr., *Duke University*
Deirdre A. Oakley, *Georgia State University*

478 **Youth Voice and Leadership in Mixed-Income Communities: Heritage Park and the Green Garden Bakery**
Ephraim Adams
D'Loveantae Allen
Mohamed Mohamed
Green Garden Bakery
Joni R. Hirsch, *Fines and Fees Justice Center*
Taryn H. Gress, *National Initiative on Mixed-Income Communities, Case Western Reserve University*
Elana Dahlberg
Alecia Leonard
Urban Strategies Inc.

490 **Reassessing Market-Rate Residents' Role in Mixed-Income Developments**
Michaeljit Sandhu, *Harvard Law School & University of California, Berkeley*

5 ENGAGING THE PRIVATE SECTOR IN INCLUSION AND EQUITY

Private Market, Public Good: Private Investment in Equity and Inclusion

510 **Opportunity for Whom? A Call for Course Correction Given the Location and Targets of Early Opportunity Zone Investments**
Aaron Seybert, *The Kresge Foundation*
Lori Chatman
Rob Bachmann
Enterprise Community Loan Fund, Inc.

524 **Rebuilding the Bond Market for Mixed-Income Housing**
Carol Galante
Carolina Reid
Nathaniel Decker
Terner Center for Housing Innovation, University of California, Berkeley

The Role of Development Entities

538 **Seven Strategies to Advance Equity, Inclusion, and Resiliency in Mixed-Income Communities**
Cady Seabaugh
Vince Bennett
McCormack Baron Salazar

558 **What Works for Building and Sustaining Mixed-Income Communities: A Perspective from the Development Community**
Vicki Davis, *Urban Atlantic*
Daryl Carter, *Avanath Capital Management, LLC*
Rosemarie Hepner, *Urban Land Institute, Terwilliger Center for Housing*

577 **A Call for Property Management Transformation to Meet the Challenges of Mixed-Income Housing**
Frankie Blackburn
Bill Traynor
Trusted Space Partners

598 **Achieving Durable Mixed-Income Communities through Affordable Housing Preservation: A Successful Model of Scattered-Site Housing Redevelopment in West Philadelphia**
Michael Norton, *Reinvestment Fund*
Karen Black, *May 8 Consulting*
Jacob Rosch, *Reinvestment Fund*

6 WHAT IS NEEDED BEYOND MIXED-INCOME HOUSING?
Comprehensive Approaches to Mixed-Income Communities

622 **Ten Urban Design Strategies for Fostering Equity and Inclusion in Mixed-Income Neighborhoods**
Emily Talen, *University of Chicago*

633 **Promising Practices to Promote Inclusive Social Dynamics in Mixed-Income Communities**
Joni R. Hirsch, *Fines and Fees Justice Center*
Mark L. Joseph, *National Initiative on Mixed-Income Communities, Case Western Reserve University*

651 **Recognizing and Incentivizing Mixed-Income Communities Designed for Health**
Sara Karerat
Lisa Creighton
Center for Active Design

666 **Mixed-Income Communities Need Mixed-Income Early Care and Education**
Matthew Tinsley
Mary Ann Dewan
Santa Clara County Office of Education

7 THE PATH FORWARD FOR GREATER URBAN EQUITY AND INCLUSION

682 **The Person-Role-System Framework as a Key to Promoting Racial Equity**
JaNay Queen Nazaire, *Living Cities*

697 **What *May* Work about the Mixed-Income Approach: Reflections and Implications for the Future**
Rachel G. Bratt, *Tufts University*

ACKNOWLEDGMENTS

Welcome to this compilation of essays focused on urban equity and inclusion. The focus of this volume is the promotion of mixed-income communities as a placed-based strategy to address poverty, segregation, and urban disparity. This volume's objective is to equip practitioners, policymakers, funders, and others with the latest thinking and tools needed to achieve diverse, vibrant racially just communities where all can experience belonging and opportunity.

The essays present the insights of contributors with a varied array of backgrounds, professions, and perspectives. They convey their latest ideas and innovative approaches and propose ways to enhance conventional approaches for advancing community change. All essays address the challenge of achieving stable communities that welcome and nurture a racially, ethnically, and socio-economically diverse population. We have urged authors to be aspirational but pragmatic about the deep challenges of our era's political, economic, cultural, and demographic realities. We hope these essays will inspire serious reflection and creative action in your own work, organizations, and communities.

You will hear from youth who launched their own business in a mixed-income development in Minneapolis, financiers who are seeking to make the case for mixed-income investment opportunities with stronger social outcomes, policymakers who are launching innovative mixed-income initiatives, entrepreneurs who are advancing housing acquisition models that promote mixed-income inclusion, private real estate developers who are adapting their operating models to better advance inclusion and equity, and scholars who present new data and analyses.

These essays were originally written and published online between April 2019 and October 2020, a timespan that saw monumental shifts in public and civic attention to the challenges of enduring structural racism and inequity in our society. We believe this makes the release of this full compilation even more timely and underscores the value of documenting these insights and implications to guide future policy and practice.

A methodological note: we have recommended that essay authors use the term "African American" when referring specifically to descendants of enslaved people in the United States and the more inclusive term "Black" when referring broadly to members of the African diaspora, including African Americans, Caribbean Americans, and Africans. In this way, we seek to acknowledge the unique history and experience of descendants of enslaved people in the United States and also the diversity of backgrounds within the larger Black community. After considerable deliberation, we have also recommended the capitalization of Black and White. Though both are labels for socially-constructed racial categories, we join organizations like Race Forward and the Center for the Study of Social Policy in recognizing Black as a culture to be respected with capitalization and White and Whiteness as a social privilege to be called out. All essays use this capitalization unless authors have expressed a different preference.

This project was led by our team at the National Initiative on Mixed-Income Communities at the Jack, Joseph and Morton Mandel School of Applied Social Sciences at Case Western Reserve University. We thank our stellar developmental editor Leila Fiester whose keen eye and craft strengthened each of the essays. We thank our wonderful project coordinator, Sherise McKinney, whose ability to manage the two of us, the many essay authors, the online and print dissemination of this work, and all the moving parts of this undertaking was remarkable and invaluable. We also appreciate the early coordination efforts of Emily Miller who helped us start this journey. We thank our dedicated administrative team Diane Shoemaker and Dawn Ellis for handling innumerable behind-the-scenes logistics that made this project possible. We are grateful to Karoline Kramer who worked with us to design and manage the What Works website where all essays were posted prior to print dissemination. Research assistance and editorial support was provided by Hannah Boylan, Grace Chu, and Donovan Young. Copy editing support was provided by Susan Petrone, and early consultation on media strategy was provided by Gabriel Charles Tyler. We thank Miriam Axel-Lute and her team at Shelterforce for publishing adaptations of several essays. The beautiful design and production of the book volume is thanks to the team of designers in the University Marketing and Communications unit at Case Western Reserve University, with specific thanks to Elizabeth Brown, Tia Andrako, and Shelby Lake. We also thank our producer, Davey Berris, at Case Western Reserve's MediaVision, for helping bring these essays to life through the creation of our podcast entitled *Bending the Arc*. Check it out to hear our conversations with authors from this volume.

We are grateful for the initiation, sponsorship and financial support of The Kresge Foundation, in particular the encouragement and guidance of Aaron Seybert, Kimberlee Cornett, and Rip Rapson. We greatly appreciate the support of the Ford Foundation for publication and dissemination of the volume, with special thanks to Amy Kenyon and Jerry Maldonado. We thank the Federal Reserve Bank of San Francisco for publishing this volume as the fifth in its What Works series. We count ourselves lucky for the collaboration and support of Laura Choi, Naomi Cytron, and Ian Galloway at the Federal Reserve Bank of San Francisco and the encouragement of David Erickson, the originator of the What Works series, now at the Federal Reserve Bank of New York. We also deeply appreciate the valuable insights and guidance of our advisory committee for this volume, with particular thanks for extensive early input from Rachel Bratt, Salin Geevarghese, Rolf Pendall, and Stockton Williams.

We approach every day aiming for our shared efforts on urban inclusion and equity to make a dent in the systemic racism and classism that too often interrupt the opportunities for transformative change. We hope that this project will contribute to small shifts in everyday routines, as well as deeper shifts in institutions and policies as we discover together how to better promote inclusive, equitable mixed-income communities. We wish you success in your own journey of learning and individual and systemic transformation.

Mark L. Joseph
Co-Editor
Leona Bevis and Marguerite Haynam Associate Professor of Community Development
Founding Director, National Initiative on Mixed-Income Communities

Amy T. Khare
Co-Editor
Research Assistant Professor
Research Director, National Initiative on Mixed-Income Communities

Jack, Joseph and Morton Mandel School of Applied Social Sciences, Case Western Reserve University

FOREWORD

The Kresge Foundation

In the fall of 2017, Aaron Seybert, the managing director of Kresge's Social Investment Practice, proposed we support the publication of a series of cutting-edge essays about the promise of inclusive, equitable mixed-income communities. At the time, many practitioners shared a growing sense of renewal, re-imagination, and hope for the nation's cities. It seemed a spark of entrepreneurial innovation had ignited possibilities unimaginable a generation ago, that a steady layering of thoughtful persistence had produced incremental progress that would powerfully aggregate over time.

That, we all know, was BC—Before COVID-19. That was before the devastation that has cost, as I write, more than 210,000 American lives and millions of jobs.

So why continue to bring forward this cache of essays? Because we believe that no matter how great the setback, the examples explored here probe how we can foster equitable, inclusive, mixed-income neighborhoods capable of anchoring our metropolitan areas for decades to come.

The collective heft of the thinking gathered together in this project of the National Initiative on Mixed-Income Communities and the Federal Reserve Bank of San Francisco suggests that this aspiration is within reach. The angle of entry is different if you are an advocate, a practitioner, an academic, or a critic. But all take their bearings from a shared sense of urgency, a recognition of profound complexity, and an ambition to deliver on the promise of equity, opportunity, and justice.

The Kresge Foundation has participated directly in Detroit's decade-long struggle to regain its bearings, set a new trajectory for inclusive recovery, and reclaim its rightful role as one of America's most iconic cities. We helped set the table for essential civic conversations—about land-use, public transportation, cultural identity, environmental stewardship, and many others. We furnished risk capital to drive private markets where they were unwilling to go. We contributed to fortified civic problem-solving capacity—in the neighborhoods, within the public sector, and among essential community development intermediaries.

In the process, it has become clear that although the degree of difficulty of Detroit's climb from the abyss was unique, its fundamental predicament was anything but. Its experiences offer powerful lessons to countless other communities about the shared challenges of 21st century urban life—from racial polarization to capital deployment strategies, from public infrastructure investment to civic engagement practices.

And most fundamentally, the Detroit experience underscores the uncomfortable truth that without carefully calibrated and cross-braided strategies to build and sustain mixed-income neighborhoods, we will return to an insidious cycle of flight, disinvestment, and decline.

The writers in this volume understand that. Addressing the complex interplay of power and inequality, history and policy, theory and practice, they furnish compelling reason to believe that we can substitute for that fate a future animated by the value of full social, economic, and political inclusion for all members of our community.

Rip Rapson
President and CEO
The Kresge Foundation

Federal Reserve Bank of San Francisco

Published in 2012, *Investing in What Works for America's Communities: Essays on People, Place, and Purpose* was an effort to provoke new ways of thinking about an old challenge: poverty in America. Conceived and produced by the Federal Reserve Bank of San Francisco and Low Income Investment Fund (LIIF), the volume attempted to answer the question teased by its title—how do we expand economic opportunity for all Americans? What works? That analysis uncovered four important observations. First, good data and analytical tools are essential to evaluating and effectively responding to the needs of low- and moderate-income (LMI) communities. Second, household financial well-being is a necessary pre-condition for multiple outcomes that drive economic resilience and mobility, such as housing stability and educational attainment. Third, financial incentives must be aligned with impact. Scarce resources should be reserved for organizations and programs demonstrating a sustained track record of success. And finally, equity and inclusion need to be centered in our work to build an economy where everyone can participate and no one is left behind.

Each of these observations were expanded upon in subsequent *What Works* volumes published over the last decade, now comprising a five-book set. At the core of each is a partnership between the Federal Reserve Bank of San Francisco and a mission-driven organization dedicated to improving outcomes for LMI communities. Beginning with LIIF, the series has now expanded to include partnerships with the Urban Institute, Prosperity Now (formerly CFED), Nonprofit Finance Fund, and finally the National Initiative on Mixed-Income Communities at Case Western Reserve University. These collaborations have yielded a rich collection of ideas that continue to inform community development policy and practice.

Authors in this volume, *What Works to Promote Inclusive, Equitable Mixed-Income Communities,* tackle a range of questions that are critical for the entire community development industry to sort through—both as we assess the outcomes of policy and practice regimes of the past 30 years and as we experiment with new models to address the legacies and current manifestations of inequitable and exclusive development patterns. Taken together, the essays point out that all of us—across sectors, disciplines, and geographies—have roles to play in catalyzing and operationalizing systems-level changes that drive racially equitable outcomes as well as inclusive decision-making processes that get us there. The events of the Spring of 2020—a global pandemic which has generated health and economic costs borne disproportionately by low-income communities and communities of color, and a global outcry in response to police brutality, structural racism, and systemic injustice, all of which constrain economic opportunity for people of color—heighten the urgency of sharpening our focus on what we can each do to advance inclusive, equitable communities. The analysis and ideas presented in this volume can help us do just this— and we encourage you to grapple with the tensions, complexities, and hard questions that are inherent to mixed-income community revitalization in service of getting us closer to an inclusive, equitable America.

A project of this scope and complexity requires visionary leadership. We are grateful to Mark Joseph and Amy Khare at the National Initiative on Mixed-Income Communities (NIMC) at Case Western Reserve University for their skillful stewardship of this effort and excellence in scholarship. We are also thankful to The Kresge Foundation, in particular Aaron Seybert, Kimberlee Cornett, and Rip Rapson, for their generous support of NIMC for this *What Works* volume and their long-standing commitment to innovative social investment. Finally, we would like to acknowledge community development leaders Nancy Andrews, Ellen Seidman, and our Federal Reserve colleague and friend David Erickson for creating this enduring platform to share ideas that advance the anti-poverty field. Continued interest in this series is a tribute to their vision and dedication to social justice.

What Works to Promote Inclusive, Equitable Mixed-Income Communities brings together leading voices in a united call for equity and inclusion, and the Federal Reserve Bank of San Francisco is excited to keep this conversation going. In addition to publishing a hard-copy version of the online volume, we are looking forward to co-hosting launch events that can bring these important essays to life through authentic dialogue. It is our hope that by amplifying the key themes of this book to a wide audience, we can invite new champions into the movement for the next generation of mixed-income communities.

Ian Galloway

Director of the Center for Community Development Investments
Regional Manager, Community Development Oregon
Co-Editor
Investing in What Works for America's Communities: Essays on People, Place, and Purpose and *What Matters: Investing in Results to Build Strong, Vibrant Communities*

Naomi Cytron

Regional Manager, Community Development
Northern California and Utah
Co-Editor
What Counts: Harnessing Data for America's Communities

Laura Choi

Vice President, Community Development, Federal Reserve Bank of San Francisco
Co-Editor
What It's Worth: Strengthening the Financial Future of Families, Communities, and the Nation

INTRODUCTION

Prioritizing Inclusion and Equity in the Next Generation of Mixed-Income Communities

Amy T. Khare and Mark L. Joseph
National Initiative on Mixed-Income Communities, Case Western Reserve University

We face an existential challenge in America. Major shifts in demographic change, housing affordability, and race and class inequality threaten to destabilize our already tenuous social fabric. As the country is becoming more diverse, it is also becoming more polarized. As our cities and some neighborhoods become more vibrant and attractive places to live, work, and spend leisure time, they also are becoming less affordable and less welcoming to people of various economic, racial, ethnic, and cultural backgrounds. In contrast, many neighborhoods and inner-ring suburbs are experiencing economic decline and depopulation, leading to increased segregation as only low-income households remain. The global COVID-19 pandemic has revealed the depths of systemic inequities and a societal moment of racial reckoning has been unleashed by horrific enduring police brutality against Black people. What America are we creating for future generations?

We, and the authors contributing essays to this volume, aspire to shape an inclusive, equitable America, where neighborhoods are places where differences are affirmed and valued, not ignored or scorned. We envision a nation where your ZIP Code is not the strongest predictor of your life chances. We envision communities strengthened by a sense of mutual prosperity rather than zero-sum competition.

We believe that the next generation of mixed-income, racially diverse communities could offer a path toward this America through greater intentionality about promoting inclusion and equity. This next generation of mixed-income communities is incredibly consequential because it offers unique geographic potential for healing and connection across differences as well as a path to mobility out of poverty. Cultivating more equitable and inclusive mixed-income communities will require a vigilant focus on broadening access to economic, political, and social opportunities, while bridging divisions of class, race, gender, and other identities. It will require new practices at the micro-level within neighborhood associations, school classrooms, community policing meetings, neighborhood businesses and local libraries as well as operational changes within institutions, private firms, and organizations. And it will require macro-level efforts required to disrupt systemic racism and classism through government policies, philanthropic strategies, and market processes.

There are mounting concerns that the mixed-income approach does more harm than good for low-income households of color, promotes displacement and exclusion, and thus should be abandoned as an antipoverty approach. We share these concerns but have not lost hope in the potential of mixed-income communities to alleviate poverty and racial segregation, to spur equitable economic development opportunities, and to generate positive benefits for households and for cities. Neighborhood revitalization efforts can clearly produce a complete physical transformation, accompanied by improvements in local amenities, safety, and residential stability. However the benefits of mixed-income neighborhood transformations are not enjoyed by all residents. Rather, low-income households often experience high levels of displacement, enduring social distance and exclusion, and minimal changes in economic opportunity.[1]

After more than two decades of planned efforts to design, build, and sustain mixed-income communities, much remains to be learned about how this approach can better advance inclusion and equity. We are very pleased to present this compilation that includes almost 40 essays in which about 90 co-authors share their latest insights, experience, and research about this crucial topic for the future of the United States.

WHAT DO WE MEAN BY "MIXED-INCOME COMMUNITIES"?

To start, we need to define what we mean by "promoting inclusive, equitable mixed-income communities." The mixed-income development approach

---

[1] Robert J. Chaskin and Mark L. Joseph, *Integrating the Inner City: The Promise and Perils of Mixed-Income Public Housing Transformation* (Chicago: University of Chicago Press, 2015); James C. Fraser, Deidre Oakley, and Diane K. Levy, Guest, "Mixed-Messages on Mixed-Income," *Cityscape*, 15 no. 2 (2013); Diane K. Levy, Zach McDade, and Kassie Bertumen, "Mixed-Income Living: Anticipated and Realized Benefits for Low-Income Households," *Cityscape*, 15 (2013).

typically has been defined as a means to address concentrated urban poverty and racial segregation by building housing and other amenities, such as parks, schools, and community centers, which intentionally integrate households of different income groups as part of the financial, physical, and operating plan.[2] Since the mid-1990s, the mixed-income development approach has engaged private real-estate developers to take on roles that historically were expected of the public sector, such as designing and building public housing and other amenities, serving as operators and property managers, and providing resident services and other community-based supports.[3]

We adopt a broader definition of mixed-income communities here. At the core of the definition is a *place-based* approach to poverty deconcentration, in contrast to the residential *mobility* approach which has recently gained renewed attention through the work of Raj Chetty and Nathaniel Hendren and their colleagues at Opportunity Insights. To complement the robust policy focus on moving individual households to better environments, we and other authors in this volume focus on how places themselves can be made more integrated, accessible, and opportunity-producing for low-income households, particularly households of color.

We also are interested in broadening the focus from mixed-income *housing* to mixed-income *communities*. This more comprehensive, holistic focus means that in addition to housing, the other elements that help a community thrive—schools, parks, community gardens, recreation centers, arts and cultural hubs, networks of neighbors, transit, and retail districts—also are necessary to develop and sustain as intentionally *inclusive* amenities.

The essays in this volume focus on three major place-based approaches to promoting mixed-income communities. The first approach is place-based, mixed-income developments in high-poverty neighborhoods, such as those created through the transformation of public and assisted housing redevelopments. Federal policies, such as those driving the HOPE VI Program

---

[2] Paul C., Brophy and Rhonda N. Smith, "Mixed-Income Housing: Factors for Success," *Cityscape* 3 no. 2 (1997); Mark L. Joseph and Miyoung Yoon, "Mixed-Income Development" in Wiley-*Blackwell Encyclopedia of Urban and Regional Studies*, (West Sussex UK: John Wiley & Sons Press, 2019).

[3] Mark L. Joseph, "Creating Mixed-Income Developments in Chicago: Developer and Service Provider Perspectives," *Housing Policy Debate* 20 no. 1, (2010), doi: 10.1080/10511481003599894.; Amy T. Khare "Privatization in an Era of Economic Crisis: Using Market-Based Policies to Remedy Market Failures," *Housing Policy Debate* 28 no. 1 (2018), doi: 10.1080/10511482.2016.1269356.

and the Choice Neighborhoods Initiative, promote the development of new housing developments that intentionally create a mix of residents across incomes and housing tenures.[4] This approach has received the most focused attention and scrutiny. About 260 HOPE VI grants were made, and there are now over 100 Choice Neighborhoods implementation and planning grantees.[5] Some well-known examples of local multi-site, mixed-income public housing transformation are the Atlanta Model, Chicago's Plan for Transformation, HOPE SF in San Francisco, and the New Communities Initiative in Washington, D.C.[6]

A second approach to promoting mixed-income communities is through inclusionary housing and zoning strategies in low-poverty neighborhoods. This approach makes it possible for low- and middle-income households to live in areas that would be generally unaffordable to them, such as suburbs and desirable city districts, which tend to be predominantly White and affluent. While tens of thousands of units have been developed nationwide, 80 percent of inclusionary zoning programs are located in just three states: California, New Jersey, and Massachusetts.[7] The majority of local inclusionary zoning programs are mandatory (per state or local law), while some allow developers to "buy out" of requirements by contributing to a local affordable housing fund. Some inclusionary housing and zoning approaches offer incentives, such as cost offsets to developers, in order to create a mix of market-rate and affordable units.[8]

A third approach aims to achieve mixed-income communities through affordable housing preservation and other strategies for preventing

---

4   Susan J. Popkin et al., *A Decade of HOPE VI: Research Findings and Policy Challenges* (Washington, DC: Urban Institute, 2004); Rolf Pendall et al., *Choice Neighborhoods: Baseline Conditions and Early Progress* (Washington, DC: Urban Institute, 2015).

5   Taryn Gress, Seungjong Cho, and Mark L. Joseph, "HOPE VI Data Compilation and Analysis," (Washington, DC: U.S. Department of Housing and Urban Development, 2016).

6   Lawrence J. Vale, *Purging the Poorest: Public Housing and the Design Politics of Twice-Cleared Communities* (Chicago: University of Chicago Press, 2013); Robert J. Chaskin and Mark L. Joseph, *Integrating the Inner City: The Promise and Perils of Mixed-Income Public Housing Transformation*; Mark L. Joseph, Garshick Kleit, R. Latham, N & LaFrance, S. (2016). HOPE SF: San Francisco's Inclusive Approach to Vale Mixed-Income Public Housing Redevelopment. *Shelterforce*. Spring 2016; "New Communities Initiative," New Communities Initiative, https://dcnewcommunities.org/.

7   Emily Thaden and Ruoniu Wang, *Inclusionary Housing in the United States: Prevalence, Impact, and Practices*, (Cambridge, MA: Lincoln Institute of Land Policy, 2017).

8   Rick Jacobus, *Inclusionary Housing Creating and Maintaining Equitable Communities* (Cambridge, MA: Lincoln Institute of Land Policy, 2015).

displacement in gentrifying areas. Gentrification occurs when an influx of more affluent households generates an increase in rents, property taxes, and general cost of living.[9] In these communities, an influx of capital—from real estate developers and investors, for instance—results in social, economic, cultural, political, and physical transformations that change the community's social dynamics. This intense level of private-market activity can lead to the physical and cultural displacement of the original residents and businesses; thus, there is a need for strategies that preserve affordable housing, locally owned businesses, traditional and historic social venues, and other local assets and ensure that original residents can benefit from the market activity (e.g., through access to capital and stable jobs).

WHAT DO WE MEAN BY "INCLUSION" AND "EQUITY"?

Racial and socioeconomic integration of residents is necessary but not sufficient to create social inclusion in a community. We define inclusion as the active, intentional, and sustained engagement of traditionally excluded individuals and groups through informal activities and formal decision-making processes in ways that build connections and share power. We believe that inclusion occurs when a social context enables people of diverse backgrounds to interact in mutually respectful ways that reveal their similarities and common ground, honor their social and cultural differences and uniqueness, and value what each individual and group can contribute to the shared environment. Through this inclusion and interaction, people can shift narratives and perceptions about "the other." Inclusion requires sustained intentionality and action.

Equity is the process of ensuring a fair opportunity for individuals and their families to thrive socially and economically. An equity focus can be motivated not just by a sense of morality and justice but also by pragmatism: inequity hurts all of us by preventing some individuals and subgroups from realizing their full potential and value in service of the greater societal good. Equity requires that people receive a more fair share of resources, opportunities, social supports, and power, given their differential needs and circumstances based on different life experiences. Equity therefore entails addressing structural disparities that exist between people of different backgrounds.

---

9   Loretta Lees, Tom Slater, and Elvin Wyly, *Gentrification*, (New York, NY: Taylor and Francis, 2008).

Equity is not the same as equality. After centuries of discrimination, the needs of historically marginalized populations may be higher than those of groups who have had privileged opportunity and power. Thus, getting a "fair share" does not mean that everyone receives the same amount of resources; rather, it means that resources are allocated in a way that promotes the attainment of a person's full potential. Success toward equity would be indicated by the decrease in social and economic disparity among people of different racial and economic backgrounds.

In a quest to treat everyone equally, mixed-income planners, developers, and practitioners may fail to appreciate how historical imbalances may require resources to be balanced in favor of traditionally marginalized populations. Without a focus on *equity*, stakeholders may miss an opportunity to meaningfully generate greater access and opportunity for low-income households and people of color.

WHAT DO WE MEAN BY RACIAL EQUITY AND INCLUSION?

Although it is not explicit in how the term "mixed-income communities" generally is framed, we are highly interested in strategies to promote *racial* equity and inclusion as well as mixing across income and class. Racial equity places priority on ensuring that people of color, particularly Blacks/African-Americans and Indigenous people, are afforded opportunities that they have historically been denied and from which they continue to be excluded.

Much of our current debate about racial equity and inclusion focuses on a fairness argument about the prevalence and durable nature of concentrated White affluence and the inequality and harm to people of color that it causes. This debate about greater racial equity largely remains in a zero-sum frame that stifles most policy discussions on the topic: What would White people have to give up in order for marginalized groups to receive more? This plays directly into the prevailing "us versus them" dynamics that are constraining the potential of America as it diversifies. These efforts remain within a deficit-oriented, charitable frame of what White people should do *for* people of color without posing the more asset-oriented question about the *value* that Blacks/African Americans and other people of color can offer to communities and to society, if they were afforded more opportunity and inclusion. White people do not just avoid and exclude people of color because they are afraid or uncaring.

Very often, White people simply do not see *value* in people of color, because of their presumed inferiority after centuries of highly successful White-supremacist framing that has seeped into policies, practices, and conventional wisdom.

In this volume, in addition to the fairness argument, we seek to elevate the economic and social value case for greater inclusion and equity. We urge a shift in the imperatives for more inclusive mixed-income communities to emphasize the value of people of color and the value of people who are economically constrained, as well as the motivating potential of a positive-sum reality whereby greater opportunity for marginalized people actually generates increased, sustained opportunities for all people.

ORGANIZATION OF THE VOLUME

We are thrilled to have compiled an array of essays that will dramatically advance our knowledge and strategies. These essays will equip policymakers, practitioners, investors, and community members with the latest thinking and tools needed to achieve more inclusive and equitable mixed-income communities. The authors and essays represent a diverse range of perspectives and topics while exploring the central theme of urban equity and inclusion through place-based strategies. The following questions framed our shared inquiry:

- How can the benefits of mixed-income community revitalization be shared more equitably?
- How can mixed-income communities be leveraged to produce a broader range of positive—indeed, transformative—individual, household, community, and societal outcomes?
- What are the most promising innovations to be expanded in the next generation of mixed-income community efforts?
- What are the greatest threats to efforts to promote more inclusion and equity through mixed-income communities, and what steps should be taken to counter them?
- What are the practical, actionable implications of current experiences and findings for policymakers, developers, investors, residents and community members, researchers, and other important stakeholders?

We have organized the essays into seven topical areas, as follows:

What is the Current Landscape of Mixed-Income Strategies?

These essays set a geographic context for the volume's discussion of mixed-income communities, exploring questions such as: Where do mixed-income communities exist and what are their characteristics? What are the trends in where mixed-income communities are emerging in metro areas? What effects do mixed-income communities have on the areas around them? Some essays in this group focus on inclusionary housing in low-poverty neighborhoods as a promising area in which to sharpen strategies for creating inclusive, equitable mixed-income communities.

What Policy Innovations Do We Need?

These essays explore the design and implementation of federal, state, regional, and local policies to advance inclusion and equity through mixed-income communities. Questions explored include: What types of policies are being advanced and at what scale? What next-generation policy innovations have the most promise for benefiting low-income populations? What are the current challenges to the design and implementation of mixed-income policies?

Advancing Innovative Approaches

These essays focus on specific strategies to preserve and create affordable housing in resource-rich and revitalizing neighborhoods and promote more economically-integrated communities. Questions explored include: How can community land trusts be more broadly and effectively used to promote a sustainable social and economic mix? How can inclusionary housing programs be resourced, strengthened, and leveraged to promote a greater level of social impact on low-income households and households of color?

Who Has a Say and Who Benefits?

These essays focus on influence and power in mixed-income interventions and how to broaden the range of beneficiaries from mixed-income communities. Questions explored include: How can cross-sector efforts generate a greater commitment to equitable development? How can residents and other community stakeholders who are traditionally excluded from influence and control participate more fully in shaping policy reform and implementation? What are some pathways to community ownership, and can they reduce the displacement effects of mixed-income revitalization? What is the best way to frame narratives about mixed-income efforts so that they engage wider audiences and generate public will for greater inclusion and equity? What special populations within mixed-income communities, such as youth, women, and fathers, require a great level of strategic attention and focus?

Engaging the Private Sector in Inclusion and Equity

These essays discuss the opportunities and challenges of harnessing market-driven private-sector investment to promote urban inclusion and equity. Questions explored here include: How do financial incentives steer development to certain populations and places? What policy strategies are being used to incentivize and facilitate investment in mixed-income projects? What are the dangers of relying on the market, and what strategies can maximize the upsides? What can be learned from private owners' and developers' perspectives, experiences, and outlook on the field?

What is Needed Beyond Mixed-Income Housing?

These essays explore how the mixed-income field is moving toward increasingly comprehensive, holistic place-making and neighborhood development, with an emphasis on amenities, resources, and services that generate well-functioning mixed-income, mixed-use communities. Questions to be considered include: Beyond housing, what other community features, such as early care and education, health and wellness, design and environmental sustainability, and social inclusion and cohesion need to be considered when designing and developing mixed-income efforts? How might mixed-income strategies be designed and implemented more holistically?

The Path Forward for Greater Urban Equity and Inclusion

While mixed-income interventions have evolved considerably over the past 30 years, we have yet to realize the potential of these place-based interventions to play a much greater part in helping to address racism, classism, and other forms of societal isolation and marginalization. In this era of increasing social disconnection and distrust, we are excited to present a wealth of new information and ideas to advance social change through greater urban inclusion and equity.

AMY T. KHARE, Ph.D., works nationally on applied research, organizational transformation, and systems change that promotes inclusion and equity within metro areas. Khare's work is inspired by her personal experience as a sibling in the disability rights movement and her professional experience working within housing and community change organizations. Khare serves as the Research Director of the National Initiative on Mixed-Income Communities and a Research Assistant Professor at the Jack, Joseph and Morton Mandel School of Applied Social Sciences, Case Western Reserve University. Khare is completing a book manuscript entitled Poverty, Power and Profit: Structural Racism in Public Housing Reform. She earned her BSW and MSW from the University of Kansas and a Ph.D. from the University of Chicago.

MARK L. JOSEPH, Ph.D. is the Leona Bevis and Marguerite Haynam Associate Professor of Community Development at the Jack, Joseph and Morton Mandel School of Applied Social Sciences at Case Western Reserve University. His research focus is mixed-income development as a strategy for promoting urban equity and inclusion. He is the Founding Director of the National Initiative on Mixed-Income Communities, which conducts research and consulting projects in cities that have included Austin, Calgary, Chicago, Cleveland, Memphis, Minneapolis, Nashville, Pittsburgh, San Francisco, Seattle, Toronto, Tulsa, and Washington, D.C. He is the co-author of Integrating the Inner City: The Promise and Perils of Mixed-Income Public Housing Transformation. He received his undergraduate degree from Harvard University, a Ph.D. from the University of Chicago, was a Post-Doctoral Scholar at the University of Chicago and a Harlech Scholar at Oxford University.

1

WHAT IS THE CURRENT LANDSCAPE FOR MIXED-INCOME STRATEGIES?

Spatial Realities, Challenges and Opportunities

These three essays expand our understanding of the geographic context and trends of mixed-income housing and communities. They also bring to light a core dilemma in the field: how to define a "mixed-income" community. Each essay takes a different approach, underscoring the importance of further debate about how best to characterize and measure mixed-income neighborhoods. Together, these three essays establish the elusiveness and complexity of achieving and sustaining mixed-income housing and neighborhoods. They reinforce the imperative of closer attention to the nuances of geographic trends in neighborhoods, across metro areas, to examine factors that may yield a more stable mix. They set a high bar for the level of sophistication and intentionality that will be required to counter the prevailing forces that promote economic and racial segregation.

In "Spatial Context: The Geography of Mixed-Income Neighborhoods," Elizabeth Kneebone, Carolina Reid, and Natalie Holmes present an analysis of the nation's 100 largest metropolitan areas to help paint a broader picture of "naturally occurring" mixed-income neighborhoods. They find that about 10 percent of the census tracts in the largest metropolitan areas meet their definition of naturally occurring mixed-income neighborhoods, far fewer than the substantial proportions that are predominantly high- or low-income neighborhoods. A promising finding is that there were nearly 1,400 more mixed-income neighborhoods in 2016 than in 2000 in the nation's major metro areas. These tracts seemed to offer more equitable access for residents from historically marginalized populations. However, the authors also document considerable "churn" as mixed-income neighborhoods shift into high- or low-income status, as well as "stickiness" among those neighborhoods that are predominantly high- or low-income. They identify metro areas that have a higher-than-average share of stably mixed-income neighborhoods and call for a closer exploration of the policy and contextual factors that could explain this outcome.

In "Attainability of Mixed-Income Neighborhoods," Elizabeth Luther, Noah Urban, Stephanie Quesnelle, and Ayana Rubio explore the existence of dense, stable mixed-income neighborhoods in eight major metro areas that share characteristics with their home city of Detroit, MI. Using their own definition of "mixed-income," which incorporates a measure of resident and job density, they find a very small percentage—only one percent—of tracts in these eight, generally weaker market metro areas, qualify as mixed-income. They conclude that it is incredibly difficult for neighborhoods in large metropolitan areas to achieve the mix and density criteria they established, although those neighborhoods that achieve the criteria appear more likely to retain these characteristics over time. Because the few dense, mixed-income neighborhoods in these metro areas exhibit profiles that are relatively distinct from each other, reflecting their respective regions' economic and demographic trends more than similarities to each other, they suggest that the most pragmatic policies to support dense, mixed-income, stable neighborhoods must be highly localized.

Turning from naturally occurring mixed-income neighborhoods to planned development, "Mixed-Income LIHTC Developments in Chicago: A First Look at Their Income Characteristics and Spillover Effects," by Raphael Bostic, Andrew Jakabovics, Richard Voith, and Sean Zielenbach, examines the Low-Income Housing Tax Credit (LIHTC) program, widely considered the most successful federal affordable housing program. Although to date LIHTC has not had the explicit aim of promoting an income mix, almost a quarter of LIHTC projects nationwide include a mix of subsidized and market-rate units. This essay presents an analysis of the characteristics and effects of mixed-income LIHTC projects in Chicago. The authors find that tenant incomes in LIHTC properties tend to be somewhat higher in gentrifying and more affluent neighborhoods than in persistently poor communities, and thus "mixed-income" LIHTC developments are not bringing much socio-economic diversity and affluence to low-income communities. They also find that while LIHTC properties in general have had positive effects on surrounding home prices, "mixed-income" LIHTC properties have more of an effect in strong neighborhoods than in weak neighborhoods. This leads them to call careful attention to the trade-offs facing LIHTC developers that seek to promote greater equity and inclusion and to recommend a focus on mixed-income *neighborhoods*, rather than mixed-income *housing*, by investing in fully-subsidized LIHTC projects housing in strong neighborhoods.

SPATIAL CONTEXT: THE GEOGRAPHY OF MIXED-INCOME NEIGHBORHOODS

Elizabeth Kneebone, Carolina Reid, and Natalie Holmes
Terner Center for Housing Innovation, University of California, Berkeley

Over the last 30 years, income and wealth gaps in the United States have widened dramatically. Incomes of the top 1 percent of households are now 40 times that of the bottom 90 percent, and the average Black household has only six cents of wealth for every dollar of wealth in the typical White household. The growing distance between the wealthy and disadvantaged has spatial implications as well, exacerbating the residential segregation of households by income in the nation's major metropolitan areas.[1]

The widening gap between rich and poor households—and between rich and poor neighborhoods—has implications for individual economic mobility as well as for the economic vitality of regions. In addition, the costs of segregation fall disproportionately on Black and Hispanic/Latinx households, widening racial inequalities even further.[2]

While segregation is the product of many interacting factors, housing policy has played an important role in creating these economic and racial disparities.[3]

---

1 Sean F. Reardon, Lindsay Fox, and Joseph Townsend, "Neighborhood Income Composition by Household Race and Income, 1990-2009," *Annals of the American Academy of Political and Social Science* 660, no. 1 (2015): 94, doi: 10.1177/0002716215576104.

2 Gregory Acs, et al., *The Cost of Segregation: National Trends and the Case of Chicago, 1990-2010* (Washington, DC: Urban Institute, 2017), 41-42.

3 Racial and socioeconomic segregation patterns emerge from a complex interplay of many factors: racial disparities in income and wealth; racial differences in residential preferences, conditional on income; socioeconomic differences in residential preferences, conditional on race; the structure of the housing market; and patterns of racial prejudice and discrimination (Reardon, Fox, and Townsend, "Neighborhood Income Composition by Household Race and Income, 1990-2009.")

High-poverty, racially concentrated neighborhoods did not "naturally" emerge—they were the product of a constellation of policy decisions at both the federal and local levels, including racial discrimination in the siting of public housing, redlining, and exclusionary zoning practices (including restrictive covenants, many of which remain in place to this day).[4] Since the 1990s, policymakers have grappled with place-based solutions to the negative consequences of concentrated poverty, and cultivating stable, mixed-income communities is now an explicit goal of U.S. federal low-income housing policy.

As a result, "mixed-income" generally is discussed in the context of efforts to intentionally redevelop the most distressed public housing projects and undo the legacy of racially concentrated poverty. However, these efforts represent only a small slice of neighborhoods across the country. While federal policies and investments—such as housing subsidies and the Affirmatively Furthering Fair Housing rule—can be important tools to bolster integration, a strategy that relies solely on policies at the federal level ignores important opportunities to use local policy levers, such as inclusionary zoning and incentives for building below-market-rate housing, to help produce more mixed-income neighborhoods. To take better advantage of these opportunities, we need a better understanding of the broader set of demographic, economic, and policy dynamics that create "naturally occurring" mixed-income neighborhoods.

In this essay, we present an analysis of the nation's 100 largest metropolitan areas to help paint a broader picture of mixed-income neighborhoods. Rather than focusing solely on neighborhoods that were the target of mixed-income redevelopment, we seek to reveal metropolitan patterns in the location and composition of economically integrated neighborhoods. Understanding where mixed-income communities exist and what they look like offers a chance to think of broader policy implications and lessons that apply outside the narrow context of public housing and engage a wider set of stakeholders in strategies to promote more integrated patterns of development.

DEFINING MIXED-INCOME COMMUNITIES

No single definition of a mixed-income neighborhood—or how to measure it—has emerged in the research or policy work on this issue. To date, research has

---

4 Richard Rothstein, *The Color of Law* (New York, NY: Liveright, 2017).

focused more on measuring segregation and inequality than on integration and equality.[5,6] Indeed, most studies leave the term "mixed-income community" intentionally vague, with the factors creating these places believed to be "the result of more organic economic and demographic dynamics."[7]

For this analysis, we developed a measure of "mixed-income" for neighborhoods that captures two distinct ideas. First, mixed-income neighborhoods need to include households with incomes across the income spectrum—in other words, it is not enough to just have a mix of middle-class families earning between 80 and 120 percent of Area Median Income (AMI). Our measure seeks to distinguish between "middle-income" and "mixed-income" neighborhoods, in which the latter includes neighborhoods that have a broad representation of households at the lower, middle, *and* higher end of the income spectrum.

Given the large geographical differences in incomes across the United States, we used a relative measure of income specific to each region.[8] Using a regional

---

5   Robert J. Sampson, Robert D. Mare, and Kristin L. Perkins, "Achieving the Middle Ground in an Age of Concentrated Extremes: Mixed Middle-Income Neighborhoods and Emerging Adulthood," *Annals of the American Academy of Political and Social Science* 660, no.1 (2015), doi:10.1177/0002716215576117; Reardon, Fox, and Townsend, "Neighborhood Income Composition by Household Race and Income, 1990-2009."

6   There are several approaches for measuring segregation, including the Gini, Theil, dissimilarity, isolation, generalized entropy, and exposure indices. Sampson, Mare, and Perkins (2015) use a variation on Douglas Massey's (2001) Index of Concentration at the Extremes (ICE) to identify mixed-income neighborhoods in Chicago. Other researchers have used the share of households in different parts of the income distribution defined by multiples of area median income (Brophy & Smith 1997). Turner and Fenderson (2006) used the latter approach with an overlay of whether any single group dominates. In addition, several authors have looked at characteristics of *housing* in defining mixed-income communities, particularly in the context of subsidized housing, including Brophy and Smith (1997) and Vale et al. (2014).

    Douglas S. Massey, "The Prodigal Paradigm Returns: Ecology Comes Back to Sociology," in *Does it Take a Village? Community Effects on Children, Adolescents, and Families*, eds. Alan Booth and Ann Crouter (Mahwah, NJ: Lawrence Erlbaum Associates, 2001); Paul C. Brophy and Rhonda N. Smith, "Mixed-Income Housing: Factors for Success," *Cityscape* 3, no. 2 (1997); Margery Austin Turner and Julie Fenderson, "Understanding Diverse Neighborhoods in an Era of Demographic Change," (Washington, DC: Urban Institute, 2006); Lawrence Vale et al., "What Affordable Housing Should Afford: Housing for Resilient Cities," *Cityscape* 16 no. 2 (2014).

7   Mark L. Joseph and Miyoung Yoon, "Mixed-Income Developments" in *Wiley-Blackwell Encyclopedia of Urban and Regional Studies*, ed. Anthony Orum (Hoboken, NJ: Wiley-Blackwell, 2016): 2.

8   Adopting regionally specific measures distinguishes our approach from other recent analyses, including Sampson, Mare, and Perkins, "Achieving the Middle Ground in an Age of Concentrated Extremes: Mixed Middle-Income Neighborhoods and Emerging Adulthood," and Cortright (2018), which depend on national thresholds.

    Joe Cortright, *Identifying America's Most Diverse, Mixed Income Neighborhoods* (Portland, OR: City Observatory, 2018).

rather than national threshold recognizes that, for example, a household earning $50,000 in Milwaukee (where the AMI is $58,000) occupies a very different place in that metro area's income distribution than a household earning $50,000 in San Francisco (where the AMI is $118,000). For each of the 100 largest metropolitan areas in the United States, we divided households into three categories relative to AMI: Those below 80 percent AMI, those between 80 and 120 percent AMI, and those above 120 percent AMI.[9] We considered a neighborhood to be mixed-income if each of these groups makes up at least 20 percent but less than 50 percent of tract households. These parameters mean that each income group has a significant but not dominant presence in the neighborhood.

Second, our definition of "mixed-income" requires that the neighborhood has at least 10 percent of its population living below the federal poverty level. In our initial analysis, we identified a number of neighborhoods that exhibited what might be called "shallow" income mixing but were largely missing poor households (e.g., they had households in each of the three income groups, but households in the bottom tier were clustered near the 80th percentile). Core to the idea of "mixed income" is that it provides increased opportunities for poor families to access the resources often present in middle-class neighborhoods.[10] By requiring "mixed-income" neighborhoods to have at least a 10 percent poverty rate, we are trying to identify those neighborhoods where poor households may benefit from the political and social capital that mixed-income neighborhoods are thought to provide.

In the analysis below, we present the data on mixed-income neighborhoods alongside data on "low-income" and "high-income" neighborhoods for comparison. We define "low-income" neighborhoods as those where at least half of the households have incomes below 80 percent of AMI. Conversely, "high-income" neighborhoods are those where the majority of the households have incomes above 120 percent of AMI. In this way, we hope to draw

---

9   We chose these income cutoffs because of their relevance in federal housing policy, particularly as it relates to eligibility for subsidy. The American Community Survey reports household income in 16 categories. We use those data to interpolate the share of households in each of our three income groups. Grouping by categories nearest the relevant income thresholds produced similar results.

10 Mark L. Joseph, Robert J. Chaskin, and Henry S. Webber, "The Theoretical Basis for Addressing Poverty through Mixed-Income Development," *Urban Affairs Review* 42 no. 3 (2007) doi: 10.1177/1078087406294043; Sampson, Mare, and Perkins, "Achieving the Middle Ground in an Age of Concentrated Extremes: Mixed Middle-Income Neighborhoods and Emerging Adulthood."

attention to the characteristics of mixed-income neighborhoods in contrast to those concentrated at either end of the income distribution.

WHERE ARE MIXED-INCOME NEIGHBORHOODS?

Of the nearly 47,000 U.S. Census tracts that make up the nation's 100 largest metro areas, just under 5,000 met our definition of a mixed-income neighborhood in 2016. That means just one-tenth of major metro neighborhoods contained a significant share of poor, middle-class, and higher-income households living in close proximity (Figure 1).

Just as growing income inequality has seen households at the top of the income distribution pull away from those at the bottom, it is much more common for households to geographically concentrate (or segregate) by income. In 2016, one-third of tracts in the 100 largest metro areas had a majority of households in the top income tier while another third were majority low-income. Put differently, two-thirds of major metro residents lived in a neighborhood dominated by one income group (30 percent in predominantly high-income areas and 37 percent in predominantly low-income tracts), making the 11 percent of residents exposed to mixed-income neighborhoods the exception rather than the norm.[11]

The (relatively slim) odds of a major metro resident calling a mixed-income neighborhood home in 2016 were the same whether that person lived in a big city or in a suburb. But while similar *shares* of urban and suburban neighborhoods qualified as mixed-income, the actual *number* of mixed-income neighborhoods in the suburbs (3,349) outstripped big cities (1,562) by more than twofold, given the larger size of suburbia compared to the primary cities that anchor these regions.[12]

While mixed-income tracts roughly track the urban/suburban divide within the nation's 100 largest metropolitan areas, much more variation exists

---

[11] Together, these three categories of neighborhoods account for 77 percent of major metro Census tracts and population. The remaining 23 percent of Census tracts do not meet our definition of mixed, nor are they dominated by a majority of high- or low-income households.

[12] In the top 100 metro areas, 68 percent of mixed-income neighborhoods are suburban, in keeping with the overall distribution of census tracts—66 percent of which are suburban—in those regions. Here, we define cities as the first-named city in the official metropolitan statistical area title, plus any other city in the metropolitan statistical area (MSA) name that has a population of 100,000 or more. Suburbs make up the remainder of the official MSA.

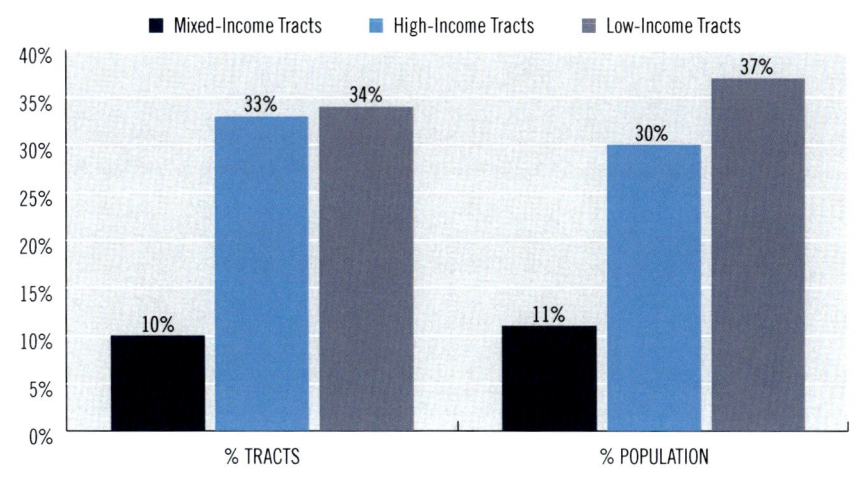

[Chart: bar chart showing shares by income category]

- Mixed-Income Tracts
- High-Income Tracts
- Low-Income Tracts

% TRACTS: 10%, 33%, 34%
% POPULATION: 11%, 30%, 37%

Source: Terner Center analysis of 2016 American Community Survey five-year estimates.

Figure 1: Share of Neighborhood by Income Category, Top 100 Metro Areas (2016)

across individual regions. The share of mixed-income tracts in 2016 reached as low as 2 percent in Bridgeport, Connecticut, and as high as 28 percent in Lakeland, Florida (Map 1). As those extremes might suggest, mixed-income neighborhoods are much more likely to be found in the Sun Belt—home to many of the nation's fastest-growing metro areas—than the Rust Belt, where the legacy of segregation and local exclusionary policies still shapes the landscape of many regions. Almost half (48 percent) of all mixed-income neighborhoods in 2016 were located in the South, compared to 18 percent in the Midwest, 17 percent in the Northeast, and 16 percent in the West (where some of the nation's highest-cost—and highest-inequality—markets are clustered).[13]

Altogether, the South accounted for 11 out of the 15 metro areas with the highest shares of mixed-income neighborhoods in 2016, with six of those regions in Florida alone. In contrast, East Coast metro areas tended to have a much lower proportion of mixed-income neighborhoods in 2016, with the share of mixed-income neighborhoods in regions like Boston, New York, and Washington, DC, falling well below 10 percent.

---

13 See, e.g., Alan Berube, "City and Metropolitan Income Inequality Data Reveal Ups and Downs through 2016," (Washington, DC: The Brookings Institution, 2018), https://www.brookings.edu/research/city-and-metropolitan-income-inequality-data-reveal-ups-and-downs-through-2016/.

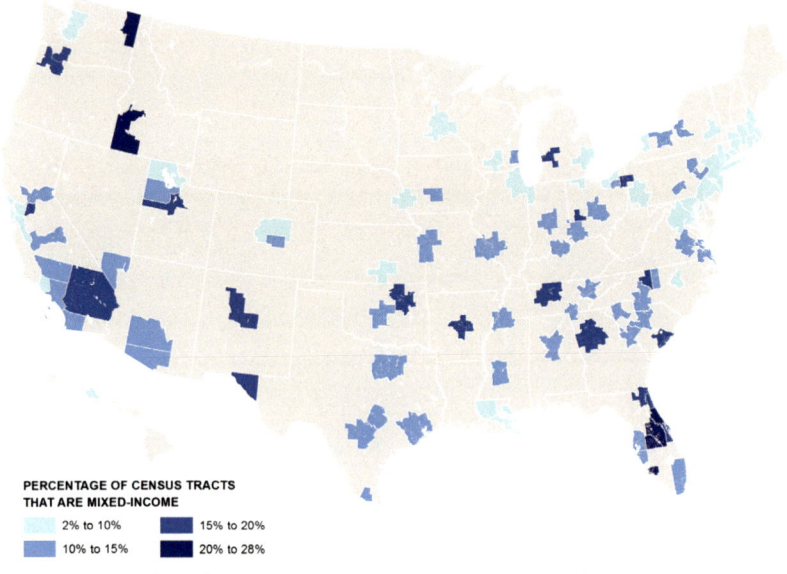

Source: Authors' analysis of 2012-2016 5-year American Community Survey data

Map 1: Share of Metro-area Tracts that are Mixed Income, 100 Largest U.S. Metro Areas, 2012-2016

That is not to say that there aren't any higher-cost, coastal markets or older, industrial Rust Belt regions performing better than average in terms of the prevalence of mixed-income neighborhoods: Portland (OR), Los Angeles, and San Diego all posted above-average shares of mixed-income neighborhoods in 2016, as did Pittsburgh, Worcester, and Philadelphia in the Northeast and Dayton, Minneapolis-St. Paul, and Grand Rapids in the Midwest.

WHO LIVES IN MIXED-INCOME NEIGHBORHOODS?

Although mixed-income tracts contain just 11 percent of the nation's major metro residents, the 23 million people living in these neighborhoods make up a strikingly representative cross-section of metropolitan America.

Twelve percent of people living in poverty in the nation's major metropolitan areas lived in mixed-income neighborhoods in 2016, along with a similar proportion (11 percent) of non-poor residents (Table 1). Likewise, roughly one in 10 White, Black, and Asian residents lived in mixed-income tracts.

Hispanic/Latinx residents posted a modestly higher share, with 14 percent residing in mixed-income neighborhoods in 2016. That rough parity stands in sharp relief compared to the entrenched disparities that exist in high-income neighborhoods—which tilt disproportionately toward White, Asian, and non-poor residents—and low-income tracts, where most major metro poor (57 percent) and Black (56 percent) residents live.

	MIXED-INCOME TRACTS	HIGH-INCOME TRACTS	LOW-INCOME TRACTS
Poor	12%	15%	57%
Non-poor	11%	40%	26%
White	10%	47%	18%
Black/African American	11%	16%	56%
Asian	9%	44%	25%
Hispanic/Latinx	14%	20%	48%
Other	12%	35%	30%

Source: Terner Center analysis of 2016 American Community Survey five-year estimates.

Table 1: Distribution of the Population Across Categories of Neighborhoods, 2016

It is true that the size of the populations represented by each of these proportions varies widely; for instance, 10 percent of the major metro White population equaled 12.1 million people in 2016, while 11 percent of the Black population equaled 3.2 million. But the relatively similar shares of each group in mixed-income tracts means that the overall makeup of these neighborhoods largely mirrors that of metropolitan America (Figure 2). People in mixed-income neighborhoods are slightly less likely to be White and more likely to be Hispanic/Latinx than the population overall, but on the whole hew closely to the racial and ethnic mix and incidence of poverty in the nation's 100 largest metro areas. In contrast, the disparities in who has typically had access to high-income neighborhoods compared to who has concentrated in (or been relegated to) low-income tracts show up in the vastly different demographic profiles of those places. Thus, mixed-income neighborhoods distinguish themselves by the more equitable access to residency they seem to provide on the basis of race and ethnicity as well as income, especially for historically marginalized populations.

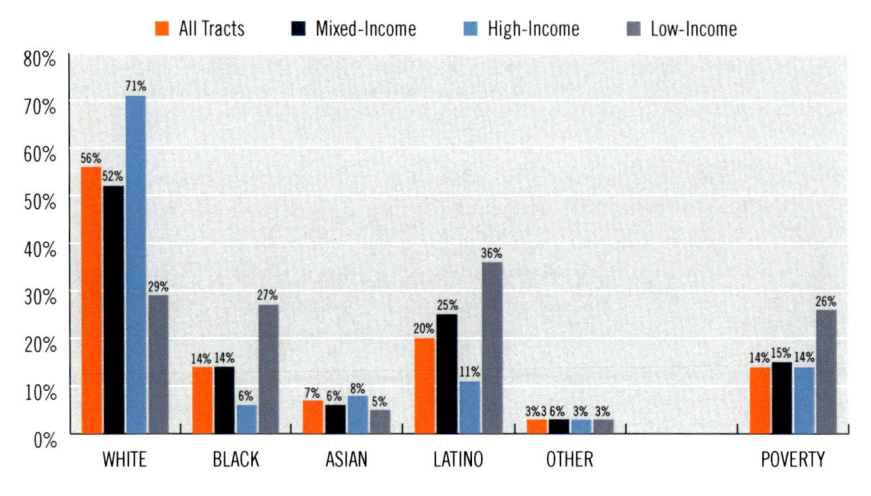

[Bar chart showing Resident Characteristics by Neighborhood Type, with categories All Tracts, Mixed-Income, High-Income, Low-Income across WHITE, BLACK, ASIAN, LATINO, OTHER, POVERTY:
- WHITE: 56%, 52%, 71%, 29%
- BLACK: 14%, 14%, 6%, 27%
- ASIAN: 7%, 6%, 8%, 5%
- LATINO: 20%, 25%, 11%, 36%
- OTHER: 3%, 6%, 3%, 3%
- POVERTY: 14%, 15%, 14%, 26%]

Source: Terner Center analysis of 2016 American Community Survey five-year estimates.

Figure 2: Resident Characteristics by Neighborhood Type (2016)

The representativeness of these neighborhoods largely holds across individual metro areas, with a few notable exceptions. For instance, compared to the overall metro area racial and ethnic composition, Whites make up a considerably smaller share than would be expected in mixed-income neighborhoods in northeastern metro areas like Springfield (MA), Bridgeport (CT), and New York, and in California metro areas like Oxnard and Bakersfield (Figure 3). In effect, people of color have higher-than-expected access to mixed-income communities in these places, although which minority groups live in mixed-income neighborhoods differs depending on the region. In the California metro areas, the lower share of Whites living in mixed-income neighborhoods is entirely offset by the higher share of Latinx in these tracts. In the northeastern metro areas of New York, Springfield, and Bridgeport, both Latinx and Black residents are over-represented in mixed-income tracts, as compared to their share of the population in the metro area as a whole.

On the other side of the spectrum, a number of metro areas in the Rust Belt and the Carolinas see Whites over-represented in mixed-income neighborhoods in comparison to the overall racial and ethnic makeup of the region. In these metropolitan areas, the greater share of White residents in these tracts is largely or entirely offset by a smaller share of Black residents. With the exception of Greenville, each of those metro areas continue to be characterized by higher-

■ Metro total ■ Mixed-Income Tracts

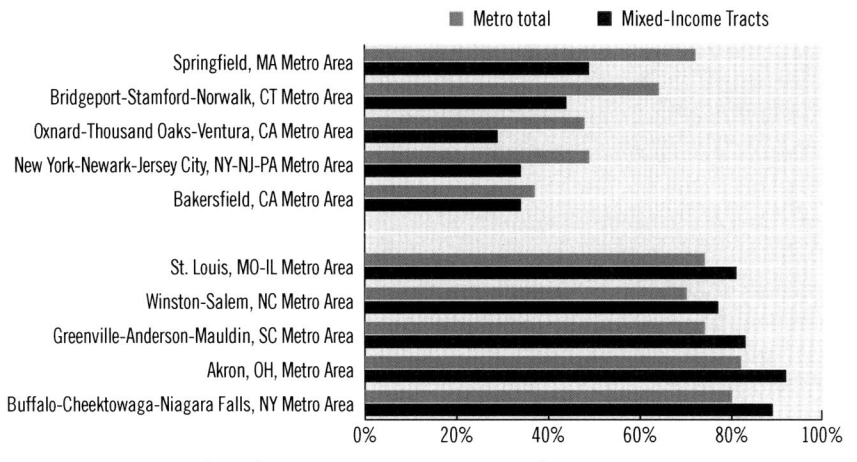

Springfield, MA Metro Area	
Bridgeport-Stamford-Norwalk, CT Metro Area	
Oxnard-Thousand Oaks-Ventura, CA Metro Area	
New York-Newark-Jersey City, NY-NJ-PA Metro Area	
Bakersfield, CA Metro Area	
St. Louis, MO-IL Metro Area	
Winston-Salem, NC Metro Area	
Greenville-Anderson-Mauldin, SC Metro Area	
Akron, OH, Metro Area	
Buffalo-Cheektowaga-Niagara Falls, NY Metro Area	

Source: Terner Center analysis of 2016 American Community Survey five-year estimates

Figure 3: Share of the Population That is White (2016)

than-average Black-White segregation.[14]

The inequalities in who has access to mixed-income neighborhoods—especially the under-representation of Blacks in mixed-income neighborhoods—has been shaped at least in part by exclusionary housing policies and practices in these regions. Local land use and housing policies also likely underlie the evidence of exclusion in the residential patterns of the roughly 90 percent of major metro residents who do not live in mixed-neighborhoods. Indeed, regions that have a higher share of people of color in mixed-income neighborhoods tend to have lower-than-average shares of tracts that qualify as mixed-income, while regions where whites are over-represented tend to post higher-than-average shares of mixed-income tracts, all of which raises the question of what is driving the barriers to both racial and economic integration. Overall, we need a better understanding of how racial segregation and discrimination influence the establishment of mixed-income neighborhoods and the role that local housing and land use decisions play in shaping where different groups of residents can and do live.

---

14 "Residential Segregation Data for U.S. Metro Areas," *Governing: The States and Localities*, accessed February 7, 2019, http://www.governing.com/gov-data/education-data/residential-racial-segregation-metro-areas.html.

HOW DOES HOUSING, INCLUDING SUBSIDIZED HOUSING, SHAPE MIXED-INCOME NEIGHBORHOODS?

Federal housing subsidies often receive attention in research and policy discussions about the geography of poverty and opportunity in the United States—both for the role they have played in driving segregation and the concentration of poverty, and, more recently, for their potential to ameliorate those patterns by increasing access to higher-opportunity neighborhoods and fostering more mixed-income communities.

Subsidized households remain much more prevalent in low-income communities. More than two-thirds of households that receive housing vouchers are located in low-income tracts, and less than 10 percent are in mixed- or high-income tracts. The same is true of Low-Income Housing Tax Credit (LIHTC) units. However, most mixed-income neighborhoods (63 percent) do contain some type of housing subsidy—most often tenant-based Housing Choice Vouchers (Figure 4). These subsidies no doubt play a role in helping the 12 percent of metropolitan poor residents in mixed-income tracts (and 15 percent in high-income tracts) gain access to these neighborhoods. In mixed-income neighborhoods where vouchers are present, they account for almost 6 percent of occupied rental units. In mixed-income tracts with LIHTC

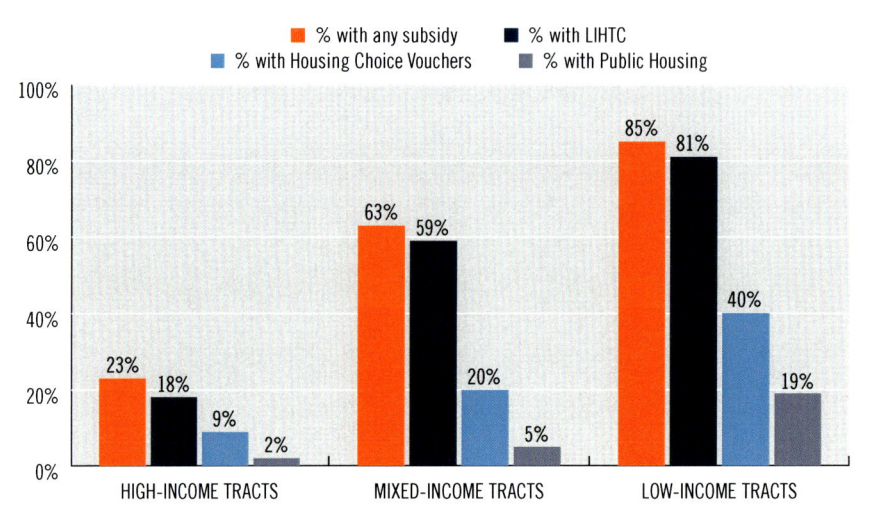

Source: Terner Center analysis of 2016 American Community Survey five-year estimates

Figure 4: Presence of Subsidies in Neighborhoods (2016)

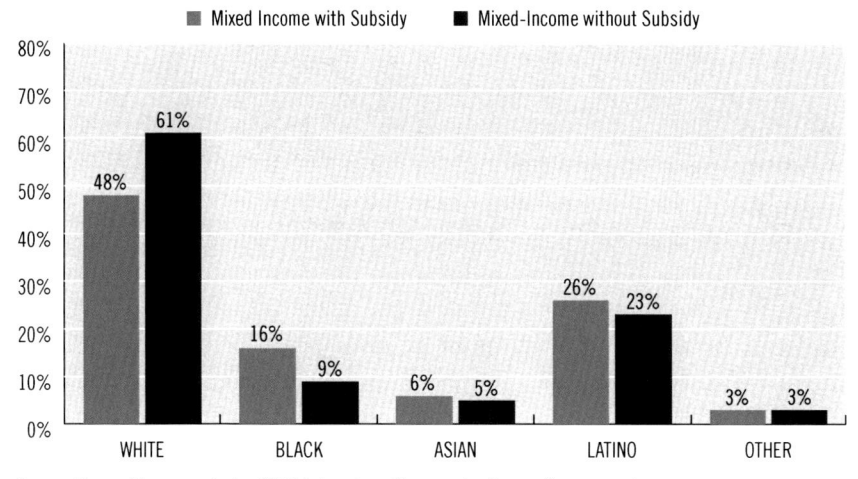

	Mixed Income with Subsidy	Mixed-Income without Subsidy

	WHITE	BLACK	ASIAN	LATINO	OTHER
Mixed Income with Subsidy	48%	16%	6%	26%	3%
Mixed-Income without Subsidy	61%	9%	5%	23%	3%

Source: Terner Center analysis of 2016 American Community Survey five-year estimates

Figure 5: Racial and Ethnic Makeup of Mixed Income Neighborhoods by Presence of Housing Subsidies (2016)

projects, below-market-rate LIHTC units make up 14 percent of occupied rental units.

The presence of subsidies in mixed-income neighborhoods seems to affect who has access to these tracts. Mixed-income tracts that contain subsidized households tend to be more racially and ethnically diverse (Figure 5). Specifically, the share of Black residents in mixed-income neighborhoods almost doubles when housing subsidies are present.

While subsidies may be one piece of the puzzle in creating many of the mixed-income communities that exist today, they are a relatively small one. A much bigger factor (and one that largely dictates where subsidies can be used in the first place) likely is the type of housing available in different kinds of neighborhoods (Figure 6). Single-family housing has dominated housing production for decades in the United States. The prevalence of single-family housing and single-family neighborhoods in the nation's major metro areas—and, more specifically, the exclusionary zoning and housing policies that have often produced these neighborhoods and driven racialized patterns of segregation—limits the development of a diverse housing stock that can support a range of incomes and household types.

Figure 6: Tract Housing Characteristics (2016)

Legend: Mixed Income | High Income | Low Income

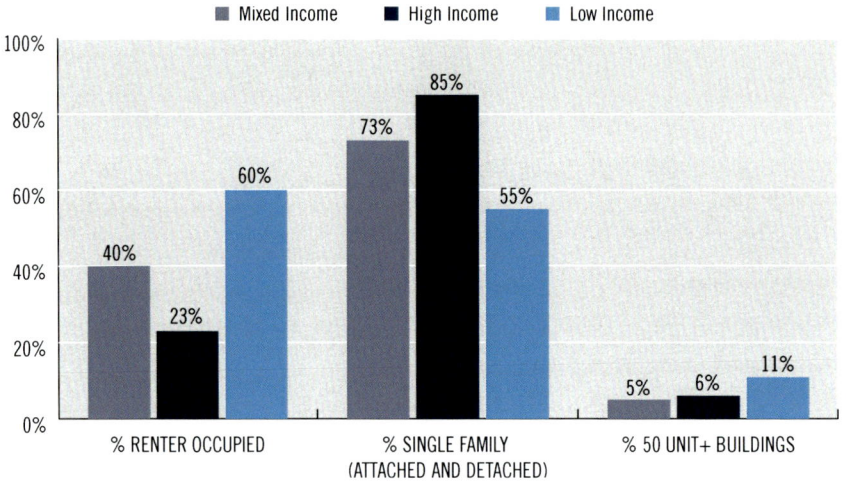

% RENTER OCCUPIED: Mixed Income 40%, High Income 23%, Low Income 60%
% SINGLE FAMILY (ATTACHED AND DETACHED): Mixed Income 73%, High Income 85%, Low Income 55%
% 50 UNIT+ BUILDINGS: Mixed Income 5%, High Income 6%, Low Income 11%

Source: Terner Center analysis of 2016 American Community Survey five-year estimates

In that context, it is not surprising that high-income tracts in the top 100 metro areas are populated predominantly by single-family homes, which are largely owner-occupied, while low-income tracts are dominated by renters and a denser, more multifamily form of development. It is likely that mixed-income neighborhoods can support a more economically diverse group of residents because these places tend to strike a middle path of housing development types. Mixed-income tracts register a relatively more balanced mix of owner and rental units and a housing stock that offers opportunities for modest density; more than one-fifth of the housing stock in mixed-income communities comes from multifamily buildings that comprise two or more units but fewer than 50.

HOW STABLE ARE MIXED-INCOME NEIGHBORHOODS OVER TIME?

The prior analysis provides important insights into where economically diverse neighborhoods exist, but a point-in-time snapshot fails to answer the critical question of how enduring these places are. Do mixed-income neighborhoods stay that way, or do they eventually become more exclusive or poor over time?

Between 2000 and 2016, the number of mixed-income neighborhoods in metropolitan America increased from 3,553 to 4,911—an uptick of 40 percent. On its face, that net gain bodes well for the expansion of more economically integrated neighborhoods over time. However, the topline numbers mask a great deal of churn within these tracts.

Of the neighborhoods that were mixed-income in 2016, just 18 percent (902 tracts) began the 2000s that way. The trajectory of neighborhoods that cycled in or out of mixed-income status between 2000 and 2016 shows how strong the pull toward income segregation tends to be. For instance, neighborhoods that lost their mixed-income status (according to our definition) after 2000 were more likely to do so because they became more heavily concentrated at one end of the income distribution. Almost 60 percent of tracts that were formerly mixed-income in 2000 transitioned to either majority low-income or majority high-income by 2016 (Figure 7).

In contrast, among neighborhoods that became mixed-income during this period, two-thirds emerged from the pool of "other" tracts (i.e., tracts that fall somewhere in the middle—not mixed-income, but not majority high- or low-income). The much smaller number of tracts that used to be majority high- or low-income but became mixed-income in 2016 suggests that the more segregated by income a neighborhood is, the "stickier" the income status of that neighborhood tends to be.

The trajectories of these neighborhoods indicate two broader trends that have reshaped the geography of poverty and opportunity in the nation's major metro areas since 2000: the revitalization (and gentrification) of an increasing number of urban neighborhoods, and the growing incidence of poverty and economic decline in the suburbs.

Of the high-income tracts that became mixed-income, more than three-quarters were located in suburban areas. This dovetails with a period in which suburbia was home to the nation's fastest-growing poor population, and the suburban poor outstripped the number of urban poor for the first time.[15] At the same time, more than half of the low-income tracts that became mixed-income were located in cities. One way to read these trends is that increased economic diversity in the suburbs created a greater mix of incomes in neighborhoods that used to be largely affluent, and greater reinvestment and population growth in cities did the same in formerly low-income areas.

---

15 Elizabeth Kneebone and Alan Berube, *Confronting Suburban Poverty in America* (Washington, DC: The Brookings Institution, 2014).

■ High Income   ■ Low Income   ■ Other

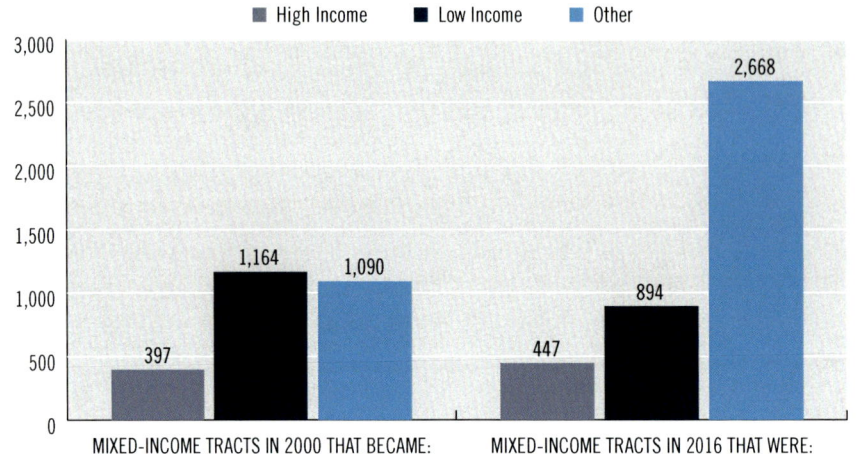

[Bar chart showing:
MIXED-INCOME TRACTS IN 2000 THAT BECAME: High Income 397, Low Income 1,164, Other 1,090
MIXED-INCOME TRACTS IN 2016 THAT WERE: High Income 447, Low Income 894, Other 2,668]

Source: Terner Center analysis of 2016 American Community Survey five-year estimates

Figure 7: The Trajectory of Tracts That Did Not Remain Mixed-Income Over Time

But those same dynamics did not just create new mixed-income communities. They also contributed to the churn in formerly mixed-income neighborhoods, furthering the concentration of both poverty and affluence and shifting the distribution of such neighborhoods across the urban-suburban continuum. Of the roughly 400 formerly mixed-income tracts that became high-income between 2000 and 2016, more than half (51 percent) were in cities. In fact, one-third of those tracts were in the cities of just five metro areas: Chicago-Naperville-Elgin; Los Angeles-Long Beach-Anaheim; New York-Newark-Jersey City; San Francisco-Oakland-Hayward, and Washington, DC-Arlington-Alexandria. On the other end of the spectrum, of the almost 1,200 formerly mixed-income tracts that became low-income, 60 percent were in the suburbs.

One result of these dual forces is a narrowing of the urban/suburban divide over this period (Figure 8). By 2016, the metropolitan balance of mixed-income and low-income neighborhoods tilted more suburban than in 2000, while high-income neighborhoods tilted slightly more urban. These trends also suggest that point-in-time snapshots of "naturally occurring" mixed-income neighborhoods often capture a temporary neighborhood equilibrium of integration in a longer-term trajectory of income sorting.

Are there ways that communities can guard against churn and boost the stability of mixed-income neighborhoods, effectively providing a bulwark against segregation pressures? At first glance, the tracts that succeeded in maintaining a mix of incomes between 2000 and 2016 do not significantly differ from those that fell in or out of the mixed-income category. In general, the underlying makeup of the housing stock, incidence of rental units, and presence of subsidies looked much the same across these groups.

However, there may be something to learn from a closer look at the regions that yielded better-than-average shares of stably mixed-income communities:

- For 15 of the nation's major metropolitan areas, at least one in four mixed-income tracts remained that way over time. Six of those regions were in California.
- The Los Angeles metro area alone accounted for 158 of metro America's stably mixed-income neighborhoods, meaning that almost half of its currently mixed-income tracts were also mixed income in 2000. The bulk of those neighborhoods (116) were spread across multiple suburban jurisdictions.
- Metro New York posted the next-largest total number of stably

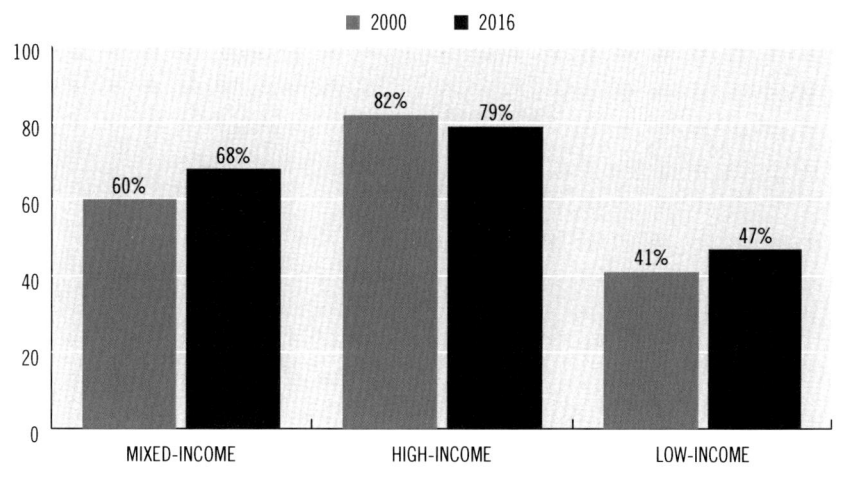

Source: Terner Center analysis of 2016 American Community Survey five-year estimates

Figure 8: Share of Major-Metro Neighborhoods Located in Suburbs, by Income Category (2000 and 2016)

mixed-income tracts overall (81), which meant that 30 percent of the region's mixed-income tracts remained stable over time. Most of those neighborhoods (54) were in urban areas.

Future research should explore what distinguishes not just these metro areas but the specific urban and suburban jurisdictions within them that have produced more enduring economically integrated neighborhoods. Delving further into these case studies could help determine what state or local policy decisions, economic dynamics, or demographic patterns have helped create—and sustain—these mixed-income neighborhoods over time.

CONCLUSIONS

Measuring the incidence and makeup of naturally occurring mixed-income communities in metropolitan America provides a framework and context for understanding how and where these pockets of economic integration emerge. There were nearly 1,400 more mixed-income neighborhoods in 2016 than in 2000 in the nation's major metro areas—an expansion in the number of economically diverse communities that could in turn help to generate the benefits of integration for more households. Moreover, where these naturally occurring mixed-income neighborhoods develop, as a whole they seem to offer more equitable access for residents from historically marginalized populations, including African Americans and those living in poverty. But these naturally occurring conditions have yet to reach a significant scale and have proven largely unstable over time. Furthermore, worsening income inequality and the "stickiness" of neighborhoods as they become more concentrated and polarized by income indicate that the forces working against naturally occurring mixed-income communities are likely to increase.

In many ways, this analysis raises as many questions as it answers about the ways in which local land use and housing decisions intersect with demographic and economic trends to shape patterns of segregation and integration. But it also offers promising pathways and examples of jurisdictions that seem to be succeeding for further exploration of the conditions and policy landscape needed to ensure that mixed-income communities not only emerge but also endure as a real alternative to the persistent pressures of segregation.

IMPLICATIONS FOR ACTION

Implications for Policy

Federal housing policy helped to create today's landscape of economic and racial segregation, and it has an important role to play in undoing that legacy. Where housing subsidies are targeted—be it through place-based investments like LIHTC or through the expansion of choice through vouchers—helps shape where low-income households can live. We find that most mixed-income neighborhoods (63 percent) contain some type of housing subsidy—most often tenant-based Housing Choice Vouchers—and that tracts that contain subsidized households tend to be more racially and ethnically diverse. This suggests that the design of housing subsidy programs, and targeting them to local housing market conditions, can make a significant difference in supporting more integrated neighborhoods. For instance, the Baltimore Regional Housing Partnership (BRHP) has a robust counseling and housing search assistance program aimed at helping Housing Choice Voucher households locate in higher-opportunity neighborhoods throughout the region. As BRHP works with voucher households pre- and post-move, it strives to foster income mixing and guard against concentrating low-income households in particular properties or neighborhoods.

However, federal subsidies are just one policy lever that should be considered alongside a broader array of public, private, state, and local tools. Local housing and zoning policies are among the most influential factors shaping housing access. Incentivizing localities to diversify the mix of housing types in all neighborhoods can foster greater economic inclusion. Inclusionary zoning, for example, can require or encourage the production of affordable units as part of market-rate development. In addition, city- or state-level sources of income discrimination protections can ensure that households with a voucher have access to fair housing choices. Policies that limit exclusionary zoning practices are also critical. For example, Minneapolis recently eliminated single-family zoning in every neighborhood to increase the supply of "missing middle" housing across the city. In Massachusetts, Chapter 40B ensures that all of its cities meet their fair share of affordable housing production by streamlining the approvals process for projects that include units targeted to lower-income households.[16] While these are just a few examples, they point to ways in which local models can facilitate the development of mixed-income communities outside of the public housing and/or federal housing subsidy context.

Implications for Research and Evaluation

Despite decades of research into the effects of concentrated neighborhood poverty on a variety of outcomes and recent evidence pointing toward the importance of neighborhood context on a child's expected earnings in adulthood,[17] we do not know *how* mixed-income neighborhoods benefit poor residents.[18] For example: are mixed-income neighborhoods good for poor children because they provide meaningful exposure to people from different backgrounds? Or because they provide access to resources and institutional capacity not present in poor neighborhoods? Or because they increase collective efficacy and political mobilization for neighborhood investments? Knowing more about which of these pathways matter would fill a central gap in our understanding of the mechanisms underlying neighborhood effects. We also need more research that accounts for the fact that neighborhoods change. We find that while low-income and high-income neighborhoods tend to be "sticky," there is a lot of churn in which neighborhoods are mixed-income over time. A deeper exploration of neighborhoods that have managed to remain stably integrated over time—and what factors have contributed to that stability—could help to more effectively direct future policymaking efforts at the local, state, and federal level.

Implications for Development and Investment

Where development and investment happens, and what kind, can have a profound influence on neighborhood change. Particularly in the context of places experiencing gentrification and a "return to the city," investments need to be coupled with tenant protections and strategies to prevent displacement. Affordable housing preservation—not just new construction—should be a

---

16 Carolina Reid, Carol Galante, and Ashley F. Weinstein-Carnes, "Addressing California's Housing Shortage: Lessons from Massachusetts Chapter 40B," *Journal of Affordable Housing and Community Development Law* 25, no.2 (2017).

17 Raj Chetty and Nathaniel Hendren, "The Impacts of Neighborhoods on Intergenerational Mobility I: Childhood Exposure Effects," *Quarterly Journal of Economics* 133, no. 3 (2018), doi: 10.3386/w23001.

18 Mark Joseph and coauthors review theory and evidence in the context of mixed-income housing developments, Mark L. Joseph, Robert J. Chaskin, and Henry S. Webber, "The Theoretical Basis for Addressing Poverty through Mixed-Income Development."

priority in neighborhoods that are seeing an influx of higher-income residents. In San Francisco, for example, the city has established a Small Sites Program, which provides loans to nonprofit organizations to buy buildings that are at risk of being sold to a private investor and converts the units to permanent affordability.

On the other hand, in neighborhoods experiencing increases in the number of poor and low-income households, policymakers and practitioners should prioritize community development investments and programs that can stabilize and support mixed-income neighborhoods. Taking steps to promote and preserve integration in such areas can help stem the emergence of new areas of concentrated disadvantage, but will require connecting housing strategies with cross-sector interventions and investments in residents and the broader community.

Implications for Residents and Community Members

The built environment is just one element of what it means to be "mixed-income." Fostering housing integration, at its core, is about the hope that doing so will also promote social integration, offer greater access to opportunity structures, and ultimately improve outcomes for low-income households and residents of color. Yet, while housing policies and investments can set the stage for integration and access, housing strategies alone are unlikely to guarantee the durability and efficacy of those conditions. Aligning services and community resources with housing interventions can help ensure that low-income families in mixed-income environments have access to employment, health, transportation, and other social services that can help stabilize individual households. At the same time, supportive services that seek to build a sense of community and belonging in otherwise transitioning and transient neighborhoods—whether urban or suburban—can promote neighborhood stability by building social cohesion across different groups of residents.

■ ■ ■

ELIZABETH KNEEBONE *is Research Director at the Terner Center for Housing Innovation at U.C. Berkeley, and a nonresident senior fellow at the Brookings Institution's Metropolitan Policy Program. Her research interests include the shifting geography of poverty in the U.S. and the ways in which the built environment shapes access to opportunity. She is co-author of the book Confronting Suburban Poverty in America (Brookings Press, 2013). Kneebone holds a master's degree in public policy from* the University of Chicago and a bachelor's degree in history from Indiana University.

■ ■ ■

CAROLINA REID is an Assistant Professor in the Department of City and Regional Planning and the Faculty Research Advisor at the Terner Center for Housing Innovation. Reid specializes in housing and community development, with a specific focus on place-based anti-poverty strategies including policies to expand access to affordable housing and homeownership for low-income and minority households, the Community Reinvestment Act, and neighborhood stabilization.

■ ■ ■

NATALIE HOLMES is a Ph.D. student at UC Berkeley's Goldman School of Public Policy. Previously, she worked at the Brookings Institution's Metropolitan Policy Program, where her work focused on the geography of poverty in the U.S., and policies and programs to support low-wage workers and families. She holds a BA from Yale College and an MPP from Georgetown University.

ATTAINABILITY OF MIXED-INCOME NEIGHBORHOODS

Elizabeth Luther
Capital Impact Partners

Noah Urban, Stephanie Quesnelle, Ayana Rubio
Data Driven Detroit

How attainable is a dense, stable, mixed-income neighborhood—one with high population density, a low poverty level, and a relatively large percentage of middle-income households—in the United States? And do neighborhoods that have achieved these characteristics maintain them over time? In 2017, researchers from Capital Impact Partners (Capital Impact), a national nonprofit Community Development Financial Institution (CDFI), and Data Driven Detroit (D3), metro Detroit's community data hub, reviewed housing and population trends in eight metro areas to address those questions. Metro areas included Atlanta, Baltimore, Cleveland, Detroit, Memphis, New Orleans, Oakland, and Pittsburgh—cities selected because Capital Impact was active there at the time of the initial study, and/or the city's economic trajectory and demographics were historically similar to Detroit's. Our study of residential and job density and income mix found that very few metropolitan statistical area (MSA) tracts are able to reach a high urban density and a balanced income mix, and even fewer are able to maintain those thresholds over time.

Our analysis' focus on residential and job density and income mix at the neighborhood level is grounded in a large body of research, including Raj Chetty et al.'s June 2014 report suggesting that the five factors most associated with upward mobility are segregation, income inequality, quality of K-12 education, social capital, and prevalence of single-parent households.[1] Capital Impact had previously explored how neighborhoods in Detroit could increase

---

1   Raj Chetty et al., "Where is the Land of Opportunity? The Geography of Intergenerational Mobility in the United States," *Quarterly Journal of Economics*.129 (4) (2014). http://www.equality-of-opportunity.org/assets/documents/mobility_geo.pdf.

Figure 1: Mixed-Income Attainability Analysis' Density and Income Mix Thresholds

Research has shown that:

- When 10 percent or more of households earn less than the poverty level, housing markets can begin to devalue.

- When 20 percent or more of households fall below the poverty level, (i.e., a Census-defined "poverty area" or a Brookings Institution-defined "high-poverty neighborhood") there can be negative impacts, such as school leaving (e.g., drop-outs and truancy) and crime.

- When 40 percent or more of households are below the poverty level, the Census defines that area as a "Category IV" (highest) area of concentrated poverty, and Brookings defines it as a "distressed neighborhood." (See: https://www.brookings.edu/research/u-s-concentrated-poverty-in-the-wake-of-the-great-recession/)

Originally, we set neighborhood income mix goals of (a) at least 40 percent of households earning middle incomes at between 50 percent and 120 percent of the Area Median Income (AMI) and (b) fewer than 10 percent of individuals living below the federal poverty line. (The U.S. Census collects data at the individual and household level. We used individual-level data for the second indicator because it was most representative and correlated well with household data.)

After a first pass, we lowered the threshold for the percentage of households earning between 50 percent and 120 percent AMI to **31 percent** to accommodate tracts in all metro areas, using the national average of 34.9 percent as a guide. Additionally, we increased the poverty rate threshold to **20 percent**, using the national average of 15.6 percent as a guide.

We also decreased the threshold of residential and job density to 20 residents plus jobs per acre and added a criterion of at least **10 households** per acre in order to ensure we were looking at residential or mixed-use neighborhoods, as opposed to job centers.

density and achieve a balanced income mix by adding new market-rate and affordable housing.[2] Our analysis further explored two findings from this research base:

- Higher residential and job density, when combined with good planning and design, can foster healthy, interactive, walkable areas with concentrations of services and amenities that support households across the income spectrum. Higher density of people generally supports the development of retail, services, health care and other facilities, and schools. As density increases,

---

[2] "Toward Inclusive Growth in Detroit," (Detroit, MI: Capital Impact Partners, October 2015) available at https://www.capitalimpact.org/wp-content/uploads/2015/10/2015-Towards-Inclusive-Growth-in-Detroit.pdf.

Figure 2: Sample Tracts in the Study

CLEVELAND'S single qualifying tract (39035160601) is located along the southern shore of Lake Erie in Lakewood, Ohio. The racial composition is predominantly non-Hispanic White (81.2% of households). Bordering the northwest edge of the city, this tract contains a number of high-rise multifamily structures that are visible from downtown. There is no subsidized housing in this tract. Widely known as the "Lakewood Gold Coast," in 2014 there was grassroots opposition to the demolition of the historic Fifth Church of Christ Scientist, which eventually was razed to make way for a large-scale mixed-use development including high-end townhomes and a "supermarket district express." Homeownership rates stayed relatively steady, as did rental rates, between 2000 and 2014.

Analysis Criteria:
- Population density/income mix: 31.5 residents plus jobs per acre, 24.8 households per acre.
- Income: 32.7% of households earn between 50% and 120% of the Area Median Income (AMI). Individual poverty rate is 7.9 percent—one of the lowest poverty rates in the study.

Stability: The Cleveland tract saw a decrease in density at both the residents plus jobs and household levels. There was a large decrease in the percentage of households earning between 50% and 120% AMI from 56.6% to 32.7%, and a slight drop in the poverty rate. The predominant race remained non-Hispanic White.

DETROIT'S qualifying tract (26163517000) lies just east of the city's greater downtown in the Lafayette Park neighborhood, home to a unique combination of high-rise apartments, condominiums, and cooperatively owned townhomes. The racial composition is predominantly non-Hispanic Black (70.8%), the only such tract in the study. The area is visibly distinct from Detroit's primary makeup of single-family neighborhoods. Fewer than one quarter of households (22.6%) own their homes, compared to a 68.4% rate at the MSA level. Nearly half of households (48.1%) experience a housing cost burden—the third-highest proportion of all tracts that qualified for the study, and more than one-third of households (36.2%) earn less than $25,000/year—the highest percentage of all tracts that qualified as having attained a mixed-income profile in this analysis. There are no subsidized affordable housing units within the tract. Between 2000 and 2014, owner occupancy decreased along with median home values, whereas its median gross rental rate increased by 10%.

Analysis Criteria:
- Population density/income mix: 21.4 residents plus jobs per acre, 13.6 households per acre.
- Income: 32.1% of households earn between 50% and 120% of the AMI. Individual poverty rate is 17.6%.

Stability: The Detroit tract saw a slight decrease in job density balanced out by an increase in household density. Like Cleveland, it also saw a large decrease in the percentage of households earning between 50% and 120% AMI (from 50.9% to 32.1%) and a 0.3% increase in poverty rate.

(continued on next page)

Figure 2: Sample Tracts in the Study (continued)

A number of **OAKLAND'S** qualifying tracts are located near Lake Merritt in the center city. One of these tracts (06001405200) roughly corresponds with the Bella Vista neighborhood just east of the lake; housing values have increased on the west side of the tract adjacent to the lake, whereas values on the east side remained markedly lower at the time of the study. This was one of five qualifying tracts in the study—all of which are located in the East Bay MSA—with a predominant race that changed between 2000 and 2014. In this case, the predominant race changed from non-Hispanic Asian to non-Hispanic White. Its Herfindahl index of racial/ethnic diversity, the third-highest of all tracts, increased between 2000-2014 from 0.72 to 0.75. Between 2000 and 2014, this tract's median home value increased by over 60%, and median gross rental rate increased by over 30%.

Analysis Criteria:
- Population density/income mix: 23.5 residents plus jobs per acre, 11.1 households per acre.
- Income: 37.2% of households earn between 50% and 120% of the AMI. Individual poverty rate is one of the lowest in the study, at 6.3%.

Stability: This tract saw limited changes in density and poverty rate, but a large drop in the percentage of households earning between 50 and 120% AMI, from 60% to 37.2%.

---

so does transit ridership, particularly once the density of residents and employees combined surpasses 30 people per acre, leading to increased access to jobs and housing for all residents.[3] Residential densities above 15 housing units per acre encourage people to walk more, leading to public health benefits.[4]

- Measures of household and per capita income can be telling indicators of a neighborhood's well-being and overall trajectory. Median household income is a common measure; others include ratios of aggregate income by quartile or quintile or measures of evenness and diversity across income categories. While there are limits to what we can extrapolate about neighborhood health from income data, evenness across proportions of lower-, middle-, and higher-income households is generally thought to affect neighborhoods positively. Some research suggests that the healthiest neighborhoods avoid high concentrations of extremes (wealth or poverty) and lower-income populations generally

---

3 "Transit-Supportive Densities and Land Uses," (Seattle, WA: Puget Sound Regional Council, February 2015), https://www.psrc.org/sites/default/files/tsdluguidancepaper.pdf.

4 Anne Vernez Moudon et al. "Operational Definitions of Walkable Neighborhood: Theoretical and Empirical Insights," *Journal of Physical Activity and Health*, 3 (1), (2006), 99-117.

benefit more from proximity to middle-income households than from proximity to high-income households.[5]

The criteria for selecting tracts initially included three primary measures of density and income mix and dozens of additional contextual measures. After the first thresholds proved either too limiting or misleading, however, we adjusted them (see Fig. 1) to identify at least one census tract in each metro area that appeared to describe the type of neighborhood we hoped to learn about.[6] In fact, the task of setting density and income mix thresholds for this analysis revealed that the thresholds used to frame some policy approaches are, perhaps not surprisingly, unreasonable for built environments in automobile-centric, lower-density, and weaker-market cities like Detroit and Memphis.

Across all selected metropolitan areas, under 1 percent of all tracts (0.6 percent, or 34 of 5,572) met the established thresholds for density and income mix.

To understand whether the 34 selected tracts were able to maintain a dense, mixed-income profile over time, we examined the 22 that met density and income mix thresholds in both 2000 and 2014 (in eight cases, comparisons over time were unavailable because the U.S. Census redrew tract boundaries during the time period). It is possible that significant shifts in population and/or demographics occurred in those places, but we cannot say without further research and analysis.

FINDINGS

Density/Income Mix

Just 34 tracts—or less than 1 percent of all tracts in the selected MSAs—exhibited both a high urban density and a balanced income mix, based on the most recent data available when this analysis was conducted. Of that number, more than half (19) are located in the East Bay area of the Oakland MSA.

---

5 Laura Tach et al., "Income Mixing across Scales: Rationale, Trends, Policies, Practice, and Research for More Inclusive Neighborhoods and Metropolitan Areas." (Washington, DC: What Works Collaborative and Urban Institute, January 2014), https://www.urban.org/sites/default/files/publication/22226/412998-income-mixing-across-scales-rationale-trends-policies-practice-and-research-for-more-inclusive-neighborhoods-and-metropolitan-areas.pdf.

6 In Oakland, only areas within the East Bay portion of the Oakland MSA were included. In Memphis, household density levels prevented any tracts from qualifying as dense mixed-income tracts, though they remained in the analysis.

Filtering for any one of the criteria yielded more tracts, however: about 9 percent of tracts met the density criterion of having at least 20 residents plus jobs per acre, and about 2 percent had at least 10 households per acre, while 62 percent of tracts met the income criterion of having at least 31 percent middle-income households and 24 percent had fewer than 20 percent of individuals below the poverty line. The universal density and poverty thresholds were more limiting than the middle-income threshold, which was contextual to each MSA.

While we were initially surprised by the small number of tracts meeting *all* criteria, their shared characteristics may offer valuable lessons for our understanding of the attainability of dense, mixed-income neighborhoods. For instance:

- The majority fall within the boundaries of the MSA's urban center, putting them near job centers, including central business districts, and anchor institutions like universities and hospitals.
- They are generally more racially/ethnically diverse than the MSAs in which they are located, measured by the Herfindahl Index of Race/Ethnicity. All—with the exception of one predominantly Black tract in Detroit and five predominantly Asian tracts in Oakland—are home to a predominant percentage of White residents, though the average percentage of White residents across qualifying tracts (56 percent) is lower than the national population average in 2014 (73 percent).
- Homeownership rates are lower, often by multiple measures, than homeownership rates nationwide and at the MSA level.
- These tracts contain a lower percentage of subsidized affordable housing than the average census tract, despite large percentages of households earning less than $25,000/year. In many cases they are geographically adjacent to tracts containing at least some subsidized affordable housing.
- In some cases, they comprise housing stock that is distinct from the surrounding tracts, such as high-rise apartments or townhomes in predominantly single-family metropolitan areas.

Stability of Density/Income Mix Over Time

The 22 "stable" tracts, i.e., those that met all density and income mix criteria in both 2000 and 2014, offer additional context for our understanding of mixed-income neighborhoods. They comprise just under two-thirds (64 percent) of all qualifying tracts, which suggests that stability of density and income mix is more attainable than not. From 2000 to 2014, on average, the stable tracts experienced the following trends:

- Job density increased from an average of 11.3 jobs/acre in 2002 to 13.6 jobs/acre in 2014.

- Household density decreased at a slower rate between 2000 and 2014 than in non-stable qualifying tracts (from an average of 14.5 households/acre in 2000 to 14.2 households/acre in 2014, compared to a change from 16.0 to 13.3 in non-stable tracts).

- The percentage of middle-income households earning between 50 percent and 120 percent AMI decreased, from an average of 56 percent in 2000 to 37 percent in 2014. Two tracts in Pittsburgh were the only areas in which this percentage increased.

- The average poverty rate in stable tracts remained below the rate in nonstable tracts, despite smaller decreases.

- The predominant racial composition remained the same in most tracts. The exceptions were in the East Bay Area of the Oakland MSA, where five measurable shifts occurred (twice from Black to White, twice from White to Asian, and once from Asian to White). The non-stable tracts did not see any shifts in the predominant racial composition, and no tracts shifted to Black, suggesting that that the Black presence and in-migration is largely excluded from these measures of stable, high-density, mixed-income communities.

- Homeownership rates remained generally stable at an average rate of 31 percent, although there does not appear to be a consistent trend at a tract-by-tract basis. Pittsburgh tracts were more likely to experience a decrease in homeownership, while Baltimore tracts were more likely to experience an increase in homeownership. Overall, homeownership rates in these tracts is less than half of the all-tract, eight-MSA average of 64 percent.

SUMMARY

Our analysis is predicated on the assumption that stable, high-density, mixed-income neighborhoods offer economic and quality-of-life benefits to those who live there—particularly to low-income residents. To that end, we explored how attainable it is for neighborhoods across the country to achieve strong urban densities and balanced income mixes over time. The short answer is that it is incredibly difficult for neighborhoods in large metropolitan areas to achieve these ideals, though neighborhoods that achieve them appear more likely to retain them than not—at least over the timespan of a decade and a half. And, perhaps not surprisingly, this less-than-one-percent of neighborhoods exhibit profiles that are relatively distinct from each other, reflecting their respective regions' economic and demographic trends more than their similarities. This uniqueness suggests that the most pragmatic policies to support dense, mixed-income, stable neighborhoods must be highly localized, at least in the short term. Those policies will need to explore how the national trends we observed are affected and can be changed by state, local, and hyper-local (i.e., neighborhood) dynamics. For instance, how can current and historic local zoning and housing policies explain why many mixed-income tracts are close to center cities, predominantly White, and limited in having subsidized housing in a particular place? We challenge practitioners and residents to seek to change those trends if they are deemed exclusionary while retaining long-term outcomes that recognize the potential benefits of density and income mix at the neighborhood level.

IMPLICATIONS FOR ACTION

Implications for Policy

Local, state, and national policies all play a role in the attainability of stable, dense, mixed-income communities. Local policymakers and neighborhood-level practitioners are the likely leaders in promoting attainability. These actors must work to understand the dynamics of density and income mixing in their communities and designate locally contextualized short- and long-term planning goals to improve them. Dynamic housing and zoning policies have the potential to yield highly accessible residential and job centers that offer residents tools to access economic mobility seem the most likely tools to further local density and income-mix goals. The most successful local policies will leverage local expertise and experience to take into account how factors such as race and ethnicity, property ownership dynamics, school quality, and other neighborhood features can work to best improve outcomes for residents, particularly low-income residents of color.

Implications for Research and Evaluation

We know that higher density and a balanced income mix can benefit residents across the income spectrum in a number of ways, but there are additional questions to explore. How have residents—specifically low-income residents of color—fared economically in comparison to the population at large in any one of the "stable, qualifying" tracts we analyzed? Why are homeownership rates so low in these tracts (compared to national/MSA trends), and what are the implications for how residents access opportunity in mixed-income areas while also gaining wealth and passing it on to future generations? Are homeownership rates simply lower in higher-density areas, and is this trend changing at all? How do these trends play out in other MSAs, and what can we learn from other cities that our analysis did not explore?

Implications for Development and Investment

We were surprised by the finding that many qualifying mixed-income tracts have low homeownership rates, relative to their MSAs, and lack subsidized affordable rental housing; we had assumed that the presence of these two housing metrics would contribute to income stability at the tract level. To some degree, this outcome could largely be a factor of the thresholds used in the analysis, as higher-density areas in the United States generally have low homeownership rates. However, we must recognize that resident turnover rates in these neighborhoods may be relatively high even as household economic measures remain steady. This set of findings also raises questions about the impact of subsidized rental housing on neighborhood stability. One development-related finding worth noting is that our qualitative research suggested that some of the dense, mixed-income tracts in this study appear to contain concentrations of housing that are unique to the metro areas in which they are located, including concentrations of cooperatives and high-rises in predominantly single-family metro areas. Developers and investors in affordable housing should seek to better understand the impacts of these relatively distinct housing structures on neighborhood trends and, where appropriate, create projects that offer residents neighborhood features that are unique at the metropolitan level.

Implications for Residents and Community Members

Residents and neighborhood-level practitioners in the 22 stable, mixed-income tracts identified through this analysis are encouraged to share how they perceive the changes in their communities in the past 20 years. Do their neighborhoods "feel" stable, and do residents perceive a benefit to the dense, mixed-income profile that we assume to be positive? Neighborhood-level practitioners and resident leaders elsewhere might look at how their neighborhood metrics compare to the density, income mix, and stability thresholds we used to conduct this analysis and discuss whether they offer direction or opportunity for their neighborhoods.

■ ■ ■

ELIZABETH LUTHER directs Capital Impact Partners' Detroit Program, leading its programmatic, policy, and research agenda in the city. The Program focuses on ensuring Detroit residents have access to the reinvestment activity taking place in their neighborhoods and the city as a whole. Most recently, Luther developed and launched the Equitable Development Initiative—an innovative program to support real estate developers of color investing in the city through training, technical assistance, and financing.

■ ■ ■

NOAH URBAN is Data Driven Detroit's Senior Analyst, tasked with managing projects, coordinating the analytical team, writing reports and blogs, and disseminating data and information. He has led projects with diverse partners including Microsoft Corporation, the U.S. Department of Health and Human Services, The Kresge Foundation, Forgotten Harvest, and Capital Impact Partners. Urban's past research efforts have focused on neighborhood change, understanding property conditions, and support mechanisms for local data intermediaries. He currently sits on the Executive Committee for the National Neighborhood Indicators Partnership.

■ ■ ■

STEPHANIE QUESNELLE is a Research Analyst at Data Driven Detroit, with a specialty on developing quantitative models to analyze data for projects. Prior to joining D3, she worked in a wide-range of analyst roles, including automotive marketing, the Department of Defense, think tanks, and academic research. Her research endeavors have included unemployment insurance programs, process improvements, mental health, early childhood development, incarceration of at-risk populations, and neighborhood change.

■ ■ ■

AYANA RUBIO is a Data Analyst at Data Driven Detroit, with a background in environmental research. At D3, Rubio provides mapping, GIS, and data support, and conducts much of the organization's health-focused research and data analysis.

MIXED-INCOME LIHTC DEVELOPMENTS IN CHICAGO: A FIRST LOOK AT THEIR INCOME CHARACTERISTICS AND SPILLOVER IMPACTS

Raphael Bostic
Federal Reserve Bank of Atlanta

Andrew Jakabovics
Enterprise Community Partners

Richard Voith
Econsult Solutions

Sean Zielenbach
SZ Consulting

Many policymakers and practitioners have embraced mixed-income housing as a key component of neighborhood stabilization and revitalization. Such developments ensure that high-quality housing remains available for low-income residents while also helping to attract more affluent, often more politically and socially connected individuals to the community. At least theoretically, the mix of enhanced social networks, increased social capital, and increased purchasing power can benefit existing residents and attract additional investment and economic activity to the area.

Most of the research on mixed-income development has focused on HOPE VI, Choice Neighborhoods, and other developments where income mixing was a deliberate goal. At the same time, many other residential developments do not have an explicit income mixing aim yet provide high-quality housing for households across multiple income levels. For example, a substantial proportion of properties financed in part with equity associated with the federal Low-Income Housing Tax Credit (LIHTC) contain a mix of market-rate and subsidized units. In Chicago alone, more than 19 percent of all LIHTC-financed developments for non-elderly households contain at least five units that are not subsidized and therefore are targeted for market-rate, presumably moderate-income or more affluent households.[1] Unlike most HOPE VI and Choice Neighborhood developments, which are specifically designed to attract residents across a variety of income levels, LIHTC properties are developed primarily to create or preserve affordable housing for low-income people. Rarely is income mixing an explicit aim.

Little research exists on the extent of income mixing within LIHTC properties, even though there are far more of this type of mixed-income property than HOPE VI or Choice Neighborhoods developments. Nationally, there are 259 HOPE VI developments containing nearly 100,000 units. There are more than 10,000 LIHTC properties throughout the country (24 percent of all such developments) that contain both subsidized and market-rate units.[2] In Chicago alone, 83 LIHTC properties have at least 5 market-rate units, and these developments contain an average of 130 units apiece (about 10,750 in aggregate).[3] For those interested in mixed-income developments, it therefore makes sense to examine more closely the characteristics of these LIHTC properties. To what extent is there a mix of incomes within the LIHTC complexes? Is it realistic to expect properties without an explicit mixed-income focus to create and sustain mixed-income communities?

More broadly, LIHTC developments frequently serve as important components of a neighborhood stabilization and revitalization strategy. It is important to understand whether LIHTC properties with larger proportions of market-rate units have greater catalytic spillover neighborhood impacts than those that contain almost exclusively subsidized units. Multiple studies have found that mixed-income HOPE VI developments have had positive spillover effects on

---

1 "LIHTC Database Access," U.S. Department of Housing and Urban Development, http://lihtc.huduser.gov.

2 Kirk McClure, "What Should Be the Future of the Low-Income Housing Tax Credit Program," *Housing Policy Debate* 29, no. 1 (2019), https://doi.org/10.1080/10511482.2018.1469526.

3 "LIHTC Database Access," U.S. Department of Housing and Urban Development, http://lihtc.huduser.gov.

surrounding housing prices, public safety, and private investment.[4] There also is a growing body of research documenting the generally positive effects of LIHTC developments on surrounding home prices.[5] It remains unclear, however, whether and to what extent a mixed-income development makes a measurable difference in the dynamics of its surrounding community. None of the studies has focused specifically on the mixed-income character of the HOPE VI or LIHTC development and its relative importance in bringing about the observed change. It is quite possible, for instance, that the observed spillover benefits resulted primarily from the replacement of poor-quality properties or vacant lots with new or significantly rehabilitated, more fully occupied, and often better-managed developments, regardless of the actual mix of incomes among the buildings' residents.

Our study aims to help fill this gap. We focus on LIHTC properties in the city of Chicago to identify the extent of income mixing in the developments, the role of local market conditions in determining that mix, and the relative impact of mixed-income versus fully subsidized properties on surrounding property values. We consider differences between LIHTC developments in relatively strong and weak local markets. Chicago's LIHTC developments tend to be located in more economically distressed communities, i.e., those with persistently high rates of poverty and unemployment. Residents of the

---

[4] See, for example, Mindy Turbov and Valerie Piper, "HOPE VI and Mixed-Finance Redevelopments: A Catalyst for Neighborhood Renewal," Discussion paper prepared for the Brookings Institution Metropolitan Policy Program, 2005; Edward Bair and John M. Fitzgerald, "Hedonic Estimation and Policy Significance of the Impact of HOPE VI on Neighborhood Property Values," *Review of Policy Research* 22, no. 6 (2005); Nina Castells, "HOPE VI Neighborhood Spillover Effects in Baltimore," *Cityscape* 12, no.1 (2010), doi: 10.2139/ssrn.1585386; Sean Zielenbach, Richard Voith, and Michael Mariano, "Estimating the Local Economic Impacts of HOPE VI," *Housing Policy Debate* 20, no. 3 (2010); William Cloud and Susan Roll, "Denver Housing Authority's Park Avenue HOPE VI Project: Community Impact Results," *Housing Policy Debate* 21, no. 2 (2011), https://doi.org/10.1080/10511482.2011.567288.

[5] See, for example, Michael H. Schill et al. "Revitalizing Inner-City Neighborhoods: New York City's Ten-Year Plan," *Housing Policy Debate* 13, no. 3 (2002), doi: 10.1080/10511482.2002.9521454; Amy Ellen Schwartz et al. "The External Effects of Place-Based Subsidized Housing," (Working paper 05-02, The Furman Center For Real Estate and Urban Policy, 2005); Amy Ellen Schwartz et al. "The Impact of Subsidized Housing Investment on New York City's Neighborhoods," (Working paper 06-02, The Furman Center For Real Estate and Urban Policy, 2006); Amy Armstrong et al. "The Impact of Low Income Tax Credit Housing on Surrounding Neighborhoods: Evidence from New York City," (Working Paper 07-02," The Furman Center For Real Estate and Urban Policy, 2007); Ingrid Gould Ellen et al. "Does Federally Subsidized Rental Housing Depress Neighborhood Property Values?" *Journal of Policy Analysis and Management* 26, no. 2 (2007), doi: 10.1002/pam.20247; Cheryl Young, "There Doesn't Go the Neighborhood: Low-Income Housing Has No Impact on Nearby Home Values," *Trulia.com* (blog), November 16, 2016; https://www.trulia.com/blog/trends/low-income-housing/; and Rebecca Diamond and Timothy McQuade, "Who Wants Affordable Housing in Their Back Yard? An Equilibrium Analysis of Low-Income Property Development," (Working Paper, National Bureau of Economic Research, 2016), RePEc:nbr:nberwo:22204.

neighborhoods containing LIHTC properties tend to be predominantly African American or Hispanic/Latinx. To the extent that mixed-income LIHTC properties can increase local property values and ultimately help attract additional investment and amenities to the areas, they can simultaneously help improve the quality of life for existing residents while making the communities more appealing to external investors.

Our analysis employs a mix of quantitative and qualitative methods, combining rigorous statistical analyses with in-depth interviews of key local developers, community leaders, and investors. Unlike many mixed-income analyses that focus on the characteristics of the people living in the developments and the benefits they may receive from such residence, we are concerned primarily with the interaction between mixed-income properties and local market dynamics. We start with a brief overview of the LIHTC program and how it has evolved within the city of Chicago. We then explore the demographic composition in a representative sample of LIHTC properties throughout the city and the factors contributing to those socio-economic patterns. Following this predominantly qualitative analysis, we pivot to a more quantitative assessment of the effects that different LIHTC properties have on surrounding property values. We augment the statistical study with brief case studies of selected neighborhoods that have a meaningful concentration of LIHTC properties; these provide a more nuanced understanding of the specific local factors that can enhance or hinder properties' spillover impacts. Finally, we discuss the policy and research ramifications of our findings.

A BRIEF OVERVIEW OF THE LIHTC PROGRAM

Established as part of the Tax Reform Act of 1986, the Low-Income Housing Tax Credit provides investors in affordable housing projects with federal tax credits equal to either 9 percent or 4 percent of the project's total eligible costs.[6] Investors can claim the credit each year for 10 years, provided that the project remains in compliance with various program regulations. The equity that the credits incentivize can support up to 70 percent of a project's total costs, significantly reducing the developer's financing expenses and enabling

---

6   The value of the credit depends primarily on the type of project being financed; in general, new construction projects can qualify for the 9 percent credits, while rehabilitation or preservation projects tend to obtain 4 percent credits.

it to maintain low rents for the property's tenants. The credits are allocated to individual projects in a competitive process administered by state housing finance agencies and cost the federal government approximately $9 billion per year.[7] LIHTC-financed properties currently account for about 90 percent of the affordable rental housing created throughout the country.[8] Through mid-2016, more than 46,500 LIHTC-financed projects containing 3.05 million units had been placed in service throughout the country.[9]

To be eligible for LIHTCs, a property must restrict rents so that (a) at least 20 percent of its units are affordable to households earning 50 percent or less of the respective area median income (AMI), adjusted by household size or (b) at least 40 percent of units are affordable to households earning no more than 60 percent of AMI. Affordability is defined as rent equaling no more than 30 percent of the threshold income level. The developer must select one of these eligibility thresholds at the outset and abide by it throughout the whole credit period. In each case, the LIHTC equity subsidizes the income-restricted units.

A 2018 legislative change to program rules now allows developers to select a third income eligibility option—permitting tenants earning up to 80 percent of AMI to be included in the project's affordability calculations, which implicitly encourages a broader mix of tenant incomes within the projects. Under the new rules, at least 40 percent of units have to be affordable to households whose *average* income is at or below 60 percent of AMI, with no tenant's income exceeding 80 percent of AMI. Again, the developer must select the income averaging option when applying for the credits. Given the newness of this option, it does not apply to any of the properties we have analyzed; therefore, none of the properties in our study include units whose rents are restricted for households earning up to 80 percent of AMI.

According to the U.S. Department of Housing and Urban Development (HUD), about 71 percent of existing LIHTC projects are located in high-

---

[7] Mark P. Keightley, "An Introduction to the Low Income Housing Tax Credit," 2018, https://fas.org/sgp/crs/misc/RS22389.pdf.

[8] "Low-Income Housing Tax Credit," Illinois Housing Development Authority, https://www.ihda.org/developers/tax-credits/low-income-tax-credit/.

[9] "Low-Income Housing Tax Credits," U.S. Department of Housing and Urban Development, https://www.huduser.gov/portal/datasets/lihtc.html.

poverty neighborhoods, and about 77 percent are in neighborhoods with high proportions of minority residents. Such concentrations are logical results of the program's rules, which increase the amount of LIHTCs available (130 percent of total eligible costs instead of 100) to projects in difficult development areas or qualified census tracts—typically areas that suffer from severe economic distress and have large proportions of racial or ethnic minorities.

While the program's regulations allow for a significant proportion of the units in a given LIHTC development to be rented at market rate, the vast majority of LIHTC-financed units historically have benefited low- and very low-income households. A 2013 analysis of 12,228 LIHTC projects in 16 different states—properties collectively containing more than 760,000 units—found that 93 percent of the units were occupied by households earning 60 percent or less of the prevailing AMI. Moreover, 40 percent of the units provided housing for extremely low-income households, those earning 30 percent or less of AMI. Still, 7 percent of the units went to households earning at least 61 percent of AMI and thus presumably did not count toward the income eligibility threshold.[10]

As we highlight below in our discussion of LIHTC properties in Chicago, some of the more recently developed LIHTC projects have higher proportions of market-rate units. The Illinois Housing Development Authority and other state and local housing authorities increasingly are factoring neighborhood dynamics into their allocation decisions, giving applicant projects additional points for their ability to contribute to broader neighborhood redevelopment strategies. This can potentially give more weight to projects in slightly stronger markets where other development activity is underway, and where market rents are high enough to make it financially worthwhile for a developer to include some market-rate units in the LIHTC property. Because of allocators' shifting geographic priorities and developers' ability under the new income averaging option to incorporate a wider range of tenant incomes in individual properties, an analysis of LIHTC tenant incomes and property spillover effects is both relevant and timely.

---

[10] "What Can We Learn about the Low Income Housing Tax Credit Program by Looking at the Tenants?" (Policy Brief, The Moelis Institute for Affordable Housing, New York University, 2012), http://furmancenter.org/files/publications/LIHTC_Final_Policy_Brief_v2.pdf.

CHARACTERISTICS OF LIHTC PROPERTIES IN CHICAGO

LIHTC developments in Chicago initially focused almost exclusively on housing low-income residents. Throughout much of the 1990s, nonprofit organizations developed or co-developed the vast majority of LIHTC properties in the city, designating virtually all of the units as "affordable" housing. Of the large LIHTC properties put into service in the city prior to 1998 (those with 100 or more units), only 7 percent had unsubsidized, "market rent" units. [11]

With the beginning of the federal HOPE VI program in 1992 and the national emphasis on de-concentrating poverty, mixed-income housing became somewhat more prevalent in Chicago. A key element of the Chicago Housing Authority's Plan for Transformation (launched in 1999) entailed demolishing multi-story public housing high-rises that had been occupied solely by extremely low-income households and replacing them with developments targeting three different types of tenants. One-third of the units would be set aside for public housing residents, another third would be reserved for other low-income residents (those below 60 percent of the area median income), and the remaining third would be priced and targeted for market-rate households.

Concurrently, many housing developers in Chicago concluded that concentrating exclusively low-income residents in LIHTC projects in lower-income neighborhoods depressed the communities' revitalization potential. Some of these developers began to include a greater mix of incomes within newly developed and rehabilitated properties. This incorporated some market-rate units in LIHTC and other affordable housing properties and provided low-income but upwardly mobile individuals whose incomes increased over time with an opportunity to remain in and stabilize the properties and the surrounding communities. The approach also provided moderate-income households with an affordable, high-quality housing option. (LIHTC regulations permit resident households whose incomes rise above 140 percent of AMI to remain in the property as long as the next available unit in the development goes to an income-eligible household—i.e., one earning 60 percent or less of AMI.)

---

11 The LIHTC data came from three sources: HUD's "LIHTC Database Access," U.S. Department of Housing and Urban Development, http://lihtc.huduser.gov/; "Low-Income Housing Tax Credit: Previously Approved Projects," The Illinois Housing Development Authority, https://www.ihda.org/developers/tax-credits/low-income-tax-credit/; and "Multi-family production," The Illinois Housing Development Authority, https://www.ihda.org/wp-content/uploads/2015/07/mfproductionApril2016.xls.

Subsequent events have increased the incentives for developers to include market-rate units. The collapse of the subprime mortgage market in the late 2000s forced many previous homeowners back into the rental market, driving up demand and thus market rents in many areas. This coincided with increasing affluence—and increased demand for market-rate housing—in some Chicago neighborhoods.[12] As part of its support for the Chicago Housing Authority's Plan for Transformation, the Illinois Housing Development Authority created a $3 million annual set-aside for developers of mixed-income projects.[13]

There are also some technical explanations for the increasing proportion of market-rate units in LIHTC developments. HUD changed the basis for its calculation of area median incomes, relying on annual American Community Survey data instead of extrapolations from the decennial census; during the great recession, this had the effect of lowering AMIs and thus reducing the rent that could be charged on the subsidized units. Furthermore, developers have to include a utility allowance in their determination of rents. The method for computing the allowance was based primarily on older, less energy-efficient properties, which often over-estimated the actual utility cost and thus further reduced the amount of rent that could be charged for the subsidized properties. Taken together, these latter two figures lowered the available income from the subsidized units and led more developers to explore the feasibility of including more market-rate units in the properties.[14]

Because of these factors, nearly half of the large new and rehabilitated LIHTC properties placed in service in Chicago since 1998 have contained at least some market-rate units. Overall, however, the proportion of market-rate units remains low. As indicated in Table 1, only 83 of the 430 non-elderly LIHTC properties placed in service from 1987 to 2016 (19.3 percent) contained five or more market-rate units.[15] Within those properties, market-rate units comprise

---

12 "Appendix: The Socioeconomic Change of Chicago's Community Areas (1970-2010)." Natalie P. Voorhees Center for Neighborhood and Community Improvement, http://voorheescenter.red.uic.edu/wp-content/uploads/sites/122/2107/10/Voorhees-Center-Gentrification-index-Oct-14.pdf.

13 Amy Khare, "Privatizing Chicago: The Politics of Urban Redevelopment in Public Housing Reforms," (PhD diss., University of Chicago, 2016), https://pqdtopen.proquest.com/doc/1799650562.html?FMT=ABS.

14 Jerry Ascierto, "Low-Cost Housing a Challenge for Midwest Developers," Affordable Housing Finance, last modified October 1, 2007, https://www.housingfinance.com/news/low-cost-housing-a-challenge-for-midwest-developers_o.

15 We have chosen five units as an effective threshold because that number suggests that the developer/project sponsor deliberately elected to include market-rate rental units in the property. A much larger number of

	ALL DEVELOPMENTS	PROPERTIES WITH 5+ MARKET-RATE UNITS	PROPERTIES WITH <5 MARKET-RATE UNITS	COOK COUNTY OVERALL
Number of Properties	430	83	347	
Average Number of Units	94	130	85	
% Market-Rate Units	7%	27%	0.2%	
Tract Median HH Income	$29,861	$32,071	$29,306	$52,827
Tract Median Vacancy Rate	13%	12%	14%	9%
Tract Median Poverty Rate	33%	31%	34%	15%
Tract Median % African American*	53.9%	63.8%	54.2%	6.0%
Tract Median Contract Rent	$745	$765	$739	$986
Tract Median Home Value	$184,500	$202,350	$181,500	$202,500

Note: Census tract data are based on American Community Survey 2012-2016 five-year estimates.
*The proportions in the subset of tracts are greater than the universe as a whole because 33 tracts contain both "mixed-income" and "conventional" LIHTC properties.

Table 1: Key Characteristics of Cook County LIHTC Properties for Non-Senior Citizens

an aggregate 27 percent of all units. In the most "mixed" of those properties, 80 percent of the units are designated as market-rate.

As Table 1 illustrates, Chicago-area LIHTC properties tend to be located in very low-income, predominantly African-American neighborhoods (see also map on next page). These communities have notably fewer moderate and middle-income households than other neighborhoods throughout Cook County. They also tend to have relatively weak real estate markets. Median contract rents in census tracts with LIHTC properties are more than 24 percent lower than the median rent for the county as a whole.

---

properties have set aside one or two ostensibly market-rate units for the property/building manager and/or office space.

What is the Current Landscape for Mixed-Income Strategies?

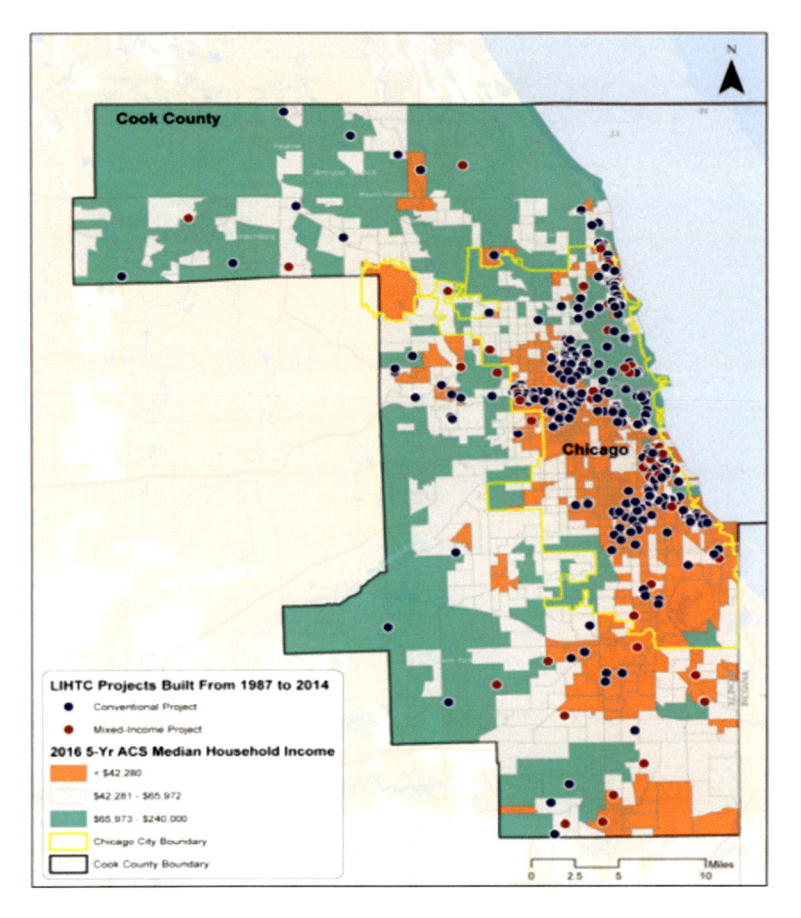

Figure 1. LIHTC Projects Built from 1987 to 2014

Tenants in Subsidized LIHTC Units

As illustrated in the following representative examples, the income levels of lower-income tenants within Chicago-area LIHTC properties vary somewhat by the location of the property and the particular emphasis of the developer.[16]

For example, the Holsten Real Estate Development Corporation owns

---

16 Because there is no single repository of property-level LIHTC tenant income data, we had to obtain that information from individual developers and property managers. Some had the information and were willing to make it available, while others did not. Those who had the information generally had it only for tenants in the subsidized units, since they have to verify those incomes for LIHTC compliance purposes. While our tenant income data are thus inherently incomplete, our conversations with local developers gave us confidence that the data generally reflect income trends in LIHTC properties throughout the market.

multiple LIHTC properties in moderate- to middle-income neighborhoods within Chicago. In large part because of the higher resident incomes in those communities, the tenants in its subsidized units tend to be earning close to the LIHTC income limit (60 percent of AMI). Local market dynamics enable the properties to accept less-poor but still qualifying low-income tenants.

The nonprofit Bickerdike Redevelopment Corporation owns and manages several LIHTC developments in West Town and Logan Square, two near-Northwest Side neighborhoods that suffered from years of economic distress but that have experienced considerable gentrification in the past 10-15 years. Most of Bickerdike's LIHTC tenants qualify as very low-income. Four-fifths make less than $30,000 annually, and 59 percent make less than $20,000 per year. The organization deliberately sets rents so they are affordable for households at or below 50 percent of AMI. Such tenants include many older individuals who are aging in place, as well as a fair number of people working low-wage and/or part-time jobs; many of these workers saw their incomes drop dramatically during the recession. Of course, this effort to target lower-income individuals has not come without costs. Bickerdike has had to search for various types of subsidies in order to support tenants earning 30 percent or less of AMI. One approach has been to convert some buildings to project-based Section 8 developments (instead of having housing vouchers subsidize individual tenant households); this is a complicated process that often necessitates re-financing the property, among other things.

Particularly in the region's very low-income communities, tenant incomes in LIHTC-financed properties often have been much lower than the properties' developers initially anticipated. Consider the properties that Brinshore, a for-profit development firm, owns and manages in West Haven (directly west of downtown) and in Grand Boulevard (south of downtown). Financed with a mix of HOPE VI, LIHTC, and federal Neighborhood Stabilization Partnership funds, the properties were designed primarily to provide affordable housing for households making 30 percent to 60 percent of AMI. The firm estimated that more than 75 percent of tenants would fall within this income range and about 20 percent would earn more than 60 percent of AMI. In actuality, the majority of residents earn 30 percent or less of AMI, and only 13 percent make more than 60 percent of AMI. Most tenants in these and other LIHTC properties the firm manages are Section 8 voucher holders, who tend to be extremely low-income. Property managers are "inundated with applications" for the

INCOME LEVEL	INITIAL ESTIMATES	ACTUAL PROPORTION
< 30% AMI	3.9%	55.7%
31-50% AMI	40.2%	22%
51-60%	36.3%	9.3%
> 60% (includes market rate)	19.7%	13%

Note: Proportions are based on tenant data as of mid-2016.

Table 2: Projected Versus Actual Income Mix in Selected Brinshore LIHTC Properties

properties, but virtually all of the applications come from very poor individuals and households; few applicants have high enough incomes to qualify for the properties' market-rate units.

Based on our conversations with LIHTC developers, lenders, and allocators in Chicago, the for-profit firm's experience is typical of LIHTC developments in the city's distressed neighborhoods. Except in relatively well-off communities, tenants in the subsidized units frequently are not earning close to the maximum income level (60 percent of AMI). In the most distressed neighborhoods, it is often challenging to find renters earning 60 percent of AMI; most earn 50 percent or less.

To a large extent, the explanation for low tenant income levels lies in changing regional economic dynamics. As one developer explains, the lower middle class in Chicago "has been gutted." The minimum wage currently equates to about 30 percent of AMI, so a person earning 60 percent of AMI needs to make about twice the minimum wage. Yet many of those better paying jobs no longer exist. Technological advancements eliminated many jobs that did not require high skill levels but paid up to $20 or $25 per hour, including many of the positions held by less-educated middle- and lower-middle-class workers. And the market simply is not replacing those jobs in the city, according to officials working to promote development in Chicago's low-income neighborhoods. As a result, ostensibly affordable rents are still quite a stretch for many LIHTC tenants.

Market-Rate Units in LIHTC Properties

The flip side is that the low real estate values in many LIHTC neighborhoods make the properties' market-rate units quite affordable. "Market rents" in many LIHTC properties are significantly lower than the citywide average but are still a bit higher than the contract rent charged for the properties' subsidized units. Consider two representative properties in the State Street corridor on the South Side. Park Boulevard contains a mix of affordable and market-rate apartments and condominiums between 35th and 37th Streets, on the site of the former Stateway Gardens public housing property. Further south in Grand Boulevard, on the site of the former Robert Taylor Homes public housing complex, Legends South consists of five separate mixed-income apartment complexes between 38th and 44th Streets. A market-rate two-bedroom apartment in Park Boulevard rents for $1,200 per month, about $200 more than the rent for a subsidized apartment in the property. Market-rate one-bedroom units in Legends South rent for $935 per month. While this is one-third higher than the $695 charged for a subsidized "affordable" unit, it is well below the $1,500 going rent for similar apartments elsewhere on the South Side. Farther south, in the historically distressed Washington Park neighborhood, three-bedroom units in LIHTC properties developed by the St. Edmund's Redevelopment Corporation (SERC) rent for $1,000 to $1,200 monthly.[17] For all practical purposes, "market rate" LIHTC units in these areas are simply "unsubsidized" or "non-income-restricted" units.

Not surprisingly, the market-rate tenants in these and similar LIHTC properties are not significantly better off financially than their neighbors living in subsidized units. The market-rate tenants in the Grand Boulevard and Washington Park properties, for instance, are much more likely to earn about 70 percent of AMI than 100 percent of AMI or more. Those tenants tend to be city employees, public transit workers, health care providers, post office employees, and other moderate-wage workers who are looking for high-quality housing at bargain prices. There are basically three categories of tenants at SERC's properties in Washington Park: individuals on fixed incomes who do not have any additional subsidies, working people with modest incomes, and Section 8 voucher holders. Those in the first and second groups can find a better market-rate apartment in SERC's LIHTC developments than they could elsewhere in Chicago.

Because the market-rate rents at most LIHTC properties are substantially lower than those at comparable properties elsewhere in the city, it is relatively easy for the LIHTC properties to attract tenants for their market-rate units.

---

17 Rents are as of mid-2016.

The units in Brinshore's Westhaven properties, for instance, rent for about $1.50 per square foot, whereas other new apartments in more affluent areas near downtown rent for more than $3 per square foot. On a larger unit, the difference in monthly rent can be more than $2,500. Brinshore's apartments are attractive, come with free parking, central air conditioning, and a washing machine and dryer in each unit, and are in close proximity to downtown and to the Rush Presbyterian Medical Center. Moreover, they represent some of the only relatively new rental units in the city's low-income, predominantly African-American neighborhoods. As the city continues to recover from the recession, rents in many of its more affluent and middle-income areas are climbing. For moderate-income households, high-quality housing in a LIHTC or other mixed-income development proves very appealing.

Whether a mixed-income property in a lower-income community remains mixed-income ultimately depends on the willingness of market-rate tenants to stay. One important factor is the quality of the property's management. Each of the LIHTC developers with whom we spoke emphasized the importance of good ongoing management in maintaining the quality of a building, attracting and retaining good tenants, and generating positive spillover benefits for its community. Good management begins with screening potential tenants. Property managers can conduct criminal background checks of prospective residents, and they often require tenants to be drug-free and either employed or attending school. The managers set and enforce rules of tenant behavior, and they are ultimately responsible for a property's physical and social condition.

Managing a property well is not easy, especially in buildings where many of the subsidized tenants have significant personal and family challenges. One developer emphasizes that "property management is very hard work, and the people doing it tend to be underpaid and undervalued." Keeping track of the qualifications and requirements of various rental subsidy programs can be difficult. "You're asking $14-an-hour employees to understand a lot of data, a lot of different layers, a lot of different reporting requirements, and a very complicated rent structure," notes a senior official at a regional property management company.

Perhaps not surprisingly, there is a fair amount of burnout and turnover among property-level personnel, which can lead to a decline in the quality of the on-site management. One developer we interviewed believes that "people get lax and less careful, and they therefore let more problematic people in and/

or don't enforce rules as diligently as they should." As standards for property maintenance and tenant behavior slip, a property can lose its luster. For developers and property management companies, figuring out how to train, support, and retain effective property managers is an ongoing concern.

In numerous LIHTC properties with a mix of subsidized and unsubsidized units, turnover among market-rate tenants tends to be lower than that among tenants in subsidized units. Within our sample, the turnover rate has been about 10 percent for market-rate units and 15 percent for the units designated as affordable. Part of the difference results from a larger proportion of tenants in the subsidized units being evicted for nonpayment of rent. Many voucher holders still struggle to come up with their required payment (set at 30 percent of their adjusted gross income), in part because they end up using their budgeted rent monies to cover other needs.

At the same time, certain properties struggle to attract and retain market-rate tenants because of the dynamics in their surrounding neighborhoods. Brinshore's Westhaven Park development is located on the site of the former Henry Horner Homes, a notoriously dangerous public housing complex. While crime in the area has declined significantly since Horner's demolition, the gangs that operated out of Horner have not left the area, and many gang members retain strong family and other ties with Westhaven Park residents. Consequently, many people still perceive Westhaven to be Horner and associate it with the public housing property's various problems. While the property is much improved from a physical perspective, crime remains a major concern—one that makes it challenging to fill the complex's market-rate units. Prospective homebuyers and market-rate renters look at Westhaven as a more affordable alternative to the hot West Loop market, but then read about the shootings that occur within the community and have second thoughts.

In short, the incomes of tenants in LIHTC properties reflect the socio-economic characteristics of the communities where the properties are located. Tenant incomes in LIHTC properties tend to be somewhat higher in gentrifying and more affluent neighborhoods than in persistently poor communities. Developers in the former areas are better able to attract tenants close to 60 percent of AMI for the properties' subsidized but non-targeted units,[18] and they generally

---

18 We are distinguishing here between subsidized units with no income targeting (i.e., < 60 percent of AMI) and those specifically targeted for households further down the income ladder (< 30 percent or < 50 per-

can charge higher rents—and therefore attract more moderate- and middle-income households—for any market-rate units in the properties. In contrast, the difference between the LIHTC rents and the market rents in weaker-market neighborhoods is not that great. For all practical purposes, "market rate" in these areas simply means "unsubsidized" or "non-income-restricted." To the extent that there is income mixing within these communities' LIHTC properties, it is among low, very low, and extremely low-income tenants. "Mixed-income" LIHTC developments therefore are not bringing much socio-economic diversity and affluence to low-income communities.

The weakness of these latter real estate markets threatens the financial viability of mixed-income properties. The prevailing market rent often is less than the cost of operating and maintaining the unit; only in "hot" real estate markets is the rent on LIHTC market-rate units close to what it costs to develop and maintain the units. The LIHTC subsidy covers about 70 percent of the costs of the affordable units but does not cover any of the cost of the market-rate units. As a result, LIHTC market rate rents in economically distressed neighborhoods are "total economic losers," in the words of an affordable housing lender with extensive experience in the city's low-income neighborhoods. In the weakest markets, a property's affordable units are effectively subsidizing the market-rate units, not the other way around.

SPILLOVER EFFECTS OF MIXED-INCOME LIHTC PROPERTIES

The presence of market-rate units within most Chicago LIHTC properties generally does not result in a broad mix of tenant incomes. But from a broader community stabilization and development perspective, is there a benefit to having market-rate units and tenants in the properties? To address this question, we considered the spillover impacts of the 430 non-senior citizen LIHTC developments that were put into service in Cook County between 1987 and 2016. We then segmented that universe of properties into two subsets: the 83 properties with 5 or more market-rate units, and the 347 other developments. We characterize the former group as the "mixed-income" LIHTC properties—or, perhaps more accurately, given the observed tenant incomes in the sample of properties discussed above, the partially subsidized properties.

---

cent of AMI, for instance). Qualified Allocation Plans often give developers additional points for targeting a portion of their units to very low- or extremely low-income households.

Methodology

To measure changes in neighborhood conditions, we focused on differences in housing price trends within certain distance bands from the LIHTC property (0–1/8 mile, 1/8–1/4 mile, and 1/4–1/2 mile). While it is impossible to capture neighborhood dynamics in a single variable, residential property values serve as a useful proxy for assessing the extent of resident and investor confidence in an area and thus both its near-term desirability and its perceived longer-term economic prospects.[19] We obtained information on all home sales in Cook County from 1997 to 2016 from DataQuick Information Systems, geocoded the properties, and determined their distance from nearby LIHTC properties. (Many of the homes that changed hands are located within half a mile of multiple LIHTC properties.)

To assess the impact of LIHTC developments on surrounding property values, we employed a modified interrupted time series approach within the aforementioned distance bands. We compared housing price trends in the years prior to the completion of the LIHTC property with the trends subsequent to the property's completion. To account for the clustering of LIHTC developments in many Chicago neighborhoods (and the resulting influence of multiple such developments on the sale price of a single home), we included a post-development variable for each LIHTC property placed in service within a given distance band, as well as a temporal variable to reflect the number of years between the completion of the original and subsequent LIHTC property (or properties).

We also incorporated census tract and property characteristic effects in our model. Certain factors (neighborhood income and racial composition, for instance) can overwhelm a housing price trend analysis, and it is impossible both to identify and control for the multitude of neighborhood- and property-specific factors that can affect prices. In essence, our model accounts for differences in home sizes and types, neighborhood socio-economic conditions, and other particular local amenities. To get at differences across certain types of neighborhoods, we ultimately stratified our sample by census tract median income as well as by the tract's proportion of African-American residents.

---

19 Sean Zielenbach, Richard Voith, and Michael Mariano, "Estimating the Local Economic Impacts of HOPE VI."

We then applied our model to the highest and lowest third of tracts within each category.[20]

Overall LIHTC Price Effects

In general, the introduction of a LIHTC development into a Chicago neighborhood has had a positive, statistically significant effect on local property values. Prior to any LIHTC property being placed in service, values within one-eighth mile of the site were about 6.7 percent lower than the Cook County average. Once the development went into service, surrounding values increased by 10.8 percentage points relative to the county average, so that they were about 4.1 percent higher than average post-development. The property value impacts dissipated over distance. Home prices up to one-quarter mile from the LIHTC development increased by 10.3 percentage points relative to the county, while properties up to one-half mile away increased in value by only 4 percentage points. These findings are outlined in Table 3.

Far from depressing surrounding home prices, the development of subsequent LIHTC properties further boosted local prices. For example, the introduction of a second LIHTC property increased prices within the one-eighth to one-fourth-mile band by another 1.5 percentage points. In other words, the first property increased prices by 10.3 points relative to the county average, and the second property increased values by 11.8 points. The introduction of a third LIHTC property boosted those values by another 3.6 points, so post-development values were 15.4 percentage points higher than their values prior to the initial LIHTC development.[21]

As indicated in Table 3, "mixed-income" LIHTC developments—those containing at least five market-rate units—have had a greater effect on surrounding home prices than more "conventional" LIHTC properties, those with four or fewer market-rate apartments. The price benefits of the

---

20 In our segmentation, high-income tracts are those with median household incomes of $65,972 or more. Low-income tracts have median incomes of $42,280 or less. "High African-American neighborhoods are those where African Americans comprise 26 percent or more of the tract's residents. Low African-American neighborhoods have 3 percent or fewer African-American residents. An extended discussion of the model, as well as the results of the various regressions, can be found in "Too Much of a Good Thing? The Effects of Concentrated LIHTC Development on Surrounding House Prices," forthcoming.

21 Because of the relatively small number of cases in which there are three or more LIHTC developments within one-eighth mile of each other, we combined the 1/8 and 1/4 mile bands in the analysis of the price impacts of three or more LIHTC developments.

# OF LIHTC PROPERTIES	DISTANCE BAND	ALL LIHTC PROPERTIES	"MIXED-INCOME" LIHTC PROPERTIES	"CONVENTIONAL" LIHTC PROPERTIES
1	0–1/8 mile	.108 ****	.148	.108 ****
	1/8–1/4 mile	.103 ****	.119 **	.104 ****
	1/4–1/2 mile	.040 **	.061	.044 *
2	0–1/8 mile	.122 ****	.200 ***	.114 ***
	1/8–1/4 mile	.118 ****	.163 ***	.114 ****
	1/4–1/2 mile	.048 **	.058	.054 *
3 or more	0–1/4 mile	.154 ****	.115	.172 ****
	1/4–1/2 mile	.077 **	.075	.085 ***

**** significant at .001 level; *** significant at .01 level; ** significant at .05 level; * significant at .10 level
Note: Within certain distance bands, the price effects associated with each type of property are greater than the overall price effects. This results from the fact that some communities have both "mixed-income" and "conventional" properties within a short distance of each other.

Table 3: Observed House Price Changes, Pre-Versus Post- Development, Resulting From Various LIHTC Properties

"mixed-income" properties have been greatest in closest proximity to the developments. Within one-eighth mile of a LIHTC property, the marginal price benefit of a "mixed-income" property was 4 percentage points greater than a "conventional" property (.148 versus .108). In areas with two "mixed-income" properties, the marginal price benefit was even greater: 8.6 percentage points (.200 versus .114). Moreover, the aggregate effect on home prices increased with the introduction of a second "mixed-income" development—a gain of 5.2 percentage points within one-eighth mile of the two properties (.200 versus .148). With the introduction of a third "mixed-income" property, the positive impact disappears. We caution against placing too much weight on this finding, however, since there were very few cases in which three or more "mixed-income" LIHTC properties are closely clustered geographically.

Effects across Different Neighborhoods

In many cases, LIHTC developments in Chicago either have converted a vacant lot into a residential property or transformed a deteriorating building into more productive use. Therefore, it was not surprising to find that LIHTC properties developed in the city between 1987 and 2016 generally have had positive,

# OF LIHTC PROPERTIES	DISTANCE BAND	"MIXED-INCOME" LIHTC—HIGH INCOME AREAS	"CONVENTIONAL" LIHTC—HIGH INCOME AREAS	"MIXED-INCOME" LIHTC—LOW-INCOME AREAS	"CONVENTIONAL" LIHTC—LOW-INCOME AREAS
1	0_1/8 mile	.317 ****	.058 **	.059	.176 ***
	1/8–1/4 mile	.224 ****	.042 **	.086 *	.168 ****
	1/4–1/2 mile	.001	.016	.100 *	.103 ****
2	0–1/8 mile	.321 ****	.042	.198 ***	.368 ****
	1/8–1/4 mile	.222 ***	.047 *	.230 **	.200 ****
	1/4–1/2 mile	.044	.024	.132 **	.152 ****
3 or more	0–1/4 mile	.221 **	.098 **	.030	.283 ****
	1/4–1/2 mile	.106 **	.056 ***	.256 ****	.193 ****

**** significant at .001 level; *** significant at .01 level; ** significant at .05 level; * significant at .10 level

Table 4: Price Effects of Different LIHTC Developments In High Versus Low Income Communities

statistically significant price impacts. We also found that Chicago's "mixed-income" LIHTC properties have had a more positive effect on surrounding home prices than the city's more "conventional" developments. Yet that finding masks significant differences across neighborhoods, as illustrated in Table 4.

Strong Markets

"Mixed-income" LIHTC properties have had much greater effects on nearby home prices in high-income neighborhoods than in low-income ones. One potential explanation is that LIHTC developments in higher-income areas almost invariably focus on transforming tougher, more problematic properties from local liabilities into more useful assets. (More appealing properties likely have been developed or earmarked for market-rate uses.) In areas that already have comparatively strong markets, the elimination of a price "depressor" may enable surrounding values to move more quickly toward the prevailing norm. Another possibility is that the inclusion of market-rate units, and the higher rents those units can generate for the developer, may help minimize any negative perception of the property among nearby residents and potential neighborhood investors. The market-rate units also may serve as an incentive for the developer/project sponsor to ensure that the property remains in good condition going forward. To continue attracting higher-paying tenants—people who presumably have more choices about where to live—the developer/sponsor may be more rigorous in tenant screening and property management.

It is important to note that "conventional" LIHTC properties have had positive spillover price effects in these areas as well. Consider the Logan Square neighborhood, which has experienced substantial, sustained gentrification in the past 15 years. Instead of representing some of the only development in the community, LIHTC developments now have become the primary means of preserving affordability for the neighborhood's lower-income residents. There is little market or anecdotal evidence to suggest that wholly affordable LIHTC properties have had any negative spillover economic effects. Some of Logan Square's more affluent newcomers challenged the development of recent LIHTC properties, including the 61-unit, fully affordable Zapata Apartments near Palmer Square, fearing negative effects on local housing prices. Yet there were few complaints once the properties were completed and leased up. The Palmer Square area has experienced continued investment, with no discernable depressing price effects, and has transformed a "sketchy" area (to quote one resident) into a development anchor for the western part of the community.

Weak Markets

Turning to LIHTC property impacts in lower-income areas, we found that "conventional" LIHTC developments, those with few or no market-rate units, have had a greater effect on property values than their "mixed-income" counterparts. This is puzzling. In theory, the inclusion of market-rate units should have marginally greater benefits for the surrounding community. Market-rate tenants typically have higher incomes than subsidized tenants, and their additional purchasing power can help support local retail and other amenities. Higher-income individuals also tend to be more politically and civically engaged, all things being equal, which could result in additional pressure being placed on local officials to improve and maintain the local infrastructure and to ensure public safety. And indeed, "mixed-income" LIHTC developments in low-income areas have larger effects on nearby property values than do "conventional" LIHTC developments located in high-income communities.

What explains the counterintuitive price effect finding in low-income neighborhoods? Multiple explanations are likely. First, the market dynamics are different in low-income areas, where prevailing prices are already low. A problematic property may not have as strong a negative effect on surrounding values, simply because of the overall weakness of the real estate market. Consequently, eliminating the liability may not result in as much of a benefit, simply because there is a lower price ceiling. While responsible developers are likely to take care in their tenant screening, there is less potential economic risk from losing a market-rate tenant in a low-income area than in a high-income area, because of the differences in rents.

Second, "conventional" and "mixed-income" LIHTC properties tend to be located in different parts of the city. As highlighted in Table 1, LIHTC properties that exclusively (or almost exclusively) target households at or below 60 percent of AMI tend to be located in higher-poverty communities. They also are more likely to have been developed in the 1980s and 1990s, when they often represented some of the only new construction the communities had seen in years. Affordable housing development was some of the only noticeable residential real estate activity in areas such as Logan Square and Washington Park in much of the 1980s and 1990s. Hispanic Housing Development Corporation and Bickerdike (both nonprofits) were two of the only developers active in Logan Square during the period. The quality of the organizations' properties, coupled with the lack of any other significant development in the area, may have magnified the impact of those LIHTC projects. Even though they were 100 percent affordable, those early projects helped convince nearby residents to invest in their own homes and encouraged others to re-consider the community as a place to live.

Third, there may be a higher amount of turnover among market-rate tenants at LIHTC properties in lower-income areas than in higher-income ones. This greater churn could limit the economic, political, and social capital benefits that more affluent households frequently generate for a community. (We do not have the data either to support or refute this hypothesis, however.)

An even more counterintuitive finding is that the impact of "mixed-income" LIHTC developments on home prices in low-income communities has increased with distance from the property. We suspect a couple of factors are at play here. There are far fewer "mixed-income" LIHTC properties than "conventional" LIHTC properties in the low-income communities (49 v. 236), and the areas where those "mixed-income" properties are located may be subject to particular (idiosyncratic) influences that have not been accounted for in our model. It also is possible that some of the lower-income neighborhoods abut communities with stronger real estate markets, and those external dynamics may be affecting home prices near the community boundaries (farther from the LIHTC properties). Consider the dynamics along the State Street Corridor in Grand Boulevard, an area that houses both the Park Boulevard and Legends South mixed-income complexes. While both developments are attractive, fully or near-fully occupied, and well-managed, neither has sparked much additional commercial or residential investment.

Despite its reasonably favorable location—residents can access the Loop easily via the expressway or the green "el" line—the State Street Corridor simply does not have the appeal of other communities on the city's South Side. Hyde Park has the University of Chicago and a well-established intellectual community. North Kenwood-Oakland sits near Lake Michigan and Hyde Park and has a longer tradition of resident engagement. The Bronzeville area in the eastern part of Grand Boulevard benefits from a tradition of African-American arts and culture, as well as a series of graceful greystones. In contrast, the State Street Corridor has struggled economically for years, with a much poorer and less stable population than other neighborhoods in the area.

Thus far, the State Street Corridor has been unable to support significant additional development. Market-rate two-bedroom apartments in the area currently rent for about $1,200 per month, or about half of the roughly $3 per square foot that local developers claim is necessary to support unsubsidized development. Not surprisingly, LIHTC and similarly subsidized housing remains the only economically viable residential development in the area. The local alderman has pushed for additional homeownership, but the likely sale prices cannot justify the development costs.

DISTANCE BAND	"MIXED-INCOME" LIHTC— HIGH AF-AM AREAS	"CONVENTIONAL" LIHTC— HIGH AF-AM AREAS	"MIXED-INCOME" LIHTC— LOW-AF-AM AREAS	"CONVENTIONAL" LIHTC— LOW-AF-AM AREAS
0–1/8 mile	.062	.147 ***	.250 ****	.053 **
1/8–1/4 mile	.098	.124 ***	.195 ***	.045 **
1/4–1/2 mile	.141	.082 **	.064 *	.004

**** significant at .001 level; *** significant at .01 level; ** significant at .05 level; * significant at .10 level

Table 5: Overall Price Effects of LIHTC Developments in Communities With High Versus Low Proportions of African-American Residents

The State Street Corridor also has struggled to attract commercial and retail activity. The demolition of the Stateway Gardens and Robert Taylor Homes public housing complexes resulted in a significant loss of population in the area, and residential density remains low more than a decade later. (There currently is enough vacant land along the corridor to support small farms.) Retail and other consumer amenities depend on an area's demographics, and the State Street Corridor does not yet have enough "housetops" to sustain such businesses.

Predominantly African-American Neighborhoods

Chicago historically has been one of the country's more racially segregated cities, with strong spatial correlations between race and income. (Predominantly African-American neighborhoods tend to be disproportionately poor.) Thus it is not surprising that an analysis of LIHTC properties' spillover impacts in low-minority and high-minority neighborhoods found results—and disparities—similar to those in high-income and low-income communities, respectively. As Table 5 illustrates, "mixed-income" LIHTC developments have had greater price effects (predominantly higher income) in areas with relatively few African-American residents than in lower-income areas with higher concentration of African-American residents. "Conventional" developments have had greater impacts in the largely African-American areas than "mixed-income" developments have.[22]

IMPLICATIONS FOR ACTION

Our study has focused on the characteristics and impacts of a subset of Cook County mixed-income developments in which income mixing was not the primary policy objective. These LIHTC properties contain a meaningful number of market-rate apartments. Unlike HOPE VI redevelopments and other affordable housing developments that deliberately aim to achieve a mix of tenant incomes, the LIHTC properties are designed primarily to create and/or preserve affordable housing for low-income renters. They may or may not have

---

22 While our findings for LIHTC properties in communities with low proportions of African Americans are statistically significant and generally consistent with what we found more broadly, it is important to not keep in mind that the analysis is based on a small number of subject properties. Only 16 LIHTC properties in Cook County are located in census tracts where African Americans comprise 3 percent or less of the population. At the same time, there are only 62 "mixed-income" LIHTC properties in tracts where African Americans represent at least 26 percent of the population, compared to 241 conventional projects in these areas. Simply put, the substantial majority of LIHTC developments in heavily African-American neighborhoods are designed almost exclusively as subsidized affordable housing.

specific income targets within their subsidized units, but any unsubsidized units have neither income targets nor rent restrictions.

While Chicago and surrounding Cook County reflect many of the dynamics affecting urban America, they are not necessarily representative of conditions elsewhere in the country. Thus, it is important to examine the tenant characteristics and spillover effects of various "mixed-income" LIHTC properties in other markets to ensure the applicability of our findings more broadly. (We are currently conducting similar research in Los Angeles.) With that caveat, we feel that our Chicago analysis has several implications for developers, investors, and policy makers:

The Financial Realities of LIHTC Developments—Including the Availability of Subsidies and Prevailing Market Rents—May Significantly Constrain a Developer's Ability to Achieve a Desired Mix of Incomes

The ultimate mix of subsidized versus unsubsidized units in a given development depends on many factors specific to the development and its market, including:

- The strength of the market. Are market-rate rents substantially greater than LIHTC rents? Is there substantial demand for more higher-end units in the area, with corresponding options for greater economic returns for the developer?
- The mission of the developer and its desire/need for an economic return.
- The type of housing credits available for the project, as 4 percent credits tend to attract less equity than 9 percent credits.
- The availability of other (non-LIHTC) subsidy for the property.
- Whether the property involves new construction or rehabilitation and, if the latter, whether it is trying to preserve existing affordable housing.

From an economic feasibility perspective, there may well be situations in which more market-rate units are necessary within a property to preserve the maximum number of affordable units. But from a community development perspective, we see little compelling evidence to suggest that market-rate units should be a regular feature of LIHTC properties.

Limits on a Property's Total Number of Developable Units May Force Hard Choices on the Amount of Income Mixing Within Those Units

Physical site constraints, zoning restrictions, and/or financial considerations may limit the number of units that can be developed on a given site. Including "market-rate" units in such developments may result in fewer subsidized units being built. If market-rate rents are high enough (likely only in strong or gentrifying neighborhoods), the presence of such units may generate enough cross subsidy for the property to support more very low or extremely low-income tenants in the affordable units. Developers and policy makers need to be mindful of these tradeoffs and be explicit about their specific goals for a given property.

The Actual Mix of Incomes within an LIHTC Property Depends Largely on Micro-Market Conditions

In Chicago, and likely in other cities with a range of micro-markets, tenant incomes in LIHTC properties generally reflect the socio-economic characteristics of the communities where the properties are located. In more affluent areas, the subsidized units tend to house residents whose incomes are close to 60 percent of AMI. Market-rate units tend to house more moderate- and middle-income households. In poorer areas, virtually all LIHTC residents tend to qualify as low-income. Tenants in subsidized units often have incomes at or below 30 percent of AMI, and the market-rate units tend to attract households earning at most 70 to 80 percent of AMI. These income ranges are nowhere near as broad as those in many HOPE VI developments, where stated policy aims included income mixing in addition to replacing distressed public housing.

Recent Programmatic Changes to LIHTC May Expand In-Building Income Mixes

The recent changes to the LIHTC program may promote greater income mixing within "conventional" properties, albeit within a range of well below 30 percent of AMI to up to 80 percent of AMI. As detailed earlier, program regulations now allow subsidized units to support households earning up to 80 percent of AMI—provided that the average tenant income in the subsidized units is at or below 60 percent of AMI. This has the potential to create more affordable housing options for low-income households (those in the 60 to 80 percent of AMI range); many of these people have full-time jobs and bring stability to the community. At the same time, the new regulation promotes greater housing options for very and extremely low-income individuals (those earning 40 percent or less of AMI). This may help reduce the dependence of these individuals on Section 8 vouchers in order to afford LIHTC units. The ultimate outcomes will be the subject of future research.

In Weak Micro-markets, LIHTC Properties Are Unlikely to Attract a Broad Mix of Incomes without Substantial Incentives to Attract Higher-Income Individuals

The economic weakness of lower-income neighborhoods often makes them relatively unattractive to households that have a wide range of choices as to where to live. In Chicago, neighborhoods such as Washington Park and the State Street Corridor have little retail and few amenities, at least in comparison to other south side neighborhoods such as Bronzeville, Hyde Park, and Kenwood. Rents in these areas are affordable to low-income people, but not low enough to attract and retain higher-income people who have the financial wherewithal to afford more appealing areas. It is unclear what, if any, subsidy would be sufficient to attract these more affluent individuals into weak-market neighborhoods. Even the market-rate townhomes associated with the Cabrini Green redevelopment, in a highly desirable area just north of the Loop, were initially priced at a 25 percent discount to other comparable units in the area to attract the desired tenants. To attract more affluent residents to LIHTC properties in areas such as Washington Park, developers likely would have to lower the "market" rents even further. But such an approach would further jeopardize the financial viability of these already fragile projects.

Allocating additional resources to attract higher-income people to LIHTC properties in weak markets therefore seems counter-productive. There is no evidence to suggest that more mixed-income LIHTC developments in these areas have greater spillover effects than wholly subsidized properties. On the contrary, we find that LIHTC properties in low-income areas that are comprised of entirely (or almost entirely) subsidized units have about twice the impact on nearby prices as do LIHTC properties with a mix of subsidized and market-rate units. And from an equity perspective, it is hard to justify additional subsidy to attract more affluent households when there remains a substantial shortage of housing affordable to low-income households.[23]

---

23 DePaul's Institute for Housing Studies calculated that demand for affordable housing in Cook County in 2016 exceeded the supply by about 182,000 units. See "2018 State of Rental Housing in Cook County" (April 5, 2018); available at https://www.housingstudies.org/releases/2018-state-rental-housing-cook-county/

In Strong Micro-markets, Within-Building Income Mixing Is Easier to Achieve for LIHTC Properties. But in Light of the Need for Affordable Units in These Communities and Limited Development Capacity, Traditional LIHTC Developments May Be More Appropriate in These Areas to Ensure That Lower-Income People Can Continue to Live in the Communities

In stronger, often gentrifying markets such as Logan Square, it is easier to attract more affluent households to market-rate LIHTC units. These mixed-income developments have greater spillover effects on surrounding housing prices than wholly subsidized properties. At the same time, these gentrifying communities typically have a growing number of quality housing options for higher-income households and an increasing shortage of affordable housing options for low-income households. A LIHTC development often is one of the few mechanisms for creating and/or preserving affordable housing.

We therefore would argue that policy-makers encourage LIHTC properties in more affluent areas to contain more subsidized units instead of fewer. As we have found, LIHTC developments containing only subsidized units have a demonstrably positive effect on surrounding property values in both weaker and stronger micro-markets. In many weaker markets, the spillover effects of subsidized-only properties are greater than those of properties with a substantial number of market-rate units. In more affluent communities, more mixed LIHTC properties tend to have greater effects on property values. Yet given the need for affordable housing in these appreciating markets, we believe that the presence of additional subsidized units in a development is worth the trade-off of lower marginal property value increases.

LIHTC Developments Can Help Achieve a Greater Mix of Resident Incomes Within a Neighborhood

The LIHTC program was not designed to promote mixed-income communities, yet individual developments can help foster that outcome. An entirely subsidized property can help ensure the continued availability of affordable housing for low-income residents of gentrifying areas, helping to alleviate the threat of displacement. All types of LIHTC properties have positive spillover effects on nearby property values. Such impacts can help strengthen weaker markets by increasing the net worth of existing owners and potentially helping to attract new residents with a wider range of incomes. In short, LIHTC developments can be important components of broader strategies to promote mixed-income neighborhoods. Trying to achieve a broader mix of incomes within specific LIHTC properties, however, is unlikely to be achievable (or economically feasible) in most of the communities where such developments are likely to be located.

■ ■ ■

RAPHAEL W. BOSTIC, Ph.D. is President and Chief Executive Officer of the Federal Reserve Bank of Atlanta. He is a participant on the Federal Open Market Committee, the monetary policymaking body of the Federal Reserve System.

■ ■ ■

ANDREW JAKABOVICS is Vice President, policy development at Enterprise Community Partners, where he oversees the Policy Development & Research team, researching issues related to affordable housing, housing and community development, housing finance, foreclosures and neighborhood stabilization, and broader housing supply and demand concerns. He has also been analyzing small multifamily properties, neighborhood change, and the demographics and socioeconomics of renter households in the United States. Prior to joining Enterprise, he served as senior policy advisor at the U.S. Department of Housing and Urban Development and as associate director for Housing and Economics at the Center for American Progress.

■ ■ ■

RICHARD VOITH, Ph.D. is President of Econsult Solutions Inc. (ESI), an economic consulting firm focusing on urban issues. Dr. Voith is also a Research Fellow at the University of Pennsylvania Institute for Urban Research. He has published widely on transportation, real estate, and economic development issues in scholarly journals and in the popular press. Dr. Voith's consulting efforts have focused a range urban issues including the impacts of HOPE VI housing on nearby neighborhoods, the impacts of transit systems on economic development, and the evolving role of technology in cities.

■ ■ ■

SEAN ZIELENBACH, Ph.D. is the President of SZ Consulting, a firm focused on community economic development throughout the country. He works with a variety of loan funds, banks, public agencies, and nonprofits on issues relating to affordable housing, development finance, poverty alleviation, and neighborhood revitalization. He focuses primarily on strategic planning, program and product development, and impact measurement. He has conducted multiple studies on the effects of various housing, commercial, and community facility initiatives in catalyzing neighborhood change.

2
WHAT POLICY INNOVATIONS DO WE NEED?

Innovations in Policy Strategies: National Strategies

These two essays explore the national policy perspective on mixed-income communities. Salin Geevarghese provides a first-hand retrospective in his essay, "Reflections on the Role of the Federal Government in Promoting Greater Urban Equity and Inclusion." How did the Obama administration approach place-based policy and what were the challenges and accomplishments? What was learned that can inform future community revitalization efforts? Geevarghese weaves a narrative describing the innovative cross-silo, cross-sector, and cross-jurisdictional approaches that were championed during the Obama administration, detailing the program and policy efforts that sought to impact how actors collaborated with one another at the local, state, and federal levels to advance place-based strategies. Based on this review, he charts a path forward for federal efforts.

In "HUD's Affirmatively Furthering Fair Housing Rule: A Contribution and Challenge to Equity Planning for Mixed-Income Communities," Katherine O'Regan and Ken Zimmerman examine the 2015 AFFH Rule's potential as a planning tool for creating equitable and inclusive mixed-income communities. They explain the framework and theory behind the Rule and consider how its focus on overcoming racial segregation offers potential connections to, and tensions with, the mixed-income strategy. O'Regan and Zimmerman assess the experience of municipalities that began early implementation of the Rule and convey their concerns about the threat posed by HUD's current suspension of it. They conclude that the AFFH Rule is a potentially innovative mechanism for realizing equity goals, especially for situations in which mixed-income efforts are insufficiently attentive to the needs of communities of color.

REFLECTIONS ON THE ROLE OF THE FEDERAL GOVERNMENT IN PROMOTING GREATER URBAN EQUITY AND INCLUSION

Salin Geevarghese
SGG Insight, LLC

As we think about how far the country has come and how far it still must go to maximize equitable outcomes for residents of all communities, the place-based policies and initiatives of the Obama Administration offer a valuable set of experiences and lessons. For leaders across the federal agencies during that time, efforts to advance place-based policies were guided by some key realities about how people and place are inextricably linked and why some regions fared better than others, both during and after the Great Recession. One is that segregation by race and income—and the unequal access to opportunity that it creates—stand in the way of equitable, inclusive, mixed-income communities in which everyone can succeed. Another is that geographically concentrated poverty, an issue that spawned the mixed-income transformation work in public-housing communities decades ago, often is racially identifiable and has enduring impacts on those who have to contend with such marginalized conditions.

Obama-era government leaders recognized that the solutions to these realities would need to be as comprehensive as the problems were complex, requiring changes to policies, interventions, and investments and the development of cross-silo, cross-sector, and cross-jurisdictional capacities and approaches. Consequently, place-based initiatives to build mixed-income communities operated simultaneously across multiple frames, policies, interventions, and investments. Leveraging place to improve social, community, and economic outcomes became the "unfinished business" of mixed-income community transformation. This essay revisits the innovations of the Obama-era housing policies and community initiatives and examines the possibilities and implications for future action.

HALLMARKS OF OBAMA-ERA EFFORTS TO ACHIEVE EQUITABLE, INCLUSIVE COMMUNITIES OF OPPORTUNITY

During the Obama Administration, approaches to "place," including strategies to create mixed-income communities, had historical antecedents. Approaching program and policy innovation from a posture of humility and engagement was important for new leaders in the federal government. Several of the strategies built on what had been learned from previous efforts (e.g., the HOPE VI program); knowledge gained through research and evaluation (e.g., of comprehensive community change initiatives and the Moving to Opportunity voucher program); and the collective wisdom of practitioners and policymakers who served as connective tissue and memory across the decades (e.g., President's Council on Sustainable Development, U.S. Interagency Council on Homelessness, Enterprise Zones-Enterprise Communities). Experience drawn from these sources underscored the inter-relationships between policies and strategies and the critical importance of cross-sector partnership to achieving positive results. During 2009-2010, considerable creativity, innovation, and commitment emerged. In particular, federal efforts to create inclusive, equitable communities during this period required deliberate efforts to work across silos, sectors, and jurisdictions.

Cross-Silo Approaches

The cross-silo approaches taken during the Obama Administration recognized the interconnectedness of issues such as housing, education, transportation, health, economic development, and climate. Silo busting became the mantra, with local practitioners and policymakers describing the challenges of federal fragmentation and imploring leaders from the vast array of federal agencies to work more effectively and efficiently together. This entailed a huge investment in interagency work, which started at the leadership level and then expanded to involve policy development, programmatic initiatives, and new modes of day-to-day management and coordination.

Silo Busting at the Federal Level

The first interagency connection began in early 2009 between leaders at the U.S Department of Housing and Urban Development (HUD), the Department of Transportation (DOT), and the Environmental Protection Agency (EPA). Their first step was to develop a set of "livability" principles to establish the values that would guide the interagency partnership. These principles included equitable and affordable housing, support for existing communities, and increased transportation choices. The principles became an organizing construct for the work on the ground, they guided program design, and they informed federal budget requests and appropriations from Congress. New interagency staff workgroups were formed, and soon representatives from the Department of Agriculture, Health and Human Services, and others joined the collaborative working sessions. The new White House Office of Urban Affairs helped recruit, corral, and direct agency staff and leaders to these gatherings in the early period. A core early focus of the expanding collaboration was to find existing programs that could be redesigned to be more symbiotic across agencies. Along the way, staff learned more about the tools and programs that existed at other agencies.

Those early leadership meetings led to the creation of the Partnership for Sustainable Communities between HUD, DOT, and EPA, the first place-based partnership to be rolled out. Each participating agency offered different resources for communities. For instance, the new Sustainable Communities Initiative (SCI), managed by HUD, represented the largest federal investment in comprehensive, integrated planning across agencies in 40 years. DOT had the TIGER competitive grant program (now known as BUILD grants), which focused on comprehensive infrastructure planning and investments that served multiple community goals. And EPA led the Brownfield Remediation program, which targeted revitalization activities including assessment, cleanup, technical assistance, and lending. The agencies worked together on program design and policy alignment, and collaborated on decision-making. Notably, all of the funding availability announcements for these competitive grant programs made similar references to the jointly crafted livability principles and other program alignment in order to signal to local communities that the agencies were purposefully collaborating.

HUD, the Department of Justice (DOJ), and the Department of Education (ED) then worked together to develop the Neighborhood Revitalization Initiative (NRI) to establish neighborhood-scale initiatives to complement the efforts at the city and regional scale. During this period, collaborators further defined language about equitable and inclusive communities. It was within the context of NRI that HUD began to design the Choice Neighborhoods Initiative, a comprehensive approach to mixed-income transformation of high-poverty public housing and assisted housing complexes.

Silo Busting Between Local, State and Federal Leaders

As these cross-silo initiatives rolled out, federal leaders looked to local governments and partners to help shape their design and target investments. The federal agencies were aware of concerns that government policies seemed to be created in a vacuum without meaningful public input and that the public comment process was inadequate. So the agencies established a more responsive process with local leaders, including an interactive web presence, a phone hotline for questions, and frequent stakeholder meetings. This desire to engage led HUD to produce and disseminate an advanced version of the Sustainable Communities Initiative's notice of funding availability, the first of its kind. The notice was essentially a five-page outline of the initial thinking about the initiative. HUD officials then held listening sessions around the country in early 2010, which generated thousands of comments and letters. This feedback informed program design and generated local interest, support, and stake in the program. Consequently, when the initiative began taking applications, an extremely high number of applicants responded—nearly 75 percent of all eligible applicants in the country, even though HUD was only able to award grants to 11 percent.

Outcomes of the Cross-Silo Approach

At the state and local levels, governmental departments began to re-consolidate and better align. The federal government's effort to bridge silos motivated some states to look for ways to do so, too. Furthermore, localities could not play federal officials from different agencies against each other, because those agencies were in closer conversation and collaboration.

Community officials had long begged the federal government to act as one enterprise supporting people and places, and cross-silo coordination helped to actualize that vision. It enabled multiple points of entry, allowing each agency's grantees to be more favorably recognized by the other agencies. For example, Preferred Sustainability Status (PSS) gave preference points in competitive grant competitions across HUD, DOT, and EPA. Promise Zones gave preference points in more than 10 agency grant competitions. Choice Neighborhoods, Byrne Criminal Justice Innovation Program (now known as the Community Based Crime Reduction Program), and the Promise Neighborhoods Initiative also gave reciprocal recognition to grant applicants. These policy innovations were not without criticism, as some communities that did not receive awards claimed that the preferencing practices layered rewards on the same grantees at the expense of others and of a sense of overall fairness. Overall, however, these innovations proved popular and helped communities push toward stronger results through more comprehensive approaches and investments.

Beyond the preferencing, cross-silo approaches also fostered better policy alignment as interagency policy review processes and practices improved. Traditionally, increased agency engagement usually created extensive delays as policies underwent multiple cycles of legal review. Requests for review also tended to come out of the blue, and comments from reviewing agencies sometimes were relatively uninformed. Because of the interagency infrastructure built for cross-silo coordination, however, the review processes became much tighter and fewer items landed on administrators' desks for review without being previously discussed.

Another important outcome of the cross-silo coordination was greater efficiency in how resources were allocated. As agencies coordinated around shared aims to achieve better alignment, synergy, and joint targeting of resources, they could saturate particular places with potential impacts. Agencies could coordinate investments to sequence them more effectively, too; for example, if might make sense for an EPA brownfields remediation grant to precede another place-based initiative operating in the same place. In this way, the federal government began to operate as a system of systems designed to advance shared results.

Cross-Sector Approaches

For these cross-silo approaches in government to achieve maximum impact, cross-sector capacity and partnership was crucial. Government cannot solve complex issues with comprehensive solutions without the help of capable partners and stakeholders in the private, nonprofit, and philanthropic sectors; nor is government always best equipped to be in the lead or to convene other partners. Therefore, cultivating, reinforcing, and institutionalizing partnership instincts and behaviors across sectors was critical for Obama-era domestic policy priorities. This was accomplished through multiple strategies, including:

- Leverage scenarios, in which private and philanthropic sector actors were encouraged to scale their risk, funding, and impact by co-investing with the public sector. Thus, for example, grant applications that included private and philanthropic funders' investments were evaluated and scored more favorably, taken as a sign of stakeholder engagement and commitment to long-term impact.

- Cross-sector participation in processes by which public, nonprofit, private, and philanthropic representatives worked together to plan, govern, and manage public resources and set priorities. For example, the SCI Regional Planning and Community Challenge grants required broad stakeholder engagement and allowed set-asides for community-based organizations' participation (e.g., in planning for land use, housing, transportation).

- Civic leadership and engagement, as residents were incentivized and encouraged to participate in the local stakeholder collaborations responsible for framing, holding, and implementing the vision for change, alongside leaders from community-based nonprofits, municipal government, metro/county agencies, and philanthropy.

- Strategic information sharing, in which federal program officers communicated with all types of informal and formal community representatives, regardless of their position, rather than limiting their contact to grantees.

- Establishing public-private partnership offices in several federal agencies, which worked to cultivate external partners, identify program and policy innovations from outside government, create information exchanges, and determine rules of engagement.

- Technical assistance, whereby high-capacity partners were identified and supported to build the implementation skills and knowledge of local actors; and,

- Proposal evaluation, with nonprofit and philanthropic leaders joining with agency leaders to assess applications and learn from each other as they scored the proposals.

Outcomes of the Cross-Sector Approach

Through cross-sector partnerships, leaders in each sector came to learn about the value propositions and unique roles of other sectors, including the tools available to them and their risk tolerance, orientation to results, political sensitivity, and motivations for taking action.

Cross-Jurisdictional Approaches

The issues that affect equity and inclusiveness in mixed-income communities do not follow jurisdictional boundaries. Racially concentrated poverty may show up in specific ZIP Codes, for instance, but the causes and impacts are not confined to neighborhood boundaries or circumstances. Furthermore, the levers and solutions to problems of equity, inclusion, and opportunity cannot be limited to what can be accomplished at the project or neighborhood scale. Housing markets, jobs, transportation and other infrastructure, economic opportunities, the environment, and health factors exist within a larger geographic dynamic and ecosystem, revealing the interconnectedness of neighborhoods, cities, and regions. Consequently, many of the Obama Administration's early, signature place-based initiatives operated at multiple jurisdictional levels. Two prominent examples of cross-jurisdictional initiatives were Strong Cities, Strong Communities (SC2) and the Partnership for Sustainable Communities (PSC).

Strong Cities, Strong Communities targeted post-industrial cities that have experienced economic and population decline, needed capacity building at the city level, and required investment beyond challenged neighborhoods. SC2 placed loaned federal staff in city halls, often in mayoral offices, to help the city manage key federal initiatives, remove federal administrative barriers that impinged on work, and assess what additional capacity-building resources were needed. The SC2 staffers also helped local government leverage resources and influence for neighborhood transformation efforts such as a Choice Neighborhoods Initiative implementation grant.

The Partnership for Sustainable Communities operated regionally, covering multiple neighborhoods, cities, and towns. It made investments across the range of policy priorities and consistent with the livability principles developed by federal collaborators in 2009, but it also acknowledged the importance of planning and investing across jurisdictional lines. PSC's grants, guidance, and capacity building aligned housing/community development, transportation, environment, and economic development strategies and resources as a way to counteract the fragmented nature of local government, which can make regional collaboration difficult if not impossible. By hard-wiring cross-jurisdictional collaboration into place-based policy and practice, PSC made it possible to use the federal government's tools to create more equitable, inclusive, opportunity-rich communities.

CHALLENGES AND SOLUTIONS

Cross-silo, cross-sector, and cross-jurisdictional approaches for creating more inclusive, equitable communities faced several challenges, particularly after the 2010 midterm election when an environment of resource scarcity, regulatory and administrative constraint, and legislative gridlock was the norm. In particular:

- As HUD sought to focus everyone's attention on the importance of increasing equity and opportunity in disinvested, marginalized, and isolated neighborhoods, some stakeholders argued that the agency's purview was broader and HUD could not target a limited number of places at the expense of others.

- Cross-silo approaches pushed up against statutory barriers, where legislation impeded interagency collaboration and broader flexibilities. For instance, the desire to hire local residents (consistent with the Section 3 obligation at HUD) for an infrastructure project ran up against rules at the Department of Transportation that forbade it.

- Cross-sector approaches revealed how the public sector's role was paramount and could not be subsumed by other sectors. The public sector's role in setting local policy conditions for action and accountability—such as requiring jurisdictions to invest in equitable and inclusive strategies as a condition of a grant program—cannot be assigned to nonprofit, private, or philanthropic partners. This includes the use of federal enforcement authority when inappropriate local actions are taken—for example, when jurisdictions subverted obligations to affirmatively further fair housing, only to be held accountable in court by the federal government. When compliance must be forced, only government possesses the hammer.

- Cross-jurisdictional efforts often encountered push-back, as some units of local government objected to other units' "intrusions" into their authority (i.e., it's my job, not yours) while also shifting blame to each other in terms of role and responsibility (i.e., it's your job, not mine).

These challenges required agency officials to build the case for why equity, inclusion, and opportunity deserve everyone's attention and why taking a more comprehensive approach would be more effective. That persuasive case-making often started with White House leadership (e.g., Office of Urban Policy), agencies (e.g., HUD) and program leaders (e.g., environmental justice,

Office of Civil Rights, Fair Housing and Equal Opportunity) whose equity emphasis is crafted into their missions but whose authorities and scope are limited. These leaders acknowledged the need for an "all-of-government" approach to equity through which all policies and levers could be brought to bear. If housing investments are not aligned with transportation and economic development investments, equitable outcomes become more elusive. However, transportation departments do not necessarily come pre-wired for engagement on equity considerations; nor is their performance measured by equity criteria. Consequently, equity champions within government had to convince other leaders to use their tools for equity, inclusion, and opportunity even when a statutory mandate did not exist. For example, when the Affirmatively Furthering Fair Housing (AFFH) rule was being developed, leaders of the Partnership for Sustainable Communities and the Neighborhood Revitalization Initiative met with AFFH rule drafters to determine ways in which, for example, the transportation and health components of the data and mapping tools could be strengthened. Because of the interagency mandates within the Fair Housing Act, AFFH leaders could persuasively engage non-housing policy leaders about the law's original intent to have all domestic agencies carry their own burden to fulfill the vision of communities that are free of discrimination and that offer maximum opportunities for all.

Another challenge came in the form of the budget appropriations process, which constrained the resources that could be dedicated to place-based approaches, especially as the political climate changed. The more these initiatives were labeled as favored programs of a particular administration, the more vulnerable they were to the political headwinds blowing against or in favor of the president. To combat these risks, the solution was to shift from an either/or, exclusive mentality to a both/and, inclusive one. For example, in the policy development process for the AFFH rule, a choice between neighborhood revitalization versus housing mobility strategies emerged. Research, practices, and legislative history were divided on this choice, as were practitioners, policymakers, and advocates. Citing the existing evidence, some advocated strongly for housing mobility while others took up the call for neighborhood revitalization, asserting that not every resident wants to move out of their community. The Obama Administration landed on a both/and approach and pushed cities and states to base plans on a recognition that both revitalization and mobility are important strategies for maximizing opportunity.

While not all issues lend themselves to both/and solutions, the goal was to expand choices rather than limit them. As the Choice Neighborhoods Initiative was being designed, for instance, policy and program designers understood that investing in housing alone would be insufficient; to maximize opportunity for residents, it would also be crucial to use Choice Neighborhoods resources to co-invest in neighborhood amenities and services. Therefore, agency officials allowed Choice Neighborhoods grant recipients to deploy HUD resources for non-housing purposes. Similarly, to optimize the development of high-quality schools to drive mixed-income community transformation, some communities were able to secure funding from both the Department of Education's Promise Neighborhoods program and HUD's Choice Neighborhoods Initiative to increase the probability of access to high-quality education within a revitalized neighborhood.

The innovations that emerged capitalized on tools the federal government possessed independent of Congressional mandates: leadership, agency alignment, administrative and regulatory relief, and capacity building. Two of the most celebrated, durable initiatives—Strong Cities, Strong Communities and Promise Zones, each of which conferred benefits but no new, direct grant dollars—enabled the federal government to press forward with available tools and, in doing so, exemplified the value proposition that government support is not just about new money but also non-financial tools and capacities. State and local governments as well as social investment and philanthropic organizations mirrored this approach as they attempted or launched parallel programs. For instance, the Partnership for Sustainable Communities, a collaboration among HUD, DOT, and EPA, prompted the State of North Carolina to reorganize its own agencies to reflect the Partnership. Similarly, local councils of government and metropolitan planning organizations with economic development responsibilities pressed the U.S. Economic Development Administration (EDA) to recognize that their efforts aligned to PSC policies and programs and therefore should qualify for consideration by EDA. Consequently, EDA accepted plans that met the agency's Community Economic Development Strategy (CEDS) criteria, even though they had been submitted for other federal agency requirements. This type of reciprocal recognition, administrative barrier removal, and technical assistance by the federal government added clear value to communities beyond grantmaking.

UNFINISHED BUSINESS: NEW OPPORTUNITIES AND DIRECTIONS FOR EQUITABLE, INCLUSIVE, MIXED-INCOME COMMUNITIES

The job of ensuring access to equitable, inclusive, mixed-income communities remains unfinished, and probably will be for some time. The country now is reeling from an unprecedented combination of a global health crisis, a deep economic recession, and widespread social unrest and disruption advancing a national reckoning on enduring structural racism. All of this is occurring in the midst of a time of high distrust and increased cynicism in our political, cultural, civic, and media institutions and an increased polarization among Americans on the basis of political, racial, and economic differences.

Despite these extreme challenges, the work of transforming communities into places for all people across all lines of difference is not at all hopeless. Indeed, the breadth and depth of the challenges should refresh our mission, strengthen our resolve, and induce a new generation of stakeholders to pick up the baton. These new leaders are already picking up the mantle of civil rights icons like Rep. John Lewis and Justice Ruth Bader Ginsberg, demanding that we deliver justice, fairness, equity, and opportunity to those who have been denied that promise.

The advantage of cross-silo, cross-sector, cross-jurisdictional, comprehensive approaches is that the roots of these efforts reach far and wide, increasing the odds that a commitment to and stake in the common enterprise and desired results will endure. To succeed, we must diligently improve on previous efforts, learning from previous mistakes and holding ourselves accountable to building on evidence about what has worked. As other essays in this volume have documented, nonprofit and philanthropic leaders and state and local actors have stepped up to deploy interventions that tackle the challenges in front of them, even without all of the necessary supports and accountability tools fully in place. They are working to fill gaps made wider by the inattentiveness of federal leaders in any given political cycle. These local and nonprofit actors have grown accustomed to compensating for an absence of leadership and innovating where they can but, when they operate with limited resources, the cost to community impact is clear. In this context, inspiration is not hard to find. The bigger challenge—and the greatest opportunity—will be to balance and manage our steps forward while maintaining the sense of imagination and innovation that brought us this far.

IMPLICATIONS FOR ACTION

Implications for Policy

Policymakers at the local, state, and federal levels can take the following steps to create stronger conditions for inclusive, equitable communities:

- To reduce governance fragmentation, align policies that affect cross-silo, cross-sector, and cross-jurisdictional approaches. This will entail incentivizing more equitable and inclusive partnerships by requiring cross-sector partners to engage in projects with distinct roles and responsibilities; more flexibility in blending and braiding resources across silos by allowing funds to be designated for shared results beyond the central purpose of the agency; and strategic barrier removal through early identification of impediments and the creation of a legislative or regulatory action plan for policy fixes.

- Confront the effects of racial and income segregation and inequality by encouraging and providing cover for local leaders to examine the effects of structural and institutional racism across systems and silos as communities plan, invest in, and implement equitable, inclusive, mixed-income community strategies. The revised 2015 Affirmatively Furthering Fair Housing rule, data and mapping tools, and guidance have been rescinded, but this—along with other federal civil rights legal frameworks—still provides guidance for those local leaders who seek to advance change in their jurisdictions.

- Position civil service government officials as a voice of continuity in times of change and as a bulwark to protect gains made for equitable, inclusive approaches. Investing in staff capacity at the local, state, and federal level to institutionalize work should be an early priority of policymakers as well as nonprofit and philanthropic partners. Training career staff on key place-based programs and policies and engaging them early in design and implementation will prove beneficial later on, when leadership churn occurs. Because these career professionals may be subjected to loyalty screens and be unfairly tested in new administrations, enshrining their efforts in legislation will help to protect their new practices, policies, and innovations.

Implications for Research and Evaluation

Researchers and evaluators have roles to play in increasing our knowledge base and our confidence in approaches to equitable, inclusive community development.

- Compared with recent work on housing mobility, evidence on the role of neighborhood revitalization as an opportunity-making strategy is more limited. Therefore, more longitudinal studies of residents of mixed-income transformation efforts are needed to determine what works. These studies will likely require funding from partnerships between the public and philanthropic sectors. Given that need for external investment, federal agencies should continue creating public-private structures for joint deliberation and decision making on research agendas.

- Increasingly, if "both/and" strategies are to prevail, we must meet the evidence standards set by the regional housing mobility movement with their seminal research findings on the importance of place. In the absence of rigorous evaluation and research, the mixed-income movement will likely be overly reliant on its most fierce advocates and practitioners to protect a place at the table for neighborhood revitalization. Advocacy must be bolstered by strong evidence that neighborhood revitalization can consistently lead to stronger economic, social, and community outcomes for all residents of mixed-income communities.

- The importance of "big data" innovations, randomized controlled trial designs and quantitative methods, and the use of large administrative data sets has emerged over the last decade, producing a great deal of knowledge on key social science questions. Government and the private sector can operate more authoritatively with interventions based on these studies' findings. These research approaches should continue, but they should also be accompanied by qualitative methods that enable us to understand the challenges of improving social and community outcomes in mixed-income communities.

Implications for Development and Investment

Developers and investors must continue to focus on physical transformations that make housing stability a platform for family success, but they also must help to create equitable, inclusive mixed-income communities by bringing all of the tools and influence they can muster for the sake of better social and economic outcomes.

- Unless developers and investors combine housing with the opportunity structures of access to high-quality "living wage" jobs, schools, transportation, and health, families in mixed-income communities will continue to have difficulty getting on a pathway to economic mobility. Housing stability is foundational and necessary, but it is insufficient for the results that communities aspire to reach.

- Although it is essential to keep attention focused on increasing opportunities for the most marginal populations, mixed-income developers, investors, and practitioners also need to make communities places where everyone can belong if they hope to sustain racial, social, and income mixing over time. To leverage the social mix as an asset, developers and investors can keep a keen eye on how social mix is sustained over time within a community, and they can fund the programming, marketing, and design work that leverages social mixing as a key asset. Policymakers may need to think differently and creatively about how to incentivize developers and investors to sustain the social mix, including flexibility with how subsidies can be used beyond low-income populations.

- Sustainable financing and funding is the next frontier. New cost-saving models are proliferating and producing a stronger evidence base than in the past. In conjunction with these advances, new models for preventing negative outcomes and achieving greater system efficiencies may enable a fresh look at how to support this work financially (e.g., by creating housing interventions that produce health benefits, leading to investments in housing by health systems).

Implications for Residents and Community Members

Residents play critical roles in completing the unfinished business of inclusive, equitable, and mixed-income communities where there is an opportunity to build assets and close racial wealth gaps.

- Existing low-income residents—often families who live in public housing—must gauge whether mixed-income communities will serve their interests directly, assessing what is and is not favorable to their circumstances. They must also join with other residents in creating a community that will support and value all members, regardless of individual circumstances.
  - To foster self-agency and self-determination, residents should be involved in making choices about design, governance, and community building for the community. Residents may need access to capacity-building resources in order to self-advocate with power.

- The pursuit of equity and inclusion cannot stop at jurisdictional borders. Residents and their leaders will need to organize and participate at decision-making tables beyond their neighborhood boundaries in order to advocate successfully for better jobs, wealth building, health services, schools, and transportation. The actors charged with managing these tables will need to make sure residents' voices and knowledge are present.
- In neighborhood redevelopment situations, not all residents will return to their former homes. Families that choose to leave should have the choice to leverage the redevelopment of their physical space into an opportunity to move elsewhere. This will require putting more effort, attention, and investment into regional housing mobility strategies and adopting both revitalization and mobility policies for residents who qualify. In addition, residents need comprehensive services and supports in these new areas beyond just housing.
- Redevelopment imposes trauma on residents, so steps must be taken to mitigate its negative effects. In particular, residents need the opportunity to protect and preserve the essential cultural identity of their community, even as gentrification and income mixing may introduce an alternative one.

- Residents of market-rate and workforce units have their own balancing act to perform in mixed-income communities. While they may choose the community because of its high-quality affordable housing, they may or may not celebrate or be well-equipped to be part of an equitable, inclusive, diverse community. Therefore, helping all residents see the advantages of living amongst racial and income diversity is key. Because our segregated existence in the United States leaves us ill-equipped for diversity and inclusion, all residents need to be engaged in the effort to determine how best to share neighborhoods and help all residents succeed in mixed-income communities.

■ ■ ■

SALIN GEEVARGHESE *is the Founding Director of the Mixed-Income Strategic Alliance and its Mixed-Income Innovation and Action Network. He is also the President & CEO of SGG Insight, LLC, a consulting firm offering comprehensive services to public, private, nonprofit and philanthropic sector leaders and organizations, and serves as a Senior Fellow at the Center for the Study* *of Social Policy (CSSP). From April 2014 to January 2017, Geevarghese served in a senior appointed leadership post as HUD's Deputy Assistant Secretary for the Office of International and Philanthropic Innovation (within the Office of Policy Development and Research) during the Administration of President Barack Obama.*

HUD'S AFFIRMATIVELY FURTHERING FAIR HOUSING RULE: A CONTRIBUTION AND CHALLENGE TO EQUITY PLANNING FOR MIXED- INCOME COMMUNITIES

Katherine M. O'Regan and Ken Zimmerman
NYU Furman Center, New York University

In July 2015, the U.S Department of Housing and Urban Development (HUD) issued its final Affirmatively Furthering Fair Housing (AFFH) Rule, perhaps the most significant fair housing initiative of the Obama Administration. This rule reflects new learning and a refined approach to the core challenge of remedying ongoing housing and development barriers that perpetuate spatial disparities in opportunity, and it represents an important planning tool for creating equitable and inclusive communities. Specific components of the rule link directly to mixed-income strategies and incentivize those that are consistent with affirmatively furthering fair housing strategies and mandates. The rule can also act as a check on mixed-income strategies that are insufficiently attentive to the needs of communities of color. The rule is under threat, and it would be a major step backward for efforts to increase *economic* as well as racial integration, were it to be dismantled.

After providing a brief background on the legal basis of HUD's rule, this essay explains the framework and theory behind the rule and how a rule aimed at overcoming racial segregation can support the creation and preservation of mixed-income communities. We lay out key details of the rule and how they connect to more equitable and inclusive planning and highlight potential connections and tensions for mixed-income strategies within the context of the rule. We then assess early experience with its approach and the threat posed by HUD's current suspension of the rule. We conclude with a discussion of implications for action (or at least attention) with respect to the rule, particularly with respect to mixed-income strategies.

THE FAIR HOUSING ACT AS A TOOL FOR INCOME MIXING THAT PROMOTES EQUITY AND INCLUSION

Background. The Fair Housing Act (FHA), enacted in 1968 in the immediate aftermath of the assassination of Dr. Martin Luther King Jr., is a robust and wide-ranging piece of civil rights legislation. As the courts have recognized, the Act is designed and has been given broad application to fully achieve "the policy of the United States to provide, within constitutional limitation, for fair housing throughout the United States."[1] As a tool to promote income-mixing strategies that promote equity and inclusion, it has both significant power and potential but also limitations, which come to the fore as one anticipates the potential use of the AFFH rule in this domain.

In enacting the FHA, Congress recognized that simply combatting future discrimination based on race, color, and other protected bases would not be enough to overcome the history of racialized policy and practices that led to dual housing markets and what the Kerner Commission (whose report was issued less than two months before the FHA's passage) recognized as "two societies."[2] To achieve this goal, the FHA went beyond anti-discrimination provisions and required the federal government to take "affirmative" steps to overcome this legacy. Specifically, it imposed on the federal government an obligation "affirmatively to further fair housing," which we refer to as the AFFH mandate.[3]

---

1   Fair Housing Act of 1968, 42 U.S.C. § 3601 (1968).

2   The Kerner Commission stated that "fundamental to the Commission's recommendations" was the need for "[f]ederal housing programs [to] be given a new thrust aimed at overcoming the prevailing patterns of racial segregation," United States Kern Commission, *Report of The National Advisory Commission on Civil Disorders* (Ann Arbor, MI: University of Michigan Libraries, 1968), https://babel.hathitrust.org/cgi/pt?id=mdp.39015000225410;view=1up;seq=2.

3   The Fair Housing Act, 42 U.S.C §3608(d) states "All executive departments and agencies shall administer their programs and activities relating to housing and urban development (including any Federal agency having regulatory or supervisory authority over financial institutions) in a manner affirmatively to further the purposes of this subchapter and shall cooperate with the Secretary to further such purposes. See also Fair Housing Act, 42 U.S.C. § 3608(e) (5). Litigation has made clear that the AFFH mandate applies to all federal investments, including the Low- Income Housing Tax Credit Program. See Re: Adoption of uniform housing affordability controls by the New Jersey Housing and Mortgage Finance Agency, 848 A.2d 1 (N.J. Super. Ct. App. Div. 2007).

This recognition of structural inequality and racism was visionary.

Given the FHA's starting point as a piece of civil rights legislation, it has an important history of grappling with the interplay between racial discrimination and policies or practices that differentiate based on income. This is seen, for example, in the Fair Housing Act's long-standing application to override local zoning rules that are intended or have the consequences of precluding the creation of affordable housing.[4] Similarly, from its earliest days, the Fair Housing Act has been applied to the process and assessment of redevelopment efforts and programs seeking to create mixed-income communities, especially when the majority of tenants who may be displaced are families of color.[5] In these and the many other situations in which the FHA has been applied, the starting point is racial impact but the significance of income disparities frequently becomes relevant.[6]

In many respects, this makes the AFFH's mandate as applied to income-mixing strategies an important and powerful but sometimes limited element in the toolkit to address constraints on equity and inclusion in housing and development policy. Given the significant interplay in the United States between race and income, the AFFH mandate has considerable relevance to when and how income-mixing strategies advance efforts to overcome our racial history and, equally importantly, when they do not. More attention is warranted to the interplay between the goals of income-mixing strategies and the AFFH mandate, and HUD's rule provides an important starting point given the strategies and approaches it prioritizes.

Of course, it must be noted that the efforts to translate the AFFH mandate into

---

4   Under the "disparate impact" theory of discrimination, the courts have long held that exclusionary zoning ordinances that lack requisite justification violate the Fair Housing Act. See, e.g., Huntington Branch, NAACP v Town of Huntington, 844 F.2d 926 (2nd Cir.), aff'd per curiam, 488 U.S. 15 (1985). The United States Supreme Court recently upheld this method of proving a Fair Housing Act violation. Texas Dept. of Housing v. Inclusive Communities Project, 135 U.S. 2507 (U.S. Super. Ct, 2015). See generally, Robert Schwemm, *Housing Discrimination: Law and Litigation* (New York: C. Boardman, 1990).

5   From its earliest days, the Fair Housing Act required assessment of racial impact in site selection and project planning in a range of subsidized housing programs, e.g., Shannon v. HUD, 436 F.2d 809 (3rd Cir. 1970) and In Re Adoption of 2033 LIHTC Qualified Application Plan, 848 A.2d 1 (N.J. App. 2003). Consistently, Fair Housing Act concerns have been raised regarding mixed income development that has not been attentive to its racial implications, e.g., Thomas C. Kost, "Hope after HOPE VI? Reaffirming Racial Integration as a Primary Goal in Housing Policy Prescriptions," *Northwestern University Law Review* 106, no. 3 (2012): 1404, https://scholarlycommons.law.northwestern.edu/cgi/viewcontent.cgi?article=1106&context=nulr.

6   The FHA centers on the consequences of policies and programs for racial or ethnic minorities, families with children, people with disabilities, and others specifically protected under the statute.

practice during the 50 years since the FHA's passage has been a halting process. The efforts to implement the AFFH provisions have met a host of political, programmatic, and other roadblocks that prevented significant advances and led to what some commentators have termed a "fundamental imbalance in [the Act's] statutory missions."[7, 8] This history informs how one should examine the AFFH rule's ambition and approach and its relationship to income-mixing strategies. This backdrop also reinforces the significance of the current fight over the rule's future.

The Rationale behind the AFFH Rule. With the 2008 election of President Obama and his appointment of Shaun Donovan as HUD Secretary, the new Administration revisited the AFFH mandate to determine how it could be revitalized as part of the Administration's broad commitment to furthering equity.[9] In doing so, the new Administration was influenced by the reality that the many deep challenges it faced as it took office—the record high rate of foreclosures, the Gulf Region's failed post-Katrina recovery efforts, and the specter of climate change—all had deep and widely recognized racial dimensions.

Against this backdrop, the new Secretary and his team started with several premises that shaped HUD's overall agenda and informed its approach to the AFFH mandate. First, they recognized that major challenges ranging from climate change to ongoing racial disparities along numerous measures of well-being required approaches that transcended public sector silos and would best be achieved by coordinated planning and integrated resource allocation. Applied to the AFFH effort, this suggested that previous approaches—which had been driven primarily by and focused on the agency's fair housing office—needed to be broadened and would require the full participation of and buy-in by the components of HUD responsible for community development and public and assisted housing. The goal was to ensure that HUD's annual distribution

---

7   Nestor Davidson and Eduardo Penalver, "The Fair Housing Act's Original Sin: Administrative Discretion and the Persistence of Segregation" (Unpublished manuscript, 2018).

8   See for a general discussion: Timothy. M. Smyth, Michael Allen, and Marisa Schnaith, "The Fair Housing Act: The Evolving Regulatory Landscape for Federal Grant Recipients and Sub-Recipients," *Journal of Affordable Housing and Community Development Law* 23, no. 2 (2015): 238, https://www.jstor.org/stable/24389794#metadata_info_tab_contents.

9   For more details on the history and context of the rule's development, see Katherine O'Regan and Ken Zimmerman, "The Potential of the Fair Housing Act's Affirmative Mandate and HUD's' AFFH Rule," *Cityscape* 21 no. 1 (2019): 89, https://www.jstor.org/stable/pdf/26608012.pdf.

of more than $40 billion to state and local governments, public housing authorities, and Native American tribes were part of AFFH implementation.[10]

Second, HUD aspired to revisit how best to define the respective roles of the federal government and state and local actors in operationalizing the AFFH mandate. Pursuant to the FHA's AFFH provisions, HUD had a legal obligation to affirmatively further fair housing, and the legal authority to take enforcement action when its grantees failed to do so.[11] But beyond that starting point, there were myriad ways of utilizing federal authority to harness state and local housing and community development capacity. Decades of poor experience with top-down, one-size-fits-all approaches to community development had inspired more locally driven and locally tailored comprehensive efforts, and state and local governments, private entities, and nonprofit groups had developed new capacities as a result.[12] In the AFFH context, this meant prioritizing the federal government's ability to set direction, articulate policy and program options, incentivize participation, and provide resources for enhancing local capacity while empowering state and local actors to take leadership in identifying best approaches tailored to local conditions.

Finally, there was a deep belief and increased appreciation of the importance and potential for robust community engagement to improve both process and outcome. While community participation had a long and mixed history in housing and civil rights practice and policymaking, HUD recognized that engagement of community groups and the broader public could make the

---

[10] In fact, the ideal approach to the AFFH mandate would move beyond HUD programs and incorporate transportation, education, and other key elements that addressed barriers to fully equal opportunity, such as with the cross-HUD-DOT-EPA Sustainable Communities Initiative that HUD led. See "Regional Planning Grants and the SCI," HUD Exchange, accessed May 16, 2019, https://www.hudexchange.info/programs/sci/.

[11] The importance of the AFFH legal obligation had been reinforced in 2007 when a federal court found Westchester County had violated the False Claims Act by falsely certifying its compliance with the AFFH mandate. See U.S. ex rel. Anti-Discrimination Center v. Westchester County, 668 F. Supp. 2d 548 (S.D.N.Y. 2009). In the aftermath of this decision, HUD engaged with the plaintiff fair housing group and the County and entered into a Consent Order that set forth actions to place the County in AFFH compliance. That Consent Order became hotly contested, and, following judicial findings that the County had violated the Order, led HUD to suspend distribution of HUD funds to the County.

[12] HUD's Choice Neighborhoods and the Department of Education's Promise Neighborhoods exemplify this newer orientation. See Raphael Bostic and Luke Tate, "Fighting Poverty and Creating Opportunity: The Choice Neighborhoods Initiative," *PD&R Edge* (blog), accessed May 16, 2019, https://www.huduser.gov/portal/pdredge/pdr_edge_frm_asst_sec_101911.html; "Promise Neighborhoods (PN)," Office of Innovation and Improvement, United States Department of Education, accessed May 16, 2019, https://oese.ed.gov/offices/office-of-discretionary-grants-support-services/school-choice-improvement-programs/promise-neighborhoods-pn/.

difference between a paper exercise and meaningful action. There were clear-cut challenges to enable meaningful and effective community engagement in the AFFH context, however. The capacity of local communities, especially low-income communities of color, to use, access, and deploy information to influence public resource allocation was highly uneven. Further, it was uncertain what data would be most useful and how it might be shared to enable community groups to participate effectively.

Each of the Administration's three premises had particular resonance given the existing state of the AFFH process. Prior to HUD's AFFH final rule in 2015, recipients of HUD formula grants mainly complied with their "affirmatively furthering" obligation through the Analysis of Impediments (AI) process.[13] Jurisdictions were required to conduct an AI to fair housing in their jurisdictions and take appropriate action to address those impediments. The AI process, however, was widely recognized as highly flawed. This was confirmed by a review by the Government Accounting Office (GAO), which in dry, objective terms made clear that the AI process was meaningless.[14] The report was particularly critical of the uneven quality of analyses that were conducted, noting that HUD did not specify the content or scope of AIs. The GAO also questioned whether AIs had any effect, given that they did not need to be submitted to or reviewed by HUD, and that many AIs were not even signed by local elected officials.

The AFFH Rule's Specifics

After nearly seven years of internal and public debate, HUD issued its final AFFH rule in 2015. The rule sought to operationalize the Administration's new approach while addressing many flaws identified by the GAO[15] and others. It delineated substantive objectives in a new way and articulated a new process

---

13 For a description of the AI process, see U.S Department of Housing and Urban Development, *Fair Housing Planning Guide Vol. 1*, (Washington, DC: United States Department of Housing and Urban Development, Office of Fair Housing and Equal Opportunity, 1996) https://www.hud.gov/sites/documents/FHPG.PDF.

14 After collecting and reviewing more than 400 AIs, the GAO found that a large share of jurisdictions did not have AIs that were current, and the GAO questioned the usefulness of many of the AIs that did exist, concluding that "[a]bsent any changes in the AI process, they will likely continue to add limited value going forward in terms of eliminating potential impediments to fair housing that may exist across the country," Government Accountability Office, *Housing and Community Grants: HUD Needs to Enhance Its Requirements and Oversight of Jurisdictions' Fair Housing Plans*, (Washington, DC: United States Government Accountability Office, 2010), https://www.gao.gov/assets/320/311065.pdf.

15 Government Accountability Office, "Housing and Community Grants"

that redefines the roles of the federal government and state and local actors. In doing so, it reworked how fair housing issues are to be incorporated into participants' planning processes and into how HUD (and potentially other) resources would be allocated. Collectively, these represented a significant shift in approach, one that directly relates to mixed-income strategies.

The Final Rule's Explanation of Core AFFH Objectives

To provide clarity of purpose, for the first time HUD's rule defines the duty to affirmatively further fair housing.

Specifically, it explains that the AFFH mandate requires "meaningful" actions to:

> …*overcome patterns of segregation and foster inclusive communities free from barriers that restrict access to opportunity based on protected characteristics.*[16]

The rule continues by articulating four objectives for the AFFH effort: (1) to address significant disparities in housing needs *and in access to opportunity* (emphasis added), (2) to replace segregated living patterns with truly integrated and balanced living patterns, (3) to transform racially or ethnically concentrated areas of poverty into areas of opportunity, and (4) to foster and maintain compliance with civil rights and fair housing laws.

By setting these four objectives, the rule makes clear that furthering fair housing can entail both place-based investments and steps to promote mobility, thus addressing perhaps the preeminent fair housing tension and embracing investment strategies in either domain that are likely to promote income mixing. Further, it clarifies that non-housing disparities are relevant to AFFH objectives and must be addressed. This more holistic focus may also incentivize mixed-income strategies as one feasible means of lowering neighborhood disparities. Finally, by including the four objectives, the rule clarifies that the specific actions to be taken by state and local actors would be determined locally rather than being dictated by HUD.

---

[16] 24 C.F.R. § 5.152 (2000), https://www.law.cornell.edu/cfr/text/24/5.152. The rule explains that "meaningful actions" means "significant actions that are designed and can be reasonably expected to achieve a material positive change that affirmatively furthers fair housing by, for example, increasing fair housing choice or decreasing disparities in access to opportunity."

The Updated AFFH Process

The rule seeks to clarify how participants should assess current conditions in their communities by replacing the much-criticized AI process and document with a standardized and very detailed Assessment of Fair Housing (AFH) tool that includes specific questions to be answered. The analysis seeks to push jurisdictions to go beyond describing patterns of segregation to assess racial and ethnic disparities in the quality of neighborhood-based services such as schools, employment, and transportation. Along a similar vein, the AFH contains a section focusing specifically on areas of racial or ethnic concentration of poverty. These analyses seek to help localities assess residential segregation through a lens that focuses on the linkage between racial separateness and inequality of opportunity and adopt strategies to increase equity and inclusion.

To facilitate that analysis, and consistent with a shift in HUD's role in the process, HUD provides detailed data publicly on all jurisdictions and their surrounding regions, including data on segregation, location of subsidized housing, and disparities in measures of opportunity. In doing so, HUD seeks to provide direction and serve as a resource to state and local actors—especially helpful to entities without significant data capability—and to "democratize" the inputs relevant to the process by making those data publicly available to all stakeholders. The rule establishes a more inclusive process by requiring a robust community engagement process, specifying several steps designed to ensure community input is incorporated into the final assessment.[17]

Importantly, unlike AIs, AFHs must be submitted to HUD, and within 60 days HUD needs to determine if the AFH is accepted.[18] Jurisdictions must reference their AFH priorities and goals in their next administrative plan required for HUD funding (e.g., consolidated plans)[19] and need to have an AFH accepted

---

17 Community input is required before the drafting of the AFH; the draft AFH must be made available for public comment. Akin to the federal rulemaking process, jurisdictions need to reference public comments in their AFH submission and explain the reasoning for not addressing specific comments in the content of the AFH.

18 Acceptance means the plan is complete and consistent with fair housing and civil rights laws. Acceptance does not deem a jurisdiction is necessarily meeting all its fair housing obligations.

19 Consolidated plans are the planning and reporting requirements for CDBG recipients. Since 1995, CDBG recipients have been required to conduct AIs as part of their consolidated plans (though the AI itself was not included or referenced in those plans). See: Raphael Bostic and Arthur Acolin, "The Potential for HUD's Affirmatively Furthering Fair Housing Rule to Meaningfully Increase Inclusion" (Paper presentation, *A Shared Future: Fostering Communities of Inclusion in an Era of Inequality*, Cambridge, MA, April 2017), https://www.jchs.harvard.edu/sites/default/files/a_shared_future_potential_for_hud_affh_in-

by HUD prior to receiving that funding. In theory, there is a direct link here between strategies proposed in the AFH and the spending of resources, at least HUD resources, though the AFH may include goals for non-HUD resources as well. Subsequent AFFHs must assess the participants' progress on their previous AFFH goals in a continuous assessment and learning loop.

Finally, in recognition that fair housing issues cross jurisdictional and agency boundaries, the final rule notes that HUD not only permits but encourages collaboration through jointly submitted AFHs. Collaboration can occur among multiple jurisdictions, as well as between jurisdictions and public housing agencies (PHAs). PHAs were not required to conduct AIs previously, so are now conducting comprehensive fair housing assessments for the first time.[20]

INTEGRATING AFFH AND INCOME-MIXING STRATEGIES

While income-mixing strategies can be important to promote equity and inclusion, they often have negative racial impacts either through displacement of a predominantly minority population or through shifts in neighborhood services and organizations that feel alienating to long-standing residents. Such actual and cultural displacement mean these strategies can have an unequal distribution of benefits and costs.[21] Income-mixing strategies adopted within AFFH may help ensure that the racial implications of these strategies are incorporated into program design up front and in subsequent assessments in a way that provides a helpful check on differential racial burdens and benefits. By way of example, one can envision how efforts to use Low-Income Housing Tax Credits (LIHTC) to redevelop a site for mixed-income housing as part of an AFH goal might need to assess and ameliorate racial impact if virtually all of the pre-existing tenants were people of color and/or with disabilities. Similarly, if the development was in an area of high opportunity that was largely White, it might require a robust approach and commitment of resources to tenant recruitment from minority communities, plus amenities designed to support them.

---

crease_inclusion.pdf.

20 Prior to HUD's final rule, PHAs self-certified that they were meeting their AFFH obligations as part of their HUD planning process.

21 For example, on displacement in HUD's Hope VI program, see Susan J. Popkin, "A Glass Half Empty? New Evidence from The HOPE VI Panel Study," *Housing Policy Debate* 20, no. 1(2010): 45, https://www.tandfonline.com/doi/pdf/10.1080/10511481003599852?needAccess=true.

The AFFH data and engagement processes also are potentially positive additions to income-mixing strategies, because they provide low-income and minority communities with tools and a process through which to participate. That buy-in can—but will not always—shape eventual outcomes. Perhaps just as importantly, there is a hope that the data will reveal over time whether such strategies contributed to increased equality of opportunity and, if they did not or did so only partially, how they might be adjusted to be more effective and overcome any negative consequences.

Moreover, by focusing on racially concentrated areas of poverty and a broader way of thinking about opportunity, the AFFH rule places mixed-income strategies in a desired lens of opportunity, not just housing. The key outcomes are not just the tenant composition of a mixed-income complex but whether and how those communities are linked to high-quality jobs, public education, public safety, transit, etc. The AFFH rule charts a course that prioritizes this broad perspective and thus helps put income-mixing strategies—at least those that share a similarly broad frame—squarely in the mix as a desirable component in a locality's approach to AFFH.

Finally, there is also an explicit aspiration in AFFH for social inclusion— not just presence—of all members of a community. This potentially helps focus mixed-income development strategies on a noted challenge: that they do not accomplish true inclusion of lower-income households.[22]

INITIAL CRITIQUES DURING THE RULE-MAKING PROCESS

While many commentators respected the substantial shifts HUD made in its approach to the AFFH implementation process, public comments were extensive and often quite heated, reflecting widely differing perceptions about the purpose, value, and desired outcomes. While some people expressed hostility or indifference to the FHA's mandate, stakeholders supportive of fair housing goals raised a range of concerns during the rule's development and after its issuance.

The fair-housing advocacy community raised significant concerns about the lack of enforcement tools and processes in the new rule, questioning whether

---

[22] Robert J. Chaskin and Mark L. Joseph, *Integrating the Inner City: The Promise and Perils of Mixed-Income Public Housing Transformation* (Chicago, IL: University of Chicago Press, 2015), 21.

HUD had struck the appropriate balance between support to state and local actors and accountability for those who did not respond meaningfully to the new process.[23] They noted the long history of segregated housing patterns sometimes reinforced by existing municipal boundaries, and observed that even well-intentioned local jurisdictions frequently faced opposition if they sought to promote integration and otherwise address fair housing challenges. Thus, fair housing critics questioned whether the rule included sufficient monitoring tools and assessment mechanisms to determine when local actors appropriately used the discretion they had been granted. This concern was exacerbated by the rule's "default approval" provision by which HUD would deem an AFH "accepted" if HUD did not disapprove or raise concerns about it within 60 days.[24] While the legal significance of this "acceptance" was uncertain, fair-housing advocates saw it as a step toward a safe harbor that might insulate entities from liability who failed to take meaningful actions.

In tension with this concern, many state and local governments and other actors responsible for complying with the new rule were skeptical that HUD would be able to embrace a more collaborative role and meet its obligation to support communities with data and technical assistance. For some HUD grantees responsible for undertaking the new process, HUD's rhetoric outstripped the reality of the process that had been set up. For example, the rule strongly encouraged collaboration between different actors and joint submission but did not provide an assessment tool designed to be used for such collaborations, nor incentives (financial or otherwise) to do so. On the flip side of the concern raised by fair housing advocates, state and local actors wondered whether HUD would support their discretionary decision making.

Finally, there were questions about scale: whether the resources at issue were sufficient to meet the AFFH objectives through the process the rule set forth. In other words, some doubted that the rule could satisfy the AFFH mandate because it neither contributed significant new resources nor changed existing statutory or regulatory terms of HUD programs to expand options that state

---

23 For a good articulation see Michael Allen, "HUD's New AFFH Rule: The Importance of the Ground Game," *The Dream Revisited* (blog), *NYU Furman Center*, (September 2015) http://furmancenter.org/research/iri/essay/huds-new-affh-rule-the-importance-of-the-ground-game.

24 See final rule, in "Federal Housing Administration (FHA): Small Building Risk Sharing Initiative Final Notice" *Federal Register* 80, no. 136 (July 16, 2015): 42105, https://www.govinfo.gov/content/pkg/FR-2015-07-16/pdf/FR-2015-07-16.pdf.

and local governments might choose. From a resource perspective, some noted that there was no *new* HUD funding available and other public resources—such as those involving transportation and education, which were larger and arguably more critical contributors to development patterns—were not subject to the rule. Others questioned whether HUD needed to provide greater flexibility in the way that HUD's existing program funds, which are significant, could be used.

The conflicting concerns about enforcement versus useful planning mirror tensions HUD grappled with internally in building a useful planning tool that also had appropriate teeth when needed. In some sense, this middle ground gave all stakeholders something to dislike. Whether HUD would be able to implement the rule in a way that provided jurisdictions with the flexibility needed for a new planning process while also holding jurisdictions accountable was an aspiration that would require adaptation following on-the-ground experience. In this and myriad other situations, the AFFH rule reflected the complexity of equity planning in the balances it struck between competing priorities and its awareness of the multiple ways that goals might be achieved. As such, it anticipated, at least implicitly, how it might be refined and improved with increased funding, engagement of other departments, and sustained attention to learning.

CURRENT STATUS: EARLY LESSONS AND THREATS

HUD issued its final rule in July of 2015, which made the first AFHs due to HUD in 2016.[25] With no existing AFHs to serve as models and an entirely new process unfolding, there was great uncertainty among grantees and HUD staff in this early stage. The rule happened to be passed when there was a particularly small group of grantees next up in the consolidated planning cycle, permitting HUD (and philanthropy) to focus attention and technical assistance on "first submitters."[26]

By January 2018, 49 AFHs had been submitted to HUD and had received an official notice of acceptance or non-acceptance. Eighteen of those submissions

---

25 The timing of a jurisdiction's AFH depends on when their next consolidated plan is due, generally running on a five-year cycle.

26 The Ford Foundation and Open Society Foundations, in particular, provided funding for technical assistance on the ground in numerous jurisdictions.

were accepted outright; 14 received initial feedback from HUD on needed improvements and were quickly resubmitted and accepted; and the remaining 17 were formally not accepted.[27] There were several potential surprises and insights from these early submissions. First, it was notable that HUD proactively provided feedback to submitters so their entries could be corrected for minor omissions and resubmitted, potentially in a learning loop for both grantee and HUD. While such a mechanism was intended by the rule, this required HUD staff to work much more in partnership with submitters toward a common goal (acceptance) than a traditional "compliance stance" would permit.

The second surprise was that HUD actually rejected a sizable number of AFHs. In the 50 years since passage of the FHA, HUD has withheld funding on an AFFH basis only a handful of times.[28] These 17 non-acceptances put more than 20 jurisdictions and public housing agencies at risk of not receiving HUD funding.[29] In their review of the 17 non-acceptances and the comments HUD provided those submitters, Steil and Kelly[30] report that the most common weaknesses cited concerned setting realistic goals that would also meaningfully advance fair housing goals, as well as creating measurable metrics for assessing progress on those goals. Eight of the 17 non-accepted AFHs subsequently were revised, re-submitted, and accepted by HUD by the time the rule was suspended.

Analysis comparing the content of these first AFH submissions to earlier AIs of the same jurisdictions provides some early indication that local jurisdictions' responses were consistent with HUD's aspirations. Steil and Kelly found that AFHs for 28 of the first submitters included more concrete and quantifiable goals and more new actions to achieve those goals than did the preceding AIs.[31] In terms of cross-silo or holistic aspirations, AFHs were more likely than AIs to contain goals related to transportation improvements; economic

---

27 Justin Steil and Nicholas Kelly, "The Fairest of Them All: Analyzing Affirmatively Furthering Fair Housing Compliance," *Housing Policy Debate* 29, no .1 (2019):85-105.

28 Alex Schwartz, *Housing Policy in the United States*, 3rd Ed. (New York: Routledge, 2014)

29 Most AFH submissions were collaborations, either between a jurisdiction and its PHA or/and multiple jurisdictions, itself a goal of the new AFFH rule. For access to early submit ted AFFHs, see: Justin Steil, "Assessment of Fair Housing by City," Department of Urban Studies and Planning, Massachusetts Institute of Technology, (May 16, 2019) https://steil.mit.edu/civil-rights-and-fair-housing-city.

30 Justin Steil and Nicholas Kelly, "Survival of the Fairest: Examining HUD Reviews of Assessments of Fair Housing," *Housing Policy Debate* (forthcoming).

31 *Ibid.*

development, such as increased workforce training or job creation; and the environment, such as improvements in air and water quality or parks. Strategies to achieve those types of goals may be most likely to increase income mixing as well, because improvements in the non-housing aspects of neighborhoods may attract residents across a broader range of incomes or might be explicitly connected to a mixed-income development strategy. The researchers also found that, on average, AFHs were more likely than AIs to contain goals for regional cooperation or coordination. Indeed, the majority of AFHs submitted to date are collaborative or joint in some fashion.

An analysis of the inclusiveness of the process, conducted on 19 of the first AFH submitters by Been and O'Regan, concluded that the public engagement processes used under the AFH requirement were much more robust, along five distinct dimensions.[32,33] For example, jurisdictions used a much more extensive set of communication channels to solicit participation in their AFH process, provided many more opportunities for participation, and adopted more accommodating engagement strategies. This included bringing the AFH conversation to where people might already be, such as community meetings on non-AFFH (but related) topics in their own communities. There was, however, great variation in the engagement practices used by jurisdictions, and, unlike other aspects of the AFFH rule, specifics of the engagement process are not prescribed within the rule (or assessment tool).

A third unexpected event occurred in January 2018 when HUD, in the context of a new Administration and under new leadership, took steps to halt the new process, leaving its future uncertain. At that time, HUD announced it was delaying implementation of the rule until October 31, 2020.[34] During the delay, jurisdictions that had not already had an AFH accepted were to return

---

32 Vicki Been and Katherine O'Regan, "The Potential Costs to Engagement of HUD's Assessment of Fair Housing Delay," *NYU Furman Center Blog*, (March 7, 2018), http://furmancenter.org/research/publication/the-potential-costs-to-public-engagement-of-huds-assessment-of-fair-housing.

33 Specifically: the number of opportunities for public engagement; the inclusiveness of those opportunities; the provision of data for assessing public engagement; documentation and consideration of the public input; and existence of cross-jurisdictional or cross-sector engagement.

34 HUD extended the AFH deadline for jurisdictions that had not had an AFH accepted and whose AFH deadline fell before October 31, 2020. For those with deadlines between January 2018 and October 2020, this provides nearly a five-year delay. See "Affirmatively Furthering Fair Housing: Withdrawal of Notice Extending the Deadline for Submission of Assessment of Fair Housing for Consolidated Plan Participants," *Federal Register* 83, no. 100 (May 23, 2018): 23928, https://www.govinfo.gov/content/pkg/FR-2018-05-23/pdf/2018-11143.pdf.

to the AI process. After fair housing advocates filed suit challenging the delay, HUD rescinded its delay of the rule but also removed the AFH assessment tool for local governments from formal use, essentially delaying implementation.[35] HUD has since announced its intent to develop a new regulation that would revise the AFFH process and AFH tool. In kicking off the process for what is known as Advanced Notice of Proposed Rulemaking, HUD cited the high non-acceptance of early submitters as part of its reasoning, as well as the burden on jurisdictions and HUD staff reviewing the new assessments. The notice requests comments on whether the AFH and its required engagement could effectively be folded into the existing consolidated planning process.[36]

As the legal battle on removal of the tool unfold, and HUD potentially undertakes a public rulemaking process, some jurisdictions are moving forward with assessments that more closely resemble AFHs than AIs, incorporating some or all of HUD's AFH assessment tool into their analysis and using robust public engagement processes to develop and revise their draft AIs. Those efforts, along with the early AFHs, are important examples of how well a process that incorporates new substantive and procedural steps dedicated to fair-housing issues and equitable opportunity might promote new approaches and improve older consolidated planning engagements.

Finally, numerous AFHs submitted before the rule's suspension either implicitly or explicitly contained mixed-income goals or strategies, affirming the potential of such a planning process to incentivize mixed-income strategies. For example, Nashville's AFH includes a mixed-income redevelopment strategy for its public housing stock, using HUD's rental assistance demonstration (RAD) program to invest in the public housing stock and to add workforce and market-rate housing.[37] Philadelphia's plan includes two mixed-income goals, one aimed at its use in areas of concentrated poverty as part of redevelopment and the second reviewing the zoning code to further incentivize mixed-income development more broadly. The plan submitted by five cities in the Kansas

---

35 On August 17, 2018, the U.S. District Court of the District of Columbia found in favor of HUD on whether the delay violated the APA. An appeal is pending. See "National Fair Housing Alliance et al versus Carson (2018)," Poverty & Race Research Action Council, (May 16, 2019) https://prrac.org/national-fair-housing-alliance-et-al-v-carson-2018/.

36 For details see "Affirmatively Furthering Fair Housing: Streamlining and Enhancements," (August 2018), https://www.hud.gov/sites/dfiles/FHEO/documents/AFFH-ANPR.pdf.

37 See Justin Steil's Fair Housing website for access to AFHs submitted to HUD before the suspension of the rule at: "Assessment of Fair Housing by City," https://steil.mit.edu/civil-rights-and-fair-housing-city.

City metropolitan area provided some of the more concrete or explicit mixed-income strategies. This plan called for increased use of federal financing tools (including LIHTC) and leveraged financing to support mixed-income housing and also noted the need for specific expensive jurisdictions in the region to provide formal incentives for mixed-income housing.

IMPLICATIONS FOR ACTION

At a time when there is growing understanding that opportunities stemming from where one lives have life-long consequences,[38] the effort to operationalize the AFFH mandate is notable. As an innovation in equity planning and how it informs the use of federal housing and community development resources to further fair housing, the AFFH rule marks a significant departure from HUD's prior approach and may also herald the potential for equitable planning in other realms.[39] As a fair-housing framework that recognizes the centrality of access to opportunity and that housing must be viewed in concert with education, transit, and other critical aspects of neighborhood vitality, it opens the door for income-mixing strategies to become more central to and integrated within approaches developed to further the AFFH mandate. In significant measure, the rule is a potentially innovative mechanism that could herald experimentation and new approaches to realize equity goals broadly.

As we assess the current state of play and look forward, we see four major areas for sustained attention and action for AFFH, particularly as it relates to mixed-income strategies.

Implications for Policy

- *Articulate More Explicit Policy Aims and Strategies that Integrate*

---

38 See, for example, Raj Chetty, Nathaniel Hendren, and Lawrence F. Katz, "The Effects of Exposure to Better Neighborhoods on Children: New Evidence from the Moving to Opportunity Experiment," *American Economic Review* 106, no. 4 (2016): 856, https://scholar.harvard.edu/files/lkatz/files/chk_aer_mto_0416.pdf; Ralph Richard Banks, "An End to the Class versus Race Debate," *New York Times*, March 21, 2018, https://www.nytimes.com/2018/03/21/opinion/class-race-social-mobility.html.

39 There is a growing body of experience and literature about efforts to incorporate equity planning in public programs (at all levels of government) that suggests potential value in broader investigation into common challenges and successes. See, for example, Federal Highway Administration, *Travel Behavior: Shared Mobility and Transportation Equity* (Washington, DC: US Department of Transportation, 2017), https://www.fhwa.dot.gov/policy/otps/shared_use_mobility_equity_final.pdf; Oregon Education Investment Board, *Equity Lens*, (2018); Jason Corburn, et al., "Making Health Equity Planning Work: A Relational Approach in Richmond, California," *Journal of Planning Education and Research* 35, no. 3 (2015): 268, https://journals.sagepub.com/doi/pdf/10.1177/0739456X15580023.

Economic and Racial Objectives. Mixed-income goals are not explicitly incorporated into the AFFH rule, yet the broad focus on opportunity creates a space within AFFH for such strategies. Especially given the rule's emphasis that housing must be seen within a broader array of components in order to create "truly integrated living patterns" and "areas of opportunity," AFFH suggests that mixed-income strategies might be refined to more explicitly adopt such goals. With growing attention to the implications of both racial and economic integration, it is incumbent on advocates, policymakers, and researchers to push further to assess and develop when and how policies that advance these goals complement each other and discern ways to address circumstances when they are in conflict.

- *The Federal Government and Its Partners Should Continue to Refine the Rule and Process.* Much like the continuous "learning loop" built into the rule for communities, HUD should continue to refine the rule and the process it delineates. Before the AFFH tool was suspended, more than 40 communities had their assessments approved by HUD, and those communities are still bound by the AFFH rule. Another set of communities are undertaking assessments that essentially mimic the full AFFH process. Much can be learned from each of these groups about what works best in the process and what is less useful. Notably, for policymakers who focus on mixed-income strategies, this is an invaluable opportunity to examine how to develop processes that, from the outset, anticipate the interplay between income and race—including by paying more attention to applicable data sources and community outreach strategies.

- *Further Develop Standards that Provide the Appropriate Balance of Discretion and Accountability in the Oversight of Local Agencies.* Especially when assessing the interplay between mixed-income and racial-equity strategies, HUD should develop performance standards that allow income-mixing strategies to be assessed within a racial equity (AFFH) lens. This may be especially important for situations in which some aspect of the mixed-income strategy has a negative racial impact and thus requires amelioration.

- *Protect the Rule from Being Dismantled.* Whatever the short-term successes or limitations of the rule, it unquestionably provides infrastructure on which to build. HUD's proposed rulemaking process could be used to radically revise the rule and assessment tool in a way that would undermine, not advance, the purposes of the rule and strategies for creating more equitable and inclusive communities. At particular risk are the rule's broader focus on opportunity (critical for increasing equity and the primary link to mixed-income strategies) and the robust community engagement process (central to greater inclusion).[40]

Implications for Research and Evaluation

- *Document and Learn from the Discussion and Adoption of Mixed-income Strategies Contained in Submitted AFHs.* Those communities that included (explicit or implicit) mixed-income development strategies in their prioritized AFFH goals could provide valuable lessons for other communities, particularly in how they articulated the connections and any tensions that arose in those discussions. Those lessons may be applicable beyond AFFH, and even beyond broader equity planning efforts.

- *Evaluate the Efficacy of Mixed-income Strategies to Reduce Segregation and Disparities in Access to Opportunity.* The experimentation occurring in AFFH and AFFH-like communities around the interplay between AFFH and mixed-income strategies could serve as an invaluable laboratory to determine how and when mixed-income strategies help to overcome patterns of segregation and reduce disparities in access to opportunity. This should include assessing whether there are tradeoffs between income and racial integration strategies, under what circumstances these occur, and what steps might be taken to align them.

- *Evaluate the Efficacy of Mixed-income Strategies in Addressing Concentrated Poverty.* The AFFH rule and process could promote a more full-fledged incorporation of mixed-income strategies into the effort to overcome ae challenge closely tied to the racialized history of housing and development policy, especially in places that are attempting to transform racially and ethnically concentrated areas of poverty,. Here, too, the research agenda should include examining how and in what ways economic integration advances the goal of transforming these areas into places of opportunity, and what (if any) constraints would be appropriate in such endeavors.

---

40 HUD's Advanced Notice of Proposed Rulemaking questioned the importance of neighborhood attributes for people older than 13 years and specifically asked for comments on whether the AFFH engagement process could be rolled into engagement for other planning purposes. See "Affirmatively Furthering Fair Housing," *Office of Federal Register.* 40713

Implications for Development and Investment

- *Develop Data-driven Approaches for Incorporating Racial-equity Ambitions into Mixed-income Strategies.* A challenge for mixed-income development and investment programs in the context of AFFH is their singular focus on income, while the AFFH mandate (like other governmental civil-rights obligations) seeks to overcome racial disparities. An opportunity exists to deepen the ways in which mixed-income development programs and investments can use data about the racial differences of target communities or goal-setting that incorporates racial-equity ambitions. Similarly, it is valuable to deepen the database that incorporates both income and racial measures to facilitate an analysis of progress on both economic and racial integration and associated well-being outcomes in terms of both race and class.

- *Broaden Mixed-income Strategies beyond Reinvestment in Lower-income Communities.* The AFFH rule recognizes that the creation of more equitable and inclusive communities requires both place-based and mobility strategies. In this regard, it offers an opportunity to consider how mixed-income strategies (which typically have been place-based and targeted in lower-income communities) might be applied to efforts that give low-income families access to existing high-opportunity places. This might be done by pairing income-mixing place-based efforts with mobility strategies and/or targeting efforts to make existing areas of opportunity truly inclusive in terms of composition and lived experience. Certainly, the evolution and refinement of inclusionary zoning strategies at the state (New Jersey), regional (Twin Cities), and local (New York City) levels, including their attention to the appropriate beneficiaries, suggests approaches that such efforts should include.

Implications for Residents and Communities

- *Cull Lessons on How Best to Develop Meaningful Community Participation, Especially in Low-income and Communities of Color.* The AFFH rule and the process it calls for signals a meaningful commitment to substantive community participation—a critical aspect of inclusion—by linking community engagement more specifically to public-sector allocation decisions. In doing so, the rule recognizes the imbalance in power and technical knowledge between community residents and other stakeholders in the process and seeks to address it by providing data to the public and ensuring that community comments are taken into account. Foundations and other entities have expanded these starting points by supporting community groups that seek to become involved[41] and holding intermediaries accountable for supporting high-quality community engagement. The promise, but also pitfall, of such participation should be carefully examined by local leaders to see whether and how it advances resident and community interest and to develop local capacity on a jurisdiction-by-jurisdiction basis *and* engage national entities or intermediaries that can help support.[42] One specific issue relevant to mixed-income strategies involves understanding when and how these efforts do and do not "make the case" for communities of color.

- With adequate support, leaders of mixed-income efforts should ensure that residents and community members fully participate in project development and management. For residents and community members, the AFFH mandate offers the opportunity to engage and seek—even demand—access to the planning processes that control very large sums of money flowing from the federal government into their communities. Under the rules, residents and community members have the right to expect that these processes are responsive to *their* questions and concern, and that the data are provided by local initiative leaders and used in ways that allow them to deepen their ability to participate.

- *Leverage the AFFH Data and AFHs for Best Examples of Data Use for Effective Community Engagement.* The AFFH tool provides maps and data meant to level the playing field and add capacity to advocates and community members, but it is quite a bit of data. Residents and community representatives who are beginning their assessment processes should be provided with information from HUD and local partners that enables them to draw upon the experiences of those who conducted the first AFHs, including noting what appears to have worked or not worked. In

---

41 Note that there is significant public funding for local fair housing groups through the Fair Housing Initiatives Program (FHIP) and Fair Housing Assistance Program (FHAP) which in 2018 resulted in $39.6 million and $23.9 million, respectively going to non-profit and local government groups (See Libby Perl, *The Fair Housing Act: HUD Oversight, Programs, and Activities* (Washington, DC: Congressional Research Service, June 2018), https://fas.org/sgp/crs/misc/R44557.pdf.) This provides at least nascent infrastructure for fair housing community engagement support.

42 In an ideal world, one would plan over a multi-year period for what local and national capacities should be created. It's noteworthy, for example, that the manner in which community groups used and applied HMDA data evolved over time.

addition, residents might glean relevant lessons from other efforts where data was made available to enhance community participation, such as the experience of the Home Mortgage Disclosure Act. Residents may find that the extensive public data in the AFFH tool will be useful in an array of processes designed to enhance community voice and interests beyond the AFFH planning process.

We conclude both on an optimistic note and by observing the challenge for future mixed-income strategies. Optimistically, while the long-run impact of the AFFH rule cannot be assessed yet, early lessons suggest there is ample reason for optimism that the rule embodies an important new approach that can and should be refined over time. We firmly believe it is possible to build on the rule and develop an approach to equitable planning inclusive of mixed-income strategies that is consistent with the understanding Congress set forth when it enacted the FHA and included the AFFH mandate as one of its two statutory goals.

The challenge is that the issues of racial equity that were central to this nation when the Fair Housing Act was enacted 50 years remain no less significant today as the nation strives to live up to its aspirations. The AFFH rule provides an opportunity for appropriate mixed-income strategies to become fully incorporated into the ongoing efforts to meet this challenge. Both the AFFH rule and this challenge are well worth pursuing.

■ ■ ■

KATHERINE O'REGAN *is Professor of Public Policy and Planning and Faculty Director of NYU's Furman Center for Real Estate and Urban Policy. She spent April, 2014 through January, 2017 in the Obama Administration, serving as the Assistant Secretary for Policy Development and Research at the Department of Housing and Urban Development. Her primary research interests are at the intersection of poverty and space—the conditions and fortunes of poor neighborhoods and those who live in them. Her recent research includes work on a wide variety of affordable housing topics, from whether the Low Income Tax Credit contributes to increased economic and racial segregation, to whether the presence of housing voucher households contributes to neighborhood crime. Her board work includes serving on the board of the Reinvestment Fund, one of the largest community development financial institutions in the U.S. She holds a Ph.D. in economics from the University of California at Berkeley and spent ten years teaching at the Yale School of Management prior to joining the Wagner faculty in 2000.*

KEN ZIMMERMAN *is a Distinguished Fellow at the NYU Furman Center. Zimmerman's research examines new forms of social advocacy and policy development in the urban environment, with a special focus on evolving mechanisms for civic engagement and innovative approaches to address growing inequality. Zimmerman, a noted policy maker, fair housing expert, and civil rights attorney, has devoted his career to justice and equality issues. Prior to joining the NYU Furman Center, Zimmerman served as the Director of U.S Programs for the Open Society Foundations, preceded by a role as part of the Obama Administration's presidential transition team for the U.S Department of Housing and Urban Development (HUD), and as senior advisor to HUD Secretary Shaun Donovan. Previously, he has served in multiple capacities including as a litigation partner for the pro bono practice group at Lowenstein Sandler PC, chief counsel to New Jersey Governor Jon S. Corzine, and founding Executive Director of the New Jersey Institute of Social Justice. Zimmerman graduated magna cum laude with a B.A. from Yale University in 1982 and earned a J.D. from Harvard Law School, also graduating magna cum laude, in 1988.*

Innovations in Policy Strategies: State and Regional Strategies

These three essays expand our understanding of the design and implementation of state and regional policy innovations. The essays address pathways that leaders in public housing authorities, state financing agencies, and state governments are taking to address segregation, exclusion, and inequity. Each essay takes a different approach to advancing inclusion and equity, underscoring the importance of further deliberation about how best to foster policy change at multiple scales. The authors underscore the extensive political barriers that make the vision for inclusive communities difficult, but not unsurmountable, to achieve. Courageous leadership, creative cross-jurisdictional partnerships, and alliances across social and political interests are key to advancing policy change.

In "California For All: How State Action Can Foster Mixed-Income Inclusive Communities," Ben Metcalf argues that leaders in state governments have a powerful role in shaping solutions for major challenges, such as systemic racism and economic inequality. Metcalf makes a compelling case by highlighting recent examples of policy change in California, where he served as Director of the California Department of Housing and Community Development. First, he describes changes in regulations and program guidelines to more equitably award public subsidies for multifamily affordable housing developments in state subsidy programs and the Low-Income Housing Tax Credit program. Metcalf also shares new legislative efforts, including the State Ministerial Streamlining Program and the California Fair Housing law, that allow new affordable housing to be built in communities that are failing to adhere to state-mandated affordable housing goals. With regard to areas that face entrenched poverty and racial segregation, Metcalf describes the new Transformative Climate Community program, which aligns climate-change interventions with work to advance positive outcomes within low-income communities of color.

In "Qualified Allocation Plans as an Instrument of Mixed-Income Placemaking," Bryan Grady and Carlie Boos explore how state housing finance agencies, or HFAs, are uniquely situated to address inclusion and equity through the administration of the Low-Income Housing Tax Credit (LIHTC) program. They argue that Qualified Allocation Plans (QAPs) provide significant latitude to distribute tax credit resources in an equitable manner that promotes mixed-income communities. According to Grady and Boos, "A plethora of challenges stand in the way: regulatory capture, institutional inertia, and political constraints, among others. But success is achievable. It just requires inciting a minor revolution in housing and development mentality and inspiring a newfound respect for the integral and innovative role of HFAs." They build off their experience in crafting policy at the Ohio Housing Finance Agency to illustrate four methods for achieving income integration.

Turning from state-level policymaking to regional approaches, "Embracing Odd Bedfellows in Odd Times: How to Sustain Financial and Political Support for Mixed-Income Communities," by Robin Snyderman and Antonio Riley, examines how partnerships across jurisdictional and agency boundaries can lead to advancements in promoting mixed-income housing. Their essay details the implementation and outcomes of the Chicago-area Regional Housing Initiative (RHI), which created more affordable rental housing options in suburban environments where jobs and quality schools are located. This effort has emerged as a replicable "workaround" of public housing policies since it provides versatility in pooling resources across agencies and jurisdictions. The essay also shares examples of recent policy shifts at the federal level that offer opportunities to scale RHI's success. The authors document how this novel approach has created a high level of regional coordination, resulting in hundreds of new housing opportunities.

CALIFORNIA FOR ALL: HOW STATE ACTION CAN FOSTER INCLUSIVE MIXED-INCOME COMMUNITIES

Ben Metcalf
Terner Center for Housing Innovation, University of California, Berkeley

> *"… [T]he new housing units would include low-income, high-density housing apartments. This would mean we would have uneducated people living in Cupertino. […T]his would make the current residents of Cupertino uncomfortable." (From a community member's PowerPoint presentation at a September 2018 City of Cupertino council hearing, providing misleading information in opposition to a proposed new housing development.)*[1]

Californians who believe that the legacies of residential segregation are behind us (or comfortably situated to the East of the Sierra Nevada Mountains) would be well served to attend a city council meeting in one of California's more exclusive coastal communities when a new affordable or mixed-income project is being proposed. Indeed, in California, where I served as director of the state Department of Housing and Community Development, we contend not only with neighborhood resistance to communities of color and new affordable housing but with a history of actions that perpetuate those patterns—as does much of the rest of the United States. Richard Rothstein's *Color of Law*, published in 2017, captures well the legacies of racially restricted housing covenants, exclusionary municipal zoning, and racist federal mortgage insurance policies that greatly shaped residential

---

1   Shirin Ghaffary, "In Apple's Hometown of Cupertino, a Debate over the Fate of an Old Mall Epitomizes Silicon Valley's Class Divide: Who Gets to Live in One of Silicon Valley's Richest Cities?," *Recode*, September 21, 2018, https://www.recode.net/2018/9/21/17883246/silicon-valley-cupertino-development-housing-apple-yimby-nimby.

patterns of development through the 20th century and into the 21st, even in a state that consistently has seen itself as progressive, innovative, and welcoming to diversity.

The consequences of those past practices and the ongoing challenges of achieving mixed-income communities today translate directly into decreased economic mobility and serve as a direct affront to the American Dream. Look no further than the ground-breaking research compiled as part of the Opportunity Atlas[2] project, a collaboration between the U.S. Census Bureau, Harvard University, and Brown University, which married federal tax data and census records for 40 million Americans over a three-decade timespan to create indicators of upward mobility at the tract level (such as increased social cohesion, higher median income, low rates of incarceration, or presence of two-parent households). The research findings suggest that, all else being equal, a family that lives in a neighborhood with above-average prospects increases a child's lifetime earnings as an adult by $200,000 and dramatically decreases the likelihood of incarceration.[3] When we overlay these findings with data showing that being Black in California correlates closely with living in a high-poverty neighborhood, the challenges ahead become clear.[4]

Remarkably, although California today would be the fifth-largest global economy in terms of gross domestic product if it were considered a country and has supported one of the longest periods of economic expansion in history, it also has the highest poverty rate in the nation when cost of living is

---

2   Opportunity Atlas, accessed June 20, 2019, https://opportunityatlas.org

3   John Ydstie, "The American Dream Is Harder to Find in Some Neighborhoods," *National Public Radio*, October 1, 2018, https://www.npr.org/2018/10/01/649701669/the-american-dream-is-harder-to-find-in-some-neighborhoods.

4   While the Opportunity Atlas data are clear that Black boys who move to higher-opportunity neighborhoods earlier in their childhood have higher incomes and lower rates of incarceration, it must be noted that Black boys are disproportionately located in neighborhoods that impede their long-term economic mobility. In addition, uniquely as compared to girls and non-Black boys, those higher-opportunity neighborhoods that most benefit Black boys appear to be ones that also have higher rates of fathers and lower rates of racial bias among Whites: "Among low-poverty neighborhoods (those with poverty rates below 10%), there are two factors that are strongly associated with better outcomes for Black men and smaller Black-White gaps: low levels of racial bias among Whites and high rates of father presence among Blacks… Less than 5% of Black children currently grow up in areas with a poverty rate below 10% and more than half of Black fathers present. In contrast, 63% of White children live in areas with poverty rates below 10% and more than half of White fathers present." See Raj Chetty et al., "Race and Economic Opportunity in the United States: An Intergenerational Perspective," NBER working paper No. 24441, National Bureau of Economic Research, (Cambridge, MA, March 2018).

considered, according to the U.S. Census Bureau.[5] And the share of households living in poverty is growing. Some 1.7 million low-income households are considered to have "worst-case housing needs" (i.e., paying more than half their income on housing costs without receiving any subsidized housing assistance), as of 2017.[6] Furthermore, notwithstanding a torrent of media attention on the remarkable gentrification (and displacement) of lower-income neighborhoods and communities of color in California, the number of neighborhoods of concentrated poverty has also been growing. Between 2000 and 2017, the growth in the poor population for California's 10 largest metros averaged 28 percent, while the growth of poor residents in high-poverty census tracts averaged 53 percent. This is experienced unequally by race and ethnicity. Two-thirds of Black and Hispanic/Latinx households in California experiencing poverty live in high-poverty neighborhoods, while only one-quarter of non-Hispanic White households experiencing poverty live in high-poverty neighborhoods.[7]

The factors that fuel this increased economic segregation by place and race are varied and include national and global trends that are generally going in the wrong direction. They include insufficient poverty-alleviating tax and federal spending policies; the collapse of unions; and, in places like California, a massive underproduction of housing over several decades, all of which have combined to price entry-level housing—both for-sale and rental—well out of reach of those who need it most. These economic factors in turn exacerbated residential patterns of racial segregation that had deep roots in state and federal policies enacted over the past century.

However, all hope is certainly not lost. A half century of intentional experimentation, kicked off in the wake of the federal War on Poverty and the Civil Rights Act, brings into focus some clear models of what works to foster diverse and inclusive communities. These can be clustered into two categories, revitalization and mobility strategies. Nationally, large-scale revitalization strategies include place-based efforts like the U.S. Department of Housing and

---

5   Liana Fox, *The Supplemental Poverty Measure: 2017*, (Washington, DC: U.S. Census Bureau, 2018), 26-27, https://www.census.gov/library/publications/2018/demo/p60-265.html.

6   California Department of Housing and Community Development, *California's Housing Future: Challenges and Opportunities*, (Sacramento, CA: California Department of Housing and Community Development, 2018), http://www.hcd.ca.gov/policy-research/plans-reports/docs/SHA_Final_Combined.pdf.

7   *Ibid.*

Urban Development (HUD)'s HOPE VI Program and Choice Neighborhoods Initiative, which focused on redeveloping existing affordable housing, as well as the Obama Administration's much-lauded Promise Zones effort. Mobility strategies that facilitate access to high-income neighborhoods include HUD's promulgation of Small Area Fair Market Rent standards to allow voucher holders access to higher payment standards in more affluent neighborhoods.

A "both/and" approach to promoting revitalization and mobility is perhaps best articulated by the Obama Administration's Affirmative Furthering Fair Housing (AFFH) rule that was promulgated in 2015. The new AFFH federal regulation aimed, in part, to redress the legacy of past governmental actions by adopting plans for the expenditure of federal funds that obligate state and local jurisdictions to take into consideration these past practices. (Under the Trump Administration's Secretary of Housing and Urban Development Ben Carson, local governments' obligation to comply with the rule was suspended pending consideration of changes to it.)

At the state level, Massachusetts' Chapter 40B program has proven successful in overriding local zoning bylaws to allow developers to build affordable housing in jurisdictions where less than 10 percent of the housing stock is affordable.[8] New Jersey's fair housing standards, though they have had a more mixed track record, were created to redress past discriminatory practices. These standards obligate towns to approve their fair share of affordable housing (or, failing that, to pay the costs of affordable housing in other jurisdictions) and created an independent Council on Affordable Housing, which oversaw those obligations and monitored local compliance.[9]

Indeed, with the retreat of federal leadership on both funding levels and fair housing, states increasingly are stepping up to push these types of efforts forward. They are doing so first by continuing the effort to conduct effective comprehensive planning—for example, by incorporating findings from plans

---

8   Since enactment of the law in 1972, there has been a 10-fold increase in the number of towns in Massachusetts that have at least 10 percent of their housing stock reserved for low- or moderate-income household. See Spencer M. Cowan, "Anti-Snob Land Use Laws, Suburban Exclusion, and Housing Opportunity," *Journal of Urban Affairs* 28, no. 3 (June 2006): 300.

9   Both of these developments emerged out of the Supreme Court's 1975 and 1983 decisions in the Mount Laurel case, which led to a set of state fair housing standards that included state mandates on local governments to approve affordable housing. These controversial regulations initially allowed wealthier towns to opt out of their obligations by paying other municipalities to build up to half their shares and did not prevent jurisdictions from exclusively serving elderly affordable households.

developed for use of federal funds that expressly take into account Obama Administration-era guidance on Affirmatively Furthering Fair Housing plans even if not mandated by HUD—and by leaning in on metropolitan planning organizations to conduct regional planning and regional growth plans that can serve as templates for local-development patterns. In California, every eight years regional governments must create Sustainable Communities Strategies that serve as regional templates for growth strategies and regional and transportation investments. They must assign housing permitting targets for homes serving different income levels to all member jurisdictions (indeed, all cities must accept at least a minimal allocation of lower-income homes, for which they must plan and zone); and, more recently, regions and cities are obligated by state law to incorporate a fair housing lens into this process.[10]

The second way states are stepping up is by building on, and innovating from, national models for revitalization and mobility. This essay focuses on efforts to further mixed-income communities under the strong leadership of former Governor Jerry Brown and current Governor Gavin Newsom. Both leaders pushed to use state power in new and creative ways to help the state address racial and economic inequities while also facilitating economic gains. As Gov. Newsom said shortly after his inauguration in 2019: "The California Dream is in peril if we don't act to address this housing crisis. The cost of housing—both for homeowners and renters—is the defining quality-of-life concern for people across this state. Housing costs threaten to erode our state's long-term prosperity and are driving hard-working Californians to look for opportunities elsewhere."[11]

---

10 The California work on regional planning—specifically, the Sustainable Communities Strategies land-use plans that all regions must create and update regularly—served as the model for federal Sustainable Communities grants that were jointly awarded by HUD, the Department of Transportation, and the Environmental Protection Agency starting in 2010 until it was defunded several years later in the wake of the Republican takeover of the U.S. House of Representatives because of concerns that it constituted federal overreach into local land-use matters. For more information on California's Sustainable Communities Strategies, see California Air Resources Board, *2018 Progress Report: California's Sustainable Communities and Climate Protection Act*, (Sacramento, CA: California Air Resources Board, 2018), https://ww2.arb.ca.gov/sites/default/files/2018-11/Final2018Report_SB150_112618_02_Report.pdf.

11 Office of Governor Gavin Newsom, "Governor Newsom Unveils Proposals to Tackle Housing Affordability Crisis," January 15, 2019, https://www.gov.ca.gov/2019/01/15/housing-affordability-crisis/.

FACILITATING MIXED-INCOME COMMUNITIES IN EXCLUSIONARY COMMUNITIES: REBALANCING STATE AFFORDABLE HOUSING INVESTMENTS

Starting in early 2017, leaders within the State of California's Department of Housing and Community Development (HCD) and the State Treasurer's office collaborated on an initiative to more equitably award public subsidies for multifamily affordable housing developments in state subsidy programs and the Low-Income Housing Tax Credit (LIHTC) program. The initiative stemmed from a concern that too many of the state's affordable housing investments were in lower-resourced areas and inadvertently might be perpetuating patterns of segregation and poverty. State officials also recognized the growing body of data suggesting improved outcomes for children in mixed-income neighborhoods, as well as the risks of litigation if they couldn't assess and defend the underlying data.[12]

Pulling together researchers from the Terner Cerner for Housing Innovation and the Haas Institute at University of California (UC) Berkeley, the Center for Regional Change at UC Davis, the Kirwan Institute at The Ohio State University, Enterprise Community Partners, and California Housing Partnership Corporation, the state launched an effort to better identify which California census tracts might be most conducive to economic mobility for children growing up in low-income families. The Opportunity Mapping effort, as it was called, identified approximately 25 evidence-based indicators in environmental, economic, and educational areas that predicted upward economic mobility. These indicators were regionally weighted and then filtered by racial/ethnic segregation and/or concentration of poverty to create a tract-level map.[13]

The results were eye-opening: Back-testing showed that 62 percent of affordable homes in large-family new construction developments that had

---

[12] A notable example is the litigation brought by the Inclusive Communities Project against the State of Texas Department of Housing and Community Affairs for its disproportionate awarding of federal Low-Income Housing Tax Credits in higher poverty communities, which ultimately worked its way in 2015 to the United States Supreme Court, see Texas Department of Housing and Community Affairs v. Inclusive Communities Project, Inc., 135 S. Ct. 2507 (2015).

[13] The opportunity mapping team's review of the literature confirmed the extent to which living in racially and ethnically concentrated areas of poverty constrained upward economic mobility and so used data on that item to filter out tracts that otherwise showed positive indicators for purposes of reflecting low and lowest resource areas.

received 9 percent LIHTC allocations from the state of California since 2003 were located in the poorest and most racially segregated census tracts—and only 7 percent of homes were located in areas with the most resources.[14]

Responding to these findings, over the course of 2018 and early 2019 the state of California enacted new regulations and program guidelines for LIHTC and other state subsidy programs that provide low-income families more options for where to live.[15] Changes included new scoring boosts for new-construction family projects proposed for high-opportunity neighborhoods over others. Projects in high-opportunity neighborhoods no longer needed to be proximate to amenities traditionally valued in the scoring process (such as grocery stores, drug stores, and schools) for which the literature had not identified improved outcomes for residents of the developments.[16] Also, in recognition of the additional costs (such as higher land values, higher permitting and impact fees, and longer approval processes) that complicate development of affordable housing in more affluent areas, program changes allowed somewhat greater subsidy levels for those projects. Accordingly, a greater share of affordable housing now is being developed in wealthier communities, pushing those communities in a mixed-income direction by opening up heretofore unobtainable opportunities for lower-income families to access affordable housing in single-family, for-sale communities that may otherwise have been entirely priced out of reach.[17]

---

14 The two types of federal low-income housing tax credits are the 9 percent and 4 percent credits. The 9 percent federal credits are much more valuable, limited in supply, and awarded through a competitive process. The 4 percent tax credits derive from a project's use of tax-exempt bond authority and are limited only by the amount of bond cap available to California. Back-testing data are from internal memorandum prepared by the Opportunity Mapping Research Team.

15 At present, two HCD-administered programs incorporate Opportunity Mapping: federal HOME funds administered by the state and state bond-funded Multifamily Housing Program (MHP) funds. Roughly $70 million in state-administered HOME funds and $560 million in MHP funds are expected to be released over the next two years. See "Notices of Funding Availability (NOFAs)," California Department of Housing and Community Development. Accessed July 11, 2019, http://www.hcd.ca.gov/grants-funding/nofas.shtml.

16 "High-opportunity" refers to the top two quintiles of census tracts that the Opportunity Mapping tool indicates to be most predictive of upward economic mobility.

17 In the initial funding year for the 9 percent low-income housing tax credit round, Mark Stivers, then the executive director of the Tax Credit Allocation Committee, estimated that only two more projects in high-opportunity areas were awarded funding than would have without the credit. However, this reflects in part the long lead time for developers to identify and prepare sites prior to submitting them for competitive funding. State officials expect to see higher rates of developments in high-resource neighborhoods going forward. No data are yet available on changes in outcomes on the state HOME program or Multifamily Home Program, but state officials are monitoring closely.

FACILITATING MIXED-INCOME COMMUNITIES IN EXCLUSIONARY COMMUNITIES: OVERRIDING LOCAL CONTROL

Increased availability of government funding to support affordable housing in high-resource areas is important but insufficient to ensure mixed-income communities in the absence of conducive sites, zoning, and politics. Fortunately, the changes to California's state funding programs were accompanied by new state streamlining authority, enacted as part of the state's 2017 Housing Package. Senate Bill 35, a highly contentious component of that package pushed by key leaders in the state senate and Governor Brown, required cities and counties to accept a new State Ministerial Streamlining Program that allows new, affordable housing to be built in communities that are not keeping pace with their state-mandated affordable housing goals. California, similar to other states with strong histories of local control of land-use policy, has seen local leaders repeatedly capturing the local political process to regulate who lives (and, more critically, who does not live) in their neighborhoods and cities. As of April 2019, only 11 of 540 cities were keeping pace with their share of the state's goal for affordable housing production,[18] thus virtually all communities are subject to streamlining.[19] Additional eligibility limitations to the State Ministerial Streamlining Program stipulate that the proposed housing conform to local zoning, be located on an infill site, and pay prevailing wages to construction workers.

The streamlining authority means that cities cannot say "no" to a mixed-income or affordable housing project, nor can they substantially de-densify it or cause it to comply with ad hoc and expensive design requirements if a developer

---

18 Since 1969, California has required that all local governments adequately plan to meet the housing needs of everyone in the community, based on demographic projections calculated at the state level. California's local governments meet this requirement by adopting housing plans that serve as the local government's blueprint for how the city and/or county will grow and develop. The state's Department of Housing and Community Development regularly reviews all local governmental zoning plans and regulatory systems to ensure that opportunities exist for private developers to build both market-rate and affordable housing.

19 The state's mapping tool for compliance with Senate Bill 35, which documents residential permit issuances for lower-income and market-rate housing compared to state housing goals, can be found on HCD's website. There are two tiers of cities that must comply with streamlining: those that are meeting their state targets for market-rate housing and must streamline developments in which residential units are primarily affordable, and those that are meeting neither their affordable nor their market-rate targets and must approve any project that has at least 10 percent of its units restricted to lower-income households. See "Housing Element Open Data Project and SB 35B Determination," California Department of Housing and Community Development, accessed July 11, 2019, http://cahcd.maps.arcgis.com/apps/View/index.html?appid=8ea29422525e4d4c96d52235772596a3.

chooses to use the streamlining provision of state land-use authority. In such an instance, the project must be reviewed in a non-discretionary fashion only for its conformance to local objective standards codified in the ordinance, and the project cannot be subject to litigation under the California Environmental Quality Act (CEQA). In addition, HCD was given express authority both to codify this policy through regulations and to enforce it as necessary in partnership with the State's Attorney General. The regulations were finalized in December 2018, and so the early impacts will need to be tracked.

These policy changes have two important intended effects: affordable projects can be built in neighborhoods and cities where they might otherwise be locally disallowed, as is too often the case in affluent, exclusive communities wary of moving toward a mixed-income neighborhood; and the projects can be built more quickly and at lower costs than might otherwise be the case.

Developers have begun to test the new regulations with early but promising results. A 130-unit affordable family housing project at 681 Florida Street in San Francisco, which made use of the streamlining authority, is expected to reduce the timeframe to receive local governmental approvals to build by six months to a year. In fact, San Francisco—along with several other large California cities— now is explicitly requiring use of some form of ministerial streamlining as a prerequisite to receiving local subsidy gap funds for affordable housing. Other projects using this new authority have now received approvals in both Berkeley and Cupertino, both infamous for their protracted entitlement processes and both of which have historically opposed denser affordable housing projects out of concerns that include the nebulous notion of "neighborhood character" or traffic impacts, which privilege existing residents over proposed residents. Ministerial streamlining is poised to bring 2,400 new units to Cupertino (half of which will be affordable to low-income households) and 142 units to Berkeley (all of which will be affordable to low-income households).

Fears that some cities might respond by comprehensively downzoning residential sites or placing moratoria on new construction have proven unfounded. Few, if any, have tried this approach because the state of California requires cities to zone for their fair share of both low-income and market-rate housing. Moreover, the state 2017 Housing Package of legislation included new authority for HCD to retain the State's Attorney General to challenge cities that sidestepped that authority. Indeed, in January 2019 the state of California brought suit against the city of Huntington Beach for its failure to comply with state housing law, including its provision of a minimum level of zoned land available for low-income housing.

The new State Streamlining Ministerial Program also has been bolstered by the enactment, effective in January 2019, of a new California Fair Housing law that fills the gap left by HUD's suspension of its Affirmatively Furthering Fair Housing rule. It does so by imposing on all California cities an obligation to consider racial equity and patterns of economic and racial segregation in both their local funding decisions and their local land-use decisions. This new legal authority gives broad latitude to the public to bring suit against cities that either fail to enable state streamlining or lack equity-oriented zoning and land-use maps to begin with (for example, by obtaining higher-density zoning conducive to building multifamily developments in neighborhoods that have historically refused anything other than single-family zoning and that disproportionately fail to house lower-income individuals or persons of color).

FOSTERING MIXED-INCOME COMMUNITIES IN RACIALLY/ETHNICALLY CONCENTRATED AREAS OF POVERTY

Efforts to give low-income communities access to opportunity cannot hinge solely on providing choices for individuals and families to relocate into exclusive communities. Nor can they focus only on mitigating the impacts of rising rents and home prices in decreasingly affordable, gentrifying neighborhoods. For those communities that have endured generational segregation and entrenched poverty, California's Transformative Climate Community (TCC) program offers another possible solution. TCC grants support community-led initiatives to tackle entrenched environmental, health, and economic concerns in California's most disadvantaged census tracts. Using a place-based, neighborhood-level, community-driven approach, the program helps bring together key community actors, including local government, advocacy groups, anchor institutions, and others, who holistically tackle the issues that contribute to poverty and segregation while also facilitating a low-carbon, climate-friendly alternative. Collaborators invest simultaneously in preserving affordable housing, improving resident mobility options, and investing in evidence-based services and key community facilities for low-income residents, generally in partnership with local government and academic researchers. The program's design draws heavily on lessons learned from the federal Strong Cities, Strong Communities initiative; the federal Promise Zones Initiative, which does not provide federal funding directly; and HUD's Choice Neighborhoods, for which demand has far outstripped limited congressionally appropriated funds.

TCC was authorized in 2016 following intense advocacy from racial equity and environmental justice organizations with concerns that California's ambitious climate-change goals, launched under Governor Arnold Schwarzenegger, ignored issues of racial equity and the realities of entrenched poverty. The state's climate-change efforts hinged on an ambitious cap-and-trade program that succeeded in lowering carbon emissions but also allowed emitters located close to poor neighborhoods to buy their way out of environmental impacts that were disproportionately affecting communities of color. In fact, a San Francisco State University study published in 2018 found that increased emissions from regulated facilities occurred more often in neighborhoods populated by people of color or low-income, less-educated, and non-English-speaking residents.[20]

TCC is funded entirely from proceeds generated through California's quarterly cap-and-trade auctions by polluters that are unable or unwilling to achieve certain regulatory targets for greenhouse gas emissions and instead purchase carbon credits. In 2016, as this program was being renewed, Governor Jerry Brown and legislative leaders faced significant opposition from the progressive left, which chafed at the lack of an equity focus, and from conservative Democrats and moderate Republicans, who disdained any increase in regulation and fees on businesses. By explicitly targeting the TCC program to the most disadvantaged census tracts—which in California happened to be overwhelmingly located in the high-poverty, high-minority, and relatively conservative San Joaquin Valley—Governor Brown and other leaders reached a delicate balance. Outgoing Fresno Mayor Ashley Swearingen, a Republican who had collaborated closely with the Obama Administration on Strong Cities, Strong Communities, a place-based initiative similar to the proposed program, was an early advocate for TCC who helped bring over reluctant moderate Assembly Democrats representing the San Joaquin Valley.

To date, almost $200 million has been deployed through one round of TCC planning grants and two rounds of implementation grants. Grant amounts have ranged from $22 million to $75 million to support efforts in neighborhoods

---

20 Lara Cushing et al., "Carbon Trading, Co-Pollutants, and Environmental Equity: Evidence from California's Cap-and-Trade Program (2011–2015)," *PLOS Medicine* 15, no. 7 (July 2018): 4.

in Los Angeles, Fresno, Riverside County, Pacoima, and Sacramento. For example, the Housing Authority of the County of Los Angeles (HACLA) is the lead grantee for the Watts Rising initiative, which received one of three TCC implementation grants in the inaugural round. The Watts neighborhood is home to a large population of individuals without legal status, for whom English is not a native language, and has a substantial Black community.[21] Watts residents have experienced historic discrimination in housing accessibility, making these two majority populations in Watts less likely to advocate for their rights as tenants or to utilize the government and legal channels available to them.

With the TCC grant, HACLA brought together a coalition of more than a dozen different civic, stakeholder, and governmental organizations to facilitate a range of interrelated investments intended to catalyze private-sector investment while benefiting existing residents. Pending efforts include redeveloping dilapidated homes in the Jordan Downs public housing development, opening 118,000 square feet of new commercial space, offering electric-vehicle car sharing and electric shuttle buses, constructing new solar initiatives, launching a new food waste prevention program to divert 300 tons from landfills, and much more. HACLA aims to prevent the displacement of low-income residents through resident education and access to legal services, creating new deed-restricted affordable housing and retrofitting existing housing stock to lower expenses. A workforce development plan is in place to connect Watts residents with new jobs created by the TCC projects; at least 30 percent of all new hires will be local, low-income residents. As one Watts resident put it, "The Transformative Climate Communities program will allow Watts to finally move away from survival mode to becoming an integrative, sustainable community."[22]

While future investments in other communities through TCC will hinge on continuing to direct cap-and-trade funds toward this purpose via the state

---

[21] Since the 1990s, Watts has seen a rapid influx of households of Hispanic/Latinx origin and is currently 73 percent Hispanic/Latinx and 25 percent Black. Almost half of the neighborhood's residents have extremely low incomes and high housing cost burdens, paying more than 35 percent of income for housing. Watts has the highest number of single-parent households in the city, and almost 50 percent of Watts' residents are 17 years old or younger (compared to 23 percent citywide). Nearly 50 percent of residents over age 25 do not have a high school diploma, and only 4 percent have a four-year degree or higher. From "Watts Rising: Transformative Climate Communities," California Strategic Growth Council, accessed July 12, 2019, http://sgc.ca.gov/programs/tcc/docs/20190201TCC_Awardee_Watts.pdf.

[22] *Transformative Climate Communities*: January 29, 2018 hearing of the California Strategic Growth Council (testimony of Watts resident).

budget process, the early successes of initial investments as in Watts will help sustain the political will.[23] Furthermore, the TCC program has been aided by federal tax reform's creation of the Opportunity Zone Program, which has significant geographic alignment with the eligible census tracts designated as disadvantaged under the TCC. In his 2018 budget proposal, Governor Newsom called for the legislature to offer conforming state tax changes to affordable housing and green infrastructure projects located in federal Opportunity Zones.

CONCLUSION AND IMPLICATIONS FOR ACTION

The challenge of creating and sustaining mixed-income communities is significant but achievable. As experiences in California illustrate, state leaders can take the mantle to devise policy interventions that are commensurate with the challenges in front of them and deploy solutions, at scale, even if federal supports diminish or are not fully in place. To succeed over the long term, however, we must be diligent about building on what has worked—learning from mistakes and holding ourselves accountable to documentable outcomes—and doubling down wherever we see momentum. To that end, highlighted below are a few key implications for future action.

Implications for Policy

While the federal government has historically led on housing matters, states can establish housing as a priority of statewide importance, and they have a powerful role to play in setting statewide and regional housing goals. States can guide innovation in land-use policy, ensure affirmatively advancing fair housing, provide resources and technical support to local governments, and hold jurisdictions accountable for plans and progress toward implementing local governments' share of the state's overall housing goals.

Implications for Research and Evaluation

Understanding and measuring progress against key data indicators is essential for achieving policy outcomes. Pulling data on economic factors into a place-based format, as has been done in developing opportunity mapping programs, is crucial for directing policy interventions, measuring outcomes, and iterating

---

23 "Governor Newsom's proposed 2019-20 budget includes $40 million for the Transformative Climate Communities program," See "2019-20 Governor's Budget," California Department of Finance, accessed July 12, 2019, http://www.ebudget.ca.gov/budget/2019-20/#/Home.

programs successfully.

Implications for Development and Investment

While it may be tempting to offer policy quick-fixes to address our most visible public problems, long-term change must include tackling root causes. The homelessness crisis in California is an instructive example. Although there may be cause to invest in shelters, the drivers of rising homelessness rates stem from the underlying lack of affordable housing supply. Root-cause solutions require inclusive intersectoral efforts. While leadership from within state government may be key to launching such initiatives, civic, academic, and business support must be incorporated to flesh out the details and ensure long-term fidelity to the vision.

Implications for Residents and Community Members

The land-use decisions that most impact mixed-income communities happen at the local level; local government should be the first point of entry for concerned residents and community members. However, given the role of land use in shaping historic patterns of segregation and the hostility of many local governments to reform, state action may ultimately be a more effective lever in facilitating mixed-income communities in otherwise exclusive jurisdictions. Organizing residents and community members and engaging at the state level with advocates and elected officials affords marginalized populations the opportunity to gain strength and influence.

■ ■ ■

BEN METCALF *is Managing Director of the Terner Center for Housing Innovation at the University of California, Berkeley. He was appointed Director of the California Department of Housing and Community Development (HCD) in 2015. Prior to joining HCD, Mr. Metcalf worked at the U.S. Department of Housing and Urban Development (HUD) in Washington, D.C., where he served most recently as an appointee of President Barack Obama in the role of Deputy Assistant Secretary of HUD's Office of Multifamily Housing Programs. Previously, he developed mixed-income and mixed-use communities with California-based BRIDGE Housing Corporation company. Mr. Metcalf earned his Bachelor of Arts in history from Amherst College and his Master in public policy and urban planning from the Harvard Kennedy School.*

QUALIFIED ALLOCATION PLANS AS AN INSTRUMENT OF MIXED-INCOME PLACEMAKING

Bryan P. Grady
South Carolina State Housing Finance and Development Authority [1]

Carlie J. Boos
Affordable Housing Alliance of Central Ohio

In the American economic and political context, housing—mixed-income or otherwise—does not blossom organically; it must be financed. However, the profit maximization inherent in traditional financing vehicles naturally steers housing development toward serving the highest-income residents possible. Too frequently, reasonable investor returns and project sustainability are incompatible not only with affordability but also broader inclusion and equity objectives like community development, population health, and resident growth.

State housing finance agencies, or HFAs, are uniquely situated to resolve this contradiction through their administration of the Low-Income Housing Tax Credit (LIHTC) program. Governed by locally written Qualified Allocation Plans (QAPs), states have substantial latitude to distribute tax credit resources in an equitable manner that promotes integrated communities.

Our experience in affordable housing, particularly in crafting policy at the Ohio Housing Finance Agency (OHFA), has shown that HFAs are organizations with sufficiently reliable resources and mission motivation—providing safe, decent, and affordable housing for all—to lead the mixed-income housing movement. OHFA policy changes illustrate how HFAs can help advance policies that promote mixed-income, racially diverse, and welcoming spaces. In this essay,

---

1   Disclaimer: Both authors were previously employed by the Ohio Housing Finance Agency. Views expressed in this essay are those of the authors alone and not necessarily those of the Ohio Housing Finance Agency, the State of Ohio, or the authors' current employers.

we describe four existing HFA methods for achieving income integration, all of which can be used independently or through a multifaceted approach. Then, we theorize about prospects for future policy implementations to further drive mixed-income development. A plethora of challenges stand in the way: regulatory capture, institutional inertia, and political constraints, among others. Success is achievable, but it requires inciting a minor revolution in housing and development mentality and inspiring a newfound respect for the integral and innovative role of HFAs.

BACKGROUND

Each state, as well as New York City, the District of Columbia, and four U.S. territories, has an HFA. Most HFAs were created by states to issue public activity bonds, established in the Tax Code of 1954, to support low- and moderate-income homeownership. Later, this role was expanded to allocating LIHTCs upon their creation in the Tax Reform Act of 1986.[2] Distinctively structured, HFAs have a wide range of responsibilities and spheres of influence. HFAs in some states are intricately woven into the political process, with leadership appointed by and responsive to governors. Others are highly independent and operate akin to socially conscious corporations. The vast majority of HFAs are members of the National Council of State Housing Agencies (NCSHA), which enables them to share best practices, learn from others in the field, and develop tools of self-governance.

While all HFAs have different roles and responsibilities, as noted above, nearly all have two core programmatic tasks: (1) issuance of mortgage revenue bonds and other financial instruments to support low- and moderate-income homeownership, and (2) administration of the federal LIHTC program. LIHTCs are indispensable for the development and preservation of affordable rental housing;[3] a 2012 report noted that the number of units financed using LIHTC was more than all public housing and federally assisted private housing

---

2 National Low Income Housing Coalition, *Advocates' Guide to Housing and Community Development Policy* (Washington: National Low Income Housing Coalition, 2019); Corrianne Scally, "States, Housing, and Innovation: The Role of State Housing Agencies" (PhD diss., Rutgers University-New Brunswick, 2007).

3 LIHTCs come in two varieties. The more valuable "9 percent" credits support approximately 70 percent of development costs but are capped by federal law and, therefore, awarded to affordable housing developers on a competitive basis. The ancillary "4 percent" credit provides a less potent subsidy, offsetting only about 30 percent of development expenses, but is only limited by the availability of tax-exempt bonds.

combined.[4] Furthermore, LIHTC was responsible for nearly all rent-restricted units placed into service in the 25 years prior to the report. According to federal data, more 3.05 million affordable housing units were produced via the LIHTC through 2016.[5] A state HFA's competitive allocation authority is determined by population, ranging in 2018 from $31 million in small states and U.S. territories to $1.07 billion in California, totaling $9.09 billion nationally.[6]

To distribute these resources, the Internal Revenue Code requires LIHTC allocators to establish a QAP that "sets forth selection criteria to be used to determine housing priorities [...] which are appropriate to local conditions." Not only must states have a QAP, federal law mandates that this plan must give preference to projects serving the lowest-income tenants, preserving affordability for the longest periods, and serving qualified census tracts as part of a concerted community reinvestment plan.[7] Additionally, projects must be evaluated on 10 criteria ranging from the length of local housing waiting lists to the energy efficiency of the project.

Notably, the Internal Revenue Code is silent on a state's responsibility, legal or otherwise, to remedy the injustices of racism and segregation. This absence is balanced by the duty to affirmatively further fair housing that permeates all aspects of federal funding recipients' housing agendas.[8] The gravity of this charge is both understood and solemnly accepted by many policymakers. Accordingly, QAPs can be steeped in the code words of desegregation ("opportunity housing") or the language of restitution ("revitalization" or "preservation"). However, significant state variation remains; for every state with an obvious commitment to equitable placemaking, there is another that concentrates more singularly on the "bricks and sticks" subsidy. Those that chart a moderate course are given the latitude to do so through a byzantine process that shields them from broader public scrutiny. This relative isolation

---

4   Jill Khadduri et al., "What Happens to Low-Income Housing Tax Credit Properties at Year 15 and Beyond?" (Bethesda, MD: Abt Associates Inc., 2012), https://www.huduser.gov/portal/publications/what_happens_lihtc_v2.pdf.

5   "Low-Income Housing Tax Credits," U.S. Department of Housing and Urban Development, accessed June 21, 2019, https://www.huduser.gov/portal/datasets/lihtc.html.

6   Notice 2018-45, 2018-21 I.R.B 620. Credits allocated to a project are awarded in 10 installments once units are placed in service.

7   Internal Revenue Code, 26 U.S.C. § 42 (2001).

8   Fair Housing Act, 26 U.S.C. § 3608 (2010).

and limited stakeholder feedback loop should be seen as an opportunity for relatively easy policy change: 20 or 30 vocal proponents of change could easily form a majority in any QAP hearing room. A written letter, a public comment, a casual coffee with a career bureaucrat are all accessible and powerful devices to shape QAP policy.

Within this overlapping regulatory framework, HFAs have extraordinary flexibility and authority to maximize the utility of the program while reflecting community needs. Leadership rests with the states, which make decisions for the LIHTC program based on a keen understanding of hyperlocal housing needs, building conditions, and economic prospects. Each state's policy agenda is intended to be collaborative, responsive, and transparent. Because the QAP process is centered in HFAs, largely operating outside the legislative process, QAP policies can be formed quickly and provide immediate resolutions to emerging market disruptions.

THE OHIO CONTEXT

OHFA is a blend of the two HFA structural extremes noted earlier, as it is neither a governmental department nor an autonomous entity; it is a quasi-independent state agency administered by an 11-member board, appointed by the governor, which selects an executive director to lead the agency's staff. The biennial QAP development process is managed by a planning, preservation, and development team and informed by the agency-wide strategic annual plan developed by the office of housing policy. For OHFA to arrive at its policy priorities, community engagement is purposeful and extensive, including legally mandated hearings, written comment periods, public forums and trainings, regional focus groups, and one-on-one meetings offered with relevant stakeholders throughout the year.

In addition to engaging with the general public, OHFA has deep ties to stakeholders who work for organizations that facilitate equitable development. The community engagement helps the QAP tackle issues ranging from affordable healthcare access to green building techniques, transit-oriented design, infant mortality prevention, anchor institution engagement, and food desert avoidance. This occurs against a backdrop of cultivating relationships with relevant stakeholders, including those from other state agencies, to break down silos and establish affordable housing as a platform for addressing other policy challenges. Active partnerships with Ohio's departments of education, Medicaid, developmental disabilities, mental health, and addiction services, in addition to the private housing and advocacy communities, further a broad agenda designed to advance the needs of low-income tenants.

The result of this work is that OHFA has funded nearly 130,000 rental units through the LIHTC program since 1987, with about 100,000 units currently subject to rent and income restrictions and undergoing routine compliance monitoring. Based on data reported to OHFA by property managers, LIHTC residents are overwhelmingly in deep economic distress, with a median household income around $13,000 per year. Furthermore, the LIHTC program serves White and Black tenants in approximately equal numbers in a state that is 82 percent White and 13 percent Black.

OHFA has been eager to serve as a policy entrepreneur, with the state's QAP emphasizing the expansion and support of mixed-income communities.[9] The totality of the QAP embodies a "both-and" approach to development that not only expands mixed-income environments but also promotes investments in legacy neighborhoods, expansion of suburban affordability, and rural access to rental stock. The agency's leadership took the position that (a) the development of mixed-income places clearly falls within an HFA's mandate; (b) despite the myriad challenges this approach necessarily invites, the potential to bridge community differences, strengthen bonds between diverse constituencies, and promote economic independence among low- and moderate-income Ohioans warrants decisive action; and (c) the legacy of racism and the deleterious impact of redlining—racially and ethnically concentrated poverty—is perched firmly atop government's shoulders and must be conscientiously and comprehensively unwound. OHFA's promotion of mixed-income development via the QAP dates back to at least 1997 and has endured through five governors and four executive directors, a testament to power of well-reasoned policy to overcome partisanship and bureaucratic gridlock.[10]

---

9 The 2019 Ohio Qualified Allocation Plan opens with the following statement of principles: "[T]his document advances the five primary policy objectives that were first articulated in this year's plan: Smart Revitalization, Portfolio Diversification, Healthy Living, Ending Homelessness and Cost Efficiency and Simplicity... We are honored to celebrate the fiftieth anniversary of the [Fair Housing Act] in the only way we see fit: with steadfast support for all those working to create diverse and accessible communities."

10 "Projects that create a mixture of market and affordable rental housing will receive 2 points," Ohio Housing Finance Agency, *1997 LIHTC Allocation Plan* (Columbus, OH: Ohio Housing Finance Agency, 1997).

How can OHFA and other HFAs accomplish these objectives? We begin with the "low-hanging fruit" before describing more multifaceted and visionary options.

METHOD ONE: BLENDING INCOMES WITHIN THE LIHTC FRAMEWORK

The easiest and most common way for HFAs to achieve some version of income integration is to require or incentivize a range of incomes inside LIHTC developments that, while significantly different from each other, all fall under the overarching "low-income" banner. This means that blue-collar workers earning 60 percent of area median income (AMI), families living on minimum-wage incomes and earning less than 30 percent of AMI (extremely low-income, or ELI), and residents whose incomes fall below 20 percent of AMI and who often survive solely on Supplemental Security Income all live in the same building. In addition, about half of Ohio LIHTC tenants have some form of further rent assistance through Section 8 or the Housing Choice Voucher program, allowing units that target higher-income populations to also serve those with little to no income. Although this distribution is more truncated than full income integration, this mix is designed to stimulate interaction between households with stable but low-wage jobs and households in more precarious economic conditions.

OHFA has long endorsed this approach to mixed-income housing development. A customized suite of financing tools makes it possible to serve ELI households while preserving the economic viability of a project:

- OHFA offers a 15 percent "basis boost" for new housing developments that set aside at least 25 percent of their units for ELI households, which ensures that additional tax credits are available to defray the reduced rents at the low end of the income bracket.[11]

- Developers are permitted to access a $75,000 developer fee supplement if they reserve over 25 percent of units for ELI households, a reflection of the additional planning and outreach services necessary to launch the development.

---

11 These policies were effective in the 2018-2019 QAP. As of this writing the 2020-2021 QAP has not been released.

- OHFA offers additional points within its competitive scoring process for both ELI targeting and incorporation of rental subsidies such as place-based Section 8 or the Section 811 Project Rental Assistance Program, both administered by the U.S. Department of Housing and Urban Development.

As a result of these incentives, 41 percent of the units in Ohio funded with competitive LIHTCs in 2018 had household income limits below the statutory maximum (i.e., 60 percent of AMI).

Income gradation is only likely to increase in coming years. The federal Consolidated Appropriations Act of 2018 permitted a new minimum set-aside called the "average income test." The average income test allows LIHTC units to serve households with incomes between 20 percent and 80 percent of AMI, provided the weighted average of income restrictions on LIHTC units does not exceed 60 percent of AMI. This allows for resources to be directed toward a wider array of populations while simultaneously facilitating deeper income targeting though self-subsidization practices, in which higher-income units are used to offset the rent losses of lower-income units. With increased income to the projects using the average income test—thanks to higher rents—more projects likely will be able to use the non-competitive 4 percent LIHTC credit, freeing up the highly competitive 9 percent credits and expanding the overall availability of housing development funds. It is now the states' responsibility to establish average income test policies that appropriately balance the integrative power of this tool with the risk mitigation necessary to protect assets until more comprehensive Internal Revenue Service guidance is released.

METHOD TWO: MEETING THE CHALLENGE OF FULL MARKET INTEGRATION

A more traditional view of income integration involves placing non-low-income, market-rate units into otherwise affordable developments. Often perceived as more challenging, evolving consumer demands and market-wide shortages are opening a window towards wider acceptance.[12]

In the HFA realm, this approach is typified by OHFA's sustained push to incorporate non-LIHTC units within tax credit communities. As noted

---

12 Kathleen McCormick, "Millennials' Preferences Are Good News for Mixed-Income Development," *Urban Land Magazine*, March 29, 2017, https://urbanland.uli.org/development-business/millennials-preferences-good-news-mixed-income-development/.

previously, in one form or another since 1997 OHFA has offered competitive scoring points to developments that construct market-rate units—i.e., those without income restrictions—alongside units reserved for low-income households. Tapping into the same self-subsidization concept described above, this ideally conserves limited state resources while aiming to achieve broader objectives of destigmatizing and demystifying other lived experiences and building egalitarian routes to shared prosperity.

The incentive's structure has evolved over time, adjusting how many market units are necessary to achieve the points required or how they will be treated by underwriters, but none proved sufficient to sway a significant number of applicants to propose fully mixed-income developments. Only about 3 percent of units in OHFA's portfolio lack income restrictions, and some of these are reserved for property managers and maintenance staff. This tepid reception was not unforeseeable, as there are many obstacles to market integration within LIHTC housing projects:

- Projects that fall outside the well-worn template of fully low-income projects embraced by developers and investors attract more skepticism and unease from investors and, therefore, a lower price in the market for their tax credits.

- During the development phase, affordable projects with market-rate units are forced to straddle an unusual debt position, stuck between two underwriting standards that make the lending risk difficult to parse and therefore result in higher interest rates than similarly situated LIHTC proposals. In an environment that champions cost containment, this trade-off could effectively act as a competitive disadvantage.

- Architects may struggle to design a unit that meets both the thriftiness demanded by use of public resources and the luxury necessary to attract a market-rate renter; reconciling these differences while honoring fair housing's equivalency spirit is a substantial challenge. Separating out non-LIHTC square footage via a condominium can ease some of these tensions, but it comes with an administrative price tag that restricts its feasibility.

- Operating an apartment building with non-LIHTC units adds complexity and potentially stiff compliance consequences during the leasing phase that are atypical for LIHTC deals. This challenge can be compounded by an expertise gap, with some affordable housing managers not yet conversant in balancing the differing needs of a blended population.

While the impact of any one of these challenges might be limited, when combined the challenges likely result in a lower equity price and unfavorable investment terms, making the deal less viable. However, these hurdles could be mitigated through social venture lending that more appropriately balances risk against outcomes and technical assistance to operators willing to take the leap.

Looking at the big picture in Ohio, QAP points for market-rate integration are currently situated within scoring categories that equally value the use of historic tax credits, design features to support older adults aging in place, and health programming. It is not surprising that, given the incentive's relatively low weight, developers are opting for more easily executable features. This impediment is compounded when cross-subsidization fails to provide sufficient income coverage for low-cost submarkets in which the economic profiles of a tax credit renter and a private tenant are essentially identical.

METHOD THREE: INTEGRATING LOW-INCOME BUILDINGS IN THRIVING NEIGHBORHOODS

Income inclusion isn't only relevant at the building level; it also is necessary at a community level. For decades, affordable housing has been concentrated in neighborhoods that lack meaningful access to self-stabilizing resources such as upwardly mobile jobs and high-quality schools. Rooted in a history of racism from redlining to white flight, the intergenerational cycle of poverty is self-perpetuating. Poor families in historically under-developed and under-financed neighborhoods lack access to the education, job opportunities, and other resources necessary to compete in the modern economy. Their low-income counterparts who may live in high-cost neighborhoods have proximity to necessary services but remain unable to earn enough income relative to their expenses to achieve self-sufficiency. Without a holistic approach that incorporates the goals of both affordability and accessibility, these generational patterns will reproduce. Encouragingly, research has shown that development of low-income housing in high-income and resource-rich communities improves many positive life outcomes for new residents while preserving quality of life for existing residents.[13]

---

13 Raj Chetty, Nathaniel Henderson, and Lawrence F. Katz, "The Effects of Exposure to Better Neighborhoods on Children: New Evidence from the Moving to Opportunity Experiment," *American Economic Review* 106, no. 4 (April 2016): 855-902, https://www.aeaweb.org/articles?id=10.1257/aer.20150572;

HFA leaders are increasingly cognizant of their responsibility to diversify the affordable housing portfolio, but simple solutions are elusive. HFAs must balance numerous and competing priorities, including assessing the proper valuation of community and culture in legacy lower-income neighborhoods, supporting the expansion of low-income households located in prosperous communities, recognizing the transformational power of capital in investment-hungry areas, satisfying legal obligations to affirmatively further fair housing, committing to the preservation of access on rapidly gentrifying blocks, facilitating mobility for families in low-income spaces, and easing the struggle of poor families in wealthy suburbs. The extent to which issues of race and ethnicity factor into these considerations, and the mechanisms by which they do so, should be honestly debated and deliberated at every opportunity.

OHFA has been recognized as a national leader in this space.[14] Reliable, localized data are invaluable to this effort. OHFA's partnership with the Kirwan Institute for the Study of Race and Ethnicity at The Ohio State University to build and continually refine a proprietary opportunity mapping system proved essential for understanding the geographic dimensions not only of opportunity but of neighborhood change in urban, suburban, and rural contexts.[15] This cataloguing of resources and liabilities provides the information OHFA uses to confront and address inequalities in the state's housing stock. While this work was not overtly focused on analyzing race and ethnicity, overlaying OHFA's opportunity maps with historical redlining maps dramatically demonstrates the undeniable link between economic landscapes and racism.

Using this rigorous tool, OHFA reconfigured its QAP to incentivize affordable housing development in economically flourishing neighborhoods. Consequently, in 2018, 40 percent of competitive LIHTC awards were situated in high- or very high-opportunity census tracts. As operationalized by Kirwan's research, these categories represent the top two quintiles of tracts based on a composite index that computes economic, educational, health, housing, and transportation conditions relative to peer tracts (i.e., urban, suburban, or rural areas). The

---

Ingrid G. Ellen, Karen M. Horn, and Katherine M. O'Regan, "Poverty Concentration and the Low-Income Housing Tax Credit: Effects of Siting and Tenant Composition," *Journal of Housing Economics* 34, (December 2016): 49-59, https://www.sciencedirect.com/science/article/pii/S1051137716300183.

14 National Council of State Housing Agencies, email message to author, April 13, 2018.

15 "Opportunity Mapping Tool," Ohio Finance Agency, accessed June 21, 2019, https://ohiohome.org/ppd/opportunitymap.aspx.

remaining investments, located in more traditional LIHTC locations, are tailored to maximize local benefits, such as strong transit infrastructure, stewardship of anchor institutions, and access to world-renowned healthcare facilities. This is the epitome of the "both-and" approach: meeting LIHTC residents wherever they are, supporting growth and autonomy, and providing them with supports that complement existing neighborhood amenities.

METHOD FOUR: ENCOURAGING HYPERLOCAL RENAISSANCE

Distinct from simply carving out islands of affordability in already stabilized neighborhoods, the renaissance method seeks to catalyze the growth of affordability and affluence simultaneously in depressed communities. Unsurprisingly, political and policy contexts make this type of neighborhood-level transformation extremely difficult to achieve, but HFAs are singularly qualified to lead the effort. At the most basic level, the Internal Revenue Code already requires tax credit allocators to give preference to developments situated within the parameters of a concerted community revitalization plan. Despite a long track record, however, the full potential of this innovative approach is only now being tested.

In 2016, OHFA created a "local initiatives" carve-out in its QAP. This reserved pool of funds gave developers the opportunity to compete for additional resources if their project contributed to a comprehensive, multi-phase or transformative community development effort. This initiative created a financing vehicle for Poindexter Phase III, a 159-unit mixed-income redevelopment of one of the nation's first public housing communities. The redevelopment was funded by a Choice Neighborhoods implementation grant and supported by an affiliate of the Purpose Built Communities network. When the final phase is completed, the refurbished neighborhood will include 450 housing units, partnerships with the City of Columbus and The Ohio State University to stimulate economic mobility, and a museum honoring the site's origins. Further, this transformational redevelopment is situated near Columbus' rapidly growing urban core, with access to abundant employment opportunities, transportation facilities, and neighborhood amenities.

Recently, OHFA moved forward with a more aggressive strategy for meeting renaissance goals. The 2019 QAP established the FHAct50 Building Opportunity Fund, which authorizes each of the state's three largest cities

(Columbus, Cleveland, and Cincinnati) to draw down $3 million in 9 percent LIHTCs (approximately $30 million in equity) over the next three years for affordable housing development. Operating outside the competitive process, this fund empowers cities to craft unique solutions without the usual scoring constraints. Instead, developments advanced under this fund must contribute to a comprehensive neighborhood revitalization plan that prioritizes income inclusivity and system-wide transformation. Further, OHFA requires each unit developed using LIHTC resources to be matched with a concurrent building permit for market-rate housing, ensuring that the projects will be placed within a growing mixed-income community.

This vision will only be realized if OHFA aggressively prioritizes current residents' growth, actively prevents displacement in the face of revitalization, and offers supports to facilitate comprehensive individual advancement. Accordingly, OHFA requires all FHAct50 Building Opportunity Fund developments to be spearheaded by a nonprofit with commitment to and leadership born from the community it serves. Moreover, each project must be accompanied by a high-impact service partnership customized to local needs, such as the development of new educational opportunities, construction of amenities to promote community health and wellbeing, or transformations in legal protections afforded to renters. These are all possibilities that are both achievable and meaningful to the population. Requiring unit configurations and building designs that equally welcome families, senior citizens, workers, and individuals with disabilities ensures that this chance to build opportunity is open to every walk of life.

As of this writing, all three FHAct50 Building Opportunity Fund cities have selected their target neighborhoods and are collaborating with residents to create long-term, sustainable development plans. While still very new, there are positive indications that the investment is being infused into gentrifying neighborhoods and communities where affordability and diversity are threatened. If these early signs are indicative of larger victories, the burden will shift back to the state to develop a feedback loop that capitalizes on momentum and replicates success. That responsiveness and malleability is both the crux of a fair housing philosophy that empowers the people it serves and a necessary foundation of any operationally achievable goal.

WHAT'S NEXT? THE REALISTIC AND THE RADICAL

How can HFAs continue to advocate for and facilitate the development of mixed-income communities? Most broadly, state HFAs must honestly assess the power they hold and the bounds of their influence, and advocates for racially and economically marginalized populations should strongly encourage such deliberations. This is, unquestionably, a state-by-state determination across political, legal, and jurisdictional dimensions.

At the programmatic level, Opportunity Zones—established in the Tax Cuts and Jobs Act of 2017—will open achievable avenues for affordable housing collaboration and leveraging that must be considered. These areas, nominated by state governors and approved by the U.S. Department of the Treasury, provide preferential tax treatment to investors who purchase assets situated within these putatively economically distressed areas. In Ohio, 320 census tracts in 73 counties are now Opportunity Zones.[16] There has been much discussion in communities nationwide about how to best leverage this new provision.[17] Stakeholders in these neighborhoods should consider ways in which this capital incentive can be used to generate broad-based prosperity. In recent months, much conversation has centered on regulations that the Internal Revenue Service will or will not place on the provision to ensure that incentivized economic activity actually takes place in designated neighborhoods and benefits current residents.[18] Proposed regulations were propagated by the Internal Revenue Service in April 2019 but were not finalized as of this writing.[19] LIHTC projects within these areas could potentially generate additional equity, as the tax benefits of an investment in affordable housing can be magnified for certain investors.[20] While this financing boost alone should naturally drive LIHTC

---

16 "Opportunity Zones," Ohio Development Services Agency, accessed June 21, 2019, https://development.ohio.gov/bs/bs_censustracts.htm.

17 Jordyn Grzelewski, "The Floodgates Are About to Open: Cuyahoga County, Cleveland Leaders Unveil Opportunity-Zone Plan," *The Plain Dealer*, March 21, 2019, https://www.cleveland.com/news/2019/03/the-floodgates-are-about-to-open-cuyahoga-county-cleveland-leaders-unveil-opportunity-zone-plan.html.

18 Mariam Rozen, "Give Us More Red Tape! Opportunity Zone Investors Implore IRS," *Financial Advisor IQ*, March 27, 2019, https://financialadvisoriq.com/c/2235593/269163.

19 Internal Revenue Service. "IRS Issues Guidance Relating to Deferral of Gains for Investments in a Qualified Opportunity Fund," News release, (April 17, 2017).

20 John Sciarretti, Michael Novogradac, and Peter Lawrence, "New Opportunity Zones Could Be Used to Finance Rental Housing," Novogradic (blog), February 23, 2018, https://www.novoco.com/notes-from-no-

development, HFAs may use the QAP to further direct the types of amenities or services necessary to bolster an emerging mixed-income neighborhood.

The central issue in how aggressive states can or should be with QAP-based policymaking is the degree to which communities and developers will pursue LIHTCs and other resources that HFAs can provide. Whether HFAs can, or should, use these tools to coax policy concessions is a valid discussion question. Theoretically, if interest in these resources is strong enough in an age of austerity, these funding streams could be used to pursue dramatic policy objectives. What if credits could only be directed to jurisdictions that repealed or blocked nuisance ordinances that compromised the housing situations of domestic violence victims? Or adopted "ban the box" legislation preventing employment discrimination against those residents who have a criminal justice background? What if suburbs could earn scoring points for their applicants by permitting density zoning or supporting transit infrastructure? What if organized NIMBY campaigns resulted in *more* points being awarded to developments fighting for affordable housing inroads in exclusionary communities? What if QAPs provided a funding set-aside to cities that promulgated inclusive zoning regulations?

To see how one of these ideas could work in practice, it is worth examining the last of these more closely. According to the Grounded Solutions Network, localities in 30 states have passed some form of inclusionary housing program that either mandates or incentivizes the creation of units affordable to low-income households within market-rate rental housing projects.[21] These policies were implemented both in urban cores and suburbs.[22] Of the latter, those in New Jersey—compelled by the state Supreme Court's *Mount Laurel* decisions—and Montgomery County, Maryland, are the most prominent.[23]

---

vogradac/new-opportunity-zones-could-be-used-finance-rental-housing.

21 "Inclusionary Housing Database Map," Grounded Solutions Network, accessed June 22, 2010, https://inclusionaryhousing.org/map/.

22 U.S. Department of Housing and Urban Development, "Inclusionary Zoning and Mixed-Income Communities," *Evidence Matters*, 2013, https://www.huduser.gov/portal/periodicals/em/spring13/highlight3.html.

23 These cases are *Southern Burlington County N.A.A.C.P. v. Mount Laurel Township* (1975) and *Southern Burlington County N.A.A.C.P. v. Mount Laurel Township* (1983), colloquially referred to as *Mount Laurel I* and *Mount Laurel II*, respectively. Southern Burlington County N.A.A.C.P. v. Mount Laurel Township, 67 N.J. 151 (1975); Southern Burlington County N.A.A.C.P. v. Mount Laurel Township, 92 N.J. 158 (1983).

The production of new housing through these programs is quite limited and, in many cases, it is more cost effective to pay an impact fee than construct the affordable units.[24] However, it might be possible to use LIHTCs to make these units more feasible, using state-level streamlined allocation techniques. At its most extreme, HFAs could theoretically condition the allocation of LIHTCs and other resources they control on the implementation of inclusionary housing policies in neighborhoods undergoing redevelopment, multiplying the policy impact of these funding streams. Alternatively, other policy options might include providing bonus resources to jurisdictions that adopt inclusive zoning policies, streamlining allocation pools exclusively for cities with mandatory affordable housing set-asides, and prioritizing consideration of neighborhoods that promote inclusive growth.

Lastly, it is worth emphasizing some of the other roles that state housing agencies can play in facilitating the work of others in policymaking. HFAs collect massive amounts of administrative data about their investments and the tenants who reside in them, allowing researchers to learn more about what is, as noted earlier, the largest source of affordable housing in America today. HFAs have legislative liaisons, communications experts, and others who can connect local stakeholders with policymakers and other audiences. Further, many LIHTC allocators also administer mortgage financing programs that support low- and moderate-income homeownership, meaning that they can be a source of expertise across tenures and income levels, and in some states also administer a wide variety of community and economic development programs, magnifying their potential impact.

CONCLUSION

With federal policy often deadlocked, states are a natural nexus for those seeking to develop equitable mixed-income communities, and HFAs are a deeply underappreciated player in that policy space. QAPs are the central instrument for HFA policymaking, channeling billions of dollars in resources annually that can be used to achieve any number of objectives. Those with an interest in inclusive and equitable placemaking should engage—actively,

---

24 Joe Cortright, "The 0.1 Percent Solution: Inclusionary Zoning's Fatal Scale Problem," City Observatory (blog), April, 4 2017, http://cityobservatory.org/the-0-1-percent-solution-inclusionary-zonings-fatal-scale-problem/.

strongly, and repeatedly—with their state's housing agency and work toward furthering those goals, and states must learn from one another to widely and rapidly adopt best practices in this arena.

IMPLICATIONS FOR ACTION

Implications for Policy

- The Low-Income Housing Tax Credit is, by far, the largest source of financing for the construction and preservation of affordable housing in the United States. Advocates and administrators must appreciate and flex the power of the QAP in remedying entrenched housing problems such as racial and economic segregation.

- Like many significant but stilted governing documents, QAPs are often created with little input from or responsiveness to the wishes of ordinary citizens. With so few stakeholders at the table, there is awesome potential for emerging grassroots movements to participate in transforming the housing legacy. Citizens, advocacy groups, and nonprofits need to attend public feedback events, initiate one-on-one meetings with QAP drafters, and use the bully pulpit to demand mixed-income results.

Implications for Research and Evaluation

- Academics and other researchers should develop and expand partnerships with HFAs. These entities have policy expertise and large administrative data sets that can serve as a source of answers to research questions. Conversely, policymakers can gain better access to emerging trends in academic analysis of housing issues.

- Just as research has been conducted on federal initiatives to create racially and economically integrated communities like HOPE VI and Choice Neighborhoods, state-level policies like the FHAct50 Building Opportunity Fund should be similarly evaluated.

Implications for Development and Investment

- Because corporate investors and syndicators are so central to the process of raising capital using LIHTCs, there should be a process for engaging these actors on the issue of mixed-income housing. If these parties become more likely to participate in such projects, there will be more funds available for both mixed-income and traditional affordable housing. Policymakers may wish to explore how to reduce investor risk, such as through equity guarantees similar to adjustors, or ways in which they can draw new, non-economically motivated investors to the table.

- Where market conditions permit, inclusive zoning should continue to be refined and advanced as one tool in a portfolio of solutions to the housing crisis. As local governments become more comfortable with the inclusive zoning model, more ambitious efforts to pair with the LIHTC should be considered, particularly those that allow private owners to create condominiums and outsource development and management functions to affordable housing experts.

Implications for Residents and Community Members

- As housing policy reaches a new level of political salience, voters should demand substantive conversations and realistic solutions about the roles of HFAs from presidential contenders, state-level office seekers, and political candidates up and down the ballot.

- Not In My Back Yard (NIMBY) is not a reasonable response to development. A person who does not like a housing proposal should demand that it be improved, not scrapped, and work to harness these investments for neighborhood-wide sustainability. Where NIMBY is rooted in misinformation, targeted education showcasing the local need for affordable housing and the success stories of past initiatives should be highlighted. Where NIMBY is a mere smokescreen for racist and segregationist ideology, that motivation should be named and confronted.

■ ■ ■

BRYAN GRADY is Chief Research Officer at the South Carolina State Housing Finance and Development Authority. He has six years of experience in program evaluation and policy development at state housing finance agencies with a research interest in alternative measures of housing affordability. Grady holds a Ph.D. in planning and public policy from Rutgers University.

■ ■ ■

CARLIE J. BOOS is the Executive Director at the Affordable Housing Alliance of Central Ohio, a nonprofit that uses research, collaboration, and advocacy to create housing solutions for Central Ohio. Previously she worked at the Ohio Housing Finance Agency overseeing affordable housing programs and setting the agency's policy agenda.

EMBRACING ODD BEDFELLOWS IN ODD TIMES: HOW TO SUSTAIN FINANCIAL AND POLITICAL SUPPORT FOR MIXED-INCOME COMMUNITIES

Robin Snyderman
BRicK Partners

Antonio R. Riley
Former HUD Regional Administrator for Region V

It was the Shakespearean character Trinculo, in *The Tempest,* who first introduced the phrase about misery inspiring acquaintance among strange bedfellows. Some say this choice of words was influenced by the poverty and overcrowded housing of Shakespeare's time—specifically, the need to find shelter even if it meant bedding down with an unexpected partner. Today, the saying typically refers broadly to unlikely alliances among politicians. These sorts of alliances are incredibly important when pursuing an agenda focused on poverty and affordable housing. In part, this is due to the reality that little in contemporary society is as inefficient and unfair as the U.S. housing delivery system. Even a small and much-needed mixed-income development is likely to face a tempest of technical, financial, and political hurdles.

In the early days of the Obama Administration, the co-authors of this essay began working together with a range of "strange bedfellows" in metropolitan Chicago on creating a more efficient strategy to increase the supply of mixed-income housing communities as part of an overall focus on viable regional housing solutions. The Regional Housing Initiative (RHI), which started in 2002, is an interagency collaboration of housing authorities and other partners. As of 2019, it has helped finance 40 housing developments, of which 33 are up and running. Seven others are nearly ready for occupancy.

The political challenges of managing the layers of local, state, and federal financing and regulations for housing are as common as the challenges of exclusionary zoning, source-of-income discrimination, and bigotry, but they are not insurmountable. RHI is promoting equitable housing solutions at a regional scale and, once sufficient administrative support and incentives are available, has demonstrated potential for even broader scale and replication.

REGIONAL SEGREGATION REQUIRES A REGIONAL RESPONSE

Encompassing more than 280 municipalities, each responsible for local housing policy and land use, and 15 public housing authorities (PHAs) serving all those towns, the Chicago area's challenges are both unique and illustrative. *The Cost of Segregation: National Trends and the Case of Chicago, 1990–2010*,[1] a landmark report published by The Urban Institute in 2017, reminds us that "Chicago's combined racial and economic segregation is among the highest in the nation":

> Blacks and whites generally do not reside in close proximity to one another in Chicago: whites are spread throughout the region except in the south and west sides, while blacks are heavily concentrated in the south and west sides and the southern suburbs" (p. viii).

The Cost of Segregation research didn't just update data on these historic trends, however. It also quantified how metropolitan Chicago's segregation patterns have handicapped the entire region, reaching beyond the people and neighborhoods most intensely harmed by institutional racism. As in other U.S. metropolitan areas, Chicago-area towns struggle with a mismatch between where low-income residents live and where public funds are concentrated. More people in poverty live in the Chicago suburbs than in the urban core, while most of the federal antipoverty programs are still designed for and provide funding within inner cities. And in the suburbs, most of the poverty is located in economically struggling communities with limited capacity to generate revenue, while other suburbs are home to some of the country's best schools and nestled in affluent neighborhoods with easy access to Chicago's extensive public transit system, forest preserves, retail life, and other amenities.

---

1 Gregory Acs et al., *The Cost of Segregation, National Trends and the Case of Chicago, 1990-2010*, (Washington, D.C.: Urban Institute, 2017). https://www.urban.org/sites/default/files/publication/89201/the_cost_of_segregation_final_0.pdf.

The report's findings demonstrated that, across metropolitan Chicago, everyone's economic prosperity, education, health, and safety are in peril regardless of one's race or income. The question then becomes how to address regional trends at a regional scale.

Mixed-income housing is an equally vital tool for revitalizing neighborhoods that are pursuing economic development and for amenity-rich communities interested in diversifying housing options. In both scenarios, however, the past failures of public housing still taint the local approval process to the extent that any multifamily rental housing proposal with an affordability component is likely to face significant "we-don't-want-Cabrini-Green-or-Robert-Taylor-Homes-in-our-backyard" resistance. Irrelevant is the fact that most of Chicago's notorious high-rises are long gone, many replaced with beautiful mixed-income housing. Community and political resistance may reflect ignorance about high-quality affordable housing or thinly veiled racial and class discrimination. In any case, it is impossible to make a dent on these issues one town at a time.

Whether the barriers to an efficient housing delivery system relate to the complexities of financing bricks and mortar with federal, state, local, public and private resources or to winning the hearts and minds of local leaders and neighbors, we are failing: The stark reality is that a family's ZIP Code still predicts future health, earnings, college graduation, teen pregnancy rate, and more. The American Dream is about everyone having opportunity to prosper, but families living in areas of concentrated poverty are unlikely to succeed.

Younger children benefit significantly when their parents can move them out of poverty, as demonstrated by the Moving to Opportunity research studies.[2] But what happens when moderate- and lower-income families with children in the Chicago area want to move to "opportunity areas"—places with good schools, jobs, transit, open space, and other amenities? The region's housing market offers them the preposterous dilemma of choosing between (a) an affordable home in a neighborhood lacking good schools and good jobs; or (b) living in overcrowded conditions, or far beyond their economic means, in a higher-resourced neighborhood. The lower a family's income, the more likely the family is to have no choice at all except to remain stuck in a racially segregated,

---

2 Raj Chetty, Nathaniel Hendren, and Lawrence F. Katz, "The Effects of Exposure to Better Neighborhoods on Children: New Evidence from the Moving to Opportunity Experiment." *American Economic Review* 106, no 4, (April 2016): 855-902

under-resourced community. Once again, everyone—children, working parents, and employers—feels the impact of the price families pay in terms of lost opportunities and higher stress at work and at home. The federal Housing Choice Voucher Program (HCV) aims to help families rent better apartments in opportunity neighborhoods by letting federal support follow tenants rather than vice versa, but there is a scarcity of opportunity-area properties, and those owners and managers are often resistant to renting to families using vouchers.

Developers and policymakers face a perfect storm of political and practical barriers when they respond to these challenges by trying to establish mixed-income housing in high-resource neighborhoods. In particular:

- The suburban policy-making process is time-consuming and unfamiliar to many developers and can therefore be excessively expensive. Even if a local mayor endorses or champions the proposal to members of the planning, housing, and city councils (who typically are volunteers), community resistance, fear, and even media drama are almost inevitable.

- Financing and political will are crucial but elusive. Even the most committed municipal partners face the challenges of staying in office while supporting needed housing developments and aligning jurisdictional and agency resources to create meaningful incentives for developers to implement local plans and priorities.

- Improvements to the federal Affirmatively Furthering Fair Housing Act and the Supreme Court's Disparate Income ruling created more tools, incentives, and restrictions to tackle segregation, but without continued federal oversight and support, local efforts to increase and diversify housing choices remain slow and tedious.

Motivated to reduce housing segregation and housing policy inefficiency, the Chicago-area Regional Housing Initiative emerged as a small but replicable and scalable "workaround" to systems and policies that are slow to accommodate demographic trends and regional needs.

RHI: A WORKAROUND TO LEVERAGE MIXED-INCOME HOUSING

RHI began in a very different housing market than we have today, at a time when stakeholders were analyzing the first regional rental market analysis to show that housing trends in the Chicago area were not accommodating suburban job and population growth. The fresh data helped prompt the Metropolitan Mayors Caucus to begin its own exploration of how mayors could take leadership to solve the "jobs-housing mismatch" problem. These mayors began working to improve the balance between housing stock, jobs, and population growth.

An important push came from the business community, when one employer who was providing his own workers with homeownership assistance asked this bold question that prompted the mayors' interest: "Why are we paying property taxes in towns that don't use those resources to help our workers afford housing options near work?" That question helped local leaders finalize their own Housing Endorsement Criteria to ensure that whatever housing policies they support serve local workers and others by providing well-managed, well-designed housing near jobs and transit.

What is RHI, and How Does it Support Mixed-Income Housing?

The Regional Housing Initiative is a financing strategy that aims to increase the range of affordable rental housing near jobs, good schools, and transit, especially in low-poverty suburban neighborhoods throughout the Chicago region. RHI enables PHAs to:

- pool and convert some of their tenant-based federal housing choice vouchers into site-based operating funds for interested developers and owners;
- attract developers who leverage additional financing to create new, mixed-income housing options in priority neighborhoods; and
- support existing market-rate properties in opportunity areas by enabling owners to set aside a portion of the apartments to serve lower-income households.

Through a competitive process, RHI selects rental housing developments to participate in the initiative and gives subsidies to some of the apartments—typically 25 percent in any one building, consistent with federal regulations.[3] Because the vouchers ensure payment of full market-rate rents, developers only charge the very low-income residents a rent that equals a third of their income. The remaining rent is covered by the participating public housing authority

---

3   PBV Regulations (24 CFR Part 983)

and guaranteed for any RHI-referred tenant who moves into the subsidized apartment during the term of the renewable contract (typically 15-year renewable terms).

Working with housing developers, owners, and managers who are selected in part for their commitment to community building, RHI supports developments that would not otherwise get built due to lack of PHA funding—such as two recently approved developments by nonprofits to provide housing, vocational, and educational services for low-income single mothers and their children. RHI's approach enhances the voucher and development capacities of smaller individual PHAs, which often struggle to find high-quality available housing for the thousands of households on their waitlists, and enables low-income families to access a new supply of housing increasingly located in the region's opportunity-area ZIP Codes. In this way, RHI typically diversifies the income mix not only in participating buildings but also the surrounding community.

Most of the region's 15 PHAs (large and small, suburban and urban) currently participate in the Chicago-area RHI, which, through modest but consistent activity since 2003, has awarded nearly 600 RHI subsidies to 40 mixed-income and supportive housing developments, providing a total of more than 2,200 apartments.

How Does the RHI Model Work?

Federally formulated housing funds, with local and state allocations, provide much-needed predictability for municipal leaders and developers dedicated to addressing local demands, especially when markets and more competitive funding opportunities are not responding to local needs. But there is a scarcity of such resources for lower-income households in opportunity area neighborhoods—i.e., those with good schools, jobs, transit, open space, and other amenities.

RHI's response to the above is an approach consistent with lessons learned from The Brookings Institution's work on Confronting Suburban Poverty in America, Living Cities' capital absorption work, collective impact efforts, and other best practices from around the country. Chief among them: work across jurisdictions, develop shared priorities, invest in capacity building, use a management "quarterback," and leverage greater private-sector investment.

RHI's approach involves navigating the priorities of diverse partners and stakeholders, political and otherwise—the "strange bedfellows" noted at the top of this essay—which include the public housing authorities; the region's metropolitan planning organization, which in this case is the Chicago Metropolitan Agency for Planning (CMAP); and the state's Housing Finance Agency (HFA). CMAP serves as management quarterback for the effort, and the participating PHAs sign onto an intergovernmental agreement. The public housing authorities' administrative plans for HUD also include common language about this regional effort.

Through one efficient and competitive process, currently managed by CMAP, RHI staff facilitate the developer outreach, application, and review process regionwide. Given CMAP's leading role in helping communities with local planning, these communications help to deter and navigate local concerns by focusing on RHI as a tool for implementing (and attracting more financing for) those local plans.

All PHAs score the proposals and select which will receive their pooled resources, using the housing endorsement criteria developed by the Metropolitan Mayors Conference along with other regional CMAP data on housing supply and demand trajectories. The selection criteria also consider the developer's ability and track record in cultivating a mixed-income community to gauge whether families from high-poverty areas will be thoughtfully integrated into the building and surrounding neighborhood. On the financial side, the criteria incentivize developers to "follow the money" by producing new rental housing options that advance local, regional, state, and federal housing and economic development objectives.

Although RHI offers a rolling application process, it also schedules reviews to help developers leverage support for other competitive housing processes, especially the state's Low-Income Housing Tax Credits. The Illinois Housing Development Authority (IHDA) provides essential support to RHI, both by providing points to developers who have secured rent subsidies and are developing in opportunity areas and by allowing RHI to undertake its reviews on a parallel track with IHDA, so developers don't have to complete separate applications in order for RHI's commitments to leverage the IHDA competitive points. Coordinating the timing and scoring reduces hurdles and increases incentives for developers to address the unmet housing demand.

Once selections are made, the PHAs manage the subsidy contracts with developers. Special operating and management agreements allow the subsidies to cross jurisdictions when necessary, but this workaround arrangement has proven challenging and inefficient as the program grows, with both the large donor PHAs and the smaller receiving PHAs pointing to a duplication of services for the same limited administrative fees. Removing this technical obstacle would make RHI far easier to replicate and scale.

RHI created a single, regional referral waitlist for lease-up and turnover of RHI-subsidized buildings, combining households from the participating PHAs' waitlists that choose to participate in RHI and identifying the buildings and subregions that interest them. Because the households on this consolidated referral list already are on the waitlists for housing choice vouchers, most are Black families currently living in segregated parts of the region. RHI staff offer basic information on educational and support services to help families choose and prepare for the move. Families referred by the larger housing authorities that work in the highest-poverty areas get preference in all new lease-ups and turnovers, as do families referred by the local PHA contributing to the development and families that work near the new site. Another important waitlist preference is for households whose members work or participate in job training within a specified radius of the site.

LOOKING AHEAD: RHI'S REPLICABILITY AND SCALABILITY

RHI's nontraditional partnerships across areas of authority and expertise, regional focus, ability to overcome political obstacles, and versatility in pooling resources across agencies and jurisdictions have made the initiative unique. RHI has demonstrated its effectiveness in diversifying the housing stock in selected areas. This tool for addressing residential segregation can be replicated and scaled, thanks to four recent federal policies and programs:

- Passage of the Housing Opportunity Through Modernization Act (HOTMA) in 2016 provided additional incentives and removed specific barriers to mixed-income housing in opportunity areas, which supports the goals of RHI.
- New language in HUD's Moving to Work Demonstration Program, which gives public housing authorities flexibility in using federal funds to increase housing choice for low-income families, now allows larger PHAs to share

- that flexibility with neighboring PHAs. This can support the effort to address housing needs regionally.
- HUD's new technical assistance for public housing authorities provides hands-on assistance, if needed, for regional PHAs to design their own programs.
- In early 2019, Congress funded the Housing Choice Voucher Mobility Demonstration Program, a new effort by HUD to encourage PHAs to help families access "communities of opportunity" by offering housing mobility support services and operating regional mobility programs. The federal program includes 500 new vouchers, giving agencies extra incentive to participate. Ideally, lessons learned will be scaled and implemented more broadly within Rental Assistance Demonstration (RAD) and other HUD programs.

Efforts to learn from and expand on the Chicago model have already begun. Baltimore's metropolitan planning organization started exploring the RHI model with six Baltimore-area public housing authorities in 2015; by 2019, 70 vouchers had been committed to opportunity-area developments. As in Chicago, all of the PHAs involved manage housing choice voucher programs, and most were already working together to minimize barriers for families interested in moving across jurisdictions. The impetus for further collaboration was a painful shortage of available housing options in neighborhoods with good schools and other amenities. Baltimore's regional effort adapted and improved the RHI model by adding more extensive mobility counseling services and a third-party administrator of subsidies. The Baltimore program is now fully operational and has received more than 10 new proposals.

CONCLUSION

For low-income people across the United States, the shortage of affordable, accessible housing options in opportunity areas causes misery of Shakespearean proportions. Such hard times often benefit from new alliances among odd bedfellows. The Regional Housing Initiative's model for financing and incentivizing mixed-income housing illustrates how these alliances can create sustainable solutions that bridge jurisdictional and agency borders, accommodate the varying capacities and resources available, and address the very different challenges faced by developers, municipal leaders, employers, and working families. Additional federal funding and incentives suggest opportunities to significantly scale up and replicate this approach.

IMPLICATIONS FOR ACTION

Implications for Policy

- *Test and Support Housing Mobility Models that Overcome Regional Barriers.* HUD's new Housing Choice Voucher Mobility Demonstration Program provides one vehicle to do so. After testing how RHI-type models can better utilize and connect with innovations offered through the Rental Assistance Demonstration, PHA consortia opportunities, Moving to Work, and HOTMA, policies should support the application of lessons nationwide.

- *Ensure that PHAs Have Sufficient Administrative Support to Promote Housing Mobility Regionally.* Operating and managing subsidies in other jurisdictions is cumbersome and expensive for all parties. Baltimore's approach eliminated this burden by using a third-party regional administrator; however, this innovation was created and funded via a lawsuit. Several mechanisms can be piloted to reduce the duplication of responsibilities when larger PHAs allow smaller PHAs to administer their vouchers in opportunity areas.

- *Create More Financial Incentives for PHAs and Developers.* Federal policy allows 20 percent of the nation's 2.2 million tenant-based vouchers to be converted into operating subsidies or project-based vouchers. If that 20 percent leverages new mixed-income development near good jobs and schools, it could amount to close to 2 million more apartments. Most PHAs underutilize this 20 percent conversion prerogative, and now that cap can be higher in opportunity areas and in RAD conversions to project-based vouchers.

Implications for Development and Investment

- *Make It Easier for Housing Developers to Follow the Money.* State housing finance agencies are in a unique position to create structure and incentives that align state tax credits and other housing programs with PHA vouchers and with municipal, county, and regional plans.

- *Pool and Redeploy Turn-over Resources.* Redirecting unused rent subsidies to new and existing opportunity area properties enables regional initiatives to support proposals that local jurisdictions could not otherwise take on, especially suburban neighborhoods.

- *Don't Hesitate to Start Small with Regional Collaboration, Allowing Evolution.* Developers and other advocates wanting to use a mechanism like RHI for leveraging resources in opportunity areas should not be daunted by the challenges of getting all the PHAs signed on up front. Chicago's 15 public housing authorities were all motivated by housing trends to explore how they could collaborate to increase the supply of housing in priority areas. With no incentives beyond good will, only three PHAs signed the original Intergovernmental Agreement to pool resources for developments that advanced the Metropolitan Mayors Caucus Housing Endorsement Criteria, but most of the early applications were submitted by supportive housing developers familiar with layered financing. Framing the whole approach via a regional leader like CMAP has also been critical to its growth, but starting small worked just fine.

Implications for Research and Evaluation

- *Identify Cost-effective Supports for Families Moving to Opportunity Areas.* Mobility counseling, while valuable, can be a costly tool. Important questions for research include: What are the differences in costs, resident experiences, and residential longevity between place-based opportunity-area models like RHI and other more traditional housing mobility strategies? How many people make the move and stay, and at what costs? What positive economic, health, and safety outcomes are experienced by parents and children?

Implications for Residents and Community Members

- *Design Regional Waitlists with the Big Picture in Mind.* There are many implications for action related to the regional waitlist for residents, neighbors, and property managers: Should there be a preference for households who live or work near the site? (That always helps with community acceptance, but doesn't necessarily help with mobility goals). What kind of pre-move information and services are most helpful? What kind of training and criteria should be formalized to best identify and cultivate housing providers to be true mixed-income community builders?

What kind of technology is most efficient? How best to work with special needs populations and supportive housing? Take time to balance the needs and goals of the future residents with those of the participating PHAs, the community, and the region.

- *Implement a Realistic and Sustainable Strategy to Overcome Community Resistance to Needed Housing Options.* The inefficiency of the housing delivery system has contributed to the sobering Brookings Institution finding that only 11 regions succeeded in generating inclusive growth between 2010-2015. This underscores the fact that good "community acceptance" messages are not enough. There is a need for additional partners and messengers to coordinate early, forming a "nimble network" that includes employers, residents, developers, housing advocates, and policymakers who promote a coordinated effort that results in acceptance by community members.

■ ■ ■

ROBIN SNYDERMAN *has been providing leadership in the housing and community development arena for 30 years. A recent Non Resident Senior Fellow with the Brookings Institution, Snyderman is also a Founder and Principal with the "collaborative management" and consulting firm, BRicK Partners, LLC. A native of the Chicago area, Robin served as housing director and Vice President of Community Development for the Metropolitan Planning Council (MPC) for 15 years, where she managed the launch and growth of several nationally recognized efforts to promote regional collaborations and secure resources for trailblazing initiatives in the areas of interjurisdictional municipal coordination, employer-assisted housing, public housing reform and local, state and federal policy innovation.*

■ ■ ■

ANTONIO R. RILEY *was appointed by President Barack Obama to serve as a U.S Department of Housing and Urban Development Regional Administrator in 2010 and served until 2017. He was responsible for overseeing the delivery of HUD programs and services to communities and evaluating their efficiency and effectiveness. Prior to joining HUD, Riley served as Executive Director of the Wisconsin Housing and Economic Development Authority (WHEDA). A graduate of Carroll University in Wisconsin and also of the Senior Executives in State and Local Government program at Harvard University's John F. Kennedy School of Government, Riley served 10 years in the Wisconsin Legislature representing Milwaukee's 18th Assembly District.*

Innovations in Policy Strategies: Local Strategies

These two essays explore the local policy perspective on mixed-income communities. In "Promoting Mixed-Income Communities by Mitigating Displacement: Findings from 80 Large U.S. Cities," Adèle Cassola looks at how municipal governments across the nation preserve affordability and prevent displacement in revitalizing neighborhoods. Her comprehensive research documents the use of tools such as condo conversion regulation, just cause eviction, inclusionary zoning, housing trust funds, affordable housing incentives, affordability covenants, community land trusts, and affordable commercial space set-asides. She finds that the most common residential interventions are voluntary inclusionary zoning and housing trust funds, both of which exist in nearly half of the cities she surveyed. Cassola highlights some key political, economic, and regulatory conditions that influence the likelihood, timing, and type of policy adoption. Her essay suggests numerous specific actions that cities can take to implement a proactive, multi-dimensional approach to preserving affordable housing.

In *"Mixed-Income Housing in New York City: Achievements, Challenges, and Lessons of an Enduring Mayoral Commitment,"* Alex Schwartz and Sasha Tsenkova provide a detailed review of New York City's extensive and exceptional efforts to create mixed-income housing. Spanning multiple mayoral administrations, New York City has been the site of ambitious efforts to create affordable housing in the midst of booming real estate market conditions which have threatened to displace major swaths of the low- and moderate-income population. Schwartz and Tsenkova make the case that mixed-income housing in New York City is notable not only due to its scale—almost 300,000 affordable units created or started in inclusionary housing projects during the past two mayoral administrations—but also its location, often in middle-class and affluent areas, and the broad economic mix of its residents. While they contend that New York City is the site of "more creative, ambitious, and durable approaches to mixed-income housing than anywhere else in the U.S.," they also draw many lessons and cautionary insights from the New York experience and share implications for mixed-income policy and practice throughout the country.

PROMOTING MIXED-INCOME COMMUNITIES BY MITIGATING DISPLACEMENT: FINDINGS FROM 80 LARGE U.S. CITIES

Adèle Cassola
Global Strategy Lab

Government efforts to promote investment in low-income neighborhoods are often guided by the policy goal of fostering long-term socioeconomic diversity. Amid a scarcity of public funding, local governments have increasingly pursued this objective through initiatives like inclusionary zoning and public housing revitalization that encourage private development but include units for a range of income levels. However, creating communities that remain broadly accessible to lower-income households and residents of color when these interventions occur requires measures that enhance housing and economic opportunities within the larger neighborhood and address the threats of physical, economic, and cultural displacement associated with increased investment.

Drawing on data from 80 of the most populous U.S. cities, this essay shows that municipal governments have embraced market-leveraging tools to address affordability in revitalizing neighborhoods but are less likely to have the regulatory, funding-based, and tenant protection measures that can mitigate attendant displacement pressures.[1] Without these mitigating policies, efforts to promote income mixing in disinvested neighborhoods risk

---

1 Data were collected in late 2016 and early 2017 through an online survey sent to a housing, planning, or community development official in each of the 146 most populous U.S. cities. Survey responses were verified and supplemented through a systematic review of cities' ordinances, plans, program descriptions, and policy documents. The 80 cities in the dataset are comparable on average to the full sample of surveyed cities across a range of demographic, fiscal, and economic indicators as well as measures of housing affordability. Data were obtained for 79 cities on residential interventions and 53 cities on interventions concerning commercial affordability and economic opportunities. The author wishes to thank the city officials who generously contributed their time and knowledge to this study. The research was supported by a doctoral fellowship from the Social Sciences and Humanities Research Council of Canada.

accelerating gentrification and displacement rather than fostering long-term socioeconomically integrated communities. The examples of cities that are intervening early and combining reinvestment with comprehensive protections for current and future low-income residents demonstrate the feasibility of more equitable approaches where local political, economic, and regulatory contexts are supportive.

TOOLS FOR BALANCING INVESTMENT WITH SOCIOECONOMIC DIVERSITY

In a market-led and fiscally constrained urban development context, achieving a balance between improving residential quality in lower-income neighborhoods and supporting existing residents' ability to remain in place is a continual challenge for city governments. Revitalization can trigger gentrification, which refers to the socioeconomic transformation of previously disinvested neighborhoods as an influx of residents with more purchasing power and different cultural and commercial practices displaces lower-income households, particularly households of color. Investment can increase the risk of direct displacement for existing residents due to unaffordable increases in housing costs, heightened eviction or landlord harassment activity, and building sale, conversion, or demolition. Investment can also lead to indirect displacement when residents who remain in a neighborhood feel alienated by the political, socio-cultural, and commercial changes associated with demographic shifts and when the loss of low-cost units prevents households from moving into an area that was previously affordable to them.[2]

---

2   John Betancur, "Gentrification and Community Fabric in Chicago," *Urban Studies* 48, no. 2 (February 2011): 383-406; Derek Hyra, "The Back-to-the-City Movement: Neighbourhood Redevelopment and Processes of Political and Cultural Displacement," *Urban Studies* 52, (2015): 1753-1773; Justine Marcus and Miriam Zuk, "Displacement in San Mateo County, California: Consequences for Housing Neighborhoods, Quality of Life, and Health," (Berkeley IGS, 2019); Peter Marcuse, "Abandonment, Gentrification and Displacement: The Linkages in New York City," In *Gentrification of the City*, ed. Neil Smith and Peter Williams, (London: Unwin Hyman, 1986); Kathe Newman and Elvin Wyly, "The Right to Stay Put, Revisited: Gentrification and Resistance to Displacement in New York City," *Urban Studies* 43, no. 1 (January 2006): 23-57; Trushna Parekh, "They Want to Live in the Tremé, but They Want It for Their Ways of Living: Gentrification and Neighborhood Practice in Tremé, New Orleans," *Urban Geography* 36, no 2 (2015): 201-220; Filip Stabrowski, "New-Build Gentrification and the Everyday Displacement of Polish Immigrant Tenants in Greenpoint, Brooklyn," *Antipode* 46, no. 3 (2014): 794-815.

The policy and advocacy literatures identify an array of tools that can mitigate the multiple dimensions of displacement and promote long-term affordability when reinvestment occurs (Table 1).[3,4]

While evaluations of these tools' effectiveness are scarce, there is evidence that policies including rent regulation, subsidized housing, legal aid for tenants, just cause eviction ordinances, right of first refusal laws, condo conversion controls, and community land trusts have preserved affordable housing or otherwise enabled some residents to remain in place when their housing was threatened.[5] Interventions that address commercial affordability and efforts to boost economic opportunities by giving residents preference for jobs created through redevelopment have also shown promise.[6] Such measures can help mitigate the disproportionate costs that gentrification and revitalization often impose on residents of color. Specifically, commercial affordability measures can tackle

---

[3] Causa Justa/Just Cause, "Development without Displacement: Resisting Gentrification in the Bay Area." (Oakland, CA: Causa Justa/Just Cause, 2014); Grounded Solutions Network. "What about Housing? A Policy Toolkit for Inclusive Growth," (Portland, OR: Grounded Solutions Network); Luke Herrine, Jessica Yager, and Nadia Mian, "Gentrification Responses: A Survey of Strategies to Maintain Neighborhood Economic Diversity," (New York, NY: NYU Furman Center, 2016); Olivia LaVecchia and Stacy Mitchell, "Affordable Space: How Rising Commercial Rents Are Threatening Independent Businesses, and What Cities Are Doing about It," (Institute for Local Self-Reliance, April 2016); Diane Levy, Jennifer Comey, and Sandra Padilla, "In the Face of Gentrification: Case Studies of Local Efforts to Mitigate Displacement," (Washington, DC: The Urban Institute, 2006); Diane Levy, Jennifer Comey, and Sandra Padilla, "Keeping the Neighborhood Affordable: A Handbook of Housing Strategies for Gentrifying Areas," (Washington, DC: The Urban Institute, 2006).

[4] This essay focuses on the sustained displacement threats that are common in neighborhoods experiencing reinvestment or revitalization. This table therefore does not include more temporary tools such as short-term financial assistance to households at risk of eviction because of overdue rent. Such assistance is a critical part of the eviction prevention toolbox more broadly, but in neighborhoods where rents are rising, the economic pressures resulting from rent increases are likely to be more enduring in nature.

[5] Myungshik Choi, Shannon Van Zandt, and David Matarrita-Cascante, "Can Community Land Trusts Slow Gentrification?" *Journal of Urban Affairs* 40, no. 3 (2018): 349-411; Mitchell Crispell and Nicole Montojo, "Urban Displacement Project: San Francisco's Chinatown," (Berkeley, CA: University of California, Berkley, 2016); Mitchell Crispell, Logan Rockefeller Harris, and Sydney Cespedes, "Urban Displacement Project: San Mateo County's East Palo Alto," (Berkeley, CA: University of California, Berkley, 2016); Caroline Gallaher, *The Politics of Staying Put: Condo Conversion and Tenant Right-to-Buy in Washington DC*, (Philadelphia: Temple University Press, 2006); Cassadra Wolos Pattanayak, D. James Greiner, and Jonathan Hennessy, "The Limits of Unbundled Legal Assistance: A Randomized Study in a Massachusetts District Court and Prospects for the Future." *Harvard Law Review* 126, no. 4 (February 2013); Newman and Wyly, "The Right to Stay Put, Revisited," 23-57; Miriam Zuk and Karen Chapple. "Housing Production, Filtering and Displacement: Untangling the Relationships," (2016).

[6] Olivia LaVecchia and Stacy Mitchell, "Affordable Space," (2016); Kathleen Mulligan-Hansel, "Making Development Work for Local Residents: Local Hire Programs and Implementation Strategies That Serve Low-Income Communities," (Oakland, CA: The Partnership for Working Families, July 2008); Leland Saito and Jonathan Truong, "The L.A. Live Community Benefits Agreement: Evaluating the Agreement Results and Shifting Political Power in the City," *Urban Affairs Review* 51, no. 2 (2014): 263-286.

the small business dislocations that have been shown to contribute to indirect displacement among Black residents of gentrifying neighborhoods in the United States,[7] and hiring requirements can create employment opportunities for workers of color in redevelopment projects.[8]

Displacement mitigation policy tools can tackle citywide challenges or specifically address displacement and economic opportunity in neighborhoods experiencing revitalization and reinvestment. This essay focuses on the latter category of interventions.

There are three main toolkits that can directly address displacement in areas at risk of gentrifying. The first involves targeting these areas geographically. Policy tools that create or preserve affordable housing or commercial space or increase economic opportunities were categorized in this study as mitigating displacement in revitalizing neighborhoods if they were aimed at or used in such areas. The second set of tools involves addressing the types of displacement that are common in neighborhoods that are attracting investment. Examples include rent regulation (which targets economic displacement due to housing cost increases) and tenant protections (which can reduce illegal evictions and other predatory landlord activity). The final set of tools includes initiatives like housing trust funds that possess the flexibility to tackle the rapid changes that can occur in appreciating areas.

Figures 1 and 2 show the percentage of survey respondent cities that had adopted each displacement mitigation tool. The most common residential interventions were voluntary inclusionary zoning and housing trust funds, both of which were in place in nearly half of cities. The vast majority of the inclusionary zoning programs in these cities offered density, height, or floor area ratio bonuses (or other land use concessions that are particularly valuable in neighborhoods where demand is increasing) in exchange for the onsite construction of below-market-rate units. Similarly, most cities' housing trust funds were financed by fees charged on private development or by property/

---

7   Lance Freeman, *There Goes the 'Hood: Views of Gentrification from the Ground Up*, (Philadelphia: Temple University Press, 2006); Daniel Monroe Sullivan and Samuel Shaw, "Retail Gentrification and Race: The Case of Alberta Street in Portland Oregon," *Urban Affairs Review* 47, no. 3 (2011): 413-432.

8   The Office of Economic and Workforce Development, "San Francisco Local Hiring Policy for Construction: Annual Report to the San Francisco Board of Supervisors," (San Francisco, CA: The Office of Economic and Workforce Development); Partnership for Working Families, "Making a Success of Local Hire," *Shelterforce* (blog). October 21, 2016; Hannah Roditi and Naomi Zauderer, "Breaking Down the Wall: Opening Building-Trade Careers to Low-Income People of Color," *Clearinghouse Rev.* 36, (200): 154.

occupancy taxes. The two most prevalent displacement mitigation tools thus leverage market demand and appreciation to address the costs of these processes for low-income households.

This strategy is appealing to local governments because it generates affordable housing resources at a time when public funding is inadequate. For example, inclusionary zoning can produce below-market-rate units without direct public subsidy in neighborhoods that are hosting market-rate investment, and fees charged on development have supported the acquisition and rent-limitation of low-cost housing in appreciating areas.[9] However, due in part to the rising costs associated with market-stimulating efforts, the below-market-rate housing units generated through these initiatives are not always affordable to long-time neighborhood residents and are not produced in sufficient quantities to meet their needs.[10] On their own, policy tools that leverage market demand to increase affordability are unlikely to counterbalance the displacement pressures associated with increased high-end development and the in-migration of more affluent households with different commercial preferences and cultural practices.

There are four complementary approaches that cities can take to reduce the adverse impacts of market-leveraging mixed-income efforts on lower-income households and increase incumbent residents' opportunities to benefit from neighborhood investment. The first involves accounting for potential displacement impacts in the initial design of redevelopment plans. For example, Seattle's Mandatory Housing Affordability Plan limits the extent of proposed rezonings for increased development capacity in neighborhoods where low-

---

9   City of Boston. "Acquisition Opportunity Program,." accessed June 19, 2019, https://www.boston.gov/departments/neighborhood-development/acquisition-opportunity-program; San Francisco Office of the Mayor, "Mayor Lee Announces Funding for Small Site Acquisition Program to Protect Longtime San Francisco Tenants," News Release, (August 11, 2014).

10 Tom Angotti, *New York for Sale: Community Planning Confronts Global Real Estate* (Cambridge: MIT Press, 2008); Leslie Bridgers, "Portland Jumps Aboard a Hot Affordable Housing Trend—Inclusionary Zoning," *Portland Press Herald*, November 15, 2015; Peter Cohen and Fernando Marti, "Searching for the 'Sweet Spot' in San Francisco," in *Whose Urban Resistance? An International Comparison of Urban Regeneration Strategies*, ed. Kate Shaw and Libby Porter, (London: Routledge, 2009); Bethany Li, "Now is the Time! Challenging Resegregation and Displacement in the Age of Hypergentrification," *Fordham Law Review* 85, no. 3 (2016): 1189-1242; Carolina Sarmiento and J. Revel Sims, "Facades of Equitable Development: Santa Ana and the Affordable Housing Complex," *Journal of Planning Education and Research* 35, no. 3 (2015): 323-336; Filip Stabrowski, "Inclusionary Zoning and Exclusionary Development: The Politics of 'Affordable Housing' in North Brooklyn," *International Journal of Urban and Regional Research* 39, no. 6 (2015): 1120-1136; Samuel Stein, "Progress for Whom, Toward What? Progressive Politics and New York City's Mandatory Inclusionary Housing," *Journal of Urban Affairs* 40, no. 6 (2018): 770-781.

Table 1: Displacement Mitigation Policy Tools

HOUSING MARKET REGULATION	RESIDENTIAL TENANT PROTECTIONS	ZONING FOR AFFORDABLE HOUSING	DEDICATED REVENUE FOR AFFORDABLE HOUSING	CREATING AFFORDABLE HOUSING THROUGH PUBLIC INVESTMENT	EXTENDING HOUSING AFFORDABILITY THROUGH PUBLIC INVESTMENT	ADDRESSING COMMERCIAL AFFORDABILITY AND ECONOMIC OPPORTUNITIES
Rent regulations	Legal aid for tenants facing eviction or harassment	Voluntary inclusionary zoning (including incentive zoning/density bonus programs)	Housing trust funds	Converting financially/physically distressed units to affordable housing	Establishing affordability covenants on unsubsidized, low-cost housing	Incentives for landlords to provide small businesses with affordable/long-term leases
No net loss policies	Right of first refusal	Mandatory inclusionary zoning	Reinvesting increased property tax revenue in affordable housing (e.g., through tax increment financing)	Affordable housing development on public land (or banking land for future affordable housing development)	Preserving subsidized housing	Assistance for historically or culturally significant businesses
Condo conversion regulations	Just cause eviction and anti-harassment laws			Other funding/incentives for affordable housing (e.g., reduced parking requirements, expedited permitting, tax exemptions, etc.)	Repair programs for owner-occupied/rental properties	Restrictions on national chain retailer locations
Short-term rental regulations					Support for decom-modified housing (such as community land trusts)	Affordable space set-asides for locally owned small businesses
					Property tax relief for owner-occupiers	Affordable space set-asides for minority-owned businesses
						Construction or retail job set-asides for neighborhood residents

income households and communities of color have a high risk of displacement.[11] Portland, Oregon's comprehensive plan similarly commits the city to anticipate and proactively reduce the costs of investment and development for vulnerable communities.[12] These principles also guided the city's strategy for investment in the historically Black neighborhood of North/Northeast Portland. The neighborhood plan was developed through substantial engagement with existing and previously displaced residents; it also included efforts to prevent displacement by providing home repair loans and grants, creating permanently affordable homes for rent and sale, and acquiring land to be used for permanently affordable housing in the future. Recognizing that past city policies reduced housing options for the neighborhood's Black population, the plan also gave preference for housing created through these new programs to residents who were at risk of or previously experienced displacement from the area.[13]

The second approach involves investing in long-term affordable housing when land values are low, so that fewer units are threatened by market forces when demand increases. Support for de-commodified housing and the construction of affordable units on public lots were among the least common tools used by respondent cities to address displacement in neighborhoods experiencing revitalization or reinvestment (Fig. 1). While this likely reflects rising land costs in areas where demand is increasing, it also highlights the importance of early intervention to preserve the ability of low-income households to benefit from investments in their neighborhoods. Establishing land banks and community land trusts before appreciation occurs can stabilize communities and shield them from market volatility. For example, a community land trust in Boston's Dudley Triangle that was established with city support as part of a neighborhood revitalization initiative has preserved affordability for residents amid heightened demand and protected them from foreclosure during market

---

11 Office of Planning and Community Development, Office of Housing, Department of Neighborhoods, and Seattle Department of Construction and Inspections, "Mandatory Housing Affordability (MHA) Citywide Implementation: Director's Report and Recommendation," (Seattle, WA: Office of Planning and Community Development, Office of Housing, Department of Neighborhoods, and Seattle Department of Construction and Inspections, February 2018); Seattle Office of Planning & Community Development, "Seattle 2035 Growth and Equity: Analyzing Impacts on Displacement and Opportunity Related to Seattle's Growth Strategy," (Seattle, WA: Seattle Office of Planning & Community Development, May 2016).

12 City of Portland, "Portland 2035 Comprehensive Plan," (Portland, OR: City of Portland, December 2018).

13 Portland Housing Authority, "North/Northeast Neighborhood Housing Strategy: Executive Summary," (Portland, OR: Portland Housing Authority.

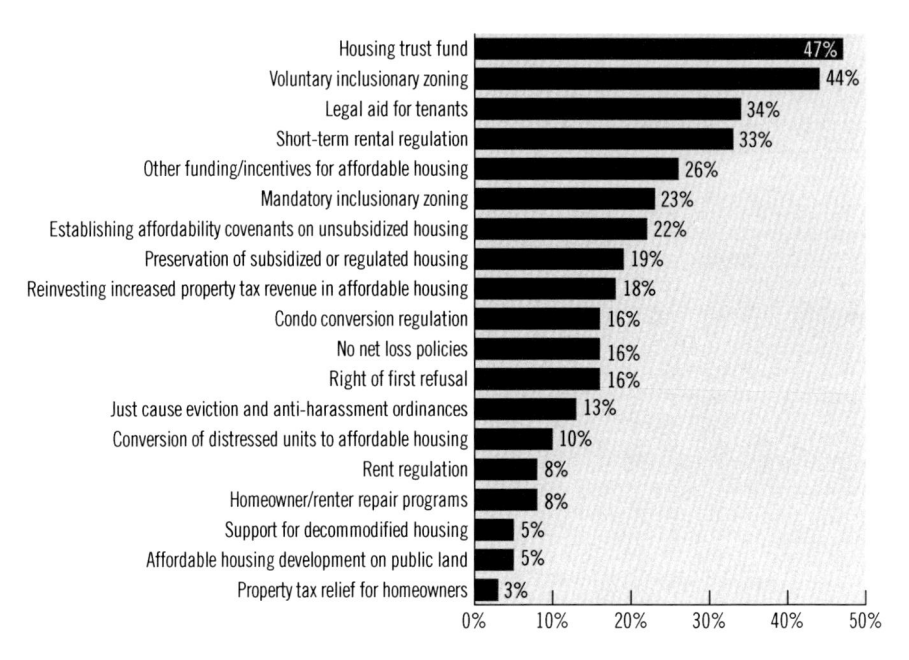

Policy Tool	Percentage
Housing trust fund	47%
Voluntary inclusionary zoning	44%
Legal aid for tenants	34%
Short-term rental regulation	33%
Other funding/incentives for affordable housing	26%
Mandatory inclusionary zoning	23%
Establishing affordability covenants on unsubsidized housing	22%
Preservation of subsidized or regulated housing	19%
Reinvesting increased property tax revenue in affordable housing	18%
Condo conversion regulation	16%
No net loss policies	16%
Right of first refusal	16%
Just cause eviction and anti-harassment ordinances	13%
Conversion of distressed units to affordable housing	10%
Rent regulation	8%
Homeowner/renter repair programs	8%
Support for decommodified housing	5%
Affordable housing development on public land	5%
Property tax relief for homeowners	3%

Figure 1: Percentage of Respondent Cities With Policy Tools to Mitigate Residential Displacement From Neighborhoods Experiencing Revitalization or Reinvestment (N=79)

downturns.[14] Because it is less expensive to invest in affordability before appreciation is advanced, early intervention can also reduce cities' reliance on strong-market tools to address displacement.

The third approach involves pairing market-leveraging efforts with measures that attenuate their ripple effects for residents of targeted neighborhoods. Relevant policy tools include protections against or legal aid in the event of harassment and evictions; regulations that limit rent increases or prevent landlords from leasing units on the short-term market; and measures that mandate one-for-one replacement of affordable units in the affected area, limit the conversion of rental units to condominiums, or assist tenants in purchasing their units when such conversions occur. Although these anti-displacement

---

14 John Emmeus Davis, "Origins and Evolution of the Community Land Trust in the United States," in *The Community Land Trust Reader*, ed. by John Emmeus Davis (Massachusetts: Lincoln Institute of Land Policy, 2010); Lee Allen Dwyer, "Mapping Impact: An Analysis of the Dudley Street Neighborhood Initiative Land Trust" (master's thesis, MIT, 2015); May Louie, "Community Land Trusts: A Powerful Vehicle for Development without Displacement," *Trotter Review* 23, no. 1 (2016).

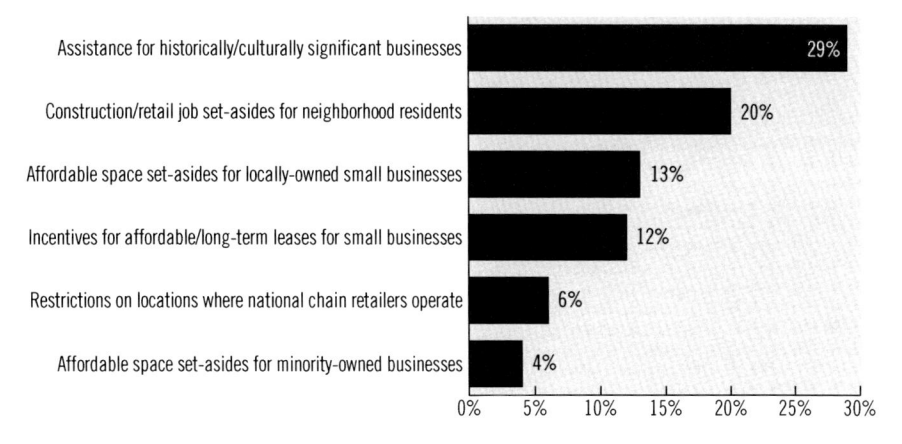

Tool	Percentage
Assistance for historically/culturally significant businesses	29%
Construction/retail job set-asides for neighborhood residents	20%
Affordable space set-asides for locally-owned small businesses	13%
Incentives for affordable/long-term leases for small businesses	12%
Restrictions on locations where national chain retailers operate	6%
Affordable space set-asides for minority-owned businesses	4%

Figure 2: Percentage of Respondent Cities Using Commercial Affordability and Economic Opportunity Tools Somewhat or Very Actively in Neighborhoods Experiencing Reinvestment or Revitalization (N=53)

tools were not in place in most respondent cities (Fig.1), the case of New York illustrates how they can be combined with market-based programs. In conjunction with its inclusionary housing programs, the city has rezoned numerous low-income neighborhoods with high proportions of residents of color for increased development capacity, raising fears of displacement.[15] The municipal government is using several mitigating tools in response. Some aim to ensure that the below-market-rate units produced in target neighborhoods are affordable and accessible to neighborhood residents: for example, public subsidies help inclusionary units reach lower-income households and half of city-assisted units are reserved for income-eligible residents of the affected neighborhood.[16] The city has also stepped up efforts to combat speculative and predatory behavior through door-to-door tenant education and legal referrals in neighborhoods with heightened displacement risk; laws that protect tenants

---

15 The Furman Center for Real Estate and Urban Policy, "How Have Recent Rezonings Affected the City's Ability to Grow?" (2010); Emily Goldstein, "New York City Needs to Stop Negotiating Rezonings from an Uneven Playing Field," *Shelterforce* (blog), May 1, 2018; Stein, "Progressive Politics and New York City's Mandatory Inclusionary Housing."

16 Rafael Cestero, "An Inclusionary Tool Created by Low-Income Communities for Low-Income Communities," *The Dream Revisited* (blog), *NYU Furman Center*, November 2015; "Mandatory Exclusionary Zoning," NYC Department of City Planning, accessed June 18, 2019; New York City Department of Housing Preservation and Development, "HPD Commissioner Torres-Springer and HDC President Enderlin Announce Housing Lottery for 25 Affordable Apartments in Brooklyn," News release, (March 27, 2017).

against harassment from owners seeking buy-outs; partnership with the state government to investigate and prosecute tenant harassment; and legislation that will, within five years, guarantee legal counsel for all low-income tenants facing eviction.[17] The city's administration also plans to create a list of rent-regulated buildings whose sale is likely to put tenants at risk of eviction, so the city can target legal assistance and other protections accordingly.[18] Although it is too early to assess these interventions' effectiveness in New York, they demonstrate a multi-dimensional approach to addressing the adverse residential impacts of market-stimulating policy tools on lower-income neighborhoods.

The final strategy involves enabling residents of revitalizing neighborhoods to benefit from employment opportunities generated by investment and keeping existing neighborhood commercial and cultural institutions viable in the face of an influx of households with different lifestyles and more purchasing power. Respondent cities did not commonly use policy tools in these categories (Fig. 2), although the majority (55%) reported using at least one tool somewhat or very actively. The example of San Francisco demonstrates how three of these tools—assistance for local businesses, restrictions on locations where chain establishments can operate, and job set-asides for residents—can target different aspects of displacement. The city combats rising commercial rents by providing financial assistance to owners of historically and culturally significant establishments and to landlords who grant them long-term leases.[19] The city has also successfully limited the presence of chain businesses and preserved independently owned establishments in commercial districts by requiring enterprises with more than 11 locations globally to acquire a special use permit before opening a store in these areas.[20] Moreover, San Francisco's jobs ordinance for city-assisted construction projects has increased the rate of

---

17 "Tenant Harassment Prevention Task Force," New York City Department of Housing Preservation and Development, accessed June 19, 2019; New York City Office of the Mayor, "Mayor de Blasio Signs Three New Laws Protecting Tenants from Harassment," News release, (September 3, 2015); New York City Office of the Mayor, "Protecting Tenants and Affordable Housing: Mayor de Blasio's Tenant Support Unit Helps 1,000 Tenants Fight Harassment, Secure Repairs," News release, (February 29, 2016); New York City Office of the Mayor, "Mayor de Blasio Signs Legislation to Provide Low-Income New Yorkers with Access to Counsel for Wrongful Evictions," News release, (August 11, 2017).

18 New York City Department of Housing Preservation and Development, "Mayor de Blasio Announces Implementation of New Law to Combat Speculators and Tenant Displacement," News release, (January 3, 2018).

19 City and County of San Francisco, "About the Legacy Business Program," Accessed June 19, 2019.

20 Olivia LaVecchia and Stacy Mitchell, "Affordable Space," (2016); "San Francisco Formula Retail Economic Analysis," Strategic Economics, accessed June 18, 2019.

local hiring for eligible projects from 20 percent in 2011 to 45 percent in 2016; although it does not specifically apply to residents of neighborhoods affected by development, the program has focused on creating opportunities for workers from lower-income areas.[21]

LOCAL OPPORTUNITIES AND BARRIERS

Although multiple strategies exist to mitigate displacement in areas targeted for investment and mixed income development, cities vary in their capacity to introduce the tools discussed in this essay.[22] Political, economic, and regulatory conditions all influence the likelihood and timing of policy adoption as well as the intensity and type of action taken. For example, local advocacy groups are crucial in putting interventions on the agenda, and a supportive electorate and progressive policy environment can increase the chances that programs are introduced. Cities where survey respondents reported very active community pressure to address affordability and displacement had more than three times the number of policy tools from Figure 1 adopted, on average, compared to those with inactive pressure (Fig. 3).[23] Moreover, a higher percentage of cities with very active pressure had legal protections for tenants, market regulation tools, and investments to create and preserve affordable housing in these areas, compared to those with inactive or somewhat active pressure. Similarly, places with the highest progressive political culture scores had each of these measures adopted more commonly than those in the middle and lowest third of the sample on this indicator, and cities with progressive policy histories (as measured by the early adoption of a living wage ordinance) were more likely to

---

21 The Office of Economic and Workforce Development, "San Francisco Local Hiring Policy for Construction"; "Labor, Law and Lessons from California: The Debate Over Local Hiring and the Rezonings," *City Limits*, accessed June 18, 2019.

22 Commercial affordability and local hiring policies are not examined in this section because the number of cities using these tools actively is too low to detect trends.

23 This section examines the following local conditions: the level of community pressure to address affordability and displacement (from the author's survey of city governments); population size and median housing value (2011-15 American Community Survey); adoption of a living wage ordinance by 2000 (categorized as early adoption) (Swarts & Vasi, 2011); state support for affordable housing (an index that assigns states one point each for permitting rent regulation and mandatory inclusionary zoning (National Multifamily Housing Council, 2017) and one additional point for each capital/production program listed in the National Low Income Housing Coalition's (2014) database of rental programs); and an index of progressive political culture that includes: the percentage of the population aged 18-44; individuals living alone or with non-relatives; same-sex partner households; women in the workforce; residents in professional, technical, educational, creative, or knowledge-based jobs; workforce members who bike or walk to work; and residents over 25 with a college degree (2011-15 American Community Survey).

have market regulations, tenant protections, and investment strategies in place.

Economic factors and locational demand also matter. Cities with the highest median housing values and largest populations, respectively, had more than two and a half times as many tools adopted as those with the lowest. Market regulations, legal protections, and inclusionary zoning policies were also in place in a higher percentage of cities in the top third of the sample on these indicators than those in the middle and lowest third. While it is possible that increased regulations and requirements lead to higher housing prices, evidence from past studies suggests that high-cost markets generate increased motivation to intervene and provide leverage to impose regulations and requirements on market actors.[24] However, strong markets also increase the cost of preserving affordable housing, and policy tools that involved investing resources to keep housing at below-market-rates in revitalizing neighborhoods were more common in cities with the lowest housing values than the highest.

External policy forces also influence cities' ability to introduce displacement mitigation measures. Survey responses and policy documents frequently referred to the role of state government in hindering, permitting, or mandating the adoption of displacement mitigation tools. Among the cities in the author's dataset, those with the highest scores on an index of state government support for affordable housing adopted nearly two and a half times as many tools as those in the lowest third and were more likely to have tenant protections and market regulations in place.

These descriptive findings are consistent with numerous case studies and multivariate analyses which show that affordable housing and equitable local development policies are significantly more common in places with a need for intervention, active advocacy group pressure, strong economic and fiscal bases, a history of progressive policymaking, a conducive state government environment,

---

24 Victoria Basolo and Corianne P. Scally, "State Innovations in Affordable Housing Policy: Lessons from California and New Jersey," *Housing Policy Debate* 19, no. 4, (2008); Pierre Clavel, *Activists in City Hall: The Progressive Response to the Reagan Era in Boston and Chicago* (Ithaca: Cornell University Press, 2010); Neil Kraus, *Majoritarian Cities: Policy Making and Inequality in Urban Politics* (Ann Arbor: University of Michigan Press, 2013); Levy, Comey, and Padilla, "In the Face of Gentrification" (2006); The Urban Institute, "Expanding Housing OpportunitiesThrough Inclusionary Zoning: Lessons from Two Counties." (Washington, DC: The Urban Institute, December 2012); Marcia Rosen and Wendy Sullivan, "From Urban Renewal and Displacement to Economic Inclusion: San Francisco Affordable Housing Policy 1978-2014," *Stanford Law & Policy Review* 25, no. 1 (2014): 121-162; Brian Stromberg and Lisa Stuevant, "What Makes Inclusionary Zoning Happen?" (2016).

and a progressive local political culture.[25] Some of these contextual factors are malleable: community advocacy can be intensified, state governments can be lobbied, and information campaigns can increase electoral support for intervention. Other conditions are more circumscribed by structural forces but can be leveraged in different ways. For instance, while cities with stronger demand have more latitude to regulate markets and impose requirements on developers, those with lower property values have greater opportunities to acquire land at a reasonable cost and preserve its affordability in perpetuity.

TOWARD A PROACTIVE AND COMPREHENSIVE APPROACH TO EQUITABLE MIXED-INCOME NEIGHBORHOODS

For those who are working to build durable socioeconomically mixed communities that support the ability of lower-income households and residents of color to benefit from investments in their neighborhoods, these findings have numerous implications. Formulating neighborhood revitalization plans that reduce displacement risks by design and investing proactively in perpetually affordable housing are fundamental strategies that can increase stability in the face of heightened demand. When demand is strong, market-reliant efforts like inclusionary zoning should be combined with measures that increase incumbent residents' chances of accessing below-market-rate units and protect them against eviction, harassment, and speculation.

A comprehensive anti-displacement approach also requires preserving the cultural and commercial amenities that incumbent residents rely on and

---

25 Victoria Basolo, "The Impacts of Intercity Competition and Intergovernmental Factors on Local Affordable Housing Expenditures," *Housing Policy Debate* 10, no. 3 (1999); Victoria Basolo, "City Spending on Economic Development Versus Affordable Housing: Does Inter🛚City Competition or Local Politics Drive Decisions?" *Journal of Urban Affairs* 22, no. 3 (2000); Cohen and Marti, "Sweet Spot"; Katherine Levine Einstein and David Glick, "Mayors, Partisanship, and Redistribution: Evidence Directly from U.S. Mayors," *Urban Affairs Review* 54, no. 1 (2016): 74-106; Katherine Levine Einstein, David Glick, and Katherine Lusk, "Mayoral Policy Making: Results from the 21st Century Mayors Leadership Survey," (Boston, MA: Boston University Initiative on Cities, October 2014); Levy, Comey, and Padilla, "In the Face of Gentrification," (2006); Paterson, Robert G. and Devashree Saha, "The Role of 'New' Political Culture in Predicting City Sustainability Efforts: An Exploratory Analysis," Working Paper Series 2010.01, Center for Sustainable Development, The University of Texas at Austin, Austin, TX, January 2010; Laura Reese and Raymond Rosenfeld, "Reconsidering Private Sector Power: Business Input and Local Development Policy," *Urban Affairs Review* 37, no. 5 (2002): 642-674; Devashree Saha, "Factors Influencing Local Government Sustainability Efforts." *State and Local Government Review* 24, no. 1 (2009): 39-48; Stromberg and Stuevant, "What Makes Inclusionary Zoning Happen?"; Anaid Yerena, "The Impact of Advocacy Organizations on Low-Income Housing Policy in U.S. Cities," *Urban Affairs Review* 5, no. 6 (2015): 843-870.

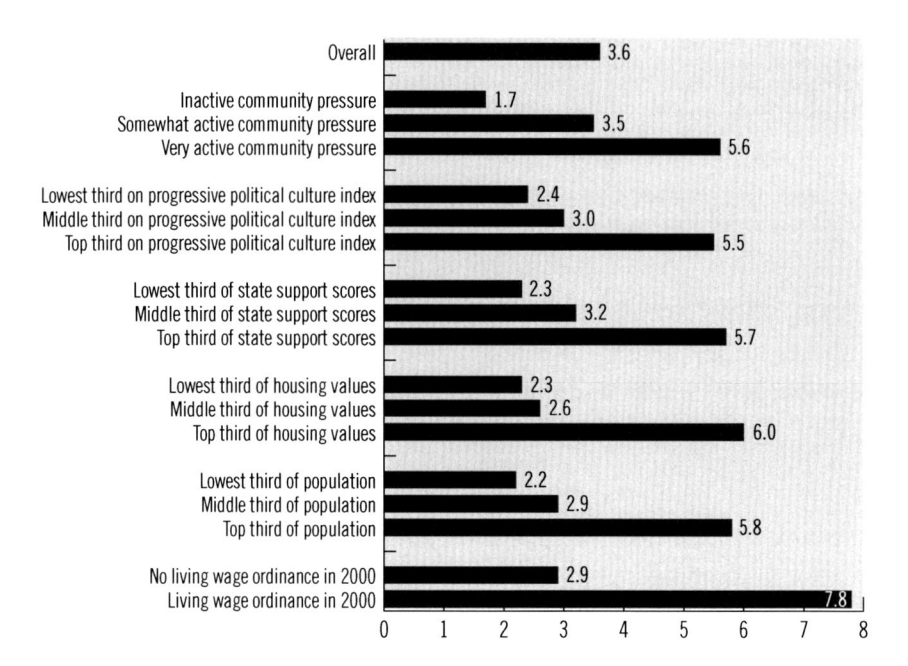

Category	Value
Overall	3.6
Inactive community pressure	1.7
Somewhat active community pressure	3.5
Very active community pressure	5.6
Lowest third on progressive political culture index	2.4
Middle third on progressive political culture index	3.0
Top third on progressive political culture index	5.5
Lowest third of state support scores	2.3
Middle third of state support scores	3.2
Top third of state support scores	5.7
Lowest third of housing values	2.3
Middle third of housing values	2.6
Top third of housing values	6.0
Lowest third of population	2.2
Middle third of population	2.9
Top third of population	5.8
No living wage ordinance in 2000	2.9
Living wage ordinance in 2000	7.8

Figure 3: Average Number of Adopted Residential Displacement Mitigation Tools by Select City Conditions

increasing their ability to benefit from economic opportunities generated in their neighborhoods. However, these tools were largely overlooked among respondent cities, possibly because direct residential displacement often takes priority in advocacy and policy agendas on tackling gentrification. When commercial affordability and local hiring tools were used in respondent cities, this was often on an ad hoc basis as opportunities arose during specific redevelopment projects. One way to increase policy activity in this area involves expanding on these case-by-case practices to create more formalized policy tools to guide equitable redevelopment. Another approach would adapt city-wide small business or hiring initiatives to the specific challenges experienced in neighborhoods at risk of gentrification.

The tools and strategies analyzed in this essay are relevant in rapidly appreciating neighborhoods facing immediate risks of displacement as well as in areas of concentrated poverty where communities are struggling to create better-quality living conditions. In both cases, the challenge is to enable current and future lower-income households to benefit from revitalization through opportunities to access housing, jobs, and affordable and culturally appropriate amenities. In neighborhoods at the early stages of reinvestment, introducing or strengthening land banks, community land trusts, and citywide tenant protections can provide a bulwark against future market volatility and speculation. Where gentrification is more advanced, resources can be marshalled to finance legal aid for tenants who are at heightened risk of eviction and to fund the acquisition of low-income housing that is at imminent risk of sale or conversion. Targeted tenant protection measures, such as those tackling buy-outs, providing information about building sales, and proactively informing residents of their rights can also address looming risks where appreciation is advancing rapidly. Whatever the circumstances of the targeted neighborhood, only by tackling this challenge through prompt action and a multi-dimensional approach will cities be able to curb the gentrification pressures associated with market-leveraging mixed-income efforts.

IMPLICATIONS FOR ACTION

Implications for Policy

- Tools that harness market conditions to create mixed-income communities should be considered one carefully designed component of a comprehensive and proactive strategy that includes preservation and tenant protection efforts. An underutilized tool that more jurisdictions should consider involves introducing specific legal safeguards for tenants against predatory landlord activities—such as improper evictions, buy-out pressure, and other forms of harassment—that often occur in areas where demand is expected to rise.

- Investing in land banks and community land trusts in weaker markets is a cost-effective way to create long-term stability for lower-income residents before appreciation occurs. Land banks should be considered when jurisdictions have the capacity to acquire and stabilize vacant, abandoned, or financially distressed properties. Authorities should require that properties subsequently returned to the market include long-term affordability provisions. Local governments should also consider donating land bank properties or other publicly owned lots to community land trusts and work to establish the regulatory, taxation, and funding provisions that will ensure the trusts' long-term sustainability and affordability.

- Dedicated revenue for affordable housing from taxes, fees, or general funds provides a flexible tool for mitigating displacement. Such funds can be marshalled to address rapidly changing conditions in gentrifying areas and tackle different dimensions of displacement, such as by financing legal aid for tenants or funding the acquisition and rent-limitation of low-cost housing. Race-conscious strategies to allocate these funds can assure that the benefits are shared by households of color.
- Addressing displacement pressure through measures that support incumbent small businesses and foster economic opportunities, such as assistance for historically or culturally significant establishments, affordable space for minority-owned businesses, and job set-asides for neighborhood residents, can help mitigate the disproportionate impact of gentrification on residents of color.

Implications for Research and Evaluation

- Researchers have an important role to play in supporting policy development, particularly through accessible and timely policy briefs that convey key lessons from existing efforts. Study respondents repeatedly indicated that city agencies value the opportunity to learn from other cities' strategies but rarely have the time and resources to create comprehensive policy inventories.
- More research is urgently needed to evaluate the impact of displacement mitigation interventions, both through in-depth case studies that can provide detail about strategies and results and quantitative work that can help identify factors associated with successful outcomes.

Implications for Development and Investment

- For-profit real estate actors should work with city officials to provide information on how to calibrate programs like inclusionary zoning in a way that achieves the government's affordability goals without deterring development and adversely affecting housing supply.
- Cities can leverage dedicated funding for capacity building, operating funds, and equity investment that can help nonprofit developers compete against for-profit actors in acquiring low-income housing that is at risk of sale or conversion in gentrifying areas.

Implications for Residents and Community Members

- Advocacy has the power to influence the political agenda, especially when it has a strong community base. Organized pressure directed at shifting political calculations on when to intervene to address displacement could lead to more proactive equitable development strategies. Attention should be given to ensure that residents of color have an equitable voice and access in advocacy efforts.

- Residents and community members should pressure local political representatives and nonprofit actors to emphasize the economic logic of early intervention to mitigate displacement when fighting to put this measure on the policy agenda.

■ ■ ■

ADÈLE CASSOLA *is Research Director, Public Health Institutions at Global Strategy Lab, York University in Toronto. She completed her Ph.D. in Urban Planning at Columbia University, where her dissertation drew on an original dataset of 80 U.S. cities to analyze how and why municipal governments address residential and commercial affordability in gentrifying neighborhoods. She also holds a B.A. in Peace and Conflict Studies from the University of Toronto and a M.Sc. in City Design and Social Science from the London School of Economics.*

MIXED-INCOME HOUSING IN NEW YORK CITY: ACHIEVEMENTS, CHALLENGES, AND LESSONS OF AN ENDURING MAYORAL COMMITMENT

Alex Schwartz
The New School[1]

Sasha Tsenkova
University of Calgary

New York City has long been a laboratory for mixed-income housing. For decades, in collaboration with nonprofit and for-profit organizations, the city has built thousands of housing units in mixed-income developments under many different programs and formats. New York is also distinctive among other cities in the United States in that its mixed-income housing is not contingent on the redevelopment of public housing or on inclusionary zoning. Whereas much if not most mixed-income housing built elsewhere in the country since the 1990s is connected to the demolition and redevelopment of public housing, often leading to a net loss of public housing, this is not the case for New York City. New York has had some form of inclusionary zoning since the 1980s, but it is a minor source of the city's mixed-income housing.

In this essay, we describe the breadth of mixed-income housing in New York City. We situate mixed-income housing within the history of New York's affordable housing programs and emphasize the variety of forms it takes and the neighborhood contexts in which it occurs. We show how

---

[1] An earlier version of this essay was presented at the Partnership for Affordable Housing International Conference at the University of Calgary in 2018. The authors acknowledge the support of the Social Sciences and Humanities Research Council of Canada.

New York's mixed-income housing ranges from luxury housing that include some units designated for lower-income households, to developments with a larger proportion of low- and moderate income-units and a much smaller share of market-rate units. We argue that New York City's case, including its experimentation with many forms of mixed-income housing, shows that:

- Mixed-income housing can be much more diverse in terms of its income composition, funding sources, and programmatic design than one might presume from a reading of the literature.

- Mixed-income housing is an ordinary, even mundane, part of the city's landscape. Notwithstanding occasional controversies sparked by particular buildings or programs, it is commonplace for people with widely varied incomes and other characteristics to reside in the same building or on the same block. In fact, the mixed-income quality of mixed-income housing may not be what defines or distinguishes the housing in the eyes of residents.

- Mixed-income housing nearly always requires government subsidy; the notion that income from market-rate units will fully subsidize the "affordable" units is rarely viable.

- The city's chronic shortage of affordable housing and broad-based support for public investment in many forms of affordable housing may allow for more creative, ambitious, and durable approaches to mixed-income housing than anywhere else in the U.S.

We conclude with a brief discussion of lessons and unresolved questions about New York's experience with mixed-income housing and implications for policy and practice in the mixed-income field.

THE RELATIONSHIP BETWEEN PUBLIC HOUSING AND MIXED-INCOME HOUSING IN NEW YORK CITY

In the rest of the United States, mixed-income housing is strongly associated with the redevelopment of public housing. Under HOPE VI and other programs, public housing authorities demolished more than 150,000 public housing developments, replacing many with mixed-income housing that includes a smaller number of public housing units and varying blends of other subsidized and market-rate housing, sometimes including owner-occupied housing.[2] New York has not demolished any of its public housing developments, however; its two HOPE VI projects upgraded the physical plants and remained 100 percent public housing.

New York's public housing encompasses aspects of mixed-income housing that are found in few other cities. First, many of New York's public housing developments have been home to households with a wider range of incomes than elsewhere. As with public housing in the rest of the country, New York's public housing accommodates many people with extremely low incomes. But unlike other places, New York's public housing has also attracted many people, including teachers and civil servants, with higher incomes. This attraction reflects the relatively high quality of many public housing developments at the time of their construction, their affordability, and in many cases their proximity to transit and other urban resources.[3] It also reflects the fact that public housing in New York City is widely dispersed, with developments located in 46 of the city's 59 community districts. While fewer moderate- and middle-income residents currently live in New York's public housing than in years past, they are still more prevalent in New York than in the public housing of other cities. For example, in 2018, earned wages were the most important source of income for 40 percent of New York's public housing residents, compared to an average of 29 percent in the 10 next-largest housing authorities in the continental U.S., and 40 percent of New York's public housing households earned at least $20,000 annually, compared to 23 percent in that comparison group.[4]

The second aspect of mixed-income public housing in New York City stems from the fact that many developments are situated in middle-class and affluent neighborhoods. While many public housing developments are located in relatively isolated low-income neighborhoods, others are found in the midst

---

2 Robert J. Chaskin and Mark L. Joseph, *Integrating the Inner City: The Promise and Perils of Mixed-Income Public Housing Transformation* (Chicago, IL: University of Chicago Press, 2015); Taryn Gress, Mark L. Joseph, and Seungjong Cho, "Confirmations, New Insights, and Future Implications for HOPE VI Mixed-Income Redevelopment," *Cityscape* 21, no. 2 (2019): 185-212; Lawrence J. Vale and Shomon Shamsuddin, "All Mixed Up: Making Sense of Mixed-Income Housing Developments," *Journal of the American Planning Association* 83, no. 1 (2017): 56-67; Lawrence J. Vale, Shomon Shamsuddin, and Nicholas Kelly, "Broken Promises or Selective Memory Planning? A National Picture of HOPE VI Plans and Realities," *Housing Policy Debate* 28, no. 5 (2018): 746-69.

3 Nicholas Dagan Bloom, *Public Housing that Worked* (Philadelphia, PA: University of Pennsylvania Press, 2008).

4 U.S. Department of Housing and Urban Development: Office of Policy Development and Research, Picture of Subsidized Households (2019), https://www.huduser.gov/portal/datasets/assthsg.html

of some of New York's wealthiest areas.[5] It isn't hard to find public housing located next door to or across the street from condominium towers with apartments that cost several million dollars each. For example, Amsterdam Houses is located across Amsterdam Avenue from Lincoln Center for the Performing Arts and the 54-story Hawthorne Parke luxury rental building, where the average monthly rent for apartments leased from January 2018 to June 2019 was $7,218.[6] The Chelsea Elliot Houses and Fulton Homes are located in close proximity to the Highline, the elevated park that has stimulated the construction of numerous luxury condos. Among them is 520 West 28th Street, designed by internationally renowned architect Zaha Hadid, where the sales price of apartments sold from January 2018 to March 2019 averaged $10.3 million.[7] New York University's Furman Center found that nearly 60 percent of New York's public housing units, as of 2017, were located in gentrifying neighborhoods and an additional 27 percent in higher-income neighborhoods.[8] The close proximity of public housing with various tiers of market-rate housing illustrate what Vale and Shamsuddin have called the "mixing-around" form of mixed-income housing[9].

In an effort to generate much-needed revenue to help finance essential renovations and other capital improvements, New York City has started to lease vacant land on selected public housing campuses for the development of high-rise housing developments—some 100 percent market-rate and others that combine luxury housing with units priced for lower-income households.[10]

---

5   NYU Furman Center, "How NYCHA Preserves Diversity in NYC's Changing Neighborhoods," http://furmancenter.org/research/publication/how-nycha-preserves-diversity-in-new-york8217s-changing-neighborhoods, (2019).

6   The real estate service StreetEasy listed 57 apartments that were leased in this building from Jan. 25, 2018, to June 6, 2019. The lowest rent was $3,295 for a studio apartment and the highest was $16,900 for a three-bedroom unit.

7   Sales data from StreetEasy, which listed 28 open-market transactions during this period.

8   NYU Furman Center, "How NYCHA Preserves Diversity"

9   Vale and Shamsuddin, "All Mixed Up."

10 New York City Housing Authority, *NYCHA 2.0: Part 1—Invest to Preserve*, (New York, NY: New York City Housing Authority, 2018), https://www1.nyc.gov/assets/nycha/downloads/pdf/NYCHA-2.0-Part1.pdf.

These efforts have been controversial, both because of the loss of open space, light, and views and because of fears that the development of market-rate housing will ultimately lead to the displacement of public housing residents.[11] That said, the fact that private developers will build luxury market-rate housing cheek by jowl with public housing underscores that public housing need not be demolished or downsized in order to make mixed-income communities possible.

MIXED-INCOME HOUSING PRODUCED UNDER MAYORAL HOUSING PLANS

Most of New York City's mixed-income housing originated from the various affordable housing programs launched by the city since the late 1980s. Starting with Mayor Koch's 10-year housing plan of 1987, New York City has invested, after inflation, more than $18.9 billion on the construction and preservation[12] of more than 450,000 units of affordable housing. Every subsequent mayor, Democrat and Republican, has allocated hundreds of millions of dollars each year for this purpose (see Figure 1). The current mayor, Bill de Blasio, set a goal of building 120,000 units and preserving 180,000 from 2014 to 2026; as of April 2019, the city had completed or started work on nearly 124,000 units.[13] De Blasio's initiative builds on Mayor Michael Bloomberg's 12-year New Housing Marketplace plan, which produced 165,000 affordable units[14].

New York's housing plans are assemblages of various programs that target different income groups and residents; they involve new construction, physical renovations, and the renewal of existing subsidies. The plans involve a range of partners, including for-profit housing developers, large nonprofit organizations, and smaller community-based organizations. The plans are funded through the city's capital budget (in the form of general obligation bonds), and also from tax-exempt and taxable private activity bonds issued by the city's Housing

---

11 Elizabeth Kim, "Facing Opposition to Redevelopment Plan, City Establishes Working Group to Decide Future of NYCHA's Chelsea Complex," *Gothamist*, October 11, 2019, https://gothamist.com/news/facing-opposition-redevelopment-plan-city-establishes-working-group-decide-future-nychas-chelsea-complex

12 Preservation refers to physical renovation and other capital improvements of existing affordable housing and to commitments to extend or renew existing subsidies so that housing can remain affordable.

13 Alex Schwartz, "New York City's Affordable Housing Plans and the Limits of Local Initiative," *Cityscape* 21, no. 3 (2019): 355-88.

14 New York City Department of Housing Preservation and Development, *New Housing Marketplace Plan*. (New York, NY: New York City Department of Housing Preservation and Development, 2010).

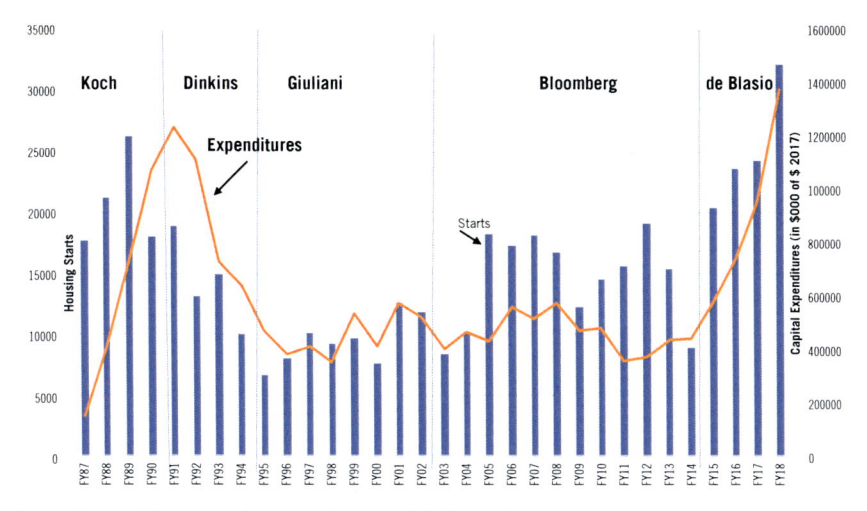

Source: Mayor's Management Report and Comptroller's Budget Report

Figure 1: Capital Budget Expenditures (In 000s of 2017 Dollars) and Affordable Housing Starts, 1987-2018

Development Corporation, federal Low-Income Housing Tax Credits, and other sources. The plans also make use of property tax abatements and inclusionary zoning, which provide private developers with financial incentives to allocate a portion of otherwise market-rate housing developments to lower-income occupancy. Under Mayor de Blasio, the city expanded its previous voluntary inclusionary zoning program with the establishment of mandatory inclusionary zoning in neighborhoods that complete a rezoning process to permit higher-density housing.

New York's housing plans have produced several forms of mixed-income housing. These vary from luxury apartment buildings in prime Manhattan neighborhoods that include some units for low- and/or moderate-income households, to developments situated in far less affluent communities that designate a higher percentage of units for such households. Virtually all mixed-income housing built over the past several decades involves some form of public subsidy. With the development of affordable housing often involving the purchase of expensive privately owned land, New York's housing programs increasingly include units for higher-income households to reduce the amount of public subsidy necessary to support low-income units.[15]

As discussed below, the mixed-income housing produced under mayoral plans varies widely in terms of the share of housing allocated to various income bands and the degree to which the housing is affordable to very-low-income people. Some mixed-income programs, especially under Mayors Koch and Dinkins, designated most units to very-low-income households (earning up to 50 percent of the area median family income), including the formerly homeless, and allocated most of the rest to moderate- and middle-income families. Other programs produced predominantly market-rate housing, with a small share earmarked for low- or moderate-income tenants. Except for formerly homeless individuals and families, who almost always receive federal Housing Choice Vouchers or other rent subsidies, the lowest-income band in New York's mixed-income programs has ranged between 40 percent and 60 percent of average median income (AMI). Unfortunately, there is no information available on the racial and ethnic composition of the mixed-income housing produced in New York City.

Most of the mixed-income housing developed over the past three decades occasioned minimal if any opposition or controversy. However, this is less true today. Some opposition involves the real estate tax exemptions given to developers of ultra-luxury housing. The city has provided more than $1 billion in exemptions for high-end housing, some but not all of which included affordable units.[16] A more recent debate has centered around the rezoning of selected neighborhoods, mostly minority and low-income, for higher density. Although these rezonings trigger mandatory inclusionary zoning that requires 20 to 40 percent of new units to be affordable to households at various income levels, critics contend that the affordability levels are not affordable enough given the low incomes of most residents, and that new market-rate development resulting from the rezoning will exacerbate the neighborhoods' affordability problems by stimulating gentrification[17] and displacing low-income residents.

---

15 Thomas J. Waters and Victor Bach, *Good Place to Work Hard Place to Live: The Housing Challenge for New York City's Next Mayor*, (New York, NY: Community Service Society, 2013), https://www.cssny.org/publications/entry/good-place-to-work-hard-place-to-live.

16 Victor Bach and Thomas Waters, "Why We Need to End New York City's Most Expensive Housing Program: Time to End 421-a," http://lghttp.58547.nexcesscdn.net/803F44A/images/nycss/images/uploads/pubs/421aReportFinal.pdf, (2015).

17 Alessandro Busa, *The Creative Destruction of New York City: Engineering the City for the Elite* (New York, NY: Oxford University Press, 2017); Michael Greenberg, "Tenants Under Siege: Inside New York

Finally, a few mixed-income developments elicited public outrage by requiring the residents of the affordable units to enter the building through a separate door and barring them from using some of the buildings' amenities.[18]

SELECTED EXAMPLES OF MIXED-INCOME HOUSING IN NEW YORK CITY

Luxury Housing with a Low- or Moderate-Income Component

Private developers have built hundreds of market-rate apartment buildings in prime sections of Manhattan and, more recently, Brooklyn that include some amount of units for people with low or moderate income. Whether through below-market-rate financing, property tax exemptions, the opportunity to build at higher densities than otherwise allowed, or a combination thereof, developers have used these incentives to build apartment buildings that are mostly market-rate but reserve up to 25 percent of units for lower-income tenants. (Sometimes these developments receive two or more such incentives.) The affordable units are assigned to eligible households by lottery. The number of people who apply for affordable units in these mixed-income units typically exceed the number of available units available by a ratio of several hundred to one.[19]

The so-called 80-20 program used tax-exempt bond financing to underwrite below-market-rate mortgages for housing that reserved 20 percent of units for households with incomes up to 60 percent of AMI, while the remaining 80 percent was market-rate. Most buildings financed under the 80-20 program also received property tax exemptions. The 421a tax abatement program, created in the 1970s and modified several times to include buildings located in particular areas of New York City,[20] required developers to designate

---

City's Housing Crisis," *New York Review of Books*, August 17, 2019, https://www.nybooks.com/articles/2017/08/17/tenants-under-siege-inside-new-york-city-housing-crisis/; Samuel Stein, "Progress for Whom, Toward What? Progressive Politics and New York City's Mandatory Inclusionary Zoning Program," *Journal of Urban Affairs* 40, no. 6 (2018): 770–781.

18 Mark L. Joseph, "Separate but Equal Redux: Resolving and Transcending the Poor Door Conundrum," in *The Dream Revisited: Contemporary Debates about Housing, Segregation, and Opportunity*, ed. Ingrid Gould Ellen and Justin Peter Steil (New York, NY: Columbia University Press, 2019), 292-94; Mireya Navarro, "88,000 Applicants and Counting."

19 Navarro, "88,000 Applicants and Counting;" Julie Satow, "Better than the Powerball: For New Yorkers Looking for an Affordable Home, the Odds of Winning a Housing Lottery are 1 in 592," *New York Times*, January 11, 2019, https://www.nytimes.com/2019/01/11/realestate/better-than-the-powerball.html.

20 Originally Manhattan below 96th Street; later extended to parts of other boroughs.

a portion of units for low- or moderate-income tenants. An example is a project at 505 West 37th Street, Manhattan. Completed in 2009, the 835-unit doorman building is located in the Hudson Yards district on the far-west side of Manhattan. Average market-rate rents in 2019 amount to $3,533, but 168 units are designated for low-income households earning no more than 60 percent of AMI.

Generally, the affordable units within 80-20 and 421a buildings are intermixed with market-rate units, although units with the best views and other amenities usually are reserved for market-rate tenants. An exception is the small number of buildings that partitioned affordable units within separate sections. This issue became particularly contentious when news came out that a mixed-income building on the west side of Manhattan had installed separate entrances for market-rate and affordable units; the latter soon became known as the "poor door."[21] The developer structured the building as two condominiums, each with its own entrance; in effect, a market-rate building situated next to a subsidized building.[22] The physical segregation of income groups within a development, symbolized by separate entrances and amenities, raised concerns that this form of mixed-income housing can stigmatize lower-income residents and undermine the potential for community building across income groups.[23]

In 2015, the city issued regulations requiring all entrances in mixed-income projects that receive tax exemptions or other subsidies to be open to all residents regardless of income.[24] However, some mixed-income buildings prohibit residents of affordable units from using amenities (e.g., gyms, storage spaces) available to market-rate residents. The physical separation of income groups is characteristic of some luxury buildings that include a component of affordable units; it is much less common in other forms of mixed-income housing.

---

21 Mireya Navarro, "'Poor Door' in a New York Tower Opens a Fight over Affordable Housing," *New York Times*, August 26, 2014, www.nytimes.com/2014/08/27/nyregion/separate-entryways-for-new-york-condo-buyers-and-renters-create-an-affordable-housing-dilemma.html?searchResultPosition=2.

22 Carol Lamberg, "Housing Priorities: Quality Is More Important Than the Number of Entrances," in *The Dream Revisited: Contemporary Debates about Housing, Segregation, and Opportunity*, ed. Ingrid Gould Ellen and Justin Peter Steil (New York, NY: Columbia University Press, 2019), 295-97.

23 Joseph, "Separate but Equal Redux"

24 Justin W. Moyer, "NYC Bans 'Poor Doors' –Separate Entrances for Low-Income Tenants," *Washington Post*, June 30, 2015, https://www.washingtonpost.com/news/morning-mix/wp/2015/06/30/nyc-bans-poor-doors-separate-entrances-for-low-income-tenants/.

MIXED-INCOME HOUSING WITH LARGER PROPORTIONS OF LOWER-INCOME UNITS

New York has sponsored many mixed-income developments that feature substantially larger percentages of low- and moderate-income units, with the top income tier targeted to households earning much less than the market-rate tenants in 80-20 or 421a buildings. Because these buildings tend to designate more units for lower income households, they often involve larger amounts of subsidy than 80-20 buildings and the like.

Mayor Koch's Construction Management Program.

One of the earlier mixed-income programs instituted in New York City was the Construction Management program. Created as part of Mayor Koch's original initial 10-year plan, Construction Management involved the gut rehabilitation of large assemblages of vacant and highly deteriorated housing in the Bronx and Harlem. There were six Construction Management developments, each involving several hundred housing units.[25] One of these projects was the New Settlement Apartments, sponsored by the Settlement Housing Fund, one of New York's largest nonprofit sponsors of low-income housing. Located in the Mount Eden section of the Bronx, the complex currently has 1,082 units. Thirty percent of the units were originally allocated to formerly homeless families, who received Section 8 vouchers to cover the rent; 40 percent were allocated to low-income families; 20 percent to moderate-income families; and 10 percent to households paying market-rate rents. Interestingly, the rents paid for the market-rate units were less than the rents paid by Section 8 vouchers. Every floor in the development includes households from all targeted income groups.[26]

The Construction Management program is one of very few mixed-income initiatives in New York City to be examined from the tenants' perspective. In focus groups with residents in two Construction Management developments in the Bronx, Schwartz and Tajbakhsh explored resident satisfaction with the developments, awareness of the mixed-income character of the developments, and degree of social interaction within and across income categories. The

---

25 Alex Schwartz and Kian Tajbakhsh, "Mixed-Income Housing," in *Revitalizing the City: Strategies to Contain Sprawl and Revive the Core*, ed. Fritz E. Wagner, Timothy E. Joder, Anthony J. Momphrey, Jr., Krishna M. Akundi, and Alan F. J. Artibise (Armonk. NY: M.E. Sharpe, 2005).

26 Carol Lamberg, *Neighborhood Success Stories: Creating and Sustaining Affordable Housing in New York* (New York, NY: Fordham University Press, 2018).

Figure 2: Hunter Point in New York City: The Largest Affordable Housing Development

researchers found that while the residents were fully aware of the mixed-income character of the developments, they did not consider it to be a defining feature. More salient were the affordability of the apartments, the location of the developments, the high physical quality of apartments, the responsiveness of property managers to their concerns, and the availability of on-site social services.[27]

Mayor Bloomberg's Mixed-Income Programs

These included three types of mixed-income projects: low- to moderate-income (80 percent AMI or below), New HOP (81 percent AMI or above) and 50/30/20 mixed-income (replacing the previous 80-20 program). Developments were located mostly in Manhattan, to capitalize on demand for mid- and higher

---

27 Schwartz and Tajbakhsh, "Mixed-Income Housing." See also Lamberg 2018 for a detailed account of the challenges in building and managing one of the Construction Management developments, as well as profiles of several long-time residents. Lamberg was the Executive Director of the Settlement Housing Fund, the sponsor of the development.

Credit: New York City Housing Development Corporation

Figure 3: Via Verde Sustainable Mixed-Income Housing in New York City

income housing. Newly built mixed-income, affordable housing set an example for sustainability, design innovation, and institutional partnerships. The

Hunter's Point South development on the Queens waterfront is the largest new affordable housing complex built in New York City since the 1970s. Envisioned as part of the City's 2012 Olympic bid, the first phase, co-developed by Related Companies, Phipps Houses, and Monadnock Construction, included 925 permanently affordable apartments and 17,000 square feet of new retail space, key infrastructure installations, a new five-acre waterfront park, and a new 1,100-seat school, while meeting national green building criteria (see Figure 2).

Another mixed-income project to come out of the Bloomberg era is Navy Green, co-developed by Dunn Development, L&M Development Partners, and the Pratt Area Community Council. Consisting of 433 units in four multi-family buildings and 23 townhouses, the development combines supportive housing for formerly homeless families, owner-occupied housing, and rental housing for several income groups. Located across from the former Brooklyn Navy Yards, the complex also includes retail space, a children's play area, open lawn, patios and gardens.

Via Verde is a sustainable residential development with 222 units of mixed-income housing in the South Bronx co-developed by Phipps Houses and Jonathan Rose Companies (see Figure 3). The project received the U.S Department of Housing and Urban Development's Award for Excellence in Affordable Housing Design in 2013. The ground floor features 11,000 square feet of retail, a community health center, and live-work units. With a 66-kilowatt, building-integrated photovoltaic system, onsite cogeneration, green roof, community vegetable gardens, green interior finishes, rainwater harvesting, and drought-tolerant vegetation, the complex is LEED NC Gold certified.[28]

Mayor de Blasio's Mixed-Income Housing Programs

Mixed-income programs rolled out by the de Blasio administration vary widely in terms of the top and bottom income levels that are targeted, the number of income tiers represented, and the distribution of units across income tiers. Two programs allow some units to be rented to market-rate tenants of any income, but three programs cap the maximum income at a specified percentage of the area median family income (from 100 to 165 percent). The lowest-income

---

28 Sasha Tsenkova, "Investing in New York's Future: Affordable Rental Housing in Mixed Income Projects," *Plan Canada* 53, no. 3 (2014): 32-40.

households eligible for the programs vary from formerly homeless people with incomes well below the poverty level to those earning 60 percent of AMI. The percentage of units allocated to the top income tier varies from 30 percent to 75 percent.

For example, the Extremely Low- and Low-Income Affordability (ELLA) program's income tiers include formerly homeless and other extremely low-income households. In one option, units must be allocated as follows: 10 percent to formerly homeless households, 10 percent to households earning up to 30 percent of AMI, 10 percent to households earning up to 40 percent of AMI, 10 percent to households earning up to 50 percent of AMI, and 30 percent to households earning up to 60 percent of AMI. Developers have the option of designating some or all of the remaining 30 percent of the units to households earning 70 to 100 percent of AMI; otherwise they must be slated for households earning up to 60 percent.[29] In the second option, 30 percent of the units are allocated to formerly homeless households, 5 percent to households earning up to 40 percent of AMI, and 5 percent to households earning up to 50 percent of AMI. As with the first option, the remaining 60 percent must go to households earning up to 60 percent of AMI, although developers may allocate up to 30 percent of the units to households earning 70 to 100 percent of AMI. The city provides $130,000 to $150,000 in subsidy per unit, depending on the overall income mix in the development. City subsidies, federal Low-income Housing Tax credits, and property tax exemptions, combined with the cash flow from the higher-income units, makes it financially viable to charge lower-income households affordable rents.

One of the first ELLA projects to be developed, by Dunn Development and L&M Development Partners, is Livonia Commons. Located in the East New York section of Brooklyn, the development includes 278 apartment in four buildings. Fifty-one units consist of supportive housing for formerly homeless families who receive services on-site from two nonprofit organizations. More than half of the units are designated for families earning below 50 percent or 40 percent of AMI. The development also includes an arts center, a legal services office, a supermarket, a pharmacy, and other retail space (see Figure 4).

---

29 Sasha Tsenkova and Alex Schwartz, "Partnerships for Affordable Rental Housing in New York City," in *Housing Partnerships*, ed. Sasha Tsenkova (Calgary, AB: University of Calgary), 37-46.

Source: Dunn Development Corp.

Figure 4: Livionia Commons

In the Mix and Match program, eligible developments must have a minimum of four income tiers. Forty to 60 percent of the units must be affordable to households earning up to 60 percent of AMI, including at least 10 percent of units serving formerly homeless households. A minimum of 10 percent of units must be affordable to households earning 30 percent to 50 percent of AMI, and the remaining 40 percent to 60 percent of the units must be affordable to households earning up to 130 percent of AMI. Units receive $10,000 to $225,000 from the city's capital fund, depending on the income designation. Developments may also receive federal Low-Income Housing Tax Credits and property tax exemptions.

New York's Mandatory Inclusionary Housing Program

This mixed-income housing program allocates the majority of units to households able to pay market-rate rents. However, it also includes households with incomes that are lower than those permitted in nearly all other inclusionary zoning programs in the United States. Moreover, the program allocates a larger proportion of units to low- and moderate-income households, and it requires affordable units to remain so permanently (i.e., affordability is not time-limited).[30] The program takes effect whenever a neighborhood (or land parcel) is rezoned for higher densities. As of January 2019, five neighborhoods, starting with East New York, had been rezoned at higher densities, thereby effectuating mandatory inclusionary housing. Rezoning proposals were in process or anticipated for six additional neighborhoods. All but one of the neighborhoods with rezoning completed or in process are located outside Manhattan, and most are predominantly low-income.[31]

There are two basic options in the mandatory inclusionary housing program.[32] Under one, developers can designate 75 percent of total floor area for market-rate units, while the remaining 25 percent must go to households with an average income of 60 percent of AMI, including 10 percent that are allocated to households earning up to 30 percent of AMI. In the second option, 60 percent of the floor area is reserved for market-rate units, and the remaining 40 percent goes to households with an average income of 80 percent of AMI. If developers choose to build the affordable units off-site at a separate location, they must allocate an additional 5 percent of total floor area to households with an average income (depending on the option) of 60 percent or 80 percent of AMI. Mixed-income housing properties are underwritten so they do not require direct city subsidy, although they may be eligible for federal Low-Income Housing Tax Credits and city property tax exemptions. However, buildings financed under other subsidy programs may be, and are, located in rezoned neighborhoods.

Mandatory inclusionary housing is the most controversial of the de Blasio administration's affordable housing programs. Although it accounts for less than 4 percent of the 39,949 units of new construction started under the plan from 2014 through the first quarter of 2019, the program has attracted far more attention and criticism than all other aspects of the de Blasio plan.[33] One criticism is that even the lowest-rent apartments are unaffordable to most low-

---

30 Emily Thaden and Vince Wang, "Inclusionary Zoning in the United States: Prevalence, Impact, and Practices" (working Paper WP17ET1, Lincoln Land Institute, Cambridge, MA, September 2017).

31 Sadef Alli Kully, "De Blasio's Sixth Year in Office Could Feature Three Neighborhood Rezonings," *City Limits*, January 7, 2019, https://citylimits.org/2019/01/07/de-blasios-sixth-year-in-office-could-feature-three-neighborhood-rezonings/.

32 "Inclusionary Housing Program," New York City Department of Planning, accessed April 14, 2020, https://www1.nyc.gov/site/planning/zoning/districts-tools/inclusionary-housing.page.

33 Alex Schwartz, "New York City's Affordable Housing Plans and the Limits of Local Initiative," *Cityscape* 21, no. 3 (2019): 355-88.

income residents. This is because the rents are set in relation to the New York metro area's median family income, which is much higher than the median income in the neighborhoods that have been upzoned.[34] A second criticism is that, while the new buildings in the rezoned neighborhoods will provide some affordable units (notwithstanding the first criticism), the construction of taller, mostly market-rate buildings will exacerbate affordability problems by driving up land prices and rents throughout the neighborhood.[35] The fact that the residents of most of the neighborhoods slated for rezoning tend to have low incomes and to be predominantly non-White has no doubt contributed to the plan's hostile reception. Some observers have suggested that the plan might have received more support if the city had also included more affluent and more White neighborhoods among those to be rezoned.[36] In any case, there is little evidence to show that the affordability pressures in the rezoned neighborhoods are any greater than in other neighborhoods of the city. On the other hand, rental pressures are acute in many neighborhoods, including many that have not been rezoned.

CONCLUSIONS

The New York City experience leads us to the following conclusions.

Mixed-income Housing Can Be a Financially and Socially Viable Form of Housing That Leverages the Private Sector to Finance a Limited Amount of Affordable Housing

The city's experience with public housing and, most especially, with the many housing programs that have been instituted under mayoral housing plans since 1986 illustrates the many ways in which mixed-income housing can be configured. It includes luxury housing located in prime Manhattan and Brooklyn neighborhoods in which about 20 percent of the units are designated for relatively low- and/or moderate-income households. It also includes developments located in lower-income neighborhoods with a larger percentage

---

34 Schwartz, "New York City's Affordable Housing."

35 Benjamin Dulchin, "Does Trickle-Down Affordability Justify the Mayor's Zoning Policy?" *Association for Neighborhood and Housing Development* (blog), https://anhd.org/blog/does-trickle-down-affordability-justify-mayors-zoning-policy, (January 24, 2019).; Abigail Savitch-Law, "Will Rezoning Cause or Resist Displacement? Data Paints an Incomplete Picture," *City Limits*, January 10, 2017, https://citylimits.org/2017/01/10/will-rezoning-cause-or-resist-displacement-data-paints-an-incomplete-picture/.

36 Savitch-Law, "Will Rezoning Cause or Resist Displacement?"

of low-income units and in which the rents charged to tenants at the top of the income tier tend to be considerably less than the market-rate rents of other mixed-income developments.

Mixed-income housing also has limitations as a vehicle for producing and financing affordable housing, however. The inclusion of market-rate units can generate a "cross-subsidy" to supplement the lower rents paid by lower-income residents. But only in limited circumstances is this cross-subsidy sufficient by itself to make the development financially viable. It may be sufficient when 80 percent of the units are reserved for market-rate units charging more than, say, $4,000 per month, and when few, if any, affordable units are designated for households with extremely low incomes. Even in these cases, the developments receive low-interest financing and tax exemptions.

Ambitious Design That Set the Bar High in Terms of Sustainable Design and Green Elements Can Be Achieved

New York projects have won design awards for excellence, innovation, incorporation of public realm, and mixed-use components that contribute to neighborhood qualities.[37] Such experiences create an image of affordable housing projects that is remarkably different from the stigma associated with public housing of the 1960s.

Mixed-income Housing Can Take Many Forms and Be Situated in Many Different Types of Neighborhoods

Physically, mixed-income housing can involve rehabilitation of existing buildings as well as new construction. It can involve walk-up buildings of six stories to towers of 30 stories or more. It can be limited to single buildings or encompass multiple structures. Mixed-income projects can be entirely residential, and they can include various types of nonresidential components too, including retail, medical offices, schools, and libraries. As noted above, New York's mixed-income housing programs feature various combinations of income groups, with the representation of market-rate units varying from 80 percent to less than 20 percent. And while it is true that mixed-income housing typically requires less subsidy in more affluent neighborhoods that command relatively high rents—rents that can "cross-subsidize" units occupied by low-

---

37 Sasha Tsenkova, "Investing in New York's Future;" Katie Honan, "New York City Selects Designers with Big Ideas for Small Lots," *The Wall Street Journal*, May 13, 2019.

and moderate-income households—with sufficient government subsidy, mixed-income housing also is viable in low-income neighborhoods.

There Is No One Way to Finance Mixed-income Housing

Nearly all of the city's mixed-income developments have received some form of subsidy from New York City; very few have been underwritten entirely from private sources. Subsidies include property tax exemptions, grants, low- or zero-interest mortgages, federal Low-Income Housing Tax Credits, and project-based Housing Choice Vouchers. One challenge for financing mixed-income housing is the difficulty of providing subsidies for households with incomes that exceed the eligibility limits for the Federal Low-Income Housing Tax Credit (60 percent of AMI) but are too low to afford market-rate rents.

IMPLICATIONS FOR ACTION

Implications for Policy and Planning

- Policy makers and planners need a commitment to long-term planning and urban policy in order to align policy instruments and deliver economically and socially viable developments.

- Mixed-income housing often requires public subsidies in order to make units affordable to very low-income households. When developments target households with very low incomes, when market rate-units account for less than about 80 percent of all units, and developments are located in neighborhoods where market-rate rents are lower than in the most expensive areas of the city, mixed-income housing almost always requires sizable public subsidy. Put differently, there is a trade-off between the depth of subsidy that can be provided and the number of affordable units that can be included in a mixed-income development, especially if the development doesn't also receive public subsidies.

Implications for Development and Investment

- Investors and developers should recognize and promote diversity of mixed-income models in terms of financing, planning, development, management, and potential to provide more inclusive neighborhoods.

- Given the variety of funding sources involved in mixed-income housing developments, planners should expect a collaborative endeavor involving

partnerships between local government and for-profit and nonprofit organizations.
- Mixed-income housing need not be restricted to neighborhoods with particular market conditions.
- Developers should understand and facilitate residents' understanding of and input on mixed-income projects at the neighborhood level. Residents and other community stakeholders may object to the development of mixed-income housing if it entails major increases in density, is seen as a catalyst for gentrification and displacement, charges "affordable" rents that most neighborhood residents still cannot afford, or segregates residents of the "affordable" units from tenants paying market rates. Developers and local governments should:
  - Ensure that at least some units in the development are affordable to low-income neighborhood residents;
  - Protect residents of nearby buildings from landlord harassment and pressure to move;
  - Rezone more affluent, predominantly White neighborhoods at higher density to avoid giving the impression that only low-income, minority neighborhoods are being upzoned.

Implications for Research and Evaluation

- Researchers and evaluators should conduct more studies and ethnographies to improve understanding of the diversity of mixed-income models and help shape strategies to promote inclusive social dynamics. Key topics to study include:
  - Social interactions within mixed-income developments;
  - Resident satisfaction;
  - The financial performance of mixed-income developments, including the degree to which higher-income units can cross-subsidize lower-income units with varying configurations of income groups and housing market conditions;
  - The social and economic benefits of mixed-income housing; and
  - The impact of mixed-income developments on surrounding communities, including the impact of increased densities associated with mandatory inclusionary zoning on neighborhood housing markets.

Implications for Residents and Community Members

- Residents and community members should organize themselves to advocate for full understanding of proposed mixed-income housing in their communities and insist that city planners and developers maximize affordability in the housing, give preference for affordable units to local residents, respect and honor the character of the existing neighborhood, and provide ongoing opportunities for input before and after the housing is complete.

■ ■ ■

ALEX SCHWARTZ is a Professor of Public and Urban Policy at the New School. He is the author of Housing Policy in the United States: 3rd Edition (Routledge, 2014) and co-author of Policy Analysis as Problem Solving: A Flexible and Evidence-Based Framework (Routledge 2019). His research has appeared in such journals as Cityscape, Economic Development Quarterly, Housing Policy Debate, Housing Studies, International Journal of Urban and Regional Research, Journal of the American Planning Association, and Journal of Urban Affairs. In addition, he is the Managing Editor for North America for the international journal Housing Studies.

■ ■ ■

SASHA TSENKOVA holds a Ph.D. in Architecture (Technical University, Prague) and a Ph.D. in Geography (University of Toronto). She specializes in urban planning, housing policy and comparative urban development. Her research and professional activities in these areas for the World Bank, Council of Europe and the United Nations include a range of housing and urban projects in more than 20 countries in Central and Eastern Europe, Latin America and Central Asia. She is the author of 25 books and research monographs and over 50 articles on urban policy, regeneration, urban sustainability and housing policy. Her scholarship is internationally recognized by a number of other prestigious awards for international scholars. www.ucalgary.ca/cities

3
ADVANCING INNOVATIVE APPROACHES

Building Mixed-Income Communities through Community Land Trusts

These two essays expand our understanding of how community land trusts (CLTs) advance inclusion and equity through a commitment to resident power in decision-making processes, robust multi-sector partnerships, and long-term financial sustainability. CLTs are nonprofit corporations that buy and preserve land in perpetuity for the preservation or development of affordable housing. They are run by a board of directors composed of community members and other stakeholders, charged with representing the interests of residents who live within and around the community. Whereas market-rate housing in revitalizing areas may spur gentrification and the displacement of low-income residents, CLTs ensure that people with low incomes continue to have an affordable place to live in the community and that their voices and participation are valued.

In "Community Land Trusts: Combining Scale and Community Control to Advance Mixed-Income Neighborhoods," Emily Thaden and Tony Pickett of the Grounded Solutions Network observe that practitioners and advocates must balance their pursuit of two goals, both of which are necessary to advance racial justice and inclusive community development. They write: "Land is power, and people united is power. Hence, we need to adopt a reconciled approach that advances both control of land at scale *and* democratic community decision-making to achieve gains for residents, neighborhoods, cities, and society. Under a CLT approach that gives equal priority to community control and impact from scale, the systems and structures of land use policy and the housing finance and real estate
industries may be fully utilized, so that communities can gain land in trust and hold CLTs accountable to their mission when scaled."

In "Multi-Sectoral Partnerships for Social and Affordable Housing: The Community Land Trust Portfolio Model," Penny Gurstein from the University of British Columbia describes a CLT in Vancouver, British Columbia that encompasses multiple sites owned by a single, multi-sector development partnership. The approach captured by Gurstein's case study enables more-expensive rental units to subsidize lower-rent units, thereby ensuring both financial stability and a mix of incomes across the portfolio.

These essays document key ingredients of mixed-income CLTs in which residents have meaningful voice, power, and leadership—places where inclusion and equity are more than just words in a vision statement. Those ingredients include strong multi-sector partnerships, active governing boards, collaborations between government officials and non-profit representatives, and investment by social finance institutions. The essays also illustrate the necessity—and the complexity—of achieving a mixture of housing tenures that are sustainable over time and underscore how important it is for practitioners, policymakers, advocates, developers, and funders to support expansion and capacity building within the CLT movement.

COMMUNITY LAND TRUSTS: COMBINING SCALE AND COMMUNITY CONTROL TO ADVANCE MIXED-INCOME NEIGHBORHOODS

Emily Thaden and Tony Pickett
Grounded Solutions Network

Community land trusts (CLTs) continue to gain ground as an innovative model for achieving permanently affordable housing through community control of the land placed in trust. Large-scale implementation of the CLT model can buffer the adverse effects of displacement through gentrification by ensuring that a lasting stock of high-quality, affordable housing remains in place even when new investments create a market-driven increase in real estate values. When CLTs control a sufficient percentage of housing in areas that are high-cost or where housing costs are rising, the neighborhood can achieve mixed-income status. This has potential to enrich residents' lives across all income levels through diverse interconnectedness and opportunities for betterment.[1]

However, research continues to reveal just how challenging it is for mixed-income communities to produce benefits for lower-income people of color. Too often, communities of color that experience new investments accompanied by an influx of more affluent and often predominately White households report that the changes work to the benefit of the higher-income White households and the detriment of lower-income households of color. Residents of color can experience social and cultural alienation and a loss of political influence, which are often expressed in sentiments such as "This is no longer my neighborhood."

---

1 Robert J. Chaskin and Mark L. Joseph, *Integrating the Inner City: The Promise and Perils of Mixed-Income Public Housing Transformation* (Chicago: University of Chicago Press, 2015).

The CLT model attempts to address both the perception and the reality of these shifts in power and culture by placing the residents of homes on the CLT's land in key leadership and decision-making positions and by putting the needs of low-income residents at the center of the CLT's mission.

A major debate among CLT practitioners and advocates involves the tradeoffs and tensions between "going to scale" with the housing portfolio and enacting "community control." People on one side of this debate make the case that increasing the number of homes held in trust is necessary both for CLTs' financial sustainability and for the production and preservation of mixed-income communities. The other side argues that ever-increasing scale may inevitably erode the community's and local residents' control in decision making—a vital part of the CLT governance model.

In this essay, we suggest that pitting the straw men of scale and community control against one another does the field more harm than good. Instead, we support a theory of change that reconciles and balances the two goals in order to create more comprehensive CLT-based approaches that advance racial justice and inclusive community development. But first, we explain the CLT model and its challenges.

AFFORDABLE HOUSING IN MIXED-INCOME COMMUNITIES DONE DIFFERENTLY: THE CLT MODEL

Unfortunately, the majority of new affordable housing developed in urban areas follows an ill-fated pattern:[2] Public funds are invested to improve disinvested communities, address poor housing conditions, and create high-quality affordable housing options. Improvements to the affordable housing stock often spur additional private real estate investments within the same area. The neighborhood is considered to be "revitalizing"—an unmanaged process that may slowly or quickly turn into gentrification. Higher property values drive up rents and property taxes, which attracts higher-income households and more private investment. This begins to push out lower-income households. Additional displacement pressure often occurs as the affordability periods for the affordable housing stock start to expire and properties revert

---

2 There are many "colder" urban neighborhoods where this pattern does not take place and revitalization stalls without attracting private investment.

to market-rate.[3] When that happens, residents of the affordable housing also get displaced.

Within this pattern there is a brief period—somewhere between revitalization and gentrification—when the community is mixed-income and, typically, more racially diverse. However, this period quickly wanes in the absence of stopgaps to prevent the pressure of displacement. Ultimately, the neighborhood may end up more segregated than it was before public investment hit the streets. CLTs provide a solution to this unanticipated consequence of development. Community land trusts are nonprofit corporations that steward community assets and provide permanently affordable housing for families and communities. CLTs acquire and secure land with a renewable ground lease (typically with a 99-year agreement) and ensure that all affordable housing on that land remains affordable in *perpetuity*. If CLTs can create a significant stock of affordable housing in neighborhoods, they act as bulwarks against gentrification and low-income resident displacement.

CLTs and "Community Control."

In his framework of displacement, Dan Immergluck defines *political displacement* as occurring when new residents belonging to racial and economic groups that have traditionally held more power move into a neighborhood and stifle the voice of long-time residents, which perpetuates economic and racial supremacy[4]. CLTs mitigate this type of displacement by placing current and future lower-income residents at the center of "community control" and decision making about neighborhood needs. Unlike most other nonprofits or community development corporations, the traditional CLT governance model operationalizes community control by being structured as a nonprofit, corporate-community membership organization whose members include all residents of CLT homes and other residents in the CLT service area. The members pay nominal annual dues and support the CLT's mission. Members have decision-making authority over major decisions.

One-third of a traditional CLT's board of directors is elected by and composed of residents living on the CLT's land. An equal portion is elected by and

---

3   Federal housing programs require that rehabbed or newly constructed housing must remain affordable for anywhere from 5-30 years, which are insufficient periods to retain the affordable housing stock over the long-term.

4   Dan Immergluck, personal communication, February 28, 2019.

Figure 1. Fast Facts About CLTs

The first CLT, New Communities, Inc., was established in Albany, GA in 1969 by local civil rights leaders, to benefit African-American* farmers who desired to advance their racial justice agenda for economic empowerment by gaining collective control over farmland and housing.

As of the end of 2016, Grounded Solutions Network estimated that there are approximately 225 CLTs in 46 states and the District of Columbia. Of those, about 60 organizations are start-ups or have no housing units. Roughly 165 CLTs have homeownership units, totaling approximately 12,000 homes. Many CLTs also have affordable rental portfolios, estimated to include 25,000 rental units.

composed of members who reside within the CLT's targeted "community" but do not live on the CLT's land. This structure balances the interests of residents of different incomes, races, cultures, and backgrounds to ensure that the uses of CLT-owned land prioritizes the needs of all members.

Through their commitment to community control, CLTs foster engagement and interconnectedness among economically and racially diverse residents to enact the CLT's mission and decide on the prioritized uses of land owned in perpetuity by the CLT. Many CLTs also actively engage the communities where they hold land in trust through community events, educational programming, and opportunities for civic engagement.

CLTs and homeownership

Depending on what the community needs, CLTs can develop rural and urban agriculture projects, commercial spaces to serve local communities, affordable rental and cooperative housing projects, or conserve land or urban green spaces. To date, however, most CLTs have focused mainly on creating homes that remain permanently affordable and thus provide successful homeownership opportunities for generations of lower-income families. The importance of this focus cannot be understated. Redlining, predatory lending, and other barriers have made homeownership through the private housing market incredibly difficult for lower-income families and households of color to attain and sustain. One study found that the probability of sustaining homeownership for longer than five years by first-time homebuyers who were low-income or people of color was equal to a coin toss—and that was *before* the foreclosure crisis.[5]

---

[5] Carolina Katz Reid, "Achieving the American dream? A longitudinal analysis of the homeownership experiences of low-income households," (CSD Working Paper 05-20, Center for Social Development, Washington University, St. Louis, MO, 2005).

By contrast, the approach used by CLTs—shared equity homeownership—invests public resources to reduce the home's initial price and then keeps the price affordable to all future homebuyers through resale restrictions. This gives the CLT a vested interest in the property and in the homeowner's success. Homes are not treated as risky and speculative investments; rather, homes are stabilizing and transformational forces. In return, the homeowners agree to sell their homes at a resale-restricted and affordable price to another lower-income homebuyer in the future. This arrangement enables the resident to own a home and build some wealth and the CLT to preserve the public's investment in making homes permanently affordable for family after family.

EVIDENCE OF CLTs' EFFECTIVENESS

CLTs have demonstrated effectiveness in increasing racial diversity and affordability; stabilizing the average household income in their neighborhoods; and maintaining middle-class ratios, education levels, and owner-occupied housing rates. Researchers have found that:

- Homeowners in CLTs across the country were 10 times less likely to be in foreclosure proceedings and eight times less likely to be seriously delinquent than homeowners across all incomes in the private market at the peak of the foreclosure.[6] Unlike many of their private-market counterparts, these residents were not displaced from their homes or their neighborhoods.

- Across 124 CLT neighborhoods in 15 states, community land trusts moderated the adverse effects of gentrification between 2000 and 2010 by increasing affordability, stabilizing housing prices, and reducing displacement, compared with similar non-CLT neighborhoods.[7] Moreover, even when gentrification is not the threat, CLTs foster a mixed-income community that grants access to opportunity and creates a thriving neighborhood for residents with modest incomes.[8]

---

6 Emily Thaden, "Stable Home Ownership in a Turbulent Economy: Delinquencies and Foreclosures Remain Low in Community Land Trusts," (Working Paper WP412ET1, Lincoln Institute of Land Policy, Cambridge, MA, 2011).

7 Myungshik Choi, Shannon Van Zandt, and David Matarrita-Cascante, "Can community land trusts slow gentrification?" *Journal of Urban Affairs* 40, no. 3 (2018): 394-411.

8 Choi et al., "Can community land trusts slow gentrification?" 394-411.

- In a study of 58 shared equity homeownership programs and 4,108 properties over the past three decades, shared-equity homes are: (1) serving low-income homebuyers and increasingly serving people of color, (2) providing affordable homes and mortgages, (3) ensuring homeownership is sustainable, (4) building wealth for families, (5) remaining permanently affordable to serve households of the same income levels over subsequent sales, and (6) retaining the public investment in affordable housing.[9]

These findings suggest that CLTs' affordable housing can withstand skyrocketing property values, land speculation, and the influx of higher-income households—making CLTs one of the best ways to stabilize neighborhoods, preserve affordability, and build community assets in neighborhoods.

If CLTs are delivering on their promises, then why aren't they proliferating? Lack of available funding is undoubtedly the biggest problem: Affordable housing requires that homes be subsidized to a below-market-rate price, and federal funds for rehabilitation and construction are not growing while costs are. In this article, however, we want to focus on another challenge that is more in our collective control to change: the false dichotomy of community control, as represented by the CLT approach, versus getting to scale.

MEET THE STRAW MEN: "COMMUNITY CONTROL" VERSUS "SCALE"

In the debate over whether CLT practitioners and advocates should focus on community *or* scale, one side says that holding considerable land in trust, containing a large number of affordable homes, is antithetical to community control. The other side insists that the time needed to cultivate real community control is a barrier to achieving scale. Grassroots groups that focus solely on community control tend to minimize efforts to build the resource systems and infrastructure that CLTs need to develop and grow their impact (e.g., enabling public policies, a pipeline of real estate assets, and financing) because these activities are perceived as removed from the communities the groups are trying to serve. Conversely, groups that focus solely on scale tend to minimize community organizing and planning, resident empowerment, community

---

9 Ruoniu Wang, Claire Cahen, Arthur Acolin, Rebecca J. Walter, "Tracking Growth and Evaluating Performance of Shared Equity Homeownership ProgramsdDuring Housing Market Fluctuations," (Working Paper WP19RW1, Lincoln Institute of Land Policy, Cambridge, MA, 2019).

ownership, and authentic place-based leadership of the CLT. The former approach fails to achieve the accumulation and development of enough land to foster mixed-income communities, and the latter approach fails to achieve enough resident empowerment and decision making to ensure that cultural and political displacement are prevented.

Two trends in current CLT development efforts exacerbate the debate. One is that more and more grassroots community groups are interested in bringing community land trusts to their communities. These grassroots efforts often are highly effective at organizing the community and garnering resident-driven plans for the CLT, but they rarely succeed in obtaining land and bringing development to fruition. When they do, it is often as a one-off small development, or the CLT ekes out a couple of homes per year. In these cases, the community organizers often misconstrue the CLT model as "operating outside of the market" or want their CLT to subvert capitalism. They don't accept the fact that developers, government staff, and real estate and housing investors are vital partners for obtaining land, funding, and financing CLT community assets—just as they are for all affordable housing development—or they fear that scaling the CLT will mean sacrificing neighborhood-based decision making. Ironically, this stance can result in community residents losing the ability to control neighborhood land, and the disappointment and distrust that follows may (unjustly) be attached to the CLT concept rather than its implementation.

Another trend is that some CLTs are being successfully established as "programs" operated by nonprofit organizations. Sometimes these programs are adept at obtaining land and producing affordable housing, but they lack meaningful community control and resident authority because they are not governed by a corporate community membership and do not have community residents and leaseholders on their boards. Because the parent nonprofit has other lines of business and existing bylaws that compete for representative governance, community control of the CLT gets scant attention, or superficial community engagement is deemed sufficient. In the worst cases, a nonprofit takes the paternalistic or racist stance that facilitating authentic community control would hinder the pace of developing and scaling up the community land trust.

A RECONCILED APPROACH: SCALING UP COMMUNITY CONTROL

We argue that scale is not the enemy of community control, nor is community and resident leadership the enemy of scaling up the number of permanently affordable homes. Without community buy-in and accountability, the resources and will to scale up will not persist, which in turn means that permanently affordable homes are unlikely to be created and preserved.

Land is power, and people united is power. Hence, we need to adopt a reconciled approach that advances both control of land at scale *and* democratic community decision making to achieve gains for residents, neighborhoods, cities, and society. Under a CLT approach that gives equal priority to community control and impact from scale, the systems and structures of land use policy and the housing finance and real estate industries may be fully utilized, so that communities can gain land in trust and hold CLTs accountable to their mission when scaled.

A reconciled approach holds the most promise for significantly impacting communities by holding racial and economic justice and integration at the heart of the CLT. Fundamentally, grassroots activists are best suited for community organizing and campaigning for political will, resources, and enabling policies that will support consistent and meaningful growth of the CLT's land holdings and affordable housing. Nonprofits that either are CLTs or have CLT programs should be doubling down on community control of land so it can be leveraged into community buy-in and leadership for advocacy, which are vital ingredients for reaching scale. Put differently, if lower-income residents and residents of color are in control of land, then the CLT can support the mobilization and empowerment of those residents and the broader community to demand land and resources from public and private entities and enable development to fulfill the needs of residents. The result can be mixed-income communities that not only survive through market pressures but thrive through diverse interconnectedness.

CLTs REALIZING A RECONCILED APPROACH: THREE EXAMPLES

The three cases that follow profile CLTs developed at different points in time by diverse actors that have, or are working to adopt, approaches that concurrently prioritize community control and scaling up. Dudley Neighbors is the story of a *grassroots organizing effort* that created a CLT subsidiary to pursue land acquisition with community control, recognizing that residents needed to garner power and control over the fate of their neighborhood. City of Lakes Community Land Trust is the story of a *coalition* that formed and decided a city-wide CLT was needed, leading to the mobilization of communities across neighborhoods and, ultimately, formation of a new community around the CLT's mission and governance. In this example, a network of CLTs across the state, along with residents and community stakeholders, effectively foster resources. Houston Community Land Trust is the story of a *local government* that is bringing political will, land, and major financial resources to the table, ushering forward the CLT idea brought forward by community groups as a needed tool. It holds promise to be the fastest-growing CLT that develops community control across neighborhoods.

These cases illustrate how CLTs can use various reconciled approaches to advance both community control and the growth of land in trust. They also support the assertion that balancing these two priorities must be an ongoing, intentional endeavor.

Dudley Neighbors, Inc. and Dudley Street Neighborhood Initiative

Like so many other inner-city neighborhoods across the country, the Dudley and Roxbury neighborhood in the city of Boston experienced extreme disinvestment in the 1970s and early 1980s. What was once an almost entirely White neighborhood in 1950 experienced White flight to such an extreme that only 14 percent of the population remained White by 1990, and the neighborhood lost roughly 40 percent of its total population. The poverty and unemployment rates for residents was almost double that of Boston. Real estate development stopped in the neighborhood, while slumlords and speculative land owners moved in to make money from operating unsafe, substandard housing and holding land. Meanwhile, waste removal companies and private companies illegally used vacant parcels as their dumping grounds.

By the mid-1980s, residents had had enough.[10] In 1984 they formed the Dudley Street Neighborhood Initiative (DSNI), a community-based planning and organizing nonprofit, to reclaim their neighborhood. DSNI's mission is "to empower Dudley residents to organize, plan for, create and control

---

10 Peter Medoff and Holly Sklar, *Streets of Hope: The Rise and Fall of an Urban Neighborhood*. (Cambridge, MA: South End Press, 1994); and *Holding Ground: The Rebirth of Dudley Street*, directed by Leah Mahan and Mark Lipman, (1996; Boston, MA: Holding Ground Productions.)

a vibrant, diverse and high-quality neighborhood in collaboration with community partners."[11] Within the decade, Dudley residents had completed a comprehensive planning process to address the 1,300 parcels of abandoned land in the neighborhood. The City of Boston adopted their comprehensive plan, which included the creation of a community land trust called Dudley Neighbors, Inc. (DNI).

In a historic act of relinquishing control to an organized community, the city granted DNI the power of eminent domain for abandoned properties within the 62 acres of the Dudley Triangle. The community land trust hired staff, including neighborhood residents and people with experience in financing and development, and they began implementing the community's plan. Today, DNI holds more than 30 acres of formerly vacant and abandoned land in trust. This land now includes 227 affordable homes and more than 10 additional homes in the development pipeline—some shared-equity and some rentals—as well as commercial space, a commercial greenhouse, urban farm, gardens, parks, and playgrounds.

Neighborhood residents continue to control development activities in the Dudley neighborhood through the formal review and approval of all new projects and by the neighborhood initiative's governance structure. Thirty-two of the seats on the Dudley Street Neighborhood Initiative's 34-member board are up for election every two years, and neighborhood residents are educated on the elections and candidates before casting their ballots. Sixteen board seats are for representatives of the racial and ethnic groups that reside in Dudley, including Blacks (4), Latinos (4), Cape Verdeans (4), and Caucasians (4), and three board seats for youth representatives. The community land trust's board is composed of nine members, of which two non-voting seats are held by state legislators. In order to prevent election fatigue, six of the nine voting members are appointed by the DSNI board, and four of those board members live or work on the land in trust. The remaining seats are appointments by the Neighborhood Council, city council member, and mayor.

Dudley Neighbors, Inc., was established to "realize a vision of development without displacement."[12] DSNI leaders established the community land trust as

---

11 Dudley Street Neighborhood Initiative, accessed August 26, 2019, https://www.dsni.org/.

12 Dudley Neighbors, Inc., accessed August 26, 2019, https://www.dudleyneighbors.org/.

a separate nonprofit subsidiary because they expected that, as the community organizing entity, DSNI would dissolve after resident leadership was cultivated, community planning was completed, and the land was acquired. They also wanted to ensure that the practical constraints of development being handled by DNI were addressed separately from the broad-based community visioning and planning process organized by DSNI. Ultimately, community members decided to continue with both entities as complementary anchor institutions so that DSNI could foster youth and resident leadership development, raise funds, and facilitate training, organizing, and community-requested programs while DNI continued acquiring land, overseeing development, and stewarding a growing portfolio on behalf of the community.

DSNI/DNI is an example of a community land trust that has kept resident control of land at the forefront without sacrificing scale in its land holdings. In fact, scaling the trust's portfolio to enact residents' vision was a primary driver of community organizing. When the long-standing Boston Mayor Tom Menino left office in 2014, DSNI and DNI advocated to ensure that eminent domain and political will for the community land trust remained intact during changes in city leadership and staff. Impressively, during the start of Mayor Martin J. Walsh's first term, John Barros—a Dudley resident, former youth leader, and current executive director of DSNI— became the city's chief of economic development.

Once deemed "undesirable" and "blighted," the Dudley neighborhood now faces encroaching pressure from private development. Luckily, through the land trust, the community continues to have the right to claim vacant land, and community control continues to grow larger and stronger. Dudley is now a mixed-income, racially diverse community that practices neighborly engagement and collective advocacy to attract resources, influence private real estate developers, maintain political will, and position long-time residents as the leaders and beneficiaries of community change. Because the community land trust ensures that there will always be homes for lower-income households, the neighborhood should remain economically and racially integrated.

City of Lakes Community Land Trust

In many ways, Minneapolis is the quintessential midwestern city. In the 1950s, new highways and inexpensive mortgages lured the mostly White middle class to the suburbs. As that trend continued into the 1980s, the city's population fell. During the same period, the Twin Cities' racial diversity increased, as churches sponsored refugees and immigrants from Cambodia, Laos, and Vietnam in the 1970s; the former Soviet Union in the 1980s; and Somalia, Ethiopia, and Liberia in the 1990s. The people who remained in Minneapolis as the suburbs grew included a larger proportion of people of color, both because of diversification overall and due to redlining in the suburbs. Minneapolis' population began to grow again in the 1990s. The city's population is now double that of 1950 and approximately 60 percent White.[13]

As the Minneapolis housing market began to heat up in 2001, driven by the growth in population and the large proportion of households needing affordable housing, a coalition formed in South Minneapolis. Members included the Powderhorn Residents Group, Seward Redesign, Powderhorn Park Neighborhood Association, and the Lyndale Neighborhood Development Corporation. Through research and community meetings, coalition members realized that the entire city could benefit from a community land trust. They incorporated the City of Lakes Community Land Trust (CLCLT) in fall 2002.[14]

As a city-wide rather than neighborhood-based community land trust, CLCLT took a different approach to engaging residents and fostering community control. CLT staff conducted intensive education and outreach to neighborhood associations and community groups, presenting the land trust as an asset or tool residents could use if they felt pressure from outside development. As Executive Director Jeff Washburne said in a 2007 interview:

> We've gone out and met with all of the Minneapolis neighborhood organizations. We went to their meetings and talked about the land trust, but didn't ask them to provide us with anything. We wanted them to see us as a community asset, but one that doesn't require any neighborhood resources. The only thing we asked of them was to think about the CLT model, particularly if there was potential for a housing development to be built in their neighborhood. Our message was, "If you and your neighbors feel that the development requires affordability—especially long-term affordability—then your

---

13 Greta Kaul, "Minneapolis is growing at its fastest rate since 1950," *MinnPost*, May 23, 2018, https://www.minnpost.com/politics-policy/2018/05/minneapolis-growing-its-fastest-rate-1950/. Minnesota State Demographic Center, "Minnesota Now, Then, When... An Overview of Demographic Change," August 28, 2019, https://mn.gov/admin/assets/2015-04-06-overview-MN-demographic-changes_tcm36-74549.pdf.

14 City of Lakes Community Land Trust, accessed August 28, 2019, http://www.clclt.org/.

neighborhood association should suggest that the developer come and talk to us." In more than one instance, neighborhood groups have told developers to talk to us before the groups would agree to move forward on a project.[15]

City of Lakes CLT has a 15-person board composed of one-third lessees and one-third community members. Approximately 350 community members across Minneapolis, along with the residents living on land in trust, form the corporate community membership.[16] By the end of 2018, the CLCLT had 272 homeownership units and four rental units maintained as permanently affordable in the trust and was on track to have about 40 more homes for sale. The proportion of CLCLT homeowners who are persons of color has reached 53 percent, compared to only 24 percent of all homeowners in Minneapolis.[17] CLCLT leaders hope to acquire more land and create as many permanently affordable homes as possible before Minneapolis becomes a runaway market like some other cities, rendering it prohibitively expensive to create mixed-income communities. They plan to rehabilitate or construct homes in neighborhoods that have not experienced major "warming" yet as well as working in areas that have already gentrified. The latter is more difficult because it costs more, but the CLT is strategically tracking tax foreclosure sales and has a program that allows prospective homeowners to find homes in the market and bring them into the CLT.

As the CLT's portfolio and number of residents increased and their relationships in the broader community has grown, a community of residents, stakeholders, and supporters has formed around the CLT and helps to drive its success. Residents have testified in public, at budget hearings, and to their city council to ensure that resources are maintained for affordable housing and directed to shared equity homeownership. Residents and community members show up when mobilized by the CLT for advocacy, and they open their homes and share their stories with policymakers and prospective funders of the CLT.

---

15 Federal Reserve Bank of Minneapolis, "A conversation with Jeff Washburne -- Director, City of Lakes Community Land Trust," accessed on August 28, 2019. https://www.minneapolisfed.org/publications/community-dividend/a-conversation-with-jeff-washburne-director-city-of-lakes-community-land-trust?sc_device=Default.

16 City of Lakes Community Land Trust, "2018 Annual Report," accessed on August 28, 2019, http://www.clclt.org/wp-content/uploads/2019/01/Final-Annual-Report_10232018.pdf.

17 Federal Reserve Bank of Minneapolis, "A conversation with Jeff Washburne," 2019.

Just as importantly, City of Lakes CLT joins with other CLTs across the state to promote partnerships and resources through their state housing finance agency, Minnesota Housing, which provides subsidies to CLTs through competitive grantmaking and mortgages for CLT homebuyers.

Now community members are calling upon the CLT for two new endeavors. One involves acquiring or creating commercial developments to be held in trust. Pressure is mounting on Minneapolis' light-rail corridors and nodes, so council members and their constituents are asking the CLT to secure land for businesses needed by the community or to help preserve commercial spaces so that small-business owners are not displaced. The hope is that the CLT can stem the tides of both economic and cultural displacement, but it is yet to be seen if the city will come up with needed financial resources for this endeavor. Second, tenant advocacy groups have asked the CLT to explore the creation and preservation of limited equity cooperatives (LECs) on land held in trust. This will not only prevent displacement of existing residents but also ensure that the land is forever dedicated to affordable housing, while the buildings will be directly governed by the LEC residents.

CLT Director Washburne sees the community requests as evidence of success. "When we started this work, racial equity and displacement were not being talked about, so we couldn't really lead with that kind of message," he observes. "Sixteen years later, we lead with the importance of community control of land for racial justice and mixed-income communities. I think we're at a turning point where we have clout with funders and can work the systems for community control. So, we want more grassroots groups telling us where to go and what to do. We want them to drive, and we'll be the horsepower."[18]

City of Houston and the Houston Community Land Trust

As community land trusts have gained attention as a tool to buffer gentrification while providing stable, permanently affordable homeownership and rental opportunities, a growing number of municipalities are taking the lead in launching CLTs. One such place is Houston, Texas. Nonprofit organizations and neighborhood groups, such as Row House Community Development Corporation and Emancipation Economic Development Council, began exploring the CLT concept in 2015 as a way to address

---

18 Federal Reserve Bank of Minneapolis, "A conversation with Jeff Washburne," 2019.

mounting concerns over realized and anticipated increases in housing values and gentrification in predominantly Black neighborhoods. Residents of the Third Ward, for instance, saw housing values climb 176% from 2000 to 2013; more recently, high-end development came with a $34 million redevelopment of Emancipation Park.[19] After listening to residents and community leaders, the city worked with Grounded Solutions Network to begin exploration and planning for a community land trust.[20]

On August 24, 2017, Hurricane Harvey hit, and the city moved into crisis mode. Well over a year later, Houston—along with the other areas affected in Texas—was still waiting to receive $5 billion in Community Development Block Grant-Disaster Recovery (CDBG-DR) funds. As noted in the *New York Times*, communities of color were disproportionally affected and hurting from the storm's impact. As Houston Mayor Sylvester Turner stated, "There are thousands of families who live in low-income communities who already were operating at the margins before Harvey, and the storm pushed them down even further."[21]

Despite the disaster, the city resumed working with Grounded Solutions Network in 2018 to develop a community land trust. The Housing and Community Development Department realized that the CLT might be a critical tool during rebuilding to serve lower-income families and communities of color who were displaced or had their neighborhoods destroyed by the storm and to help bring racial equity and economic integration to rebuild Houston neighborhoods. They worked to align other local resources, policies, and tools with the future CLT. This effort included using the Houston Land Bank to usher properties over to the community land trust and planning to bring multimillion-dollar funding to CLT development through Tax Increment Reinvestment Zones. After working with Grounded Solutions and other consultants to build out the framework and business model, the city then created a new nonprofit organization, the Houston Community Land Trust.

---

19 Leah Binkovitz, "In Houston, A Radical Approach to Affordable Housing," *Urban Edge Blog*, June 6, 2018, https://kinder.rice.edu/2018/06/06/houston-radical-approach-affordable-housing.

20 Grounded Solutions Network, "Community Land Trust Business Plan," accessed on August 28, 2019, https://www.houstontx.gov/council/committees/housing/20170201/community-land-trust.pdf.

21 Manny Fernandez, "A Year after Hurricane Harvey, Houston's Poorest Neighborhoods Are Slowest to Recover," *New York Times*, September 3, 201, https://www.nytimes.com/2018/09/03/us/hurricane-harvey-houston.html.

City leaders realized that the CLT could not be a governmental entity; rather, it had to be an independently governed nonprofit and advocate on behalf of the communities where it works to ensure the CLT is sustainable beyond political changes. In partnership with community stakeholders, city staff held community events to inform and gather input from community members and stakeholders. Over the course of a year, the board of directors was recruited, the first two staff were hired, and the CLT has broken ground on its first three homes. Leaders expect to add over 50 homes by the end of 2019 while staff and board members continue to convene public education events, conduct outreach to resident groups, and build relationships with leaders in the neighborhoods where the CLT will work.

The Houston CLT is positioned to be the fastest-growing CLT in the nation due to the enabling policies, resources, and city support. However, the CLT has the daunting task of building resident leadership and community control as it grows and works in different neighborhoods across Houston. Similar to City of Lakes CLT, the intent is to partner with community organizations and neighborhood groups, offering a tool that communities can deploy to build high-quality, affordable housing that will last in disinvested or disaster-hit areas and in areas facing gentrification and displacement pressures. Over time, the CLT plans to create a corporate community membership and adopt a new board structure (once they have residents), ensuring resident leadership and representation from the various neighborhoods where they hold land in trust. The CLT also plans to organize and mobilize communities to ensure that the resources and political will for community control of land in trust creates a mixed-income, racially integrated Houston that lasts long into the future.

LESSONS LEARNED

Whether they are building homes in recovering, revitalizing, gentrifying, or high-opportunity areas, all of the CLTs profiled here have created or are fostering the creation and preservation of mixed-income communities in which households not only have a *place* but also a *say* over the fate of their neighborhood(s). What can we learn from these examples about using a reconciled approach?

Community Engagement and Control Will Manifest Differently Due to Varying Context

Because of the differences in how each CLT was established, "community" is defined differently and, therefore, "community control" is manifested differently—at least in part—in each example. Part of the difference lies in how residents and other members of the community interact with the community land trust. For the Dudley Neighborhood Initiative, residents of the neighborhood (lessees and non-lessees of the CLT) are literally walking by or on the land held in trust every day. They are organized by the parent nonprofit, DSNI, to direct land disposition strategies, and residents of CLT properties have meaningful board representation. For City of Lakes, residents of CLT properties have formed a new community around the organization, representing the various neighborhoods where they live as part of the CLT's membership, governance, and advocacy. Place-based communities call upon City of Lakes CLT to influence neighborhood development and, if they are members, approve of CLT developments. For Houston, the nonprofit CLT has just been born, so there are no residents on land held in trust yet. But community members are being informed and engaged so the CLT can form a board with resident representation and neighborhood groups can influence the CLT's development. In time, all three CLTs arguably will have meaningful community engagement and accountability to residents on land held in trust and in the broader community.

Regardless of Context, Larger Land holdings Translate to Increased Community Control

Focusing solely on governance and authority misses a critical component of "community control" that comes to light if we ask "How much of the community *geographically* do community members and residents control?" Under the mission and obligations of a CLT, meaningful land holdings allot residents and community members more power. For instance, DSNI and DNI serve a small geography, but they are a force to be reckoned with for private development efforts that attempt to come into their neighborhood. City of Lakes CLT does not have the same levels of local political and financial support. This could be due their larger service area even though they have a slightly larger and faster-growing portfolio than DNI. Meanwhile, if the Houston CLT grows at the clip expected, the CLT's residents and community membership have the potential to organize and influence private development as well as local policy and resources (even if the political will fades in the future). Larger land holdings mean that the community controls more—both in terms of community development and political capital.

Community Organizing Groups and CLTs Should Maximize Their Distinctive Roles

A lesson learned from both DSNI and DNI as separate entities—and City of Lakes CLT now partnering with tenant advocacy groups—is that community organizing and the CLT are effective complements. Remember, CLTs are nonprofits that have made a *permanent* commitment to stewarding land for the community, so they must be perceived as reliable, productive, and effective to policymakers and funders. Grassroots community groups can do more confrontational organizing, running short-term campaigns that use direct tactics to apply political pressure for funding and policies. Consequently, grassroots community organizing groups are more often going to be better off if they remain the steadfast advocates for a CLT rather than trying to become a nonprofit CLT that does development. We believe grassroots groups will get further in their goals if they find a nonprofit partner with the capacity to house the CLT and steward the land under community control.

CLTs and Their Stakeholders Should Adopt "Inside-Outside" Advocacy Strategies for Enabling Policies and Obtaining Revenue

Unfortunately, efforts to build enabling policies and obtain dedicated revenue for CLTs are not happening in many of the localities that would benefit from CLTs. In the absence, scale remains modest (even in the case studies). Using a reconciled approach, CLTs should adopt an "inside-outside" advocacy strategy whereby residents, community members, and advocates organize campaigns for policies and funding from outside of government, while the staff and board of the CLT lead or participate in coalitions to set strategic policy goals, coordinate stakeholders, and partner with policymakers inside government. Organized communities can push policymakers and government leaders to prioritize resources for the CLT (and to require permanent affordability when resources are deployed) and to pass enabling legislation for equitable land use and mixed-income community development. Hence, CLTs should celebrate—even cultivate—the role of residents and community members as mobilizers, organizers, and advocates. Ultimately, CLTs will not proliferate if they are simply competing against other affordable housing nonprofits for scarce existing resources. Instead, they need to mobilize communities to build an infrastructure that reliably produces land in trust and a greater number of permanently affordable homes.

IMPLICATIONS FOR ACTION

Adopting a reconciled approach that values both community control and meaningful land in trust will maximize creating or maintaining mixed-income communities by community land trusts. We call upon the field to never forget that land is power *and* people united is power. Below are recommendations for how to advance both.

Implications for Policy

- As CLTs are developing or pursuing sustainability, dedicated funding sources and enabling policies should be developed in tandem, which requires educating policymakers and elected officials on CLTs. This may include establishing local sources and policies (see below), as well as prioritizing permanent affordability for competitive federal funding programs, such as HOME or the Community Development Block Grant Program.
- CLTs and their stakeholders need to analyze which enabling policies and funding sources are most practical in their local and state political contexts. For instance, in places with local housing trust funds, the CLT and its stakeholders could work to ensure that the fund requires or prioritizes lasting affordability. For places using tax increment financing, CLTs and stakeholders should advocate for ensuring that a portion of homes created with Tax Increment Financing funds are permanently affordable and stewarded by the CLT. Community land trusts and stakeholders also should advocate for new and existing land banks to provide a pipeline of discounted or donated land. Lastly, CLTs and advocates should promote inclusionary housing policies that require affordable homes to be placed in trust.

Implications for Research and Evaluation

- Research on variations in organizational structures, governance structures, community memberships, and resident and community leadership and engagement activities should examine the impact on "community control" and growth.
- Further research on housing in community land trusts should examine whether it buffers the adverse effects of gentrification as well as creates and

maintains mixed-income communities.

- Researchers should assess the economic feasibility of a rent-to-shared equity homeownership fund. The field must pursue innovative financing strategies that minimize the reliance on subsidies to expand the affordable housing produced by CLTs, such as the Vancouver Community Land Trust (see companion essay by Penny Gurstein). Although in its nascent conceptual stage, Grounded Solutions Network hopes to explore the feasibility of a fund that would pursue single-family acquisitions in relatively low-cost markets that are on the cusp of gentrification and facing displacement pressures. The homes would be rehabbed and rented to families with a local CLT as the responsible "landlord." In three to 10 years, when the value of homes in the private market has appreciated, the rented homes would be converted into shared-equity homes held by the CLT. After debt is repaid in the conversion, the appreciation effectively provides the subsidy to cover the difference between the market-rate value of the home and the discounted purchase price that a lower-income family can afford. If a fund like this proves feasible, it could substantially generate homes on land in trust that are community controlled and result in mixed-income neighborhoods.

Implications for Development and Investment

- CLTs need to prioritize community participation and leadership in the disposition strategies for land in trust, and they must partner with grassroots groups to garner the necessary resources for the community's development vision to come to fruition.

- CLTs also need to maintain partnerships and collaboration with government offices, political officials, funders, and financial institutions for their ongoing sustainability.

- The field needs to shift from reliance on public funds to program-related investments and private financing by creating unique funding structures to advance scale, such as (1) acquisition funds and (2) single-family rent-to-shared equity homeownership funds (see above).

Implications for Residents and Community Members

- Residents and community members of the CLT should join the corporate community membership, assume leadership positions, and engage in land disposition decisions whenever possible.

- Residents and community members should advocate for the CLT to build political will, secure financial resources, and pass enabling policies that will increase community-controlled land and developments.

■ ■ ■

EMILY THADEN, Ph.D. is the Director of National Policy & Sector Strategy at Grounded Solutions Network, which is a national nonprofit membership organization consisting of community land trusts, inclusionary housing programs, and nonprofits that create and steward housing with lasting affordability. Her relevant research has been published in Housing Studies, Urban Geography, Journal of Architectural and Planning Research, Social Science Quarterly, Shelterforce, and numerous reports published by the Lincoln Institute of Land Policy. She received her masters and doctorate in applied community research from Vanderbilt University and her bachelors from New York University. She is also currently on the Board of Commissioners for Nashville's housing authority, the Metropolitan Development & Housing Agency.

■ ■ ■

Currently serving as Chief Executive Officer for the Grounded Solutions Network, **TONY PICKETT** has been described by collaborators as innovative; thinking about and achieving equitable outcomes in a comprehensive and cross-disciplinary manner. Under his leadership Grounded Solutions is advancing a new racial equity focused agenda for its policy and capacity building work, to increase the scale and impact of housing programs with lasting affordability. Tony is a graduate of the Cornell University School of Architecture, Art and Planning with a more than 35-year professional career as a successful architect and shared equity affordable housing development practitioner.

MULTI-SECTORAL PARTNERSHIPS FOR SOCIAL AND AFFORDABLE HOUSING: THE COMMUNITY LAND TRUST PORTFOLIO MODEL

Penny Gurstein
University of British Columbia

The crisis that started in the U.S. mortgage markets in 2007-2008 exposed the vulnerabilities of housing markets, especially for low-income households and people marginalized by race and ethnicity. Subsequently, interest has grown[1] for initiatives that encourage cross-sector efforts to create affordable and mixed-income housing that minimizes "poverty traps."[2] Governments have used public-private partnerships (PPPs) to leverage the private sector's financial resources and expertise, and these efforts have succeeded in achieving economies of scale and scope (although there are concerns that PPPs will increasingly lead to the privatization of government responsibilities). Consensus has been growing in North America and elsewhere, however, that a broader multi-sectoral approach is needed—one that includes the for-profit and nonprofit sectors[3] and community involvement. Through jointly determined goals and consensus-based decision making, these partnerships deliver housing, provide governance, and build the relationships needed for sustainability. This essay focuses on portfolio community land trusts (CLTs), in which multiple sites are owned by a single, multi-sectoral development partnership, as a model for achieving both mixed-income and affordable housing options that include a range of housing types and income groups.

---

1 Kathleen Scanlon, Christine Whitehead, and Melissa F. Arrigoitia, eds., *Social Housing in Europe*, (Chichester, UK: Wiley Blackwell, 2014).

2 A poverty trap is a self-reinforcing mechanism that causes poverty to persist.

3 Nonprofit housing is rental housing that is owned and operated by community-based, nonprofit organizations or by governments to serve households with low to moderate incomes. Most nonprofit housing agencies receive some form of financial assistance from government to enable them to offer affordable rents.

WHAT ARE COMMUNITY LAND TRUSTS?

Community land trusts, which began in the state of Georgia in the late 1960s, are locally based nonprofit organizations that acquire and hold land for the benefit of communities. The intention is to provide land that can be perpetually available for affordable housing. By holding the land for community interests, CLTs separate the value of the land (usually the most expensive component) from the buildings developed on the land, effectively removing the land from the real estate market. A typical CLT is registered as a nonprofit organization, formed at the grassroots level, and controlled by its members through a board of directors made up of residents and community representatives. The CLT retains ownership of the land, grants the rights to use that land through long-term leases, and ensures perpetual affordability by setting limits to resale values and/or controlling rents.

Because the land value is not part of the costs of CLTs, secure and affordable housing can be realized for a range of income levels. CLTs' flexibility allows for diverse tenures and mixed incomes in a project that can include home ownership, co-operative housing membership,[4] and rental units for households from low to middle incomes. CLTs can level the playing field for low-income, marginalized individuals to access and sustain affordable housing in the face of market pressure.

CLTs vary widely in their organizational structure and purpose, but they all share these features: nonprofit status, community leadership, multiple ownership partners, and perpetual affordability. CLTs do not focus on a single project located on a single parcel of land; they are committed to actively acquiring and developing land holdings to increase the supply of affordable housing under their stewardship. Because CLTs provide housing for low-income people and often redevelop blighted neighborhoods, in the United States they are eligible to receive a charitable designation from the Internal Revenue Service.

CLTs IN CANADA

While CLTs have a long-standing tradition in Europe,[5] the United States, and

---

4   Co-operative housing offers a mix of market-value units and geared-to-income units in a fixed ratio or funded from a subsidy pool. Subsidies vary annually based on a household's income.

5   Including planned communities on leased land, such as the Garden City movement in the United Kingdom

other places,[6] they are less established in Canada, with only a handful operating across the country. In Canada, there is no federal legal framework for CLTs as in the United States, where the conditions and defining features of CLTs are enshrined in law.[7] Lacking government oversight, the community land trust model evolved into a flexible approach to providing affordable housing using different housing strategies to meet a variety of community needs and goals. This flexibility makes the Canadian context a particularly promising opportunity for innovation around using CLTs to promote more inclusive and equitable mixed-income communities.

Thus far, two CLT models have been advanced in Canada:

- Co-operative CLTs ensure the long-term affordability of co-op housing, a form of housing membership based on a share purchase, which grants members the right to occupy a housing unit within a jointly owned complex.
- Lease-to-own CLTs enable low-income households to become homeowners by counting their rent toward a down payment, while the land is held as a CLT through a long-term leasehold agreement.

After World War II, the Canadian government had a robust housing agenda that included building social[8] and co-operative housing and providing tax incentives for the development of rental housing. After the mid-1990s, federal policies focused on encouraging home ownership. Until recently, however, federal intervention was largely absent from the housing market,[9] and responsibility for addressing the housing needs of low-income households fell to provincial governments and nonprofit housing organizations.

In British Columbia, this situation resulted in the formation of a variety of provincial, municipal, and nonprofit partnerships to deliver housing. In cities such as Vancouver, where the lack of affordable housing is so acute it affects all segments of the population, these partnerships explored solutions to keep the cost of land low and ensure perpetual affordability. One example, described

---

6   Such as "moshav" communities on lands owned by the Jewish National Fund in Israel

7   Section 213 of the Housing and Community Development Act of 1992 governs CLTs.

8   "Social housing" refers to rental housing that may be owned and managed by the state, by nonprofit organizations, or by a combination of the two, with the aim of providing affordable housing for low-income citizens such as seniors, disabled individuals, and single-parent families.

9   The federal ruling party elected in 2015 won on a platform to develop a national housing strategy and to work with the provincial governments to address homelessness and lack of affordable housing.

in the case that follows, was the first co-operative CLT in North America, and its innovations are applicable to many other locales. In particular, the multi-site portfolio approach enables this CLT to be self-sustaining because it allows the development partnership to build market-rate housing that can be used to cross-subsidize the affordable housing.

CASE STUDY OF A PORTFOLIO CLT IN VANCOUVER, BRITISH COLUMBIA[10]

The Starting Point

Planning for the Vancouver Community Land Trust Foundation (Land Trust)[11] project began in 2012. Because city leaders and policymakers viewed the lack of affordable housing as a priority in Vancouver, they convened a task force to develop recommendations; members include policymakers, housing association leaders, private developers, and academic experts. The task force focused on affordability solutions for moderate-income households earning between $21,500 CAD[12] (single) and $86,500 CAD (combined) annually. A key recommendation proposed leveraging the city's considerable land assets by leasing land at a nominal rate to create new social and affordable rental housing. The task force's report also identified community land trusts as a potential vehicle for creating affordable rental and ownership options.

The study and recommendations prompted city government, in August 2012, to issue a call for proposals to create new affordable housing on six city-owned sites. The Land Trust,[13] three nonprofit housing organizations (one subsequently

---

10 The case study research was conducted by Kristin Patten as part of her master's degree coursework at the School of Community and Regional Planning, under the guidance of a Steering Committee composed of Penny Gurstein, School of Community and Regional Planning (supervisor); Thom Armstrong, the Co-operative Federation of B.C.; Jill Atkey, the B.C. Non-profit Housing Association; Mike Lewis, Canadian Centre for Community Renewal; and the B.C.-Alberta Social Economy Research Alliance (BALTA). See: Kristin Patten, *Vancouver Community Land Trust Foundation: Examining a model for long-term housing affordability*, (Vancouver, BC: UBC School of Community and Regional Planning, 2015), http://scarp-hrg.sites.olt.ubc.ca/files/2018/09/Vancouver-Community-Land-Trust-Case-Study-April-2015.pdf.

11 The idea for the Land Trust Foundation was modeled on an Australian co-operative housing initiative, Common Equity Housing Ltd.: https://www.cehl.com.au.

12 Canadian dollars

13 The Land Trust was formed in 1993 by the Co-operative Housing Federation of B.C. The first properties were co-operatives, operating on lands owned by the provincial government that were transferred to the Land Trust.

dropped out), and a co-operative housing society, supported by two social finance institutions,[14] submitted a successful multi-sectoral partnership proposal; B.C. Housing, the provincial housing agency, joined the partnership later to provide direct funding.[15] In June 2019, along with the federal government renewing subsidies for existing nonprofit and co-operative housing in BC, they also committed funds for subsidies for low-income residents of the Land Trust.[16]

Project Design

The Land Trust is a nonprofit organization established by the Co-op Housing Federation of BC (CHF BC). The two nonprofit housing organizations that are involved participate as corporate members of the Land Trust. The Land Trust is the lead decision maker for the consortium of partners that negotiated agreements with the city and is taking the lead in matters of governance.

The partnership's design centers around a multisite portfolio approach that will provide 358 units of subsidized rental townhomes and co-operative apartment units on four sites. All of the sites are on the east side of Vancouver, with three clustered together close to the Fraser River. Nonprofit and co-operative housing organizations will operate the units for a diverse array of tenants, with each site housing different resident populations:

- The first site, managed by a nonprofit housing organization, will provide 48 one-bedroom units with support services for people with mental illness and/or addiction. About half of the units will rent for $571 USD, the provincial shelter rate, and the other half will rent at the low end of market rate, for an average of $740 USD per unit.

---

14 Social finance is an approach that mobilizes private capital to deliver a social dividend and an economic return. See: "Social Finance," Government of Canada, accessed October 19, 2019, https://www.canada.ca/en/employment-social-development/programs/social-finance.html.

15 The Land Trust comprises Fraserview Housing Co-op, for low- to moderate-income families; Sanford Housing Society, providing supportive housing for those with mental health and substance abuse issues; and Tikva Housing Society, primarily for Jewish low- to moderate-income adults and families. VanCity Credit Union, New Market Funds, and B.C. Housing provided funds, and the City of Vancouver provided the land.

16 This now ensures that half of the homes will be affordable to households with incomes of $60,000 CAD or less. Before the subsidies, only a quarter of the units were affordable to these households. See: Frances Bula, "Experts question funding levels, rollout of federal housing announcements," The Globe and Mail, August 13, 2019, https://www.theglobeandmail.com/canada/british-columbia/article-experts-question-rollout-of-federal-housing-funds/.

- The second and third sites will offer two types of housing: 32 two- and three-bedroom townhouses and 188 one- to three-bedroom apartments for low- to moderate-income adults and families, half of which will receive some form of subsidy. Some of these units will be managed by a nonprofit housing organization and others by a cooperative housing organization. Target rents will start at the provincial shelter allowance rate of $426 USD per month for a single-parent family, with an average rent of $941 USD for a three-bedroom unit.

- At the fourth site, 90 one- to three-bedroom units renting at 90 percent of market rate will cross-subsidize the lower-priced units at other sites.

It is anticipated that the population of the project will be racially and ethnically diverse, given the diversity of Vancouver residents, who include recent immigrants from Southeast Asia (e.g., the Philippines) and South Asia (e.g., India, Pakistan and Sri Lanka), and immigrants and refugees from the Middle East and Africa.

Overall, the average cost to renters will be 76 percent of market rate, ranging from 23 percent of market rate for households receiving income assistance to 90 percent of market rate for moderate-income households. Commercial retail units will be sold with pre-paid, 99-year sub-leases, and the income generated will be used to reduce the amount required to finance the whole project. The CLT anticipates operating surpluses that can be used for future affordable housing projects. These surpluses will be split 50-50 between the community land trust and the City of Vancouver.

The design of the project raises questions about the extent to which a multisite portfolio model might be used to promote mixed-income housing. In this case, while the overall portfolio has units geared toward an array of income levels, the sites and buildings are segregated by income. Combining income levels on a single site greatly raises the financial and logistical complexity of any project but possibly increases the social and economic impact on residents and the surrounding neighborhood. This is a tradeoff that deserves more consideration from owners of multisite portfolios. What are the benefits and challenges of income mixing within sites in a portfolio model?

Governance

The Land Trust has the lead in decision making; the nonprofit partners have input into decisions but do not have as much autonomy as they would have if developing their own property. The project centralized control even more by shifting from the initial concept of a master land lease with subleases to nonprofit partners to a single-lease model. The single-lease model is advantageous to nonprofit housing organizations, because the Land Trust primarily holds the project's risks. However, the nonprofit housing organizations lose some degree of control over their units.

To accommodate this situation, the Land Trust and the nonprofit housing organizations created a Portfolio Administration Agreement that outlines how decisions will be made, specifies roles and responsibilities, and distinguishes between portfolio-level and partner-level responsibilities. The operating partners are responsible for managing and operating their own housing, including repair, maintenance, capital replacement funds, utilities, insurance, etc. Tenants are selected by each nonprofit housing organization according to criteria outlined in the Agreement (for example, Vancouver residents have priority).

Partnership

The fact that the Land Trust could pull stakeholders together across sectors to create this project was due to a history of partnership-building efforts involving the Vancouver-area nonprofit housing sector and municipal and provincial governments spanning two decades, following the federal government's drastic reduction in support for nonprofit housing. Stakeholders in the nonprofit housing sector realized they had to find new ways to deliver affordable housing, which led to social-public partnerships, collaborations between municipalities and social actors, and social-public-private partnerships as well as strong partnerships within the nonprofit community.[17] By the time the Vancouver Land Trust project came about, the partners were all committed to collaborative endeavors and had sufficient capacity and mission to move the project forward.

---

17 For example, the B.C. Non-profit Housing Association, the provincial umbrella organization for the non-profit housing sector composed of over 600 member societies, and the Co-operative Housing Federation of B.C., made up of 260 housing co-ops and associated organizations across British Columbia, have partnered in forming Housing Central to coordinate their efforts. This has made it easier for nonprofit and co-operative housing societies to work together.

Nonetheless, the complex nature of this project created delays in negotiations with city representatives who were concerned about the risks involved in partnering with such a venture. Numerous city departments—including planning, housing, legal, and real estate—were part of the negotiations, and when new representatives from these departments became involved they had to be brought up to speed on CLTs and the project.

Financing

Placing multiple sites under the umbrella of one CLT creates efficiencies in developing and operating the project and enables the higher-rent units to subsidize units on the lower end of market rents, thereby ensuring a mix of incomes among the tenants. The CLT gains further affordability through a discount arrangement with the City of Vancouver, which leases the land to the Land Trust for 99 years at a nominal rate.

The strong involvement of social finance institutions was critical to the Land Trust's affordability. VanCity Credit Union,[18] the largest member-owned credit union in Canada, provided the impetus for the project to evolve from concept to feasibility. The community investment department of VanCity provided construction financing[19] for the design and permitting phases. VanCity also brought New Market Funds[20] into the project, providing access to private capital from investors looking for competitive financial returns and community benefit. The continuum of social financing involved in this endeavor includes grants from venture philanthropy partners that are tied to specific outcomes; "impact first" investments (e.g., partner equity, co-investor equity) that prioritize community impacts; blended investments in which financial returns and community benefits share equal status; and mortgage financing from government or a social finance institution.

While this CLT has many features shared by other CLTs, there are some distinct differences. Instead of the land being owned by a community organization, the City of Vancouver retains ownership of the land over the long term. The city also is ensuring perpetual affordability within the lease agreement between the

---

18 VanCity Credit Union has a social-purpose real estate fund that aims to build the capacity of organizations to undertake social purpose real estate projects. Social-purpose real estate encompasses property and facilities owned and operated by mission-based organizations and investors for the purpose of community benefit.

19 Estimated at $57.34 million CAD

20 New Market Funds's mission is to deliver investment opportunities with lasting community benefit.

city and the Land Trust, something that CLTs usually ensure on their own.

Impact on Residents

The Land Trust project is scheduled for completion in 2019, and as of mid-2019 residents had not yet moved in. Thus, it is too early to determine how this type of mixed-income development will affect social relations across populations of residents. The co-operative and nonprofit organizations each have their own way of managing their existing projects. Nevertheless, each housing organization is developing plans to create social events and activities and is working with the other organizations to encourage mixing of residents. Except for the townhouses, all of the other buildings have common indoor and outdoor spaces where such activities can occur.

Next Steps. The project is already being lauded as an innovative approach in Canada to delivering affordable housing through the CLT model because it ensures that land in cities such as Vancouver, where rising costs are making housing unaffordable, will remain at a fixed price and serve the common good. The Vancouver Affordable Housing Agency (VAHA),[21] a city agency, has announced that the Land Trust will develop seven more pieces of city-owned land, resulting in approximately 1,000 more affordable rental units by 2021. Continuing the mixed-income focus of the target population for the overall project, the new homes will be targeted to individuals and families earning between $30,000 and $80,000 CAD annually.

The need to consider new partnership models for housing delivery has been increasingly evident in the nonprofit and co-op housing sectors. Although nonprofits and co-ops have expressed concern about their ability to retain autonomy and obtain value for equity that they bring into the partnerships, the Vancouver Land Trust model is appealing because it provides clarity around roles and responsibilities. Replication of the model will require commitment from government and social finance institutions in collaboration with nonprofit and co-operative housing organizations.

---

21 "VAHA and City announce Community Land Trust will build 1,000 units of affordable rental housing on City land," City of Vancouver, accessed October 19, 2019, https://wayback.archive-it.org/8849/20190105073730/https://vancouver.ca/news-calendar/vaha-and-city-announce-community-land-trust-will-build-1000-units-of-affordable-rental-housing-on-city-land.aspx.

LESSONS FROM THE VANCOUVER CASE STUDY

The Vancouver CLT model has many benefits. The portfolio approach enables economies of scale and cross-subsidization of units, which allows for a mix of incomes in the housing and ensures that low-income residents have affordable units. The long-term lease provided by the city ensures affordability into perpetuity. The financing model allows the nonprofits involved to significantly leverage their equity through a variety of non-governmental financing products and sources. The relationships within the nonprofit sector, the public sector, and the social finance institutions that were built up over decades allowed for the confidence and trust needed to collaborate on this project and achieve its goals. Because the Land Trust will assume long-term stewardship of the project, the partners have confidence that the perpetuity of housing affordability will be ensured. These factors have resulted in a model that does not require ongoing operating subsidies from government except for the very-low-income residents. In fact, the Land Trust anticipates having surpluses, half of which will be reinvested in developing more projects while the remainder goes to the City of Vancouver. The city also sees the ability to leverage their land asset as an opportunity to create new affordable units within the initial project and over time through reinvestment of the operating surplus.

There are significant challenges in implementing such a project, too. Decision making in complex relationships can be difficult. Because the Co-operative Housing Federation of B.C. is the lead partner, the other nonprofits do not have the autonomy they would have in developing their own property. In addition, managing a mixed-income development requires ongoing monitoring by the housing organization to track fluctuating incomes. Because of the considerable challenges and risks in managing a CLT housing development, the organizations that govern the development require ongoing capacity building and resources for management and community development.

Another challenge lies in achieving housing affordability for very-low-income renters without relying on government funding as the primary source of capital. Moreover, current CLTs can do little to benefit the most impoverished segment of the Vancouver population, Indigenous people.[22], [23] Due to the effects of

---

22 In Canada, the Indigenous populations are called First Nations or Aboriginal. In the United States, they are called Native Americans.

23 In 2018, Indigenous people constituted 2.2 percent of the Vancouver population but 40 percent of its

colonization, members of this population often have multiple mental and physical barriers and substance abuse issues that prevent them from accessing market housing, and they would benefit greatly from affordable, supportive housing. However, the federal government's funding of support for Indigenous communities is exclusively targeted to Indigenous reservations, and the CLTs are located outside the reservations. A better solution would also require significant investment by both the federal and provincial governments in access to housing both on and off reservations.[24]

The city's decision to take a portion of the operating surplus to use for new affordable rental housing also poses a challenge to the Vancouver Land Trust development because it decreases the CLT's ability to increase affordability of existing units. There has been a change in political and administrative decision making within the city since the terms of the Land Trust were set, however, which is making it easier to negotiate more favorable terms for future CLT projects.

CONCLUSION AND IMPLICATIONS FOR ACTION

Community land trusts as outlined in this case study can be adapted to diverse contexts. The approach allows for affordable mixed-income housing into perpetuity, not just affordable housing for the first residents to benefit. If scaled up, it can offer whole neighborhoods where stable housing prices will be ensured, allowing for thriving mixed-income communities. However, CLTs challenge the basic premises of the private real estate market, and without a supportive government regulatory framework and a collaborative working relationship between all levels of government and the housing providers, CLTs could become sidelined and underutilized. Full support for the implementation and durability of the CLT model will require a cultural change in citizens' attitudes towards housing, from housing as a commodity to housing as a social good that promotes local and national stability and prosperity. The implications that follow outline some actions that can help ensure CLTs' ability to produce affordable housing in perpetuity.

---

homeless population. See: Travis Lupick, "Vancouver's Indigenous people are again heavily overrepresented among the city's homeless, count finds," *Georgia Straight*, May 1, 2018, https://www.straight.com/news/1068636/vancouvers-indigenous-people-are-again-heavily-overrepresented-among-citys-homeless.

24 Since 2017, the provincial government has invested heavily in supportive modular housing for homeless people, providing 2,000 units across B.C. including 600 in Vancouver.

Implications for Policy

- Build more specificity in CLT governance and operational agreements about the roles that all partners—government, the nonprofit sector, and financial institutions—have in decision making and implementation.
- Expand the amount and variety of subsidies available to help expand the ability of community land trusts to generate housing for the most low-income and marginalized populations.
- Develop policy that encourages or requires incorporation of Indigenous groups as a target population for mixed-income CLT developments.

Implications for Research and Evaluation

- There is a need to greatly expand research and evaluation on CLTs in Canada, including conducting pre- and post-development studies, post-occupancy evaluations, and ongoing documentation to learn about the portfolio CLT model's strengths and weaknesses and any emerging opportunities or threats to the model's viability.
- Conduct more comparative research on various models of CLTs, including evaluations of how well they meet the housing needs of the most low-income and marginalized populations. It is especially important to learn which elements of CLTs enable projects to successfully house the lowest-income populations. Include attention to levels and implications of racial and ethnic diversity as well.

Implications for Development and Investment

- Involve innovative financial institutions in directing their financial resources toward the acquisition or construction of land and buildings for mixed-income housing to be developed and managed by nonprofit housing associations, thus building the nonprofit sector's capacity to advance a social mission through housing development.
- In negotiations with governments and other landholders, specify that the land used for CLTs must be used for affordable housing in perpetuity.
- Develop knowledge and capacities, such as organizational and financial management, within nonprofit organizations and co-ops so they can work effectively within CLT partnerships.
- Establish clear governance and management structures to facilitate

partnership among a mixture of housing organizations, each of which serves different populations.

Implications for Residents and Community Members

- Where a CLT exists, make sure that residents and community members across income, tenure, race, and ethnicity and other demographic lines have formal roles in making decisions, monitoring implementation, and holding the CLT accountable.

- In communities where there is no CLT and community members are concerned about increasing development, rising rents, and the possibility of displacement, engage in collective action to approach local institutions and government representatives for support in establishing a local CLT.

■ ■ ■

PENNY GURSTEIN, Ph.D. *is Professor and immediate past Director at the School of Community and Regional Planning and the Centre for Human Settlements at the University of British Columbia. She is founding Director of the Housing Research Collaborative a community of housing researchers, providers and policy makers focused on understanding systemic impediments in the housing system and the development of models to address housing unaffordability. She is co-chair of the Pacific Housing Research Network and a registered member of the Canadian Institute of Planners. Dr. Gurstein has been appointed to the Board of Commissioners of BC Housing Management Commission from 2018 to 2021.*

Inclusion and Equity through Inclusionary Housing

These three essays explore housing acquisition models that promote affordability, equity, and inclusion for low-income families in "opportunity neighborhoods"—places with strong resources, especially high-performing schools. The approaches described here largely circumvent opposition to locating affordable housing in affluent, predominantly white communities by purchasing existing housing rather than constructing new units. And, motivated by recent research on how housing mobility affects young children, the models also focus on boosting educational outcomes for children in low-income families.

In "Beyond Counting Units: Maximizing the Social Outcomes of Inclusionary Housing," Amy Khare, Emily Miller, Mark Joseph, and Shomon Shamsuddin seek to expand our aspirations for the potential social impact of inclusionary housing programs. The essay provides an overview of inclusionary housing policy implementation nationally, delving into stated policy aims and the ways in which implementation actually occurs, as well as detailing local and state jurisdiction adaptations. The authors then make the case for activating the full potential of inclusionary housing to build social capital and expand economic opportunity. Providing a proposed framework for how social outcomes might be achieved as well as specific recommended strategies, the authors construct a vision for how stakeholders can build on the platform of inclusionary housing to leverage greater impact.

In "High-Opportunity Partner Engagement: Creating Low-Income Housing Options Near Good Schools," Peter Kye and Megan Haberle of Poverty & Race Research Action Council and Laura Abernathy and Scott Kline of the National Housing Trust (NHT) provide an overview of the acquisition mode. The authors highlight four such efforts around the United States before looking more deeply at NHT's HOPE model, featuring preliminary lessons from its first pilot acquisition project in Coon Rapids, MN.

In "The MTO Fund: Harnessing the Market to Promote Opportunity and Inclusion," Hans Buder, the Founder of The MTO Fund, presents the case for an innovative approach to designing and financing a housing acquisition model. He and his partners have carefully crafted a comprehensive approach with high-touch mobility counseling, social services, community building, and crisis intervention while promising a market-rate return to investors. This model offers the possibility of groundbreaking scalability in the inclusionary housing arena.

BEYOND COUNTING UNITS: MAXIMIZING THE SOCIAL OUTCOMES OF INCLUSIONARY HOUSING

Amy T. Khare, Emily K. Miller, and Mark L. Joseph
National Initiative on Mixed-Income Communities, Case Western Reserve University

Shomon Shamsuddin
Tufts University

The mixed-income development strategy attempts to address concentrated urban poverty and racial segregation by building housing and other amenities, such as parks, schools, and community centers, in ways that intentionally integrate households of different income groups as part of the financial, physical, and operational plan. Place-based neighborhood revitalization initiatives and residential mobility programs are two of the most common housing strategies for income mixing. Since the 1970s, a third approach—inclusionary housing, or inclusionary zoning—has also become a mainstream policy strategy in the United States. Inclusionary housing aims to produce affordable housing and facilitate residential integration of households representing a variety of incomes and housing tenures within developments and neighborhoods.

Inclusionary housing policies tie the creation of affordable homes for low- and moderate-income households to the construction of market-rate housing or commercial development.[1] As a simple example, an inclusionary housing program might require developers of a new residential project to sell or rent 10 to 20 percent of the new units to low-income residents at an affordable rate.

---

[1] Kriti Ramakrishnan, Mark Treskon, Solomon Green, *Inclusionary Zoning: What Does the Research Tell Us about the Effectiveness of Local Action*, (Washington, D.C: Urban Institute, 2019); Lisa Sturtevant, *Separating Fact from Fiction to Design Effective Inclusionary Housing Programs*, (Washington, D.C:

Inclusionary housing policies are largely under the jurisdiction of state and local governments. Development firms seek to build new market-rate housing, and in exchange state and local jurisdictions compel firms to offer affordable housing as part of the zoning and housing approval process. Those affordable units are typically included in the same building, block, or neighborhood as a new market-rate housing project. Inclusionary housing policies also may generate revenue for local governments to directly produce or operate affordable housing outside of new market-rate developments.

Inclusionary housing is most useful in areas where the real estate market does not naturally provide housing affordable to low- and moderate-income households, such as in majority-White areas of concentrated wealth. Inclusionary housing also helps to address gentrification in areas where the market is attracting higher-income newcomers in ways that are displacing existing households, such as in communities of color that are becoming more attractive to White households.

To date, inclusionary housing policies have aimed to achieve two primary goals. First, inclusionary housing can contribute significantly to the supply of affordable housing. During an era in which federal funding for public and assisted housing is being cut, inclusionary housing programs are on the rise. Second, inclusionary housing can address residential racial and economic segregation. Inclusionary housing policies weave the creation of affordable housing into the development of housing for the private market. If new housing development occurs in areas that will attract market-rate buyers and renters, then the creation of affordable options in those same markets could benefit households that would not otherwise be able to live there.

In reality, however, the primary beneficiaries of inclusionary housing units have not been households of low or extremely low income and/or people of color, which are most often the populations with fewer housing options.[2] This is because most inclusionary housing programs tend to serve households earning between 60 percent and 120 percent of Area Median Income (AMI)—and, in many communities, renter households of color are disproportionately represented in income groups that fall below 60 percent of AMI.

Center for Housing Policy, 2016); Emily Thaden and Ruoniu Wang, *Inclusionary Housing in the United States: Prevalence, Impact, and Practices*, (Cambridge, MA: Lincoln Institute of Land Policy, 2017).

2   "Inclusionary Housing," Grounded Solutions, accessed October 7, 2020, https://inclusionaryhousing.org/.

We believe inclusionary housing programs should elevate a third goal of promoting social outcomes alongside affordable housing creation and desegregation. By social outcomes, we specifically mean greater social inclusion and economic advancement for low- and moderate-income residents. With greater attention to social outcomes, inclusionary housing may also be a more effective pathway for localities to advance racial equity so that housing opportunities for people of color can be created and sustained in neighborhoods where they have been denied access due to racist government policies and racial discriminatory practices.[3]

In this essay, we propose a framework to guide the development and operations of inclusionary housing policies in order to promote social inclusion and economic advancement. We believe that working toward these social outcomes will achieve positive impacts across entire metropolitan areas—not only among low- and moderate-income individuals and families who live in affordable housing units but also within the general public, which benefits from living in more inclusive, equitable communities. To make our case, we briefly review the history of inclusionary housing, introduce a social outcomes conceptual framework, consider ways to operationalize that framework, and present implications for policy and practice.

THE POLICY CONTEXT FOR INCLUSIONARY HOUSING

Inclusionary housing policies were first initiated in the 1970s as a movement by local governments responding to decreased federal resources for affordable housing development.[4] Inclusionary housing programs also developed to counteract zoning policies that excluded affordable housing—for example, by requiring low-density development, outlawing multi-family units, and enacting minimum lot size requirements.

Inclusionary housing policies exist as part of a complex system of state and local land use, zoning, and planning. Legal authority to regulate land use exists within state governments, counties, and municipalities. Large variations

---

[3] Richard Rothstein, *The Color of Law: A Forgotten History of How Our Government Segregated America*, (New York: Liveright Publishing, 2017).

[4] Nico Calavita and Alan Mallach, eds., *Inclusionary Housing in International Perspective: Affordable Housing, Social Inclusion, and Land Value Recapture*, (Cambridge: Lincoln Institute of Land Policy, 2010).

in state land use policy means that some states have broad power over local jurisdictions, whereas other states delegate significant power to municipal governments to determine the permitted use of land in what is considered "home rule."[5] The variation makes inclusionary housing a particularly "local" mixed-income policy strategy, since there is no federal policy framework. This factor becomes important as the housing and community development field clarifies and advances in its capacity to effectively advance mixed-income innovations that promote equity and inclusion.

Inclusionary housing started in localities, such as Montgomery County, Maryland and Palo Alto, California, where regional growth pressures created a focus on both economic integration and sustainable environmental land practices.[6] Its popularity spread, especially in areas with extensive real estate development, escalating housing costs, and innovative municipal governments that seek to ensure housing and economic opportunities for existing, low-income residents. By the mid-1990s, inclusionary housing policies had been enacted in a small number of affluent and progressive jurisdictions, the majority of which are in California, Massachusetts, and New Jersey.[7]

Along with other supply-side housing programs, inclusionary housing became especially important in the 2000s once the federal government decreased funding for any new public and assisted housing production. With increased progress on urban revitalization and a growing market demand in the downtown neighborhoods, inclusionary housing policies were enacted in order to use market-driven development to address the challenges of gentrification and rising unaffordability.[8]

The motivations and constraints of inclusionary housing are best understood by seeing it as part of a broader movement of neoliberalization that shifts the responsibility for providing affordable housing from the public to the private domain.[9] While local and state governments struggle to address affordable

---

5 Calavita and Mallach, *Inclusionary Housing*

6 Calavita and Mallach, *Inclusionary Housing*

7 "Where Does Inclusionary Housing Work?," Grounded Solutions, accessed September 29, 2020, https://inclusionaryhousing.org/inclusionary-housing-explained/what-is-inclusionary-housing/where-does-it-work-3/.

8 Calavita and Mallach, *Inclusionary Housing*

9 Samuel Stein, "Progress for Whom, Toward What? Progressive Politics and New York City's Mandatory

housing shortages and meet the needs of local residents, private development firms are increasingly expected to carry out roles traditionally held by the public sector. Neoliberal policy frameworks typically involve the roll-back of federal funding for needed goods and services, such as affordable housing, along with the roll-out of local and state policies that require or encourage roles for the private sector. As a neoliberal mixed-income housing policy, inclusionary housing is closely tied to the broader economic and political context, which generates particular policy parameters and constraints. The boom and bust cycles of the real estate market make inclusionary housing units more economically feasible during times of market expansion.

KEY COMPONENTS OF INCLUSIONARY HOUSING PROGRAMS

Inclusionary housing policies are implemented in many different ways, depending on local housing priorities and contexts.[10] Central features of an inclusionary housing program include: set-aside percentages, income targeting, in-lieu fees, length of affordability and monitoring, and housing incentives.

Set-Aside Percentage

Set-aside percentage refers to the percentage of affordable housing units required by law to be allocated to low- or moderate-income households. Typically, most of the new affordable housing units that are built through inclusionary housing are sited within a development that has a majority of market-rate units. For example, a building may be 80 percent market-rate units and 20 percent affordable housing units. A commonly used set-aside is 10 percent, but statutes have used percentages anywhere from 5 percent to 35 percent.

In many cases, the set-aside percentage is universally applied across the entire geography of the municipality or state. However, some local ordinances have different set-aside percentages for specific zoned areas in order to address historical exclusion, disinvestment, gentrification, and displacement. Some local ordinances, such as that of the City of Baltimore, also increase set-aside percentages for development projects that receive significant public subsidies.

Inclusionary Housing." *Journal of Urban Affairs* 40, no. 6 (2018): 770-781.

10 Mukhija et al., "The Tradeoffs of Inclusionary Zoning: What Do We Know and What Do We Need to Know?" *Planning Practice and Research* 30, no. 2 (2015): 222-235.

Income Targeting

Income targeting refers to the population of households that are targeted as the beneficiaries of the affordable housing. The range can include very-low-income households, defined as households with incomes less than 50 percent of AMI; low-income households, defined as households with incomes less than 80 percent of AMI; or moderate-income households, which can include households with incomes from 80 percent to 120 percent of AMI.

Some ordinances describe affordability levels in flexible terms, giving developers discretion about whom to serve. Given the option, developers often choose to price the units toward more moderate-income households with the aim of making the project more financially viable. Some municipalities require developers to divide the affordable units equally among households across a range of different incomes. For example, the local ordinance in Irvine, California requires that developers equally divide the set-aside units among households with incomes below 50 percent, those between 51 and 80 percent, and those between 81 and 120 percent.

Alternatively, programs may attempt to reach the most economically vulnerable populations by targeting households under 60 percent of area median income. For example, Los Angeles created a voluntary inclusionary housing program called the Transit-Oriented Communities Incentive Program in which developers can choose from three options: make a relatively large percentage of units affordable at 80 percent of AMI, a modest percentage of units affordable at 60 percent of AMI, or a smaller percentage of units affordable at 30 percent of AMI. As of February 2020, half of the affordable units planned through the program are affordable at 30 percent of AMI.

In-Lieu Fees

Local governments often give developers of new projects a choice between building affordable units or paying an in-lieu fee to opt out of providing them. Developers often chose to pay the fees so they can avoid the higher costs and complexity of incorporating affordable units or to avoid the challenges of integrating low, moderate, and higher-income households in the same housing community. Some affordable housing advocates criticize these fees as a loophole that allows developers to side-step requirements that would otherwise directly produce affordable units.[11]

Local municipalities use the revenue generated through in-lieu fees in various ways: to create and operate affordable housing in other buildings or neighborhoods, sometimes in areas that remain racially segregated and economically disinvested;[12] to build affordable units for people with special needs; or provide deeper rent subsidies for the lowest-income households.

Length of Affordability and Monitoring

Inclusionary housing programs are considered a sustainable approach to creating affordable housing because they can ensure the units' long-term affordability (e.g., at least 30 and up to 99 years) or even perpetual affordability.[13] Local governments have the ability to tailor the length of the affordability period to their needs, priorities, and housing market demands.

Housing Incentives

Most state and municipal statutes include offsets or incentives that compensate developers for the costs associated with meeting inclusionary requirements, either by reducing the cost or increasing the return to the developer. The goal is to mitigate the negative financial effect of the inclusionary housing program. Offsets and incentives come in different forms, such as density bonuses, fee waivers or exemptions, height bonuses, parking reductions, and expedited permitting. These cost offsets are politically and economically important because they acknowledge the negative financial burden on developers for compliance with inclusionary requirements.

Local municipalities may determine it is necessary to contribute additional public subsidies in order to make inclusionary housing development more attractive and feasible. These public resources may be indirect in the form of

---

11 Benjamin Schneider, "CityLab University: Inclusionary Zoning," CityLab, July, 17, 2018.; "Where Does Inclusionary Housing Work?," Grounded Solutions, accessed September 29, 2020, 2019, https://inclusionaryhousing.org/inclusionary-housing-explained/what-is-inclusionary-housing/where-does-it-work-3/; Rolf Pendall, Robert Puentes, Jonathan Martin, *From Traditional to Reformed: A Review of the Land Use Regulations in the Nation's 50 largest Metropolitan Areas*, (Washington, D.C: Brookings Instition, 2006).

12 Calavita and Mallach, *Inclusionary Housing*; Thaden and Wang, *Inclusionary Housing*

13 Schwartz et al., *Is Inclusionary Zoning Inclusionary? A Guide for Practitioners*, (Santa Monica: RAND Corporation, 2012).

tax abatements on the affordable units, below-market-rate construction loans, tax-exempt mortgage financing, discounted or no-cost land, and tax increment financing to generate additional for targeted local investment. Governments may also offer direct subsidy, such as through city funds from Community Development Block Grants and state housing bonds financing.

OUTCOMES FROM INCLUSIONARY HOUSING PROGRAMS

It is difficult to evaluate inclusionary housing programs' success in producing more affordable housing and residential integration, because of the relative lack of research and evaluation in this policy arena and because local approaches are so varied and therefore not comparable. Here's what we do know about progress in achieving the two primary goals of inclusionary housing.

Affordable Housing Production

Inclusionary housing is becoming more prevalent: Today, 886 jurisdictions in 25 states have enacted an inclusionary housing program or policy, compared with just 487 jurisdictions in 2014.[14] Despite nationwide increases in recent years, however, the majority of inclusionary housing programs are concentrated in just three states: California (17 percent of the national total), Massachusetts (27 percent), and New Jersey (45 percent).[15] Limited information exists about the national production of affordable housing units using inclusionary housing approaches, and there is no system for tracking the total number of affordable housing units produced or the total revenue generated through in-lieu and impact fees across jurisdictions. Thaden and Wang, who conducted the most notable recent study about the production outcomes of inclusionary housing on a national scale in 2017, documented a total of 172,707 units of affordable housing created through inclusionary housing policies since the earliest programs were enacted in the mid-1970s.[16]

Research on state and local jurisdictions shows that inclusionary housing policies will deliver more units in strong markets when the creation of units

---

14 Thaden and Wang, *Inclusionary Housing*.

15 "Where Does Inclusionary Housing Work?," Grounded Solutions, accessed September 29, 2020, https://inclusionaryhousing.org/inclusionary-housing-explained/what-is-inclusionary-housing/where-does-it-work-3/

16 Thaden and Wang, *Inclusionary Housing*.

is mandated and when active political support exists to enforce policies.[17] However, variation in unit production also is greatly influenced by whether jurisdictions provide the option of in-lieu fees. Affordable housing is mostly provided to households that earn 60 to 120 percent of the area median income, ultimately excluding extremely low-income families.[18] Many of the affordable units produced nationwide are affordable homeownership units, rather than rental units.[19]

Residential Integration

The field lacks information about the extent to which inclusionary housing approaches have reduced residential segregation and promoted residential integration. No dataset provides clear evidence about the extent to which affordable and marketrate units are integrated either within newly constructed housing projects or within neighborhoods ripe for market-rate development. The question of the effectiveness of inclusionary housing policy to generate residential integration is largely based on specific state and local policy parameters, such as whether units were required to be distributed within buildings, proximate blocks, and surrounding neighborhoods.[20] In smaller-scale studies of local programs, research has found that participants living in units created by inclusionary housing policies tended to be located in low-poverty neighborhoods that had higher-performing schools.[21] Schwartz et al.[22] found through a case study of 10 inclusionary housing programs that affordable units

---

17 Diane K. Levy, Zach McDade, and Kassie Dumlao, *Effects from Living in Mixed-Income Communities for Low-Income Families: A Review of the Literature*, (Washington, D.C: Urban Institute, 2011).; Jesse Mintz-Roth, *Long-Term Affordable Housing Strategies in Hot Housing Markets*, (Cambridge: Joint Center for Housing Studies at Harvard University, 2008); Mukhija et al., "The Tradeoffs of Inclusionary Zoning"; Sturtevant, *Separating Fact from Fiction*; Thaden and Wang, *Inclusionary Housing*

18 Stockton et al., *The Economics of Inclusionary Development*, (Washington, DC: Urban Land Institute, 2016); Schwartz et al., *Is Inclusionary Zoning Inclusionary?*

19 Thaden and Wang, *Inclusionary Housing*.

20 Levy, McDade, and Dumlao, *Effects from Living*; Mintz-Roth, *Long-Term Affordable Housing*; Mukhija et al., "The Tradeoffs of Inclusionary Zoning";Sturtevant, *Separating Fact from Fiction*; Thaden and Wang, *Inclusionary Housing*.

21 Ingrid Gould Ellen and Keren Mertens Horn, Do Federally Assisted Households Have Access to High Performing Public Schools? Civil Rights Research (Washington, D.C: Poverty & Race Research Action Council, 2012); Alexandra Holmqvist, "The Effect of Inclusionary Zoning on Racial Integration, Economic Integration, and Access to Social Services: A Davis Case Study," MS diss., (University of California, Davis, 2009).

22 Schwartz et al., *Is Inclusionary Zoning Inclusionary?*

tended to be built in neighborhoods that were already racially and economically diverse as compared to majority-White, affluent neighborhoods.

MAXIMIZING THE SOCIAL OUTCOMES OF INCLUSIONARY HOUSING

We believe that inclusionary housing policy and practice can be enhanced to promote more impactful social outcomes. If affordable housing is to be a strong platform for improving various dimensions of well-being, such as health, education, and economic mobility, then changes are needed to how inclusionary housing is designed and implemented. Given the levels of investment and the extent of societal need, we believe that affordable housing production and residential integration in and of themselves should not be seen as sufficient outcomes.

Because inclusionary housing operates through the mechanism of market rate development, newly constructed affordable housing units often are located in neighborhoods where market dynamics attract capital investment. These neighborhoods may feature amenities that are especially valuable to low-income households, such as high-quality schools, employment options, retail services, and access to public transportation. Given the proximity to resources that inclusionary housing facilitates, households living in units created through inclusionary programs may have greater opportunities for advancement, such as income and wealth generation.

Increasing proximity to opportunities, resources, and amenities is only the first step toward addressing economic and racial inequities and advancing more inclusive, equitable mixed-income communities. Meaningful access to and sustained engagement in those resources and amenities are also necessary to improve the lives of low- and moderate-income residents. Furthermore, inclusionary housing programs can provide opportunities for the development of stronger social networks and understanding among people of different economic and racial backgrounds. Higher-income residents have much to gain from connections with residents of inclusionary housing units, especially when those interactions lead to dismantling the racial and economic biases often perpetuated by people with economic resources.

Our vision is that low-income residents perceive and experience a meaningful improvement in quality of life following their move into affordable housing, as well as concrete changes in their social and economic mobility. We believe that social inclusion and economic advancement should be more strategically promoted so that low-income households can benefit more fully from living in inclusionary housing. Furthermore, this greater attention to social inclusion and economic advancement should be undergirded with an explicit commitment to advancing racial equity.

Social Inclusion

Like other mixed-income housing approaches, inclusionary housing presents an opportunity for greater social inclusion of low- and moderate-income residents in economically diverse housing and communities. We understand social inclusion to be "the active, intentional, and sustained engagement of traditionally excluded individuals and groups through informal activities and formal decision-making processes in ways that build connections and share power [....I]nclusion occurs when a social context enables people of diverse backgrounds to interact in mutually respectful ways that reveal their similarities and common ground, honor their social and cultural differences and uniqueness, and value what each individual and group can contribute to the shared environment."[23]

The co-location of market-rate and affordable units does not ensure social inclusion, however; it simply achieves residential integration. It is possible, and in fact likely, that low- and moderate-income residents living in homes created through inclusionary housing may still experience a sense of exclusion and marginalization, given than many buildings are designed with a small proportion of affordable units. Low-income renters in other mixed-income environments have experienced "incorporated exclusion," reporting a sense of stigma, discrimination, and isolation in their economically integrated housing complex and the broader neighborhood.[24] By proactively seeking to mitigate exclusion and promote social inclusion, inclusionary housing developments may increase the likelihood that low- and moderate-income residents experience a sense of belonging and connection that builds their social capital and enhances their quality of life.

---

23 Amy T. Khare and Mark L. Joseph, "Prioritizing Inclusion and Equity in the Next Generation of Mixed-Income Communities," in *What Works to Promote Inclusive, Equitable Mixed-Income Communities*, eds., Mark L. Joseph and Amy T. Khare (San Francisco: Federal Reserve Bank of San Francisco, 2020).

24 Robert J. Chaskin and Mark L. Joseph, *Integrating the Inner City: The Promise and Perils of Mixed-Income Public Housing Transformation*, (University of Chicago Press, 2015).

Economic Advancement

Most inclusionary housing programs do not include strategies to directly promote economic mobility—for example, by providing access to career opportunities, financial literacy programs, or connecting youth with after-school or extracurricular activities. Yet, inclusionary housing often is located in neighborhoods with access to high-quality schools, transit, and employment opportunities. These neighborhoods could actually enhance possibilities for low-income people to obtain living-wage jobs and better health care supports and to attend high-performing schools, all of which could contribute to long-term financial well-being. Because inclusionary housing programs are extremely localized and context-specific, opportunities exist for creative interventions that may help remove the multiple barriers to economic advancement for low-income households.

Racial Equity

We consider racial equity to be the condition in which race no longer predicts life opportunities and outcomes. Racial equity places priority on ensuring that people of color are afforded opportunities that they have historically been denied and from which they continue to be excluded; it centers the interests of people of color so that they "receive a more fair share of resources, opportunities, social supports, and power, given their differential needs and circumstances based on different life experiences."[25] Racial equity is defined as "both an outcome and a process."[26] As a process, it means that people of color are actively engaged in creating and implementing policies, programs, and practices that have an impact in their lives. As an outcome, it means that race no longer determines how people access important resources, such as a safe home and amenity-rich neighborhood.[27]

In most jurisdictions, inclusionary housing operates as a race-neutral policy. This means that affordable housing is not targeted for particular populations

---

25 Khare and Joseph, "Prioritizing Inclusion and Equity"

26 This definition is advanced by the Center for Social Inclusion.

27 "Equity is not the same as equality...Equity requires that people receive a different share of resources, opportunities, social supports and power, given their differential needs and circumstances based on different life experiences" (Khare and Joseph, "Prioritizing Inclusion and Equity"). For more resources, see the Annie E. Casey Foundation, Racial Equity and Inclusion Action Guide, Government Alliance on Race and Equity (GARE); Othering and Belonging Institute, University of California Berkeley; and Living Cities.

based on racial, ethnic, and cultural identity; nor is it used to stall gentrification in areas where people of color are actively being displaced by market conditions that are attractive to White incoming homebuyers. Without making a commitment to racial equity and instead operating as a race-neutral policy, however, inclusionary housing may not achieve desired outcomes for residential integration—and may, in fact, join other race-neutral housing and community development policies that actually exacerbate harm for low-income households of color.[28] For example, mid-century highway expansion and home mortgage policies tended to benefit the mobility of White households out of the central city and into suburbs in ways that disproportionately harmed communities of color.[29] More recently, home lending laws and policies have created a system of devaluing homes and businesses within Black communities.[30]

Conversely, inclusionary housing policies that seek to advance racial equity may be part of a broader approach to address structural racial disparities in housing opportunities at the municipal, regional, and state levels. Government officials who oversee inclusionary housing could prioritize a focus on race to ensure that people of color, particularly African Americans, are afforded housing opportunities that they have historically been denied and from which they continue to be excluded.

There are many ways to advance racial equity within inclusionary housing. Often, the developers have flexibility on the unit sizes and choose to build units that are smaller, such as studios and one-bedrooms, for the inclusionary portion. However, local ordinances can require or encourage the construction of apartments that match the typical household sizes of people of color, which often include multiple generations living together. In Cambridge, MA, for example, the inclusionary housing program encourages developers to provide affordable three-bedroom units, and in developments of 30,000 square feet or larger the ordinance *requires* the creation of three-bedroom units.

---

28 Rothstein, *The Color of Law*

29 Kenneth Jackson, *Crabgrass Frontier: The Suburbanization of the United States*, (Oxford University Press,1987); Alice O'Conner, "Swimming Against the Tide: A Brief History of Federal Policy in Poor Communities." In Ronald. F. Ferguson & William T. Dickens, eds., *Urban Problems and Community Development* (Washington, D.C.: Brookings Institute Press, 1999):77-137.; Thomas J. Sugrue, *The Origins of the Urban Crisis: Race and Inequality in Postwar Detroit*, 2nd ed. (Princeton: Princeton University Press, 2014).

30 Andre Perry, *Know Your Price Valuing Black Lives and Property in America's Black Cities*, (Washington, D.C.: Brookings Institution Press, 2020).

Another race-conscious strategy is to establish marketing and applicant selection policies that proactively encourage information sharing, applications, and leasing practices that reach people of color. For example, the San Francisco Mayor's Office of Housing and Community Development has a detailed marketing requirement that developers publish a notice of new inclusionary housing units in at least five local newspapers published by and on behalf of people of color. Amy Khare and Stephanie Reyes recently authored two guides outlining an array of strategies for advancing a racial equity focus in inclusionary housing programs.[31]

SOCIAL OUTCOMES FRAMEWORK FOR INCLUSIONARY HOUSING

We offer the following social outcomes framework for inclusionary housing to provide guidance to policymakers and practitioners as they seek to increase the social impact of inclusionary housing strategies. The framework has three stages—stabilize, fortify, and advance—which we define and explore here.

Stabilize

The first stage is for policymakers and practitioners to recognize the trauma and life challenges with which many low-income households have grappled for most, if not all, of their lives and to be more intentional about making operational and programmatic choices that establish durable stability through inclusionary housing. For people whose everyday living is characterized by a constant state of uncertainty and risk, living in high-quality, affordable housing can provide an essential foundation for achieving stability and predictability.

To promote more impactful social outcomes, inclusionary housing programs can do more to ensure that low-income households' lives are as stable as possible. Three strategic imperatives are to: (a) establish a culture of belonging and support, (b) be proactive about eviction prevention, and (c) take a comprehensive approach to social supports and services for residents.

A Culture of Belonging and Support. Beyond providing high-quality affordable housing, developers and managers of inclusionary housing properties can

---

[31] Amy T. Khare and Stephanie R. Reyes, *Advancing Racial Equity in Housing and Community Development: An Anti-Racism Resource Guide for Transformative Change*, (Cleveland, OH: National Initiative on Mixed Income Communities, Grounded Solutions Network, 2020); Stephanie R. Reyes and Amy T. Khare, *Advancing Racial Equity in Inclusionary Housing Programs: A Resource Guide for Policy and Practice*, (Cleveland, OH: National Initiative on Mixed Income Communities, Grounded Solutions Network, 2020).

do more to engender a culture of belonging and support in which residents are encouraged to feel a sense of home and stability. There can be a natural tendency on the part of inclusionary housing providers to prioritize marketing and customer service to higher-income residents, who are seen as cross-subsidizing the lower-income households. Conversely, lower-income households, particular African Americans and other residents of color, can be perceived as being fortunate to have secured the inclusionary unit and expected to instantly conform to the norms and expectations of the building and neighborhood. For some low-income households, adapting to the new environment may be a largely seamless transition. But those who wrestle with a variety of life challenges need greater support, starting with an explicit indication from property management that the household is truly welcome as part of the new community. Since most property managers are trained to be vigilant about transgressions and carry their own implicit biases about poverty and race, intentionality about staff recruitment, selection, training, and accountability is essential to ensure an authentic sense of welcome, belonging, and stability.

Eviction Prevention and Proactive Problem-Solving. Beyond an initial sense of welcome and belonging, inclusionary housing programs should explicitly identify resident challenges early and take measures to prevent eviction. This starts with efforts to educate residents about tenant expectations, rights, protections, and support, including a thorough explanation of lease compliance, information and access to tenant advocates and resources, and information about emergency rental assistance. Ideally, housing operators, property managers, maintenance staff and other partners will receive training and support for trauma-informed practices and implicit bias so they will recognize and pay attention to early signs of household challenges and have constructive techniques for engaging and supporting tenants, thereby avoiding more extreme measures that might jeopardize the tenant's housing.

A Comprehensive Approach to Household Stabilization. A comprehensive array of supports and services to help address household barriers and challenges also helps to increase household stability. In most cases, inclusionary housing providers have limited resources to do any more than manage high-quality and secure housing, so this imperative requires them to form partnerships and connections with other organizations that have the resources and capacity to support residents' needs and aspirations. Property staff should be given the information and means to connect residents to appropriate local systems of care and support, such as social services or employment services. Proactive communication and outreach from the housing provider to local organizations, to learn about existing programs and to establish contacts and processes for referring households, is essential. Comprehensive support also includes attention to systems and structures—such as social welfare agencies or local police and security—that may be a source of destabilization and marginalization for residents. It may be well beyond the scope of most inclusionary housing providers to directly change these systems, but helping households navigate these systems can be a key to stability.

Fortify

Living in inclusionary housing can make it easier for low-income households not only to "hold steady" and weather setbacks but also prepare for positive change. Having put in place a foundation for stabilizing low-income households, inclusionary housing programs can do more to strengthen households' readiness for change and growth by promoting: (a) a growth and aspirational mindset at the individual level; (b) bonding and bridging social ties at the social level; and (c) meaningful voice and agency for residents to shape and influence their housing and community environment at the structural level.

A Growth and Aspiration Mindset. Years, decades, and often generations of living in precarious housing and insecure neighborhood environments and dealing with stigmatizing systems often predisposes low-income households to a scarcity mindset that prioritizes risk avoidance and the management of limited resources. This mindset, along with the realities of living every day with complex trauma, can prevent residents of inclusionary housing units from being mentally prepared to take advantage of the new opportunities and resources available to them. Thus, a key component of fortifying low-income households for change is to make housing staff more sensitive to the scarcity mindset so they can complement the environment's stability with a consistent sense of aspiration and possibility, backed up by specific resources and activities that support growth.

Bonding and Bridging Social Ties. For many residents, connection to a supportive social network is the key to readiness for personal growth and development. This connection can include bonding social ties that provide social support, motivation, and accountability, and bridging ties that provide a connection to information and resources. Many residents, across income levels, may be uninterested or resistant to establishing relationships with their neighbors, for a variety of reasons. But inclusionary housing programs can provide places and opportunities to galvanize a sense of community and common purpose among residents of different social and economic backgrounds who are inclined to seek and provide neighborly connection and support. Over time, consistent efforts to build a welcoming sense of community can attract a broader range of residents. In addition to community-building activities in the inclusionary housing area, housing staff can identify community organizations and institutions that offer a setting for residents to connect to one another, such as local businesses, religious communities, neighborhood schools, or community centers.

Promoting Resident Voice and Agency. In addition to a scarcity mindset and social isolation, another barrier to readiness for change is a sense of powerlessness to influence the surrounding environment. This is another area where longstanding experiences of marginalization and exclusion may leave residents unprepared to engage in and benefit from the opportunities of an inclusionary housing environment. This also is an area where property management and other staff may have been trained and encouraged to take a more authoritarian, top-down approach to establishing an environment of rules and order. Alternatively, housing staff can engender a sense of greater agency and influence through one-on-one interactions that invite input and feedback, collective activities at which residents' ideas are solicited, and connections to community-based efforts to address neighborhood challenges and opportunities.

Advance

Inclusionary housing programs can serve as a springboard for low-income residents' personal growth and economic mobility by facilitating improvements in health, wellness, earnings, career development, and asset-building. Three key strategic imperatives are to support: (a) knowledge and skill building, (b) coaching and mentoring, and (c) strategies that help residents advance toward a living-wage income, a career, and the acquisition of wealth and assets.

Education and Skill Building. For low-income residents who are able to work, the predominant focus is often on simply landing and maintaining a job to generate income. And for those with pressing income needs and an inconsistent work history, securing steady employment is a crucial first step for household stability. The next step of personal and economic advancement requires access to opportunities for further education and skill-building, however. This is another area in which forming strong partnerships with educational institutions, workforce development organizations, and local employers could be a critical support provided by inclusionary housing programs.

Coaching and Mentoring. For residents looking to advance along their educational, professional or entrepreneurial pathway, one-on-one coaching and mentorship can be a valuable complement to formal education and programs. Particularly for residents who do not have extensive experience in the formal employment sector, having a consistent and trusted source of information, counsel, motivation, assistance with decision-making, and accountability can make a major difference. The mentoring can come from formal programs or informally, through neighbors or community members. Inclusionary housing programs can look for opportunities to make these connections for residents who are ready to take a next step in personal advancement.

Support for A Career Trajectory and Asset Acquisition. An ultimate phase of the process of moving from housing stability to economic mobility involves establishing a career trajectory in a particular employment sector and role, and building assets and wealth to complement employment income. These social outcomes are well beyond the attention and focus of most inclusionary housing programs. However, we believe that all of the investment and energy to create high-quality, affordable housing in vibrant neighborhoods will be underleveraged if a similar investment is not made to generate personal growth and economic mobility for the residents who are ready. This focus adds an additional dimension to the partnerships established to help provide supports to stabilize residents, with additional connections to supports such as job training, career coaching, financial literacy, matched savings accounts, and entrepreneurial programs and with formal channels to local job and career opportunities.

City and state government staff can support the creation of an opportunity pipeline for residents of affordable housing units built through inclusionary housing policies. For example, public institutions might offer these households greater access to resources such as free or reduced college tuition, job training, and health and wellness programming. Through these additional resources, residents may start to overcome the barriers to transcending poverty.

IMPLICATIONS FOR ACTION

The social outcomes framework outlined here has several implications for the policies and practices that involve inclusionary housing programs and their designers, developers, investors, researchers, and residents.

Implications for Policy

- *Move from Race-Neutral to Race-Conscious Policies.* Inclusionary housing programs should have income targets that match those of renter households of color within the local area. Policies also should require or encourage the construction of unit sizes that match the household sizes of renter households of color. These two priorities will help advance racial equity within inclusionary housing programs.

- *Prioritize Low-Income People as Much as Unit Production.* Inclusionary housing programs should require housing developers to articulate their commitment to and strategy for achieving social outcomes beyond affordable housing production. These commitments can be articulated in clear selection criteria for interested developers; detailed information about expectations for activities and strategies to stabilize, fortify, and advance the well-being and mobility of low-income households; and technical assistance provided to support the design of social programs.

- *Build Partnerships.* Inclusionary housing programs should establish connections with social service agencies, community-based organizations, workforce development agencies, and other organizations that can partner with housing developers to provides the necessary supports and services to help stabilize, fortify, and advance low-income households.

Implications for Development and Investment

- *Expand the Commitment Beyond Housing.* Housing developers should broaden their vision for the social outcomes of their inclusionary housing efforts, hiring senior staff with experience and capacity in comprehensive community collaborations and supporting their efforts to undertake creative partnerships that have a positive impact on low-income households.

- *Focus on Social as Well as Financial Returns.* Banks and finance agencies should broaden expectations for the outcomes of their investments in inclusionary housing projects, providing additional funding for the design, staffing, and implementation of social programs and partnerships and requiring developers to track and report on a broader array of social outcomes.

Implications for Research and Evaluation

- *Broaden the Focus of Research to Examine the Social Outcomes of Inclusionary Housing.* Existing research on inclusionary housing tends to focus on affordable housing production and how these programs affect local housing markets, rather than on the experiences of individuals who live in the housing. In order to inform more effective policy and practice, researchers must focus on resident experiences and outcomes.

- *Improve Inclusionary Housing Programs' Data Collection Methods and Systems.* Inclusionary housing programs should provide resources and technical assistance for routine data collection and tracking of resident characteristics and well-being, capitalizing on existing data collection processes such as annual income recertifications.

Implications for Residents and Community Members

- *Hold Inclusionary Housing Developers and Property Managers Accountable for Cultivating an Environment of Inclusion and Opportunity.* Residents of all income levels and social background stand to benefit from a housing and community environment in which all residents are encouraged and supported to stabilize their lives, fortify their capacity for change, and advance their personal growth. If residents recognize the tremendous potential of an inclusionary housing environment and hold housing operators accountable to strong aspirations and strategies, this will provide a key source of support and pressure to leverage the full potential of inclusionary housing.

- *Take the Lead, Along with Other Neighbors, to Promote an Inclusive and Welcoming Sense of Community.* Residents have a crucial role to play in achieving a sense of inclusion and opportunity. Residents can invest in making connections and engage in meaningful and supportive interactions with neighbors across lines of race and class.

■ ■ ■

AMY T. KHARE, Ph.D., works nationally on applied research, organizational transformation, and systems change that promotes inclusion and equity within metro areas. Khare's work is inspired by her personal experience as a sibling in the disability rights movement and her professional experience working within housing and community change organizations. Khare serves as the Research Director of the National Initiative on Mixed-Income Communities and a Research Assistant Professor at the Jack, Joseph and Morton Mandel School of Applied Social Sciences, Case Western Reserve University. Khare is completing a book manuscript entitled Poverty, Power and Profit: Structural Racism in Public Housing Reform. She earned her BSW and MSW from the University of Kansas and a Ph.D. from the University of Chicago.

■ ■ ■

EMILY K. MILLER, MSSA is a doctoral student at the Jack, Joseph, and Morton Mandel School of Applied Social Sciences at Case Western Reserve University. She has research and consulting experience in promoting inclusion and equity through mixed-income community development. Her current research interests include collective and community trauma, and how environments can promote resilience to protect against the development of complex trauma. She received undergraduate degrees in Sociology and Anthropology from DePauw University and her Master of Science in Social Administration from Case Western Reserve University.

■ ■ ■

SHOMON SHAMSUDDIN, Ph.D. is an Assistant Professor of Social Policy and Community Development at Tufts University. He studies how social problems are redefined by policies to address urban poverty and inequality. His research examines the effects of local and federal housing policy on socioeconomic mobility for poor families. In addition, he studies barriers to educational attainment for low-income students. Prior to joining Tufts, Shomon was a National Poverty Fellow at the University of Wisconsin-Madison and the U.S. Department of Health and Human Services. He holds a Ph.D. from MIT, M.Arch. from Yale University, and Sc.B. from Brown University.

■ ■ ■

MARK JOSEPH, Ph.D. is the Leona Bevis and Marguerite Haynam Associate Professor of Community Development at the Jack, Joseph and Morton Mandel School of Applied Social Sciences at Case Western Reserve University. His research focus is mixed-income development as a strategy for promoting urban equity and inclusion. He is the Founding Director of the National Initiative on Mixed-Income Communities, which conducts research and consulting projects in cities that have included Austin, Calgary, Chicago, Cleveland, Memphis, Minneapolis, Nashville, Pittsburgh, San Francisco, Seattle, Toronto, Tulsa, and Washington, D.C. He is the co-author of Integrating the Inner City: The Promise and Perils of Mixed-Income Public Housing Transformation. He received his undergraduate degree from Harvard University, a Ph.D. from the University of Chicago, was a Post-Doctoral Scholar at the University of Chicago and a Harlech Scholar at Oxford University.

HIGH-OPPORTUNITY PARTNER ENGAGEMENT: CREATING LOW-INCOME HOUSING OPTIONS NEAR GOOD SCHOOLS

Peter Kye and Megan Haberle
Poverty & Race Research Action Council

Laura Abernathy and Scott Kline
National Housing Trust

It is well established that place matters. School quality, employment, health, and life opportunities are shaped by the neighborhoods in which we live. All too often, however, low-income people of color live in neighborhoods that lack the benefits found in areas of opportunity. Despite the potential of initiatives such as the Housing Choice Voucher (HCV) program to open up areas of opportunity to low-income residents, most voucher holders lack real housing choice and remain concentrated in poor and racially segregated neighborhoods. To counter this, resident mobility programs have emerged to enable voucher holders to move to a broader range of neighborhoods, where they can access high-performing schools and other vehicles of economic mobility. Some positive reforms to the HCV program, such as the Small Area Fair Market Rent rule, have also begun to address the historic tendency of government housing programs to replicate segregated patterns and to gradually improve access to opportunity.

While there is a strong need to continue voucher program reforms, there also is a great need for complementary initiatives to address the insufficient supply of available housing in opportunity neighborhoods where many voucher holders hope to move. "High-opportunity areas" are generally defined as having low rates of poverty and access to high-quality schools, jobs, and other resources and amenities that make a community desirable. More needs to be done to expand neighborhood access and to ensure that when voucher holders seek to move to such areas, they are able to find and access units. But new housing construction in high-opportunity areas is often weighted down by discriminatory zoning delays and litigation costs that deter many affordable housing developers from entering these markets. In an effort to avoid these issues and to create mixed-income properties that give families with HCVs real choices in where they live, several housing acquisition programs focus specifically on areas of opportunity.

This opportunity-based housing acquisition work currently is being pioneered in various forms by an array of mission-driven actors, including affordable housing developers, public housing authorities (PHAs), and private foundations. This essay reviews the housing acquisition approach to providing greater access to opportunity and highlights promising models. We focus in particular on the National Housing Trust's (NHT) innovative High Opportunity Partner Engagement (HOPE) initiative (developed with the support of the JPMorgan Chase Foundation and The Kresge Foundation), which we hope will become a model for a community of practice among housing developers.

THE IMPORTANCE OF PLACE FOR CHILDREN

There is strong evidence that neighborhoods can affect residents' life outcomes. These neighborhood effects are especially strong for young children. In a compelling study that corroborates the observations made by housing mobility counselors over the years, Raj Chetty, Nathaniel Hendren, and Lawrence Katz found that moving to low-poverty neighborhoods had a strong causal effect on the life outcomes for young children below the age of 13.[1] In the mid-1990s, the U.S. Department of Housing and Urban Development (HUD) launched the Moving to Opportunity (MTO) experiment. Designed to evaluate whether moving from high-poverty to low-poverty areas could improve life outcomes for low-income families, MTO offered a randomly selected subset of very low-income families in high-poverty neighborhoods vouchers and counseling to help them move to low-poverty areas. Children in the MTO demonstration who moved from high-poverty to low-poverty neighborhoods exhibited higher rates of college attendance and higher earnings as young adults, were more likely to

---

1 Raj Chetty, Nathaniel Hendren, Lawrence F. Katz, "The Effects of Exposure to Better Neighborhoods on Children: New Evidence from the Moving to Opportunity Experiment," *American Economic Review*, 106, no. 4 (2016): 856, http://dx.doi.org/10.1257/aer.20150572.

live in better neighborhoods as adults, and were less likely to be single parents than MTO children who were not in the experimental group. The recorded benefits were greater the younger the child's age at the time of the move, and every additional year a child spent in a better neighborhood environment improved long-term outcomes and prospects for upward economic mobility.[2]

One of the key ways in which neighborhoods affect life outcomes is through schools. Since most children attend school based on where they live, an important benefit of moving to a higher-opportunity neighborhood is the ability to attend high-performing schools. In addition, greater student diversity can benefit both these movers and the community at large. Attending a diverse school is positively associated with higher academic achievement in math, science, language, and reading.[3] These benefits accrue to students in all grade levels but are greatest in the middle and high school years, suggesting that these benefits accumulate over time. Integrated, diverse schools tend to have more resources, stable student populations, and more experienced and highly qualified teachers than schools that are racially and socioeconomically isolated.[4] Students who attend diverse schools are more likely to graduate from high school, enter and graduate from college, and possess workplace readiness and interpersonal skills needed for the modern economy. Attending diverse schools as a child can also make individuals more likely to choose to live in a diverse neighborhood as adults.[5]

AN ACCESS TO OPPORTUNITY CRISIS

Far too many families lack access to the higher-opportunity communities that provide economic mobility and educational opportunity. Widening economic inequality and a lack of affordable housing, particularly in high-opportunity areas, make it difficult to achieve upward economic mobility. While housing prices have increased, the supply of affordable housing has not. Indeed,

---

2   *Ibid.*

3   Roslyn Arlin Mickelson, "School Integration and K-12 Outcomes: An Updated Quick Synthesis of the Social Science Evidence," Washington DC: National Center on School Diversity (2016), https://files.eric.ed.gov/fulltext/ED571629.pdf.

4   *Ibid.*, 3.

5   Jennifer Ayscuse, Erica Frankenberg, and Genevieve Siegel-Hawley, "The Complementary Benefits of Racial and Socioeconomic Diversity in Schools" (2017), https://school-diversity.org/pdf/DiversityResearchBriefNo10.pdf.

there is a shortage of affordable housing for extremely low-income renters (renters whose household incomes are at or below the federal poverty level or 30 percent of the area median income) in every state, and the majority of extremely low-income renters are cost burdened[6] in every state.[7] In addition, the legacy of racial segregation persists through concentrated poverty and a lack of opportunity in many neighborhoods. Neighborhoods are key in transmitting this disadvantage across generations.[8]

Despite the goals of the HCV program, it has largely failed to meaningfully disrupt residential segregation and the intergenerational transmission of poverty.[9] In particular, the HCV program fails to provide enough families with access to areas with high-quality schools. Analysis of the HCV program shows that, on average, voucher holders live near schools that perform well below the median in their state. Despite the goals of the HCV program, voucher households generally do not live near schools that are higher-performing than households that receive other forms of housing assistance.[10] The shortcomings of the voucher program have serious implications for racial equity, as voucher holders disproportionately are people of color.[11]

Theoretically, HCVs should help low-income families choose housing on the open market. However, a variety of issues prevent the program from realizing

---

6 I.e., 30 percent or more of the household's monthly gross income is dedicated to housing.

7 Andrew Aurand et al., "The Gap: A Shortage of Affordable Homes," Washington, DC: National Low-Income Housing Coalition (March 2019), https://www.novoco.com/sites/default/files/atoms/files/2019_gap_shortage_of_affordable_homes_031419.pdf.

8 Patrick Sharkey, *Stuck in Place: Urban Neighborhoods and the End of Progress toward Racial Equality*, Chicago: University of Chicago Press (2013), 19.

9 Stefanie DeLuca and Peter Rosenblatt, "Walking away from the Wire: Housing Mobility and Neighborhood Opportunity in Baltimore," *Housing Policy Debate* 27, no. 4 (2017): 520, https://doi.org/10.1080/10511482.2017.1282884; Deborah Thrope, "Achieving Housing Choice and Mobility in the Voucher Program: Recommendations for the Administration," *Journal of Affordable Housing* 27, no. 1 (2018): 145, https://www.nhlp.org/wp-content/uploads/2018/05/AH-27-1_11Thrope.pdf; Alicia Mazzara and Brian Knudsen, "Where Families with Children Use Housing Vouchers: A Comparative Look at the 50 Largest Metropolitan Areas," Washington, DC: Center on Budget and Policy Priorities and Poverty & Race Research Action Council (2019), https://www.cbpp.org/research/housing/where-families-with-children-use-housing-vouchers.

10 Ingrid Gould Ellen and Keren Horn, "Housing and Educational Opportunity: Characteristics of Local Schools near Families with Federal Housing Assistance," Washington, DC: Poverty & Race Research Action Council (July 2018), https://prrac.org/housing-and-educational-opportunity-characteristics-of-local-schools-near-families-with-federal-housing-assistance/.

11 "Who Lives in Federally Assisted Housing?" (2012), https://nlihc.org/sites/default/files/HousingSpotlight2-2.pdf.

its potential to allow families to choose to live in a full range of neighborhoods. While there is a need for more affordable housing generally, the failures of the program in providing access to opportunity are not simply about market conditions. Rather, they fall into three general areas: (1) the features and priorities of the HCV program itself as it is designed by HUD and administered by public housing authorities; (2) a lack of widespread informational and counseling services to help tenants access areas outside those where public housing tends to be concentrated; and (3) a lack of balance in where affordable units are located and of landlords willing to rent to voucher holders.

This essay focuses primarily on solutions to the third aspect of the problem—the need for additional units in high-opportunity, low-poverty areas to be made available to voucher holders—by describing strategies for increasing the availability of such housing by acquiring existing buildings. We believe that housing policy should address each of these three areas in complementary fashion in order to help the HCV program fulfill its promise. Because the barriers and solutions in these areas interrelate, this section provides broader context on these issues within the HCV program.

Families searching for housing often contend with a lack of information about high-opportunity neighborhoods throughout their regions, racial and ethnic discrimination, and the refusal of landlords to rent to voucher holders ("source-of-income discrimination, which is especially pervasive").[12] Moreover, families facing market constraints and tight search periods often may be more concerned with finding any place to live than with focusing on high-opportunity neighborhoods. Payment standards also may be insufficient to cover the rent in low-poverty neighborhoods.

Serious structural problems also prevent families from moving to neighborhoods with high-quality schools and other opportunities. Limited interjurisdictional public housing authority (PHA) cooperation may prevent families from being able to effectively exercise the portability feature of the HCV program. In the face of constraints, PHA staff may spend their limited time and energy simply finding housing for as many families as possible in any neighborhood rather than on a more resource-intensive search for housing in a high-opportunity area. Moreover, the system by which HUD evaluates the performance of PHAs focuses on administrative performance (e.g., voucher utilization rates, rent

---

12 Thrope, "Achieving Housing Choice and Mobility in the Voucher Program," 151-153.

payment calculations, client income verifications) while placing little emphasis on desegregation and deconcentrating poverty. This creates a disincentive for PHA staff to spend time helping families relocate to opportunity areas and finding landlords who welcome voucher holders.[13] Mobility programs have been established around the country to address the obstacles that stand in the way of moving to better neighborhoods. These programs provide supportive services that help voucher holders overcome challenges to finding housing in low-poverty areas and can help participants more fully realize the potential of the HCV program. These programs provide housing search assistance to help families fully understand how the HCV program works, assist with security deposits, and connect renters with landlords who will accept vouchers. The services also may include pre-move counseling on such topics as credit and budgeting and can help make tenants more attractive to landlords. In some instances, program participants may receive post-move counseling to help ease the transition to new areas. Such programs have been successful in areas such as Dallas, Chicago, and Baltimore, where they originally resulted from litigation. For example, in Baltimore, families who participated in a mobility program and successfully moved lived in neighborhoods with dramatically lower poverty rates and higher-performing schools.[14] Mobility programs are beginning to gain attention elsewhere as effective interventions that help families access better life opportunities. The experience of many voucher holders who have participated in such programs attests to the potential of housing mobility to improve lives.

CONNECTING FAMILIES TO OPPORTUNITY THROUGH HOUSING ACQUISITION

While the counseling programs described above help to address many of the barriers that residents face in accessing high-opportunity areas, complementary *site-based* strategies that increase the supply of affordable units in a targeted way are also an important component in providing low-income families with access to such neighborhoods. Affordable housing may be especially difficult to find in such areas, in part because of the continuing imbalance in the

---

13 Stefanie DeLuca, Phillip M. E. Garboden, and Peter Rosenblatt, "Segregating Shelter: How Housing Policies Shape the Residential Locations of Low-Income Minority Residents," *The Annals of the American Academy of Political and Social Science* 647, no. 1 (2013): 287, https://doi.org/10.1177/0002716213479310; Thrope, "Achieving Housing Choice and Mobility in the Voucher Program," 152.

14 Stefanie DeLuca and Peter Rosenblatt, "Walking away from the Wire," 522.

geographic location of government-subsidized housing[15] as well as barriers such as zoning restrictions on multifamily construction.[16] Site-based strategies that rely on mission-driven housing developers to expand the supply of affordable housing can protect tenants from discrimination based on their source of income and ease the administrative burden that public housing authorities and mobility programs would otherwise face in building relationships with landlords who are willing to accept vouchers.

Increasing recognition of the need to give families the choice to live in high-opportunity areas and to increase the supply of affordable housing in such areas has sparked pioneering efforts to create low-income housing in areas of opportunity. The details of each model differ but the underlying concept is straightforward: The targeted acquisition of existing buildings in neighborhoods with amenities, resources, and good schools will help expand the supply of affordable housing and preserve the long-term affordability of units. Introducing a number of low-income families into these acquired buildings will help create mixed-income, diverse buildings and communities and can help children attain better outcomes over the course of their lives. By creating a pipeline between PHAs and specific properties, this approach can also complement mobility counseling programs in expanding access to opportunity neighborhoods that were previously largely inaccessible for these families.

The emerging housing acquisition models offer several practical advantages over more conventional approaches to providing affordable housing. Acquiring existing housing in areas with high property values often is more financially feasible than developing new housing in such areas, because there is no need for expensive new construction. In comparison to new construction, acquisition can also help reduce the threat of community opposition derailing a project. Traditionally, acquisition has been most financially and logistically advantageous in areas where affordable housing already is concentrated or when used as a means to prevent displacement; this is partly due to the lack of successful models for opportunity-focused acquisition. In a promising turn, however, a number of opportunity acquisition models have taken root and are beginning to thrive.

---

15 Ingrid Gould Ellen and Keren Mertens Horn, "Housing and Educational Opportunity."

16 Ingrid Gould Ellen, Keren Mertens Horn, and Yiwen Kuai, "Gateway to Opportunity? Disparities in Neighborhood Conditions among Low-Income Housing Tax Credit Residents," *Housing Policy Debate* 28, no. 4 (2018): 576, https://doi.org/10.1080/10511482.2017.1413584.

EMERGING OPPORTUNITY ACQUISITION MODELS: AN OVERVIEW

Opportunity acquisition strategies have gained interest among an array of entities in both the public and private sectors. Such initiatives are still relatively rare, with ample room for this field to grow, and these early efforts are significant in part because they provide models from which others can learn. In this section we provide an overview of several of these initiatives and then explore more deeply the NHT HOPE model. It is our hope that this initiative will inspire a new community of practice among housing developers, as more of them build on these models and engage in opportunity acquisition.

NHT's High Opportunity Partner Engagement Acquisition Model

The National Housing Trust's HOPE initiative acquires existing market-rate rental housing in areas with high-quality schools and then allocates a portion of these units to low-income choice voucher holders. This strategy aims to show that coordination between housing providers and local housing authorities, with an intentional focus on access to good schools, can lead to permanent increases in educational achievement. HOPE will introduce low-income families into existing properties as turnover occurs. Over time, these all-market-rate properties will become mixed-income buildings as voucher holders move into vacant units. Because vouchers are introduced as natural attrition occurs, no existing market-rate tenants will be displaced in the process. NHT is working with local partners in a number of states and closed on its first transaction in 2017 in Coon Rapids, Minnesota. At the time of this writing, NHT has renovated the building and is currently in the process of leasing vacated units to voucher holders.

The Moving to Opportunity Fund

Another variant of this financing model, the Moving to Opportunity (MTO) Fund, is a real estate fund focused on improving access to good schools for extremely low-income families with young children living in areas of concentrated poverty, while delivering market-rate returns for investors. MTO seeks to acquire class A multifamily properties in communities with top schools and voluntarily reserve 20 percent of units for voucher holders. The MTO Fund is a for-profit real estate investment operation coupled with an affiliated nonprofit that will focus on service delivery. The MTO Fund will target properties in the largest 20 metropolitan areas and hold properties long-term.

The MTO Fund also provides a variety of supportive services such as mobility counseling, family counseling, and support for children. Initially, the fund is seeking to partner with foundations to fund a pilot before expanding to attract mainstream investors such as pension funds that are looking for conservative long-term investments. For an in-depth discussion of the MTO Fund rationale, strategy, and implications, please see the essay by Hans Buder in this volume.

Baltimore Regional Project-Based Voucher Program

Project-based vouchers are an important key in a new effort to connect low-income families to opportunity in the Baltimore region. The Baltimore Metropolitan Council is working with and PHAs in the Baltimore region to pilot a new regional PBV program. This initiative was partly modeled on the Regional Housing Initiative developed in the Chicago area (For more on the Chicago RHI, see the essay by Robin Snyderman in this volume). The Baltimore Regional Project-Based Voucher Program uses project-based vouchers pooled from PHAs throughout the Baltimore region. Affordable housing developers can apply for subsidies to create housing in areas of opportunity (through existing homes, rehabilitation, or new construction) in five participating jurisdictions. The program uses criteria developed by BRHP to designate high-opportunity census tracts as locations for developments, with a focus on access to high-quality public schools, jobs, and neighborhood safety. At least two-thirds of vouchers awarded through the Regional PBV program must be in high-opportunity areas. Tenants are selected from a waiting list from a housing mobility program administered by BRHP and must receive mobility counseling before and after their move.

Housing Authority-led Affordable Opportunity Housing Acquisition

In the Seattle area, the King County Housing Authority (KCHA) is an example of a public housing authority that has embraced housing acquisition as a mobility strategy. Over the last 20 years, KCHA has acquired or developed thousands of housing units. Targeted acquisitions are generally older multifamily developments where KCHA limits rent growth and introduces project-based HCVs for 15 to 20 percent of the units. KCHA collaborated with partners in 2010 to rank census tracts across five opportunity categories: education, economic health, housing, transportation and mobility, and health and environment. KCHA's site-based affordability strategy focuses on increasing the supply of subsidized housing options in opportunity areas; the majority of units are located in high or very-high opportunity areas. Of these units, 28 percent house extremely low-income voucher holders. Acquisitions generally are financed through private debt, with Low-Income Housing Tax Credits (LIHTC) utilized where significant rehabilitation or new construction is required.[17]

Each of the models described above focuses on expanding the supply of affordable housing in high-opportunity areas and connecting tenants to such housing, indicating how this can work with different actors, financing structures, and geographies. We now turn to a deeper look at one of these models—NHT's HOPE program—to describe the specific opportunities and challenges it has encountered and the lessons it may present for opportunity acquisition as a whole.

THE HOPE MODEL: A DEEPER LOOK

In 2017, NHT launched HOPE to provide affordable housing options near high-performing schools.[18] Although NHT acknowledges that access to high-quality education is not the only measure of opportunity, the intent of the HOPE model is to test a financing mechanism for acquiring properties in those areas, which traditionally are difficult for low-income renters to access. Partnering with local organizations in communities across the country, NHT is identifying, bidding on, and acquiring market-rate, multifamily rental properties in communities that meet the education criteria. Working with public housing authorities to introduce HCVs in 20 percent of the apartments, NHT and its partners are making this high-opportunity housing affordable to low-income residents.

Apartments eligible for HOPE acquisition require minimum rehab (about $5,000 to $10,000 per unit) and are in a high-quality school district, meaning one in which the primary elementary school (a) has as rank of seven or above (meaning "good" or "excellent") in the GreatSchools[19] index; (b) outperforms

---

17 Stephen Norman and Sarah Oppenheimer, "Expanding the Toolbox: Promising Approaches for Increasing Geographic Choice," working paper, Cambridge, MA: Joint Center for Housing Studies of Harvard University (2017), https://www.jchs.harvard.edu/research-areas/working-papers/shared-future-expanding-toolbox-promising-approaches-increasing.

18 The HOPE initiative is supported by The Kresge Foundation and the JPMorgan Chase Foundation.

19 GreatSchools provides a snapshot of school quality. Although components included within a school's rat-

its peers in at least two of the following three subject areas: math, reading, and science (as reported by GreatSchools); and (c) appears in the top quartile of the relevant state's ranking of all elementary schools. In addition, NHT and its partners prioritize properties with family-sized units, helping to ensure that low-income children gain access to the high-quality education available. While HOPE promotes NHT's mission of providing low-income individuals and families the opportunity to live in quality neighborhoods with access to opportunities, it also is a successful housing finance model with a required internal rate of return of only 8.5 percent. Properties that will work for the HOPE model are not just those that provide access to good schools, they are properties on which it is economically feasible to meet the market-rate acquisition price based on allowable voucher rents.

For the first HOPE property, NHT and CommonBond Communities (an affordable housing developer based on Minneapolis) successfully acquired Pine Point Apartments, a 68-unit market rate property in Coon Rapids, Minnesota, with access to excellent elementary schools. This $6.8 million project included a $1 million renovation with a focus on unit and common-area enhancements. Pine Point Apartments are accessible to public transportation, retail and other neighborhood amenities through a bus stop at the property's entrance that provides service to downtown St. Paul and Minneapolis.

Hoover Elementary, a high-performing school rated eight by GreatSchools at the time of acquisition, is the elementary school that serves Pine Point Apartments. Children from the property have two choices for middle school. Northdale Middle School is a high-performing middle school, scoring seven on the Great Schools Index. Northdale's test scores are well above the state average, and its Black, Hispanic/Latinx, and Asian students significantly outperform their peers statewide. The property management team at Pine Point strongly encourages middle school-aged residents to attend Northdale. Students may also elect to go to Coon Rapids Middle School. Although not as high-performing as Northdale, the school does have a number of high-performing programs. At the time of acquisition, Coon Rapids Middle School science and math programs performed in the Northdale range (indeed, a higher percentage

---

ing may vary according to the availability of data, the index score is based on five ratings of the school: test scores, student or academic progress, college readiness, equity rating, and advanced courses. GreatSchools ratings follow a 1-10 scale, with 10 the highest and 1 the lowest. For more information, please visit "About Us," GreatSchools, accessed May 21, 2019, https://www.greatschools.org/gk/about/.

of students at Coon Rapids Middle School pass Algebra I than at Northdale), and Black and Hispanic/Latinx students significantly outperform their peers across the state in reading, math, and science.

As discussed later in this essay, competing with market-rate developers is the most significant challenge in this work. While NHT has engaged partners across the country to identify prospective properties, Pine Point was the first property that met HOPE's criteria for providing access to good schools, was financially feasible for introducing vouchers, and—most importantly—on which NHT was not outbid by another developer. Eighteen months after acquiring the property, 14 apartments were currently occupied by families with HCVs, meaning that a full 20 percent of the total units in the market-rate, high-opportunity property are occupied by low-income families. In 2018, NHT hired Dr. Ann Owens, an Associate Professor of Sociology and Management at the University of Southern California, to conduct a preliminary study of Pine Point and its role in helping low-income families access opportunity. In May 2018, Dr. Owens visited Pine Point to meet with five of the six families with HCVs that had moved into the property at that time. Of the five families interviewed for this study, four are headed by single mothers with children living in the home. One head of household is retired, one was not employed, and the other three held at least part-time, low-wage jobs in retail, customer service, or food service. Most of these residents have faced numerous challenges throughout their lives, including family poverty and instability in childhood, exposure to personal and neighborhood violence, limited educational opportunities, homelessness, relationship instability, deployment to war, emigration from war-torn home countries, and health problems.

Although it is too early to tell how or if the children in these families are benefitting from the local high-performing schools in which they are now enrolled, residents evaluated their experience at Pine Point and in the Coon Rapids neighborhood positively. Many, however, were still learning about the community as they had been living in the area for fewer than seven months at the time of Dr. Owen's interviews.

NHT's success in acquiring Pine Point and making it available to families with HCVs, and the success of any developer wanting to provide opportunity to low-income families through a similar approach, depends on having a strong local partner. In the case of Pine Point, CommonBond provided invaluable knowledge of the local real estate market that NHT, as a national organization, does not have. In addition to identifying properties that fit HOPE's high-opportunity and financing requirements, a savvy local partner can also help negotiate a purchase prior to a property being placed on the market, which increases the rate of success. NHT's experience is that bidding on eligible properties on the open market generally is unsuccessful for this model, as potential market-rate buyers, many of whom may plan to perform modest rehab and increase rents, can offer higher purchase prices. Pine Point was identified and purchased through CommonBond's local and professional relationships, sparing both NHT and its partner the challenges of competing with market-rate bidders.

Just as important as a strong relationship with a local development partner is a candid, trust-based relationship with the local PHA. For this critical role, NHT again relies on a local development partner who either has an existing relationship or is well-positioned to foster one. In the case of Pine Point, CommonBond's relationship with the local PHA has been critical to securing residents with vouchers. In fact, it was the PHA's initial support of the proposed project that encouraged NHT and CommonBond to pursue the project. When Pine Point was acquired, it was fully occupied by market rate-renters. Even as natural attrition occurred and units became available to families with vouchers, it took several months before these families moved in. NHT also recognized that some of the delay in renting to low-income families was the result of transitioning to a new management company. When the property was acquired, a new management company took over and, as can be expected with any change in management, it took some time to become familiar with the newly acquired property and establish new operating systems. Once that transition period was over, families with vouchers were quickly able to move into the property and NHT has delivered early on its goal of making 20 percent of the apartments affordable to low-income renters.

In addition to these lessons learned through the Pine Point acquisition, there are risks associated with the HOPE model, primarily on the property identification and financing levels. These risks include difficulty identifying housing projects that meet NHT's high-opportunity criteria, properties with sale and rehabilitation prices too high for the financing model to be feasible, and inability to secure sufficient equity to generate the requisite number of affordable units. While NHT is minimizing the first and second risks by working with strong local partners who know the local real estate market, the potential lack of low-cost equity needed to successfully compete for these high-opportunity properties remains the greatest challenge. NHT has taken steps to address the challenge by securing $6 million from The Kresge Foundation for low-cost equity, enabling NHT—either as owner/developer, co-developer, and/or investor—to quickly bid on properties. NHT is in the process of securing more commitments of debt that can be invested as equity or subordinate debt into HOPE projects. Additionally, NHT has a $20 million line of credit from UBS, with a favorable interest rate, that can be used as low-cost debt to acquire properties. Finally, NHT is a member of Housing Partnership Equity Trust, a Real Estate Investment Trust (REIT) that provides low-cost equity to its members to acquire and preserve affordable housing. NHT has successfully used this REIT financing in the past and hopes to continue to do so.

The possibility that rents approved for HCV properties may not be comparable to market rents is another risk in many places. NHT is reducing this risk by identifying properties in areas where the approved voucher rents equal market rents, including areas that have moved to higher Small Area Fair Market Rents (SAFMRs). Recently implemented by HUD in 24 metropolitan areas characterized by high voucher concentration and vacancy rates (with the opportunity for other areas to adopt them voluntarily), SAFMRs recognize that the higher rents of some neighborhoods result in higher payment standards for vouchers in higher-cost areas, and thus increase the number of homes economically feasible for acquisition through the HOPE model.[20] PHAs also have the ability to increase their payment standards in higher-cost opportunity areas in order to help facilitate moves to those areas.

CONCLUSION

As affordable housing and opportunity become increasingly out of reach for low-income residents, and as racial and economic segregation persist, new strategies are needed to create mixed-income communities that expand access to the amenities, resources, and schools that can lead to upward mobility. The

---

20 HUD requires the use of SAFMRs in 24 metropolitan areas that met all five of the following selection criteria: (1) at least 2,500 HCVs under lease in the metropolitan FMR area; (2) at least 20 percent of the standard-quality rental stock within the metropolitan FMR area is located in ZIP Codes where the SAFMR is more than 110 percent of the metropolitan area FMR; (3) at least 25 percent of families with HCVs live in concentrated low-income areas; (4) the percentage of renters with vouchers living in concentrated low-income areas, relative to the percentage of all renters within these areas over the entire metropolitan area, exceeds 155 percent; and (5) the vacancy rate for the metropolitan area is greater than 4 percent. Other areas may adopt SAFMRs or exception payment standards voluntarily.

National Housing Trust's HOPE initiative, along with several other models, has the potential to improve racial and economic equity in society by creating pathways to opportunity for many low-income households. The focus that HOPE places on access to good schools has the potential to create a lasting positive impact for children who move to new neighborhoods. Going forward, housing acquisition programs can build on lessons from the current set of initiatives and should also carefully consider issues such as financing, leasing policies, affirmative marketing strategies, and the services provided to families who choose to move. If executed well, housing acquisition programs that create low-income housing options in quality neighborhoods can be a powerful tool to create access to opportunity.

IMPLICATIONS FOR ACTION

Implications for Policy

- As policymakers grapple with growing concern over high housing costs and structural inequality, housing acquisition models offer one potential way to improve equity and inclusion for low-income families, especially families of color. Policymakers should consider increasing support for these models in order to expand choice and opportunities for low-income families of color. Assembling financing to acquire unrestricted properties on the market is a significant challenge. Policymakers therefore should work to expand the subsidies available while taking steps to ensure that both current and future funding streams adequately support affordable housing in high opportunity areas. Such support to organizations and PHAs seeking to acquire property could help make acquisition more financially feasible.

- Policymakers also should consider a broader set of policy initiatives to complement opportunity acquisition, such as measures to improve the effectiveness of the Housing Choice Voucher program in furthering housing choice, laws banning discrimination based on source of income, and increased funding for housing mobility programs that provide comprehensive counseling and other supportive services that help voucher holders successfully move to high opportunity neighborhoods. The recently passed Housing Mobility Demonstration Act, which provides $25 million in funding for PHAs seeking to establish mobility programs, is a promising step in expanding mobility.

- Finding a home with a housing voucher is challenging. Affirmative marketing programs that provide for increased outreach to voucher holders with children to make them aware of options in acquired properties could streamline and ease the frustrating search process for these families even more. Interaction with housing and other social service agencies was critical in facilitating these families' moves to Pine Point, so maintaining and strengthening these connections will be important in helping future tenants make opportunity moves.

Implications for Research and Evaluation

- The housing acquisition models discussed here offer additional opportunities to assess the effects of moving to new neighborhoods on the long-term educational, economic, and health outcomes for low-income residents, particularly for children. The HOPE and MTO Fund models provide an opportunity to explore the role of high-performing schools in inclusionary programs.

- Evaluation of these models' financial feasibility and sustainability will be important for attempts to replicate acquisition efforts.

Implications for Development and Investment

- These emergent housing acquisition models have potential to alter the way that private developers and investors approach the creation of mixed-income developments. If the models are financially sustainable, they have the potential to encourage innovation and greater investment into opportunity areas, thereby helping to deconcentrate poverty, redress racial segregation, and create more mixed-income communities. Developers, investors, and PHAs should go beyond "business as usual" to explore new financing models.

Implications for Residents and Community Members

- Low-income families who choose to move with a voucher to housing in a high-opportunity neighborhood may benefit from increased educational and other opportunities and may experience improved mental and physical health. Neighborhoods and schools also will benefit from increased diversity, especially if efforts are made to cultivate a welcoming, inclusive environment.

- As preliminary interviews with new Pine Point residents indicated, additional supports, including holistic case management, social activities, and neighborhood and school orientations could further benefit families as they transition into Pine Point and the surrounding neighborhood.

■ ■ ■

PETER KYE is a Law and Policy Associate at PRRAC focusing on housing and environmental justice issues. Mr. Kye earned his J.D. from the University of Virginia School of Law in 2016. During law school, he received the Mortimer Caplin Public Service Award and interned at the Legal Aid Justice Center, Community Legal Services of Philadelphia, and the New York Legal Assistance Group. Mr. Kye received his B.A. from the College of William & Mary in 2013, where he studied Government and Sociology. He is a member of the New York State Bar.

■ ■ ■

MEGAN HABERLE is Deputy Director of the Poverty & Race Research Action Council, where she has worked since 2012. She specializes in policy designs, public education, and technical assistance relating to government programs and civil rights, with a focus on advancing fair housing and environmental justice. She is a graduate of Columbia Law School, where she was an Executive Editor of the Columbia Journal of Environmental Law, and Swarthmore College, where she studied anthropology.

■ ■ ■

LAURA ABERNATHY joined the National Housing Trust in 2010 and currently serves as the State and Local Policy Director. In this role, Abernathy oversees the Trust's work on state and local public policy initiatives in all 50 states, working with elected officials, government employees, and advocates from around the country to shape public policy that promotes local affordable housing preservation, strengthens communities, and provides access to opportunity for low-income families. Laura holds a B.A. in Economics and English Literature from Franklin & Marshall College and a Master's degree in Urban and Regional Planning from the University of Florida, where she specialized in Housing, Community, and Economic Development.

■ ■ ■

SCOTT L. KLINE is Vice President of the National Housing Trust and Senior Vice President of NHT Communities. Scott oversees a team of developers and asset managers responsible for acquisition efforts throughout the United States on behalf of NHT Communities which involves identifying preservation opportunities, negotiating site control with owners, developing project concepts and finance plans, coordinating due diligence processes, securing financing, and the asset management *of acquired properties. Kline earned an M.B.A. in Real Estate Development and Urban Planning, from American University, Washington, D.C. and also holds a B.B.A in Finance, from George Washington University, Washington, D.C.*

THE MTO FUND: HARNESSING THE MARKET TO PROMOTE OPPORTUNITY AND INCLUSION

Hans Buder
Moving to Opportunity Fund

Despite decades of persistent effort, the challenges confronting community development practitioners in the housing space are perhaps greater than ever. There are 4.25 million low-income children growing up in neighborhoods of concentrated poverty; the country is in the grip of a crushing affordability crisis, with families in the bottom income quintile spending more than half of their income on rent;[1] and social mobility, which rose steadily throughout the postwar period, has been declining for almost 40 years.[2] The federal government currently spends almost $50 billion a year on housing-related programs for low-income families,[3] but with ballooning federal deficits and a notable lack of broad-based political will, the prospects for significant spending increases are limited. Given these realities, we are left with two operative questions. First, how can we increase the impact of existing expenditures by using those dollars more effectively—in other words, how can we do more with what we already have?

---

1   Jeff Larrimore and Jenny Schuetz, "Assessing the Severity of Rent Burden on Low-Income Families," Board of Governors of the Federal Reserve System: *FEDS Notes* (December 22, 2017), https://www.federalreserve.gov/econres/notes/feds-notes/assessing-the-severity-of-rent-burden-on-low-income-families-20171222.htm.

2   Jonathan Davis and Bhashkar Mazumder, "The Decline in Intergenerational Mobility After 1980," working paper 17-21, Opportunity & Inclusive Growth Institute, Federal Reserve Bank of Minneapolis, MN (2017), https://www.minneapolisfed.org/institute/working-papers/17-21.pdf.

3   In 2018, federal spending on housing-related programs for low-income families included: $22 billion for the Housing Choice Voucher program, $11.5 billion for Project-Based Section 8, $7.3 billion for public housing, and $8.1 billion (in foregone tax revenue) for the Low-Income Housing Tax Credit program. This equates to roughly 8 percent of all non-defense discretionary spending, which totaled $610 billion in 2017. See: "Housing," Center on Budget and Policy Priorities, accessed May 22, 2019, https://www.cbpp.org/topics/housing; Corianne Payton Scally et al., *The Low-Income Housing Tax Credit*, Washington, DC: Urban Institute (September 2018), https://www.urban.org/sites/default/files/publication/98761/lihtc_past_achievements_future_challenges_finalized_0.pdf.

And second, how can we bring additional resources to bear by harnessing market mechanisms and leveraging private capital? This essay describes one particular strategy for achieving these goals, outlining an "opportunity acquisition model" that has been consciously designed to attract capital from mainstream institutional investors by fusing frameworks drawn from real estate private equity with best practices from mixed-income development, and sharing new research that details the life-changing benefits that exposure to high-opportunity neighborhoods can have for low-income children. Still in its infancy, the mission of our organization, The Moving to Opportunity Fund (MTO Fund), is to pioneer a scalable impact-investing model capable of putting low-income children born into concentrated poverty on the path to college, by providing access to service-enriched, mixed-income housing in high-opportunity communities with top-ranked public schools—and to so do while delivering market-rate returns for investors.[4] What follows is a brief overview of our approach and its underpinnings. A preliminary section outlines the growing disconnect between research findings, and the manner in which traditional affordable housing strategies are being implemented. The second section explains the rationale for a private-sector solution, underscoring the magnitude of the potential impact. The third section represents the heart of the essay, outlining our vision for the MTO Fund in greater detail and providing an overview of key components of the model: our approach to family recruitment, the mobility counseling and supportive services we intend to offer, and our investment strategy. A fourth section identifies the constraints imposed by our double-bottom-line approach and walks through how we designed our model to satisfy those constraints and maximize our potential impact. The essay concludes with an examination of our anticipated operational challenges and a final section proposing implications for action.

TRADITIONAL PLACE-BASED AFFORDABLE HOUSING: A DISCONNECT BETWEEN RESEARCH AND PRACTICE

These days it is virtually impossible for an informed American to get through the week without encountering a commentary lamenting rising social inequality and declining social mobility. Perhaps even more alarming, however, is the rise of residential segregation by income, which has been increasing for nearly

---

[4] "Overview," The MTO Fund, accessed May 22, 2019, https://www.mtofund.org/.

four decades.[5] Put simply, upper- and lower-income Americans are less and less likely to live near one another, to be friends with one another, to coach Little League together, or to send their kids to the same schools. And while the ramifications are troubling across the board, the consequences of this growing segregation are particularly disturbing at the bottom of the income distribution, as evidenced by the fact that the number of low-income Americans living in neighborhoods of concentrated poverty *more than doubled* between 2000 and 2014.[6] A robust body of social science evidence demonstrates that growing up in this kind of concentrated poverty is extremely damaging for low-income children—resulting in higher dropout rates, negative health outcomes, and diminished economic mobility.[7]

And yet, rather than combating the problem, federal housing programs have instead substantially exacerbated it. Indeed, despite the research findings, traditional place-based affordable housing models such as the Low-Income Housing Tax Credit program (LIHTC), public housing, and Project-Based Section 8 continue to provide financing for housing that is almost exclusively low-income, rather than mixed-income, and that is overwhelmingly concentrated in higher-poverty neighborhoods, trapping kids in failing schools and perpetuating the cycle of poverty. The numbers are striking. For all of the buzz in community development circles about mixed-income development, 95 percent of units in LIHTC-financed properties are low-income units,[8] and most public housing projects are essentially 100 percent low-income. The school quality findings are equally dismal. The average LIHTC development feeds into a public school ranked in the 31st percentile, in which 67 percent of students qualify for free or reduced-price lunch, and the average public housing and

---

5   Richard Fry and Paul Taylor, "The Rise of Residential Segregation by Income," Washington, DC: Pew Social & Demographic Trends (August 2012), https://www.pewresearch.org/wp-content/uploads/sites/3/2012/08/Rise-of-Residential-Income-Segregation-2012.2.pdf; Gregory Acs et al., "The Cost of Segregation: National Trends and the Case of Chicago, 1990-2010," Washington, DC: Urban Institute (March 2017), https://www.urban.org/research/publication/cost-segregation/view/full_report.

6   Elizabeth Kneebone and Natalie Holmes, "*U.S. Concentrated Poverty in the Wake of the Great Recession,*" Washington, DC: Brookings Institution (March 2016), https://www.brookings.edu/research/u-s-concentrated-poverty-in-the-wake-of-the-great-recession/.

7   George C. Galster, "The Mechanism(s) of Neighbourhood Effects: Theory, Evidence, and Policy Implications," in *Neighbourhood Effects Research: New Perspectives*, eds., Maarten van Ham, David Manley, Ludi Simpson, and Duncan Maclennan, London, UK: Springer, Dordrecht (2012): 23-56, https://link.springer.com/content/pdf/10.1007%2F978-94-007-2309-2.pdf.

8   Amy Roden, "Building a Better Low-Income Housing Tax Credit," *Tax Notes* (April 2010): 210, http://www.aei.org/wp-content/uploads/2011/10/TaxNotesRodenApril2010.pdf.

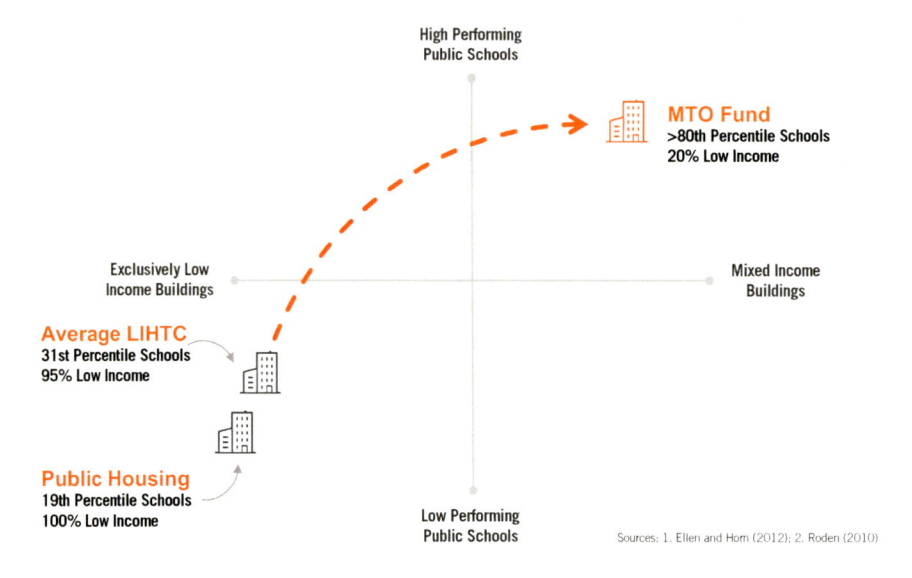

Figure 1. Housing Interventions—School Quality and Income Mix

Project-Based Section 8 sites feed into schools that rank in just the 19th and 28th percentiles, respectively (See Figure 1).[9] Perhaps unsurprisingly, given this bleak portrait, traditional place-based affordable housing models do not meaningfully enhance economic mobility for low-income children: they neither raise lifetime earnings for kids nor narrow the achievement gap in education.[10]

Fortunately, recent research demonstrates that housing interventions that provide low-income children with access to high-opportunity neighborhoods have the potential to be incredibly effective in combating inter-generational poverty and promoting social mobility—findings that have important implications for place-based approaches. In the most high-profile of these studies, a 2015 re-analysis of outcomes for children in the Moving to Opportunity (MTO) experiment, Harvard economist Raj Chetty and his colleagues found that low-income children randomly assigned to move out of

---

9   Ingrid Gould Ellen and Keren Mertens Horn, "Do Federally Assisted Households Have Access to High Performing Public Schools?" Washington, DC: Poverty & Race Research Action Council (November 2012), http://furmancenter.org/files/publications/PRRACHousingLocationSchools.pdf.

10 Robert Collinson, Ingrid Gould Ellen, and Jens Ludwig, "Low-Income Housing Policy," NBER Working Paper Series, Working Paper 21071, National Bureau of Economic Research, Cambridge, MA (April 2015), https://www.nber.org/papers/w21071.pdf.

public housing and into private rental housing in lower-poverty neighborhoods before the age of 13 had 31 percent higher incomes in early adulthood and were 32 percent more likely to attend college, with girls being three times more likely to be married and 26 percent less likely to be single mothers.[11] These headline statistics are all the more remarkable in light of the fact that MTO was a fairly weak treatment: three-fifths of families moved to neighborhoods that were still quite segregated (80 percent minority), there was no budget for mobility counseling or supportive services, and kids in the treatment group attended schools ranked in just the 19th percentile (versus 15th percentile schools for children in the control group).[12] Additional research has drawn a more explicit link between opportunity-oriented strategies and educational achievement. In one notable study analyzing low-income children randomly assigned to scattered-site public housing units located in market-rate properties in Montgomery County, Maryland, Heather Schwartz of the RAND Corporation showed that children assigned to housing in neighborhoods feeding into low-poverty schools cut the math achievement gap in half over five to seven years in elementary school.[13] And thanks to the recent publication of a new online mapping tool by Raj Chetty and his colleagues, these findings on the linkages between neighborhoods and economic mobility are now remarkably actionable for practitioners. This tool, The Opportunity Atlas, employs data on 20 million Americans born between 1978 and 1983 to show us the current income of American adults who grew up in a particular census tract, controlling for factors such as income, race, and gender.[14] In other words, we can now look at metro areas across the country and pinpoint on an extraordinarily granular level the precise neighborhoods that have historically generated the greatest economic mobility for particular demographic groups, for example, children of low-income parents.

---

11 Raj Chetty, Nathaniel Hendren, and Lawrence F. Katz, "The Effects of Exposure to Better Neighborhoods on Children: New Evidence from the Moving to Opportunity Experiment," *American Economic Review* 106, no. 4 (2016): 880, https://www.aeaweb.org/articles?id=10.1257/aer.20150572.

12 Lisa Sanbonmatsu et al., "Neighborhoods and Academic Achievement: Results from the Moving to Opportunity Experiment," Working Paper no. 11909, The National Bureau of Economic Research, Cambridge, MA (2006), https://www.nber.org/papers/w11909.pdf.

13 Heather Schwartz, "Housing Policy Is School Policy: Economically Integrative Housing Promotes Academic Success in Montgomery County, Maryland," Washington, DC: The Century Foundation (2010), https://tcf.org/assets/downloads/tcf-Schwartz.pdf.

14 "The Opportunity Atlas," The Opportunity Atlas, accessed May 22, 2019, https://www.opportunityatlas.org/.

THE CASE FOR A PRIVATE-SECTOR SOLUTION

All of this begs the question: How can we build on this research to create a pathway out of poverty for children in low-income families? Policy change would seem to be a natural starting point, but unfortunately, from a political standpoint, residential mobility and opportunity-oriented strategies historically have been a cause without a constituency, either on the right or the left.[15] Nor is substantial support likely to be forthcoming from the philanthropic sphere, as major foundations such as MacArthur and Ford are ending their active involvement as champions for housing strategies. And even if this were not the case, the endowments of even the largest foundations pale in comparison to the resources required. By process of elimination, what remains is private capital—a massive untapped resource in the affordable housing space. Simply put, this is where the money is. Investing activity in real estate investment trusts (REITs) and closed-end real estate vehicles alone tops $200 billion a year[16], dwarfing both government expenditures on place-based affordable housing programs and the $408 million[17] a year in housing-related grantmaking by foundations. Indeed, a single pension fund, the California Public Employees Retirement System, has significantly more assets under management—$340 billion—than the top 50 U.S foundations combined.[18] And, while major investors are increasingly paying lip service to so-called ESG (environmental, social, and governance) considerations, this capital is overwhelmingly returns-driven and largely impact-agnostic. The challenge, then, is as follows: to design an investment product that can compete for meaningful allocations of mainstream institutional capital, virtually none of which is currently being leveraged in a purposeful way to improve outcomes for low-income children.

---

15 This may be beginning to change, as evidenced by recent bipartisan Congressional support for a limited mobility pilot demonstration, but the politics of the issue remain fraught.

16 Preqin, *Preqin Quarterly Update*: Real estate Q1 2018, accessed June 5, 2019, https://docs.preqin.com/quarterly/re/Preqin-Quarterly-Real-Estate-Update-Q1-2018.pdf; "Historical Offerings of Securities", Nareit, accessed June 5, 2019, https://www.reit.com/sites/default/files/IndustryData/HistOff1812.pdf

17 Based on 2015 grants data, the most recent year for which full data were available, in the Foundation Center database as of May 12th, 2019. The figure includes 13,666 grants classified by the Foundation Center as being in support of "Housing Development" with a U.S.-based recipient organization, where the funder was a community foundation, independent foundation, or company-sponsored foundation. While the Foundation Center database is not comprehensive, it contains 2015 grant-level data on 63,724 foundations, including the largest and most active funders.

18 "CalPERS Investment Fund Values," CalPERS, accessed May 22, 2019, https://www.calpers.ca.gov/page/investments/asset-classes/trust-level-portfolio-management/investment-fund-values; "The Foundation Center," The Foundation Center, accessed May 22, 2019, https://foundationcenter.org/.

THE VISION: THE MTO FUND

Informed by research described above, MTO's vision is to raise a social impact real estate fund to provide low-income families across the country with access to service-enriched, mixed-income housing in high-opportunity communities with high-performing public schools, leveraging Housing Choice Vouchers and forgoing a portion of our investment management fees to cover program costs and deliver a market-rate financial return. The MTO Fund will specifically target neighborhoods that feed into top-ranked schools and that have historically provided low-income children with significant economic mobility, pursuing an opportunity acquisition strategy to circumvent "NIMBY" ("not-in-my-backyard") barriers by acquiring existing market-rate apartment buildings with private financing. Properties will be held for the long term, with 20 percent of the units voluntarily reserved for voucher families with young children. We are initially targeting foundations (for either program-related or mission-related investments), Community Reinvestment Act-motivated banks, and high-net-worth investors, but our ultimate goal is to create a scalable impact investing model with broader appeal—one that can compete head-to-head with mainstream investment managers for major allocations of institutional capital.

The MTO Fund will have a "core-plus" profile, acquiring substantially stabilized, class A properties in the top 20 metro areas in the United States and employing typical core-plus leverage (approximately 50 percent loan-to-value). We will hold properties for the long term, adopting an open-end fund structure to provide investors with ongoing liquidity while maintaining housing stability for families in the program. The Fund will target risk-adjusted market-rate returns for core-plus multifamily real estate, with an estimated 8 to 11 percent internal rate of return, net of fees. In order to achieve these returns, we will proactively manage the properties in the portfolio, upgrading common areas and gradually renovating unit interiors every five to 10 years on a staggered schedule. And unlike other models, which couple an opportunity acquisition approach with a naturally occurring affordable housing (NOAH) strategy aimed at artificially holding down rent increases, we will manage our market-rate units like a traditional operator, aggressively pushing rents to grow net operating income and increase net asset value.

In order to fill our inclusionary units, we will engage in targeted outreach to identify families who fit our selection criteria: extremely low-income families with young children who have household incomes of 30 percent of Area Median Income (AMI) or below, have qualified for a Housing Choice Voucher, and are currently living in census tracts of concentrated poverty (30 percent poverty rate or higher). Wherever possible, we will conduct this outreach by working in conjunction with established local partners, whether that be a mobility program (as in Dallas, where we are partnering with the Inclusive Communities Project), a nonprofit service provider, or a local housing authority. Families who express interest after this initial outreach will attend small-group information sessions in which they will receive a detailed description of the program. Subsequently, families will participate in one-on-one mobility counseling sessions, in which counselors will perform a life resource assessment, analyzing transportation needs, childcare arrangements, family stability, and financial health, and helping families think through the implications of an opportunity move. At the end of the recruitment process, families will enter a lottery and be placed on a waitlist.

Families who ultimately enter the program will participate in a high-touch supportive services program organized around four pillars. The first pillar is a mobility counseling program, which will feature both pre-move and post-move counseling. In the pre-move phase, the counselor will help families prepare for the move, cataloguing strengths and assets that the family can draw upon for their transition; mapping out alternative resources and arrangements that can substitute for existing support systems; facilitating introductions to school staff, service providers, and other families in the new community; and supporting families as they iron out details such as transferring their voucher between housing authority jurisdictions and enrolling school-age children in the school system. Post-move, the counselor will help families navigate the transition by tracking children's academic progress, conducting home visits, and providing customized support for parents organized around regular goal setting and goal monitoring. The second pillar is service connection. In order to keep costs to a manageable level, instead of recreating complex direct services programs our approach will be to refer families to established local service providers with particular areas of specialization, such as mental health, substance abuse, etc. The third pillar of the program focuses on community building, with the goal of helping families establish strong social networks and systems of social support in their new community. This will be a multi-pronged effort: families in the program will be paired with a similarly situated "buddy" family, small group dinners will be organized with individuals from the broader community, and the property management team will work to foster a sense of community at the building level by organizing events and other programming. Finally, the fourth pillar is crisis intervention, which builds on findings from the housing mobility literature showing that manageable crises such as job loss and health problems can quickly spiral. A key responsibility for our counselors will be proactive intervention to address potential threats to housing stability.

We believe this model has the potential to be incredibly impactful. A favorite "gotcha" question that wealth managers like to ask social entrepreneurs in the impact investing space goes something like this: "This is interesting, but could you put $100 million to work behind this strategy?" For most the answer is no, and the implication is clear: "You're a rounding error—we would be wasting our time with this." In our case, however, the answer is a resounding "yes"—many, many hundreds of times over. There are 1.8 million low-income children in families with Housing Choice Vouchers, and on average they attend bottom-quartile schools.[19] And there are *1.94 million units* in large multifamily properties located in school districts ranked in the 80th percentile or higher, based on state test scores.[20] For those of us accustomed to seeing a program officer blanch at a $2 million program-related investment request, it can be easy to lower one's sights. We need to remember that the market has the potential to aggregate capital on a massive scale, provided we play by its rules. Indeed, a *single* core-plus real estate fund, launched by private equity giant Blackstone in 2014, now has $32 billion in assets under management, with plans to reach $60 billion within two years.

THE CONSTRAINTS IMPOSED BY OUR DOUBLE-BOTTOM-LINE APPROACH

As noted above, the MTO Fund has a double-bottom-line mission: to put low-income children born into concentrated poverty on the path to college by providing them with access to service-enriched, mixed-income housing in communities with top-ranked public schools while delivering market-rate returns for mainstream institutional investors. Both facets of that mission

---

19 Barbara Sard and Douglas Rice, "Realizing the Housing Voucher Program's Potential to Enable Families to Move to Better Neighborhoods," Washington, DC: Center on Budget and Policy Priorities (January 2016), https://www.cbpp.org/sites/default/files/atoms/files/11-9-15hous.pdf; Gould Ellen and Mertens Horn, "Do Federally Assisted Households Have Access to High Performing Public Schools?"

20 MTO Fund analysis of U.S. Department of Education and U.S. Census Bureau datasets.

imposed key constraints as we were designing our model. In this section we highlight four of those constraints and describe how they influenced several foundational design decisions.

The Strategy Must Address the Challenge Posed by NIMBY Political Opposition in High-Opportunity Neighborhoods

To state the obvious, efforts to create affordable housing in high-opportunity neighborhoods typically encounter significant NIMBY opposition from residents. Ground-up development requires discretionary public approvals, thus NIMBYs effectively have veto power over new construction projects. Given that we are targeting affluent communities with top-ranked public schools, this was a particularly relevant consideration for us, and one that factored heavily into the design of our model. Our approach was to eschew development and focus exclusively on the acquisition of existing properties. An opportunity acquisition strategy of this kind effectively circumvents formalized NIMBY opposition because, unlike ground-up development, acquiring an existing property is a purely private transaction involving no public approval process of any kind.

The Property Must Be Held for an Extended Period of Time in Order for Low-Income Families to Benefit

The second major constraint in our model is the need to hold properties for an extended period of time so that low-income children have access to a high-opportunity neighborhood and its amenities throughout their childhood. Because our model contemplates renting to families with Housing Choice Vouchers in situations in which the maximum voucher subsidy does not fully cover the market rent, we cannot sell the property in the near term because a buyer would re-tenant the property with a higher-paying household. (Even if the voucher *does* fully cover the rent, this would remain a concern in most markets because source-of-income discrimination against voucher families is legal in 37 out of 50 states.[21]) Nor could we add a deed restriction tying the hands of a future buyer, because this would significantly lower the resale value of the property, resulting in a below-market return for investors.

---

21 "Expanding Choice: Practical Strategies for Building a Successful Housing Mobility Program; Appendix B: State, Local, and Federal Laws Barring Source-of-Income Discrimination," Poverty & Race Research Action Council, last modified January 30, 2019, https://www.prrac.org/pdf/AppendixB.pdf.

If we cannot sell the property in the short term, and we cannot add a deed restriction, we need a structure that will allow us to remain in control of the property while providing investors with liquidity (i.e., the ability to withdraw their capital). For our initial investments, we are building in a planned re-capitalization after five to seven years, with fresh investors buying out our initial investors at a mutually agreed-upon valuation (and with the Fund retaining its role as the investment manager).[22] Longer-term, however, our solution is to create an open-end fund structure. In this structure, properties are appraised on a quarterly basis, at which point investors have the opportunity to make withdrawals based on the current fair market value of the properties held by the fund. Managers of open-end funds are perpetually fundraising, with new investors joining an entrance queue. Withdrawal requests are then satisfied by back-filling with new investors from the queue. Thus, an open-end structure of this kind will allow us to provide our investors with ongoing liquidity while holding the property for the long term and maintaining fidelity to our social impact mission.

To the Greatest Extent Possible, the Offering Should Resemble an Investment Product That Already Exists to Facilitate Widespread Acceptance within the Industry

The asset-management industry is highly standardized, and the gatekeepers for the largest pools of capital have established a defined taxonomy for particular types of investments—replete with elaborate return benchmarks, industry standard fee guidelines, and expectations about what kinds of structures are "market" or "out of market." Whether we like it or not, any investment product cooked up in the lab that strays too far from these boxes is destined to be dead on arrival. In the world of institutional real estate investing, there are essentially four such boxes, corresponding to different points on a continuum of risk and return: core, core-plus, value-add, and opportunistic strategies. Value-add and opportunistic strategies are an imperfect fit for our model, because we would never be able to consistently deliver the high returns that they target without adopting their buy it, fix it, sell it approach—an approach precluded by our social impact mission, as detailed above. On the opposite end of the risk spectrum, core funds, which use an open-end fund structure and which make conservative, long-term investments rather than three- to five-year

---

22 Initial investments will be structured as single-asset LLCs, with the goal of contributing those properties into an eventual open-end fund at fair market value.

flips, represent a better model to emulate; however, their focus on brand-new properties stresses the economics in our model and limits the percentage of units that can be reserved for low-income families. A better fit for our approach is a slightly modified version of a core strategy, known as core-plus. Core-plus funds share many of the characteristics that make a core strategy an interesting fit for what we are trying to do—a focus on current income, a bias toward longer-term hold periods, and an open-end structure—but while they target high-quality, class A properties, those properties are slightly older than true core products, which will allow us to reserve 20 percent of the units for low-income families.

In Order to Achieve Meaningful Scale, the Investment Product Must Provide Investors with a Market-Rate Financial Return

Unfortunately, while there is an effectively infinite supply of return-driven private capital, the universe of investors willing to accept a concessionary return is vanishingly small,[23] which means that in order for an impact investing model to achieve meaningful scale it needs to deliver a market-rate return. This poses a challenge in our case, because there are two significant costs associated with our model: (1) foregone revenue on the low-income units (to the extent the Housing Choice Voucher does not fully cover the market rent), and (2) the cost of the mobility counseling and supportive services that we intend to provide. In theory, several parties could potentially cover these costs, including investors, philanthropists, the government, and the investment manager. Shifting these costs onto the investor is out, for the reasons we have just discussed. While we will likely need some start-up funding for our services program, in order for the approach to be scalable and self-sustaining, we made the conscious decision to design a model that covers these costs without ongoing philanthropic support. Of the parties remaining, we have the government picking up most of the tab, although—to return to the first of the two questions that framed this essay—we accomplish this not by seeking new subsidy but by making more effective use of a program already in place, the Housing Choice Voucher Program. Since we are targeting class A properties in high-opportunity areas, the maximum voucher subsidy will usually only cover 70-85 percent of the market rent; for families who can only contribute $350-500 a month in rent, this represents

---

23 In fact, pension funds, which represent the largest bucket of institutional capital, are expressly forbidden from making concessionary investments by U.S. Department of Labor guidelines.

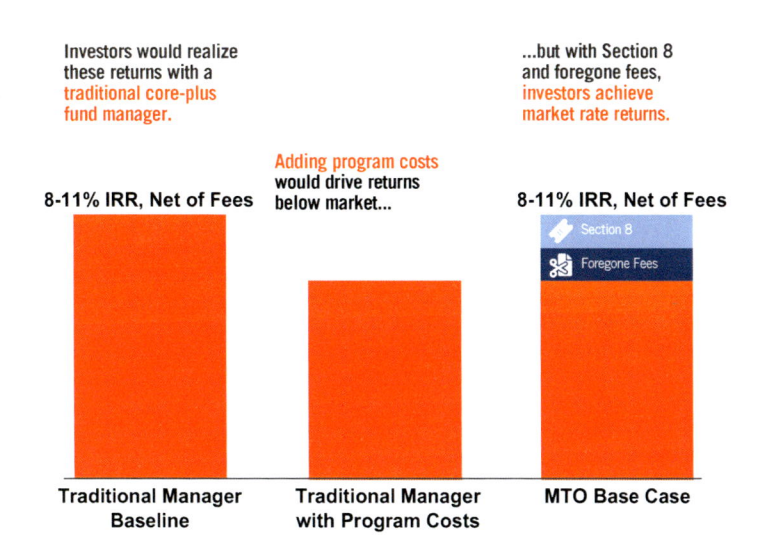

Figure 2. The MTO Fund's Financial Model

[Bar chart with three bars:]
- **Traditional Manager Baseline**: 8-11% IRR, Net of Fees. "Investors would realize these returns with a traditional core-plus fund manager."
- **Traditional Manager with Program Costs**: "Adding program costs would drive returns below market..."
- **MTO Base Case**: 8-11% IRR, Net of Fees (Section 8 + Foregone Fees). "...but with Section 8 and foregone fees, investors achieve market rate returns."

a massive subsidy and puts us within striking distance.[24] We have identified a number of return-enhancing mechanisms that can help to cover the remaining costs—from property tax abatements to tax benefits for taxable investors—but the most straightforward option, and the one we use in our base case modeling, is simply to run the Fund as a social enterprise and charge slightly lower investment management fees to investors, thereby shifting the residual cost onto the investment manager. From a returns perspective, net operating income will be lower due to the added costs, but we make up for that with savings on fees, with the math penciling to the exact same net-of-fee return that an investor could expect from investing in the identical property with a traditional impact-agnostic manager.

OPERATIONAL CHALLENGES TO OVERCOME

What Is the Highest Proportion of Low-Income Households That Can Be Included without Meaningfully Increasing Turnover Costs or Depressing Rents on the Market-Rate Units?

---

24 In markets with local payment standards or ZIP Code-based payment standards (so-called Small Area Fair Market Rents), the voucher will often fully cover the rent, even on newer class A properties in high-opportunity areas.

The single greatest operational challenge in our model will be integrating households from two distinct ends of the economic spectrum: class A renters and families with Housing Choice Vouchers (whose incomes average just 23 percent of the area median).[25] Complicating the task is the fact that market-rate renters in the affluent, high-opportunity areas we are targeting are predominantly white, while the majority of our voucher families will be racial and ethnic minorities. To put it simply, one of the key questions at the heart of our approach is: Will higher-income residents be tolerant of living alongside lower-income minority families with young children, or will they demand a discount for doing so? It is critical we take steps to ensure that the new income and racial mix does not impair the marketability and financial performance of the property, but our goal is to do so in a manner that avoids the kind of "incorporated exclusion" that has led to alienation among low-income households in other mixed-income models.[26] We are planning a multi-pronged approach on our initial investments, which includes starting out with smaller buildings, partnering with a boutique property management firm known for its high-touch approach, and leveraging the relationships that we establish through our services program. Longer term, our goal is to take property management in-house in order to develop a dedicated training program for front-line staff and to have greater touch at the property level.

How Can We Combat Social Isolation and Help to Build Community?

There are two important tasks before us from a community-building standpoint. First, how can we combat social isolation among the low-income families in the program as they seek to navigate the unfamiliar cultural milieu of a high-opportunity neighborhood? (Although, truth be told, research has shown that this may be less of a concern than one might expect.[27]) Second, more aspirationally, how can we help to foster relationships between voucher families and individuals from the broader community without making those interactions feel forced or awkward? While the specifics undoubtedly will evolve over time, the core of our approach will be proactive and sustained

---

25 "Assisted Housing: National and Local (2017 data)," U.S Department of Housing and Urban Development, accessed May 22, 2019, https://www.huduser.gov/portal/datasets/assthsg.html.

26 Robert J. Chaskin and Mark L. Joseph, *Integrating the Inner City: The Promise and Perils of Mixed-Income Public Housing Transformation*, Chicago, IL: University of Chicago Press (2015): 159.

27 Xavier de Souza Briggs, Susan J. Popkin, and Jon Goering, *Moving to Opportunity: The Story of an American Experiment to Fight Ghetto Poverty*, New York, NY: Oxford University Press (2010): 254.

attention to community building, with the goal being to help families establish strong social networks and systems of social support in their new building and community. Families will be paired with a similarly situated "buddy" family in the program; small group dinners with members of the broader community will be organized to create space for mutually beneficial relationships that bridge lines of class and race; and the property management team will work to create community at the building level by organizing events and other programming.

How Can We Help Low-Income Families Adapt to the Loss of the Support Systems They Relied on in Their Old Neighborhood?

Moving can be a disruptive experience for any family, and for a low-income family an opportunity move can be especially so, because low-income families are more heavily reliant on informal arrangements for basic needs such as transportation and childcare. Admittedly, dealing with this challenge will be a continual learning process for us over the next several years, but in an attempt to set ourselves up for success our model incorporates an extremely extensive post-move mobility counseling program, with a far higher-touch staffing model than even the most successful housing mobility programs and with ongoing support for families throughout their tenure in the program.

IMPLICATIONS FOR ACTION

Implications for Policy

- Research consistently demonstrates that providing low-income families with access to housing in high-opportunity neighborhoods generates substantial savings for governments at all levels, in the form of higher tax revenue, lower healthcare costs, and reduced expenditures on everything from prisons to social services.[28] To encourage impact investors and developers to provide affordable housing options in these areas, states and local governments should consider implementing a pay-for-success approach, providing a small monetary reward for each year that a low-income child is housed in a high-opportunity neighborhood. Pay-for-success contracts have often been criticized for their bespoke nature and high transaction costs, but

---

28 Dan Rinzler et al., "Leveraging the Power of Place: Using Pay for Success to Support Housing Mobility, working paper 2015-04," San Francisco: Federal Reserve Bank of San Francisco (2015), https://www.pr-rac.org/pdf/LeveragingThePowerOfPlace2015.pdf; Chetty, Hendren, and Katz, "The Effects of Exposure to Better Neighborhoods on Children: New Evidence from the Moving to Opportunity Experiment."

this situation presents an opportunity for a state or municipality to craft a far more streamlined and scalable model—one that is open to all property owners within the jurisdiction and is predicated on a pre-defined payment structure based on the magnitude of the savings identified by researchers. The end result would be a win-win for all involved: investors would receive a modest degree of financial compensation for providing affordable housing in hard-to-access opportunity areas[29]; low-income children in the families touched by the program would enjoy dramatically enhanced economic mobility; and because the savings generated would be greater than the cost of the pay-for-success payments, the program would have no net cost associated with it and, in fact, would save the government money.

- Existing policy incentives in the affordable housing space are geared almost exclusively toward the LIHTC and Project-Based Section 8 programs and should be expanded to support the efforts of social entrepreneurs seeking to leverage mainstream private capital through acquisition-based strategies. For example, eligibility for real estate tax abatement programs and low-cost affordable housing-oriented debt products typically requires onerous 30- to 50-year deed restrictions, which are unworkable when acquiring a market rate property. However, with some additional flexibility, these programs could easily be modified to accommodate a more market-driven approach while still maintaining reasonable protections to safeguard their underlying social objectives.

- While the availability of Housing Choice Vouchers provides a key boost to the feasibility of our model, the voucher program has several significant and well-known flaws. Reforms aimed at addressing some of these shortcomings—for example, more widespread adoption of Small Area Fair Market Rents and the passage of source-of-income protection laws—could attract other groups to help take the model to scale and could do as much to advance the goals of income and racial integration and equality of opportunity as any proposal outlined in this volume.

- Given the overall demographic make-up of the voucher population in our target markets, an extremely high proportion of the children in our program

---

29 The magnitude of the financial incentive here would not need to be large. Even if the pay-for-success payments enhanced the internal rate of return by 50 basis points (0.50 percent), it would substantially increase the universe of financially feasible projects, allow for deeper affordability targets, and alter the behavior and site selection of impact-agnostic investors and developers.

are likely to be racial minorities[30]; and as such, are likely to encounter subtle forms of subconscious racial bias (and potentially incidents of overt racism) that could blunt the positive impact of the move or even impel their parents to leave the neighborhood altogether. Social science indicates that these biases can be manifested in a variety of forms: on the part of teachers, who tend to have lower expectations for minority students, which become a self-fulfilling prophecy[31]; on the part of school administrators, who tend to give black children more severe discipline than their peers for similar infractions[32]; and on the part of local law enforcement and community members at large, with research showing that minority children report feeling less safe in white neighborhoods due to the increased scrutiny that they often receive.[33] Therefore, housing-focused policies are necessary but not sufficient. Unless we take steps to address these subconscious biases, the opportunity and economic mobility that the children in our program enjoy will remain, at least in some measure, constrained.

Implications for Research and Evaluation

- Through a research partnership with the Urban Institute and the National Initiative on Mixed-Income Communities, the MTO Fund's pilot investments will represent the first dedicated effort to measure the effect of a mixed-income or inclusionary housing model on rents and turnover among market rate renters. Refining our understanding of those impacts will be critical for assessing the financial viability of various place-based mixed-income models.

- Unlike inclusionary zoning models, which reserve affordable units for families at higher levels of area median income (only 2 percent of such

---

30 As an example, in Dallas, one of our initial target markets, 94 percent of individuals in households with Housing Choice Vouchers are racial or ethnic minorities. The corresponding figure at the national level is 69 percent. "Assisted Housing: National and Local (2018 data)," U.S Department of Housing and Urban Development, accessed May 22, 2019, https://www.huduser.gov/portal/datasets/assthsg.html.

31 Seth Gershenson and Nicholas Papageorge, "The Power of Teacher Expectations," *Education Next* 18, no. 1 (2018): 66.

32 Nathan Barrett et al., "Discipline Disparities and Discrimination in Schools," *Brown Center Chalkboard (blog)*, Brookings Institution (November 20, 2017), https://www.brookings.edu/blog/brown-center-chalkboard/2017/11/20/discipline-disparities-and-discrimination-in-schools/.

33 Sandra E. Garcia, "Black Boys Feel Less Safe in White Neighborhoods, Study Shows," *New York Times* (August 18, 2018) www.nytimes.com/2018/08/14/us/black-boys-white-neighborhoods-fear.html.

programs target households below 50 percent of AMI[34]), the MTO Fund will seek to integrate extremely low-income families with Housing Choice Vouchers into otherwise market-rate, class A properties. This research will help to inform practitioners and policymakers about the social and financial implications associated with incorporating deep affordability targets into market rate properties—be it through acquisition, tax credit financed mixed-income development, or more ambitious forms of inclusionary zoning.

Implications for Development and Investment

This model represents a call to action to impact investors to set a higher bar for target neighborhood selection, income mix, and attention to a more comprehensive array of supports.

- Given that the acquisition of an existing property circumvents the discretionary public approval process (and the attendant NIMBY veto) associated with new construction, opportunity acquisition models of this kind represent an important alternative for impact investors seeking to equalize access to high-opportunity neighborhoods.

- Asset managers frequently lament the lack of impact-oriented investment opportunities capable of absorbing significant allocations of capital. An opportunity acquisition strategy along the lines described here has the potential to help fill this gap in the market. Indeed, as noted above, there are 1.8 million children in families with Housing Choice Vouchers, and 1.94 million *units* in large multifamily properties located in top-quintile public school districts, so the opportunity to achieve impact at scale and to put significant capital to work is substantial.[35] However, the very quality that makes real estate such a compelling opportunity in this regard—its inherent capital intensiveness—also makes it challenging to finance pilot-stage efforts aimed at developing promising new concepts into investable opportunities. Unfortunately, in the nascent impact investing ecosystem there is currently a dearth of mission-driven institutional investors with the capacity and motivation to invest in early-stage efforts to test novel supply-side housing

---

34 Brian Stromberg and Lisa Sturtevant, "What Makes Inclusionary Zoning Happen?" (2016), http://landuselaw.wustl.edu/Articles/Inclusionary%20Zoning%20Rept%202016.pdf.

35 Barbara Sard and Douglas Rice, *Realizing the Housing Voucher Program's Potential to Enable Families to Move to Better Neighborhoods*.

strategies. Foundations, which often devote grant dollars to "field-building" efforts in the impact investing space, should consider that charge more broadly when it comes to housing. As noted above, it is not that foundations need—or have the financial capacity—to *directly* address the nation's housing challenges through their housing investments; rather, they should focus on seeding promising new strategies that have the potential to yield substantial downstream impact but would otherwise struggle to attract pilot funding.

Implications for Residents and Community Members

- Research clearly shows that providing low-income children with access to mixed-income housing in high-opportunity neighborhoods has life-changing benefits. In making these moves, however, low-income families in the program will often be stepping significantly outside of their comfort zone. Maximizing the benefits of the program will require support, advocacy, and self-reflection on the part of neighbors in the building and the broader community to ensure that lower-income residents feel welcomed and included as full and valued participants in the life of the community. For their part, the low-income households will need to draw upon resilience and open-mindedness and demonstrate some willingness to adapt to the norms and expectations of the building and community.

■ ■ ■

HANS BUDER *is the founder of the Moving to Opportunity Fund, prior to dedicating himself to the Fund full time, Buder was a project manager at McCormack Baron Salazar, his responsibilities included underwriting new tax credit developments across the country and helping to manage the transformation of the Alice Griffith public housing project in San Francisco into a mixed-income community through the HUD Choice Neighborhoods Program. Prior to his work there, Buder served as Associate Director of Acquisitions at Long Wharf Capital, a Boston-based real estate private equity firm (and the former private real estate arm of Fidelity Investments), where he closed on real estate acquisitions with a total capitalization in excess of $350 million. Buder holds an MBA from the Stanford Graduate School of Business, a Masters in Public Administration from the Harvard Kennedy School of Government, and a Bachelor of Arts from Duke University.*

4
WHO HAS A SAY AND WHO BENEFITS?

Activating Community Change: Voice, Power and Influence

These three essays seek to lift up the role community members play in the community change process, highlighting how their successful participation can lead to the preservation and creation of mixed-income communities.

In "Community Building and Neighborhood Associations: Strategies for Greater Mixed-Income Inclusion," in Seattle's HOPE VI Neighborhoods, Stephanie Van Dyke and Ellen Kissman present an in-depth review of the evolution of the Seattle Housing Authority's approach to mixed-income community engagement. The Seattle Housing Authority (SHA) has taken a strategic approach to mixed-income inclusion throughout its 25-year history of redeveloping public housing through the federal HOPE VI program. SHA has created staff positions for "community builders" who are dedicated to weaving connections among residents, and has reimagined the roles of neighborhood associations, going beyond conventional purposes to attempt to leverage them as unifiers that bring homeowners and renters together. The authors describe the mixed-income communities where these strategies have helped to forge common ground among residents, and created environments where community members have opportunities to contribute meaningfully to their neighborhoods. The authors distill SHA's inclusion strategy, writing, "Making a mixed-income community requires more than taking some acres of land, building...housing for people at different income levels, and leaving the rest to chance. To lay the groundwork for resilient, safe, welcoming communities, developers of mixed-income communities should strive to create the conditions for people to move outside the comfort zones of their class, culture, or race, and find common ground, mutual respect, and trust."

In "Weinland Park, Columbus, Ohio: Building Community as a Neighborhood Transitions to Mixed-Income," Kip Holley, Matthew Martin, and Stephen Sterrett document the achievements of the Weinland Park Collaborative (WPC), a partnership of public, non-profit, and private entities that includes The Ohio State University. They describe how property acquisition, renovation, and construction in Weinland Park catalyzed the area's transformation from the neighborhood with the city's highest violent crime rate and highest concentration of project-based Section 8 housing into a mixed-income, mixed-race neighborhood. The essay describes how a household survey conducted by Ohio State's Kirwan Institute for the Study of Race and Ethnicity helped identify five demographically distinct resident clusters. Analysis of resident perspectives by cluster revealed a nuanced understanding of different attitudes and perceptions among sub-groups of residents who share common life experiences. Using maps that portray areas of the neighborhood perceived as safe and unsafe by survey respondents, Kirwan researchers generated provocative insights about ways in which neighborhood perceptions were dramatically different by race and household make-up. The essay describes the difficult conversations the survey results provoked among residents and presents implications for effective mixed-income community building.

Ralph Rosado's essay, "The Role of Community Benefits Agreements in Increasing Equity and Inclusion" examines the benefit and necessity of active community voice and participation in holding developers accountable, demonstrating the immense power that communities hold and the importance of ensuring community members are involved throughout the development process. Rosado presents a case comparison of pathways taken in Los Angeles and New York to demonstrate the complex political stories behind community benefits agreements, and the resulting necessity of transparency in order to ensure continued housing affordability and remain true to a community's unique needs and values.

COMMUNITY BUILDING AND NEIGHBORHOOD ASSOCIATIONS: STRATEGIES FOR GREATER MIXED-INCOME INCLUSION IN SEATTLE'S HOPE VI NEIGHBORHOODS

Stephanie Van Dyke
Seattle Housing Authority

Ellen Kissman
Consultant

From 1997 to the present, under the auspices of the federal HOPE VI program, Seattle Housing Authority (SHA) has transformed three large public housing communities, New Holly, Rainier Vista and High Point, from concentrated public housing to mixed-income communities. HOPE VI was based in the theory that people with low incomes would be more likely to thrive when they could live in safe, well-designed, well-managed neighborhoods with access to good schools, parks, community organizations, stores, jobs, transportation options, social services, and neighbors with a wide range of incomes. As other authors in this volume have noted, recent research by Raj Chetty and his colleagues has been particularly influential in demonstrating the profound positive impact on low-income children who are able to grow up in communities of opportunity.

SHA's experience over the last 20-plus years indicates that the HOPE VI theory of change has merit, as long as there is continuing attention to sustaining all the elements that make strong communities. Making a mixed-income *community* requires more than taking some acres of land, building a lot of housing for people at different income levels, and leaving the rest to chance.

To lay the groundwork for resilient, safe, welcoming communities, developers of mixed-income communities should strive to create the conditions for people to move outside the comfort zones of their class, culture, or race, and find common ground, mutual respect, and trust. Seattle Housing Authority has tested a variety of approaches and evolved new practices along the way to that end. In this essay, we explore some of those approaches and lessons learned, focusing on the role of two elements of ongoing organizational infrastructure: neighborhood associations and dedicated staff community builders.[1]

In the early planning of these neighborhood transformations, SHA anticipated a number of significant challenges including attracting and retaining middle-income neighbors; finding common ground for connection and engagement across class, culture, race, and language differences; and empowering neighbors to advocate for themselves to shape their neighborhood's identity. As the communities came into being, SHA began to better understand other challenges including:

- Sustaining effective social services for vulnerable families and, in particular, strong, engaging, positive activities for youth;
- Cultivating and maintaining shared responsibility for keeping public spaces—parks, pathways, alleys, community gathering spots—safe and welcoming for all;
- Sustaining the commitment to community among residents over time as the first residents move away and new people move in; and
- Ensuring that every entity that has a role in managing the community buys into a shared vision of community and makes decisions in accordance with that vision.

As described below, over time SHA developed new structures and practices to address these challenges.

---

[1] This essay was informed by interviews with a small group of people who lived and shaped the transformation of these communities in different ways. The authors extend our gratitude to George Nemeth and Carol Wellenberger of SHA's development and asset management departments; Willard Brown, former senior property manager of New Holly, Rainier Vista, and High Point; Tom Phillips, former manager of the High Point redevelopment; Joy Bryngelson, former community builder at New Holly and Yesler Terrace; Heather Hutchison, former HOA administrator at High Point; Terry Hirata, current High Point senior property manager; Asmeret Habte, current High Point community builder; Jeniffer Calleja, current Rainier Vista community builder; Sakina Hussain, current Rainier Vista homeowner; and Ed Frazier, current Rainier Vista renter.

THE SHA STRATEGY FOR TRANSFORMING ENCLAVES OF POVERTY INTO THRIVING NEIGHBORHOODS

The federal HOPE VI grant program began in the early 1990s to transform failing public housing communities. The program was intended to replace worn-out, poorly designed, and poorly constructed public housing and reconnect these isolated, often high-crime enclaves of poverty with the surrounding community, physically and socially. Seattle Housing Authority seized the opportunity HOPE VI brought to remake three of its four World War II-era garden communities—Holly Park, Rainier Vista, and High Point—from the ground up.[2] In concert with government agencies, residents, and other partners, SHA envisioned and created plans for equitable, resilient, and sustainable mixed-income neighborhoods woven back into the fabric of the city.

These efforts directly affected 300 acres within the City of Seattle—the largest in-fill developments Seattle had seen in decades. Over a period of about 25 years, 2,068 extremely low-income homes have been replaced, and 1,346 low-income homes and 1,491 market-rate homes have been added. New parks, libraries, medical clinics, and other community facilities have been built. While each community has unique features, all of the redevelopments have the following inter-related elements in common.

Inclusive, Equitable Development

Features include:

- Full replacement of the public housing stock affordable to households with incomes below 30 percent of area median income; any units that were not replaced on site were replaced elsewhere within the city limits;
- The addition of rental housing affordable to households with incomes at 50, 60, and 80 percent of area median income, along with market-rate and affordable homeownership;
- New housing with design features and supportive services customized for seniors;

---

[2] In 2010 HOPE VI was replaced by the Choice Neighborhoods Initiative, which broadened the redevelopment focus to the entire neighborhood in which a public housing was located and bolstered investments in education, workforce development, and supportive services. SHA is transforming its fourth and last World War II-era community, Yesler Terrace, with two federal implementation grants totaling $30 million under the Choice Neighborhoods Initiative.

	NEW HOLLY	RAINIER VISTA	HIGH POINT
Acres	102	67	120
Redevelopment timeline	1997-2006	1999-2016	2000-2010
Location in Seattle	Rainier Valley	Rainier Valley	West Seattle
Units pre-redevelopment (100% public housing)	871	481	716
Units post-redevelopment	**1414**	**895**	**1529**
Rental units			
Public housing	400	251	350
Affordable (low-income)	288	226	250
Any income level	16	48	104
Senior units (rental)			
Low-income, independent living	80	78	75
Low-income, assisted living	100		
Any income, assisted living	54		156
For people with disabilities		22	
For sale units			
Income-qualified	112	59	56
Any income level	364	211	538

Figure 1: By The Numbers: Hope VI Redevelopment in Seattle

- Housing choices for residents of the community prior to redevelopment, including the right to stay in or return to the rebuilt community;
- Comprehensive attention to the supportive-service needs of low-income residents of the community before, during, and beyond the redevelopment;
- Ongoing support for low-income residents to achieve their educational and economic goals and to eliminate barriers to their participation in community activities and governance; and
- Authentic community engagement in planning and design, involving residents of the public housing community and of the surrounding neighborhood.

People-Centered Design

Priorities include:

- Overcoming stigma of "the projects" with housing for people with a wide range of incomes spread throughout the community, designed so that the low-income housing is not readily distinguishable from the rest of the housing stock and so people on different points on the economic spectrum, living side by side, have informal opportunities to meet and get to know each other as neighbors;

- Connecting the street grid to that of the surrounding neighborhood and making the streets function for pedestrians, bikes, and public transit as well as cars;

- Increasing density to match the surrounding neighborhood, which leveraged the value of the land to help fund the building of affordable housing and community facilities;

- Health-focused building design, including state-of-the-art environmental sustainability and green building;

- Easily accessible, well-designed, safe open spaces: each neighborhood has several new public parks, including community gardens, small pocket parks, and a large central park accessible to all; and

- Community gathering spaces and facilities of various scales and types designed to welcome the neighborhood at large, including new libraries, medical clinics, community centers, and formal and informal gathering spaces, built in partnership with local government or nonprofit institutions.

Organizational Infrastructure

Examples include:

- Community builders: full-time SHA staff members who help bring neighbors together. Community builders have a broad mandate to empower neighbors to engage with each other, foster mutual understanding and support, and participate in community governance;

- Homeowners associations to integrate homeowners into the new community, in addition to traditional HOA functions such as insuring and maintaining properties; and

- Mechanisms for managing and maintaining open spaces. These mechanisms evolved over time as SHA grew to understand the impact open-space management has on operating costs and how the community functions. We look more deeply at this feature below.

WHO LIVES IN THESE COMMUNITIES? FOSTERING COMMUNITY WITHIN A HIGHLY DIVERSE POPULATION

New Holly, Rainier Vista, and High Point neighbors—before and after redevelopment—have been exceptionally diverse in language, race, culture, religion, ability, age, gender, and family composition. The addition of units at several affordability levels introduces diversity in income, and the introduction of homeownership brings diversity in tenure. Low-income households usually are renters, although there are some lower-income homeowners through Habitat for Humanity-type programs.

Residents, particularly the residents of low-income housing, come from around the world, predominantly East Africa and Southeast Asia. They often have limited English proficiency. Many lack formal education in their native language. They may have been here for a generation, or have arrived within the last few years. They bring their religious and cultural traditions and ways of daily life, which can be profoundly different from each other and from the dominant culture in the United States. Often their journey to the United States was protracted, difficult, and filled with loss and trauma that has left lasting scars.

Many of the low-income families have children. Some families have six or more children, as is normal in their culture. As a result, these communities are home to a great many children and youth. Helping young people connect across cultures and engage in positive activities is, of necessity, a community-building priority. Many others are elders or people with disabilities with varying levels of supportive-service needs to remain independent and active.

Many low-income residents, whether U.S. or foreign-born, are employed, sometimes at more than one job; go to school or employment training programs; and frequently demonstrate remarkable perseverance in overcoming barriers to achieve a measure of economic stability.

The neighbors in the market-rate homes also are a mix of races, ethnicities, and countries of origin. They tend to be of working age or newly retired and of sufficient means to afford expensive market-rate housing in Seattle. Some have or are planning to have children. Some choose to live in these communities because of the diversity and their mixed-income nature; others like the location, design, or price point.

THE SHA APPROACH TO COMMUNITY BUILDING

SHA chose to invest in community building as an essential element of redevelopment projects. Without deliberate attention to fostering positive neighborhood interactions among such a diverse population, SHA was concerned that the new communities would not live up to their potential as places where low-income residents would find the quality of life and opportunities that were not available in the old public housing. SHA's approach to community building is by necessity multi-faceted, organic, and—to the degree resources permit—comprehensive. One goal is to nurture integration within each neighborhood across lines of tenure (renter/homeowner), income, race, ethnicity, and culture.

Over time, SHA learned the value of having organizational infrastructure to support community building. Organizational infrastructure differs in each community, reflecting lessons learned over time, as described below. All of the approaches SHA has put in place—including SHA staff, other on-site entities managing property (e.g., senior housing buildings), and on-site programmatic or social services—work best when they are well-coordinated with each other. The organizational infrastructure always includes a community builder.

Community Builders

In each redevelopment, SHA employs a community builder charged with working to build positive relations among neighbors before, during, and after the physical transformation of the site. The community builder's daily tasks can include encouraging people to volunteer for or come to events, coordinating one-time events, organizing ongoing "affinity groups" around a topic or issue that many people share (e.g., traffic), promoting neighborhood leadership development, responding to a community crisis (e.g., a shooting), conferring with property management or the Community Police Team officer about neighborhood issues, and getting accurate and timely information out about opportunities, events or incidents through multiple channels in multiple languages.

A significant portion of the community builder's time is straightforward volunteer management—finding people who want to help out in various ways, linking them up to work that needs to be done, and keeping them interested and engaged in the life and issues of the community. As Sakina Hussain, a homeowner at Rainier Vista, notes, "having the position of a community builder, a person who can champion things, organize events, send email blasts and the like, is essential. Most of the work is volunteer powered, so there needs to be one person whose job it is to hold it all together."

Homeowners Associations

Each community has one or more homeowners association(s), chartered under Washington State laws and regulations. SHA set up the HOAs to:

- Establish mechanisms for a high standard of property maintenance and control over the appearance of properties for the long term. Each HOA has instituted design standards and guidelines;

- Limit the conversion of homeownership units to rentals;

- Give homeowners a stake in management and maintenance of the community's public spaces in order to spread the cost and responsibility over the entire community, allowing SHA to keep its limited resources focused primarily on the low-income housing and its residents; and

- Unify the community through joint contracts between SHA and the HOA for landscaping and some building maintenance functions, such as window washing or roof and gutter cleaning.

In general, under state charters HOA roles and responsibilities do not include community building. SHA added engagement with SHA and other entities in the community to the legally required minimum mandate of HOAs in order to use them as part of the infrastructure for building community. The HOAs give homeowners a collective voice with other residents, property owners, and SHA in community-wide issues, and they provide a channel for homeowners to work together with all neighborhood residents on shared projects and issues.

With intention, an HOA can be an effective vehicle for informing new homeowners about their community. When SHA deliberately used the HOAs to inform homeowners about the mixed-income nature and diversity of the community from the very start, homeowners became (and remain) more interested and involved in community building with their renter neighbors.

New Holly was SHA's first mixed-income redevelopment and the first in which the agency had set up an HOA. As former SHA Association Liaison Carol Wellenberger noted, "the learning curve was steep." Successful home sales at New Holly were proof-of-concept that middle-income people would buy into places that used to be stigmatized as "the projects." This in itself was a significant accomplishment, not to be taken for granted. But it was only after some time that SHA also recognized the opportunity that HOAs represented to help bring together homeowners and renters.

Willard Brown, former senior manager of New Holly, Rainier Vista, and High Point during each community's redevelopment, highlighted the importance of using HOAs for community building through shared responsibility for maintenance. At Rainier Vista, this took the form of long-term leases of three small parks to the HOA, while SHA retained responsibility for the large Central Park and several other open spaces. "SHA worked closely with the HOA to prepare them," Brown explained. "Then, the HOA stepped up, raised some funds, and installed playground equipment. We jointly developed a Good Neighbor Agreement to ensure that the parks would be open to all. This instilled in the HOA the sense that their community included Rainier Vista renters, too."

With support from their community builder, renters and homeowners in the first redevelopment phase (called New Rainier Vista) formed a Multicultural Community Committee to hold cross-cultural events, potlucks, and other activities to bring people together. SHA worked with realtors to market the new neighborhood as a multicultural community. The HOA included information about the Multicultural Committee (now called the Community Building Committee) in its welcome materials for new neighbors. The community as a whole has adopted "multicultural community" as their community identity.

The effects of this early preparation can still be felt. For example, Sakina Hussain, the Rainier Vista homeowner and an active member of both the HOA and the Community Building Committee, has supported cross-cultural engagement using her grant-writing skills:

> *In 2017, I wrote a grant for the Vietnamese Senior Group, who are mostly renters, to the City of Seattle Department of Neighborhoods to pay for extra food and bring in some Lion Dancers for a Tet celebration. We got the grant. The celebration was held on a*

weekend day and widely publicized. More people from different cultural and ethnic backgrounds came than in previous years.

Rainier Vista is bisected by a major thoroughfare running north-south through the community. Because home construction on Rainier Vista's east side stopped for several years after the Great Recession, SHA decided to create two HOAs. This allowed the homeowners on the west side to assume control of their HOA in a timely fashion. A second HOA was established for Rainier Vista East several years later. A consequence of this decision is that the scale of each organization is small, fostering participation among more homeowners. Another result is that the homeowners, especially those on the east side, tend to focus on their side of the neighborhood, making community building for the whole community a bit more challenging.

At High Point, SHA faced its most difficult marketing challenge to bring in homeowners, and the HOA approach reflects that situation. New Holly and Rainier Vista are located in Seattle's Rainier Valley, the most diverse area of the city. Buyers in these neighborhoods already expect to live among a wide variety of people. In contrast, High Point is located in the predominantly White area of West Seattle. This public housing development historically had the deepest stigma of the three sites, with a long-standing reputation as a crime hotspot. Instead of focusing on diversity and multi-culturalism, High Point was primarily marketed to homeowners as a green community. In addition to an HOA, two other entities were created at High Point as organizational infrastructure evolved to sustain the community. We discuss these entities next.

HIGH POINT INNOVATIONS

Infrastructure innovations at High Point included an Open Space Association and a Neighborhood Association.

High Point Open Space Association

For New Holly, SHA's first redevelopment, SHA assumed management and maintenance responsibility for all the open spaces built on SHA land, and even for an adjacent City of Seattle Parks Department recreational field. This proved expensive and unsustainable. At New Rainier Vista, SHA took a first step toward sharing this cost with other property owners in the community by dividing ownership responsibility for the open spaces with the HOA. At

Rainier Vista East, SHA took a slightly different approach, retaining ownership of all the common area parks but entering into a cost-sharing agreement with the HOA for maintenance of all the common areas. This ensured a consistent standard of maintenance for all the open spaces and the potential for some economies of scale in maintenance resources.

At High Point, open space management required a fundamentally different approach. The area is in an environmentally sensitive watershed of Longfellow Creek, an urban salmon spawning stream undergoing restoration. The site's landscape was carefully designed with an integrated system to manage storm water runoff—a big part of High Point's green identity. The system includes a three-acre human-made pond for storm water management, storm water swales along streets and sidewalks, porous pavement, many mature trees, and a generous amount of land (12.5 acres, about 10 percent of the site) allocated to parks, open spaces, and community gardens of various sizes located throughout the neighborhood.

According to Tom Phillips, former High Point redevelopment manager, "When we started to plan for managing the community, we realized that High Point's unique green features called for launching an association that would have the resources and authority to make the 120-acre site look really good."[3] Beyond maintaining an attractive appearance, which was important for home sales, was a commitment to maintaining these features in an organic way with low environmental impact. This required careful and ongoing attention to *how* the open spaces are managed, and, therefore, additional oversight.

SHA created a formal structure for sharing and sustaining this vision, as well as spreading the responsibility and cost for common-area upkeep among all property owners in the neighborhood. Every unit on site is assessed the same amount; SHA pays dues for the units it manages, as do the other property owners. The Open Space Association focuses on the details of property maintenance and budgets. Decision-making authority for the Open Space Association is vested in a volunteer board of directors consisting of three homeowner representatives appointed by the HOA, three SHA representatives, and one representative for the other on-site property owners. Staff support for the Open Space Association is contracted out to a firm that also manages the

---

[3] Tom J. Phillips, *High Point: The Inside Story of Seattle's First Green Mixed-Income Neighborhood*, (Splashblock Publishing, 2013).

HOA. Compared to all the other approaches, this approach puts SHA and the homeowners on the most equal footing.

High Point Neighborhood Association

The intent of the Neighborhood Association was "to officially create an organization that would work to break down the class, income, and ethnic barriers we anticipated would be present in the new community," Phillips said. "Our idea was that this entity would focus on building social networks, including through events such as community potlucks, clubs for mutually shared interests, block parties, and so on."[4] This association's governing board was to be made up of a 50/50 mix of homeowners and renters elected by residents, though that mix was never achieved in practice. (Finding people, especially renters, who wanted to participate in an ongoing committee proved too difficult; it was easier to find people to volunteer for specific events or short-term tasks.)

The Neighborhood Association as a stand-alone entity was short-lived. Funding for the Neighborhood Association initially came from a small fee captured on each property sale, and when the state legislature allowed authority to levy the fee to expire, a replacement revenue source had to be found. In addition, the Neighborhood Association on its own could not find affordable insurance coverage for community events. For these practical reasons, the Open Space Association's annual dues were increased slightly to make up the lost revenue and the Neighborhood Association evolved into a standing committee of the Open Space Association. This also solved the insurance problem, as the Open Space Association could add event coverage to its policy at minimal cost.

COMMUNITY-BUILDING CHALLENGES AND SOLUTIONS

Community building is a complex, organic, ever-changing process, and organizational infrastructure alone—while necessary—is not sufficient to guarantee that redeveloped public housing projects will become true communities. This section explores how having community builders and the various associations has addressed key challenges.

Meeting and Managing Homeowner Expectations in Mixed-Tenure Communities

People who buy homes in communities with HOAs understand that they

---

4   Phillips, High Point.

are also agreeing to a set of rules that govern what they can do with their properties, particularly building exteriors and yards. One of the advantages of living in a community with an HOA is the implied promise that these rules will help the community retain its character and value over time. In SHA's HOPE VI communities, SHA is also a member of the HOA, responsible for ensuring that its properties meet HOA rules. This has several important implications, such as:

- Property maintenance: Homeowners expect that SHA-maintained rental properties and public spaces will always look as good as the homeowner's properties. This is a higher standard of maintenance than was typically achieved in 100 percent public housing communities, given tight public housing funds. Over time, SHA has gotten used to the neighborly oversight and has become better at planning for the additional workload and expense, but it remains a challenge.

- Property (and people) management: SHA property managers are responsible for ensuring that tenants abide by both SHA and HOA rules for how to use porches and yards. Prior to redevelopment, for example, typically a few residents would use their outdoor spaces for long-term storage. Even though this was technically not permitted, property managers often would choose to prioritize other lease enforcement issues and let this infringement go. With homeowner vigilance in redeveloped communities and underlying HOA rules, as well as lease terms, property managers have to work with residents to stop this practice. This has opened up several issues. For example, in some of the cultures represented in the community, it is inappropriate to keep certain items (such as shoes) in the home; and some large families living in small houses have struggled to find room for all of their belongings inside. So, some exceptions for outside storage have had to be made.

Promoting Stronger Neighboring

In addition to the interpersonal dynamics one might find in any neighborhood, residents of mixed-income communities need to negotiate a wide variety of worldviews and cultural expectations about what constitutes acceptable behavior in the neighborhood's public spaces. Having organizational infrastructure in place for residents to come together, explore their differences, and arrive at common understanding is one way for a community to deal with the tensions that can arise. For example, in the early days of the Rainier Vista East HOA, several homeowners raised concerns with the HOA board that a multiracial group of teens using the playgrounds wasn't adequately supervised.

Community-Building Infrastructure Pays Off When Difficult Things Happen

A shooting occurred in Rainier Vista just before Community Builder Jen Calleja started her job, followed by widespread vocal concerns about safety and finger-pointing about who was to blame. The tragic event and its chaotic aftermath had the potential to tear the community apart. Jen spent much of her energy in the months that followed working to rebuild trust among homeowners, renters, and SHA. She also had to work on rebuilding trust among young people, parents, and police.

Calleja began by listening to the youth to hear what they needed to avoid getting caught up in violence. Then she engaged the mothers of teens targeted by neighbors and the police as the source of the problem, and convened elders to provide a way for them to air their concerns.

Several changes were made as a result:

- SHA hired a youth engagement specialist who works at Rainier Vista and New Holly to provide ongoing capacity for high-quality youth programming.
- Residents came together to deal with one contributing factor—cars speeding around the Central Park. They developed physical changes to the street grid, which interrupted the circle that intruders were driving around. This effort required residents to work with the City of Seattle to close off part of a street with bollards and speed bumps. Residents also raised funds to create a pavement-to-park project on that section of road, which included a pavement mural painted by neighborhood youth. This project was so successful, and participants had so much fun, that two more mural projects were planned.
- Property management did its part with better lease enforcement of families with gang-involved members who were opening the door to the community for gang activity.

The 30 or so homeowners at that meeting had a long discussion about who these teens were (i.e., Rainier Vista residents or from elsewhere), whether what they were doing was actually inappropriate or causing anyone or any property harm, and the harm that might come to the teens if the police were called. In the end, the homeowners left with a deeper understanding of what it means to live in a multicultural community and encouragement to get to know their neighborhood teens and their parents so that they would feel comfortable interacting with them as neighbors. (As recalled by Ellen Kissman during her time as President of the RVE HOA.)

Cultural sensitivity is required in community building programming as well. Heather Hutchinson describes some of the dynamics she encountered at High Point:

> *What brings people together in most communities? Pets, music, arts activities, sports. Typical programming in these areas doesn't really*

work for the Somali community. Dogs are not a positive thing in their culture. For conservative Somalis, programs where girls and boys play together aren't acceptable. Ongoing programming that doesn't take these kinds of things into account doesn't reach that many people."

Heather described one particularly successful event that she attended and felt participants enjoyed, one of the quarterly neighborhood nights out. These events always had a theme and sharing of food, and were open to everyone but usually attended by renters. This event was attended by about 15 people, "a fantastic cross-section. Participants were given prompts to talk about themselves with others. It allowed them to feel creative, open up, and bond with each other," Hutchinson said.

Enabling Renters' Self-Advocacy

Prior to redevelopment, all three communities had a formal resident council that, among many other purposes, gave residents a structure through which to articulate their issues and concerns and to advocate for their needs with SHA and other agencies, such as social service providers or the police department. In reimagining these communities, the exclusively renter-focused resident council structure was not maintained; planners hoped it would no longer be needed and would be replaced by organizations that included all types of residents (e.g., High Point Neighborhood Association and Rainier Vista Community Building Committee). In practice, these new structures did fulfill many of the functions of the resident councils, because renters and homeowners often have many interests and concerns in common. However, there are situations when their interests diverge and residents need a voice of their own in their relationship with landlords. Since renters don't have a formal association or council, they may seek help from the community builder to support their organizing and advocacy.

Juggling the Demands Placed on Community Builders

Because community builders are trusted, readily accessible, and work for SHA, low-income residents sometimes look to them for help finding social-services support or resolving conflicts with property management. Sometimes community builders help low-income neighbors with urgent problems either directly or through a referral to other resources, but the demand for this kind of service support can pull community builders' attention away from their work of bringing the community together. Joy Bryngelson, former SHA community builder at New Holly and Yesler Terrace, describes the challenge:

> *In working with low-income residents, there is often a pull toward basic social work. Someone comes to you with an urgent concern about their kid or making rent, you can't just ignore that and say, "Here's a great volunteer opportunity for you," or "Why don't you come to the neighborhood event?" You need to do something practical and focused on responding to that particular urgent need. And from a community building point of view, building trusted and respectful relationships with people is actually for the good of the community as a whole. Attention does need to be paid to sustaining a culturally relevant social services infrastructure. When the necessary supports and resources are not in place, or if there's a cultural gap, the community builder can be drawn more toward the urgent needs of the individuals and families in crisis, and not have the bandwidth to focus on the longer-term work of building community and neighborhood development.*

Finding Sustainable Funding for Community Building

Community building is never finished. As SHA Senior Housing Developer George Nemeth notes, "Community building requires continuous, active engagement to instill a sense of ownership, especially among the renters, that this is their place and that they can care for it. That builds confidence and hope." This means that the funding to support the community builder and activities also must never end. With each redevelopment, SHA has gotten better at accounting for the expense as part of setting up the community-building organizational infrastructure. However, since SHA's share comes from ever-decreasing federal funds, the challenge of finding funding is never finished.

The funding challenge also pertains to supportive social services, another key element of community building (though not addressed in this essay). Mixed-income communities will always have a large proportion of low-income residents, even as individual residents move on and new people move in. A robust, comprehensive, culturally sensitive supportive-services infrastructure to address basic needs and support residents' economic self-sufficiency goals is essential. People who are hungry, looking for work, concerned about their teen getting in trouble, or struggling to pay the rent are not going to want to hear about, much less participate in, community activities or decision making. The lack of adequate, sustainable funding for social services puts a strain not only on low-income families but also the whole community.

Over time, homes are sold and newcomers move in. The HOAs and other associations provide some institutional memory about the unique nature of these communities and can help transmit community identity. Several people interviewed for this essay noted that keeping the vision of a mixed-income community alive takes ongoing effort. This visioning has to be deliberate, inclusive, and revisited from time to time as conditions change.

COMMUNITY BUILDING: WHAT SUCCESS LOOKS LIKE

Joy Bryngelson describes designing community building events as "a bowl of mixed nuts. Some people like the cashews, others the macadamias or pecans. You need variety so that there's something for everyone." With the support of the community builder and active, committed volunteers, each community has benefited from a program of varied and frequent activities open to everyone.

The breadth and depth of diversity in these communities, in the context of our current divisive political and social environment, makes community building across the vast divides of culture and class particularly challenging—but also increasingly necessary. The connections forged among people through fun activities and shared interests can serve the community well in times of crisis. For example:

- At High Point, when Seattle Public Schools attempted to change the boundaries for elementary school assignment in a way that would have sent neighborhood children to two different schools, High Point residents—renters and homeowners—organized and successfully advocated that their neighborhood remain in one school's assignment area.

- In February 2017, about 200 New Rainier Vista residents (mostly homeowners) who were concerned about the impact of the Trump Administration's anti-immigrant policies on their Muslim neighbors, sent a letter to everyone in the community saying, in part, "As we watch the rising tide of fear in our nation, as we listen to preposterous hate speech and rhetoric from this President, our hearts are cracked wide open. Today, we want to say loudly and clearly that if they target Muslim Americans, or any member of our diverse community, they target all of us; for we stand together as one." In response, several Muslim neighbors hosted a thank-you potluck and invited everyone in the community, which hundreds attended.

Out of these interactions grew a community-wide cultural celebration on Eid-Al-Fitr, the end of Ramadan, in summer 2017. The community hopes to make this an annual tradition.[5]

The fact that SHA communities have come together several times in trying circumstances is due, at least in part, to the investment in community building infrastructure described here.

New Holly, Rainier Vista, High Point are fundamentally different places now. SHA's initial ambitious visions and hopes for community building may not always have been achieved. As George Nemeth notes, "At High Point we had dreams of blocks of homeowners and renters living together as neighbors separated only by a driveway, becoming friends, and forming mentoring relationships. We thought that if that didn't happen, we would have failed. It didn't happen, mostly. But we didn't fail either. The lesson is to focus on something more basic: people recognizing each other as neighbors, seeing each other as human beings and not strangers across lines of class, race, or ethnicity."

Nemeth continues, "It matters that low-income people live in safe, beautiful places where they are exposed to opportunity and have access to the regular services that someone in a city should expect—libraries, safe parks—that they didn't necessarily have in public housing." Adds Tom Phillips, "The whole tenor of High Point is different. Parents let their kids go outside and play. People are civil to each other. The residents aren't living with the chronic stress from fear of violence; it's a better situation for them physically and mentally."

IMPLICATIONS FOR POLICY AND PRACTICE

Implications for Policy

- Mixed-income communities created under HOPE VI or its successor program, Choice Neighborhoods, will always have a significant percentage of low-income residents. Building strong, cohesive communities is easier when households in poverty have their basic needs met. Community building in mixed-income communities occurs in a context where, in our current

---

5 Sources for this anecdote include interview with Shakina Hussain and Monica Guzman, "'We know they would stand up for us.' How good neighbors are helping South Seattle Muslims lose their fear in the Trump era." *The Evergrey*. March 30, 2017, https://theevergrey.com/muslims-losing-fear-trump-era/

social safety net orientation, housing authorities have an important role in bringing services to their public housing residents through partnerships and other means. As long as this system continues, housing authorities and their partners must advocate for sustained means of addressing the barriers that people who have historically been marginalized face that could prevent full participation in their neighborhoods. These barriers include child care, economic insecurity, cultural norms, and English proficiency.

Implications for Research and Evaluation

- Evaluation partners should create protocols and surveys for measuring community connectedness that developers and managers of mixed-income communities can use to measure the success of their community-building investments. Indicators of community include people caring about each other and being comfortable around people who are different from themselves; people chatting when they meet on the street; and neighbors knowing their neighbor's children's names and going out of their way to check on each other when someone might need extra help.[6]

- Assessing the status of mixed-income developments every two or three years would help illuminate how these places function as communities over time. In addition to assessing community connection, periodic surveys should help residents and property managers understand community concerns, such as whether residents feel safe and empowered to solve problems together, and whether the services and facilities offered meet their needs. This type of attention would be a useful step in sustaining ongoing community engagement.

Implications for Development and Investment

- Developers of mixed-income communities should be deliberate and clear about their vision for community building. George Nemeth and Carol Wellenberger articulated a series of questions developers should consider: "Is it general neighborliness, people knowing each other? Is it the formation of friendships between residents that extend beyond the public spaces in the community? Is it developing a shared culture of expectations for how people behave and interact with each other? Is it strong enough bonds to permit community-based problem solving? Is it being "just like any

---

6 (Joy Bryngelson, pers.comm.)

other neighborhood?" How does the vision account for differences among residents including ownership stake (renters and homeowners), race, language, class and culture?

- Developers should ensure that all partners who join the project (e.g., home builders or realtors) also understand and can convey the vision to incoming residents.

- Developers should position homeowner associations as a mechanism for setting the tone and expectations around community norms, especially during the period before the developer turns control of the association over to the homeowners themselves. Through the homeowners association, a developer can establish practices on themes such as, "This is one community, not renters versus owners"; "This is a multicultural community with respect for all cultures"; and, "This is a listening and problem-solving community, not a finger-pointing one."

- Operating budgets for communities undergoing redevelopment should include an adequately funded community-building line item prior to, during, and after redevelopment to ensure reliable financial resources for ongoing community building.

Implications for Residents and Community Members

- Residents and community members should advocate for ongoing organizational capacity for community building support, such as a staffed position of community builder or the equivalent. Neighborhood organization does not happen by itself; it requires intention, commitment, and sustained effort. In other Seattle neighborhoods and probably most other places that don't have community builders, neighborhood organizations emerge and disappear as local issues change and as motivated, committed people come and go. Having a dedicated community builder gives the communities described in this essay ongoing support for community members to organize and advocate together on issues they care about. Even a handful of residents who are willing to put in the time to make community building events happen, with the support of a community builder, can increase the likelihood that neighbors will get to know each other and form a stronger sense of community.

- Residents and community members of all backgrounds can reap the rewards of community building. As Heather Hutchinson observes, "The people who live in these communities are getting a richer, more rewarding experience than they would get elsewhere." A goal of community building is to create places where residents, regardless of tenure, understand the opportunities available and feel welcome and able to take advantage of them.

■ ■ ■

STEPHANIE VAN DYKE was responsible for overseeing neighborhood revitalization including development of affordable housing, community facilities, parks and public infrastructure. She is leading the redevelopment of Yesler Terrace public housing site into a transit-oriented mixed-income urban neighborhood. Three neighborhood efforts, Lake City, High Point, and Rainier Vista, resulted in 2,600 new homes for seniors, families, and people with disabilities of all incomes. She launched the homeWorks project at the Seattle Housing Authority which carried out successful occupied rehabilitation of 22 low income housing high rise buildings. Van Dyke has a Master of Arts degree in Public Administration from the University of Washington, a Bachelor of Arts degree from Harvard University and completed an apprenticeship in carpentry with Carpenters Local 131.

■ ■ ■

ELLEN KISSMAN is a planner and policy analyst with more than 30 years of experience in Seattle. She has worked for the City of Seattle and the Seattle Housing Authority. Since 2006, her consulting practice has served the public and nonprofit sectors, offering grant-writing, research, program evaluation, and project management services to government and nonprofit sector clients. Kissman was part of the Seattle Housing Authority team that brought more than $100 million in funding awards to the Seattle area. She contributed to successful HUD grant applications for redevelopment at Rainier Vista, High Point, Lake City Village, and Yesler Terrace. Kissman has a Master of Public Health in Environmental Health degree and a Master of Science in Urban Planning degree from Columbia University and a Bachelor of Arts from The Evergreen State College.

WEINLAND PARK, COLUMBUS, OHIO: BUILDING COMMUNITY AS A NEIGHBORHOOD TRANSITIONS TO MIXED-INCOME

Kip Holley
The Ohio State University

Matthew Martin
The Columbus Foundation

Stephen A. Sterrett
Consultant

The Weinland Park neighborhood of Columbus, Ohio, has evolved from an area with the city's highest violent crime rate and highest concentration of project-based Section 8 housing into a mixed-income, mixed-race neighborhood. Since 2010, the Weinland Park Collaborative (WPC), a partnership of public, non-profit, and private entities, has cultivated that evolution and empowered the residents through a place-based and people-centered approach to providing investment and support. A baseline survey of residents in 2010 provided a valuable snapshot of neighborhood conditions that helped to guide WPC's investments. A follow-up survey in 2016 not only documented the changes in Weinland Park but also revealed the differing perspectives of the residents who make up this diverse neighborhood. In addition, applying innovative mapping techniques, the survey literally illustrated how Black and White residents perceive "safe" and "unsafe" areas of the neighborhood differently. While Weinland Park is one neighborhood geographically, it is not necessarily one community socially.

The 2016 survey has helped neighborhood leaders and WPC members understand the further challenge of creating a mixed-income, mixed-race *community* in which people develop authentic relationships across barriers of income, education, race, and gender. This article describes how the innovative survey and principles of equitable and inclusive community development are being used to transform Weinland Park into, as one observer suggested, "a safe place where people can come together and leave their status behind."

THE EVOLUTION OF WEINLAND PARK

Weinland Park is a compact urban neighborhood of about 30 square blocks that is adjacent to the Columbus campus of The Ohio State University (Ohio State) and about one and one-half miles north of downtown. The neighborhood's western border is High Street, the city's main north-south commercial corridor. Developed in the first decades of the 20th century as the city grew northward, Weinland Park's population peak was 8,521 in 1950, nearly twice what it was in 2010. The eastern portion of today's Weinland Park was part of a Black neighborhood, extending south and east, that resulted from redlining and other housing discrimination. That old Black neighborhood was fragmented by construction of the interstate highways and urban renewal in the 1950s and 1960s. As the suburbs developed, White residents left, and nearby manufacturing jobs vanished, Weinland Park had a steady decline in population to 4,386 in 2010. The population was 46 percent White, 36 percent Black, 12 percent Hispanic, 3 percent Asian, and 4 percent other. Housing renovation and new construction since the last Census likely puts the current population closer to 4,900. The 2020 Census will most certainly document the neighborhood's first population increase in 70 years.[1]

In the 1970s and early 1980s, many old townhomes and rowhouses were renovated to develop some 500 units of scattered-site, project-based Section 8 housing. Unfortunately, the Section 8 housing was poorly managed, had a high turnover rate, and contributed to the growing crime problem. The crack epidemic of the late 1980s added to the problem, as did a violent drug gang based in the neighborhood through the mid-1990s.

In response to the public safety concerns, deteriorated housing, and aging public infrastructure in the urban neighborhoods around Ohio State's campus, the

---

[1] For more background on Weinland Park, see Tamar M. Forrest and Howard Goldstein, Weinland Park Evaluation Project. (Columbus, OH: College of Education and Human Ecology, The Ohio State University, 2010).; *Weinland Park Demographic Analysis.* (Columbus, OH: The Kirwan Institute for the Study of Race and Ethnicity, The Ohio State University, 2012).; *Weinland Park Story Book* (Columbus, OH: The Wexner Center for the Arts, The Ohio State University, 2014).

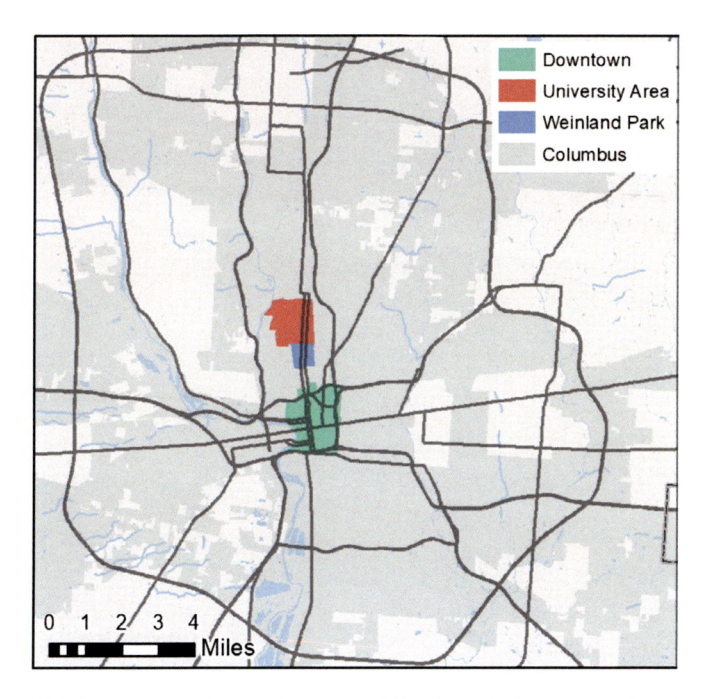

Figure 1: Weinland Park's Proximity to the Ohio State University's Main Campus and Downtown Columbus

University and the City in 1995 jointly funded development of a comprehensive improvement plan with significant public input. At the same time, Ohio State created Campus Partners for Community Urban Redevelopment as its non-profit community development corporation to spearhead the planning and to implement key revitalization initiatives. In 2001, Campus Partners negotiated an agreement with the private owners to acquire their entire portfolio of project-based Section 8 housing, which included the properties in Weinland Park. Campus Partners and Ohio Capital Corporation for Housing (OCCH), a statewide financial intermediary for affordable housing, developed a strategy to preserve the government-subsidized housing. In 2003, OCCH acquired the portfolio and created Community Properties of Ohio (CPO) as a non-profit property management company. Over the next six years, CPO invested $30 million in the extensive rehab of the units in Weinland Park, instituted effective management and public safety measures, and reduced the turnover of residents. These actions planted the seeds of a mixed-income neighborhood by securing long-term affordable housing as a cornerstone of the revitalization effort.

In 2004, the City of Columbus, in cooperation with the newly formed Weinland Park Community Civic Association (WPCCA), launched a two-year community planning process to develop the *Weinland Park Neighborhood Plan*. Central to the plan was a vision that Weinland Park become a mixed-income neighborhood. In 2008, the JPMorgan Chase Foundation and The Columbus Foundation jointly funded a grant to Campus Partners to develop a strategy to realize that vision. Among the factors that favored Weinland Park's evolution to a mixed-income neighborhood were:

- Proximity to Ohio State, downtown, and higher-opportunity neighborhoods and the University's role as an anchor institution;
- Relatively well-maintained housing stock along with remediated "brownfield" land that could attract new housing construction;
- Access to public transportation and freeways;
- A significant supply of well-managed government-subsidized housing that would remain affordable to low-income families for years to come; and
- The continued population growth of Columbus and central Ohio.

If crime and the distressed conditions of the neighborhood could be addressed, existing residents, including those in the subsidized apartments, would be more likely to stay and new residents would be attracted to Weinland Park.

Campus Partners proposed a bold place-based and people-centered strategy. Central to the strategy was a collective impact model with multiple partners and a broad approach that focused on expanding opportunities for affordable housing, while creating the conditions for development of renovated and new market rate housing. The approach included improving opportunities for existing residents and expanding their input. In 2010, the Weinland Park Collaborative (WPC)[2] was formally launched with nearly two dozen members, including the University, the City, The Columbus Foundation, JPMorgan Chase Foundation, Cardinal Health Foundation, United Way of Central Ohio, social service agencies, a private developer, and the Weinland Park Community Civic Association. Weinland Park Collaborative members met monthly to share information, consult with residents, and guide public, philanthropic and

---

2   For more on the WPC, see: *Weinland Park Collaborative Progress Report*. (Columbus, OH: Weinland Park Collaborative, 2013).; *Weinland Park Collaborative Progress Report 2013-2015*. (Columbus, OH: Weinland Park Collaborative, 2016).

Figure 2: Vision For Weinland Park Created Through Study Circles

private investments in dozens of programs and activities in the areas of resident engagement, housing, workforce development, early childhood and elementary education, public safety, youth development, health, and community art. The philanthropic funding partners each maintained their own decision-making processes for neighborhood investments, but those decisions were informed by the discussions within the WPC.

To activate a weak private housing market, WPC initially invested federal and philanthropic funds in the acquisition of properties that had been foreclosed and abandoned due to the Great Recession. WPC partner organizations subsequently renovated and constructed more than 135 single-family homes for affordable housing, including exterior home repair grants to more than 70 existing income-eligible homeowners. By 2015, neighborhood improvements were visible and the private real estate market began rebounding with construction underway on new market rate houses on a vacant remediated brownfield site. In 2016 and 2017, construction of market rate apartments and condominiums began on the brownfield site and along the High Street corridor.

The Annie E. Casey Foundation joined as a national partner of the WPC in 2013, integrating Casey's Family-Centered Community Change initiative with the Weinland Park work. One objective of the WPC was to improve opportunities for low-income families who would continue to occupy CPO apartments even as new and renovated housing attracted more affluent neighbors. Casey's initiative brought a clearer strategy and additional resources to working with low-income families. It uses a two-generation approach that emphasizes the need to serve children and their caregivers at the same time to help both succeed in breaking the cycle of generational poverty. WPC partners involved in the Casey initiative have used a coaching model to assist families and to focus on the healthy development and education of children and on the parenting skills, job readiness, and financial security of adults.

From its inception, the WPC has emphasized resident engagement and empowerment, working to build the capacity of the Weinland Park Community Civic Association. A key early initiative was a series of study circles designed "to create a vision for building a more livable Weinland Park community." With support from the WPC, the civic association in 2013 engaged a consultant from Everyday Democracy to train neighborhood residents as facilitators for the study circles. These facilitators then led study circles involving more than 80 neighborhood residents. The summary from the study circles was expressed in a poster design (Figure 2) that captured key words from the visioning discussions. The word most often used was "connectedness." The residents who participated in the study circles shared that they felt more connected to their neighbors and they appreciated the diversity of life experiences among participants.

While the neighborhood vision reflected the experience of the study circle participants, the ongoing challenge for the WPCCA and WPC's partner organizations has been to maintain the "connectedness" among the wider population of residents even as new and renovated housing brings in new residents and as some existing residents, particularly in market rate rental housing, leave the community. The Weinland Park Community Civic Association and WPC have attempted to realize this vision by cultivating a mixed-income, racially-diverse community where people connect with each other and develop authentic relationships. We define authentic community relationships as those in which participants share openly and honestly from their lived experiences and contribute meaningfully to the common good. We believe such relationships should be conducted in an understanding and inclusive manner. While long-time neighbors can often develop personal relationships and friendships with others like themselves, we also must promote community relationships that permit us to interact positively with people we may not know well and whose life experiences may be much different than our own.

Over the years, the Weinland Park Community Civic Association and WPC have encouraged community relationships and resident empowerment through a variety of initiatives. For example:

- The WPC has brought all of its housing-related projects before the WPCCA's Housing Committee for review and has actively encouraged private developers to do the same. The committee's recommendations about issues such as project size, location, and design are taken seriously in the city's formal review processes for housing and zoning.
- The WPC provided staff support to neighborhood volunteers who led the Weinland Park Community Civic Association, its committees, and many of its projects.
- Ohio State's Wexner Center for the Arts has engaged neighborhood teenagers and local artists in projects to record, illustrate and publish residents' memories of the neighborhood in the *Weinland Park Story Book* and to help change the public perception of Weinland Park through billboard art.
- WPC and its partners have supported a more informal network of CPO residents, a resident-led youth football team and cheerleading squad, an annual neighborhood festival that draws some 500 people, and activities in the neighborhood elementary school.

Weinland Park Community Civic Association's leaders, most of whom are homeowners, have consistently supported an inclusive approach to resident engagement, recognizing that deliberate efforts are needed to involve low-income people and renters. While some older homeowners have multi-generational roots in the neighborhood, the fact that no more than 10 percent of the neighborhood is owner-occupied has made the wellbeing and stability of renters crucial to maintaining neighborhood home values. As a result, homeowners in Weinland Park have tended to promote engagement among their neighbors who rent and have often advocated on behalf of renter interests, as well as their own.

AN INNOVATIVE SURVEY HIGHLIGHTS DIFFERENCES

At the request of the WPC and with funding from The Columbus Foundation, Ohio State researchers in 2010 conducted a comprehensive, in-person survey of 441 residents, representing 26 percent of the households in Weinland Park. The survey covered demographics, housing and mobility, access to basic needs, neighbor interaction, public safety, education and child development, economic wellbeing, and more, providing baseline data on neighborhood conditions and residents' attitudes. This snapshot of the neighborhood helped to guide the WPC's investments and programming decisions. Survey responses included the following highlights:

- Only 18 percent of respondents had full-time employment, 26 percent worked part-time, and 36 percent were unemployed. The remaining were homemakers, retired, or receiving disability payments. Health-related issues were reported as the number one barrier to employment. WPC partner organizations offer job readiness programs, but barriers of health, transportation, childcare, and illegal drug use have made economic self-sufficiency a challenging goal for many residents.

- Half the households contained an individual diagnosed with one or more chronic conditions of asthma, diabetes, high blood pressure, heart disease, and obesity, while 38 percent of households had an individual with a diagnosed mental health condition. The WPC promoted community health resources to residents and encouraged cooperation among local health providers to better serve the neighborhood. Moms2B, an innovative program addressing prenatal health, was founded in Weinland Park and, after several years of intensive work, the neighborhood was no longer a hot spot for infant mortality.

- Respondents identified unsupervised neighborhood youth as a major public safety problem in the neighborhood. The WPC established a collaborative program of special-duty Columbus police officers, a local neighborhood agency specializing in counseling and treatment for youths and their families, and the county juvenile court system. The goal was to respond quickly and divert juvenile offenders to immediate opportunities for counseling and treatment, rather than send them through the court system. The program was successful, but far fewer juveniles were identified as offenders than had been expected. The perception among many residents that unsupervised young people were a major problem was found to be inaccurate.

With support once again from The Columbus Foundation, Ohio State's Kirwan Institute for the Study of Race and Ethnicity conducted a follow-up survey in 2016[3] that replicated and modified portions of the 2010 survey to understand changes in the neighborhood. Kirwan staff collected 422 usable responses. The results indicated the demographic composition of Weinland Park had remained stable since 2010 and the Black population of the neighborhood had remained around 1,000, despite an increase in Latinos and the first growth in the White population in several decades. Overall, residents reported that the appearance and safety of Weinland Park were improving and that they felt that they were influencing decisions affecting the neighborhood. There was an increase in the perception that children are safe when playing outside. The financial wellbeing of residents was improving. While the survey helped to confirm many of the positive changes in Weinland Park as a whole, the survey also revealed that not all residents share the same lived experience and perceptions.

The Kirwan Institute staff analyzed and mapped the survey results to examine the variation in experiences and attitudes of different groups, or clusters, of residents. The results of this cluster analysis help illuminate the challenges of creating a community where people develop authentic relationships across lines of demographic difference. Kirwan staff used two-step cluster methods to determine if discrete groups exist within the neighborhood. After running more than 100 simulations of the data, they determined that nine demographic factors created reliable clusters: age, sex, race, highest attained education, type of housing, time in the neighborhood, employment status, student status, and children in the household. While the clusters correlate with demographic factors, such as race and education, the clusters reveal a much more nuanced understanding of different attitudes and perceptions among sub-groups of residents who share common life experiences. Using the nine demographic factors, five cluster groupings were identified:

- Neighborhood Core (31 percent of respondents)—These are the most typical neighborhood residents: working-class renters with a high school diploma and children in the household. Eighty-eight percent are in the labor force, but only 29 percent are employed fulltime. Eighty-two percent are Black.
- Educated Workforce (19 percent—Residents with bachelor's or post-

---

[3] Zachary E. Kenitzer, *A Portrait of Weinland Park: Results and Analysis of the 2016 Weinland Park Collaborative Neighborhood Survey*. (Columbus, OH: The Kirwan Institute for the Study of Race and Ethnicity, The Ohio State University, 2017).

graduate degrees, who may be renters or homeowners. Eighty-eight percent are in the labor force, with 57 percent employed fulltime. Eighty-one percent are White.

- Buckeye Undergrads (18 percent—Traditional undergraduate students at Ohio State. All are renters. Seventy-nine percent are in the labor force, but only 12 percent work fulltime. Sixty-eight percent are White, and 20 percent are Black.

- Aspirational Families (14 percent—These residents have children, live below the poverty level, tend to rent with housing assistance, and typically have a high school diploma or are pursuing one. Ninety-three percent are Black.

- Boomers and Independents (14 percent—These residents are typically older and moving toward retirement with no children in the households. This cluster also includes disabled residents not in the labor force. Sixty-two percent are Black, and 14 percent are White.

The survey report found differences in perceptions and conditions among these clusters, resulting in a richer understanding of the life experiences of the people who reside in the neighborhood. As it turns out, resident experiences and perspectives vary widely, even within the same racial groups, economic classes, and age cohorts. Among these findings were:

- Some 40 percent of Aspirational Families felt they had a "great deal" of input on community decisions, and 28 percent agreed they had a "fair amount." (This compares with 29 percent and 28 percent, respectively, for the Neighborhood Core; 33 percent and 22 percent for Boomers and Independents; 13 percent and 37 percent for Educated Workforce; and 7 percent and 19 percent for Buckeye Undergrads).

- The percentage of each cluster who agreed the neighborhood is getting "better" was 81 percent of Educated Workforce, 80 percent of Aspirational Families, 75 percent of Boomers and Independents, and 73 percent of Neighborhood Core. Of the Buckeye Undergrads, 47 percent agreed it was getting better, while 51 percent felt it had "not changed much," likely reflecting their short tenure in Weinland Park.

- Between 45 percent and 49 percent of Aspirational Families, Neighborhood Core, and Boomers and Independents reported daily interaction with neighbors. Slightly less than one-third of Buckeye Undergrads and Educated Workforce reported daily interaction.

- Approximately one-quarter of Boomers and Independents and Neighborhood Core reported attending the neighborhood civic association meetings. Their primary reasons for attending were to be engaged and to meet neighbors. Slightly more than one-sixth of Educated Workforce and Aspirational Families reported attending the meetings. For Educated Workforce, the primary reasons to attend were to be informed and to be engaged. For Aspirational Families, the primary reason was to be informed.
- The Educated Workforce and Buckeye Undergrads were very satisfied with the neighborhood, while the other clusters were moderately satisfied.
- The Educated Workforce cluster was the most trusting of police, while the Neighborhood Core and Aspirational Families were the least trusting of police.
- The Aspirational Families cluster felt most safe in the neighborhood, while the Buckeye Undergrads felt the least safe.
- The Boomers and Independents cluster was the most food insecure and the most likely to experience homelessness.
- If rents continue to rise, the Neighborhood Core cluster may become cost-burdened for housing (meaning the residents are spending more than 30 percent of their income on housing). The Buckeye Undergrads have the highest cost-burden for housing.

The statistical analysis that resulted in these five clusters brought significantly more nuance to the understanding of who lives in the neighborhood, bringing greater contrast and clarity than simply characterizing residents based on race or class alone. In doing so, the cluster analysis also produced a much better understanding of what civic engagement looks like across Weinland Park, and how changes in the neighborhood have impacted residents differently, highlighting the groups that are most vulnerable to experiencing housing instability as market conditions continue to evolve.

To further understand the differences that residents have in their perception of neighborhood safety, Kirwan staff used an applied methods approach. Survey respondents were asked to identify specific areas in Weinland Park where they feel most safe and least safe. With the location data collected in the survey software, Kirwan staff turned the data points into geographic coordinate points for analysis and then created raster maps for each cluster, race, and sex subgroup. The areas of green on each map in Figures 3 through 6 are areas where there are positive perceptions of safety; areas of red signify areas perceived as unsafe. The darker the respective green or red, the more people selected that area. The map in Figure 7 compares the areas of the neighborhood where females feel unsafe and where males feel unsafe. The maps illustrate distinct differences in perception between Black and White respondents, among the clusters, and between men and women.

Figure 3 combines the perceptions of all residents regarding which areas of the neighborhood they deem "safe" and "unsafe." Residents in general viewed the High Street commercial corridor, which has a market orientation to the university campus, and major neighborhood landmarks as "safe." The bright red area along Summit Street was the location of a carryout store that attracted loitering and illicit activities. The red along North Fourth and North

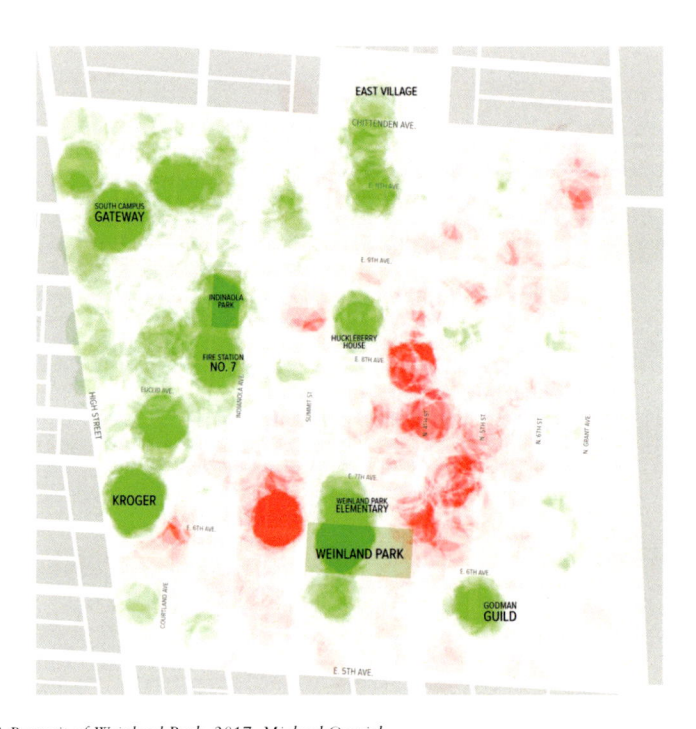

Source: A Portrait of Weinland Park, 2017. Michael Outrich

Figure 3: Map of Overall Perception of Safety

Fifth streets is an area with a significant number of CPO apartments inhabited primarily by Black families.

Figure 4 illustrates the perceptions of Black respondents regarding the areas they viewed as "safe" and "unsafe." Generally, they felt safe throughout the neighborhood.

Figure 5 shows the perceptions of White respondents. While White residents felt "safe" along the High Street corridor and neighborhood landmarks, their perception of being "unsafe" in the interior of the neighborhood where African-Americans are the majority was even more pronounced than in Figure 2.

By not including follow-up questions to ask why residents identified particular parts of the neighborhood as unsafe, the survey avoided eliciting explicit statements from respondents about fear associated with race or class. The

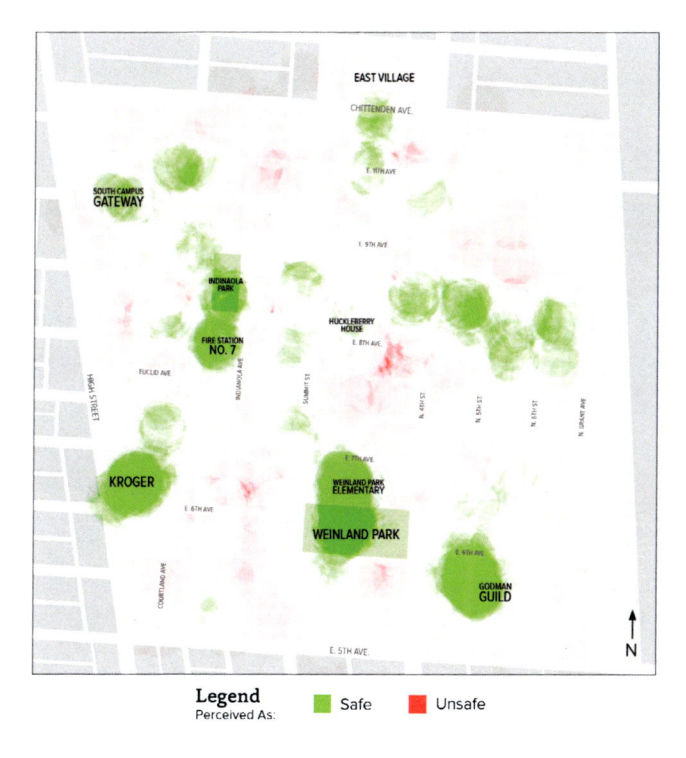

Figure 4: Map of Black Residents' Perception of Safety

Figure 5: Map of White Residents' Perception of Safety

result is a potentially more transparent portrayal of the unconscious biases of residents, even among White residents who claim to value a more diverse and inclusive sense of community. As a result, the maps have provoked ongoing dialogue among neighbors not only about public safety, but also about how to build a deeper sense of community across racial and economic differences in a neighborhood that is now more integrated in a variety of ways than ever before.

Just as revealing and perhaps more surprising than the differences in perceptions of safety between Black and White residents are the nuances across resident groups illuminated by these maps. Figure 6 shows the maps of safety perceptions for each of the clusters side by side. These maps reveal inherent racial patterns as well as differences within the three clusters composed primarily of Black residents. The older adult cohorts of Boomers and Independents and Neighborhood Core both identified a few specific places in the neighborhood as unsafe, while the Aspiring Families cluster appears to

Neighborhood Core

Educated Workforce

Buckeye Undergrads

Aspiring Families

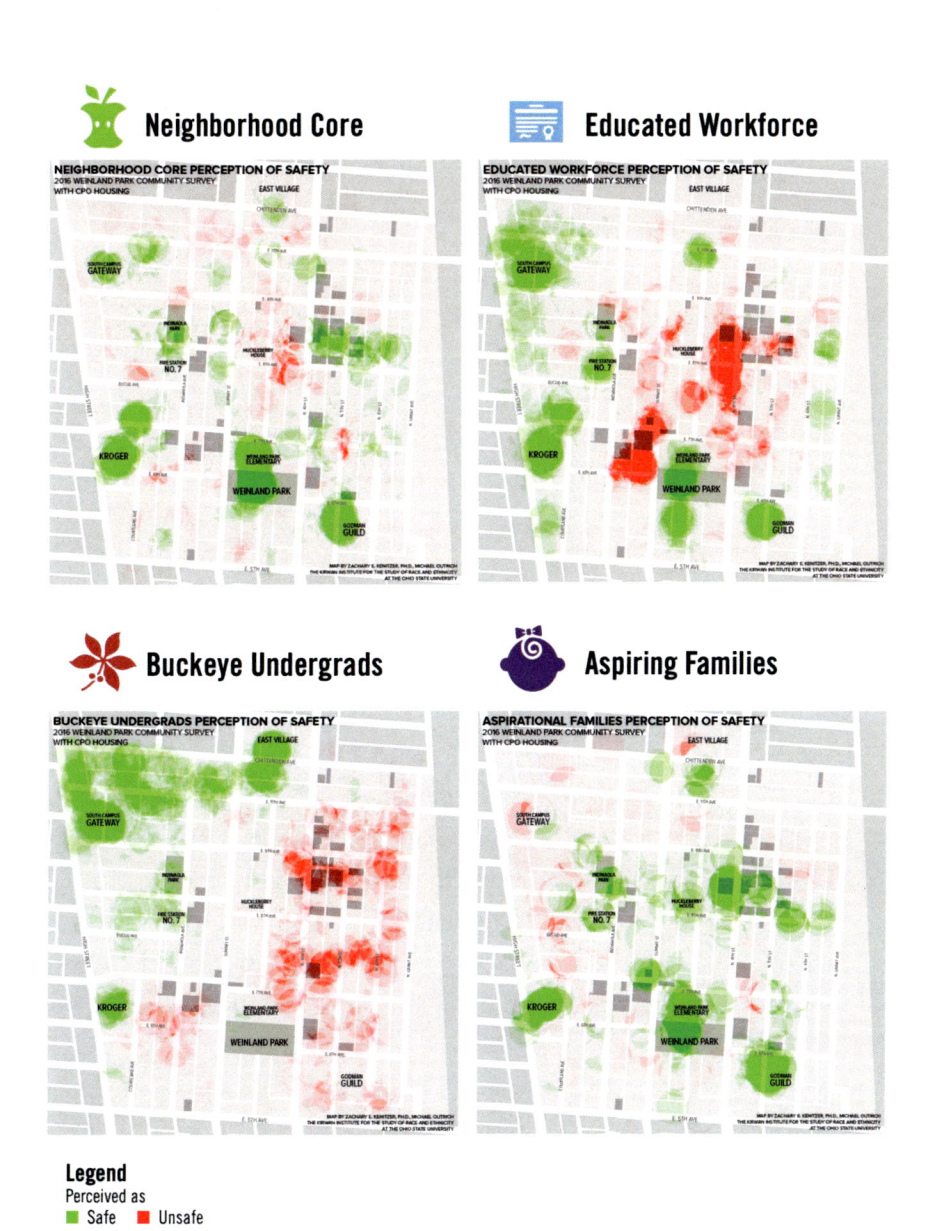

Legend
Perceived as
- Safe
- Unsafe

Figure 6: Perceptions of Safety By Neighborhood Cluster

(continued on next page)

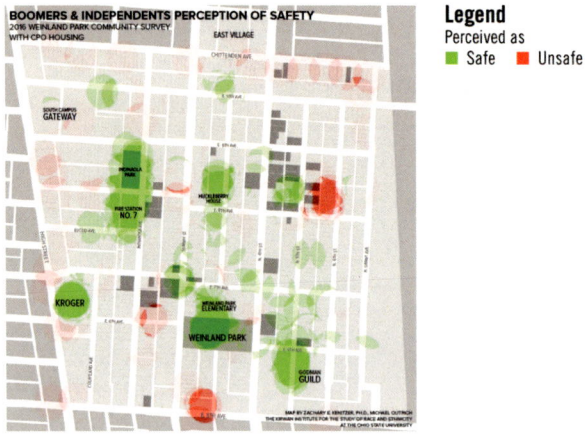

Figure 6: Perceptions of Safety By Neighborhood Cluster

have identified the fewest unsafe areas of any group in the neighborhood. Not surprisingly, Buckeye Undergrads consistently identified the part of Weinland Park most adjacent to campus as safe, and it was the only group that didn't specifically identify the park and elementary school near the center of the neighborhood as a safe place. The Kroger grocery is the one place identified by all clusters as a safe place. Perhaps ironically, it is also the place in the neighborhood where residents are most likely to interact with neighbors and members of all clusters.

Figure 7 illustrates the differences between perceptions of safety among men and women by highlighting areas that each gender perceives to be more unsafe than the other gender. Based on the survey responses, women generally tend to perceive the periphery of the neighborhood as more safe than men do, while men tend to view the core of the neighborhood as more safe than women do. Interestingly, there also appears to be a noticeable contrast between how women and men perceive prominent public spaces such as the elementary school and the park. While men perceive the area around the entrance to the school to be more unsafe than women do, women perceive the part of the park with the playground as more unsafe than men do. It is also worth mentioning that one of the last remaining corner stores in the neighborhood was located across the street from the park. While women perceive the side of the street

Legend

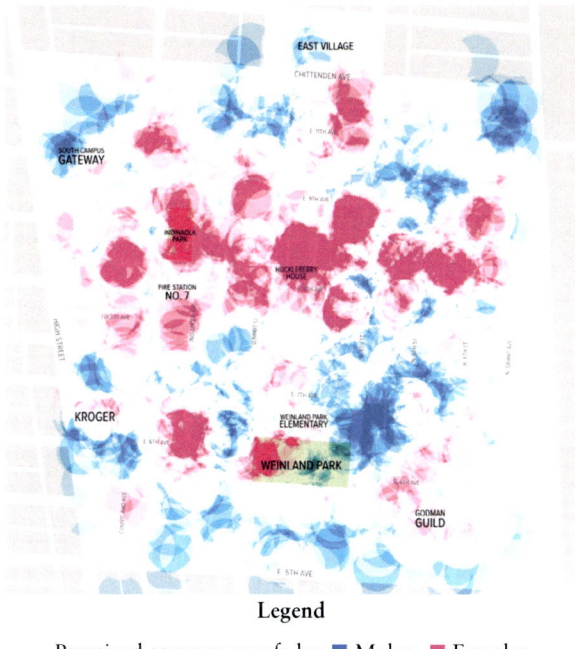

Perceived as more unsafe by ■ Males ■ Females

Figure 7: Map Showing Differences Between Male and Female Perceptions of Unsafe Areas

with the park to be more unsafe, men perceive the side of the street with the corner store to be more unsafe.

In mid-2017, Kirwan Institute staff members prepared a formal presentation of the survey results specifically designed to encourage understanding and dialogue about the meaning and implications of the results. The staff presented to a general meeting of the civic association involving approximately 60 residents—a broad cross-section of the neighborhood, although homeowners and Whites were more heavily represented. The survey results with the clusters and maps generated a great deal of discussion, often uncomfortable for participants. Reactions were strong, but mixed. While community members were generally excited to engage in the conversation about diversity and opportunity in the neighborhood, the various clusters and the idea that perceptions of the neighborhood might differ based on those clusters was a difficult topic for some. The most heated comments focused on the maps of residents' perceptions of safety. Some Whites disputed the maps showing that, in general, White residents felt least safe in the areas of the neighborhood where most Blacks live (Figure 5) and the map that indicated, in general, that Blacks had far fewer areas of the neighborhood where they felt unsafe (Figure 4). Other residents, both White and Black, asserted that their personal views differed from the cluster that appeared to represent them.

The Kirwan staff made the formal presentation to additional groups involved in Weinland Park, including CPO residents and WPC members. In general, the more diverse the audience was, the more wide-ranging and emotional the discussion. The emotion in the dialogue was a sign of the level of honest discussion about these difficult topics. The purpose of the presentation was not to determine whose perceptions were correct, but to begin a process of understanding the variety of experiences and attitudes among neighbors and why perceptions of safety differed so noticeably across the neighborhood. The strong reactions to the presentation, however, underscored the importance of sharing survey results in a format accessible to a general audience, preparing for a structured dialogue that permits people to feel safe when talking about difficult topics such as race, and allotting adequate time for the discussion.

CREATING AN INCLUSIVE COMMUNITY: THE PATH AHEAD FOR WEINLAND PARK

Since 2017, Weinland Park's population has continued to grow due to market rate housing construction on a former brownfield site on the neighborhood's eastern edge and along the High Street corridor on the western edge. The leaders of the civic association have changed. Although the new officers remain committed to an inclusive community, resident involvement in civic association meetings and similar activities has slowed due to fewer neighborhood crises and some exhaustion from a decade of civic activism. Having achieved success in Weinland Park, many of the WPC partners have turned their attention to other distressed Columbus neighborhoods. Key place-based partners, such as the University and Community Properties of Ohio, remain engaged. The Annie E. Casey Foundation will conclude its investment in 2020, but CPO and other partners are committed to sustaining and expanding in geographic scope the most effective two-generation strategies.

In Weinland Park, new structural challenges to inclusivity are related to the neighborhood's growing popularity. As the neighborhood improvements have become visible, more people are choosing to live in Weinland Park. While that is positive, rising rents and housing costs throughout central Ohio are impacting Weinland Park as well. There is limited land on which to add more affordable housing in the neighborhood. It also remains a challenge to successfully engage the Black men in Weinland Park who are connected to the women and children living in the CPO apartments but who, for a variety of reasons, are not on the apartment lease. One factor in this disconnect may be their lack of stable housing. In addition, more needs to be done to reach the Hispanic/Latinx residents and other immigrant families for whom language or immigrant status may be barriers.

As the physical infrastructure and housing market in the neighborhood continue to transform through development of vacant lots and increased sale prices for owner-occupied homes, the neighborhood has begun to face new challenges and predicaments. Non-profit organizations are considering ways to sustain their most successful programs and services as the aggregate amount of funding decreases each year, despite ongoing need among low-income seniors and families.

Weinland Park now must deal with an overly simplistic misperception across Columbus that it is all but gentrified, although it continues to have one of the highest concentrations of subsidized housing in the city. This has resulted in confusion and dissonance among institutional stakeholders and policymakers. Residents who have lived in the neighborhood for more than a few years recognize that the social challenges are morphing into more complicated forms of division. New residents, especially those of the recently built market rate, suburban-style development, are barely aware of the diverse racial and economic composition of the neighborhood, and they understandably do not appreciate the civic effort that has gone into the revitalization of the past two decades.

CONCLUSION

Over the past decade, the Weinland Park Collaborative and Weinland Park Community Civic Association invested in improving the housing and physical conditions of Weinland Park and in generating greater opportunity and empowerment for the residents. Due in part to the national and local economy, market conditions, and its location, Weinland Park evolved into a racially diverse, mixed-income neighborhood relatively quickly. The WPC and WPCCA have been intentional in attempting to create an inclusive community within the neighborhood. The 2016 neighborhood survey identified important differences in life experiences and perceptions among the residents of Weinland Park that must be validated and accepted if we are to develop the authentic relationships that comprise a community. The survey did not spell out the next steps, however, and even with the best of intentions, authentic relationships aren't developed overnight. Over time, the proximity of people in a neighborhood can create some sense of community as adults and children interact in the elementary school, at the grocery store, in the park, and during neighborhood festivals and other social activities. The insights from a tool such as the 2016 neighborhood survey, paired with well-planned public dialogue, holds promise for speeding up the process of defining an inclusive community for a particular neighborhood and the steps for getting there. As the people of Weinland Park and their institutional partners "take a breath" and consider what has been accomplished, their challenge in the next few years is to reflect on the insights from the 2016 survey and consider organizing a neighborhood-wide dialogue. These discussions would include long-term residents and the many new residents to reaffirm their vision for the neighborhood and to identify the steps needed to get there.

The promise of inclusive community-building in Weinland Park is only possible because of effective efforts to make diverse economic and racial proximity possible. Truly successful revitalization must build on those accomplishments by weaving together a heterogeneous social cohesion that has been largely discouraged or elusive throughout the history of neighborhood development in America. Consistent civic engagement and iterative research have helped surface many of the biases that present obstacles to building inclusive community. Many of the structural forces that make integrated housing difficult to achieve are being discussed on a regional level for the first time. These are all ingredients that will be necessary in order to move beyond old prejudices and injustices.

While Weinland Park has made undeniable progress in fulfilling the vision of a mixed-income, racially diverse neighborhood, much work remains to cultivate a cohesive multicultural community. Many of these challenges are related to people's habits of creating community around racial and economic similarities. Robert Putnam[4] pointed out that greater diversity often disrupts existing

---

4   Robert Putnam, "E Pluribus Unum: Diversity and Community in the Twenty-first Century. The 2006 Johan Skytte Prize Lecture." Scandinavian Political Studies, 30, no. 2 (2017).

feelings of solidarity that are based on homogeneity. In a study by the U.S. Department of Housing and Urban Development, ethnographers found that in the face of greater diversity, residents in some neighborhoods tended to align around social identities (homeowners vs. renters, length of tenure, etc.).[5] They also found that certain rules and regulations from the housing authority worked to preserve social boundaries. A general consensus among those who study mixed-identity neighborhoods, however, is that these are learned behaviors and activities that can and have been unlearned in many communities. Community engagement frameworks that prize recognizing and sharing assets and skills, creating space for mystery and lifelong learning, and empowerment through community leadership can be found in resources such as Kip Holley's *The Principles of Equitable and Inclusive Civic Engagement*[6], John McKnight and Peter Block's *The Abundant Community*, and the Annie E. Casey Foundation's *Making Connections* series. These frameworks can provide useful guidelines for developing a more expansive view of "community."

As community-building continues in Weinland Park, the civic association leadership and the WPC partners aspire to embrace this diversity of race, income, education and gender as a gift and a source of strength. As social capital is continuously built, new connections between people will unlock their capacities for growth, wellbeing, and benevolence. In turn, these connections generate strong attachments to communities and a commitment to making them better places to live for everyone.

IMPLICATIONS FOR ACTION

Implications for Policy

- *Prepare for more deliberate and intensive community engagement* in mixed-income neighborhoods to resolve civic issues, because residents bring more diverse experiences and perspectives to the public square.
- *Build the capacity of neighborhood civic leadership* to engage effectively with public and private partners, to provide the most useful advice,

---

5 U.S. Department of Housing and Urban Development. "Mixed-Income Community Dynamics: Five Insights From Ethnography." *Evidence Matters*, Spring 2013.

6 Kip Holley. *The Principles for Equitable and Inclusive Civic Engagement: A Guide to Transformative Change*. (Columbus, OH: The Kirwan Institute for the Study of Race and Ethnicity, The Ohio State University, 2016).

and, ultimately, to take responsibility for sustaining the neighborhood initiatives. This could involve providing staffing support for neighborhood representatives and holding community discussions at times and locations convenient for neighbors.

- *Commit to long-term engagement and support* by public and private partners, particularly those in the role as anchor institutions. The challenges of distressed neighborhoods and the processes for developing mixed-income communities will require well more than a decade of investment.

- *Develop policies for the inclusive use of public and private community spaces.* Local governments can support powerful and sustainable community dialogue in diverse communities by creating policies that ensure inclusive access and belonging in public spaces and developing "community use" policies for corporate or privately-owned community gathering places such as grocery stores and plazas.

Implications for Research and Evaluation

- *Develop the research tools* to define terms such as "mixed-income" and "inclusive community" and to measure the progress toward these social goals.

- *Map survey data* to more effectively illustrate and understand the social groups that compose a mixed-income neighborhood and their varying perspectives.

- *Translate the research data and analysis* into strategies and information that policymakers, civic leaders, and citizens can apply in their work. This may require the development of new techniques, such as the cluster analysis and mapping data described in this paper, to communicate research findings.

Implications for Development and Investment

- *Cultivate a deeper understanding* of the neighborhood's history, built environment, and social groups so that new developments and investments are widely accepted and are seen as benefiting the whole neighborhood. The diversity of a mixed-income neighborhood may require a variety of both formal (i.e., legally mandated) and informal processes for seeking resident input and acceptance on a project.

- *Remain engaged with the neighborhood.* As a new project becomes part of the neighborhood's fabric, the developer becomes a neighbor and remains responsible for maintaining an appropriate level of communication with civic leaders and other neighbors. This is especially critical in a neighborhood like Weinland Park where only 10 percent of residents are homeowners. Although a variety of rental products exist to provide housing for individuals and families at various price points, the regular turnover among student and family rental units makes building civic history and maintaining momentum a constant challenge. This also is one reason for the burnout among homeowners who have invested years of involvement on behalf of an ever-changing group of neighbors.

- *Pay attention to the placement of private amenities within mixed-income neighborhoods.* As developers conceive of market rate projects, they must consider the impact that private assets and amenities can have on reinforcing the gaps between economic "haves" and "have nots" in increasingly diverse settings. One poignant example is the swimming pool included in the most recent market rate apartment development in Weinland Park. As a private amenity reserved exclusively for use of residents of that particular apartment community, the pool and clubhouse symbolize the divide between those in the neighborhood with agency and those whose access to recreational opportunities like swimming pools have historically been limited.

Implications for Residents and Community Members

- *Participate in honest community dialogues about community data and trends.* Sometimes the results of surveys and other analyses may generate emotional discussions about the meaning of the data, particularly regarding difficult issues such as those involving community change, public safety, and structural racism. It is very important for community members to interact around these issues intellectually and emotionally, so they can better understand the experiences their neighbors have had that shape differing attitudes and perceptions. Civic leaders should use the data and dialogue to more effectively represent their neighborhood.

- *Use frameworks of shared opportunity and community assets to approach questions of public safety and greater diversity.* Building a sense of "connectedness" within increasingly diversifying neighborhoods can be essential for effective community planning. By framing sometimes difficult conversations related to race, income, and community change in terms of *shared* assets and goals, community members can help confront biases and plan for more equitable policies.

- *Take advantage of everyday opportunities for authentic relationship-building.* Community members experience challenges related to community diversity on an everyday basis. Therefore, it is important that neighbors make the discussion of challenges and opportunities part of their ongoing community conversations. While the forms and venues of conversations may vary, it is important for residents to engage in them both intellectually and emotionally so that community members can grow and change through their experiences together.

■ ■ ■

KIP HOLLEY is a Research Associate at The Kirwan Institute, where his primary areas of focus are using community engagement, social capital and civic leadership to promote racial equity. During his time at The Kirwan Institute, Holley has worked on a variety of civic engagement related projects with partners from areas as diverse as Central Ohio, Detroit, and California's Central Valley. He is a graduate of The Ohio State University, having received a MSW from the College of Social Work and a B.S in City and Regional Planning from the Knowlton School of Architecture.

■ ■ ■

MATTHEW MARTIN supports the philanthropic purpose of The Columbus Foundation and its donors through community research, evaluation, and grantmaking in order to strengthen and improve the community for all its residents. He guides the foundation's place-based neighborhood revitalization strategy, and works closely with a number of supporting foundations, including the Ingram-White Castle Foundation and the Central Benefits Healthcare Foundation. With a background in city and regional planning, and racial equity research, Martin brings relevant insight to much of the data interpretation and analysis undertaken by the grantmaking team and The Columbus Foundation's community partners.

■ ■ ■

For more than four decades, **STEVE STERRETT** has worked in journalism, public relations and community development. From 1994 to 2010, he was community relations director of Campus Partners, the non-profit community development corporation affiliated with The Ohio State University. He has provided staff support for the Weinland Park Collaborative (WPC) from 2010 through 2019. WPC is a coalition of 20 philanthropic, non-profit, educational, public and private entities that have worked together to foster a mixed-income, diverse urban neighborhood in Columbus, Ohio.

THE ROLE OF COMMUNITY BENEFITS AGREEMENTS IN INCREASING EQUITY AND INCLUSION

Ralph Rosado
Rosado & Associates, Jorge M. Pérez Metropolitan Center

Since 2001, community groups, labor unions, and other organizations have negotiated community benefits agreements (CBAs) with developers and/or city and county governments to prevent low- and moderate-income households of color with limited political and social capital from being displaced by the gentrification that can accompany large-scale, market-rate development and to improve overall community conditions.[1] CBAs are based on the premise that potentially disruptive real estate development projects should significantly improve the quality of life for residents in lower-resourced neighborhoods; in return, the groups representing residents support the projects' requests for government approvals and/or public subsidies. These agreements make land use approvals contingent on developers committing to providing public benefits such as affordable housing, local hiring, job training and apprenticeship programs, daycares, health clinics, and new parks. Just as importantly, the coalition building that occurs through the negotiation process can help expand the capacity of individuals and organizations to promote equity and inclusion in their locales.

For low-income communities and communities of color where residents usually are not fully engaged in planning and land-use regulatory processes, CBAs provide a mechanism for investing public funds in previously neglected areas

---

1   Ralph Rosado, "What Will the Neighbors Say? How Differences in Planning Culture Yield Distinctive Outcomes in Urban Redevelopment: The Example of the Community Benefits Agreement Trend," (Phd diss., University of Pennsylvania Press, 2015), https://repository.upenn.edu/cgi/viewcontent.cgi?article=2935&-context=edissertations.

for the benefit of current residents.[2] The degree to which CBAs serve the most vulnerable residents varies, however, according to the relationships that exist between local elected officials, civic organizations, and residents.[3] In CBAs characterized by *inclusion*, civic coalitions emerge and are seen by local elected officials as respectable, influential parties insistent upon and capable of engaging in transparent negotiations over public benefits. In CBAs developed through *political patronage*, private negotiations result in benefits being captured by politically connected neighborhood elites who negotiate on their own behalf.[4]

This essay analyzes and compares two influential CBAs to illustrate the negotiation dynamics and outcomes of the two different approaches. These examples have attracted considerable attention from policymakers, developers, activists, and the media and have influenced many subsequent agreements across the United States. The first example, involving the L.A. Live project in Los Angeles, California, resulted from extensive collaboration among dozens of local organizations and exemplifies an inclusive relationship between local elected officials and civic players. The second example, the Atlantic Yards project (now known as Pacific Park) in New York City's Brooklyn Borough, is among the most controversial CBAs. This agreement reflects a political patronage relationship in which some local organizations were excluded from the negotiating table while others were hand-selected or, in one instance, created solely for the purpose of supporting the CBA.

L.A. LIVE (LOS ANGELES)

Context

L.A. Live, located on a 27-acre parcel in Los Angeles' Figueroa Corridor, encompasses a sports and entertainment arena, two hotels, a theater, apartment

---

2   Sherry R. Arnstein, "A Ladder of Citizen Participation," *Journal of the American Institute of Planners* 35, no.4 (1969): 216-224; Sheila Foster, "Justice from the Ground Up: Distributive Inequities, Grassroots Resistance, and the Transformative Politics of the Environmental Justice Movement," *California Environmental Law Review* 86 (1998): 831-837; Alejandro Esteban Camacho, "Mustering the Missing Voices: A Collaborative Model for Fostering Equality, Community Involvement and Adaptive Planning in Land Use Decisions," *Stanford Environmental Law Journal* 24, no.3 (2005): 15-36.

3   Margaret Weir, "Power, Money, and Politics in Community Development," in *Urban Problems in Community Development*, eds. Ronald R. Ferguson and William T. Dickens, (Washington, DC: Brookings Institution Press, 1999), 139-192.

4   Rosado, "What Will the Neighbors Say?"

buildings, and a retail complex. This project had two phases: creation of the Staples Center arena, which was completed in 1999, and construction of the Los Angeles Sports and Entertainment District.

Situated at the intersection of five redevelopment project areas, the Figueroa Corridor was shaped by the (now defunct) Los Angeles Community Redevelopment Agency (LACRA). The southern part of the Corridor lies within a redevelopment area established in the 1960s in an effort to keep the University of Southern California (USC) at its South Los Angeles location by allowing the institution to expand its campus borders and eliminate surrounding community blight. With the help of the LACRA, USC became the largest landowner in the Corridor, with a real estate portfolio of over 100 properties, many of which are devoted to student housing.

To the north, development pressures on the Figueroa Corridor have emanated from the redevelopment of downtown Los Angeles. Downtown L.A. ranks among the city's most racially, ethnically, and economically diverse neighborhoods as well as one of its fastest-growing ones. According to the 2010 Census, downtown L.A.'s population is almost evenly divided between residents who are Asian American (23 percent), Black (22 percent), Latinx (25 percent), and non-Hispanic White (26 percent).

The Staples Center, located immediately north of the Los Angeles Convention Center, hosts over 250 events and nearly four million guests annually. It is home to the Los Angeles Lakers and the Los Angeles Clippers of the National Basketball Association, the Los Angeles Kings of the National Hockey League, and the Los Angeles Sparks of the Women's National Basketball Association. The Staples Center was developed by the L.A. Arena Land Company through a complex, $375 million deal involving private and public funding. Billionaire Rupert Murdoch's Fox Group purchased a 40 percent interest in the arena; the developer obtained a $70 million combination grant and loan package; and the office-supply company, Staples, Inc., paid for naming rights.

The L.A. Arena Company and Anschutz Entertainment Group (AEG) own and operate the Staples Center. In 2000, AEG announced plans to develop a theater, two convention hotels, a convention center expansion, apartments, retail stores, restaurants, and nightclubs around the Staples Center site. Officials and nearby business owners considered this second phase of development essential to the revitalization of Los Angeles. The need for significant land use variances and city subsidies provided the community leverage to negotiate one of the most comprehensive CBAs made to date.

Negotiations

A diverse coalition formed to negotiate the CBA with the L.A. Arena Company in 2001. The Figueroa Corridor Coalition for Economic Justice (FCCEJ) is comprised of representatives of more than 30 community organizations, including environmental groups, church groups, health organizations, and immigrants' and tenants' rights supporters. Strategic Action for a Just Economy (SAJE) and the Los Angeles Alliance for a New Economy (LAANE) provided organizational and political support to the coalition and community members.

FCCEJ members were motivated in part by frustration that city officials had adopted the Staples Center's construction plan with limited community input. Over 200 residents, many of them low-income Latinx immigrants, were displaced from their homes by the construction of a parking lot for the arena. Once the center opened, the residents who remained coped with traffic and parking challenges, nighttime noise, and drunk drivers. Moreover, the construction deal gained the support of The Hotel Employees and Restaurant Employees local union and the Los Angeles County Federation of Labor when the developer verbally promised to pay a living wage and remain neutral in the event of a union organizing drive.[5] After the developers obtained their subsidies and variances from the city, however, they argued that they were not subject to the living-wage requirement. They stalled on signing an agreement that would hold employers neutral when workers consider unionizing, and they claimed they had no authority to tell their tenants to sign one. Only after the unions staged a fight were the developers forced to keep their oral promises. Community activists hoped that a written CBA in phase two would help ensure the delivery of benefits—specifically, a guarantee of affordable housing, funding for parks, local hiring, and a living-wage clause.

Members of the FCCEJ coalition banded together because they realized that, despite having different missions, they shared mutual interests and might find strength in numbers. Strategic Actions for a Just Economy, one of the

---

[5] Julian Gross, Greg LeRoy, and Madeline Janis-Aparicio, *Community Benefits Agreements: Making Development Projects Accountable*, (Good Jobs First and the California Partnership for Working Families, 2015), https://www.goodjobsfirst.org/sites/default/files/docs/pdf/cba2005final.pdf.

coalition's lead organizations,[6] brought other groups on board and organized 300 tenants who lived in the area. This grassroots base played a key role in winning the agreement, which was oriented largely to their needs, and establishing a long-term community development strategy for the Figueroa Corridor that continues today. Meanwhile, the Los Angeles Alliance for a New Economy—which enjoyed a reputation for political effectiveness because of the living-wage campaign it had spearheaded[7]—cultivated union support. The unions negotiated their agreement separately from the CBA to comply with federal guidelines on labor negotiations, but the labor and community coalitions stayed united in their strategy and demands. When disagreements stymied the progress of the janitors' union, community negotiators stood in solidarity with labor. In turn, labor chimed in on issues such as affordable housing, which affects their members but was not explicitly on their agenda.[8]

Although Anschutz Entertainment Group leaders initially said they would deal solely with the LACRA, a desire to line up city approvals quickly in an election year—and evidence that the LACRA and city council would not approve the project without organized labor's support—prompted the developer to meet with the coalition's representatives. The parties reached an agreement over five months, ending in May 2001. The signatories worked together over the next several months to secure government approvals and, ultimately, significant public subsidies for the project.[9]

The influential CBA contract was a legal document specifying the developer's cooperation with and financial contribution to a variety of measures. FCCEJ members signed a separate cooperation agreement pledging not to oppose the L.A. Live project. The CBA was then incorporated into the development and disposition agreement between the L.A. Arena Company and Anschutz Entertainment Group and the local government, making it enforceable by the city as well as by the contracting community groups.[10]

---

6 Lee Romney, "Community, Developers Agree on Staples Plan," *Los Angeles Times*, May 31, 2001, https://www.latimes.com/archives/la-xpm-2001-may-31-mn-4715-story.html.

7 James Goodno, "A Movement Takes Shape," Los Angeles Alliance for a New Economy, March 2004, Accessed January 29, 2012.

8 Romney, "Community, Developers Agree on Staples Plan."

9 Patrick McGreevey, "Subsidies May Aid L.A. Live," *Los Angeles Times*, June 14, 2008, https://www.latimes.com/archives/la-xpm-2008-jun-14-me-anschutz14-story.html.

10 Los Angeles Community Redevelopment Agency, accessed January 18, 2012, http://www.crala.org/inter-

The agreement includes provisions committing the developer to ensure a mix of housing by setting aside 20 percent of the project's total housing units as affordable housing for qualified households and by making $650,000 in interest-free loans available to local nonprofit housing developers to build new mixed-income housing. In addition, the agreement assured labor protections: At least 70 percent of the permanent jobs to be created by the project—including those offered by tenants— required a living wage or better. The developer also had to create a local hiring and job training program for workers displaced by the arena who reside within three miles of the project and/or in low-income areas citywide. Finally, the agreement required the allocation of $1 million for the creation or improvement of parks within a mile of the project.

It can be challenging to monitor the implementation of the developer commitments contained in a CBA. A recent analysis[11] of the L.A. Live CBA reveals that the developer complied with the commitments, with the possible exception of the targeted hiring commitment, which was not thoroughly documented. Other commitments were achieved after the agreed-upon deadlines. Still, as the analysis demonstrates, CBAs can be a tool for community groups to ensure that developers follow through on their commitments when government monitoring and enforcement are inadequate.

ATLANTIC YARDS (NEW YORK CITY)

Context

Atlantic Yards is a $4.9 billion mixed-use, mixed-income residential and commercial development project proposed for the low- and mid-rise brownstone neighborhood of Prospect Heights in Brooklyn, New York. Known throughout most of the 1900s for its ethnic diversity, combining residents of Italian, Irish, Jewish, German, and Greek ancestry, Prospect Heights currently is recognized for its mixed black and white culture. Earlier this decade, the racial makeup of the neighborhood was 47 percent White, 30 percent Black, 7 percent Asian, and 4 percent from two or more races. Latinx individuals of any race compose approximately 12 percent of the population.

---

net-site/index.cfm.

11 Nicholas J. Marantz, "What Do Community Benefits Agreements Deliver? Evidence from Los Angeles," *Journal of the American Planning Association* 81, no. 4 (2015): 251-267.

In December 2003, Forest City Ratner (FCR), one of the nation's largest developers and managers of commercial and residential real estate, announced plans to construct a 19,000-seat arena for the New Jersey Nets professional basketball team along with housing, office suites, retail space, a hotel, a parking garage, and thousands of apartments intended for an economically diverse array of households at the Vanderbilt Railyards site in downtown Brooklyn. The proposed 22-acre project would be New York City's largest development in a quarter century and the largest development in Brooklyn history. It was initially expected to take a decade to build.[12]

FCR purchased the air rights over roughly 11 acres of Metropolitan Transportation Authority (MTA) rail yards, and an additional 13 acres were subject to state condemnation for FCR's use pursuant to eminent domain laws. At the time, the MTA, Mayor Michael Bloomberg, and Brooklyn Borough President Marty Markowitz all endorsed the project. Perhaps not surprisingly for a development of such size, however, the project also generated immediate skepticism and controversy.[13] FCR embarked on a campaign to win support for the project, and as part of that campaign raised the idea of a community benefits agreement.

Negotiations

The community benefits agreement that emerged in 2005 for the Atlantic Yards project marked the first noteworthy and controversial deviation from the prototypical CBA scenario found in Los Angeles and appeared to set a precedent for some of the New York City CBAs that would follow. Beginning in July 2004 and continuing over several months, FCR convened meetings with select social justice and labor groups.[14] As community activists learned

---

12 Charles V. Bagli, "Deal Is Signed for Nets Arena in Brooklyn," *New York Times*, March 4, 2005, https://www.nytimes.com/2005/03/04/nyregion/deal-is-signed-for-nets-arena-in-brooklyn.html

13 Nicholas Confessore, "The People Speak (Shout, Actually) on Brooklyn Arena Project," *New York Times*, October 19, 2005a, https://www.nytimes.com/2005/10/19/nyregion/the-people-speak-shout-actually-on-brooklyn-arena-project.html.; Nicholas Confessore, "To Build Arena in Brooklyn, Developer First Builds Bridges," *New York Times*, October 14, 2005b, https://www.nytimes.com/2005/10/14/nyregion/to-build-arena-in-brooklyndeveloper-first-builds-bridges.html.; Jarrett Murphy, "The Battle of Brooklyn," *Village Voice*, July 12, 2005, https://www.villagevoice.com/2005/07/12/the-battle-of-brooklyn/.

14 The ultimate signatories to this agreement were: All-Faith Council of Brooklyn, Association of Community Organizations for Reform Now (ACORN), Brooklyn United for Innovative Local Development (BUILD), Downtown Brooklyn Neighborhood Alliance (DBNA), Downtown Brooklyn Educational Consortium, First Atlantic Terminal Housing Committee, New York State Association of Minority Contractors, and Public Housing Communities.

about the negotiations underway, however, considerable controversy over the process emerged.[15] One of the organizations, Brooklyn United for Innovative Local Development (BUILD), was formed shortly before negotiations began, ostensibly in time to serve as one of the negotiating entities, and folded in 2012, shortly after the arena opened.[16] Other groups that had taken positions against the project, such as Develop Don't Destroy Brooklyn and the Prospect Heights Action Coalition, did not participate in the discussions, although there is disagreement about whether they were excluded or refused to participate.[17] As a result, only groups already committed to the project engaged in discussions. Residents opposed to the scale and nature of the project found themselves without a seat at the table.

While negotiations over the CBA were proceeding, Forest City Ratner was also negotiating with the city and state about the governmental processes that would be used to review the proposal.[18] Under the city's usual procedures, the community board would hold a hearing on the project and then recommend approval or disapproval of the project to the borough president, who in turn would hold a hearing before making a recommendation to the city planning commission, which would be required to hold a hearing. If the commission approved the project, the city council would then hold a hearing before voting on the project. But New York State's Urban Development Corporation law gives the Empire State Development Corporation (ESDC)[19] the power to

---

15 Alair Townsend, "Neighborhood Extortion," *Crain's New York Business*, November 8, 2004, Accessed January 28, 2012; Patrick Gallahue, "Tout of Bounds—Ratner Forces Apt. Sellers to Hype Nets Arena," *New York Post*, June 16, 2004, https://nypost.com/2004/06/16/tout-of-bounds-ratner-forces-apt-sellers-to-hype-nets-arena/; Nicholas Confessore, "A Nod for Atlantic Yards, and Then a Lawsuit," New York Times, December 9, 2006a. https://www.nytimes.com/2006/12/09/nyregion/09yards.html.

16 Dan Rosenblum, "Bruce Ratner-Financed Community Group Goes out of Business Two Months after His Arena Opens," *Next City*, November 15, 2012, https://nextcity.org/daily/entry/key-atlantic-yards-org-to-close.

17 Hugh Son, "Owner Neglecting Nets, Say Critics," *New York Daily News*, November 29, 2004, https://www.nydailynews.com/archives/boroughs/owner-neglecting-nets-critics-article-1.611337; Bertha Lewis, "Supporting Atlantic Yards: 'Simply Not Enough Housing in Brooklyn,'" *City Limits Weekly*, July 31, 2006, https://citylimits.org/2006/07/31/supporting-atlantic-yardssimply-not-enough-housing-in-brooklyn/.

18 Nicholas Confessore, "Arena Complex Shrinks by 5% in Latest Plan," *New York Times*, April 1, 2006b, https://www.nytimes.com/2006/04/01/nyregion/arena-complex-shrinks-by-5-in-latest-plan.html; Nicholas Confessore, "State Approves Major Complex for Brooklyn," *New York Times*, December 21, 2006c, https://www.nytimes.com/2006/12/21/nyregion/21brooklyn.html.

19 The umbrella organization for New York's two principal economic development public-benefit corporations, the New York State Urban Development Corporation and the New York Job Development Authority.

override local zoning and other laws and processes under certain circumstances. In March 2005, the city and ESDC signed a memorandum of understanding with the developer that recognized ESDC's power to override the city's land-use review procedure. The effect was to eliminate the legal role that Community Board 6, the Brooklyn Borough president, the city planning commission, and the city council otherwise would have had in deliberations over the project.

Although the ESDC's authority over the development foreclosed any official role for the community boards and removed the requirement for public hearings in review of the proposal, FCR continued to negotiate privately with organizations over a community benefits agreement. In June 2005, with Mayor Bloomberg as an official "witness," representatives of Forest City Ratner and eight community-based organizations signed the CBA, the first in New York City. Unlike the LA Live CBA negotiations, which involved dozens of community groups, many of which did not originally support the project, the Atlantic Yards CBA signatories all openly supported the project before signing on.

The CBA aims to promote the creation of mixed-income, economically and environmentally healthy communities by setting aside 50 percent of all residential units for low-income families; agreeing to allocate 35 percent of the construction work to minority-owned businesses and 10 percent to women contractors hired during construction; developing a program to find job placements for hard-to-employ youth; establishing a committee to address short- and long-term environmental issues and reporting periodically to the coalition on mitigation measures; agreeing to open a health care center and a senior citizens center within the project; agreeing to lease at least 15 percent of the gross retail leasing space to qualified community-based businesses; and setting aside six acres of open space on the project site for free use by the public.

The ESDC approved the project in August 2006, and in December 2006 the Public Authorities Control Board—consisting of Governor George Pataki, House State Assembly Speaker Sheldon Silver, and Senate Majority Leader Joseph Bruno—approved the project. The project's ground breaking occurred in early 2007. Controversy over the negotiation process has dogged the project, however.[20] By the time the Barclays Center arena opened in September 2012 as the centerpiece of Atlantic Yards and the home of the Brooklyn Nets, the

---

20 Townsend, "Neighborhood Extortion;" Gallahue, "Tout of Bounds—Ratner Forces Apt. Sellers to Hype Nets Arena;" Confessore, "A Nod for Atlantic Yards, and Then a Lawsuit."

project had experienced years of lawsuits.[21] Moreover, the 2008 economic downturn led FCR to delay construction of the residential buildings at Atlantic Yards, prompting fears that the affordable housing units they were to contain would never be built.[22]

Substantial progress on the project has occurred since 2014, following an infusion of funding from Greenland Holding Group, a Chinese development company. As of 2019, six of the project's buildings are under construction or completed. About 800 of the 6,400-plus planned apartments are deemed affordable, and the eight-acre park component is under construction. The project's original master plan, prepared by famed architect Frank Gehry, remains the guiding vision for the development, but individual components (including the potential to house Brooklyn's largest office tower on the site) remain in flux.[23] Changes to the site plan require approval from the ESDC. As the project's most prominent and longstanding critic, Norman Oder of Develop Don't Destroy Brooklyn, argues, however, "No matter the issue—affordable housing, arena operations, eminent domain, construction, changes in the project, provision of open space…there's one consistent issue: accountability."[24] Citing this particular CBA as an example, Lance Freeman, a prominent researcher, cautions that CBAs, in the hands of governmental and private parties not acting in good faith, can serve as an undemocratic way to insert the semblance of community input into a planning process.[25] The project, rebranded by the developer as Pacific Park Brooklyn in July 2014, is now expected to be completed in 2035.

---

21 Charles V. Bagli, "Slow Economy Likely to Stall Atlantic Yards," *New York Times*, March 21, 2008, https://www.nytimes.com/2008/03/21/nyregion/21yards.html.

22 Michael Daly, "As Vows Fade in Atlantic Yards, So Do Housing Hopes," *New York Daily News*, March 23, 2008, https://www.nydailynews.com/new-york/brooklyn/vows-fade-atlantic-yards-housing-hopes-article-1.290331; "BrooklynSpeaks sponsors file for stay of construction at Atlantic Yards site," Brooklyn Speaks, accessed December 5, 2019, http://www.brooklynspeaks.net/sponsors-file-for-stay; Michelle Higgins, "First Condos Soon for Sale at Barclays Center Site," *New York Times*, June 12, 2015, https://www.nytimes.com/2015/06/14/realestate/first-condos-soon-for-sale-at-barclays-center-site.html?ref=todayspaper.

23 Amy Plitt, "A Decade on, Brooklyn's Pacific Park Megaproject Is Finally Realized," *Curbed New York*, August 18, 2016, https://ny.curbed.com/2016/8/18/12417328/pacific-park-brooklyn-megaproject-update.

24 Plitt, "A Decade on, Brooklyn's Pacific Park Megaproject Is Finally Realized."

25 Plitt, "A Decade on, Brooklyn's Pacific Park Megaproject Is Finally Realized."

CONCLUSION

The L.A. Live and Atlantic Yards examples show that community benefits agreements, when arrived at through a transparent, community-involved negotiation, offer an opportunity for individuals and groups that have been historically excluded to flex greater power and influence over major decisions that shape their lives. The process of negotiating CBAs can help residents and community groups lay the groundwork for real estate projects in their neighborhoods that produce mixed-income, mixed-use developments and promote a higher quality of life, especially for the communities of color in which the projects are often located. In addition, the capacity building and coalition development involved in negotiating such agreements can serve as a platform for ongoing community efforts to advance inclusion and equity.

Conversely, a CBA can preclude meaningful community engagement and ultimately benefit mainly well-connected political elites at the expense of addressing critical community needs. As a result, instead of serving as harbingers of more inclusive planning processes, CBAs actually might make it possible to mask a lack of transparency and community involvement in land use processes across the United States.

IMPLICATIONS FOR ACTION

Implications for Policy

- Local government officials can promote more equitable development by requesting local hiring, living wages, affordable housing, and other public benefits as part of project approval processes for large projects that receive public subsidies.
- Local government officials can encourage and facilitate CBA negotiations. They can also help civic organizations, which often have small staffs, monitor the implementation of CBA commitments.

Implications for Research and Evaluation

- Researchers should monitor how well the signatories to a CBA are following through on their commitments, as the literature on this subject is sparse.

Implications for Development and Investment

- Developers should offer to include community benefits in their development agreements or enter into CBAs with affected residents and groups, especially if a project is potentially disruptive or costly to local governments in terms of development incentives.

Implications for Residents and Community Members

- Residents and civic groups should seek legal help prior to negotiating for benefits; it is important to know how local, state, and federal laws empower and/or constrain opportunities for CBAs.
- Negotiators should get commitments in writing to help avoid broken promises.
- The most effective negotiations and monitoring of benefits occur when groups work as a coalition of mutually supportive civic players.

■ ■ ■

RALPH ROSADO, Ph.D., AICP, is Village Manager of North Bay Village, Florida, as well as Senior Fellow at the FIU Metropolitan Center, and an instructor in graduate and professional programs at the University of Miami and Florida International University. Rosado holds a Ph.D. in City Planning from the University of Pennsylvania, with a focus on Neighborhood Revitalization, Economic Development, and Affordable Housing; a joint Master's degree in Public Policy and Urban Planning from Princeton University, where he was elected as the first Hispanic in Princeton University's history to serve as President of the university's Graduate Student Government for Public Affairs; and a Bachelor of Arts degree in English from Florida International University's Honors College. While in graduate school, at the invitation of President George W. Bush, Rosado served as a White House Graduate Intern with the United States Department of Housing and Urban Development.

Confronting Exclusion through Changing the Narrative

These three essays explore the importance of shifting the narrative about race, segregation and opportunity in order to make progress on fostering inclusion and equity.

In "How Do Fish See Water? Building Public Will to Advance Inclusive Communities", Dr. Tiffany Manuel examines how widespread apathy and outright resistance to mixed-income development can be traced to a deep seeded history of racism and inequality in the U.S. She writes, "Unlike climate change, health care, education or other social "issues" that are well-understood as requiring public intervention, racial and economic segregation operates so ubiquitously that it is often ignored as a "thing" to be solved. It just is." Manuel argues that public buy in is essential to an inclusive future. She dissects the beliefs and attitudes underlying the acceptance of segregation, demonstrating the conflicting narratives of scholars working to promote inclusion, with those of the community members they hope to influence, and proposing practical principles for action in reshaping and mobilizing public will to fight exclusion.

In "Changing the Narrative and Playbook on Racially Concentrated Areas of Poverty", authors Edward Goetz, Anthony Damiano, and Rashad Williams, challenge pervasive deficit-based narratives in public policy and research that posit low-income, racially concentrated areas, or Racially Concentrated Areas of Poverty (RECAPs) as the U.S Department of Housing and Urban Development has termed them, as essentially deficient and requiring strategies that would disperse and transform their economic and racial composition. The authors examine traditional approaches to community development and identify the flaws inherent in so-called mobility strategies. They use the case study of an advocacy group in Minnesota to explore the ways in which community assets can be centered to empower grassroots solutions that are not reliant on mobility or gentrification. The essay examines how to shift policy by illuminating long-standing bias and putting the focus on inequitable systems and segregation in affluent White communities. The essay shares implications for how actors at the levels of policy, research, and community can work towards fundamentally altering how community development in RECAPs is discussed and practiced.

"Addressing Resistance to Mixed-Income Communities through Empathetic Planning Techniques" by Aly Andrews and Sydney VanKuren presents an innovative approach to addressing the unconscious biases that can motivate community members' opposition to mixed-income developments in their communities. They provide an overview of the psychological phenomenon behind common arguments to mixed-income development and posit "empathetic planning" as a method to help community members recognize their fears and underlying beliefs in order to move past them. They emphasize that: "Empathetic planning is not about manipulating community members... It is about getting members of the public to become self-aware of their own framing—and putting that framing aside—to make decisions for the future of their community."

HOW DO FISH SEE WATER? BUILDING PUBLIC WILL TO ADVANCE INCLUSIVE COMMUNITIES

Tiffany Manuel
TheCaseMade

> "There are these two young fish swimming along, and they happen to meet an older fish swimming the other way, who nods at them and says, 'Morning, boys. How's the water?' And the two young fish swim on for a bit, and then eventually one of them looks over at the other and goes, 'What the hell is water?'"
>
> —David Foster Wallace[1]

Cultivating more equitable and inclusive communities is challenging work. In addition to the technical challenges of fostering such communities, there is the added conundrum of how to build public support for policies and investments that make equitable and inclusive development possible. On the public will-building front, this work is made exponentially tougher because it generally means asking people to problematize an issue—racial and economic segregation—that they do not see as a problem threatening the values and vitality of the communities in which they live. Unlike climate change, health care, education, or other social "issues" that are understood as requiring public intervention, racial and economic segregation operates so ubiquitously that it is often ignored as a "thing" to be solved. It just *is*. When people are asked explicitly to reflect on the high level of concentrated segregation that characterizes their communities and

---

1 David Foster Wallace, *This Is Water: Some Thoughts, Delivered on a Significant Occasion, about Living a Compassionate Life* (New York: Little, Brown and Company, 2005).

to consider the well-documented negative consequences of people living so separately, many struggle to "see" this as a compelling policy problem with the same shaping force of other issues requiring national attention. Perhaps most importantly, they struggle to see their stake in shaping solutions and supporting policies that cultivate more equitable and inclusive places. Because segregation is so fully woven into the environments around us, we behave like fish—ignoring the water surrounding us.

More often, segregation and its consequences are understood from a set of distinctive public narratives (or commonly shared beliefs that dominate the public discourse).[2] Those narratives are: (1) *consumer preferences and racial difference* (i.e., the idea that people make rational choices to live with others who are like them, especially in the context of race); and (2) the narratives of *individual responsibility and mobility* (i.e., poor people wanting to move to better neighborhoods need only earn their way there via hard work and perseverance). When people use these narratives to reason about segregation, it becomes infinitely tougher for them to think constructively about solutions that foster inclusion, especially around race and income. To build stronger public support, advocates of mixed-race and mixed-income policies must carefully navigate these narratives to make a much stronger case for why segregation and inequity are problems that deserve and require a more thoughtful collective response.

There is good news on the horizon for advocates who have tried for decades to elevate the issue of racial and economic segregation on the political and policy agendas. The policy window on equitable and inclusive community development practices is open now, as political will grows nationally to address the severe shortage of affordable housing, gentrification, and displacement concerns. Whether this is a moment to make real progress on how we address segregation or just a wrinkle in time, however, depends mightily on how we make the case for relevant solutions and how we are able to show how those

---

2   "Public narrative is a form of social reproduction in all societies, invisibly woven into the fabric of everyday life. These shared systems of meaning, mostly taken for granted and unremarked, exist as themes or stories in our consciousness. They give coherence to group experience, particularly how the world works. Expressed in legal codes, the arts, mass media, and corporate discourse, core narratives provide the necessary mental models, patterns, and beliefs to make sense of the world and explore our place within it." See: Corrina Wainwright, *Building Narrative Power for Racial Justice and Health Equity*, Edited by Bisola Falola and Steffie Klinglake, (Open Society Foundations, July 2019), 4. https://www.opensocietyfoundations.org/publications/building-narrative-power-for-racial-justice-and-health-equity.

solutions relate to a very long list of pressing social issues already on the political agenda.

THE PUBLIC DISCOURSE ON POVERTY, RACE AND PLACE

> *"My longstanding advice to ambitious people trapped in stagnant communities—move, for God's sake!"*
>
> —Kevin Williamson[3]

An explicit public conversation about poverty, race, and place is making its erratic way across the country and creating a perfect storm for policy action. A perfect storm always arises from a rare combination of unpredictable factors. This current political storm seems to be stimulated by at least three significant factors: a particularly challenging presidential administration that has polarized the nation around issues of race and inequality; a rapidly "browning America"[4] that is changing how Americans see themselves; and the spatial dynamics of the economic inequality that is widening the income and wealth gap. By themselves, these issues could sustain gale-force winds in the public consciousness, but they have been accompanied by a larger colluding force: a national housing crisis. The severity of the national shortage of housing is driving up housing costs across the country and upending communities that have long been home to low-income residents and many people of color, displacing them to the outer edges of many cities and raising the visibility of gentrification.

While these topics have always been fodder for debate and analysis in academic circles, they have not typically led the nightly news or played out in contentious parent-teacher association meetings. Yet today, in a very explicit way, that is exactly what is happening across the United States. On the one hand, we are seeing the onslaught of racist attacks by President Trump on cities like Baltimore (which he labeled "a disgusting, rat and rodent infested mess"[5]). On the other hand, we are seeing rebuttals by anti-racism advocates who

---

[3] Kevin Williamson, "More Garbuttiana," *National Review*, April 15, 2016, www.nationalreview.com/article/434100/white-working-class-donald.

[4] zra Klein, "White Threat in a Browning America," *VOX*, July 30, 2018,. https://www.vox.com/policy-and-politics/2018/7/30/17505406/trump-obama-race-politics-immigration.

[5] Meredith McGraw, "President Trump heads to Baltimore, a city he called a 'rodent infested mess,'". ABC News September 12, 2019, https://abcnews.go.com/Politics/president-trump-heads-baltimore-city-called-rodent-infested/story?id=65570278

also point to the vast racial and economic disparities across communities but see the culprits as a toxic cocktail of white supremacy, advanced capitalism, and a system of interlocking policies of exclusion. The fervor on both ends of this spectrum is elevating these issues in the public discourse and challenging advocates to understand how best to steer the conversations toward concrete policy actions that could make a difference.

As this dynamic has played out, contentious battles over the siting of affordable housing in neighborhoods large and small are erupting, as everyday people try to make sense of the rapidly changing racial, economic, and spatial dynamics playing out in their communities. Issues like zoning and land use policy—typically of interest only to local policy wonks—today bring people out to community meetings with almost as much passion as local football or baseball games.

Despite the challenges of wading into the erratic eye of this storm, housing and community-development practitioners are doing so because this political environment represents one of the best opportunities we have had in years to advance a real conversation about the interlocking institutional policies that have reinforced racial and economic boundaries in the United States. With better data and evidence in hand about what works to create and sustain inclusive communities, housing and community-development advocates are pushing hard to position solutions against the backdrop of these broader social forces.

WHAT'S DRIVING THE CONVERSATION IN HOUSING AND COMMUNITY DEVELOPMENT?

> *"Developers say that perhaps the toughest impediment to new housing construction is local opposition, especially if the proposed construction site is in a safe neighborhood with good schools."*
>
> —Ana Beatriz Cholo[6]

Housing and community-development practitioners have made the development and preservation of high-quality affordable housing a reality

---

6   Ana Beatriz Cholo, "Why Affordable Housing Doesn't Get Built: Developers often face public opposition, regulatory barriers and financial risks," *Huffington Post*, Feb. 6, 2016, https://www.huffingtonpost.com/entry/affordable-housingcalifornia_us_56cf4b61e4b03260bf75e01e.

in many neighborhoods across the country. We know that housing is the foundation for creating stable, healthy communities. We know that housing is key to addressing economic inequality, because housing remains the primary way that Americans build wealth. And we know that housing is a key mechanism for dismantling racial and economic segregation. Much progress has been made in addressing tough issues, such as racial and economic segregation, by bringing mixed-income developments to neighborhoods. Blighted neighborhoods have been turned into bustling ones and other, more affluent, neighborhoods are now home to low- and moderate-income families who would otherwise not be able to afford to live in those communities.

While much progress has been made, it is disheartening to see how many families across the nation still do not have a decent, affordable place to live, the extent to which many neighborhoods are still racially and economically segregated, and how difficult it continues to be to tap existing housing policies and programs to create more equitable outcomes and inclusive communities.

The housing and community development fields have been increasingly explicit about naming the goals of equity and inclusion as priorities and collaborating with other sectors (e.g., health, education, transportation), recognizing that a good portion of our very well-intended efforts have reinforced, rather than upended, patterns of racial and economic segregation in communities. Consequently, we are learning from each other about how to create more inclusive communities and developing greater sophistication in piloting strategies that advance more equitable and inclusive communities.

From the vantage point of housing and community-development practitioners, the public discourse about the relationship between poverty, race, and place has been problematic in and of itself. Anyone who has been to a neighborhood meeting on the siting or zoning of affordable housing in the last 10 years knows well how much misinformation and implicit bias is allowed to stand in for informed deliberation.[7] When the thorny issues of racial and economic segregation come up in the media, arise in community meetings, or require public comment in other community forums, rarely is there enough depth of understanding to move those conversations toward support for useful policy

---

7 Jillian Olinger, Kelly Capatosto, and Mary Ana McKay, *Challenging Race as Risk: How Implicit Bias Undermines Housing Opportunity in American—and what we can do about it*, (Columbus, OH: Kirwan Institute, 2016), http://kirwaninstitute.osu.edu/wp-content/uploads/2017/02/implicit-bias-housing.pdf.

solutions. Much of this has to do with the narratives that undergird public thinking about these issues.

From the expertise in communities, as well as a growing body of framing research on poverty and inequality, we know quite a lot about the narratives Americans use to think and talk about these issues. For example, whereas housing and community-development practitioners view the relationship between poverty, race, and place as a result of broader systems and structural issues, the narrative circulating in broader public discourse often is quite different. In public discourse, poor neighborhoods are seen as a function of the flawed people who live there: people who fail to take advantage of the opportunities that exist in America and who fail to live up to the community values around hard work, grit, and determination. As the logic goes, poor people are understood to be poor because they make "poor choices" and, by extension, the fact that they are disproportionately Black or Latinx gets attributed to a broader narrative about racial or cultural difference.

Moreover, the public narrative often posits that people need to take more initiative to address their own challenges—to move when rents are too high, to get more education or job training when wages are too low to pay for the desired quality of housing or neighborhood amenities, and more generally to make better life "choices." This perception makes it difficult to engage people in advocating for inclusive policies, programs, and investments that have equity built into them. Because the public narrative tends to attribute racial disparities in housing to individual choices rather than to the structural dynamics of social and economic inequality, it reinforces ambivalence toward supporting a stronger set of policies, programs, and investments that would ameliorate these issues. We see this playing out in housing policy today, as polls across the country show increasing support for the idea that people ought to have decent, affordable housing yet the public response to policies that would help has been lukewarm. Policies supporting fair housing enjoy widespread public support in principle, but there has been virtually no public appetite for enforcement and stronger engagement. Instead, when the public conversation moves to policy solutions on an issue people believe to be fundamentally about individual "choices," the commentary is unforgiving. Reactions often take the shape of the comment in , which responded to a NYTimes article describing the Trump Administration's virtual shut-down on the implementation of Affirmatively Furthering Fair Housing (AFFH) policy.

The New York Times

: TheUpshot

Trump Administration Postpones an Obama Fair-Housing Rule

By Emily Badger and John Eligon

Jan. 4, 2018

> **Katie**
> Atlanta   Jan. 4, 2018
>
> This is great news and I hope the rule is eventually abolished. If you can't afford to live on, say, Jupiter Island, Florida then you have no right to demand that the Island build lower cost housing to accommodate you. Discrimination in the sale or rent of housing should never be tolerated but it's a very different thing to say that there is some affirmative duty for every community to directly reflect the nation's racial and ethnic diversity even if that means forcing low income housing into Chappaqua. That is governmental overreach of epic proportions.
>
> 25 Recommend   Share   Flag

Figure 1

It also is worth acknowledging that even in discussions of poor White communities, the public message about solutions tends to be the same: Take personal responsibility and move to a place that you can afford:

> "The truth about these dysfunctional, downscale communities is that they deserve to die. Economically, they are negative assets. Morally, they are indefensible... The white American underclass is in thrall to a vicious, selfish culture whose main products are misery and used heroin needles. Donald Trump's speeches make them feel good. So does OxyContin. What they need isn't analgesics, literal or political. They need real opportunity, which means that they need real change, which means that they need U-Haul."[8]

---

[8] Kevin D. Williamson, "The Father-Führer," *National Review*, March 16, 2016, https://www.nationalreview.com/magazine/2016/03/28/father-f-hrer/

If there is any good news on this front, it is that Americans consistently support the broad ideals behind inclusive mixed-race and mixed-income communities. A 2013 Urban Land Institute study found that 62 percent of Americans surveyed said they "would prefer to settle in mixed-use communities,"[9] and a follow-up study in 2015 found that 66 percent "would rather live in a community with a mix of cultures and backgrounds."[10] In terms of equity concerns, polling finds that Americans generally feel empathetic towards those who are economically struggling,[11] believe in the ideals of policies meant to address racial discrimination in housing, and, when given sample scenarios, can identify the kinds of behavior that violate things such as fair housing laws.[12] Similarly, polling on affordable housing more generally finds that Americans believe deeply in the idea that everyone should have decent, affordable housing in communities that are thriving. Some polls also have found general support for the idea that local governments can do more to advance housing options.[13]

---

9   Urban Land Institute, *America in 2013*. (Washington, DC: Urban Land Institute, 2013), https://uli.org/wp-content/uploads/ULI-Documents/America_in_2013_web.pdf.

10 Urban Land Institute, *America in 2015*. (Washington, DC: Urban Land Institute, 2015), http://uli.org/wp-content/uploads/ULI-Documents/America-in-2015.pdf.

11 See for example, a national poll in 2017 commissioned by the Strong, Prosperous, and Resilient Communities Challenge (SPARCC), How Local Leadership Can Drive Prosperity for All, available at: SPARCC, "How Local Leadership Can Drive Prosperity for All," accessed on November 24, 2019, http://www.sparcchub.org/wp-content/uploads/2017/03/SPARCC_Poll-Results_Report.pdf. We should be careful to note that Americans also say that the poor should do more to "help themselves," "get jobs," and "stop using/abusing government programs." For example, a 2016 poll conducted by Princeton Survey Research Associates for the American Enterprise Institute and Los Angeles Times compared contemporary attitudes about the poor with the same polling questions they used in 1985, finding a persistence in the perception among Americans that the poor overuse government benefits and "prefer to stay on welfare," despite a significantly reduced set of benefits offered as part of the public's social safety net.

12 Martin D. Abravanel and Mary K. Cunningham, *How Much Do We Know? Public Awareness of the Nation's Fair Housing Laws*, (Washington, DC: HUD Policy Development and Research, 2002), https://www.huduser.gov/publications/pdf/hmwk.pdf.

13 See, for example, a poll commissioned by the Housing America Campaign and the National Association of Housing and Redevelopment Officials (NAHRO), http://www.nahro.org/sites/default/files/searchable/Zogby.pdf (last visited September 28, 2018); a series of regional polls across the country are reporting similar results. For example, a 2017 poll of the Denver region (sponsored by a group of Denver residents, developers, and advocates called All in Denver) showed wide support for affordable housing and project-based subsidies among likely 2018 voters. See: Jon Murray, "Armed with a poll, affordable housing advocates want Denver to accelerate—or expand—its $150 million plan," *Denver Post*, May 3, 2017, www.denverpost.com/2017/05/03/armed-with-a-poll-affordable-housingadvocates-want-denver-to-accelerate-or-expand-its-150-million-plan/.

A 2017 poll of the Gulf Coast region (conducted by the University of New Orleans and sponsored by nonprofit housing advocates HousingNOLA, Greater New Orleans Foundation, and Enterprise Community Partners) found that "housing was the second leading issue voters said they want candidates in the election to address." See: Jessica Williams, "Poll: Affordable housing is No. 2 issue on minds of New

On the other hand, these polls also find that Americans are deeply distrustful of government, skeptical that government agencies can positively impact tough social issues like racial discrimination,[14] and are hard-pressed to personally advocate for new governmental policies. Moreover, many of the same people who say in polls that they favor affordable housing fail to support affordable housing developments when they are proposed in nearby neighborhoods, use coded language to stand in for racial stereotypes to justify their opposition, fail to support local or national legislation that would make it possible to build, create, or preserve existing mixed-income housing, and fail to support the organizations trying to diversify the landscape of their neighborhoods.

The shallow nature of the public discourse on these issues does not reflect an absence of evidence or data that validates a perspective that emphasizes racial and economic inclusion. In study after study, scholars have demonstrated through rigorous research that neighborhoods of concentrated poverty have lower odds of advancing the life outcomes of the people who live there. For example, in a series of studies led by Harvard economist Raj Chetty and his colleagues at the Equality of Opportunity Project, researchers found that racial and economic segregation reduces intergenerational economic mobility (i.e., the likelihood that children of low-income families will, as adults, earn higher incomes than their parents). From this kind of research, we know so much more about the way in which systems can create or reinforce disadvantage as well as about the impact of policies that have the potential to produce better population-level outcomes. We also know that although living next to affluent people does not, in and of itself, improve outcomes for low-income families, the institutional pathways to opportunity are more visible in places where affluent people reside—ultimately, where better schools, jobs, transportation, community investment and a deeper bench of resources for wellness already exist.[15] Without these pathways to opportunity, whole neighborhoods and groups of people can get locked out of the opportunity for advancement. Fortune.com essentially drew the same conclusion when it headlined a story

---

Orleans voters," *New Orleans Advocate*, Sept. 19, 2017, https://www.nola.com/news/article_33b10676-fe9b-5440-bf2f-04664bd299df.html.

14 Thomas Suh Lauder and David Lauter, "Views on poverty: 1985 and today," *Los Angeles Times*, August 14, 2016, https://www.latimes.com/projects/la-na-pol-poverty-poll-interactive/.

15 Robert Chaskin, Amy Khare, and Mark L. Joseph, "Participation, Deliberation, and Decision-Making: The Dynamics of Inclusion and Exclusion in Mixed-Income Developments," *Urban Affairs Review* 48, no. 6 (2012): 863–906.

on the widening racial wealth gap with "Blacks and Latinos Will Be Broke in a Few Decades."[16]

POPULAR NARRATIVES AT ODDS WITH THE SCHOLARLY DISCOURSE

I have written extensively about the deep-seated narratives that reduce support for affordable housing and inclusive communities' work when we do not effectively navigate around them (i.e., the narratives of individual responsibility, mobility/choice, and racial difference).[17] The dominance of these narratives creates formidable and consistent opposition to calls for equity as they get lifted up in public discourse. When we examine the narratives on racial and economic segregation in particular, the difference between the scholarly discourse (evidence-based) and those shaping the broader public square is striking.[18] Below, I outline some of the ways in which public narratives about segregation differ from those advanced by scholars who study and write about these issues.

Public Narrative: Segregation Is a Historical Artifact in Post-Racial America
Scholarly Narrative: Segregation Is a Driving Force Fueling Continued Disadvantage

Scholars understand segregation as a contemporary problem that has long-term consequences, however, the public conversation often gets mired in segregation as a historical artifact or something related to the civil rights era of the 1960s with little relevance to the inequalities that characterize so many communities today. The connection to that era in public thinking allows many people to dismiss the conversation because they want to believe the problem was solved long ago, when this country enacted anti-discrimination laws and set up public agencies to adjudicate civil rights complaints. So, when confronted with the ideas that Americans continue to live very racially and economically

---

16 Josh Hoxie, "Blacks and Latinos Will Be Broke in a Few Decades," *Fortune*, September 19, 2017, http://fortune.com/2017/09/19/racial-inequality-wealth-gap-america/.

17 For example: Tiffany Manuel, "Who Gets to Live Where and Why? The Answer to This Question May Be Settled By How Strategic Our Narratives Become," *Shelterforce*, January 30, 2018, https://shelterforce.org/2018/01/30/gets-live-answer-may-settled-narratives/.

18 Praxis Media Productions, *Fair Game: A Strategy Guide for Racial Justice Communications in the Obama Era* (Praxis Project, 2011).; and Drew Volmert et al., *Mixing it Up: Reframing Neighborhood Socioeconomic Diversity*, (Washington, DC: FrameWorks Institute, 2016), https://frameworksinstitute.org/pubs/mm/mixingitup/Knight_MessageMemo_Final_2016.pdf.

separate lives, many dismiss the implications because: (1) they see themselves and the communities in which they live as post-racial[19] (i.e., the "*I don't see color*" conversation); (2) many do not want to see themselves in racial or class terms (i.e., the "*aren't we all really the same*" conversation); and (3) whites increasingly see themselves as the "victims" of racial discrimination (i.e., the "*what about reverse discrimination*" conversation).

Thus, continued calls to action on racial and economic segregation in this context meet with exasperation by a public that has grown tired of reliving it. This makes calls for continued vigilance on this issue seem dated and irrelevant, especially in a contemporary, so-called "post-racial" America.

Public Narrative: Segregation Is about People of Color
Scholarly Narrative: Segregation Is about Systems That Affect All of Us

Many scholars on the issue of segregation think and talk about segregation as being rooted in systems and policies that were intentionally designed to be exclusionary. To follow this line of reasoning and its implications would mean that many Americans would have to acknowledge their own (or their loved ones') participation in unjust systems, and they might also be led to acknowledge how they have benefitted from systems that intentionally excluded other people. Looking critically at the research evidence might also mean acknowledging that people have some role to play in undoing those systems and possibly even remediating past harms to others. To avoid this situation, racial and economic segregation gets annexed in the public imagination as being solely about people experiencing poverty, or about people of color, rather than collectivized to draw out the bigger implications for all of us. This allows many people to view any solutions (even policies to promote equitable and inclusive development) as being zero-sum and benefitting only "other" people, even when those policies could improve outcomes for everyone.

Public Narrative: Segregation Is a Function of Consumer Preferences
Scholarly Narrative: Segregation Is a Function of Bad Policymaking

Scholars understand racial and economic segregation as a problem that is dynamic, caused by a complex set of factors and with many negative

---

19 Nikole Hannah-Jones, "The End of the Postracial Myth," *The New York Times Magazine*, November 15, 2016, https://www.nytimes.com/interactive/2016/11/20/magazine/donald-trumps-america-iowa-race.html

consequences when not addressed. Much of the scholarly literature focuses on the instrumental role of public policy in creating and perpetuating segregation.[20] The public conversation, however, often fails to problematize segregation because Americans largely view segregation as a perfectly reasonable stance taken by interest-maximizing consumers. As the logic goes, people acting as consumers make choices that maximize their preferences. Some people will choose to live with others more like them while others may have a stronger appetite for diversity and choose to move to racially or economically diverse neighborhoods. Any explicit attempt to shift consumer preferences toward diversity is shunned as "social engineering." When understood in this way, the public conversation lacks substance about how the systems around us create, incentivize, and shape consumer preferences and how those preferences could be shifted to produce more equitable outcomes.

Public Narrative: Segregation Is a Motivator for Social and Economic Mobility
Scholarly Narrative: Segregation Is a Barrier to Social and Economic Mobility

Although scholars understand segregation (and especially concentrated poverty) as having negative impacts, the public conversation understands racial and economic segregation as a motivation for the hard work and social acceptance that eventually leads to economic and social mobility. As with public views of poverty more generally, segregation is thought to be a motivator for the poor to "earn" their way into thriving neighborhoods because, as the logic goes, there is no stronger motivation for hard work than the goal of "escaping" a poor or dilapidated neighborhood.

Public Narrative: Segregation Is Remedied by Integration
Scholarly Narrative: Segregation Is Remedied by Policies Intentionally Meant to Drive Equity and Inclusion

In the past, policies tackling segregation would have aimed for "integration." Today, many people—especially in communities of color—resist that language, based on the negative impact that past attempts at integration have had on those communities' self-determination. The disappearance of minority-owned businesses, professional associations, and entire communities that emerged out of the legacy of discrimination has been painful. As a result, the idea of

---

20 Richard Rothstein, *The Color of Law: A Forgotten History of How Our Government Segregated America*, (New York: Liveright Publications, 2018).

integration is now perceived among many communities of color as something to be avoided because it means the *loss* of something (racial and ethnic identity) versus *gaining* something (being welcomed fully into the fabric of local communities). Moreover, popular discussions of the value of integration focus almost exclusively on the benefits that are thought to accrue to people of color who are able to interact with Whites, but they rarely highlight how the interaction with people of color also benefits Whites and other groups. Without a more balanced appreciation of the mutual benefits of inclusion (not integration), the public conversation limits the ability of both Whites AND people of color to see the advantages of engaging on this issue.

Public Narrative: Segregation Needs No Government Intervention
Scholarly Narrative: Segregation Requires Government Intervention

Scholars see government policy interventions aimed at structures and systems as the most effective way to solve housing and community-development problems. While the popular narrative can acknowledge that government has some responsibility for improving neighborhood conditions and has a regulatory role to play in the housing market in particular, it also frames government intervention as inefficient, ineffective, and, in some cases, even counterproductive. This is especially true when the conversation is narrowed specifically to affordable housing. The term "affordable housing" is a highly racialized term often conflated with "public housing"—something the public largely considers a government failure.[21] This association makes government intervention more problematic to a public that already lacks confidence in government's ability to solve social problems.

MAKING A STRONGER CASE FOR INCLUSIVE MIXED-INCOME, MIXED-RACE COMMUNITIES

Despite the growing evidence base about when and under what conditions mixed-race and mixed-income communities meet their intended goals, public understanding remains relatively shallow. Housing and community-development practitioners must navigate carefully around the narratives that dominate public thinking and thoughtfully reframe the narrative about segregation for a wide range of community stakeholders and strategic

---

21 Rothstein, *The Color of Law.*

partners. While there are many ways to build public will on these issues, a few fundamental principles are essential.

Lead with a Strong Narrative of Interdependence That Highlights the Inter-reliance of All Racial and Economic Groups in the Region/Nation

As we noted above, mixed-race and mixed-income communities tend to be discussed primarily in terms of benefits to the low-income families and people of color whose lives will be positively impacted by greater access to amenities, social networks, better resources, and the like. Framed and discussed in this way, Whites and higher-income residents do not see what they gain from the success of such efforts. Yet, as much of the research has shown, Whites and higher-income residents benefit substantially from inclusive housing and community development policies. Acknowledgement of mutual benefits is key to elevating this conversation. As we make the case for inclusionary policies, perhaps more than anything else our task is to help people from all walks of life affirmatively connect to the ways in which we all benefit from the policies of inclusion. In particular, lifting up the value of *interdependence* has been shown to be effective in empirical research evaluating how we can shift the narrative.[22]

Research on a wide variety of issues, including housing, shows that messages that lead with values more consistently position these issues as *collective* problems that, when solved, have *collective* benefits for all.[23] Values help people get up and over the perspective of separate fates or the inclination to see problems and solutions as relating to "those people." Values-based messaging can be especially important as housing and community development advocates often need to gain support for policies and programs that are targeted to less influential constituents—low-income families, people experiencing homelessness, racial/ethnic minorities, seniors, and others.

The narrative of interdependence conveys a strong value proposition for mixed-race and mixed-income communities. A key example comes from Housing Illinois, a statewide campaign initiated to build public will around affordable housing. Their campaign's lead, We Need the People Who Need Affordable

---

22 Moira O'Neil and Julie Sweetland, *Piecing it together: A framing playbook for affordable housing advocates*, (Washington, DC: FrameWorks Institute, 2016), http://www.frameworksinstitute.org/assets/files/housing/enterprise_housing_playbook.pdf.

23 Tiffany Manuel, "Who says your frames are better than mine? Making the case for strategic framing by using the power of experimental research," *New Directions for Youth Development*, 124, (2009): 71-82.

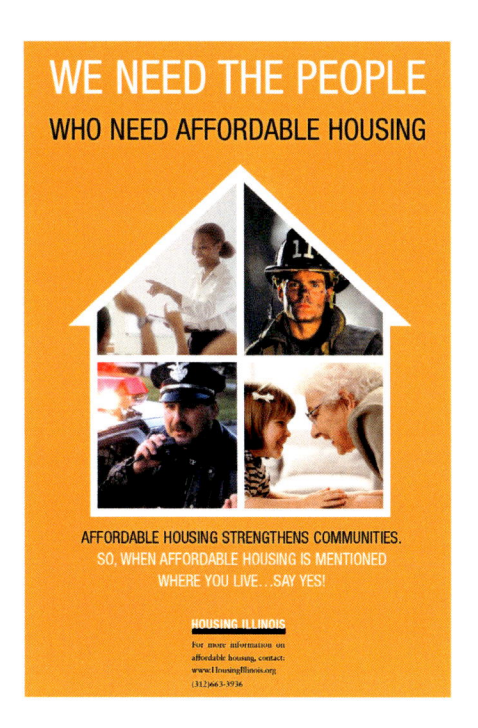

Figure 2

Housing (Figure 2), communicates a strong value of interdependence and repositions the listener—even the low-income families who will directly benefit from the availability of affordable housing—as part of the conversation. This lifts low-income families up as valued (i.e., needed in this community) and also reminds many Whites and other higher-income families that *their* success or fate is intertwined with that of others in the community.

Similar efforts around the country are beginning to emerge, such as the example below from the Workforce Housing Partnership on Martha's Vineyard, asking people to think about how they benefit from inclusive mixed-income housing.

Position Mixed-Race and Mixed-Income Communities as Smart Investments in the Long-Term Future of the Region Rather Than as a Response to the Housing "Crisis," Segregation, or the Challenges of Concentrated Poverty

Advocates for mixed-race and mixed-income communities often talk about them as resolving the broader "crisis" of affordable housing and/or addressing the challenges of racial and economic segregation. While that may be the

> **Figure 3. The Smartest Investment We Can Make in Our State's Future is Securing a Foundation of Strong Communities and Stable Homes for all Minnesotans.**
>
> In Minnesota, we enjoy vibrant communities and a dynamic economy—built on livability and affordability—that give us a strong competitive advantage, nationally and internationally. Our local businesses attract dedicated employees, our colleges and universities recruit high-caliber talent, and our towns and neighborhoods boast strong and welcoming communities.
>
> Our homes are the foundation of our flourishing communities; they fuel the engine of our economy. No one thrives if we price out young adults who have the talent and skills to strengthen our businesses. No one thrives if businesses leave the state because they can't attract and retain a workforce. No one thrives if families struggle to put a roof over their heads. The more Minnesotans who succeed, the more Minnesota will thrive—and we have proven that we have the will, the creativity, and the solution to do so.

motivation, most people do not naturally see or problematize those broad concerns in the same way. Moreover, even when they do see housing as a crisis and/or segregation as problematic, they often default to the dominant public narratives of individual responsibility, mobility, or racial difference as solutions.

Instead, position policies that foster mixed-race and mixed-income communities as smart investments to shape a prosperous future for the community and the region. As an investment, focus the conversation on both the ROI (return on investment) and the SROI (social return on investment). The key to making the case for smart investment is being specific about what those social returns are likely to be—for example, a stronger economy and better-educated workforce—and how they help position the broader community for long-term gains. This approach also helps to mitigate criticism about the public subsidy often needed to finance some portion of these developments.

A good example of this approach comes from Minnesota, where in August 2018 the Governor's Task Force on Housing released a report, *More Places to Call Home: Investing in Minnesota's Future*,[24] to kick off a campaign called Prosperity's Front Door. The report and the naming of the campaign avoided the crisis- and problem-driven messaging that typically pervades this kind of effort and instead offers a narrative (see Figure 3) that lifts up the effort as

---

24 The Governor's Task Force on Housing, *More Places to Call Home: Investing in Minnesota's Future*. (Minnesota: The Governor's Task Force on Housing, 2018), http://mn.gov/gov-stat/pdf/Housing%20Task%20Force%20Report_FINAL.pdf

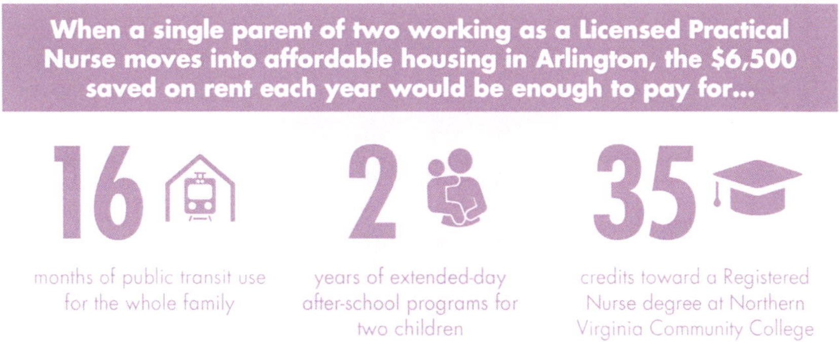

When a single parent of two working as a Licensed Practical Nurse moves into affordable housing in Arlington, the $6,500 saved on rent each year would be enough to pay for...

16 months of public transit use for the whole family

2 years of extended-day after-school programs for two children

35 credits toward a Registered Nurse degree at Northern Virginia Community College

Figure 4

smart, forward-looking, asset-based, and benefit-producing.

A second example is the social returns report[25] created for Clarendon Court, a mixed-income development in Arlington Virginia, which showed both the return on investment in the development and the social returns that accrued back to the surrounding neighborhood (see Figure 4). Using multipliers, researchers were able to quantify returns from residents who made strong use of the surrounding transit system, took advantage of after-school programs, and returned to school at the local community college.

Position Equity Concerns as Addressing the Consequences of Inaction and as Part of a Broader Set of Policy and Systems Changes

Even when policies that foster mixed-race and mixed-income communities are framed as an "investment in our future," advocates still must position equity issues as part of the conversation. Personal stories can be useful if done well, but they become problematic when they do not implicate a wider range of community actors, policies, and systems as part of the story. Our task is to position equity in the story by raising the inclination most people feel to address inequality across places—i.e., the popular notion that there should be fairness everywhere—and also by showing the negative consequences for everyone when

---

[25] Enterprise Community Partners, *More Than A Home: Investing Together to Create Opportunity* (Columbia, MD: Enterprise Community Partners, Inc., 2017), https://www.enterprisecommunity.org/download?fid=8006&nid=5922

we fail to address the disadvantages of some. Useful tactics include building a case for inclusion based on the economic costs of racial segregation to the whole community,[26] the negative impacts of restrictive local housing policies on all home values and regional economic growth,[27] and the talent communities are excluding when they let racial segregation limit access to good schools.[28]

A good example of this principle in action comes from the Metropolitan Planning Council (MPC) in Chicago (see Figure 5), which published a report on the Cost of Segregation[29] that framed economic and racial segregation as detriments that have "strangled opportunities for millions of people." This framing enabled MPC to highlight the equity concerns inherent in the issue and to raise it productively in the public conversation.

Work to Diversify Perceptions about Who Benefits Directly from Mixed-Race and Mixed-Income Communities

People often oppose inclusive development because of who they fear will be drawn to it. We know that when groups that are perceived to benefit from a proposed policy are not considered "deserving," the likelihood of public support significantly diminishes.[30] "Stereotypes and negative perceptions of what an affordable housing dweller looks like don't help," writes journalist Ana Beatriz Cholo. "Potential neighbors fear that the low-income inhabitants will drive 'junkers' and mar their pristine suburban landscape. The newcomers have too many children, and, of course, the building will resemble a Soviet housing project."[31] Therefore, the need to broaden understanding of who benefits from mixed-income policies is critical. This does not mean we need to mask who

---

26 "The Cost of Segregation," Metropolitan Planning Council, accessed January 28, 2018, http://www.metroplanning.org/costofsegregation/default.aspx?utm_source=%2fcostofsegregation&utm_medium=web&utm_campaign=redirect.

27 Paavo Monkkonen, "Understanding and Challenging Opposition to Housing Construction in California's Urban Areas," (Housing, Land Use and Development Lectureship & White Paper, UC Center Sacramento, Sacramento, CA, Dec. 1, 2016).

28 Alex Bell et al., "Who Becomes an Inventor in America? The Importance of Exposure to Innovation," http://www.equality-of-opportunity.org/assets/documents/inventors_summary.pdf, (2017).

29 Metropolitan Planning Council, *The Cost of Segregation*, (Chicago, IL: Metropolitan Planning Council, 2017), https://www.metroplanning.org/uploads/cms/documents/cost-of-segregation.pdf.

30 Anne Schneider and Helen Ingram, "Social Construction of Target Populations; Implications for Policy and Practice," *The American Political Science Review* 87, no. 2 (June 1993): 334-347.

31 Ana Beatriz Cholo, "Why Affordable Housing Doesn't Get Built"

Figure 5. Metropolitan Planning Council: The Cost of Segregation

"Everyone deserves an opportunity to earn a living—and the economy is better off when everyone participates in it. Yet not everyone in the Chicago region has the same pathway to economic success. Over generations, policies and practices have set up barricades in and around Chicago, ultimately leading to a region where people of different races and incomes live separately from one another. Some of these boundaries can be seen on a map. Others are invisible yet powerful barriers that affect local public school performance, business investment, workers' preparation for today's jobs, and what kinds of employment—if any—are available within a reasonable commute of where a person can afford to live. Like bricks in a wall, these decisions have stacked up over decades, and individuals, communities, and our entire region are living with the consequences.

Economic and racial segregation has strangled opportunities for millions of people. Disinvestment has devastated entire city neighborhoods and suburban villages, towns, and cities. Lack of diversity also hurts affluent communities, where limited housing options often mean that young people cannot afford to return when starting their own families, retirees cannot afford to stay, and valued employees are priced out.

Add it up, and it's clear that segregation holds back the entire region's economy and potential—and whether we realize it or not, it's costing all of us. Our social fabric and our economy will be stronger if we all have more opportunities to live, work, and go to school with one another."

---

the intended beneficiaries are. Our task is to widen the public's understanding of who benefits and to help a wider range of community stakeholders see how they benefit from such policies.

The Massachusetts Smart Growth Alliance took this tack in advocating for stronger public support of equitable development in their Great Neighborhoods campaign. The alliance's campaign features stories about stakeholders who are impacted by the need for housing and the shortage of affordable housing, positioning them as part of a broader story of smart investment. For example, the story of Bryan Bryson, an MIT professor and resident of a mixed neighborhood in Dorchester, Massachusetts, underscores not just his past struggles to find housing but the importance of the mixed-income community in which he now lives and the structural need for local zoning reform.[32]

---

32 The Massachusetts Smart Growth Alliance, "Why we need zoning reform: Meet Bryan," *Great Neighborhoods* (blog), November 24, 2019, https://ma-smartgrowth.org/news/the-human-cost-of-bad-zoning-meet-bryan-bryson/.

Reframe the Conversation away from the Public Narratives That Frequently Backfire and Reduce Public Support

A final note about the specific words that tend to dominate messaging on these issues. We know that people most often associate the terms "mixed-income housing" and "affordable housing" with very negative and highly racialized stereotypes. These conceptions are very narrow and, without added explanation, quickly limit public thinking about the importance of affordable housing issues, the ways in which housing is connected to other issues, and—most importantly—options for change. While it is not possible to completely avoid using these terms, it is best wherever possible to use language that connects to stakeholders' chief concerns and values. Talk about how much a 'home' means to people and how deeply affected people are by the quality of the homes, neighborhood resources, and the environment that surrounds them, for instance. Avoid phrases like "moving to opportunity" or "housing choices," because they can trigger public narratives about personal responsibility, mobility, and racial difference.

Finally, because the terminology of "racial and economic segregation" is easily dismissed by many as not relating to them and as dated, it can be tempting to avoid talking about these issues or to finagle with the terminology. No matter what we call it, just acknowledge that the real challenge is not so much the label but the fundamental challenge in how we think about segregation. Not everybody sees segregation as a problem (some actually like the idea of living with people more like themselves); not everybody wants to acknowledge the driving forces behind it; and few understand the full implications of why talking about segregation is useful. So, we'll have to work a bit harder to re-introduce these topics to a public audience that is not terribly excited about the conversation needed to transform policy. Our task is to take the time constructively to lead the conversation so that people see themselves as part of the problem *and* the enormous benefits to them of solving the problem.

CONCLUSIONS

In this essay, I have argued that our attempts to build inclusive communities that explicitly address racial and economic segregation will not advance very far or very quickly without a concomitant effort to build public will to support this work. While polls show that Americans agree in principle with the ideals of racial and economic inclusion, we also know that the public support to manifest those ideals is often tepid. Making the stronger case for policies and investments that foster inclusive mixed-race and mixed-income communities is certainly not a salve for all that is challenging in terms of organizing public support. Strategic case making[33] is critical for building the bigger tent we need to gather the resources that could help. More specifically, we need to get much more strategic in how we engage public audiences about poverty, place, and race.

The good news is that we are being called into a national conversation. While there are many challenges in how that conversation is taking place, there is equally compelling evidence to suggest that these challenges can be overcome. First, let's get serious about countering the dominant public narratives that constrain both the popular discourse and, ultimately, our ability to advance meaningful policy solutions. Second, let's reassert the relevance of race in the context of housing and community development but reframe the conversation in a way that offers Americans a better way to understand how they benefit from the continued struggle to resolve these issues. Third and finally, as we make a stronger case, we should also be organizing allies on both sides of the aisle like never before. If we truly believe in the values of equity and inclusion embedded in mixed-race and mixed-income development policies, doubling down on our case making and leaning forward on our organizing efforts should be among our highest priorities.

More specifically, our task overall is to help people "see" racial and economic segregation: (1) as a cross-cutting problem that affects us all; (2) as something that is deeply relevant today, affecting a whole range of issues we are trying to address through other policy solutions; and (3) as solvable through policies and investments that advance community-building strategies like mixed-race and mixed-income development.

IMPLICATIONS FOR ACTION

Implications for Policy

- Policymakers must make stronger, consistent, and intentional use of equity frameworks that help to evaluate how proposed policy solutions across issue areas (transportation, housing, education, etc.) will affect existing

---

33 "Resources," TheCaseMade, accessed November 24, 2019, https://www.thecasemade.com/resources.

patterns of racial and economic segregation across and within communities. Those impacts must then be broadly communicated to help strengthen a constructive public conversation that prioritizes and legitimizes a focus on reducing segregation.

- Policymakers must also be more intentional about diversifying the mechanisms used to gather community input and feedback on policy development. Even in local politics, public feedback mechanisms heavily represent the interests of more privileged constituents, often leaving out many people who might have alternative points of view. In a world of complex problems, the most meaningful solutions are created when people of different backgrounds, strengths, and skill sets put their minds together. Not only do we strengthen the efficacy of the solutions when we diversify the process, we also help build the public resolve to lean in and participate meaningfully and constructively.

Implications for Research and Evaluation

- Researchers must use data and research evidence to reinforce narratives that emphasize solutions rather than being problem- or crisis-focused, and promote those that frame overcoming segregation as an outcome that benefits everyone.

- Institutions, organizations, and individuals involved in research and evaluation should use the findings not only to engage and inform public conversation but to build public will. This means being open to an intentional process of translating those findings into narratives that have the express purpose of empowering people to act. It is important to say here that the goal of this translational process should never be to politicize the conversation or to engage in partisan politics—people need to have the freedom to act as their own beliefs inform them to—but the research findings can be presented in ways that help people get excited about the possibility for change. In other words, the findings can be presented in ways that build people's sense of agency.

Implications for Development and Investment

- Developers and investors must actively engage and listen to community residents and stakeholders, not just to expedite investment and community planning plans but to build the trust that undergirds stable and inclusive communities.

- Investors who engage in real estate and community development projects must become more intentional, data-driven, impact investors. That is, they should assess their investments both in terms of their ability to drive profits but also their ability to foster more equitable and inclusive places. And those investments must be assessed both on the front end (as new developments are proposed) as well as on the back end (after investments have been made). This kind of assessment offers up the ability to evaluate the long-term impacts of their investments. Moreover, and most importantly, it offers up the opportunity to report those impacts—both the financial returns and the social returns, on those investments. Social returns, such as their ability to cultivate multi-use, multi-racial, more inclusive developments, help to focus and prioritize the public conversation on the narrative of inclusion.

Implications for Residents and Community Members

- Advocacy and community organizing groups must be proactive in aggressively engaging nontraditional audiences who often oppose equitable development. This means working to engage new champions for equity by focusing on how we build stronger ties across sectors, factions, political parties, and community organizations.

- Advocacy and community organizing groups must refocus on powerful storytelling that positions how inclusive communities work to the benefit of a great many people in their communities. As such, this storytelling must strategically focus on telling the "story of us" and recruiting a wide range of community members to reinforce the narrative of interdependence in our stories. As more people begin to see themselves reflected in our narratives of change, it offers up new possibilities for cultivating inclusive policies.

> *"The point of the fish story is merely that the most obvious, important realities are often the ones that are hardest to see and talk about..."*
>
> —David Foster Wallace[34]

---

34 David Foster Wallace, *This Is Water*

TIFFANY MANUEL is the President and CEO of TheCaseMade, a public benefit corporation dedicated to helping leaders powerfully and intentionally make the case for systems change. With more than 25 years of experience in the non-profit, government, and private sectors, she works with changemakers and innovators across the U.S., who are building communities equitable, diverse, and inclusive communities. Dr. Manuel is passionate about using the insights harvested from this work to increase opportunities for public involvement with issues of poverty, inequality and social exclusion. Dr. Manuel earned her doctorate and master's in public policy from the University of Massachusetts Boson, a master's degree in political science from Purdue University, and a bachelor's degree from the University of Chicago.

CHANGING THE NARRATIVE AND PLAYBOOK ON RACIALLY CONCENTRATED AREAS OF POVERTY

Edward G. Goetz, Anthony Damiano, and Rashad A. Williams

Center for Urban and Regional Affairs, University of Minnesota

Social science research on urban conditions has for several decades now focused on areas of concentrated poverty. These neighborhoods, growing in number since the 1970s, are places where economic marginalization is most widespread and deepest. Research has documented the prevalence of these areas[1] and their impact on life chances.[2] Indeed, the "neighborhood effects" literature that has dominated urban scholarship and public policy for the past three decades is in large part a response to the existence of these neighborhoods. In this essay, we examine the efforts of community-based activists from low-wealth communities of color to respond to what they see as the problems and limitations of this dominant approach to the issue of urban and regional equity. The work of these activists attempts to achieve three separate objectives: (1) changing the narrative around economically disadvantaged communities of color from the deficiencies of those neighborhoods to the systems of racism and discrimination that produce extreme levels of spatial inequality in American urban areas; (2) redirecting policy away from mobility strategies aimed at moving people out of such communities and into "opportunity neighborhoods," to initiatives that target

---

1 Paul Jargowsky, *Concentration of Poverty in the New Millennium*, The Century Foundation and Rutgers Centre for Urban Research and Education, (Washington D.C: The Century Foundation, 2013).; Daniel T. Lichter, Domenico Parisi, and Michael C. Taquino, "The Geography of Exclusion: Race, Segregation, and Concentrated Poverty," *Social Problems* 59, no.3 (August 2012): 364-388.

2 Ludwig, Jens, Greg J. Duncan, Lisa A. Gennetian, Lawrence F. Katz, Ronald C. Kessler, Jeffrey R. Kling, and Lisa Sanbonmatsu. "Neighborhood Effects on the Long-Term Well-Being of Low-Income Adults." *Science* 337, no. 6101 (2012): 1505-1510.

the social, political, and economic processes producing regional inequities; and (3) changing the way decisions are made about these communities by asserting the expertise of residents about their own lives and insisting upon the presence and participation of those residents in policymaking.

THE "OPPORTUNITY" FRAMEWORK

Concentrated poverty has been an explicit concern for federal urban policy since at least 1996, when then-Secretary of Housing and Urban Development Henry Cisneros called it "urban America's toughest challenge."[3] The issue has dominated urban scholarship, as well, over this time period. Beginning in 1987 with William Julius Wilson's *The Truly Disadvantaged,* social scientists and urban planners have focused on communities of concentrated poverty.

The racialized nature of concentrated poverty—the fact that Black households in poverty are many times more likely to live in neighborhoods of concentrated poverty than are poor White households—has also been a central concern of scholars and policy makers. Communities of concentrated poverty became the reference point for an entire "neighborhood effects" literature aiming to demonstrate the impacts of these neighborhoods on residents' long-term quality of life, including health and economic mobility.[4] In 2015, when the U.S Department of Housing and Urban Development (HUD) established rules[5] for how local governments were to affirmatively further fair housing (AFFH), the agency included specific requirements to identify "racially or ethnically concentrated areas of poverty [RECAPs] within the jurisdiction and region" and to identify factors that contributed to the emergence of such areas.[6] While the AFFH rule was ostensibly created to examine patterns of racial/ethnic segregation within regions, there was no mention by HUD in the guidelines of the necessity to analyze the segregation of Whites or the

---

3   Henry Cisneros, *Regionalism: The New Geography of Opportunity.* (Washington, DC: U.S. Department of Housing and Urban Development, 1995).

4   Junia Howell, "The Unstudied Reference Neighborhood: Towards a Critical Theory of Empirical Neighborhood Studies," *Sociology Compass* 13, no. 1 (2018).

5   Office of the Secretary, HUD, "Affirmatively Furthering Fair Housing, A Rule by the Housing and Urban Development Department," *Federal Register* 80, no. 136 (July 16, 2015): 42271, https://www.federalregister.gov/d/2015-17032

6   Office of the Secretary, HUD, "Section 5.154 (d)(2)(ii) and (d)(3)," *Federal Register* 80, no. 136 (July 16, 2015): 42355.

concentration of affluence.

Single-minded attention to RECAPs is illustrative of diagnostic myopia governing the approach to problems of segregation,[7] an argument that can be made more generally about the vast literature on neighborhood effects, arguing that "the nearly exclusive analytical focus on [disadvantaged neighborhoods] has the unintentional consequence of downplaying the role that advantaged neighborhoods play"[8] in producing and perpetuating regional inequality.

A policy paradigm has emerged from this discursive focus, one that references a "geography of opportunity"[9] and the need to facilitate the movement of people out of RECAPs and into such "opportunity neighborhoods." This "opportunity paradigm" dominates much of contemporary housing and community development practice. Shifts in housing policy have come to emphasize the dispersal of subsidized housing and the mobility of low-income households out of these areas and into neighborhoods of opportunity as a means of addressing problems of concentrated poverty. Governments, prodded by fair housing advocates who disapprove of subsidized housing construction in low-income communities of color, pursue policies of dispersal and mobility. State housing finance agencies modify their qualified allocation plans[10] for the Low-Income Housing Tax Credit (LIHTC) program so as to increase the number of projects developed in "opportunity neighborhoods."[11] Foundations such as MacArthur and Ford have oriented their giving to support the access of disadvantaged families to opportunity areas and to support "opportunity mapping" so that local policy stakeholders are clear about where such opportunity does and does not exist. With the emergence of various national nonprofits focused on

---

[7] Taylor Shelton, "Rethinking the RECAP: Mapping the Relational Geographies of Concentrated Poverty and Affluence in Lexington, Kentucky," *Urban Geography* 39, no.7 (2018): 1070-1091.; Edward G. Goetz, Rashad A. Williams, Anthony Damiano, "Whiteness and Urban Planning," *Journal of the American Planning Association* 86, no. 2 (2020): 142-156.; Junia Howell, "The Truly advantaged: Examining the Effects of Privileged Places on Educational Attainment," *The Sociological Quarterly* 60, no. 3 (2019): 420-438.

[8] Junia Howell, "The Truly advantaged: Examining the Effects of Privileged Places on Educational Attainment," *The Sociological Quarterly* 60, no. 3 (2019): 420-438.

[9] George Galster and Sean P.Killen, "The Geography of Metropolitan Opportunity: A Reconnaissance and Conceptual Framework," *Housing Policy Debate* 6, no.1 (1995): 7-43.

[10] Bryan P. Grady and Carlie J. Boos, "Qualified Allocation Plans as an Instrument of Mixed-Income Placemaking," in *What Works to Promote Inclusive, Equitable Mixed-Income Communities*, eds. Mark L. Joseph and Amy T. Khare (San Francisco: San Francisco Federal Reserve, 2020).

[11] Carolina K. Reid, "Rethinking 'Opportunity' in the Siting of Affordable Housing in California: Resident Perspectives on the Low-Income Housing Tax Credit," *Housing Policy Debate* 29, no. 4 (2019): 645-669

the opportunity agenda, such as Opportunity Insights, the adoption of the opportunity framework by longer-standing initiatives such as Poverty & Race Research Action Council, and the national reach of continued research[12] on the benefits of moving to opportunity, it is clear that a small industry has emerged with the objective of seeing that low-income families are able to move out of their neighborhoods and, presumably, into opportunity.

FINDING VALUE IN THEIR COMMUNITIES

For activists in low-wealth neighborhoods and communities of color, the opportunity paradigm presents a set of interesting questions. What does the opportunity paradigm say, for example, about their communities, other than that they are places to leave? If public and philanthropic investment is channeled into opportunity neighborhoods and into mobility programs, what does this mean for investment in communities that experts feel lack opportunity? How is opportunity being conceptualized and measured, and do these practices presuppose conditions in communities of color?

Activists in these communities identify the narrative around RECAPs as a deficit narrative.[13] The assumption of mobility programs is that movement from these neighborhoods is widely desired by residents and should be supported through targeted subsidies. This approach to policy has the effect of stigmatizing low-wealth communities of color, branding them as deficient and problematic. By orienting our analysis and policy on RECAPs and on facilitating the escape from RECAPs, we problematize and stigmatize these communities. This discourse and associated advocacy provide a rationale both for redevelopment and displacement, and for housing policy that focuses on mobility (i.e., moving people out of RECAPs) rather than one focused on investment, neighborhood stability, and a "right to stay put."[14]

Increasingly, some residents of such communities are expressing both

---

12 "Moving to Opportunity (MTO) for Fair Housing Demonstration Program," accessed August 28, 2020, https://www.nber.org/mtopublic/.

13 Nelima Munene Sitati, "Speaking Up on Race, Housing, and Opportunity in Minnesota," *Shelterforce*, January 11, 2019, https://shelterforce.org/2019/01/11/speaking-up-on-race-housing-and-opportunity-in-minnesota/.

14 Chester Hartman, "The Right to Stay Put," In *Land Reform, American Style*, eds. Charles Geisler and Frank Popper (Totowa: Rowman and Allanheld, 1984), 302-318.

resentment and resistance to such a narrative and are beginning to more assertively present a counter-narrative about the value of their communities and about the policy responses that they consider to further regional equity. In this paper we examine the work of community organizations in the Twin Cities region of Minneapolis-St. Paul to redefine regional equity in ways that include "building the economic, cultural, political, human and social capital of the places people of color already call home."[15]

AN ALTERNATIVE TO THE MOBILITY/OPPORTUNITY FRAMEWORK

The emerging community-based response to the opportunity framework has a discursive element, a policy element, and a political element. Discursively, the dominant narrative that identifies RECAPs as the central problem of regional equity is being challenged. In policy terms, the dominant paradigm focusing on mobility (moving people to "opportunity") is being challenged. In political terms, residents of low-wealth communities of color are demanding a place at the table when decisions about their communities are being made.

Resistance to the opportunity framework's negative narrative has been seen, for example, in the context of public housing redevelopment. Residents of public housing in cities across the country actively resisted the demolition and/or redevelopment of their homes and pushed back against the deficit narrative about their communities.[16] These residents attempted to establish a counter-narrative about their neighborhoods as a "homeplace" where the "common project of living" is pursued in often close-knit communities.[17] Attempts to assert their communities as places of value and worth defending was a common theme across many cases of tenant resistance to public housing demolition.[18]

---

15 Equity In Place, *Equity In Place: Investment, Access, Opportunity*. July 15, 2015. Available from author.

16 Edward G. Goetz, "The Audacity of HOPE VI: Discourse and the Dismantling of Public Housing," *Cities* 35 (2013): 342-348.

17 Lynne C. Manzo, Rachel G. Kleit, and Dawn Couch, "Moving Three Times is Like Having Your House On Fire Once":The Experience of Place and Impending Displacement Among Public Housing Residents," *Urban Studies* 45, no.9 (2008): 1855-1878.; Right to the City Alliance. *We Call These Projects Home: Solving the Housing Crisis From the Ground Up*. Brooklyn, NY: Right to the City Alliance, 2010.

18 John Arena, *Driven from New Orleans: How Nonprofits Betray Public Housing and Promote Privatization* (Minneapolis: University of Minnesota Press, 2012).; Amy L. Howard, *More than Shelter: Activism and Community in San Francisco Public Housing* (Minneapolis: University of Minnesota Press, 2014).; Martine August, "It's All About Power and You Have None: The Marginalization of Tenant Resistance to Mixed-Income Social Housing Redevelopment in Toronto, Canada," *Cities* 57 (2016): 25-32.; Amy L. Howard and Thad Williamson, "Reframing public housing in Richmond, Virginia: Segregation, resident resistance

More recently, tenant activists in several cities across the country are fighting deficit narratives being applied to their communities. In San Francisco, for example, conflict between ostensible allies, the Yes In My Backyard (YIMBY) activists and tenant's rights activists, has erupted over housing policy decisions and definitions of equitable development. California housing activists have for years tried to reduce barriers of exclusionary zoning in order to make affordable housing more widely available. Conflicts have arisen when certain YIMBY activists and organizations have conflated the fears expressed by low-income communities of color of gentrification due to upzoning with the exclusionary NIMBYism of affluent White communities.[19] Rejecting the YIMBY vs. NIMBY binary, community activists have developed their own narratives about what equitable investment looks like in their communities.[20] These tensions came to a head in 2018 when tenant activists from communities of color were shouted down by YIMBY activists for expressing concerns about a state-level zoning bill.[21] In particular, the community advocates were concerned that the bill lacked sufficient protections for gentrifying communities. Rally speaker Shanti Singh, a member of the local chapter of the Democratic Socialists of America (DSA), tweeted afterward:

> "What I saw today happen to Black, Latinx, and Asian activists from working-class SF communities when they tried to speak about their struggle ... was absolutely infuriating and pathetic. Shouted over by White people. Is there a more perfect encapsulation of our urban history?"[22]

We also see the assertion of a counter vision of regional equity in the efforts of activists in several cities to establish "community preference" policies that would enhance the chances of residents to resist their own displacement and to

---

and the future of redevelopment," *Cities* 57 (2016): 33-39.; Antonio Raciti, Katherine A. Lambert-Pennington, and Kenneth M. Reardon, "The Struggle for the Future of Public Housing in Memphis, Tennessee: Reflections on HUD's Choice Neighborhoods Planning Program," *Cities* 57 (2016): 6-13.

19 Joe Fitzgerald Rodriguez, "SB 827 Rallies End with YIMBYs Shouting Down Protesters of Color," *The San Francisco Examiner*, April 5, 2018.

20 Florian Oppilard, "Resisting the Politics of Displacement in the San Francisco Bay Area: Anti-gentrification Activism in the Tech Boom 2.0.," *European Journal of American Studies* 10, no. 3 (2015).

21 Rodriguez, "SB 827"

22 Toshio Meronik, "YIMBYs Exposed: The Techies Hawking Free Market 'Solutions' to the Nation's Housing Crisis." *In These Times*, May/June 2018, http://inthesetimes.com/features/yimbys_activists_san_francisco_housing_crisis.html.

remain in their communities. In New York City, community activists support the city's policy of community preference. Rafael Cestero, President and CEO of The Community Preservation Corporation, sees community preference as a way "to recognize the claims of those who want to stay and to participate" in the redevelopment of historically marginalized communities, and to "rebuild the fabric of a neighborhood."[23] Residents of low-wealth communities of color in Seattle, WA, for example, urged their city council to create a policy that gives residents priority access to subsidized housing built in their neighborhoods:

> *We are of the Central District, the CID, and Rainier Valley [neighborhoods in Seattle]. These neighborhoods are our home, because we were not permitted to settle wherever we wanted to in Seattle due to redlining and covenants. We built strong communities with networks of civic institutions, houses of worship, and businesses that met our cultural needs. Our networks do not survive when our constituent base is dispersed, yet such networks are essential in an equitable city, and essential to ensuring that Seattle can become the safe and welcoming place for all that we aspire to be but aren't yet.*[24]

Initiatives to enhance the ability of residents to stay in their communities enjoy strong support in a number of cities.[25] The efforts of residents to recognize the value of their communities and to preserve their place in those communities is a form of resistance to the opportunity framework. Often, it is met with paternalistic assurances that policymakers know better what is good for these communities[26] or the hostility of those claiming that (re)development will

---

23 Natalie Bicknell, "Community Resident Preference: Policy and the Fight Against Displacement in Seattle," *The Urbanist*, July 23, 2018, https://www.theurbanist.org/2018/07/23/community-resident-preference-policy-and-the-fight-against-displacement-in-seattle/.

24 Bicknell, "Community Resident Preference"

25 Henry Grabar, "Obama Administration to San Francisco: Your Anti-Gentrification Plan Promotes Segregation," *Slate*, August 17, 2016, https://slate.com/business/2016/08/a-local-preference-affordable-housing-plan-in-san-francisco-might-violate-the-fair-housing-act.html; Phillip Jankowski, "Austin Task Force Trumpets 'Right to Return' Policy to Fight Gentrification," *The Statesman*, November 28, 2018, https://www.statesman.com/news/20181128/austin-task-force-trumpets-right-to-return-policy-to-fight-gentrification.

26 Henry Cisneros, "A New Moment for People and Cities," In *From Despair to Hope: HOPE VI and the New Promise of Public Housing in America's Cities*, ed. Henry G. Cisneros and Lora Engdahl (Washington, DC: Brookings Institution Press, 2008), 3-14.; Renee Glover, *AHA Lessons Learned* (blog), August 17, 2008, ahalessonslearned.blogspot.com/2009_08_01archive.html.

improve these neighborhoods[27] or the antagonism of fair housing advocates who see in these efforts a threat to fair housing goals of integration.[28]

ASSERTING A DIFFERENT VISION OF REGIONAL EQUITY IN MINNEAPOLIS–SAINT PAUL

In the following pages we present a case example of community organizations working in low-wealth communities of color attempting to assert a vision of regional equity that does not label their own communities as problems to be fixed and that does not revolve around policies and incentives to facilitate the movement of people out of those communities. The analysis centers on the work of a coalition of place-based, housing, and advocacy groups called Equity In Place (EIP). We rely on observational analysis, participant observation, informant interviews, and public document review. One of the authors observed EIP meetings and sat in on the meetings of the region's Fair Housing Advisory Committee (FHAC) over a period of 12 months when EIP fought to get its vision of regional equity recognized by regional and federal housing officials. The Center for Urban and Regional Affairs (CURA) at the University of Minnesota, where the authors work, collaborated with EIP during the events described here.

"Equity In Place"

EIP first arose in response to the Metropolitan Council's decennial regional plan, *Thrive MSP 2040*. The Metropolitan Council is the regional planning body of the Minneapolis-Saint Paul metropolitan area and *Thrive MSP 2040* is the Council's 30-year growth plan (which the Council creates anew every 10 years). As a prelude to *Thrive MSP 2040*, the Council conducted a Fair Housing Equity Assessment[29] that, in accordance with HUD's directives, placed strong emphasis on the identification of both RECAPs and "high opportunity areas."[30] EIP activists pushed back by offering two specific reframings, the "White Proximity Model" and the "racially concentrated area of affluence."

---

27 Rodriguez, "SB 827"

28 Catherine Hart, "Community preference in New York City," *Seton Hall Law Review* 47 (2017): 881-912.

29 Metropolitan Council of the Twin Cities, 2014. *Choice, Place, and Opportunity: An Equity Assessment of the Twin Cities Region*. Saint Paul, MN. https://metrocouncil.org/Planning/Projects/Thrive-2040/Choice-Place-and-Opportunity.aspx.

30 Interview #9.

The White Proximity Model

Throughout the FHAC process, EIP members were honing their message and fleshing out a discursive strategy that would challenge the opportunity framework's deficit narrative. After a Metropolitan Council meeting in 2015 in which "tipping points" were cited as a concern, the concept of the White Proximity Model was formulated by three EIP activists. The White Proximity Model attempts to summarize the practical implications of the opportunity framework and the mobility policy recommendations that flow from it. As Figure 1 depicts, opportunity was, in the eyes of the EIP activists, often implicitly synonymized with Whiteness. This implicit valorization of White places as high opportunity further stigmatizes low-income communities of color while obscuring the structural forces that perpetuate racial inequality. The graphic is an attempt to distill and amplify what EIP regarded as the paternalistic and racially based assumptions embodied in opportunity and mobility policy, and to make it visually obvious. While the problematic logic of the White proximity mindset seemed to evade the comprehension of fair

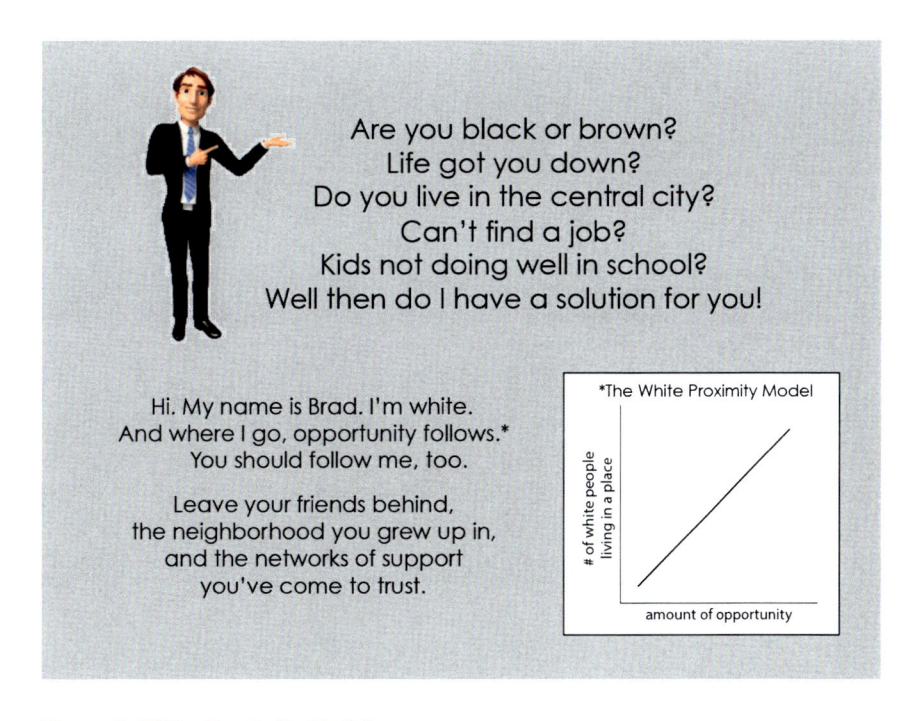

Are you black or brown?
Life got you down?
Do you live in the central city?
Can't find a job?
Kids not doing well in school?
Well then do I have a solution for you!

Hi. My name is Brad. I'm white.
And where I go, opportunity follows.*
You should follow me, too.

Leave your friends behind,
the neighborhood you grew up in,
and the networks of support
you've come to trust.

*The White Proximity Model

(y-axis: # of white people living in a place; x-axis: amount of opportunity)

Figure 1: White Proximity Model

housers and policymakers, its dog whistles were deafening to EIP and the constituents it represented.

With the introduction of the White Proximity Model into the lexicon of local planning and policymaking in the Minneapolis–Saint Paul region, EIP effected a conceptual and discursive shift that would no longer grant Whiteness invisibility in discussions of what constitutes "opportunity."

Racially Concentrated Areas of Affluence

EIP activists also mounted an attack on the preoccupation of policymakers, both federal and local, with RECAPs. As one EIP activist indicated during the 2040 regional planning process, the group:

> …highlighted the failure of systems to name racially concentrated areas of wealth as also being segregated, as these tend to be mainly affluent White communities. In identifying areas with White concentrations of wealth, we sought to dispel the myth that some areas are poor because people of the same race live together and that certain races prosper when they live together. The real reason why communities of color living together are poor is because of the discrimination that occurs when these communities choose to live together, and that is what needs to be solved for.[31]

Researchers at the Center for Urban and Regional Affairs, one of the partner organizations in EIP, took the idea of examining areas of concentrated White affluence and produced an analysis of Racially Concentrated Area of Affluence (RCAA).[32] The study examines the prevalence and characteristics of RCAAs in the 50 largest metropolitan areas of the U.S. We accepted EIP's argument that the spatial patterns of White affluence in American metropolitan areas are an equally important facet of racial/economic segregation in the U.S., and their attempt to change the public narrative about "problematic" neighborhoods in the region, to surface the privilege and advantage of White affluence in the region, and to spur investigation of spaces of White affluence and the social,

---

31 Nelima Sitati Munene, "Speaking Up on Race, Housing, and Opportunity in Minnesota," *Shelterforce*, January 11, 2019, https://shelterforce.org/2019/01/11/speaking-up-on-race-housing-and-opportunity-in-minnesota/.

32 Edward G. Goetz, Anthony Damiano, Rashad A. Williams, "Racially Concentrated Areas of Affluence: A Preliminary Investigation," *Cityscape* 21 no. 1 (2019): 99-123.

political, and economic structures that create and perpetuate them.

RCAAs are more than just the other end of the segregation continuum in American metropolitan areas. They also represent the economic returns to living in predominately White places, and they highlight the importance of examining wealthy White places in particular. As such, they shift the analytic gaze away from low-wealth communities of color and toward what has served as the unexamined reference neighborhood in urban politics, the White middle- and upper-middle-class community.[33] EIP's objective in naming RCAAs as an object for analysis was to reveal widely held policy positions that assume "the normality and superiority of White middle-class space."[34]

Figure 2 shows that the advantages of Whiteness are not equally experienced but, in fact, redound more abundantly to the wealthy than to the working class. Following Shapiro,[35] we argue that property wealth through homeownership in majority White space is the chief factor for the wide disparity in wealth between Whites and Blacks. The exclusivity of high-end White space is the primary driver of wealth disparities and is a system that self-perpetuates. Property wealth begets better education, it finances greater investments in human capital, and it allows for intergenerational transfer of wealth that solidifies class standing and related advantage. It is, as a result, one of the most visible mechanisms of White supremacy.

The model in Figure 2 estimates the marginal effect between Whiteness and home values in the census tracts of the largest 50 metropolitan areas in the U.S. at various median household income levels after controlling for other characteristics associated with home values. Each of the lines shows that as the percentage White in census tracts increases, so does the median home value. Three things are noticeable in the graph. First, the benefits of Whiteness, though in place across the spectrum of tracts, are greatest where Whiteness is concentrated. That is, the relationship between Whiteness and property wealth is non-linear, with the positive relationship becoming steeper where percentage White is the highest. Second, this pattern is most pronounced for higher-income

---

[33] Goetz, Williams, and Damiano, "Whiteness and Urban Planning"

[34] Junia Howell, "The Unstudied Reference Neighborhood: Towards a Critical Theory of Empirical Neighborhood Studies," *Sociology Compass* 13, no. 1 (2018).

[35] Thomas Shapiro, *Toxic Inequality: How America's Wealth Gap Destroys Mobility, Deepens the Racial Divide, and Threatens Our Future*, (New York: Basic Books, 2017).

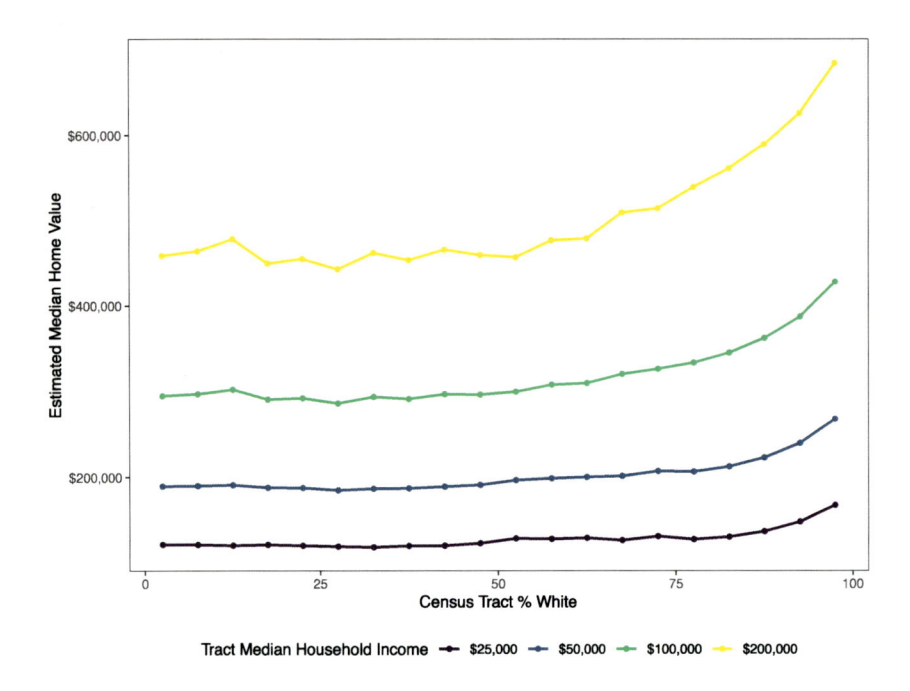

Figure 2: Estimated Median Home Values By Census Tract Percentage White At Different Median Household Income Levels

tracts. Finally, the point of inflection (i.e., the degree of "Whiteness" necessary to trigger exponential benefits) is lower in wealthier neighborhoods than it is in low-income neighborhoods. That is to say, the benefits of Whiteness are greater in the most affluent communities.

The hope of EIP activists is that the concept of racially concentrated areas of affluence will move scholarship on urban problems away from an exclusive concern for low-wealth communities of color and their dynamics, and toward a more holistic consideration of the entire range of communities within metropolitan areas, including the systems of structural and institutional racism that produce concentrated poverty and concentrated wealth, Black segregation, and White segregation. An expansion of scholarship of this type could inform a different policy perspective among public officials and philanthropic funders, allowing for a wider range of approaches to solving issues of regional equity than is currently employed within the opportunity paradigm.

Politically, the concept of racially concentrated areas of affluence is an example of flipping the script. By introducing it into their advocacy work, EIP succeeded in broadening the scope of fair housing analysis in the Twin Cities, producing a situation in which a fair housing analysis had to take into account segregation at both ends of the continuum. In the case we present below, we show how fair housing analysis in the Twin Cities moved away from what EIP advocates argued was a framework that problematized low-wealth communities of color and ignored segregation among affluent Whites. The concept of racially concentrated areas of affluence became a way for advocates to assert that the forces that produced concentrations of poverty were the same that produced concentrations of wealth. As we outline below, this was instrumental in the ability of community activists to effectively argue that fair housing policy must encompass a broader range of concerns than local policymakers initially envisioned. Specifically, EIP was able to force an analysis that acknowledged both the value of existing low-wealth communities of color and the problems associated with concentrated White affluence.

Reconceptualizing Regional Equity through Fair Housing Analysis

Tensions around the idea of "opportunity" and the racial dimensions of equity implied in the RECAP formulation intensified in 2014 when a fair housing legal challenge in the Twin Cities provided a chance for EIP to build power and advance its vision of fair housing and racial equity. The case arose from a complaint brought by three Minneapolis neighborhood organizations and a regional fair housing organization centered in the Minneapolis suburbs. The complaint alleged that Minneapolis and St. Paul failed in their obligations to affirmatively further fair housing by building a disproportionate amount of affordable housing in high-poverty communities of color or RECAPs.[36] This challenge echoed previous cases in other parts of the country.[37] According to EIP, however, none of the organizations initiating the Minneapolis–Saint Paul case had a reasonable claim to speak on behalf of the communities named in the lawsuit. The neighborhood organizations, while being located in more disadvantaged neighborhoods, had boards and staff disproportionately

---

36 Metropolitan Interfaith Council on Affordable Housing, n.d

37 See for example, *In re Adoption of 2003 Low Income Housing Tax Credit Allocation Plan*, 848 A. 2d 1, 5 (N.J. Super. Ct. App. Divi. 2004), and *Inclusive Communities Project, Inc. v. The Texas Department of Housing and Community Affairs*, Complaint filed March 28, 2008, U.S. District Court, Northern District of Texas, Dallas Division. 3:08-CV-546-D, 12.

composed of White homeowners at the time of the complaint.[38] In fact, the question of whether city-funded neighborhood organizations truly reflected the demographics of their communities had been an on-going issue in Minneapolis.[39] This question of representation, especially in wealth and racial/ethnic terms, raised red flags among EIP organizers who immediately voiced concerns about the complaint. As one organizer working in low-wealth communities of color explained, "This began to raise alarm bells. It was like they were doing this over our heads, without us."[40]

It was not just demographics per se that alienated many of the community-based organizations in the EIP coalition; it was also the accompanying deficit narrative around low-wealth communities of color that accompanied the complaint.[41] As one EIP activist has written:

> *The narratives about these neighborhoods usually focus on the negative: their poverty, low-performing schools, etc. Through our work and experience, however, we know that the people who live in these communities benefit from the cultural connections and social networks they create… In my community of Brooklyn Park and Brooklyn Center [two northern, inner-ring suburbs of Minneapolis], which have some of the fastest growing Racially Concentrated Areas of Poverty, there are many ethnic microbusinesses—immigrant-owned enterprises that provide culturally specific goods and services—that are able to thrive because of the critical mass of immigrant residents.*[42]

Most of the conversations around the places and spaces were focused on crime, poor schools, and other social pathologies which according to many community-based organizations fail to consider the historical patterns of disinvestment that lead to racialized disadvantage in the first place. From EIP's summary of the process: "The complaint assumed that affordable housing

---

38 Interview #6

39 Miguel Otarola, "Minneapolis Wants to Tie Funding to Neighborhood Groups to Their Diversity," *Minneapolis StarTribune*, January 28, 2019, http://www.startribune.com/minneapolis-wants-to-tie-funding-of-neighborhood-groups-to-their-diversity/504949652/.

40 Interview #6.

41 Interview #6.

42 Munene, "Speaking Up on Race"

investments contribute to too many people of color living in poor communities. It ignored the historical and present-day institutional and structural racism that forced people of color into those communities."[43] Moreover, EIP activists felt the fair housing complaint illustrated how low-income communities of color are sidelined in conversations around housing justice and the vulnerable status of these communities is used as a way to discredit residents and their organizers as knowledgeable about issues pertaining to their communities.

Soon after the complaint was filed, EIP members began a campaign to pressure both regional and national HUD officials for a seat at the table as the complainants who brought the suit negotiated with local officials of Minneapolis and St. Paul accused of violating fair housing law. This campaign included a combination of "inside game" and "outside game" pressure tactics.[44] Strategies included a letter-writing campaign as well as calls and direct meeting with then HUD Secretary Julian Castro and HUD Region 5 officials. Several state elected officials had also signaled their support of the complaint. EIP took time to meet with each of those legislators and offer their view that the lawsuit was misguided. The goals of these encounters were to explain to HUD administrators and elected officials that the complainants did not represent residents who were most impacted by the lawsuit and who were not granted a seat at the decision-making table, and to advocate that officials commit to a process that included communities of color. Through this consistent pressure, EIP members were able to build relationships with HUD officials. HUD was receptive to these concerns and agreed to include EIP in the resolution of the complaint.

The parties reached a voluntary compliance agreement (VCA) in May of 2015. The parties agreed to amend the 2014 Regional Analysis of Impediments (AI, a HUD fair housing planning document) to address the concerns of the complainants. In the past, the AI process was performed solely by local government officials from the 13 entitlement districts located in the Twin Cities metro area:

> *Typically, [the fair housing committee] consisted of 12 White bureaucrats sitting around a table. Again, if you are thinking about*

---

43 Equity in Place, EIP *Evaluation* (unpublished, 2018).

44 Karen Chapple and Edward G. Goetz, "Spatial Justice through Regionalism? The Inside Game, the Outside Game, and the Quest for the Spatial Fix in the United States," *Community Development* 42, no.4 (2011): 458-475.; David Imbroscio, "Shaming the Inside Game: A Critique of the Liberal Expansionist Approach to Addressing Urban Problems," *Urban Affairs Review* 42, no. 2 (2006): 224-248.

this from the standpoint of, "Oh, this is something we have to do,' as opposed to, 'How do we do this in a way that's as meaningful as it can be?"... It shouldn't be those 12 people making decisions necessarily, around how we identify barriers to fair housing.[45]

Due to the concerns of EIP, as well as HUD's interest in ensuring the viability of the process, a second advisory body was formed which was called the Fair Housing Advisory Committee (FHAC). The FHAC was a first-of-its-kind committee that would advise in writing an addendum to the 2014 AI.[46] Due to their lobbying efforts, EIP was given seats on the FHAC. The final make-up of the FHAC consisted of five members representing local governments, four representing the complainants, and four representing EIP; the remainder of participants were chosen by the facilitators from organizations not aligned with any of the above groups.[47]

The VCA specified several tasks for the FHAC. These included the job of recommending a consultant to write the AI Addendum, provide input on the scope of the AI analysis, and provide recommendations about the specific strategies needed to overcome impediments to fair housing. The FHAC met for a series of 12 monthly meetings between March 2016 and May 2017.

In the background of this conversation was a heated discourse between differing visions of fair housing. The conflict between EIP and the complainants mirrors a larger debate in housing policy between the relative merits of investing in affordable housing in disadvantaged communities and using scarce resources to invest in affordable housing in wealthier, Whiter "high opportunity" communities.[48] The complainants aligned themselves with the view that their neighborhoods already had their "fair share" of affordable housing and that claimed that more subsidized housing in those neighborhoods would concentrate poverty. EIP, on the other hand, aligned themselves more

---

45 Interview #3, local government official.

46 HUD Case 05-15-0007-6

47 Chip Halbach, *A New Approach to Fair Housing Community Engagement.* (Minneapolis, MN: Minnesota Housing Partnership, 2017), http://www.mhponline.org/images/stories/docs/research/A-New-Approach-to-Fair-Housing-Community-Engagement.pdf.

48 Galster and Killen, "The Geography of Metropolitan Opportunity"; Edward G. Goetz, *The One-way Street of Integration: Fair Housing and the Pursuit of Racial Justice in American Cities* (Ithaca, NY: Cornell University Press, 2018).; Kirk McClure, "The Prospects for Guiding Housing Choice Voucher Households to High-Opportunity Neighborhoods," *Cityscape* 12 no. 3 (2010): 101-122.

closely with the view that while mobility is important, it is also important to build affordable housing in disadvantaged communities that often disproportionately suffer from poor housing conditions, disinvestment, and high housing cost burdens on the one hand and are vulnerable to gentrification and displacement on the other.

EIP had a profound impact on the process and was able to achieve several important wins during the AI Addendum planning process. First, they were able to persuade others on the committee about the problematic framing of communities of color using narrative storytelling and personal experience. As Sandercock[49] states, when there is a power imbalance between planners and disadvantaged communities, personal narrative and storytelling become important sources of knowledge and power in planning. One housing organizer from St. Paul shared with FAHC members problems that she had had with housing stability in her own life. She talked about how her family had been displaced multiple times in the past several years. She noted that she didn't have a choice to move, but was constrained by living wherever she can afford:

> *Most wealthy people don't have to think about those things. Frogtown is beautiful and the culture is vibrant and now outsiders get to choose to replace me. Talking about race and why people of color or people with low incomes feel dispossessed as if resources dictate their decisions for them is a critical aspect of the conversation.*[50]

EIP also secured a mandatory anti-racism training for all members of the FHAC. According to the evaluation report prepared for HUD and our interviews with participants, the training was well received by stakeholders, including HUD officials. One HUD official said, "I went into the meeting thinking, 'I'm hip, liberal, and open minded,' but there were so many things I didn't know and hadn't thought about. There were a lot of things that pushed me a bit which was really powerful."[51]

In addition to centering disadvantaged communities and their history in

---

[49] Leonie Sandercock, "Out of the Closet: The Importance of Stories and Storytelling in Planning Practice," *Planning Theory & Practice* 4, no. 1 (2003): 11-28.

[50] EIP member, Fair Housing Advisory Committee Minutes, July 27, 2016.

[51] EIP member, Fair Housing Advisory Committee Minutes, April 19, 2017.

the planning process, EIP sought to influence the outreach and engagement part of the planning process. Instead of hiring a single, outside consultant to lead the engagement process, EIP insisted instead that organizations with pre-existing ties to the community be used. EIP believed this would improve trust and the quality of engagement. EIP secured $71,000 in micro-grants for community organizations throughout the Twin Cities metro area for community engagement, with a focus on reaching low-wealth communities of color as well as immigrant communities. Organizations participating in the FHAC that represented immigrant communities noted that many of their constituents are undocumented and that they would feel more comfortable voicing their concerns to these trusted voices rather than to an unknown outside facilitator. EIP noted in its evaluation of the process that "with more local control and less reliance on generic narratives, we could better challenge the … narrative that segregation was the main fair housing issue in the region. Instead, we elevated the real concerns of people of color."[52] To EIP organizers, gentrification and displacement were fair housing concerns, and they fought for those issues to be considered by the FAHC as fair housing issues. In the view of EIP, the original AI focused almost exclusively on concentrated poverty and neighborhood decline while ignoring how gentrification disproportionately affects communities of color and the ability of people of color to remain in their neighborhoods. It took the efforts of EIP to broaden the scope of the discussion about what issues should and should not be considered a part of fair housing. As a result, the final recommendations for the AI Addendum included specific policy goals to mitigate gentrification and displacement.

CONCLUSION AND IMPACT

EIP's work has had concrete impacts on the conversation around regional equity in the Twin Cities of Minneapolis and Saint Paul. Discursively, EIP was able to effectively undermine the stigmatizing narrative of concentrated poverty and the unstated assumptions behind the opportunity paradigm. Both the White Proximity Model and the concept of RCAAs helped to reset the regional conversation, directing policymakers away from an exclusive focus on low-wealth communities of color. Politically, EIP activists were able to get community residents to the decision-making tables for a range of policy

---

52 Equity in Place, *EIP Evaluation* (unpublished, 2018).

decisions, from transportation and sustainability to housing.[53] Their work has produced policy impacts as well. The group was able to convince federal housing officials to broaden and to deepen their understanding and analysis of regional inequities, to expand notions of acceptable policy response beyond mobility and concerns about deepening pockets of concentrated poverty, and to raise more fundamental questions of discrimination and power differentials.

EIP's campaign for reframing regional equity originates in a desire to assert the value of existing low-wealth communities of color, and in response to an opportunity paradigm that too often locates the policy problem within those communities and the policy solution in the movement of households out of those communities. As such, the group is arguing for regional and racial equity approach that acknowledges existing assets within low-wealth communities of color, including local business with cultural connections to existing residents. It is, in essence, a "Right to the City" position, a demand that the integrity of the community be recognized and their place in the community be safeguarded.

The group is agnostic on the specific question of mixed-income communities— pointing out, in effect, that racially concentrated areas of affluence demonstrate that segregation *per se* should not be equated with disadvantage.[54] The disadvantages of low-wealth communities of color, they argue, are not a result of segregation but of the historic and contemporary forms of racism that exploit communities of color. Thus, the EIP position neither accepts nor denies the argument for mixed-income communities, either the fairness case or the utilitarian justification as outlined by Khare and Joseph[55] in the introductory essay of this collection. Instead, EIP's position operates within a paradigm that asserts the fundamental dignity of low-wealth communities of color and demands that dignity be acknowledged and defended by public policy and community development initiatives.

---

53 Edward G. Goetz, "Transit Expansion and the Pursuit of Equity in Development and Growth in Minneapolis-St. Paul, Minnesota," in *Community Livability: Issues and Approaches to Sustaining the Well-Being of People and Communities*, eds. Fritz Wagner and Roger W. Caves (Milton Park, UK: Routledge, 2019), 113-122.

54 William A. Darity Jr., and A. Kirsten Mullen, *From Here to Equality: Reparations for Black Americans in the Twenty-First Century* (Chapel Hill, NC: University of North Carolina Press, 2020).

55 Amy T. Khare and Mark L. Joseph, "Introduction: Prioritizing Inclusion and Equity," in *What Works to Promote Inclusive, Equitable Mixed-Income Communities*, eds. Mark L. Joseph and Amy T. Khare (San Francisco: San Francisco Federal Reserve, 2020).

In the context of gentrification and displacement pressures, the EIP position aligns with the objective of mixed income communities in that it is meant to ensure that changes in the housing market do not result in a complete neighborhood turnover. This alignment, though, results from a desire to maintain a claim to community rather than a belief in the intrinsic utility of mixed income communities.

IMPLICATIONS FOR ACTION

Implications for Policy

The work of EIP and other organizations across the country suggest an approach to housing and community development policy that moves away from the "opportunity paradigm" emphasizing the integration of people of color into White space, and instead focuses on building capacity and power with communities of color. This implies greater emphasis on local, collective ownership of land and assets, such as community land trusts for housing and businesses. It implies, too, policies like "community preference" that recognize the ties residents have with their communities and allows residents preference for subsidized housing units built in their neighborhoods to offset racially disparate patterns of displacement.[56] The set of policies offered by Steil and Delgado[57] under the concept of "anti-subordination planning" are also applicable in that they are meant to center "the agonistic relations that structure democracy and questions the legitimacy of customs and policies that rationalize the social position of established groups."[58]

Implications for Research and Evaluation

The work to challenge the opportunity paradigm suggests a number of research approaches. First, it demonstrates the importance of scholarship not just on RECAPs and segregated communities of color but on White communities as well, and on the advantages and sociopolitical dynamics of exclusionary White

---

56 Rafael Cestero, "An Inclusionary Tool Created by Low-Income Communities for Low-Income Communities," in *The Dream Revisited: Contemporary Debates About Housing, Segregation, and Opportunity*, eds. Ingrid Ellen and Justin Steil (New York: Columbia University Press, 2019).

57 Justin P. Steil and Laura H. Delgado, Limits of Diversity: Jane Jacobs, the Just City, and Anti-Subordination, *Cities* 91 (August 2019): 39-48.

58 Justin Steil, Antisubordination Planning, *Journal of Planning Education and Research* 1, no. 10 (August 2018):1-10.

affluence, where the returns to Whiteness are greatest. Though we have begun an examination of racially concentrated areas of affluence[59] there is much more to explore about the segregation of White affluence, including the regional differences we found in the prevalence of RCAAs, and the social, economic, and political conditions associated with these types of neighborhoods.

Investigating the potential linkages between RCAAs and RECAPs is another important avenue for research. Shelton[60] examined RCAAs in Lexington, KY and found that high-poverty communities of color and areas of exclusive White affluence are linked by "flows of property ownership and rent extraction" that channel capital from the former to the latter. Similarly, Taylor[61] noted in her history of the FHA that exclusive White suburbs and deteriorating central city neighborhoods were "dialectically connected" during the postwar period of suburbanization. National media outlets, such as City Lab, have reported on the idea as well, placing a spotlight on the need for a more comprehensive assessment of metropolitan inequities.[62]

Implications for Development and Investment

EIP's reframing of regional equity implies a development and investment strategy that does not focus on enhancing or forcing the access of low-income people of color to so-called opportunity neighborhoods. Instead, investments in affordable housing development should continue to occur in communities where households are paying large portions of their income for substandard and low-quality housing. Affordable housing investments should also be responsive to patterns of gentrification and displacement pressures, allowing for true affordability so that residents can, if they so choose, remain

---

59 Edward G. Goetz, Anthony Damiano, Rashad A. Williams, "Racially Concentrated Areas of Affluence: A Preliminary Investigation," *Cityscape* 21 no. 1 (2019): 99-123.

60 Taylor Shelton, "Rethinking the RECAP: Mapping the Relational Geographies of Concentrated Poverty and Affluence in Lexington, Kentucky," *Urban Geography* 39, no.7 (2018): 1070-1091.

61 Taylor, Keeanga Yamhatta. *Race for Profit: How Banks and the Real Estate Industry Undermined Black Homeownership*. Chapel Hill: The University of North Carolina Press, 2019.

62 Alana Semuels, "Where the White People Live," *The Atlantic*, April 10, 2015, https://www.theatlantic.com/business/archive/2015/04/where-the-white-people-live/390153/; Alexis Stephens, "How the Rich Benefit from Handouts More than the Poor," *Next City*, April 14, 2015. https://nextcity.org/daily/entry/rich-benefit-handouts-to-the-poor; Lawrence Lanahan, "How Do We Get White People Out of Their 'Racially Concentrated Areas of Affluence'?" *Zocalo, Public Square*, July 31, 2019. https://www.zocalopublicsquare.org/2019/07/31/how-do-we-get-white-people-out-of-their-racially-concentrated-areas-of-affluence/ideas/essay/.

in neighborhoods where they have built social support networks, and where they have cultural and familial connections. Simultaneously, development and investment that challenges the economic exclusionism of White, affluent communities should also be supported.

Implications for Residents and Community Members

EIP's work demonstrates the importance of a three-pronged approach to challenge the opportunity framework. EIP sought to change the ways in which low-wealth communities of color are talked about within policy circles, and by doing so they surfaced the unexamined role that exclusive communities of White affluence play in maintaining spatial inequalities. This work had direct implications for the policy solutions that were considered in the areas of housing, community development, and infrastructure investment in the Twin Cities. Finally, their insistence on a place at the table has established an expectation in the region that residents do possess an expertise about their lives and their communities that must be considered in policymaking.

■ ■ ■

EDWARD G. GOETZ *is professor of urban planning at the Humphrey School of Public Affairs and Director of the Center for Urban and Regional Affairs at the University of Minnesota. His research focus is housing policy and community development. His most recent book is The One-way Street of Integration: Fair Housing and the Pursuit of Racial Justice in American Cities, published by Cornell University Press.*

■ ■ ■

ANTHONY DAMIANO *is a Ph.D. Candidate at Humphrey School of Public Affairs at the University of Minnesota and a research assistant at the Center for Urban and Regional Affairs (CURA). He specializes in quantitative methods, reproducible research and geographic analysis. His research focuses on housing policy, neighborhoods, race and inequality.*

■ ■ ■

RASHAD AKEEM WILLIAMS *is a Ph.D. student studying black political theory and urban planning at the University of Minnesota's Humphrey School of Public Affairs. His research and teaching explore the moral bases for corrective racial justice at the municipal level and the range of policies that might constitute reparations in the planning context.*

ADDRESSING RESISTANCE TO MIXED-INCOME COMMUNITIES THROUGH EMPATHETIC PLANNING TECHNIQUES

Aly Andrews
Project Management Advisors, Inc.

Sydney VanKuren
Farr Associates

Imagine a young woman who wants to move back to her hometown to care for her ailing mother: Despite having a steady job and a college education (and the accompanying student debt), she cannot find any rental apartments near transit and must reluctantly purchase a condo that she cannot really afford. On the other side of the country, imagine an aging man active in his community: He cannot afford his mortgage payment and manage the upkeep of his home but lacks options to downsize and stay in the neighborhood that he loves.

Engaged, productive individuals like these are facing this tough situation every day; they have a meaningful reason to live in a community, but there are too few housing choices for them there. A lack of choice creates spatial inequalities in urban environments. This spatial inequality is seen across the country, from wealthy communities looking to exclude renters (and the perceived stigma that comes with them) and homogeneous communities actively opposing newcomers of different races and ethnicities, to legacy or shrinking communities experiencing population decline and economic disinvestment, and everything in-between.

These issues are well known to planners and have received much attention, yet they persist. Why is it so difficult to both create and sustain communities with a mix of incomes, rental versus owned homes, and racial and ethnic populations?

One reason is that humans are hard-wired to expect no change and, if change does occur, to go into a kind of high alert and resist it. People's willingness to embrace change—even essential change—directly affects our ability to achieve diverse, inclusive, and equitable communities. In particular, community residents often perceive people of different races and incomes as "others" or "different" and view their presence as a change, and therefore a threat, to their environment.

Because plans for mixed-income development frequently meet with community opposition to change, it is essential to understand the factors that can lead to biases and how those biases inform community resistance to inclusive mixed-income communities. Planners, property managers, service providers, community organizations, and others involved with mixed-income communities can then take steps to counteract these biases and level the playing field. The technique proposed here to encourage more inclusive, equitable mixed-income communities is called empathetic planning, which is defined as planning that elicits empathy from community members during a public-engagement planning process in order to move community planning goals forward.

UNDERSTANDING HEURISTICS AND THEIR IMPACT ON COMMUNITY CHANGE

Communities often identify long-term goals such as "sustainable economic growth in the form of more fair-wage jobs" or "healthy, walkable communities." While these goals are universally understood as "desirable," planners in these communities often face members unwilling to accept the planning changes necessary to achieve these goals (e.g., an economically and racially diverse resident workforce population and dense, mixed-use development, respectively).

Why is this? Our evolutionary past has shaped the stunning range of ways in which we perceive and respond to change. As individuals, we are for change when it fits our worldview, when it is in our self-interest, or when our peer group sees it in the same way. We are against change if it is imposed on us, if it is perceived as leaving us worse off in any way, or if it occurs too fast.

An understanding of the most common biases we experience—and the complex and nuanced ways in which we perceive change—is essential to making better decisions and for diverse communities to thrive. While we often think of human brains as being "logical," research by Nobel Prize-winning psychologists Daniel Kahneman and Amos Tversky instead reveals a brain that often gets things wrong. We each want to believe that we (that is, our brains) make rational decisions, but limited, conflicting, and/or unavailable information forces our brains to rely on shortcuts that bias our decisions. To make decisions with limited or conflicting information, our brains rely on heuristics, defined as "simple procedure[s] that [help] find adequate, though often imperfect, answers to difficult questions,"[1] often by substituting a simpler question. This process occurs without us being aware of the substitution our brains have made.

For example, if you wanted to determine the circumference of a circle, your brain is likely to replace the indeterminate number pi (3.1415 . . .) with the number 3 and to round up slightly. Or, rather than go through the laborious process to determine which political candidate's position is in your best interests, you may instead vote for the person you consider more likeable—or perhaps the person your friend is voting for. The mental errors caused by these simplified information processing strategies are called cognitive biases.[2]

In addition to heuristics that affect almost everyone, our receptivity to change also varies with age. Put simply, as youths we embrace change before we have the wisdom to judge its merits. As seniors with the wisdom to judge the merits of change, we may begin to lose interest in it. Across cultures, adolescents exhibit a triad of routine behaviors: "(1) increased novelty seeking; (2) increased risk taking; and (3) a social affiliation shift toward peer-based interactions."[3] The "adolescent brain continues to mature well into the 20s,"[4] suggesting that novelty seeking and risk taking—traits that favor change—may play an outsized role during this period. Other research has identified three age-related developments that make us, on average, more resistant to change as we

---

1 Daniel Kahneman, *Thinking, Fast and Slow* (New York: Farrar, Straus & Giroux, 2013), 98.

2 Richards J. Heuer, *Psychology of Intelligence Analysis* (Washington, D.C.: Central Intelligence Agency, 1999). Available at www.cia.gov/library/center-for-the-study-of-intelligence/csi-publications/books-and-monographs/psychology-of-intelligence-analysis; accessed August 3, 2017.

3 Sara B. Johnson, Robert W. Blum, and Jay N. Giedd, "Adolescent Maturity and the Brain: The Promise and Pitfalls of Neuroscience Research in Adolescent Health Policy," *Journal of Adolescent Health* 45, no. 3 (2010): 216-21.

4 Johnson, Blum, and Giedd, "Adolescent Maturity and the Brain."

age: (1) decreased intellectual curiosity;[5] (2) reduced tolerance for ambiguity, leading us to seek closure;[6] and (3) higher self-esteem when expressing attitudes that avoid risk and uncertainty.[7]

The recognition of how age affects our receptivity to change poses a dilemma for community planners and others seeking public input. Many proposals for community change are first introduced in neighborhood meetings, which, as a practical matter, are attended by three types of people: the civic-minded, the passionate, and those who have time to attend. The passionate category includes people on both sides of an issue; however, the loss-aversion heuristic indicates that opponents of change are twice as emotionally committed as proponents.[8] Meetings that skew either younger or older may embrace or reject change out of step with the proposal's merits. Should we honor the effort of those people who bothered to show up to a meeting by assuming that room to be representative of the larger community? Or should we adjust our conclusions to compensate for age-related perceptions of change? When the changes we need to get to a preferred future require action by those in power today but have large implications for the next generations, who should make those decisions?

Heuristics and biases are particularly applicable to planning because public participation inherently asks people to make quick judgments in uncertain situations. Research helps explain why people default to "no" when asked if a particular change or proposed design is suitable for their community. Faced with an impossible question to compute, the brain substitutes the question at hand—"What types of housing are appropriate for this area of your community?"—with easier ones they can solve for: "Do I want that type of housing near me? Do I want the type of people whom I associate with that housing as neighbors?" The brain does not have time to analyze whether its associations are stereotypical and discriminatory; it makes the best decision possible with the information at hand.

---

5 Brent W. Roberts, Kate E. Walton, and Wolfgang Viechtbauer, "Patterns of Mean-Level Change in Personality Traits across the Life Course: A Meta-Analysis of Longitudinal Studies," *Psychological Bulletin* 132, no. 1 (2006): 1-25.

6 John T. Jost, Jack Glaser, Arie W. Kruganski, and Frank J. Sulloway, "Political Conservatism as Motivated Social Cognition," *Psychological Bulletin* 129, no. 3 (2003): 33975.

7 Alain Van Hiel and Lieven Brebels, "Conservatism Is Good for You: Cultural Conservatism Protects Self-Esteem in Older Adults," *Personality and Individual Differences* 50, no. 1 (2011): 12023. www.sciencedirect.com/science/article/pii/S0191886910004320; accessed July 3, 2017.

8 "Loss aversion," Behavioraleconomics.com, accessed July 3, 2017, www.behavioraleconomics.com/mini-encyclopedia-of-be/loss-aversion/.

Table 1 summarizes some of the most common heuristics that community members are likely to apply when making decisions in community meetings, and the extent of bias they may cause.

HEURISTIC	DEFINITION	POTENTIAL BIASES
Loss Aversion "Loss is worse than gain"	Most people prefer to avoid a loss rather than acquire an equal gain, and they value the magnitude of the loss as twice the value of the gain.	People who are given incentives to meet a goal up front and then told they must give back the incentive if they fail to meet the goal are significantly more likely to meet the goal than people given the incentive only after meeting the goal.
Framing "Glass half empty vs. glass half full"	People respond differently to the same choice depending on how it is framed (i.e., how they perceive and comprehend the situation).	When option A is presented in a favorable light and option B is not, people tend to choose option A over B. If option B is presented more favorably than A, people are likely to choose B instead.
Anchoring "Planting information"	Information, even totally unrelated to the question at hand, can seed thoughts and affect conclusions.	Asking people to guess the answer to the problem "1x2x3….x8 = ?" yields significantly lower numbers than asking the same question but ordering numbers "8x7x6…x1 = ?" despite the answer to these questions being the same: 40,320.
Diversification "Seeking variety"	People are more likely to diversify when asked to make a simultaneous choice than when making sequential choices.	When asked to choose six snacks for the next three weeks, people tend to diversify their snack choices significantly more than when they are asked in each of three separate weeks to pick six snacks.
Decoy "Choosing between similar options"	When given a choice of three options, people tend to choose one of the two most similar to each other.	If people are given a choice of A or B and then C is introduced, and C is similar to but not better than B, people will prefer B.
Representativeness "The risk of relying on a small sample size"	People often interpret what they see in a small sample size as representative of a larger sample size.	People will extrapolate what they typically see around them on a daily basis to other people or areas they are not familiar with.
Availability "Ease of recollection"	When something is easier to recall, it sticks out in people's memories as seemingly more common than it actually is and therefore has a disproportionately large impact on decision making.	When asked which is more common, A or B, people tend to identify the option they remember most easily—even if the alternative actually is more common.

continued on next page

HEURISTIC	DEFINITION	POTENTIAL BIASES
Status Quo Bias "Stay the course"	People tend to stick with what they already know.	All else being equal, people tend to choose the default option rather than analyze the costs and benefits of alternatives.
Escalation of Commitment "Justifying additional investment"	After committing resources to something, people tend to use the initial commitment as justification to commit additional resources, regardless of whether it would be more prudent to withdraw commitment.	A community that has invested heavily in option A is less likely to choose the more beneficial option B if the choice involves abandoning A.

Table 1. Typical Heuristics and the Biases They May Cause[9]

EMPATHETIC PLANNING: A STRATEGY FOR ADDRESSING HEURISTICS

Empathy is the ability to understand and share the feelings of another person, usually based on experience, context, emotions, goals, and motivations.[10] Empathetic planning acknowledges that heuristics and cognitive biases are a factor in how community members engage in planning and compensates for them by eliciting empathy from community members as part of the community engagement process. Specifically, empathetic planning incorporates exercises that help participants feel empathy toward those impacted by their preferences. The idea is to have people who oppose change recognize that the "others" being affected by their preferences are actually more like themselves than they realize. In fact, their opposition to change might be excluding the very people they want and need in their communities in order to achieve long-term sustainability goals.

Empathetic planning offers a method to level the playing field in communities that have already identified positive goals such as greater health and happiness, reduced greenhouse gas emissions, and increased economic development. When people in these communities are considering proposals that help meet their

---

9   See Appendix for examples of images used to demonstrate these heuristics. Images credited to Douglas Farr. *Sustainable Nation: Urban Design Patterns for the Future* (Hoboken, NJ: Wiley & Sons, 2018).

10 *Merriam-Webster*, s.v. "empathy," accessed Aug. 2, 2018,

goals (for example a higher-density, mixed-income development near transit), there may be some opposition. If so, it may be beneficial to make the biases explicit and let people in the community decide whether and how to correct for them. Often, the act of examining a situation from someone else's perspective shows people that their perspectives are not very far apart or may have been close at an earlier point in time. This can help community members identify people with differing viewpoints as part of their "tribe," rather than someone to treat as an outsider.

Empathetic planning is *not* about manipulating community members. It is about leveraging behavioral science to help members of a community overcome subconscious heuristics to reach the community's self-identified goals. It is about getting members of the public to become self-aware of their own framing—and putting that framing aside—to make decisions for the future of their community. As planners, we know this is important. Planning decisions related to community-vision projects tend to be on decades-long timelines, and although current community members participate, the impact may apply more directly to future generations and/or people other than the participant.

It is worth noting that professional planners benefit from empathetic planning, too. Understanding how a person's brain solves a difficult problem (i.e., by replacing it with an easier one) can help planners better anticipate how a community is likely to react to a proposal, understand why some community members are so averse to change, and be prepared to facilitate tense discussions successfully. Ideally, planners who use empathetic planning techniques will also experience empathy toward current and potential community members during the planning process.

Moreover, planners have their own heuristics and cognitive biases that influence their work. When crafting a polling process, for example, planners may demonstrate "optimism bias" by "consistently overstat[ing] expected success and downplay[ing] expected failure."[11] By using empathetic planning techniques, planners can better understand potential pitfalls and compensate for them. This topic is revisited in the last section on implications for policy.

---

11 "Persuasive Patterns Card Deck," Brain Utilities ApS, accessed Aug. 3, 2018, https://shop.ui-patterns.com/product/ui-patterns-card-deck/.

USING EMPATHETIC PLANNING TO ADDRESS HEURISTICS

Empathetic planning can be applied in many ways. Farr Associates[12] is actively adjusting the technique and has so far used it as a public engagement technique in conjunction with image preference surveys to help community members define the community character that they deem appropriate. The guidance and examples that follow, drawn from our experiences, illustrate how empathetic planning can be combined with familiar public outreach methods to address some of the common heuristics identified earlier. As the examples show, empathetic planning has enabled us to subtly transition community conversations from focusing on specific building types and density to describing the kind of community residents want—discussions that more accurately addressed social infrastructure, community character, and culture. Put another way, the conversations have shifted from being about *form* to being about *people*.

Loss Aversion

Experts observe "that the pain of losing is psychologically about twice as powerful as the pleasure of gaining."[13] The effect of this heuristic is that the human brain becomes a terrible appraiser of potential changes, routinely miscalculating the relative value of what could be gained or lost. Thus people will go to great lengths to oppose a new, high-quality housing project that would replace a terrible but familiar one, even if the community has much to gain from the project, because they perceive the change as a loss. With empathetic planning, public participation exercises can leverage loss aversion to help build consensus. For instance, group exercises can start by giving each group an incentive, such as a voucher for free ice cream, up front that participants keep if they meet the goal of reaching consensus but must give back if they do not reach consensus.

A subset of the loss aversion heuristic is the "endowment effect," which centers on property ownership. Residents often value something they own (e.g., a single-family home, a car) more than something they do not own (e.g., a small condo, transit options, access to a diverse mix of land uses and mixed-use buildings). Thus when participants in a long-term community planning meeting are asked what sorts of housing should be available in their community in the

---

[12] Farr Associates is a firm of optimistic architects and planners in Chicago who are passionate about urbanism, sustainability, and leading by example.

[13] "Loss aversion," Behavioraleconomics.com

future, responders are likely to assign more value to the types of housing they currently own than to those that they do not own. This translates into a belief that other people want what they have, and therefore an assumption that the supply of what they currently own should grow to meet an imagined demand. In this way, the current community's ownership characteristics could limit future community members' choices. The empathetic planning process can address this situation by clearly articulating the bias and reminding people who resist the change of a time in their lives when they couldn't afford the housing they now have and needed the proposed alternatives.

Framing

People respond differently to the same choice depending on how it is framed. How questions are worded and presented can lead to drastically different frames of mind—and, therefore, drastically different preferences. For example, imagine a community meeting about a 100-unit mixed-income development proposing 40 percent low-income units and 60 percent market-rate units. The planner could ask, "Do you approve of a mixed-income development that has 40 percent low-income units?" or the planner could ask, "Do you approve of a mixed-income development that has 60 percent market-rate units?" The difference in framing between these two questions does not affect how many low-income versus market-rate units will be available. However, people do not answer equally in favor of each. The framing heuristic suggests that people will be more likely to choose the option that prioritizes what the community values. In communities that seem hesitant to introduce mixed-income projects, framing the question in terms of how many market-rate units are included may result in more support than the same question framed in terms of how many low-income units are included.

Anchoring

The typical brain is biased in favor of the first information received on a given topic. Therefore, the order in which information and questions are presented can skew participants' answers. Even information unrelated to the topic at hand can have an impact. In research experiments, for example, when researchers first ask subjects how old their parent is and then ask for the answer to a complicated math problem, subjects tend to respond with a relatively large number, but when researchers precede the math problem with a question about how old the subject's child is, subjects tend to respond with a relatively smaller number.

Empathetic planning can leverage this heuristic to anchor participants' thinking about a particular aspect of inclusive, mixed-income development. For example, in 2016 Farr Associates' urban design studio worked on a regional transit-oriented development planning project in the Chicago metropolitan region in which we surveyed public-meeting participants in three adjacent communities for their preferences on building types and development density. This project included an image preference survey in which residents were shown images of urban developments and asked whether each development type was appropriate for their community. Often, such real-time preference polls begin with a warm-up question (e.g., "What is your favorite type of food—pasta, meat and potatoes, dessert?"), which planners use to solicit information about the audience's characteristics and habits. However, it is important to note that these questions are not neutral by default and could very easily influence respondents' decision making throughout the rest of the survey. For example, asking an audience of mostly middle-aged Caucasian men about their favorite food—and hearing everyone in the room answer similarly—may give people a false sense of community homogeneity.

Farr Associates used the warm-up question as a chance to anchor people's thinking about what types of people use different housing types. We asked the question: "What was your first home as an adult?" Possible answers included a friend's couch, a room in a parent/family member's home, a shared apartment, an apartment alone, or an owned condominium or house. This question reminded participants that, though they may now live in an owner-occupied, single-family home and oppose multifamily rental housing, at one time they may have needed that housing option. As expected, 52 percent, 56 percent, and 62 percent of respondents from each of the three polled communities answered that they first lived in a rented apartment after leaving their childhood home. We cannot know exactly what effect this attempt at anchoring had on the survey responses, because this was not a controlled experiment and we posed the question to all three communities involved in this project. Perhaps it achieved our goal of eliciting a positive experience with diverse housing types. This question also might have prompted participants to think about other people they know who are in the "first-home-as-a-young-adult" stage and recognize that single-family homes are not perfect for all households all the time.

Not every question should aim to be anchoring. In fact, sometimes it is important to actively avoid anchoring. In the Chicago example, for instance, after the warm-up question we carefully avoided questions that posed an "A or B" dichotomy (e.g., "Which development is better, type 1 or type 2?") in favor of evaluating each option individually, because we have found that A or B dichotomies tend to anchor people's responses by providing extra context. In other words, people may choose B simply because they like B *more* than A, even though they may find both A and B perfectly acceptable for their community.

Diversification

The diversification heuristic suggests that people are more likely to diversify when asked to make a simultaneous choice than when making sequential choices. For example, imagine a project that covers a large portion of a community. If a planning or urban design team asks the community, or even the project's client or steering committee, to choose what types of housing are most appropriate across the whole community all at once, people will seek more variety and diversify their choices more than if they were asked the same housing choice questions about one sub-district this week and another sub-district next week. The act of choosing all at once offers the brain a chance to see bias toward a particular answer, whereas when the question is asked over and over, people often don't see the pattern in their selection of a narrower set of responses.

A substantial amount of research shows that a bias toward diversification may be sub-optimal in some cases (e.g., when investing finances in individual savings plans). However, encouraging diversification in communities where diverse housing choice is an explicit goal (e.g., places with people aging in place, diverse places experiencing racial and/or economic disparities, etc.) could help communities offer a wider selection of housing types on the spectrum between single-family homes to multi-family high-rises (aka Missing Middle housing options).

This same heuristic suggests that people are more likely to diversify across a larger portion of a community or multiple areas than a smaller portion or single area. Proposals for a single site elicit feelings of finality, as if there is only one opportunity for that site. In contrast, projects that involve a larger area allow people to understand that they can put "a little over here, a little over there." One way to trigger this heuristic is to make an analogy between diversity in a community's housing and diversity in breakfast menus. Imagine explaining to a community: "Think of diverse housing types the way you think about breakfast: you may want cereal most days, and you may not want quiche today, but you probably want quiche this weekend. So we are going to put some quiche over here. Because most of us have breakfast every day, having something different every now and then is not so scary."

Decoy

Architects and planners often present several different schemes—typically, three—to a client for consideration before pursuing final project design. However, research shows[14] that when two of three presented options are very similar to each other, responders tend to pick one of those two similar options. When this happens, designers may be unintentionally skewing the choices made by their clients. Of course, most designers have a preferred scheme, based on project constraints, personal tastes, and other priorities. Imagine a case in which an architect presents three schemes: one that is a solid choice; a second that is completely different from the first; and a third that is very similar to the second design but with insignificant differences and was only included to give the client a greater choice. The decoy heuristic dictates that the client is most likely to pick the first of the similar options that was presented. Empathetic planning seeks to remove this bias from decision making by offering three completely different schemes.

Representativeness

Community members often assume that what they experience in their immediate surroundings (e.g., a lack of parking) represents what everyone else in their community experiences. Empathetic planning combats this heuristic by using community-specific anecdotes as well as research examples in planning discussions. The anecdotes and examples remind participants that, while the room may be occupied by people who appear similar demographically and economically, other community members exist who are different and therefore have different housing choices available to them, and those people must be represented even if they aren't physically in the room. It is ideal to have a name and a face associated with these diverse experiences, because seeing someone's face and hearing them express their experiences and emotions significantly increases the biological and neurological levels of empathy that observers experience.[15]

---

14 Kahneman, *Thinking, Fast and Slow*.

15 Yudhujit Bhattacharjee, "The Science behind Psychopaths and Extreme Altruists," *National Geographic*,

Farr Associates encountered this situation in public meetings held as part of the regional transit-oriented development planning project in Chicago mentioned earlier. After the audience revealed a strong preference for owner-occupied, multifamily housing developments but against the same type of development if it were rental-occupied, a young woman who looked as if she could be the relative of anyone in the room stood up and declared that, by strongly preferring owner-occupied housing, the audience had excluded her. She revealed that she had moved back to the community, her hometown, to care for her ailing mother. Despite having a steady job and a college education (and the accompanying student debt), she could not find any affordable rental apartments near transit. She reluctantly ended up purchasing a condo that she could not afford so she could be near her mother and the transportation needed to keep her job. After this testimony, the project team again asked participants their preferences. While people still preferred owner-occupied housing, fewer opposed the rental-occupied housing option.

The project team concluded the polling session with a final trio of slides. The first slide contained a chart of median incomes by profession, showing how much (and therefore what type) of housing different individuals could afford. The second slide asked whether participants know anyone working in the professions listed in the chart, and the third slide asked for which of those professions housing should be affordable.[16] People's responses on which professions' housing should be affordable directly mirrored which professions they knew people in. For example, if 8 percent of people said they knew food prep employees, 8 percent of people indicated that food prep workers should be able to find housing affordable to them within the study area. The correlation between responses about knowing and providing housing for each employee type suggests that anchoring people's thoughts on the actual people behind a housing type, rather than a hypothetical tenant whom they don't know, may result in people responding more favorably to providing those folks with affordable choices in their community.

Because this was not a controlled study, we have no metric with which to measure the effect our slides had on the outcome of the exercise; however,

---

January 2018, https://www.nationalgeographic.com/magazine/2017/08/science-good-evil-charlottesville/.

16 In this context, "affordable" referred to having any type of housing choice without paying more than 30 percent of one's income on housing.

we believe that reminding responders of the people behind housing types is a powerful way to communicate the need for diverse housing choices within a community.

Availability

When people who face a decision recall information from memory to help make that decision, some memories stick out and are easier to recall than others, regardless of their relevance or accuracy in the current situation. Those easier-to-recall memories have a disproportionately large impact on decision making, even if they are not accurate. For example, community members' understanding of their neighborhood's characteristics, such as crime levels, may be disproportionately influenced by what the media reports and how often the community members consume those media. Community members in an area where a violent crime occurred in the past may be more likely to think crime is a current issue of concern, even if recent crime statistics show an increase in safety. This distinction between perceived and actual crime is important, because the urban design and policy solutions are different for each. Empathetic planning addresses this heuristic by providing accurate, relevant data and discussing how the proposed planning project may influence those findings.

Status Quo Bias

People often prefer to keep the conditions with which they are familiar when faced with changes that are hard to imagine or understand, such as a proposal to have different types of housing to accommodate more economically, racially, and socially diverse households in the community. This bias often plays out in the form of opposition to new, mixed-income housing that would introduce lower-income residents and residents of color into a higher-income, predominantly White neighborhood. The existing residents may be sympathetic to the concepts of equity and inclusion but equally (or more) driven to preserve the status quo. Empathetic planners can counteract this heuristic by making the choices transparent and discussing the implications with decision makers.

Escalation of Commitment

Community members (including municipal staff) may reject a sustainable best practice if it entails altering something in which the community or municipality has invested money. For example, community members may not want to include in a master plan a recommendation to move curbs and reformat the roadway if the street in question was just repaved. Or politicians may choose to patch a deteriorating highway, even if tearing it down and constructing a new and different route would provide better roads and reconnect low-income neighborhoods with higher-income communities and resources, simply because of the city's historic investment in the roadway. Empathetic planning can address this by informing participants about the economic concept of a sunk cost: a cost that an ongoing project has incurred and can no longer be recovered and therefore should not be considered when making future investment decisions. Empathetic planning also ensures that the stories of all affected communities contribute to the decision-making process—which, in the example above, would include how construction of the original highway divided and cut off a community and how re-siting the road could lead to a more vibrant future.

Empathetic planning could have much wider applications than the examples given here. For example, any community outreach facilitator, such as a planner or developer, might find empathetic planning useful in public engagement workshops and exercises. Participatory art, which often already has an empathetic component, is another great application. For example artist Candy Chang, whose installations examine "the dynamics between society and the psyche,"[17] often provides ways for community members to connect with each other's humanity (Figure 1).

In all applications, however, it is important not to use empathetic planning techniques to manipulate an audience to agree to what planners want. Instead, planners should acknowledge that audience members come into a meeting with heuristics affecting their judgments and decisions. With that knowledge, it is up to planners and other facilitators to decide how to address the heuristics and whether (and how much) to compensate for the cognitive biases they create. Some planners might be most comfortable simply educating community members about these biases and letting them compensate as they see fit. Others, as in the examples presented here, attempt to compensate for the biases and obtain honest, accurate feedback about community preferences by leveraging the very heuristics that cause them in the first place.

Empathetic planning is not a silver bullet for overcoming opposition to inclusive and equitable development. Sometimes communities will still discriminate. Democratic participatory engagement processes such as the

---

17 Candy Chang, accessed December 4, 2019, http://candychang.com/.

Figure 1. A sample of Candy Chang's participatory art exhibits. Clockwise from top left: "Street Notes," "Before I Die," "Post-It Notes for Neighbors," and "I Wish This Was." Source: Farr, 2018.[a]
Copyright Farr Associates

---

[a] Farr, *Sustainable Nation: Urban Design Patterns for the Future*.

ones discussed here can easily be commandeered to serve those who organize to block diverse, equitable communities. It can be difficult if, even after the removal of cognitive biases that result from heuristics, the community reveals that it still does not want certain types of people in its community. However, this empathetic planning model lays a strong foundation for inclusivity by framing discussions around people—people whom those in the opposing group likely know and love—and in the best terms for those involved.

IMPLICATIONS FOR ACTION

Implications for Policy

Community planning is only one application of the empathetic approach; another might be "empathetic policymaking." Policymakers need to be aware of cognitive biases and the role these shortcuts play in their work. For example, the status quo bias may cause policymakers to keep applying the same processes and pathways to diverse situations. The desire to look for patterns can blind policymakers to the fact that each community is different and one policy or planning solution does not fit all.

Similarly, when public participation is not representative of a community (e.g., only 10 people show up to a public meeting), policymakers may become vulnerable to the availability and/or anchoring heuristics and subconsciously give those voices a larger-than-necessary influence.

It is important to remember that a multidisciplinary team of people working on a policy meant to benefit mixed-income communities will likely all come to the table with these cognitive biases at work. By recognizing this and acknowledging an attempt to put them aside, policies can more directly benefit those they are supposed to help and avoid unintended consequences.

If a policy is up for a public vote, voters are also susceptible to these same biases. A policy that recognizes how people are likely to react and can counteract those reactions may have more success on election day. It is interesting to note that the Trump Administration policy that every additional regulation needs to result in the removal of two other regulations directly addresses the loss aversion heuristic. The loss of one freedom (i.e., whatever the regulation applies to) is outweighed by the gain of two more (i.e., the removal of two other regulations).

The application of empathetic policymaking could also apply to a campaign effort supporting the policy. Because voters also are susceptible to biases, a policy that involves voting for a tax increase (which often triggers the loss heuristic) could be coupled with a campaign that frames the benefits gained as double the value of the tax (thereby balancing out the loss aversion heuristic).

Implications for Research and Evaluation

Future applications of empathetic planning should include efforts to measure effects. We collected anecdotal findings that empathetic planning reduced resistance to transit-oriented design in a regional planning project in the Chicagoland region, but we do not know exactly how our questions triggered empathy or whether our questions were the reason respondents favored housing types they had previously opposed.

It may be useful to incorporate knowledge about negotiation techniques into empathetic planning to help community members identify and explain their wants, needs, and underlying motivations for supporting or opposing a particular plan or design. According to former hostage negotiator Chris Voss, people feel most comfortable starting with "no."[18] After saying no, people are more comfortable revealing what they actually want, because they feel they are in a position of power. It is interesting to think about applying this idea to survey questions. What are the effects of getting to "no" with a room full of neighbors divided on a community issue? How can that be incorporated into the wording, order, and discussions of survey questions and other planning tools? Hearing "no" for an answer also positions planners in a position of being able to ask "why not," which can help uncover the biases that are influencing people's thinking and choices.

Implications for Development and Investment

Planners and urban design professionals who are trying to develop equitable, inclusive mixed-income communities should understand how heuristics and cognitive biases influence public engagement and choices both for and against proposed changes. In particular, planners should:

- Take community participants' biases into account when articulating choices and posing questions;

---

18 Chris Voss and Raz, Tahl, *Never Split the Difference: Negotiating As If Your Life Depended On It* (New York, NY: Harper Business, 2016).

- Begin preference surveys with a question that neutralizes biases (e.g., by eliciting positive experiences with diversity);
- Offer three totally different schemes to reduce bias in participants' selection process;
- Use specific-area or comprehensive plans as opportunities for diversification, as they present a greater variety of choices over a larger portion of the community;
- Include community-specific examples of diverse experiences and contexts in planning discussions to remind participants of all the perspectives that represent the community.

Universities, continuing education providers, and advanced certification programs should consider including behavioral science into their curricula to ensure that the next generation of planners is informed and competent about using empathetic planning techniques. It is important to understand that people's responses can be irrational or illogical. Such training could result in a better understanding of why people behave the way they do, which in turn could result in more choices about inclusive, equitable mixed-income communities being made with the most sensible decision making possible.

Implications for Residents and Community Members

Communities exposed to empathetic planning may have greater expectations about what they should demand from governmental and planning professionals who are trying, with good intentions, to create opportunities for positive change but may do so with more conventional methods. When communities start demanding something different, it can raise questions that encourage planners to re-evaluate their ways.

A community meeting that discusses heuristics might be one of the first times residents are confronted with their own racial biases. It also may be one of the first times they heard first-hand accounts of how fellow community members experience discrimination. Through experiences with empathetic planning, members of communities can start to ask questions, learn about their own ignorance, and start to develop conscious awareness that leads to anti-racist actions. Most people are not actively racist or discriminatory, and many see themselves as allies thus, empathetic planning is one way to invite dialogue around these issues.

ALY ANDREWS is currently a Project Manager and real estate consultant at Project Management Advisors, where she expertly manages the details of various architecture and construction projects and communicates them to the rest of the project team. Andrews worked at Farr Associates from 2014 to 2018 as an urban designer and planner. With a background in architecture, urban planning and design, her work at Farr focused on improving community engagement, tactical interventions, transit-oriented development, pedestrian and bike mobility, and resilient neighborhoods.

SYDNEY VANKUREN joined Farr Associates in 2015, focusing on sustainable urbanism projects and management of The Pattern Project, a Farr Associates initiative to accelerate change around decarbonization strategies. When working on the book Sustainable Nation: Urban Design Patterns for the Future (2018) by Doug Farr, she realized just how much power local communities and local actors have in shaping the future of their neighborhoods. She focuses on providing neighborhoods with tools that will help them create a sustainable future, faster.

VanKuren has professional experience in biology, research analysis, science communication, and environmental planning and policy. She holds a bachelor's degree in Natural Resources as well as a master's degree in Urban Planning and Policy. She is an EcoDistricts Accredited Professional. In 2017, she joined the Board of the Center for Neighborhood Technology's Young Innovators.

APPENDIX

Availability
(ease of recollection)

R _ _ _ _ _
R a b b i t
R a c e
R a i n
R e g r e t
R i c e
R o c k e t
✓

_ _ r _ _ _
T o r n a d o
F o r g e t
?
?
?
?
✗

Anchoring
(multiplying numbers)

8 x 7 x 6 x 5 x 4 x 3 x 2 x 1 = ?

1 x 2 x 3 x 4 x 5 x 6 x 7 x 8 = ?

Naive diversification
(picking snacks)

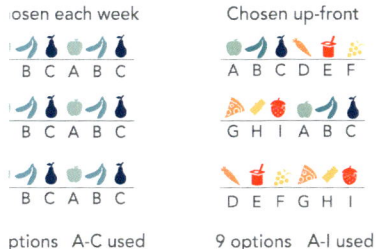

Chosen each week
B C A B C
B C A B C
B C A B C
ptions A-C used

Chosen up-front
A B C D E F
G H I A B C
D E F G H I
9 options A-I used

Decoy
(choice of three)

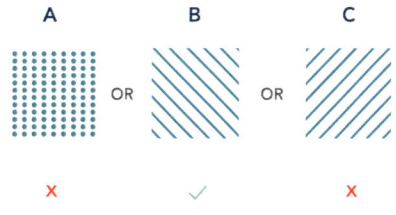

A   B   C
   OR   OR
✗   ✓   ✗

Who Has A Say and Who Benefits?   435

Representativeness
(the risk of relying on a small sample size)

Everyone is yellow

Escalation of commitment
(justifying additional commitments)

U.S. Military Involvement

Status quo bias
(stay the course)

START → END

Loss aversion
(loss is worse than gain)

100% PAIN FROM LOSS
50% PLEASURE FROM GAIN

Who Benefits? Focus on Special Populations

These essays delve into issues concerning specific populations within mixed-income communities, including black women leaders, black fathers, youth, and market-rate residents.

Akira Drake Rodriguez and Majeedah Rashid tackle three big objectives in their essay, "Black Feminist-Centered Community Organizing as a Framework for Developing Inclusive Mixed-Income Communities: Nicetown CDC's Village Network and Outreach Initiatives in Philadelphia." First, they define and elevate Black feminist politics and organizing as essential and powerful forces for greater inclusion and voice in mixed-income communities. Second, they explain the important differences between community development and community organizing approaches to urban revitalization and assert that both are necessary for equitable change. Third, they spotlight the success of the Nicetown Community Development Corporation in the Nicetown neighborhood in central Philadelphia and demonstrate the influence that Black feminism has had on the trajectory of that community.

In "Untapped Assets: Developing a Strategy to Empower Black Fathers in Mixed-Income Communities," Clinton Boyd, Jr. and Deirdre Oakley draw attention to the specific challenges faced by Black men, particularly those who are fathers, in mixed-income communities. They enumerate ways in which Black fathers are formally and informally prevented from being full participants in the lives of their children and full contributors to the flourishing of their communities. They offer specific policy and practice propositions to embrace and benefit from all that Black fathers can offer.

We are thrilled to lift up a focus on the experiences of youth in a mixed-income development by centering the voices of youth themselves in "Youth Voice and Leadership in Mixed-Income Communities: Heritage Park and the Green Garden Bakery," co-authored by youth contributors Ephraim Adams, D'Loveantae Allen, and Mohamed Mohamed; Joni Hirsch and Taryn Gress from the National Initiative on Mixed-Income Communities; and Elana Dahlberg and Alecia Leonard of Urban Strategies Inc. (USI). Green Garden Bakery is an innovative social enterprise at Heritage Park, a mixed-income development in Minneapolis. Conceived of and created by youth residents of the development with support from USI staff and local partners, the bakery emerged out of young residents' desire to use the baking and gardening skills they were learning through a USI program to improve the community's access to nutritious food and to generate local employment. The reflections of youth spotlighted in this essay convey the challenges of stigma and division that can emerge in a mixed-income community as well as the positive role youth can play to disrupt those dynamics. The authors also share insights about the impacts of Green Garden Bakery on youths' own sense of self and community involvement. As one youth shared: "Being a part of Green Garden Bakery, it brought me out of my comfort zone and I realized there are so many cool people around the community, like I should've known them back then, and it's like what have I been doing this whole time?" The essay concludes with advice from the young authors to their peers and adults, with insights about pushing through initial discomfort to get to more meaningful and nurturing interactions.

In "Reassessing Market-Rate Residents' Role in Mixed-Income Developments," Michaeljit Sandhu takes an incisive look at the role and perception of residents of market-rate units. He points out that much of the research and discussion of mixed-income communities focuses on the needs and outcomes of low-income households, reflecting planners' hope that market-rate residents could play "a powerful social and structural role in the lives of their lower-income neighbors." However, after reviewing the existing evidence on perspectives and experiences of residents of market-rate units—including his own qualitative study—Sandhu asserts that: "In many cases, market-rate residents, rather than their low-income neighbors, have become the primary beneficiaries of the sites' social and structural features. Empirical evidence suggests that market-rate residents are as likely to enforce stigmas and use their social connections, market power, and political influence to their advantage as to support and engage with their lower-income neighbors." Sandhu suggests generates implications for stronger thinking and action to leverage more inclusive benefits from "class-desegregated settings."

BLACK FEMINIST-CENTERED COMMUNITY ORGANIZING AS A FRAMEWORK FOR DEVELOPING INCLUSIVE MIXED-INCOME COMMUNITIES: NICETOWN CDC'S VILLAGE NETWORK AND OUTREACH INITIATIVES IN PHILADELPHIA

Akira Drake Rodriguez
University of Pennsylvania

Majeedah Rashid
Nicetown Community Development Corporation

Sustaining inclusive mixed-income communities requires fostering both community development and community organizing. We define community development as the mobilization of resources towards improving community assets, while we define community organizing as the mobilization of resources towards achieving social change, often through political participation. Unfortunately, communities often feel tension between the two approaches, and organizations tend to focus on one strategy to the detriment of the other. We believe both approaches must be implemented concurrently to foster inclusive mixed-income communities, particularly in cities that are finally experiencing growth after decades of decline and disinvestment. For disinvested communities that are majority Black, we advocate for a community organizing approach centered in Black feminist politics, which includes acknowledging, valuing, and cultivating leadership by Black women. We believe that the values articulated by Black feminist politics, such as validating and empowering the knowledge and traditions of local communities, allows for sustained community organization for social change while also providing opportunities for developing the physical and social capital of communities. Black feminist-centered community organizing can help to mitigate the tension between community organizing and community development strategies.

This essay examines the case of the Nicetown Community Development Corporation (NTCDC) and members of the organization's Village Network in Philadelphia. Black residents who had long been active in Nicetown formed the CDC in 1999 to foster inclusive urban planning and planning education in the area as the city's economy was on the upswing. Much of the organization's programmatic success stems from intentionally focusing on the role of Black women—a population that has long provided leadership in the community despite being marginalized by most community development practitioners. The case of NTCDC and its Village Network members experience illustrates two themes:

- *Focusing Simultaneously on Community Development (i.e., Improving the Built Environment) and Community Organizing (i.e., Increasing Local Residents' Consciousness, Agency, and Leadership around Community Needs) Contributes to a More Inclusive Mixed-Income Community.* Using a framework developed by Shane R. Brady and Mary Katherine O'Connor in 2014, we analyze the strategies and tools that NTCDC and Village Network members used to build community, plan, mobilize, and translate positive outcomes into future organizing on behalf of an equitable, inclusive mixed-income community, and we compare them to the more widely used but narrowly focused asset-based community economic development (ABCD) model;[1] and

- *Black Feminist Political Organizing Offers an Effective Framework for Inclusive Community Development.* This framework values the contributions made by woman-led households and community networks—resources that greatly influence society and culture but are often ignored by other community development approaches—and builds on these strengths and lived experiences to mobilize residents.[2] We apply concepts from Black

---

[1] Shane R. Brady and Mary Katherine O'Connor, "Understanding How Community Organizing Leads to Social Change: The Beginning Development of Formal Practice Theory," *Journal of Community Practice* 22, no. 1–2 (April 3, 2014): 210–28, https://doi.org/10.1080/10705422.2014.901263.

[2] Fayola Jacobs, "Black Feminism and Radical Planning: New Directions for Disaster Planning Research," *Planning Theory* 18, no. 1 (February 2019): 24–39, https://doi.org/10.1177/1473095218763221.

feminist politics to contextualize NTCDC's mission and approach, not to exclude other racial and gender groups but to apply a framework that directly addresses and elevates one of the most vulnerable demographics in urban communities.

Together, these themes suggest ways in which community development efforts can become more effective in producing inclusive mixed-income communities. First, this essay will provide background and context on the differences between community organizing and development while establishing how Black feminist politics mediate between the two strategies. Next, we will discuss the case of Philadelphia and the origins and mission of the Nicetown CDC. Finally, we will provide illustrative examples of how NTCDC and its Village Network members stick to a core set of strategies to foster inclusive communities in the changing city.

MOVEMENT CONTEXT: COMMUNITY ORGANIZING, DEVELOPMENT, AND BLACK FEMINIST POLITICS

Historically, as cities' tax bases and populations declined with the onset of urban deindustrialization, community development organizations often felt forced to choose between politically oriented community organizing (delivered through community-based organizations, or CBOs)[3] and asset-based community economic development (delivered through community development corporations, or CDCs).[4] Black feminist politics, meanwhile, emerged with a focus on the specific needs and contributions of Black women and children. In order to understand why these approaches work well together to create inclusive, equitable mixed-income communities, it helps to know how each strategy for social change evolved.

Community Organizing

Community organizing is a practice for changing society in ways that improve

---

3   Paul Bunyan, "Partnership, the Big Society and Community Organizing: Between Romanticizing, Problematizing and Politicizing Community," *Community Development Journal* 48, no. 1 (January 1, 2013): 119–33, https://doi.org/10.1093/cdj/bss014.; James DeFilippis, Robert Fisher, and Eric Shragge. "What's Left in the Community? Oppositional Politics in Contemporary Practice," *Community Development Journal* 44, no. 1 (July 30, 2007): 38–52, https://doi.org/10.1093/cdj/bsm010.

4   Bunyan, "Partnership, the Big Society and Community Organizing;" Defilippis, Fisher, and Shragge, "What's Left in the Community?"

outcomes for previously marginalized members.[5] It is a strategic approach for building and exerting political power in contexts where certain groups are systemically excluded from political representation. Community organizing lays the groundwork for sustaining core values over time by fostering and creating a community consciousness, literally "building community."[6]

Community organizing's origins lie in urban industrialization, when community-based organizations such as Settlement Houses and social workers provided charitable works, goods, and services to impoverished neighbors.[7] These organizations also acted as middlepersons and advocates for impoverished people, helping to create the first set of social welfare policies during the New Deal.[8] Settlement Houses often worked with White immigrant communities; as Black communities grew they also received aid, although less of it.[9] Community organizing during the early Progressive Era created the foundations for what came to be called poor people's politics. Impoverished groups had not had political representation in the form of policy directly benefitting their interests, and community organizing created a suite of social welfare policies that directly addressed the needs of some while exacerbating the needs of others.[10]

Community Development

Community development evolved out of community organizing in the mid-20th century in response to declining urban populations and lagging private investment that made government intervention necessary. The New Deal and other social welfare policies were explicitly designed to mitigate urban

---

5 Brady and O'Connor, "Understanding How Community Organizing Leads to Social Change."

6 Adrienne C. Goss, "Toward a Village Consciousness: Organizing in the African American Cultural Tradition," *Journal of Black Studies* 46, no. 8 (November 1, 2015): 797–816, https://doi.org/10.1177/0021934715608110; Saul David Alinsky, *Rules for Radicals : A Practical Primer for Realistic Radicals* (New York: Vintage Books, 1989).

7 Terry Mizrahi, "The Status of Community Organizing in 2001: Community Practice Context, Complexities, Contradictions, and Contributions," *Research on Social Work Practice* 11, no. 2 (March 2001): 176–89, https://doi.org/10.1177/104973150101100204.

8 Alice O'Connor, "Origins: Poverty and Social Science in The Era of Progressive Reform," in *Poverty Knowledge*, Social Science, Social Policy, and the Poor in Twentieth-Century U.S. History (Princeton University Press, 2001), 25–54, https://doi.org/10.2307/j.ctt7s5p3.5.

9 Karen Ferguson, *Black Politics in New Deal Atlanta* (Chapel Hill: University of North Carolina Press, 2002).

10 Michael B. Katz, *The Undeserving Poor: America's Enduring Confrontation with Poverty: Fully Updated and Revised* (Cary, United States: Oxford University Press, Incorporated, 2013), http://ebookcentral.proquest.com/lib/upenn-ebooks/detail.action?docID=1389039.

unrest from high job and housing losses, particularly as experienced by men in the unstable labor market.[11] These policies are best categorized as people- and place-based community development, with the overwhelming focus on developing individuals and places through workforce training, guaranteed mortgages for homeownership, and large-scale public works projects to stabilize employment and income while also producing new residential and commercial spaces within cities.[12]

Unfortunately, these federal policies segregated programming for Whites and Blacks administered by state and local bureaucrats, whose prejudices often created differential benefits for each group. The individualistic emphasis on job training and mortgage assistance was helpful in lifting the White middle class out of the Great Depression but did little for the increasingly Black urban denizens during the economic restructuring of the postwar era. Many community development strategies have continued to prioritize middle-class norms of homeownership, nuclear family household composition, and post-secondary school completion, even if these methods don't benefit Black communities in the ways they benefit White ones.[13]

Black Feminist Politics and Planning

Growing post-industrial cities favored policies that privileged the individual over the community, capital over labor, and agglomeration over redistribution. This neoliberal turn in social welfare policy translated into a direct attack on the livelihoods of the most disenfranchised and vulnerable,[14] including and especially single Black women with children. For them, the dismantling of the safety net of welfare, public housing, public education, subsidized health care,

---

11 Sheila D. Collins and Gertrude Schaffner Goldberg, *When Government Helped: Learning from the Successes and Failures of the New Deal* (Oxford, United States: Oxford University Press, Incorporated, 2013), http://ebookcentral.proquest.com/lib/upenn-ebooks/detail.action?docID=1538401.

12 Don Parson, *Making a Better World: Public Housing, the Red Scare, and the Direction of Modern Los Angeles* (Minneapolis: University of Minnesota Press, 2005).

13 Meghan Kuebler and Jacob S. Rugh, "New Evidence on Racial and Ethnic Disparities in Homeownership in the United States from 2001 to 2010," *Social Science Research* 42, no. 5 (September 1, 2013): 1357–74, https://doi.org/10.1016/j.ssresearch.2013.06.004; Donald R. Haurin and Stuart S. Rosenthal, "The Influence of Household Formation on Homeownership Rates across Time and Race," *Real Estate Economics* 35, no. 4 (2007): 411–50, https://doi.org/10.1111/j.1540-6229.2007.00196.x; S. Michael Gaddis, "Discrimination in the Credential Society: An Audit Study of Race and College Selectivity in the Labor Market," *Social Forces* 93, no. 4 (2015): 1451–79.

14 Zenzele Isoke, *Urban Black Women and the Politics of Resistance*, (New York: Palgrave Macmillan US, 2013).

and other entitlements warranted a political response that met their particular needs. Black feminist politics sought to fill that gap in several ways.

First, Black feminist organizing is committed to creating and sustaining "oppositional knowledge"—i.e., using knowledge of places as a tool for resistance and resilience in the post-industrial city.[15] Oppositional knowledge leverages spatialized networks of knowledge banks to aggregate and synthesize information across a specified geographic area. In what Carol Stack refers to as "survival strategies," the limited resources of spatially adjacent households are pooled to increase each individual's chance of survival.[16] Oppositional knowledge of households, resources, and strategies across a geographic area can empower and validate the decision-making autonomy of vulnerable individuals as well as promote great social mobility. An organization that collects and takes seriously the community's oppositional knowledge (as opposed to the top-down practices often deployed by traditional community development organizations) is more likely to build community and cultivate trust.

Second, Black feminist politics addresses a core set of priorities that have long been central to the Black feminist tradition:[17] high-quality and affordable or free education, fair and safe labor opportunities (and the ability to get to them), clean and safe neighborhoods with high-quality services, and affordable and safe housing. All of these priorities fall within the purview of urban and regional planning[18] and thus require a political response. Creating and implementing a plan to achieve these political priorities, using community trust and oppositional knowledge, is a key part of Black feminist organizing's approach to mobilizing communities for social change.[19] By sticking with the core political values of home, education, health, and social mobility, residents can mobilize *independently* of publicly convened, top-down planning meetings to advocate for their own interests from the bottom up.

Infusing Black feminist politics into a community organizing approach calls

---

15 Patricia Hill Collins, *Black Feminist Thought : Knowledge, Consciousness, and the Politics of Empowerment* (New York: Routledge, 2000).

16 Carol Stack, *All Our Kin: Strategies for Survival in a Black Community* (New York: Basic Books, 1983).

17 Collins, *Black Feminist Thought: Knowledge, Consciousness, and the Politics of Empowerment*; Duchess. Harris, *Black Feminist Politics from Kennedy to Obama*, 2nd ed. (New York : Palgrave Macmillan, 2011).

18 Jacobs, "Black Feminism and Radical Planning."

19 Brady and O'Connor, "Understanding How Community Organizing Leads to Social Change."

for centering Black women's leadership and engagement and intentionally engaging a diverse range of perspectives on community goals within Black femme interests—including those of young, elderly, queer, disabled, immigrant, and trans women.[20] Elected officials also serve an important role in empowering community members by translating oppositional knowledge into policies and programs and by advocating for Black feminist interests and policies. In centering a diverse mix of Black womens' perspectives in community organizing efforts, particularly in mixed-income communities, we can pay more attention to what Khare, Joseph, and Chaskin refer to as the "enduring significance of race" in structuring residential experiences.[21] This diversity of Black women leaders can help to mitigate the secondary marginalization that can occur within disenfranchised communities.[22]

GEOGRAPHIC CONTEXT: PHILADELPHIA AND NICETOWN

Philadelphia's population reached a peak of nearly 2.1 million in 1950 before declining to a post-industrial-era low of 1.5 million in 2000. As the city redevelops a thriving and diverse economy, community development and community organizing have both evolved, and mixed-income communities have become increasingly common. Growth has been uneven in the last two decades, however. Map 1 displays the changes in household income from 2008—just before the foreclosure crisis that hit Black households at twice the rate of White households in the city—to 2017.[23] During that decade, some census tracts' median household values in the city decreased by 32 percent while others increased by 137 percent in the same period. The red highlighted portion of NTCDC's designated service area shows both sides of this spectrum: A few tracts saw values appreciate by about 30 percent, while some saw values

---

20 "About Our Work!—Uplifting the Narratives, Leadership, and Lived Experiences of Trans People of Color," Trans Women of Color Collective, accessed May 20, 2020. https://www.twocc.us/about/.

21 Amy T. Khare, Mark L. Joseph, and Robert J. Chaskin, "The Enduring Significance of Race in Mixed-Income Developments," *Urban Affairs Review* 51, no. 4 (July 1, 2015): 474–503, https://doi.org/10.1177/1078087414537608.

22 Cathy J Cohen, "Punks, Bulldaggers, and Welfare Queens: The Radical Potential of Queer Politics?," in *Black Queer Studies*, eds. E. Patrick Johnson and Mae G. Henderson (Duke University Press, 2005), 21–51, https://doi.org/10.1215/9780822387220-003.

23 Svenja Gudell, "Homes in Black Neighborhoods Twice as Likely to Be Underwater as Homes in White Neighborhoods," *Zillow Research* (blog), January 11, 2017, https://www.zillow.com/research/negative-equity-race-q3-2016-14063/.

decrease by 30 percent. While household values varied dramatically across the service area, household income was a bit more uniform: Map 2 shows that most household income across the Nicetown census tracts either decreased or remained flat between 2008 and 2017. Many areas in Philadelphia experienced these simultaneous increases in household value while incomes remained flat or unchanged, creating increasing housing burdens in a high-poverty city. This housing insecurity and vulnerability makes it difficult for organizations to sustain community mobilization and advocacy in high-need areas.

Post-industrial Philadelphia has a bifurcated economy powered by low-wage service jobs and underemployed workers and high-wage, white-collar professionals. The metropolitan area is home to several universities, two teaching hospitals, and a wide range of pharmaceutical and chemical companies.

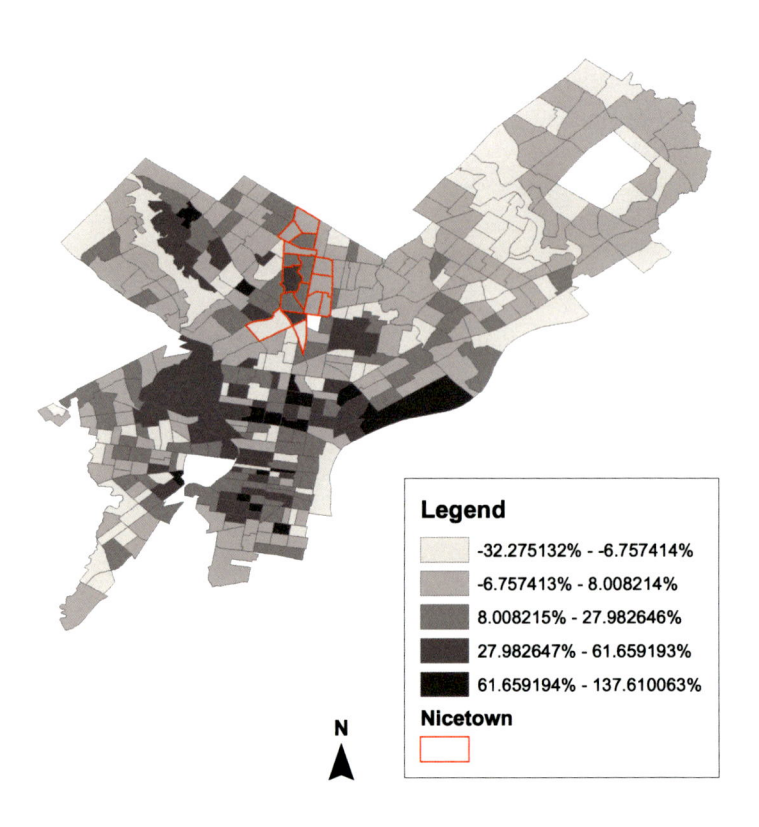

Map 1. Changes in Median Home Value in Philadelphia from 2008 to 2017

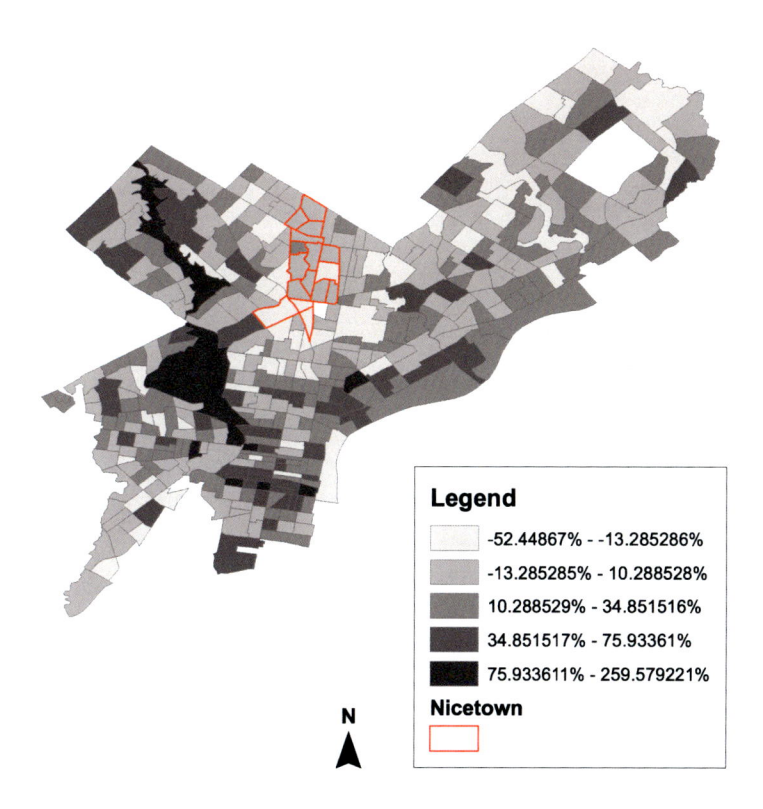

Map 1. Changes in Median Household Income in Philadelphia from 2008 to 2017

City policies are concomitant with those of a growth machine, privileging the needs and development of downtown property owner and business interests, often to the detriment of social services and policies that would stabilize outlying residential areas. The city offers a 10-year tax abatement for new construction and renovation, a reduced business privilege tax (while the regressive individual wage tax remains stable), and a number of business improvement districts that provide disproportionately strong amenities to high-rent areas in the city.

Population changes in Philadelphia have altered the practice of community organizing in different communities. In communities near downtown and the universities, membership in longstanding organizations is changing and new organizations are emerging to reflect the shifting demographics. For instance, instead of working to oppose an urban renewal project or protest the shuttering of a manufacturer, community organizations and residents in those areas are working *with* real estate developers and corporate interests to create business improvement districts and other neoliberal policy mechanisms. Sometimes these alliances result in community organizations that are full of homeowners whose interests favor property value appreciation, regressive property tax policy, and extensive use of the carceral state and poverty criminalization to maintain these interests.[24] Thus, tensions between community development and community organizing strategies are appearing with increasing frequency in mixed-income areas of the city.

Nicetown, historically a working-class neighborhood in North Philadelphia, just 10 miles from center city, is seeing some unevenness in its own economic growth while still lagging behind the growth of the city overall. Once home to many factories and Eastern European immigrant households, Nicetown transitioned into a majority-Black community in the middle of the 20th century. The neighborhood has two primary schools and one high school, several parks and green spaces, a transit center for the city's regional rail system, and multiple subway stations. Excluding the newly-renovated transit center, very few of these places and spaces have seen funding committed from local, state, and federal government. The community also has strong connections to advocates of Black feminist organizing: City Council members Cindy Bass and Cherelle Parker are Black women who cover Council districts within or adjacent to Nicetown, and Kendra Brooks, a Nicetown resident and community organizer, successfully ran for a City Council At-Large seat under the Working Families Party, the first third-party candidate in over half a century. All three women advocate for policy initiatives that reflect Black feminist organizing priorities while remaining committed to Black feminist core values.

NICETOWN CDC'S MISSION AND FOCUS

The Nicetown Community Development Corporation (NTCDC)'s mission is "to dynamically improve the quality of life in Nicetown and surrounding communities by establishing sustainable community economic development." The statement continues: "We fulfill our mission with a holistic and inclusive approach to goals and objectives that prioritize public safety; mobilization

---

24 Robert E. Thibault, "Between Survival and Revolution: Another Community Development System Is Possible," *Antipode* 39, no. 5 (December 7, 2007): 874–95, https://doi.org/10.1111/j.1467-8330.2007.00556.x.

through 're-education' and training; affordable housing development; commercial corridor revitalization; arts & culture, and land care."[25]

NTCDC focuses on homelessness prevention but takes a holistic approach to meeting individual and community needs. By addressing community development needs, such as affordable housing development and commercial corridor revitalization, *and* community organizing needs, such as mobilization through re-education, the organization straddles the divide between the need for material and political progress. Figures 1 and 2 illustrate the array of information and services provided by NTCDC.

NTCDC'S CORE FEATURES

Nicetown Community Development Corporation educates and mobilizes the community in several ways that make it more inclusive and equitable, some of which use community organizing tactics and some that focus on community development. The components include a Neighborhood Advisory Committee (NAC); a Village Network and drop sites; community surveying, needs assessment, and planning; financial autonomy; and a commitment to what we have framed as a Black feminist approach to developing leadership in the community, particularly among young residents.

Neighborhood Advisory Committee

Neighborhood Advisory Committees (NACs) are funded by the City of Philadelphia's Division of Housing and Community Development to inform residents about city programs. NTCDC established a NAC in Nicetown to function as its comprehensive planning arm, providing ongoing education and encouraging community participation and collaboration. The NAC's outreach strategy, conducted via telephone, social media, door-to-door canvassing, service area briefings and community meetings, special events, and a quarterly newsletter, was developed "to help improve quality of life as it relates to housing, poverty, neighborhood conditions, unemployment and associated problems," NTCDC materials state. "The goal is to connect with residents, businesses, schools, and various community and faith-based organizations, and enhance our capacity to serve low-moderate income residents throughout the service area."[26]

---

25 "About Nicetown CDC," accessed June 30, 2019, http://www.nicetowncdc.org/.

26 "Nicetown CDC."

Figure 1. Excerpt of NTCDC NAC Quarterly Newsletter, January-April 2019

Village Network and Drop Sites

For marginalized households in Nicetown, a number of different organizations and places offer goods and services not provided by the public sector. However, navigating this network is difficult, particularly for new or elderly residents, or residents with limited mobility. To address this need, NTCDC established a Village Network that identifies individuals and locations who have agreed to help disseminate important information, which NTCDC staff hand deliver or email to them. The distribution points change in response to an ongoing assessment of neighborhood needs and use of space and place, but they include block captains, business associations, elected officials, faith- and community-based organizations, agencies, schools, hospitals, private businesses and other information exchange locations ("drop sites"). To date, the NTCDC/NAC has identified more than 130 drop sites in its service area. Networked approaches to community organizing are not new. However, this local, scaled-down approach is an improvement on the traditional network strategy because it incorporates the organization's ongoing commitment to surveying and assessing

Source: NTCDC Brochure

Figure 2. NTCDC'S Efforts to Educate and Mobilize the Community

community needs.[27] These survey efforts are coordinated through social media, network listservs, and the Neighborhood Advisory Committee.

Community Surveying, Needs Assessment, and Planning

With funding from the Neighborhood Advisory Committee, NTCDC surveys the community frequently to assess community needs. Housing stability, childhood health and development, and community healing and responses to gun violence have surfaced as needs most frequently articulated by the interviewees. One purpose of surveying is to draw people out of their homes and into the community. For a neighborhood where nearly one in three residents are living at or below the poverty line, and with homeowners facing disproportionately high foreclosure rates, these interpersonal interactions can have broader community benefits on health and wellness, according to Sandra Harmon, NTCDC's data and outreach coordinator. "We see a lot of people, particularly seniors, living in silence not knowing that help is available ...

---

27 Robert Kleidman, "Community Organizing and Regionalism," *City & Community* 3, no. 4 (2004): 403–21, https://doi.org/10.1111/j.1535-6841.2004.00096.x.

feeling ashamed, embarrassed, any number of things you can feel when you're impoverished," Harmon says.

The hard work of conducting methodologically rigorous and iterative community surveys pays high dividends as it strengthens the organization's commitment to neighborhood diversity and inclusiveness. The surveys reach out to all residents across age, class, gender, ability, mobility, and housing tenure boundaries, literally "meeting people where they are," as Harmon puts it, "from business owners who are needing to organize, right down to someone who is substance addicted and in need of some resources." The organization takes a proactive approach to ensuring that marginalized interests are represented by going out to different community events and spaces, while also understanding that these surveys must be conducted at different literacy levels, in different formats, and address a range of needs.

NTCDC also uses survey results to inform planning and programming. NTCDC Executive Director Majeedah Rashid is certified by the local Citizen's Planning Institute (CPI);[28] she is a steering committee member of two of the city's district planning groups and brings a significant amount of planning expertise and tools to NTCDC's programming. In this way, local community planning serves as an entry point to broader community and political mobilization and household and community empowerment, and is an important contributor to producing social change.[29] When surveys underscored the community's concern with housing, for example, NTCDC obtained grants from local foundations and the Philadelphia City Planning Commission (PCPC) to create community plans for mixed-income, mixed-use, transit-oriented developments; worked with local designers to create renderings and hold charrettes; and ultimately managed to secure Low-Income Housing Tax Credits and over $40 million in financing for Nicetown Court I and II. When the development and construction of the buildings encountered some community resistance to the proposed rent scheduled, NTCDC responded by meeting the community where they were, holding a listening session, and increasing the number of units that could accept

---

[28] The Citizens Planning Institute is a seven-week course free to all Philadelphia residents that provides instruction on core urban planning concepts. After completing the course, CPI graduates are engaged in citywide and community planning processes as stakeholders and encouraged to train other community members.

[29] Brady and O'Connor, "Understanding How Community Organizing Leads to Social Change."

Housing Choice Vouchers.[30] The buildings, finished in 2016, contain 90 rental units as well as ground-level retail options, a medical office, a fitness center, and a new green space. This development certainly expands the community's resources, but the rents—$573 per month for a one-bedroom unit, and $937 for a four-bedroom—are far above median rental prices in the neighborhood and above the rent-burden threshold of many household incomes.

Financial Autonomy

Unlike older community-based organizations and CDCs, which had to accept government grants and contracts to provide social services in low-income communities as urban populations and tax revenues declined, the relatively new NTCDC has not relied on public or philanthropic money for its core operations, except for federal grants for weatherization and affordable homeownership programs. Instead, NTCDC finds that its leaders' ability to maintain strong personal networks in the community generates a great deal of in-kind donations. NTCDC often gets free consultations from local design companies, donated goods and services for its annual Nicetown Giveback Festival, and subsidized catering from local restaurants. This relative independence means that the organization can take on controversial political stances but also leaves NTCDC increasingly dependent on its leadership. Other community organizations in Nicetown have also found that independence from public funding—either by choice or because city, state, and federal administrations are an unstable source of funding for social welfare—gives them more leeway to address individuals' ongoing material needs while also supporting the community's need for recreational and assembly space. For instance, the Giving of Self Partnership (GOSP), which serves low-income households in the adjacent West Oak Lane neighborhood, purchased a large building on the border of the Nicetown and West Oak Lane neighborhoods. It draws most of its revenue for programming from renting rooms to churches, day care providers, and party organizers.

Leadership Development

NTCDC was founded by Black men and women but is currently only employing Black women in leadership positions. Black women-led households dominate the Nicetown community, but there also is a large elderly population and growing youth population. NTCDC and other Village Network members

---

30 Staff, "Community Tension Prompts Walkout at Nicetown CDC Meeting," *WHYY*, January 22, 2013, https://whyy.org/articles/nicetown-cdc-meeting/.

rely heavily on the community to act as leaders of organizations; virtually all of the leaders live in or near Nicetown. Not only does this provide a level of comfort and accountability for residents and community organization leaders, it also provides the needed context to interpret surveys and needs assessments and translate them into effective programming.

NTCDC'S VILLAGE NETWORK IN ACTION

As the examples that follow illustrate, NTCDC deploys its core components and its combination of community organizing, community development, and Black feminist political strategies to fill funding gaps in community programs; ensure that low-income legacy residents have power and resources in a neighborhood where many community organizations are stretched to and beyond their limit; and empower residents to mobilize around their immediate needs.

Financial Autonomy to Support Leadership Development

Funding streams for local, state, and federal programs and initiatives are notoriously unreliable because priorities tend to change every time a new leader assumes office. When public funding ends for programs that Nicetown residents rely on, NTCDC and its Village Network step in to fill the gap as best they can. The Nicetown branch of the public library is a good example. Located in an unassuming building on a commercial strip at the intersection of North Broad Street and Hunting Park Avenue, it is one of the city's libraries with a mission to "advance literacy, guide learning, and inspire curiosity."[31] Fred Ginyard, the Director of Programming for the North Central cluster of the public library system of Philadelphia, works with programming staff to fulfill this mission but also understands the library's broader role in the community. "We are the only free space with programming in the neighborhood," he says. "There isn't any [other] space that you're not going to get chased out of."[32] Sustaining an above-and-beyond mission is difficult in a community short on resources, but Nicetown library staff have received microgrants from the central branch for programs that serve the community's specific needs, including a series of youth theater camps and open-mic nights that were instrumental in building community and in building the space of the Nicetown library branch. Although

---

31 "About the Library," Free Library of Philadelphia, 2020, https://libwww.freelibrary.org/about/.

32 Fred Ginyard, Interview with Fred Ginyard, In-person, June 10, 2019.

funding for the open-mic night has lapsed, Nicetown Library continues to hold it with an entry fee, using audio equipment purchased with the grant.

Obtaining Resources for Nicetown Residents

NTCDC uses the Village Network and drop site arrangement with 130 partners to connect Nicetown residents with an array of in-kind goods, services, supports, and opportunities. Reflecting priorities aligned with Black feminist politics, these resources center on items and services often most needed by women and families, such as food banks, childcare, training, and part-time work opportunities. For example, a parishioner at Provision of Grace World Mission Church (a Village Network member) who has connections to the national organization YouthBuild helped the church obtain programmatic funding to train local youth to rehabilitate occupied and vacant homes in the neighborhood. Residents of low-income neighborhoods often have weak ties to outside resources, but the network created and maintained by NTCDC helped make that linkage on behalf of Nicetown youth and families.

Before organizing residents, NTCDC must first overcome counter-pressures rooted in the neighborhood's history, urgent current needs, and residents' sense of disconnection from the community. These barriers reflect a core tension between community development and community organizing in mixed-income communities notes Rhona Austin, who runs State Senator Sharif Street's Nicetown office. Communities like Nicetown experienced disinvestment and demobilization while other parts of the city experienced growth and revitalization. Residents are aware of how this affected the neighborhood— especially how public policy undermined the neighborhood's economic status. The long history of redlining and mortgage discrimination in Black communities, the stagnant wages and job opportunities, the declining quality and availability of affordable housing, and the ongoing threat of environmental pollution and health hazards that come with living in a neighborhood designed for industrial use all combine to create fewer household resources available to meet greater community needs. In that context, it isn't surprising that residents might resist showing up "to sit in a meeting [to] talk about a building across the street," Austin notes. "How can you think about the community needs when you are too busy thinking about your own?"[33] Working residents might also be too tired to take on another project; often, meetings that are meant to

---

33 Rhona Austin, Interview with Rhona Austin, In-person, June 10, 2019.

mobilize and inform all community members are attended mostly by those who have free time not dedicated to work or domestic duties. "You would have the same 15 people out of a neighborhood of 500 show up," Austin observes.

NTCDC's response is to frame community organizing as an immediate solution to residents' own needs. The organization and its Village Network partners take pride in preemptively addressing the concerns of local households and consistently providing goods and services that promote housing stability. Many of the organizations have weekly food pick-ups, clothing drives for holidays and the beginning of school, and semi-annual days dedicated to utility bill forgiveness, record expungements, or other high-cost legal and administrative functions. At the onset of the foreclosure crisis, for instance, NTCDC canvassed homeowners in areas at high risk of foreclosure, including two neighborhoods just north of Nicetown, to provide information on foreclosure diversion and assistance. Their rationale, informed by Black feminist politics, was that freeing up the emotional and mental bandwidth of heads of single-parent households would lead to more participation and engagement in community actions.

CONCLUSIONS

The field of housing and community development can learn a great deal from the experiences of organizations in communities such as Nicetown. Inclusionary mixed-income communities require an iterative, community-driven, resource-mobilizing approach to organize long-term and newly arriving residents over time. Community organizations working in areas where mixed-income development is occurring must increase funding independence and shift away from the often-conservative philanthropic foundation and nonprofit funding complex in order to maintain accountability to and flexibility for the changing community's needs. Focusing limited organizational resources on both community development and community organizing is difficult, but the benefit is inclusionary, responsive programming for communities that have both traditional and nontraditional options for community development. Centering Black feminist political values and leadership is an effective means of mitigating between this tension emerging from opposing community organizing and development priorities. This long-term investment in community will help to build trust, enhance educational outreach and community participation, and mobilize and empower residents to contribute to social change for marginalized communities.

IMPLICATIONS FOR ACTION

Implications for Policy

- Policy makers should legitimize and support the networks, foci, and spaces needed to sustain Black feminist "oppositional knowledge" and should maintain and increase funding allocated to key Black feminist political interests, such as education, care, housing, and mobility.

- Local, state, and federal policies should:
  - Include funds for surveying, community building and organization, and implementing community plans;
  - Emphasize and provide funds for grassroots programming to sustain innovative strategies, such as the Village Network; and
  - Counteract the pitfalls of funding community organizations—e.g., the emphasis on short-term service funding—by specifying funding for community organizing and community development activities.

- City governments can create dedicated streams of funding for community organizations that support multiple forms of data collection, by implementing a system similar to Neighborhood Advisory Committees.

Implications for Research and Evaluation

- Measures of success for community development should not only focus narrowly on individual mobility but also on community-wide measures of empowerment and autonomy.

- Researchers should engage in Participatory Action Research (PAR) and Community- Based Participatory Research (CBPR) to account for their own biases and produce research reflective of community needs and empowerment goals.

- In keeping with the PAR/CBPR methods, researchers can conduct research and evaluation through local organizations and schools, engaging citizens in collecting data and using data for decision making (i.e., linking planning and empowerment).

- Researchers and policy makers should accommodate longer evaluation timelines for programs and interventions in order to capture impacts and outcomes in neighborhoods with high rates of disadvantage and poverty, which make outcomes difficult to ascertain. At the same time, researchers should build local research capacity and phase out their own direct investigation in order to avoid creating "permanent laboratories," a longstanding issue involving social science in marginalized communities that undermines trust and induces research fatigue.

Implications for Development and Investment

Investment and development strategies should be diverse enough to account for multiple economy types while also offering balanced approaches to development for renters and homeowners alike. Maintaining neighborhood affordability while attracting market-rate investment is difficult. The Nicetown Courts model with service-providers, medical, retail, and political offices on the ground floor mixed with residential units in a transit-oriented development is a great means of attracting development while addressing housing needs. Other targets for investment include:

- Cooperatives (for both business and homeownership/renters), which foster empowerment and address material needs at the same time. Cooperatives can also create employment opportunities with greater autonomy than other traditional job-training and workforce development programs.
- Community land trusts (CLTs), which allow nonprofits and governments to issue leases on land but not to sell the property. This creates permanent affordability, by limiting the ability to profit from real estate sales.
- Using a block grant model to leverage the power of larger organizations to attract funding and issuing microgrants for community proposals to support businesses and provide start-up capital.

Implications for Residents and Community Members

- Residents and community members must continue to hold community organizations accountable to their service areas and to changing political, economic, and social interests and realities.
- Residents and community members need to support organizations that innovate by participating in surveys, meetings, and leadership training and opportunities.
- Based on this case study, community organizations should consider the following when building inclusive mixed-income communities:
  - Foster empowerment and engagement by legitimizing "oppositional knowledge;"

- Create space for people to gather and legitimize their own networks;
- Tap into local funding to support community planning efforts and ongoing surveying and needs assessment;
- Implement a Village Network model that stretches the definition of community—consider partnering with educational and other anchor institutions as a means of creating weak ties in the neighborhood; and
- Maintain ongoing educational opportunities in nontraditional spaces (such as parks, cafes, and laundromats) to engage wider segments in the community as an initial step of community building and empowerment.

■ ■ ■

AKIRA DRAKE RODRIGUEZ is a Joint Lecturer at the University of Pennsylvania's Weitzman School of Design and School of Social Policy & Practice. Her research examines the politics of urban planning, or the ways that disenfranchised groups re-appropriate their marginalized spaces in the city to gain access to and sustain urban political power. Using an interdisciplinary and multiple method approach, her research engages scholarship in urban studies, political science, urban history, black feminist studies, community development, urban policy, and critical geography using both qualitative and quantitative data and methods. This research agenda is particularly relevant in these politically unstable times, where cities continue to marginalize underrepresented minority groups by defunding public institutions, promoting urban policies that subsidize their displacement while limiting affordable housing options, and continuing the funding and support of a militarized police force.

■ ■ ■

Born and raised in North Philadelphia, PA, **MAJEEDAH RASHID** is Chief Operating Officer of Nicetown CDC, responsible for overseeing the administration and operations of the non-profit's projects. Following a career in health information management, Rashid earned her Master's degree in Community Economic Development from the University of Southern New Hampshire, paving the way for her to become a champion of community engagement in the Nicetown neighborhood. She also dedicates her time to serving as an advisor to a number of community initiatives, including the Philadelphia Department of Commerce Neighborhood Economic Development Advisory Council, LaSalle University President's Community Advisory Council, and the Philadelphia City Planning Commission.

UNTAPPED ASSETS: DEVELOPING A STRATEGY TO EMPOWER BLACK FATHERS IN MIXED-INCOME COMMUNITIES

Clinton Boyd, Jr.
Duke University

Deirdre A. Oakley
Georgia State University

> "Throughout history, the powers of single black men flash here and there like falling stars, and die sometimes before the world has rightly gauged their brightness."
>
> —W.E.B. Du Bois

These words culled from the pages of W.E.B. Du Bois's riveting text, *The Souls of Black Folks*,[1] merit careful contemplation. While the promise and perils of mixed-income public-housing transformation are well-documented,[2] Black men have received limited scholarly attention on the subject. If Black men are referenced in the mixed-income literature, it occurs in a "color-blind" fashion, whereby authors eschew direct racial references when describing them. The result can be an insidious deficit narrative. When value-laden descriptors such as "alcoholics," "drug addicts," "drug dealers," and "gang bangers" are used, they operate as implicit racial codes, further vilifying Black men. In this essay, we consider Black men, particularly fathers, in a positive, aspirational light.

---

1 W.E.B. Du Bois, *The Souls of Black Folk* (New York: Dover Publications, 1903).

2 Robert J. Chaskin and Mark L. Joseph, *Integrating the Inner City: The Promise and Perils of Mixed-Income Public Housing Transformation* (Chicago: University of Chicago Press, 2015).

Our essay describes how Black fathers can serve as assets to their children, families, and neighborhoods in mixed-income community settings. We focus on Black fathers in this essay given their persistent exclusion from government housing programs, their limited visibility in place-based, anti-poverty initiatives, and the recent evidence documenting Black fathers' far-reaching positive influence on Black boys in their communities. Moreover, since policies and programs often overlook the unique needs of young parents, this essay prioritizes Black fathers ages 16 to 24. To provide a solution that addresses these omissions, we describe the basic tenets of a father-focused, family-centered program for young Black fathers. We first review how systemic racism in the area of housing policy has historically constrained opportunities for Black fathers.

HOW DID WE GET HERE?

Systemic racism is the structure by which governmental policies, bureaucratic procedures, and cultural dynamics converge to deliberately advantage Whites and chronically disadvantage people of color, particularly Blacks.[3] Black American descendants of slavery have been subjected to unique forms of racialized oppression across generations, leading to long-standing calls for reparations to acknowledge, redress, and bring closure to their grievances.[4] Far from static, systemic racism has taken various forms since the founding of the American Republic. Whether it be American slavery, state-sanctioned apartheid in the form of Jim Crow segregation, or the more covert racism that emerged in the post-Civil Rights era, the overarching objective of these racial regimes were to oppress Blacks. The cumulative effects of systemic racism have also resulted in Black households having considerably less wealth than their White counterparts, even after accounting for educational attainment and employment status.[5] Housing discrimination on account of race is a particular form of systemic racism, one that has long ruptured the social fabric of Black families and created distinct obstacles for Black fathers.

---

3   Joe R. Feagin, *Systemic Racism: A Theory of Oppression* (New York: Routledge, 2006).

4   William A. Darity and A. Kirsten Mullen, *From Here to Equality: Reparations for Black Americans in the Twenty-First Century* (Chapel Hill: University of North Carolina Press, 2020).2020

5   Darrick Hamilton, William Darity, Jr., Anne E. Price, Vishnu Sridharan, and Rebecca Tippett, *Umbrellas Don't Make It Rain: Why Studying and Working Hard Isn't Enough for Black Americans* (Oakland, CA: Insight Center for Community Economic Development, 2015), http://www.insightcced.org/wp-content/uploads/2015/08/Umbrellas_Dont_Make_It_Rain_Final.pdf.

Exclusionary Housing Policies and Black Fathers

Once Aid to Dependent Children (ADC) was established under Title IV of the Social Security Act of 1935, "suitable home" policies denied housing assistance to unmarried mothers if a man resided in the household. State governments admonished unmarried mothers for not raising their children in marital households, which was the cultural ideal until the mid-twentieth century.[6] Black mothers were disproportionately affected by these "man-in-the-house" rules, as a larger share of them bore children out of wedlock and married less frequently than White women. In her seminal book, *Poverty Knowledge: Social Science, Social Policy and the Poor in Twentieth-Century U.S. History*, Alice O'Connor further notes that, in some instances, Black fathers moved out-of-state so their families could secure public assistance and subsidized housing.[7]

The welfare programs of the Great Society also failed to incorporate Black fathers in efforts to eliminate poverty. Not even the alarmist report on the "negro family" by Daniel Patrick Moynihan, the former Assistant Secretary of Labor, could persuade the Johnson Administration that "fathers should be supported by public policy."[8] Keeping with tradition, instead, the federal government continued to channel its antipoverty supports directly through Black women and children, thus, excluding Black fathers yet again.

The trend in exclusionary public housing policies entered a new phase in the 1980s and 1990s during the "War on Drugs." Under the guise of reducing drug-related criminal activity in public housing, several federal housing policies were enacted that legally prohibited individuals with criminal records from residing in public housing. Low-income Black men arrested or convicted of nonviolent drug offenses bear the brunt of this distinct form of legal housing discrimination. The families of formerly incarcerated Black men pay a hefty price as well. For example, families receiving housing subsidies can be evicted from public housing for allowing returning citizens to reside in their households. Opportunities for Black fathers to successfully reunite with their children are thwarted as a result of these "one strike and you're out" laws.

---

6 Andrew J. Cherlin, *The Marriage-Go-Round: The State of Marriage and the Family in America Today*, 1 edition (New York: Vintage, 2010).

7 Alice O'Connor, *Poverty Knowledge: Social Science, Social Policy, and the Poor in Twentieth-Century U.S. History* (Princeton: Princeton University Press, 2001).

8 Ta-Nehisi Coates, *We Were Eight Years in Power: An American Tragedy* (New York: One World, 2017), 225.

The collateral consequences of restrictive public housing policies also have implications for Black fathers seeking housing in mixed-income communities, primarily those who are less educated, economically disadvantaged, and returning citizens. For example, local housing authority administrative procedures often require that relocated public housing residents pass a rigid eligibility screening before securing housing in mixed-income communities.[9] In particular, criminal background and employment verification checks are administered to determine housing eligibility for former public housing residents and other low-income individuals. Since Black men have some of the highest imprisonment and unemployment rates in the country,[10] these screenings will have a profound impact on Black fathers trying to obtain housing in mixed-income communities.

Additionally, motivated mainly by concerns related to safety, security, and "ghetto" behavior, housing managers have codified stringent rules into rental leases to regulate the behaviors of relocated public housing residents and other low-income renters.[11] For example, leaseholders (typically women) can be evicted from their housing unit for failing to report a change in household composition. This "zero-tolerance" policy becomes a challenge for leaseholders considering whether to jeopardize their housing security to maintain a relationship with their formerly incarcerated relative or intimate partner if they allow him to move into their residence. As leaseholders know all too well, if it is discovered that someone living in the housing unit is not listed on the household roster, their odds of being evicted skyrocket immediately. Former public housing residents and other low-income renters believe that such regulatory rules were explicitly instituted to monitor the foot traffic in and out of their homes, mainly because they are perceived as "problem

---

9   Naomi J. McCormick, Mark L. Joseph, and Robert J. Chaskin, "The New Stigma of Relocated Public Housing Residents: Challenges to Social Identity in Mixed-Income Developments," *City & Community* 11, no. 3 (September 2012): 285–308, https://doi.org/10.1111/j.1540-6040.2012.01411.x.

10 William M. Rodgers, "Race in the Labor Market: The Role of Equal Employment Opportunity and Other Policies," *RSF: The Russell Sage Foundation Journal of the Social Sciences* 5, no. 5 (December 2019): 198–220, https://doi.org/10.7758/RSF.2019.5.5.10.\uc0\u8221{} {\i{}RSF: The Russell Sage Foundation Journal of the Social Sciences} 5, no. 5 (December 2019

11 Robert J. Chaskin and Mark L. Joseph, "Contested Space: Design Principles and Regulatory Regimes in Mixed-Income Communities in Chicago," eds. Barrett A. Lee et al., *The ANNALS of the American Academy of Political and Social Science* 660, no. 1 (July 2015): 136–54, https://doi.org/10.1177/0002716215576113.

households."[12] As another point of emphasis, the federal HOPE VI and Choice Neighborhoods mixed-income housing initiatives primarily target social service supports to minority women and their children.[13] Since Black men are characterized as the "undeserving poor," it is extremely rare for Black fathers to receive support services.

EMPOWERING BLACK FATHERS IN MIXED-INCOME COMMUNITIES

The time has come for a radical reconceptualization of how we engage Black fathers in U.S. housing policy initiatives. Despite being depicted as uncommitted parents by the media,[14] Black fathers are integral components of their families and communities. Chetty, Hendren, Jones, and Porter's study, *Race and Economic Opportunity in the United States*,[15] is particularly instructive on the asset potential of Black fathers. Using data on 20 million children and their parents, the report provides compelling evidence that the presence of Black fathers can help reduce income and incarceration disparities between Black and White boys.

According to the report, upon reaching adulthood, Black boys earn less money than White boys of similar initial economic status. This income gap holds even among Black boys raised in the most affluent neighborhoods and born into the wealthiest families. The racial disparities in income even cut across neighborhoods and regions. Moreover, the report highlights the pervasiveness of downward mobility in the Black community. For example, compared to White boys, Black boys born into higher-income families are more likely to become poor once they become men. The opposite is true for White boys, as those born into low-income households move up the income ladder at higher rates than Black boys.

Additionally, the probability that Black men whose parents were millionaires

---

12 McCormick, Joseph, and Chaskin, "The New Stigma of Relocated Public Housing Residents."

13 Kirk Harris, "Fathers from the Family to The Fringe: Practice, Policy, and Public Housing," in *Public Housing and the Legacy of Segregation*, eds. Margery Austin Turner, Susan J. Popkin, and Lynette A. Rawlings (Rowman & Littlefield Publishers, 2008), 203–19.

14 Travis Dixon, "A Dangerous Distortion of Our Families" (Oakland, California: Color of Change, December 2017).

15 Raj Chetty et al., "Race and Economic Opportunity in the United States: An Intergenerational Perspective" (NBER Working Paper No. 24441, National Bureau of Economic Research, Cambridge, MA, 2018).

(top 1 percent of the income distribution) would be incarcerated was equivalent to that of White men raised in households netting roughly $36,000. The report also indicates that on an average day, approximately 21 percent of all Black men born to the most impoverished families are incarcerated.

The report's authors underscored three factors that facilitate higher rates of upward mobility for Black boys, all of which have implications for Black boys growing up in mixed-income communities. First, the racial disparities in outcomes between Black and White boys are relatively smaller in low-poverty neighborhoods. Second, Black boys fare better in low-poverty neighborhoods where Whites exhibit lower levels of racial bias. Third, Black boys earn more and are incarcerated less, as adults, if Black fathers are a defining characteristic of their childhood communities, implying that the presence of Black fathers has a neighborhood-level influence that transcends family relations.[16]

Chetty and his colleagues also note that racial disparities in incarceration rates and individual earnings are relatively low between Black women and White women. However, the authors underscore that, due to Black men's lower earnings, higher imprisonment rates, and lower marriage rates than White men, the *household* incomes of Black women pale in comparison to White women. As a result, Black girls are less likely to be raised in higher-income households than White girls. Therefore, it is reasonable to conclude that Black fathers' positive influence on Black boys will also help to improve the household financial standing of Black girls and women.

To promote greater racial equity and inclusion in mixed-income communities, we propose that a father-focused, family-centered program should be strategically embedded into mixed-income community strategies. We contend that the place-based program ought to target Black boys, a sub-population highly vulnerable to the effects of systemic racism.[17] We recognize that Black girls would also benefit from strategies designed specifically to meet their needs and opportunities. However, while this essay focuses on the needs of Black boys, as stated above, we expect that the benefits of greater engagement from more stable, well-prepared fathers would benefit their daughters as well

---

[16] Chetty et al., "Race and Economic Opportunity."

[17] Candice L. Odgers, Sachiko Donley, Avshalom Caspi, Christopher J. Bates, and Terrie E. Moffit, "Living alongside more affluent neighbors predicts greater involvement in antisocial behavior among low-income boys," *Journal of Child Psychology and Psychiatry* 56, no. 10 (2015): 1055-64.

as their sons. The mixed-income community context gives Black boys whose families can secure housing in these developments access to a low-poverty community with high-quality amenities. Building on this, Black fathers should be proactively engaged and supported as critical agents in the effort to create more equitable communities.

Focus on Young Black Fathers. Young parents between the ages of 16 to 24 have been largely neglected by researchers, policymakers, and practitioners.[18] Young parents face obstacles such as inadequate access to childcare, low levels of social support, economic insecurity, housing instability, and limited access to educational services and career development opportunities.[19] While these challenges affect all subcategories of young parents, empirical evidence suggests that young Black fathers confront obstacles unlike those experienced by other young parents.

Systemic inequities in education, employment, and the criminal justice system illustrate the previous point. Due to their negative educational experiences from preschool to 12th grade,[20] many young Black fathers can easily find themselves disconnected from the very academic institutions viewed as conduits to future prosperity. As it pertains to employment, labor market discrimination has contributed to young Black males being unemployed, underemployed, and jobless at rates that far exceed their White male peers.[21] Because of racial disparities in their educational and employment outcomes, over 30 percent of Black males between 20 to 24 years of age are out of school and out of work. In cities like Chicago, the figure is nearly 50 percent.[22]

Concerning the criminal justice system, it is a well-known fact that Black men

---

18 Annie E. Casey Foundation, *Opening Doors for Young Parents* (Baltimore, MD: Annie E. Casey Foundation, 2018), https://www.aecf.org/resources/opening-doors-for-young-parents/.

19 Nathan Sick, Shayne Spaulding, and Yuju Park, *Understanding Young-Parent Families* (Washington, DC: Urban Institute, 2018).

20 Rhonda Tsoi-A-Fatt, *We Dream A World: The 2025 Vision for Black Men and Boys* (New York, NY: Open Society Foundations, 2010), https://www.opensocietyfoundations.org/uploads/f0b30746-a906-40e8-b527-05363775685a/we-dream-a-world-20110104.pdf.

21 Ronald B. Mincy, *Black Males Left Behind* (Washington, DC: Rowman & Littlefield Publishers, 2006).

22 Teresa L. Córdova and Matthew D. Wilson, *Lost: The Crisis Of Jobless and Out Of School Teens and Young Adults In Chicago, Illinois and the U.S.* (Chicago, IL: Great Cities Institute, 2016), https://greatcities.uic.edu/wp-content/uploads/2016/02/ASN-Report-v5.2.pdf.

are incarcerated far more than any other U.S. demographic group.[23] Racially discriminatory policies and policing practices are often cited as causes for Black males' overrepresentation in the criminal justice system. What is less well-known, however, is the fact that 20 percent of Black men, incarcerated for a minimum of 10 years, enter prison between the ages of 18 to 24.[24] For the 40 percent of Black fathers in state and federal prisons,[25] many of whom are young parents, a criminal record can constrain their employment prospects, prevent them from securing stable housing, and preclude them from participating in public assistance programs. Moreover, the nearly 74,000 Black fathers who re-enter society every year lose $600 million or more in collective annual earnings.[26] For Black fathers in economic straits, many feel that the mothers of their children purposely deny them access to their offspring due to their financial shortcomings.[27]

All of these challenges have additional implications for young fathers who have open child support orders and are required to contribute financially to their children's upbringing. The interrelationship between poverty, incarceration, and child support warrants consideration. An Urban Institute study of child support administrative data in nine states determined that 70 percent of child support debt was owed by noncustodial parents making less than $10,000 annually,[28] many of whom are young Black fathers with limited education.[29]

---

23 Michelle Alexander, *The New Jim Crow: Mass Incarceration in the Age of Colorblindness* (New York: The New Press, 2012).

24 Leigh Courtney, Sarah Eppler-Epstein, Elizabeth Pelletier, Ryan King, and Serena Lei, *A Matter of Time: The Causes and Consequences of Rising Time Served in America's Prisons*. (Washington, DC: Urban Institute, 2017), https://apps.urban.org/features/long-prison-terms/a_matter_of_time_print_version.pdf.

25 Lauren E. Glaze and Laura M. Maruschak, *Parents in Prison and Their Minor Children* (Washington, DC: U.S. Department of Justice, 2010), https://www.bjs.gov/content/pub/pdf/pptmc.pdf.

26 Mark L. Joseph, "Understanding the Economic Costs of Incarceration for African American Males," in *Social Work with African American Males: Health, Mental Health, and Social Policy*, ed. Waldo E. Johnson, Jr. (Oxford University Press, 2010), 311–24.

27 Kathryn Edin and Timothy J. Nelson, *Doing the Best I Can: Fatherhood in the Inner City* (Berkeley: University of California Press, 2013).

28 Elaine Sorensen, Liliana Sousa, and Simone G Schaner, *Assessing Child Support Arrears in Nine Large States and the Nation*. (Washington, D.C.: Urban Institute, 2007), https://www.urban.org/sites/default/files/publication/29736/1001242-Assessing-Child-Support-Arrears-in-Nine-Large-States-and-the-Nation.PDF.

29 Elaine Sorensen, *Obligating Dads: Helping Low-Income Noncustodial Fathers Do More for Their Children* (Washington, DC: Urban Institute, 1999), http://webarchive.urban.org/UploadedPDF/sf_2.pdf.

These men are also willing but financially unable to provide for their children.[30] To compensate for their inability to support their children monetarily, many low-income Black fathers provide the mothers of their offspring with informal and in-kind support instead.[31]

Child support enforcement utilizes several punitive tactics whenever fathers fall behind on their court-ordered payments. The penalties for child support noncompliance range from license revocation to financial penalties to incarceration, all of which negatively affect the employment outcomes and economic stability of nonresident fathers.[32] Estimates suggest that 14 percent of child support debtors are incarcerated by the time their children reach the age of nine.[33] Noncustodial parents are still responsible for their child support payments while incarcerated, despite being unable to meet their financial obligations. Their child support debt mounts uncontrollably as a consequence. Typically, fathers enter prison with $10,000 in child support debt and exit with $20,000 in arrears.

Despite their unfortunate circumstances, parenthood can serve as a positive, motivating force in the lives of young Black fathers. When young Black fathers properly embrace their parental responsibilities, they may be motivated to offer their children a life they never had.

PROGRAM COMPONENTS

Given the shortage of structured supports and activities for youth and young adults in mixed-income communities,[34] our proposed fatherhood program aims to promote more reliable social connections between young Black fathers, their children, their families, and other community members. Our ultimate objective

---

30 Ronald B. Mincy and Elaine J. Sorensen, "Deadbeats and Turnips in Child Support Reform," *Journal of Policy Analysis and Management* 17, no. 1 (1998): 44-51.

31 Jennifer B. Kane, Timothy J. Nelson, and Kathryn Edin, "How Much In-Kind Support Do Low-Income Nonresident Fathers Provide? A Mixed-Method Analysis," *Journal of Marriage and Family* 77, no. 3 (June 2015): 591–611, https://doi.org/10.1111/jomf.12188.

32 Mincy, *Black Males Left Behind*.

33 Elizabeth Cozzolino, "Public Assistance, Relationship Context, and Jail for Child Support Debt," *Socius* 4 (January 1, 2018): 2378023118757124, https://doi.org/10.1177/2378023118757124.

34 Robert J. Chaskin, Florian Sichling, and Mark L. Joseph, "Youth in Mixed-Income Communities Replacing Public Housing Complexes: Context, Dynamics and Response," *Cities* 35 (December 2013): 423–31, https://doi.org/10.1016/j.cities.2013.03.009.

is to create a well-organized community context whereby supportive activities and resources are available to young fathers and their offspring.

Inclusion Criteria

Young Black fathers between the ages of 16 to 24 are the target population for our proposed program. Additionally, since there is a tendency in social science research to gloss over the internal diversity of Black fathers,[35] our program model focuses on three types of young Black fathers: 1) resident fathers, 2) non-resident fathers, and 3) "social fathers," father figures with a social, rather than biological, relationship to the children under their supervision. Given the empirical evidence cited earlier about the importance of non-resident and non-familial Black fathers in the lives of Black boys, our program will allow us to simultaneously engage these distinct groups of young fathers.

Core Operations

Enrolling a broad range of young fathers in our program would be a top priority. Therefore, we would deploy an array of outreach and recruitment efforts to accomplish this aim. We would conduct targeted street outreach within mixed-income communities and recruit young fathers from venues that they frequent. Since much has been written about the extent to which young adults "loiter" within mixed-income communities,[36] sustained and purposeful outreach efforts will be made to recruit young fathers "hanging out" in their own neighborhood. Young fathers also will be recruited through community organizations, local service providers, and other community anchor institutions operating in or near mixed-income communities. Once young fathers have been identified and expressed interest in the program, they will be asked to attend an orientation session to learn about the program from a Fatherhood Ambassador, a staff member who will support and mentor the young fathers. Program enrollees will also be incentivized to recruit other young fathers into the program. Program graduates will also be called upon to promote the program within their networks.

Fathers would participate in a cohort-based, peer support group. Family policy

---

35 Maria S. Johnson and Alford A. Young, Jr., "Diversity and Meaning in the Study of Black Fatherhood," *Du Bois Review: Social Science Research on Race* 13, no. 01 (2016): 5–23, https://doi.org/10.1017/S1742058X16000047.

36 Mary Pattillo, *Black on the Block: The Politics of Race and Class in the City*, Reprint edition (Chicago, Ill.: University of Chicago Press, 2007); Chaskin, Sichling, and Joseph, "Youth in Mixed-Income Communities."Reprint edition (Chicago, Ill.: University Of Chicago Press, 2007

researchers have identified this particular service delivery format as an effective strategy for engaging fathers in parenting programs.[37] The cohort-based, peer support groups would provide "safe spaces" for Black fathers to be emotionally vulnerable[38] and would be offered daily during traditional and non-traditional work hours. Intensive case management supports would also be offered to enrolled fathers. Case managers would aim to help address any support needs of young fathers and also identify their personal and parental strengths, which could be leveraged to promote them as assets to other young fathers and community members. Case managers would continue to work with the young fathers for at least a year following cohort completion. The program would recruit staff who are well-positioned to build strong relationships with the young fathers, in particular those who have overcome life challenges like those encountered by program participants.

In the spirit of promoting family togetherness, monthly father-son events would be organized to create opportunities for young fathers to bond with their sons. These events would range from community beautification projects to educational activities to game nights to sports outings. Bi-monthly events for the whole family would be organized to ensure that the daughters, co-parents/partners, and extended family members of young fathers also benefit from the program.

Content Areas

The curriculum of the father-focused, family-centered program would consist of three primary content areas: 1) personal development, 2) career acceleration, and 3) system disruption.

The personal development aspect of the curriculum would help young fathers learn how to respond to discrimination, strengthen problem-solving skills, set goals, remain optimistic, manage stress, improve their overall health, enhance the quality of their co-parenting relationships, and learn developmentally appropriate parenting skills.

---

37 Robin Dion et al., *Parents and Children Together: The Complex Needs of Low-Income Men and How Responsible Fatherhood Programs Address Them*. (Washington, DC: Mathematica Policy Research, 2018), https://www.mathematica.org/our-publications-and-findings/publications/parents-and-children-together-the-complex-needs-of-low-income-men-and-how-responsible-fatherhood.

38 Alford Young Jr., "Safe Space for Vulnerability: New Perspectives on African Americans Who Struggle to Be Good Fathers," in *Boys and Men in African American Families*, eds. Linda M. Burton et al. (Springer, 2017), 173–83.

Supplemental father-centered home visiting services will also be offered to program enrollees. Home visiting programs have traditionally helped to support maternal health and early child development, mainly among children age five and under. Recent empirical evidence also documents that fathers benefit from home visiting programs.[39] It is our hope that young fathers enrolled in our program will also derive value from the home visiting services they receive.

Expectant and young fathers with children under the age of one will especially benefit from participating in home visiting services. Given America's alarming Black-White infant mortality gap,[40] Black fathers can play a critical role in not only reducing infant mortality but also improving maternal health.[41] The content offered to young fathers through our home visiting model will ensure that they can insightfully engage with child health care providers at prenatal care visits and well-baby clinic visits. This portion of our home visiting model will also educate young fathers on how to best support the mothers of their children in improving their own health outcomes during these medical visits. Ultimately, we hope to empower young fathers to become advocates both for the health of their children and the mothers of their children.

Identifying the developmental stages of infants and toddlers can be a challenge for young fathers, given that they also find themselves at a developmental crossroads. For young Black fathers specifically, "a lack of knowledge about child development" often causes them "to doubt their ability to provide paternal caregiving for their young children."[42] Since the average young father has children under the age of five,[43] evidence-based home visiting programs

---

39 Sandra McGinnis et al., "Engaging At-Risk Fathers in Home Visiting Services: Effects on Program Retention and Father Involvement," *Child and Adolescent Social Work Journal* 36, no. 2 (April 1, 2019): 189–200; Shannon Self-Brown et al., "The Impact of SafeCare® Dads to Kids Program on Father Maltreatment Risk and Involvement: Outcomes and Lessons Learned from an Efficacy Trial," *Child Abuse & Neglect* 83 (September 2018): 31–41, https://doi.org/10.1016/j.chiabu.2018.06.014.

40 Keisha L. Bentley-Edwards et al., "How Does It Feel to Be a Problem? The Missing Kerner Commission Report," *RSF: The Russell Sage Foundation Journal of the Social Sciences* 4, no. 6 (2018): 20, https://doi.org/10.7758/rsf.2018.4.6.02.

41 Michael C. Lu et al., "Closing the Black-White Gap in Birth Outcomes: A Life-Course Approach," *Ethnicity & Disease* 20, no. 1 0 2 (2010): S2-62–76.\\uc0\\u8221{} {\\i{}Ethnicity & Disease} 20, no. 1 0 2 (2010

42 Waldo E. Johnson, Jr., "Social Work Strategies for Sustaining Paternal Involvement among Unwed Fathers: Insights from Field Research," *Professional Development: The International Journal of Continuing Social Work Education* 5, no. 1 (2002): 77.

43 Sick, Spaulding, and Park, "Understanding Young-Parent Families."

can be utilized to promote the physical, cognitive, social, and emotional development of their young children. Therefore, the other aspect of our home visiting program will ensure young fathers understand the developmental milestones of their young children.

Career acceleration services—such as access to job training, job placement, career coaching, and business development—would be offered to young fathers while they are participating in cohort-based, peer support groups. These services will help young fathers to increase their earning potential and accumulate wealth.

To reach the goals associated with this objective, we plan to forge strategic partnerships with broader community and governmental agencies to assist young fathers in improving their educational and employment outcomes. Case managers will be responsible for establishing such partnerships. Working with existing community-based providers, a parallel set of program strategies would be developed to provide support to the sons of the fathers in the program.

The system disruption component of the curriculum will introduce young fathers to a robust learning environment geared towards analyzing each tier of America's governmental apparatus. This facet of the curriculum will also help young fathers to strategically engage in the political process at all levels of government. Ideally, these group sessions will equip young fathers with the tools, information, and resources they need to advocate for structural changes in the institutions and systems that shape opportunity in their communities. The goal is to help young fathers confront the macrostructural forces that perpetuate race-, gender-, and class-based inequality within mixed-income communities.

CONCLUSIONS

Black fathers typically do not benefit from the types of supportive services routinely offered to women and children in mixed-income communities. This has a great deal to do with systemic racism in exclusionary U.S. housing policy. Nonetheless, research indicates that Black fathers play a vital role in their families and communities. Therefore, we conclude that empowering Black fathers is a compelling way to leverage them as assets in mixed-income communities.

IMPLICATIONS FOR ACTION

Implications for Policy

Several policy initiatives could have an outsized effect in removing barriers to opportunity for Black fathers in mixed-income communities.

- *Several Federal Housing Policies Should Be Amended.* Specifically, key aspects of the Anti-Drug Abuse Act of 1988, the Cranston-Gonzalez National Affordable Housing Act of 1990, the Housing Opportunity Program Extension Act of 1996, and the Quality Housing and Work Responsibility Act of 1998 should be amended. These laws prevent returning citizens (disproportionately Black men) from residing in government-assisted housing; permits the eviction of families receiving housing subsidies if a member of their household was once incarcerated; and disqualifies evicted leaseholders from receiving housing subsidies for three years.[44] These heavy-handed policies undermine housing stability for reentering Black fathers and place them on the path of homelessness. The punitive nature of these policies also undercuts the prospect of family reunification for those tenants receiving federal housing subsidies in mixed-income communities.

- *The Federal Child Support System Should Be Revamped.* First, the federal Office of Child Support Enforcement should create a national database that collects race, gender, and socioeconomic information on who has unpaid child support debt. Currently, the federal government does not collect such demographic data.[45] Having this information will help to definitively determine whether Black fathers disproportionately face stiffer penalties for child support noncompliance compared to fathers of different races and ethnicities. Second, the Personal Responsibility and Work Opportunity Reconciliation Act (PRWORA) of 1996 should be amended. At the present time, PRWORA does not guarantee that noncustodial parents (disproportionately Black fathers) will have lawfully enforceable access to their children if they have an open child support order. This policy change will improve the chances of never-married, nonresident fathers having unrestricted access to their children in instances where mothers

---

[44] Silva, "Collateral Damage: A Public Housing Consequence of the 'War on Drugs,'" *UC Irvine Law Review* 5 (2015): 783–812."

[45] David J. Pate, Jr., "The Color of Debt: An Examination of Social Networks, Sanctions, and Child Support Enforcement Policy," *Race and Social Problems* 8, no. 1 (March 2016): 116–35, https://doi.org/10.1007/s12552-016-9167-8.

are denying them visitation access. Third, child support enforcement practices for noncompliance—such as license revocation, financial penalties, and incarceration—should be reconsidered. The overarching objective of the official child support system is allegedly to promote child well-being. However, the current structure of the federal child support system perpetuates racial inequality,[46] undermines family cohesion,[47] and has been flawed since its inception.[48]

- *The Marijuana Opportunity Reinvestment and Expungement (MORE) Act Should Become a Federal Law, Subject to Revision.* In addition to the bill's other key provisions, the MORE Act prohibits individuals convicted of marijuana-related offenses from being denied all forms of public assistance. The MORE Act also establishes expungement and resentencing processes for individuals with marijuana-related convictions. The race-conscious element of the proposed bill will strongly benefit Black men, as they have been disproportionately affected by the botched "War on Drugs." Another significant provision of the MORE Act is the creation of the "Community Reinvestment Grant Program," which offers job training, reentry services, legal aid for civil and criminal cases, and substance treatment services to those individuals most harshly affected by mass incarceration. Fatherhood organizations serving Black men would largely benefit from the "Community Reinvestment Grant Program," as they would have access to additional funding to support their programs.

- *The Federal Jobs Guarantee Development Act Should Become a Federal Law.* The proposed bill seeks to end unemployment, underemployment, and chronic joblessness by ensuring all working-age citizens have access to jobs that provide non-poverty wages, on-site job training, and fringe benefits.[49] If enacted, the federal jobs program would be piloted in 15

---

46 Tonya L. Brito, David J. Jr. Pate, and Jia-Hui Stafanie Wong, "I Do for My Kids: Negotiating Race and Racial Inequality in Family Court Symposium: Critical Race Theory and Empirical Methods Conference," *Fordham Law Review* 83, no. 6 (2015): 3027–52.\\uc0\\u8221{} {\\i{}Fordham Law Review} 83, no. 6 (2015)

47 Kathryn Edin et al., "Taking Care of Mine: Can Child Support Become a Family-Building Institution?," *Journal of Family Theory & Review* 11, no. 1 (2019): 79–91, https://doi.org/10.1111/jftr.12324.

48 Earl Johnson, Ann Levine, and Fred Doolittle, *Fathers' Fair Share: Helping Poor Men Manage Child Support and Fatherhood*, 1 edition (New York: Russell Sage Foundation, 1999)

49 Mark Paul et al., "A Path to Ending Poverty by Way of Ending Unemployment: A Federal Job Guarantee," *RSF: The Russell Sage Foundation Journal of the Social Sciences* 4, no. 3 (2018): 44, https://doi.org/10.7758/rsf.2018.4.3.03.

high-unemployment communities and regions to assess its impact. While the proposed bill will help American adult citizens, it will be especially impactful for young Black fathers facing limited job prospects, higher than average unemployment and underemployment, and various forms of labor market discrimination.

- *The Maternal, Infant, and Early Childhood Home Visiting (MIECH) program Should Be Expanded to More Intentionally Focus on Fathers.* In the United States and abroad, home visiting programs are used as tactical tools to provide family-focused supports to families with young children. However, mothers and children have traditionally been the beneficiaries of these services, while fathers are rarely integrated into home visiting programs. Consequently, children may be deprived of opportunities to establish meaningful relationships with their fathers during early childhood, which is considered the most developmentally important stage in the life course.

Implications for Research and Evaluation

Too few fatherhood programs have been rigorously evaluated to gauge their effectiveness, especially those for which racial or ethnic minorities are the target population. Additionally, when evaluations are carried out, researchers may not select the appropriate measurement items when assessing program outcomes, nor may they properly account for how contextual factors might affect fathers' experiences in the program. Evaluation periods also tend to be short, and they rarely track child outcomes alongside fathers. To fill these gaps:

- Our father-focused, family-centered program would be piloted and would undergo a process and outcome evaluation.
- Our evaluation would use a mixed methods approach. The qualitative component would allow fathers to detail their experiences in the research trial in ways not possible if we solely rely on close-ended measurement instruments.

Acknowledging the internal diversity among fathers, our measurement items will be sensitive to the unique ways residential, non-residential, non-biological young Black fathers engage with their children.

Implications for Development and Investment

- Community benefit agreements (CBAs) should be established between mixed-income community residents and real estate developers to incorporate features that would promote quality-of-life improvements that would benefit Black fathers. CBAs could commit to include well-designed and state-of-the-art community centers and wellness centers, for example. Black fathers could utilize these spaces for a wide variety of constructive, family-centered activities. There should also be a commitment to provide family-sustaining jobs to residents who are chronically jobless, unemployed, and underemployed. Black fathers would disproportionately benefit from this particular CBA, as Black men are overrepresented in low-wage occupations, underrepresented in high-wage jobs, and are outside the labor market more than their peers because of labor market discrimination.[50] Financial resources should also be committed to community-based advocacy organizations working to advance social change.

Implications for Residents and Community Members

- Fathers should form their own peer affinity groups to support each other and to organize themselves to effectively influence formal local resident councils and neighborhood associations in their mixed-income communities.

- Fathers should work together to create a positive action and marketing campaign to help debunk the myth of the "deadbeat" Black father.[51] These campaigns should also emphasize how Black fathers are contributing to the healthy development of their children.

■ ■ ■

CLINTON BOYD, JR., *is a Postdoctoral Associate in the Samuel DuBois Cook Center on Social Equity at Duke University. His areas of interest include race and ethnicity, poverty and inequality, urban sociology, social policy, and parenting and African American families. Dr. Boyd primarily studies how the life course events of African American men affect their experiences as fathers. His research*

---

50 Darrick Hamilton, Algernon Austin, and William Darity Jr., *Whiter Jobs, Higher Wages: Occupational Segregation and the Lower Wages of Black Men* (Washington, DC: Economic Policy Institute, 2011), https://www.epi.org/files/page/-/BriefingPaper288.pdf.

51 Roberta Coles and Charles Green, eds., *The Myth of the Missing Black Father* (New York: Columbia University Press, 2009).

also explores ways to strengthen father involvement in evidence-based home visiting programs. The National Institute of Health, Doris Duke Charitable Foundation, Chapin Hall at the University of Chicago, and early childhood non-profit organization, ZERO TO THREE, have supported his research in these areas. He earned a Ph.D. from Georgia State University, an MA from DePaul University, and a BA from Concordia University Chicago.

■ ■ ■

DEIRDRE OAKLEY is a Professor of Sociology at Georgia State University, and is the Editor-in-Chief of City & Community, the country's flagship peer-review journal of urban sociology. Her research focuses on how urban social and racial disadvantages are often compounded by various local, state and federal policies. Dr. Oakley has provided Congressional Testimony about public housing to the Financial Services Committee. She received her B.A. in American History from Bowdoin College, M.A. in Urban Geography and her Ph.D. in Sociology from SUNY-Albany.

YOUTH VOICE AND LEADERSHIP IN MIXED-INCOME COMMUNITIES: HERITAGE PARK AND THE GREEN GARDEN BAKERY

Ephraim Adams, D'Loveantae Allen and Mohamed Mohamed
Green Garden Bakery

Joni R. Hirsch
Fees and Fines Justice Center

Taryn H. Gress
National Initiative on Mixed-Income Communities, Case Western Reserve University

Elana Dahlberg and Alecia Leonard
Urban Strategies, Inc.

> "Being with the Green Garden Bakery, it helped us have our voices heard. Also I know it helped influence some people in the community's voices to be heard as well. We as youth don't know everything, but at the same time the adults don't know everything, so it's like we can both share our own inputs about life and benefit each other. Having our own input on our community helps a lot."[1]

---

[1] The quotes in this essay are from youth living in the Heritage Park mixed-income development in Minneapolis, MN, who are leaders with the Green Garden Bakery. We are grateful to the youth for taking time to share their perspectives. We thank Elana Dahlberg and Alecia Leonard of Urban Strategies, Inc. and Joni Hirsch of the National Initiative on Mixed-Income Communities for conducting focus group conversations with the youth.

Research on youth development underscores the importance of reducing young people's risky behavior while also helping them develop the skills and competencies they need to succeed throughout their formative years and into adulthood.[2] Youth, particularly those in adolescence, have potential to be great connectors in their communities. Cultivating young people's leadership skills, showcasing their talents, and empowering them to contribute positively to their community also can shift community-wide perceptions about youth and promote a culture in which they are valued members of the community.

For those reasons, it is important to promote youth development in any community. In the neighborhood transformation context in particular, mixed-income redevelopment can be leveraged to enhance youth development. Ideally, as the community gains housing stability and quality, increased neighborhood safety, and improved neighborhood facilities—including schools and youth programs—young people will provide an important source of vision, voice, leadership, and inspiration.

Unfortunately, challenges within mixed-income communities often mean that young people are not included in redevelopment planning or implementation. Residents of mixed-income communities can be diverse in income, race, ethnicity, culture, and language, and often experience unequal access to opportunities and resources, as well as different expectations around norms. Across these differences, community members hold varying perceptions about young people and their role in the community. Due to factors such as individual bias, targeted policing, and unequal access to supports and resources, low-income youth, particularly youth of color, may feel stigmatized and become targets of surveillance and exclusion.[3] Programs for youth may be overshadowed by a focus on supports for adults and young children. Adolescents also are frequently the focal point of conflicts involving behavior and delinquency,[4] so

---

2 Peter L. Benson, "Developmental assets: An overview of theory, research, and practice," in *Approaches to Positive Youth Development*, eds. Rainer K. Silbereisen and Richer M. Lerner (London: Sage), 35-58; Peter L. Benson et al., "Positive youth development: Theory, research, and applications," in *Handbook of child psychology: Theoretical models of human development*, eds. Richard M. Lerner and William Damon (Hoboken, NJ: John Wiley & Sons, Inc.), 894.

3 Susan Clampet-Lundquist et al., "Moving teenagers out of high-risk neighborhoods: How girls fare better than boys," *American Journal of Sociology* 116 no. 4, (2011): 1154-1189.

4 Robert J. Chaskin, Florian Sichling, and Mark L. Joseph, "Youth in mixed-income communities replacing public housing complexes: Context, dynamics and response," *Cities* 35 (December 2013): 423-431.

programs that do focus on them may emerge as a reaction to these problems rather than from a desire to build on youth as a community asset.

Nonetheless, a recent scan of the field found some exemplary efforts to promote positive youth development in mixed-income communities.[5] One is the Green Garden Bakery (GGB) in Heritage Park, Minneapolis, an innovative model of social entrepreneurship within a mixed-income community that invests in youth leadership, and one that has produced positive outcomes for participating youth and for the broader community. Green Garden Bakery's story illustrates how helping to create and support youth development opportunities can promote personal development and agency; build social skills and connections across race, class, and age groups; shift negative perceptions about youth; minimize the challenges that unengaged youth can present for the community; and minimize stressors youth may face in a mixed-income setting. This essay was written in partnership with D'Loveantae Allen, Ephraim Adams, and Mohamed Mohamed, three of the young community members who help to advance the work of the Green Garden Bakery today.

> *"For me living in a mixed income community… Everyone should know everyone else's perspectives. Some people are lower class and some people are higher class. I don't want to go around… having to see people of higher class, like homeowners, judge people from the lower class because that will make the lower class feel, like, really bad. And some people might need more help than others and if you don't need help, why don't you go out of your way to help somebody else?"*

THE HERITAGE PARK COMMUNITY

Heritage Park Apartments in Minneapolis, Minnesota, is a mixed-income housing development constructed as a part of a master plan for the transformation of a former public housing site. The redevelopment was led by McCormack Baron Salazar, and support for human capital development and community programs has been provided by Urban Strategies, Inc. The development now includes for-sale homes, senior housing, high-end condominiums, and affordable homeownership opportunities. The

---

5   Emily Miller, Taryn Gress, and Alex Curley, *Promoting Positive Youth Outcomes in Mixed-Income Developments: Scan of the Field #3* (Cleveland, OH: National Initiative on Mixed-Income Communities, 2020).

neighborhood offers bicycle and walking trails, a public library, 24 acres of park land, some retail and commercial businesses, and a neighborhood school. However, food access is a common concern for residents, with limited options for obtaining fresh food in close proximity to the neighborhood.

Heritage Park is home to more than 3,000 residents, 45 percent of whom are children and youth under the age of 18. Most homeowners in Heritage Park are White, while most renters in Heritage Park are African American or Black, including East African, Somali, and Oromo residents. The ethnic diversity in this community presents challenges around cultural understanding and inclusivity, especially among adults.

Economic differences among the neighborhood's residents fall along racial lines: While the median income for White households is around $78,750, the median income for Black households is $19,676. The economic differences are reflected in the observation of one GGB participant, who said: "In our community we have … a higher-middle-class area on one side, then like a lower-class [area]. I'd say I'm from like from the lower-class area. I wish that people would know what it's like and how it feels … I wish people knew all different sides of us, all the perspectives."

THE GREEN GARDEN BAKERY

> *"As a teen growing up in North Minneapolis there's a lot of trouble I could have gotten into. Thank God for Green Garden Bakery. It gave me something to do other than just being outside all day. I wanted to make my own money and help other people. I think I have learned more here than I learned at school."*

The Green Garden Bakery was founded in 2014 by youth in Heritage Park who recognized they had acquired new skills after participating in years of cooking and gardening education offered by Urban Strategies, Inc., along with other community partners. Several youth developed a healthy vegetable-based dessert cake recipe during cooking classes, using excess green tomatoes from a Heritage Park garden, and set a goal of making $500 for a friend who had recently suffered a terrible incident and been paralyzed. They sold the green tomato cake at a local festival and ending up raising over $1,500. The youth decided to donate one third of their profits to their friend, reinvest one third into the supplies needed to do more sales, and use the last third to compensate themselves for their hard work. The program still uses this financial model today, donating a third of their profits, allocating a third to supplies, and using the remaining third to compensate youth.

Since 2014, with continued support from Urban Strategies, the youth have developed a business model, expanded their business, and capitalized on their skills to generate more teen employment in the neighborhood. Today, more than 150 youth are involved in the bakery at some level, as sales and marketing leads, entrepreneurs, and graphic design apprentices among others, and many more are interested in joining. The young employees still bake green tomato cakes, along with additional baked goods that meet a variety of health and dietary restrictions and preferences, using vegetables they grow in their garden. The youth sell their baked goods to customers around the community at farmer's markets, local co-ops, and small businesses; customers can also place online orders.[6]

The program has expanded to include a curriculum for younger children, so they can start building business and leadership skills from a younger age. This approach makes it possible for siblings from age 5 to 19 to work together for several years in the program, while also preparing the older youth to transition into adult leadership roles. The next step for GGB is to create a neighborhood-based retail bakery and commercial kitchen space to serve the Heritage Park community and beyond.

IMPACT

Participating in Green Garden Bakery gives young people in Heritage Park an important anchor in their community, as this reflection by a co-founder attests:

> *Looking back, the most impactful moment of my future was in third grade when I walked past a healthy cooking class for kids in my community. I was hooked. Even after losing my housing in the community and moving around all over the city, I would find my way back to that cooking class every day after school. Soon after, I was introduced to gardening. At first I hated getting my shoes dirty, but I remember the first day I liked the garden. It was when one of*

---

[6] For more information about Heritage Park, The Green Garden Bakery, and other positive youth development strategies implemented there, see Miller, Gress, and Curley, *Promoting Positive Youth Outcomes in Mixed-Income Developments*.

the master gardeners taught me about Japanese beetles and how to catch them in a bucket so they didn't eat our corn. For some reason I was totally fascinated.

In a couple of years, my friends and I started Green Garden Bakery, but things didn't get much easier in my life as the years went on. I was hit by a car while crossing the street and had to be resuscitated outside of our community space. I received a traumatic brain injury and was out of school for a few months. The first and last people to visit me at the hospital were my Green Garden Bakery teammates. Not long after that I lost one of my best friends and my father was murdered outside my house. I still showed up to Green Garden Bakery that same day.

Other benefits described by youth include feeling like a valued, contributing member of the community, which leads to a sense of empowerment, pride, and affirmation; feeling better connected to, understood, and appreciated by adults (especially for youth who have felt stigmatized on the basis of race, income, and age); and feeling that they now have a voice in their community. In the youths' own words:

Better Communication Skills

"I was one of those people who loved to talk but at the same time was shy, so unless you approached me I would not say a word to anybody. I would never approach anyone. So being involved in GGB helped me get out of my comfort zone, it's helped me with my communication skills. I'm able to approach people easier. There are times when I still have trouble, and I'm still getting used to that, but it's more comfortable now. So it's easier for me to communicate with people and my teammates."

Connectedness

"Green Garden Bakery has helped me make relationships with a lot of people, kids and adults. So from the kid aspect of it, we kind of work in the engagement office, and there's a back door, so a kid will come up and knock on the back door to get a snack and we'll get him a snack. And for adults, I mean, when I'm at a sale I get to meet new people and hand out business cards."

Feeling Supported

"Green Garden Bakery has been a support system and another family while mine was grieving. It turned out that my coping mechanism was the garden—gardening was my happiness, life, renewal, and hope. I will graduate high school this year, just received a Beat the Odds Scholarship through the Children's Defense Fund, and plan to go to college to study urban agriculture and food law."

Feeling Known

"We've been able to be more in touch with the adults, we've been able to go out into the community, but we're based at Heritage Park, so even the people at the leasing office if I walked by they would say 'Hello Ahmad,[7] how is your day,' and they would know me, and it would be good to know them back. And then also some of the times we're doing back-to-school events, some of the adults that would live in the neighborhood would, know who I am. If they saw me in a random area, they would be, like, okay if I need help I'm going to go to this guy. And it just feels good."

Feeling Valued

"Once I joined Green Garden Bakery I got more involved with it, like the neighborhood clean-up and stuff like that, cleaning up the environment for Earth Day, community drives where we'd give gift bags to the kids. And the kids knew I was involved in GGB so they'd come up to me and ask, 'Could you go grab me a snack,' because we'd give out snacks to the kids. And it kind of just felt good hearing stuff like that from them."

Self-Affirmation

"On October 30th we were picking up leaves from people's front curb … to help out our garden. Someone drove past us while we were picking them up, and she wanted to participate as well, so she said she would leave some bags out in front of her curb in a little bit and we could come and pick them up. And she told us as we were doing it she was proud. And I don't know about anyone else but that made me feel empowered, like I'm doing something."

---

7   Names in the quotes and resident descriptions have been changed for privacy.

Engagement

"I've lived in Heritage Park basically my whole life, so I already knew basically everyone, a lot of the kids. [But] for me, I think Green Garden Bakery made me more involved in the community."

Awareness of Community Strengths

"Being a part of Green Garden Bakery, it brought me out of my comfort zone and I realized there are so many cool people around the community, like I should've known them back then, and it's like what have I been doing this whole time?"

Some of the impacts have extended to participants' families. As one participant explained, the "passion for success" that Green Garden Bakery inspires is spreading: "My younger brother is spending nine months in a juvenile detention center. He was really struggling after losing his father and calls me every week. He always asks about Green Garden Bakery and tells me how he tells the other boys about how his sister runs a business and was on TV once. He gets out in a few months, and he wants to help in the garden this summer to stay out of trouble."

The bakery's effect on the larger community has been equally powerful. GGB has created opportunities for adults and youth to connect and engage across lines of difference, which has changed how some adults view young people, especially youth of color. For example, "Bill," a homeowner who lives in a single-family home on the western boundary of the neighborhood, had always liked the neighborhood's appearance, diversity, and close proximity to downtown, but he didn't like the frequent incidents of vandalism, property crime, and teens and young adults fighting in the neighborhood park. Bill initially believed these problems were tied to youth and low-income renters living at Heritage Park Apartments, but his interactions with neighborhood youth through the Green Garden Bakery debunked those assumptions. Reflecting now on GGB and how he feels about the neighborhood after living there for seven years, Bill said: "[GGB] is a great program. I've purchased desserts from them and they are phenomenal. I often drive down Van White [Memorial Blvd.] and see [young people] out in the garden. Now I'm proud and upbeat."

IMPLICATIONS FOR ACTION

There are numerous implications for policymakers, practitioners, researchers, evaluators, and funders when it comes to supporting youth development opportunities in mixed-income communities. The main one we want to highlight in this essay, however, is the importance of lifting up the voices of youth when considering how to empower and support them. In that vein, youth who live in Heritage Park offered the following guidance to their peers:

- *Get Involved.* "Your voice isn't going to be heard unless you're doing something. So any community givebacks or picking up weeds or something, help and share your opinion," one GGB participant says. Adds another, "Just do something out of the ordinary that you know you wouldn't do to get out of your comfort zone, because … getting to know and do different things is really fun actually."

The youth also offer this advice to adults:

- *Talk to Kids and Teens and Let Them Know They Are Being Heard.* It's especially important to ask whether youth need help. Even if they say no, if it looks like they're struggling then help them anyway. Be persistent.
- *Give Encouragement.* As children become adolescents they tend to receive less encouragement, even while they are trying to act more mature. "That little push of encouragement actually goes a long way—even if we don't express it—and makes us want to do better."
- *Help Youth Learn from Their Mistakes.* Tell them when they're in the wrong as well as when they're doing things right: "It'll make them feel like they did a really good thing and they'll empower themselves after that."
- *Lift up the Fact That Youth Contribute Positively to the Community.* "For youth to feel empowered, they have to actually feel like they're actually doing something," one participant said. Another added "They could do other stuff … even little stuff like being a translator for older people can make them feel like they're doing stuff for the community."
- *Hold Community Events to Reinforce a Sense of Belonging.* "In Heritage Park we have National Night Out, that's a really big event. The whole neighborhood comes together in this big field—preschoolers all the way to elders—and then we just all have a good time, talk to each other."

A participant in the Green Garden Bakery sums up this advice with one clear and compelling observation: "Continue to encourage us and uplift us, because our voices cannot be heard if we're silent. And if we don't have no type of motivation from not even our own parents or any other adult or guardian, what's the point?"

■ ■ ■

EPHRAIM ADAMS *is the sales lead for Green Garden Bakery's Executive Team. He is a 17yr old senior at Hopkins High School. Adams has lived in Heritage Park since 2011 with his mother and 3 siblings. His older brother is on the alumni board of Green Garden Bakery and his younger siblings are currently going through Green Garden Bakery's workforce program. He is one of the oldest members of GGB's current executive team so stepping up as a leader has been really important to him. Adams is known for exerting positive behavior and communication with others around him, which helps him with talking to customers at sales and public speaking. You never would have guessed how shy he was before Green Garden Bakery! Adams is currently applying for college and would like to pursue a field in computer science. His highlight of his summer was catering an event for GGB this summer at a Google workshop. It exposed him to lots of new people in the technology field. Adams says, "Being at GGB is truly a blessing. Being able to learn different variety of skills helped shape who I am and there is only more to come."*

■ ■ ■

D'LOVEANTAE ALLEN *is a sales lead for the Green Garden Bakery's Junior Executive Team. He is 14 years old, has lived with his mom and two younger siblings in Heritage Park since 2006, and is a Freshman at Hope Academy High School. He is the youngest member of GGB's junior executive team but his age doesn't define his leadership within the sales and marketing teams. He excels at engaging with customers, adding wit and humor to GGB's social media posts, and running promotions at sales to help sellout. He also is GGB's grammar king and helps manage the business email account and proofread materials. Besides his involvement in GGB, Allen spends a lot of time babysitting his baby brother and sister, tutoring fellow students at Hope Academy, and plans to play basketball for Hope this year. When Allen gets older he wants to become an astronomer and study space because it amazes him how vast and unknown it is. He first was exposed to astronomy when he was 8 years old and his mom needed to bring him to her class at a local community college because she had nobody to watch him. The class just happened to be astronomy, he answered one of the professors questions correctly, and has been hooked ever since. Allen says "working at GGB has been life changing, I truly enjoy the place I work and the people I spend my time around on and off the clock."*

■ ■ ■

MOHAMED MOHAMED is the entrepreneurship lead for Green Garden Bakery's Executive Team. He is a 17yr old senior at Hopkins High School. Both Mohamed's mom and grandma have homes in Heritage Park and he is the oldest of 5. Mohamed first got involved in Green Garden Bakery's production crew after participating in cooking class but it wasn't until he stepped up into a leadership position that he found his strengths in GGB's entrepreneurship administration and operations work. Mohamed likes thinking big picture and asking the tough questions (or most questions for that matter). Along with GGB, Mohamed plays football (and is an avid football fan) and often watches his new baby brother. Currently, Mohamed is applying for college and would like to pursue a career in engineering, business, or a related STEM field. Mohamed says "GGB has helped me grow so much over the past two years, I've become so much more confident and mature through my experiences as a leader in the community."

■ ■ ■

JONI R. HIRSCH is a Policy and Program Associate at the Fines and Fees Justice Center where she delivers hands on technical assistance and support to jurisdictions working to reform their local use of criminal justice-related fines and fees. Previously, at the Center for the Study of Social Policy and National Initiative on Mixed-Income Communities, she managed a team of community builders who designed and implemented network-building strategies in public housing communities slated for mixed-income redevelopment. Prior to her work with NIMC, Hirsch's work centered on fair housing policy. Hirsch holds a BA from Amherst College and a Masters in City Planning from UC Berkeley.

■ ■ ■

TARYN H. GRESS, MSSA, is the Strategic Director of the National Initiative on Mixed-Income Communities (NIMC) at Case Western Reserve University. She provides strategic direction of the applied research center and has led NIMC research on three Scans of the Field studies, a study of 259 HOPE VI sites and supported numerous other research and consulting projects on mixed-income communities and is currently leading NIMC's strategic support of the Cuyahoga Metropolitan Housing Authority's mixed-income planning effort in the Woodhill Homes Estates in Cleveland, Ohio. Gress came to NIMC from The Civic Commons, a community and civic engagement organization serving Northeast Ohio. She has also worked with Cleveland community-based nonprofits Slavic Village Development, America SCORES Cleveland, and The Ohio State University Extension in Cuyahoga County. Gress holds a Bachelor of Arts from the College of Wooster and a Master of Science in Social Administration from Case Western Reserve University.

■ ■ ■

ELANA DAHLBERG is the Project Manager for Urban Strategies, Inc. in Heritage Park. Ms. Dahlberg has been working for USI for the past six year and oversees USI's Minneapolis program initiatives and partnerships. Ms. Dahlberg is responsible for human capital development among Heritage Park residents and provides the technical support to the youth leaders who develop Green Garden Bakery. Prior to joining Urban Strategies, Inc. Ms. Dahlberg was developing out of school time youth programming for a local community center in the neighborhood. Ms. Dahlberg has a Masters of Social Work and Nonprofit Management Certificate from the University of MN.

■ ■ ■

ALECIA LEONARD is a Regional Vice President who provides overall strategic and operational direction for USI's sites in Minneapolis, MN, Pittsburgh, PA, Tulsa, OK, and Columbus, OH. Leonard previously served as the Director of Resident Development and Training where she trained staff on USI›s case management model and led the rollout of LEARN to all USI sites. Prior to joining Urban Strategies, Alecia worked as a research assistant with the Center for Urban and Regional Affairs at the University of Minnesota. Leonard holds a Master's degree in Social Work from the University of Minnesota in St. Paul, MN and a Bachelor's degree in Social Work from Bethel University.

REASSESSING MARKET-RATE RESIDENTS' ROLE IN MIXED-INCOME DEVELOPMENTS

Michaeljit Sandhu
Harvard Law School & the University of California, Berkeley

Kristen,[1] a White woman in her mid-40s, works as a paralegal for an anti-discrimination law firm and lives with her daughter and longtime boyfriend. Diya is a South Asian woman in her late 30s; she stays at home to take care of her son, while her husband works for a tech company a few miles from their apartment. Tom works in tech, too; he's a White man in his early 30s, recently married, and shopping for a home to buy. All three have household incomes well above the median for the parts of northern California where they live, and all three have chosen to rent market-rate units in mixed-income developments. As prospective tenants, they were each told that their developments would include a substantial number of subsidized renters, and they still chose—without any remembered reluctance—to move in. Unlike their lower-income neighbors, they all make enough to live at many other places close by. From my interviews with these residents, it is clear that their reasons for moving to mixed-income sites varied: convenience to work, access to good schools, reasonable price, proximity to friends and family. But, while they express no qualms about the mixed-income model, they haven't reflected much on their own role at the sites and the benefits it offers to them. "I haven't really thought of that." "I haven't noticed anything." "Um, good question…"

What role do residents of market-rate units play in mixed-income developments? One of the challenges in answering that question is that the category "market-rate resident" conveys as much as it conceals. Used uncritically, the phrase becomes a stereotype, a stand-in as misleading as the pejorative terms too often associated with poor people, particularly poor

---

[1] To protect anonymity, names are pseudonyms and some identifying features have been altered.

people of color. In reality, the characteristics of "market-rate residents" vary widely, depending in large part on the development in question and its immediate surroundings. An ethno-racially homogenous area might attract market-rate residents whose background closely mirrors that of subsidized residents, while a heterogeneous area or a recently redeveloped one might be home to greater diversity. A tight housing market might drive up costs, making market-rate residents high-income by any standard, whereas a loose market might mean that market-rate residents earn as much as subsidized households do in another area. A development in close proximity to a high-quality school might attract market-rate residents with children, whereas one located near a university might attract college students or young faculty without them. There is no doubt that all of these axes of difference—race, ethnicity, class, family status, and many more—matter in how market-rate residents make their lives at the vast range of mixed-income developments across the United States.[2] But the wide range of market-rate residents does not imply that the category is meaningless: the mixed-income model was designed and developed with the hope that market-rate residents, regardless of their other characteristics, could play an influential social and structural role in the lives of their lower-income neighbors.

Surprisingly, then, since the start of the federal HOPE VI Program over 25 years ago and the spread of the mixed-income model up through today's Choice Neighborhoods Initiative, policymakers, practitioners, and researchers have devoted relatively little attention to those who can afford market-rate units. Instead, they have focused on the promise and practice of class desegregation for residents of subsidized units, justifying the creation of mixed-income developments on the purported benefits for those with low or no incomes and studying the sites primarily to discern their impact on reducing poverty and racist exclusion.[3] In the few direct examinations of market-rate residents that

---

[2] Jill Khadduri and Marge Martin, "Mixed-Income Housing in the HUD Multifamily Stock," *Cityscape: A Journal of Policy Development and Research* 3, no.2 (1997): 33–69.; Lawrence J. Vale and Shomon Shamsuddin, "All Mixed Up: Making Sense of Mixed-Income Housing Developments," *Journal of the American Planning Association* 83, no. 1 (2017): 56–67.

[3] Paul C. Brophy and Rhonda N. Smith, "Mixed-Income Housing: Factors for Success," *Cityscape: A Journal of Policy Development and Research* 3, no. 2 (1997): 3–31.; Alex Schwartz and Kian Tajbakhsh, "Mixed-Income Housing: Unanswered Questions," *Cityscape: A Journal of Policy Development and Research* 3, no. 2 (1997): 71–92.; Robert J. Chaskin and Mark L. Joseph, *Integrating the Inner City: The Promise and Perils of Mixed-Income Public Housing Transformation* (Chicago: University of Chicago Press, 2015), 23-43.; Javier Ruiz-Tagle, "The Broken Promises of Social Mix: The Case of the Cabrini Green/Near North Area in Chicago," *Urban Geography* 37, no. 3 (2016): 355.

do exist, researchers have emphasized the outsized expectations placed on them: they are expected to be role models, job sources, and agents of social control for their lower-income neighbors, while providing higher rent payments that cross-subsidize the affordable units and social, economic, and political capital to support organizations, institutions, and business in the surrounding neighborhood.[4] Few, if any, market-rate residents fully match this ideal. In fact, in many cases, market-rate residents, rather than their low-income neighbors, have become the primary beneficiaries of the sites' social and structural features. Empirical evidence suggests that market-rate residents are as likely to enforce stigmas and use their social connections, market power, and political influence to their advantage as to support and engage with their lower-income neighbors.[5]

Is it a mistake, then, to position market-rate residents as central to the expected benefits of mixed-income developments? In this brief essay, I disaggregate the many expected and actual roles of market-rate residents in mixed-income communities in order to reframe the broader value of mixed-income development as a strategy. On a smaller scale, my aim is to emphasize that desegregation is a relational concept, one that demands that market-rate residents get at least as much normative and empirical scrutiny as poor people have faced. In short, I argue that by better understanding market-rate residents and their perspectives, motivations, and biases, we—policymakers, researchers, and members of the public—can better grasp the structural value of mixed-income developments and reevaluate their social goals. First, I flip the traditional focus of the mixed-income housing literature and frame the developments in terms of the role that market-rate residents are expected to play at the sites. Next, I synthesize empirical findings about how market-rate residents actually play out their roles at mixed-income developments. Finally, I draw out the effects of making market-rate residents such a singular

---

4   Mark L. Joseph, Robert J. Chaskin, and Henry S. Webber, "The Theoretical Basis for Addressing Poverty Through Mixed-Income Development," *Urban Affairs Review* 42, no. 3 (2007): 369–409.; Edward G. Goetz, "Desegregation in 3D: Displacement, Dispersal and Development in American Public Housing," *Housing Studies* 25, no. 2 (2010): 137–58.

5   Erin M. Graves, "The Structuring of Urban Life in a Mixed-Income Housing 'Community,'" *City & Community* 9, no. 1 (2010): 109–31.; Naomi J. McCormick, Mark L. Joseph, and Robert J. Chaskin, "The New Stigma of Relocated Public Housing Residents: Challenges to Social Identity in Mixed-Income Developments," *City & Community* 11, no. 3 (2012): 285–308.; Martine August, "Negotiating Social Mix in Toronto's First Public Housing Redevelopment: Power, Space and Social Control in Don Mount Court," *International Journal of Urban and Regional Research* 38, no 4 (2014): 1160–80.; Chaskin and Joseph, *Integrating the Inner City*.; Ruiz-Tagle, "The Broken Promises of Social Mix," 353–72.

source of mixed-income success. I conclude with suggestions for practitioners, policymakers, researchers, and residents of mixed-income developments.

EXPECTATIONS

What role are market-rate residents expected to play at mixed-income sites? Socially, people who can afford market-rate rents and home prices have been framed, in theory if not in practice, as necessary to help ameliorate the myriad harms poor people experience as the result of living in areas of concentrated poverty. In Wilson's canonical account, poor people, particularly poor Black people, are forced to live in neighborhoods marked by a surfeit of crime and a lack of well-paying jobs and role models of social norms around school-going, job-seeking, and stable relationships.[6] These problems are particularly potent for residents of public housing developments, who have long been among the most isolated and impoverished poor people.[7] Thus, the hope is that in a class-desegregated setting—which, because of longstanding racial disparities in wealth, might lead to racial desegregation as well—market-rate residents would provide social control, share their job networks, and act as role models for their neighbors living in subsidized units.[8]

In other words, because they can afford market-rate prices, market-rate residents are endowed with a whole range of additional, presumptively positive characteristics. To see the centrality of market-rate residents to mixed-income developments, it is worth disaggregating their expected characteristics, even if few policymakers, practitioners, or researchers would expect any single resident to contain all or even most of them. First, market-rate residents are

---

[6] William Julius Wilson, *The Truly Disadvantaged: The Inner City, the Underclass, and Public Policy*, 2nd ed. (Chicago: University of Chicago Press, 2012), 56.

[7] Adam Bickford and Douglas S. Massey, "Segregation in the Second Ghetto: Racial and Ethnic Segregation in American Public Housing, 1977," *Social Forces* 69, no .4 (1991): 1011–36.; Ann Owens, "Housing Policy and Urban Inequality: Did the Transformation of Assisted Housing Reduce Poverty Concentration?" *Social Forces* 94, no. 1 (2015): 325–48.; Douglas S. Massey and Nancy Denton, American Apartheid: Segregation and the Making of the Underclass, (Cambridge: Harvard University Press, 1993).; Richard Rothstein, The Color of Law: A Forgotten History of How Our Government Segregated America, (New York: W.W Norton & Company, 2017).

[8] Brophy and Smith, "Mixed-Income Housing: Factors for Success," 3–31.; Khadduri and Martin, "Mixed-Income Housing in the HUD Multifamily Stock," 33–69.; Schwartz and Tajbakhsh, "Mixed-Income Housing: Unanswered Questions," 71–92.; Joseph, Chaskin, Webber, "Theoretical Basis," 369–409.; Mark L. Joseph, "Is mixed-income development an antidote to urban poverty?" *Housing Policy Debate* 17, no. 2 (2006): 209-234. Goetz, "Desegregation in 3D," 137–58.

presumed to be law-abiding and rule-following; their positive impact on social control at the sites is premised on their ability to embody "mainstream" or "middle-class" norms around job-going, school attendance, and neighborhood monitoring. Second, market-rate residents are expected to form bridging and bonding relationships with their lower-income neighbors.[9] By virtue of geographic proximity, market-rate residents are expected to befriend subsidized residents and share with them life skills and job contacts.[10] Third, there is an assumption that market-rate residents will be part of networks with ample job opportunities well-suited to their subsidized neighbors' skills. Although Wilson insisted that cross-class networking be paired with "the creation of macroeconomic policy designed to promote…a tight labor market" if poor people are to find well-paying jobs,[11] mixed-income developments have been constructed without a macro-level push to create economic opportunities for poor people. As such, they are implicitly premised on the notion that jobs are there if only wealthier people tell poor people where to find them and how to land and keep them. Fourth, market-rate residents are expected to influence, but not be influenced by, their neighbors in subsidized units. Put another way, there is an assumption that any social effects at mixed-income sites will be unidirectional, with residents of market-rate transferring social capital to their neighbors in subsidized units but not the other way around.[12] And, relatedly, market-rate residents are assumed to be content with receiving no tangible advantages from living at the sites other than a prime location at an attractive price. Indeed, the idea that residents of subsidized units might share skills, provide networks, or exert other influences, "positive" or not, on the residents of market-rate units is largely unconsidered.

Structurally, market-rate residents are expected to provide social, political, and economic capital to keep mixed-income developments and the neighborhoods that surround them stable and sustainable. Again, Wilson provides the prototypical story of communities that lost middle and working-class residents:

---

9 Sako Musterd and Roger Andersson, "Housing Mix, Social Mix, and Social Opportunities," *Urban Affairs Review* 40, no. 6 (2005): 761–90.; Hilary Silver, "Mixing Policies: Expectations and Achievements," *Cityscape: A Journal of Policy Development and Research* 15, no. 2 (2013): 73–82.

10 Rachel Garshick Kleit, "HOPE VI New Communities: Neighborhood Relationships in Mixed-Income Housing," *Environment and Planning A* 37, no. 8 (2005): 1413–41.

11 Wilson, *The Truly Disadvantaged*, 151.

12 Erin M. Graves, "Mixed Outcome Developments," *Journal of the American Planning Association* 77, no. 2 (2011): 143–53.

"The increasing exodus of [higher-income] families made it more difficult to sustain the basic institutions in these neighborhoods (including churches, stores, schools, recreational facilities, etc.) in the face of increased joblessness caused by the frequent recessions during the 1970s and early 1980s and changes in the urban job structure."[13] By returning or replacing these higher-income residents, the argument goes, the local economy and institutional ecosystem will be revived: Market-rate residents will provide a higher tax base, so that schools can be better funded; they will offer existing businesses a wealthier clientele, so that shops can stay afloat and hire more local workers, and help to attract new businesses to the area; and they will form a core constituency with the time and income to contribute to neighborhood organizations and institutions so they can provide services and promote political priorities.[14]

A similar logic applies to mixed-income developments constructed in already-affluent neighborhoods: Rather than having an influx of poor people lead to out-migration of wealthier households, mixed-income developments offer the opportunity for controlled class desegregation that minimizes the risk of local decline due to a decreased wealth base or, implicitly, racist flight by wealthier, White residents fearful of poorer people of color.[15] On a smaller scale, there also is an expectation that market-rate residents will help to supplement shallow subsidies for their lower-income neighbors, stepping in to fill the gap of reduced funding from the local, state, and federal government.[16]

In short, market-rate residents are expected to be structural salves for their new neighborhoods. Again, a number of expectations are worth disaggregating. First, the mixed-income model is partly premised on the idea that an influx of higher-income residents will not result in the detrimental displacement of lower-

---

13 Wilson, *The Truly Disadvantaged*, 137.

14 Brophy and Smith, "Mixed-Income Housing: Factors for Success," 3–31.; Joseph, Chaskin, Webber, "Theoretical Basis," 369–409.; Loretta Lees, "Gentrification and Social Mixing: Towards an Inclusive Urban Renaissance?" *Urban Studies* 45, no. 12 (2008): 2449–70.; Goetz, "Desegregation in 3D," 137–58.; Lawrence J. Vale, *Purging the Poorest: Public Housing and the Design Politics of Twice-Cleared Communities* (Chicago: University of Chicago Press, 2013).

15 Mark Davidson, "Spoiled Mixture: Where Does State-Led 'Positive' Gentrification End?" *Urban Studies* 45, no. 12 (2008): 2385–2405.; James C. Fraser et al., "HOPE VI, Colonization, and the Production of Difference." Urban Affairs Review 49, no. 4 (2013): 525-56.; Vale, *Purging the Poorest*.

16 Khadduri and Martin, "Mixed-Income Housing in the HUD Multifamily Stock," 37; Schwartz and Tajbakhsh, "Mixed-Income Housing: Unanswered Questions," 75; Alistair Smith, *Mixed-Income Housing Developments: Promise and Reality*. (Cambridge: Harvard Joint Center for Housing Studies, 2002), https://www.jchs.harvard.edu/sites/default/files/w02-10_smith.pdf.

income families.[17] Mixed-income projects built on the sites of former public housing now strive to replace all of the subsidized units that are redeveloped, but even when original low-income residents are forced to move the hope is that they will use vouchers or other forms of subsidy to find other class-desegregated settings to live in.[18] Second, market-rate residents are expected to value the same sorts of institutions, businesses, and organizations as their subsidized peers. In other words, it is assumed that a store where those with money to spare shop will also serve those struggling to get by. Relatedly, there is an assumption that market-rate and subsidized residents utilize their neighborhoods in the same ways, with both assumed to find most of their needs met in the areas immediately around their homes.[19] Finally, there is an expectation that market-rate residents will see themselves as long-term and stable residents in the community, deeply engaged in the project of community uplift or maintenance. Put another way, while many advocates of subsidized housing expect residents to want social mobility—to move in, move out, and move up from subsidized units to market-rate homes—the hope is that market-rate residents will stay put. One potential benefit for market-rate residents, and one way to keep them around, is the possibility of building equity in a home, if the mixed-income development includes homeownership. Even here, however, the benefit can be seen as a risk: Market-rate residents might expect to build less equity at a site that includes a substantial number of low-income residents than they would in a market-based, class-sorted neighborhood. As in their social roles, then, market-rate residents are expected to invest substantially in the structural success of mixed-income developments and their surrounding without receiving much of a return.

---

17 Davidson, "Spoiled Mixture," 2385–2405.; James C. Fraser, Robert J. Chaskin, and Joshua Theodore Bazuin, "Making Mixed-Income Neighborhoods Work for Low-Income Households," *Cityscape: A Journal of Policy Development and Research* 15, no. 2 (2013): 89.

18 Robert J. Chaskin et al., "Public Housing Transformation and Resident Relocation: Comparing Destinations and Household Characteristics in Chicago," *Cityscape: A Journal of Policy Development and Research* 14, no. 1 (2012): 183–214.; Vale, *Purging the Poorest*.

19 Laura M. Tach, "Diversity, Inequality, and Microsegregation: Dynamics of Inclusion and Exclusion in a Racially and Economically Diverse Community," *Cityscape: A Journal of Policy Development and Research* 16, no. 3 (2014): 13–45.; Chaskin and Joseph, *Integrating the Inner City*, 192-216.; Christopher R. Browning et al., "Socioeconomic Segregation of Activity Spaces in Urban Neighborhoods: Does Shared Residence Mean Shared Routines?" *RSF: The Russell Sage Foundation Journal of the Social Sciences* 3, no. 2 (2017): 210–31.

Evidence

Do market-rate residents living in mixed-income developments meet these expectations? By and large, no. There is little evidence that market-rate residents form strong connections with their neighbors or provide them with job contacts.[20] Although there is stronger support for successful social control at mixed-income sites, it is not clear that market-rate residents are directly responsible for the documented decreases in crime and increased feelings of subjective safety.[21] Indeed, one of the more optimistic early accounts of the benefits of income mixing on social control comes from a study of Lake Parc Place, a 100% subsidized development in Chicago that mixed extremely low- and low-income residents and included a very vigilant private management company.[22] In terms of indirect, structural interventions, the role of market-rate residents is mixed: Their presence is correlated with better-maintained sites and greater attention to services in the surrounding neighborhood, but displacement or exclusion of subsidized residents may play as much role as market-rate residents' investments.[23]

What, then, do market-rate residents do at mixed-income developments? Three clusters of empirical findings help create a more realistic image of their behavior. First, market-rate residents often receive better treatment than their subsidized neighbors. Although property managers played only a peripheral role in the expectations for mixed-income developments, they have turned out to be pivotal players in structuring social life at the sites.[24] At many mixed-

---

20 Kleit, "HOPE VI New Communities," 1413–41.; Graves, "Mixed Outcome Developments," 143–53.; Chaskin and Joseph, *Integrating the Inner City*, 124-156.

21 Graves, "The Structuring of Urban Life" 109–31.; Chaskin and Joseph, *Integrating the Inner City*, 157-191.

22 James E. Rosenbaum, Linda K. Stroh, and Cathy A. Flynn, "Lake Parc Place: A Study of Mixed income Housing," *Housing Policy Debate* 9, no. 4 (1998): 703–40.; Laura M. Tach, "More than Bricks and Mortar: Neighborhood Frames, Social Processes, and the Mixed-Income Redevelopment of a Public Housing Project," *City & Community* 8, no. 3 (2009): 269–99.; Shomon Shamsuddin and Lawrence J. Vale, "Hoping for More: Redeveloping U.S. Public Housing without Marginalizing Low-Income Residents?" *Housing Studies* 32, no. 2 (2017): 225–44.

23 James C. Fraser and Edward L. Kick, "The Role of Public, Private, Non-Profit and Community Sectors in Shaping Mixed-Income Housing Outcomes in the US," *Urban Studies* 44, no. 12 (2007): 2357–77.; Sean Zielenbach and Richard Voith, "HOPE VI and Neighborhood Economic Development: The Importance of Local Market Dynamics," *Cityscapes* 12, no. 1 (2010): 99–131.; Sean Zielenbach, "Assessing Economic Change in HOPE VI Neighborhoods." *Housing Policy Debate* 14, no. 4 (2003): 621–55.; Laura M. Tach and Allison Dwyer Emory, "Public Housing Redevelopment, Neighborhood Change, and the Restructuring of Urban Inequality," *American Journal of Sociology* 123, no. 3 (2017): 686–739.

24 Graves, "The Structuring of Urban Life," 109–31.; Chaskin and Joseph, *Integrating the Inner City*.

income developments, it is common for subsidized renters to face substantially stricter rules imposed by private management companies and, in sites with voucher holders and public housing residents, by the local housing authority. For example, the behavior, household upkeep, and family history of subsidized renters are routinely probed as part of the admissions process, while most applicants for market-rate units are subject only to a standard rental history.[25] Furthermore, once at the site, subsidized renters regularly describe market-rate residents reporting them and management citing them, often for minor rules violations.[26] Even when the rules are identical, as is the case at many Low-Income Housing Tax Credit (LIHTC) developments, and applied with relative parity, market-rate and subsidized residents face different risks: If rule enforcement becomes burdensome, market-rate renters can often afford to leave, whereas subsidized renters are constrained by their more limited housing options to comply.[27]

In structural terms too, market-rate renters often are treated better than their subsidized neighbors. Indeed, it is common for market-rate residents to pay below-market prices for their units because developers are determined to attract them to the sites.[28] In weak markets, there even is cross-subsidization of market-rate rents by subsidized units, which often have access to state subsidies.[29] In contrast, subsidized renters are subject to careful examination of their finances so that they do not pay less than they could or exceed income limits.[30] And, increasingly, public housing residents are also subject to

---

25 Vale, *Purging the Poorest.*

26 Graves, "The Structuring of Urban Life," 109–31.; August, "Negotiating Social Mix in Toronto's First Public Housing Redevelopment," 1160–80. ; Chaskin and Joseph, *Integrating the Inner City*; Ruiz-Tagle, "The Broken Promises of Social Mix," 355.

27 Susan Clampet-Lundquist, "HOPE VI Relocation: Moving to New Neighborhoods and Building New Ties," *Housing Policy Debate* 15, no. 2 (2004): 415–47.; Graves, "The Structuring of Urban Life,'" 114, 122.; Peter Rosenblatt and Stefanie DeLuca, "'We Don't Live Outside, We Live in Here': Neighborhood and Residential Mobility Decisions Among Low-Income Families," *City & Community* 11, no. 3 (2012): 254–84.; Stefanie DeLuca, Philip M.E. Garboden, and Peter Rosenblatt, "Segregating Shelter: How Housing Policies Shape the Residential Locations of Low-Income Minority Families," *The ANNALS of the American Academy of Political and Social Science* 647, no. 1 (2013): 268–99.

28 Chaskin and Joseph, *Integrating the Inner City*, 89-91.; April Jackson, "Barriers to Integrating New Urbanism in Mixed-Income Housing Plans in Chicago: Developer, Housing Official, and Consultant Perspectives," *Housing Policy Debate* 28, no. 5 (2018), 1–32.

29 Brophy and Smith, "Mixed-Income Housing: Factors for Success," 28; Khadduri and Martin, "Mixed-Income Housing in the HUD Multifamily Stock," 33–69.; Graves, "The Structuring of Urban Life,'" 121.

30 Vale, *Purging the Poorest.*

minimum rents, regardless of whether they have any income at all.[31] Ironically, then, developments that are justified in terms of their benefits for the truly disadvantaged end up catering to the relatively privileged in practice.

Second, there is little evidence that market-rate residents regularly develop trusting, transformative relationships with their neighbors in subsidized units. This is true whether the mixed-income development is built on the site of former public housing, where subsidized renters might already have strong ties to each other,[32] or is new construction, with a neighborhood formed from scratch[33]. In some cases, this failure is relatively benign: In my interviews with market-rate and subsidized renters, many specifically sought out a place where people "mind [their] own business" and keep to themselves. A strong and active community was seen as a disruption to the quiet of a self-contained home life, rather than desirable in itself. In other cases, the failure to form ties can be more intentionally antisocial: market-rate residents, without the buffer of physical distance from the poor, sometimes resort to social distancing, stereotyping and stigmatizing those they perceive to be subsidized renters. This discriminatory behavior can be even more deleterious when there are racial differences at the site.[34] In those cases, perceptions that all Black residents are subsidized residents can lead to racial discrimination compounding class discrimination, making the sites particularly unwelcoming for poor people of color. Again, in practice, the sites may create harm for those they are designed to help.

This should not imply that relationships at mixed-income developments are always, or even often, antagonistic. In residential settings, the norm for tie formation has long been homophily: like attracts like.[35] As such, it should

---

31 Alicia Mazzara, "Trump Plan to Raise Minimum Rents Would Put Nearly a Million Children at Risk of Homelessness," *Off the Charts (blog), Center on Budget and Policy Priorities*, April 27, 2018, https://www.cbpp.org/blog/trump-plan-to-raise-minimum-rents-would-put-nearly-a-million-children-at-risk-of-homelessness-0.

32 Kleit, "HOPE VI New Communities," 1413–41.; Chaskin and Joseph, *Integrating the Inner City*.; Ruiz-Tagle, "The Broken Promises of Social Mix," 353-72.

33 Michaeljit Sandhu. "Confounding Categories: Market-rate Residents' Motives for Moving to Class Desegregated Developments." (unpublished manuscript, October 15, 2019).

34 Amy T. Khare, Mark L. Joseph, and Robert J. Chaskin, "The Enduring Significance of Race in Mixed-Income Developments," *Urban Affairs Review* 51, no. 4 (2015): 474-503.

35 Herbert J. Gans, "Planning and Social Life: Friendship and Neighbor Relations in Suburban Communities," *Journal of the American Institute of Planners* 27, no. 2 (1961a): 134–40.; Herbert J. Gans, "The Balanced Community: Homogeneity or Heterogeneity in Residential Areas?" *Journal of the American Institute of Planners* 27, no. 3 (1961b): 176–84.; Herbert J. Gans, *The Levittowners: Ways of Life and Politics in a*

come as no surprise that in mixed-income developments, as in neighborhoods mixed on other bases, so-called micro-segregation amongst those with different identities is common.[36] In many cases, demographic differences between market-rate and subsidized renters mean that members of each have little leverage to form connections across class cleavages. For example, Graves[37] describes a development in Boston where the market-rate population is made entirely of households without children; they struggle to foster ties with subsidized families, whose children many see as nuisances. In Seattle, Kleit[38] describes a development filled with a diverse array of residents but with clear differences in ethno-racial background, education-level, marital status, family size, and languages spoken between the subsidized and market-rate populations. Additionally, at some sites, market-rate residents are clustered in units away from subsidized residents.[39] In those cases, design politics reinforces micro-segregation.

Finally, market-rate residents often are on a much different capital trajectory than their subsidized neighbors. Although there is little research on why market-rate residents move to mixed-income developments,[40] my own study of two sites in northern California suggests that market-rate residents rarely move to mixed-income developments with the intention of staying indefinitely or forming long-term ties. Whereas the subsidized renters I spoke with often felt stuck in place, particularly in Silicon Valley's extremely tight rental market, nearly every market-rate renter I interviewed intended to move sooner rather than later.[41] In fact, given the small price discount at the sites compared to

---

New Suburban Community (New York, NY: Columbia University Press, 1982), 153-181.; For a more recent test of this expectation, see: John R. Hipp and Andrew J. Perrin, "The Simultaneous Effect of Social Distance and Physical Distance on the Formation of Neighborhood Ties," *City & Community* 8, no. 1 (2009): 5–25.

36 Kathy Arthurson, "Operationalising Social Mix: Spatial Scale, Lifestyle and Stigma as Mediating Points in Resident Interaction," *Urban Policy and Research* 28, no.1 (2010): 49-63.; Tach, "Diversity, Inequality, and Microsegregation," 13–45.; Derek Hyra, "Mixed-Income Housing: Where Have We Been and Where Do We Go From Here?" *Cityscape: A Journal of Policy Development and Research* 15, no. 2 (2013): 123–34.

37 Graves, "The Structuring of Urban Life,'" 109–31.

38 Kleit, "HOPE VI New Communities," 1421.

39 Kleit, 1413–41.; Chaskin and Joseph, *Integrating the Inner City*.; Vale, *Purging the Poorest*.

40 For an exception, from the perspective of non-residents see: David P. Varady et al., "Attracting Middle-Income Families in the Hope VI Public Housing Revitalization Program," *Journal of Urban Affairs* 27, no. 2 (2005): 149–64.

41 While poor, non-subsidized renters commonly experience housing instability, eviction, and homelessness,

other market-rate developments in the area, many saw the sites as places for saving up to move up. This precluded them from making the social and structural investments expected of them. But, although the hope for moving out may run contrary to the expectations of mixed-income boosters, it is in line with broader societal expectations: The American dream continues to include homeownership as an essential component. By falling in line with broader norms, market-rate residents are prevented from meeting the expectations for them at mixed-income developments.

In theory then, mixed-income developments ought to try to attract residents who are committed to the model of social and structural uplift they are premised upon. Indeed, some suggest that developments that include a portion of condos or stand-alone for-sale units might attract residents seeking deeper investments.[42] But the existing empirical evidence does not find that market-rate homeowners are any more likely to create strong ties to their neighbors or neighborhoods than market-rate renters.[43] Even in those developments where homeownership options are available to market-rate residents, their ability to be mobile—to sell if the site becomes burdensome—means they are unlikely to engage in the community on equal terms with their neighbors in subsidized units, who often are locked in place by the dearth of affordable housing. When residents in a mixed-income community share a sense of "linked fate" because of a common race, the disjuncture between poorer and richer residents' visions of their community can create class-based conflicts.[44] There simply isn't a strong set of motivations for market-rate residents to engage with their communities on equal terms with their subsidized neighbors. So, in practice, they continue to look out for their own interests instead of investing in the mixed-income model.

---

poor, subsidized renters tend to have longer tenures, even when they live in places that they consider less than ideal. See: Matthew Desmond, "Eviction and the Reproduction of Urban Poverty," *American Journal of Sociology* 118, no. 1 (2012): 88–133.; Matthew Desmond, *Evicted: Poverty and Profit in the American City*, 1st ed. (New York, NY: Crown Publishers, 2016).

42 Lawrence J. Vale, "Comment on Mark Joseph's 'Is Mixed-income Development an Antidote to Urban Poverty?'" *Housing Policy Debate* 17, no. 2 (2006): 267.

43 Kleit, "HOPE VI New Communities," 1413–41.; Chaskin and Joseph, *Integrating the Inner City*.

44 Mary Pattillo, "Negotiating Blackness, for Richer or for Poorer," *Ethnography* 4, no. 1 (2003): 61–93.; Mary Pattillo, *Black on the Block: The Politics of Race and Class in the City* (Chicago: University of Chicago Press, 2007); Fraser, Chaskin, Bazuin, "Making Mixed-Income Neighborhoods Work," 83–101.

EFFECTS

What is the effect of this mismatch between expectations and evidence? Mostly, it seems to be disappointment with the mixed-income model.[45] But, once the focus is shifted from subsidized residents' expected benefits to market-rate residents' expected contributions, it becomes clear that there never was much chance that mixed-income developments would ameliorate the myriad problems facing people who live in areas of concentrated poverty.[46] If more market-rate residents were attracted to the sites by a desire to advance the social and structural premises of the mixed-income model, perhaps the outcomes would be different. But, even then, there would be the risk of positioning market-rate residents as saviors of their neighbors or salves for the harms of concentrated poverty—replacing explicit prejudice with paternalism. For some, the lack of unqualified success at mixed-income developments has led beyond disappointment to disillusionment: They insist that the mixed-income model is simply a way for developers to earn profits, market-rate residents to gain access to gentrifying neighborhoods, and poor people to get displaced, with a few exceptions who manage to get by strict admissions standards.[47]

As demonstrated above, this disappointment and disillusionment may be more the product of unrealistic expectations than irredeemable failure. Shifting scrutiny to market-rate residents can demonstrate empirically that poverty, inequality, and segregation are not properties that adhere to particular people or places, but relations: They implicate the relatively privileged as much as the truly disadvantaged and demand engagement and action across categories and classes. Still, it is notable that nearly all the residents I spoke with, across income categories, expressed enthusiasm for their mixed-income sites: They

---

45 Thomas D. Boston, "The Effects of Revitalization on Public Housing Residents: A Case Study of the Atlanta Housing Authority," *Journal of the American Planning Association* 71, no. 4 (2005): 393–407.; Goetz, "Desegregation in 3D," 137–58.; Mark L. Joseph, "Cityscape Mixed-Income Symposium Summary and Response: Implications for Antipoverty Policy," *Cityscape: A Journal of Policy Development and Research* 15, no. 2 (2013): 216.; George C. Galster and Jurgen Friedrichs, "The Dialectic of Neighborhood Social Mix: Editors' Introduction to the Special Issue," *Housing Studies* 30, no. 2 (2015): 175–91.

46 Joseph, Chaskin, Webber, "Theoretical Basis," 369–409.

47 Rowland Atkinson, "Padding the Bunker: Strategies of Middle-Class Disaffiliation and Colonisation in the City," *Urban Studies* 43, no. 4 (2006): 819–32. ; Fraser and Kick, "Role of Public, Private, Non-Profit and Community Sectors," 2357–77.; Lees, "Gentrification and Social Mixing" 2449–70.; James DeFilippis, "On Spatial Solutions to Social Problems," *Cityscape: A Journal of Policy Development and Research* 15, no. 2 (2013): 69–72.; August, "Negotiating Social Mix in Toronto's First Public Housing Redevelopment," 1160–80.; Vale, *Purging the Poorest*.

provided safe, stable, affordable housing. As one market-rate renter put it, the value of a mixed-income development is simply that "it helps people that need a place to live and keeps them in a decent neighborhood." As DeFilippis[48] notes, housing policy is too often about too much. The hope that a well-designed, well-maintained home can solve for a range of social and structural problems, from joblessness to racial prejudice to health disparities, may be too utopian. Perhaps, for mixed-income developments, providing affordable housing in a relatively desegregated setting should be seen as a strong enough start.

IMPLICATIONS FOR ACTION

Implications for Research and Evaluation

Scholars need to expand empirical inquiries in a number of new directions:

- *Determinants of Development.* Most of the national data on the mixed-income model is descriptive, showing that the stock is large and varied.[49] More work is needed to explain the reasons for this variation. More research also is needed to show how developments typically get funded and sited. These studies will help to show the conditions necessary to convince surrounding residents that mixed-income housing belongs in their neighborhoods. In other words, it might offer models for effecting class desegregation that supporters of the mixed-income model can subsequently take up.

- *Role of Market-Rate Residents.* Many questions about market-rate residents remain un-posed and unanswered. The narrow focus on the poor in urban sociology and housing policy is a perennial problem, but it is especially jarring in the mixed-income context, because market-rate residents are such an essential part of the model. We still don't have detailed answers to many basic questions about these residents, such as: Why do they move to mixed-income developments? What are their expectations and intentions? How do they engage socially and economically with the mixed-income sites and surrounding neighborhoods? What are the economic, health, and social consequences for them of living in a class-desegregated setting?

---

48 DeFilippis, "On Spatial Solutions to Social Problems," 69–72.

49 Khadduri and Martin, "Mixed-Income Housing in the HUD Multifamily Stock," 33–69.; Vale and Shamsuddin, "All Mixed Up," 56–67.

Implications for Policy

Policymakers should celebrate the mixed-income model as a success insofar as it builds affordable housing and as a continued challenge insofar as it doesn't, on its own, create equitable communities.

- *Focus on Structural Success.* For politicians and policymakers, one way to address the disappointments of the mixed-income model is to emphasize their structural value. Given the perennial lack of affordable housing and the continuing patterns of segregation by class and race, the scale of the mixed-income model should be celebrated. Furthermore, it should be positioned, as it already is in the context of inclusionary zoning programs, as a way for areas that are attractive to market-rate development to also counteract the effects of economic segregation.

- *Address Social Disappointment.* At the same time, there is a need to seriously grapple with the social shortcomings of the sites. Since it is now clear that the mere fact of class desegregation won't result in reduced inequality, policymakers should shift their focus to the potential for robust, inclusive integration. In other words, instead of seeing the sites as places where market-rate residents aid their subsidized neighbors, understanding them as intentional points of meeting—places where people share space across class cleavages—will help us promote and measure the sites' social success in more nuanced ways.

Implications for Development and Investment

For investors and developers, the focus must be on creating equity in both siting and site management decisions.

- *Equitable Siting.* There is a pressing need to economically integrate minority neighborhoods with high concentrations of poor people and, at the same time, a need to open up wealthier, Whiter communities that have long excluded poor people of color by blocking the construction of affordable housing. Meeting market-rate residents where they already are and attracting them to areas they've long since left will require careful scrutiny of siting policies. Following California's recent efforts to create a more equitable distribution of LIHTC-funded projects,[50] investors and developers

---

50 Ben Metcalf, "California For All: How State Action Can Foster Inclusive Mixed-Income Communities," in *What Works to Promote Inclusive, Equitable Mixed-Income Communities*, eds. Mark L. Joseph and Amy

can take the lead in distributing their mixed-income projects across communities with a range of class and race compositions.

- *Equitable Policies.* For practitioners working at existing mixed-income developments, the changes needed are straightforward. Once the assumption that market-rate residents are symbols of social and structural success is discarded, it should be clear that all residents, regardless of income or race, ought to be treated with respect as valued and contributing members of the mixed-income community. At the sites, this means that market-rate and subsidized residents should have access to the same units, be subject to the same rules, have similar influence on site management, and receive the same treatment by development staff.

- *Equal Information.* Leasing agents ought to inform all prospective movers to the sites that they will be home to both market-rate and subsidized renters. Making residents aware of this feature from the outset might help dissuade the most discriminatory from applying, and it will also allow all residents the opportunity to ask questions, voice concerns, and express commitment before moving in—all factors that management might take into consideration when deciding whom to lease or sell to. In a loose housing market, this tactic risks reducing demand, but it also may attract residents who ultimately stay for longer tenures.

Implications for Residents and Community Members

Residents of mixed-income developments and members of the surrounding neighborhoods should see mixed-income communities as an opportunity for greater intentionality about the potential impact of such diverse settings for collective self-governance. In order for the mixed-income model to generate high-quality, stable, safe affordable housing, neighbors need not build strong ties across their differences or create community. But they should see the decision *not* to strive for a more inclusive and engaged community as a choice, rather than an inevitable product of self-interest or social norms. Collective conversations about belonging, rulemaking, and site governance can help create spaces for shifts in perspective. In short, the work of building a desegregated, democratic site will require regular opportunities for connection and reflection among all residents, regardless of background.

T. Khare. (San Francisco: Federal Reserve Bank of San Francisco). https://case.edu/socialwork/nimc/sites/case.edu.nimc/files/2019-08/Metcalf_California%20for%20all.pdf.

■ ■ ■

MICHAELJIT SANDHU *is a Ph.D. student in Sociology at the University of California, Berkeley and a JD student at Harvard Law School. He is interested in why people move, what segregation is, and when democracy works.*

5
ENGAGING THE PRIVATE SECTOR IN INCLUSION AND EQUITY

Private Market, Public Good: Private Investment in Equity and Inclusion

Federal, state, and local policymakers have created a set of complex policies, incentives, and mandates intended to steer private development to particular populations and places. These market-centered housing and community development policies aim to address the shortcomings of relying on pure market approaches to meet the needs of low- and moderate-income people. These essays examine the opportunities and challenges inherent in policies that expand capital with the intent of fostering mixed-income neighborhoods and consider how they might be reformed to increase inclusion and equity.

In "Opportunity for Whom? A Call for Course Correction Based on Early Opportunity Zone Investments," Aaron Seybert, Lori Chatman, and Robert Bachmann describe how the intent of the Opportunity Zones (OZ) legislation has not yet been actualized. OZ is a relatively new tax incentive, delivered in the form of "special treatment" of capital gains, which encourages private investors to invest capital into low-income census tracts. However, most of the investments to date have not been in areas of greatest need. According to the authors, "Despite the glimpses of potential benefits represented in the examples we have featured, however, an untold number of Opportunity Zone funds currently being formed are decidedly *not* impact-oriented....While we believe that the fate of Opportunity Zones is neither inevitably good nor inevitably bad, we do think we are at an important juncture and it is still within our collective power to shape the tool as a force for good." Through specific examples, the authors demonstrate how OZ could advance its intended purpose across geographies and at scale. Without future reforms, however, Opportunity Zones may actually exacerbate the wealth inequality gap, rather than narrow it.

In "Rebuilding the Bond Market for Mixed-Income Housing," Carol Galante, Carolina Reid, and Nathaniel Decker argue for the use of tax-exempt bonds—otherwise known as 80-20 deals—as a method to finance mixed-income housing. These projects combine market-rate units (usually 80 percent of total units) and affordable units (usually 20 percent of the units reserved for families at or below 50 percent of the area median income) in a single deal funded

through tax-exempt private activity bonds. This financing approach has been used to generate and preserve low-cost, income-restricted housing in both higher-income and gentrifying neighborhoods. As Galante, Reid, and Decker argue, the advantages are clear: "Expanding public- and private-sector capacity to arrange 80-20 deals would tap into an underutilized funding stream without reducing the resources for 100-percent affordable projects. Furthermore, as cities increasingly turn to inclusionary zoning and other policies to expand the supply of affordable housing, 80-20s may help make more projects financially feasible." Current examples of 80-20 projects in New York, Texas, and Minnesota illuminate how successful they have been in boosting the financial viability of mixed-income projects and expanding affordable housing in higher-resourced neighborhoods. These case study examples show how 80-20 projects may help local stakeholders overcome NIMBY objections while at the same time aligning with the policy framework
of the Affirmatively Furthering Fair Housing rule.

OPPORTUNITY FOR WHOM? A CALL FOR COURSE CORRECTION BASED ON EARLY OPPORTUNITY ZONE INVESTMENTS

Aaron Seybert
The Kresge Foundation

Lori Chatman
Enterprise Community Investment, Inc.

Robert Bachmann
Enterprise Community Loan Fund, Inc.

Something has gone wrong in America. Starting in the early 1980s, following a three-decade decline in America's wealth gap, the household income per-capita gap between the wealthy and poor reversed its positive trajectory and began a steady rise toward the current alarming level of inequality.[1] By 2016, the country's wealthiest households held 77 percent of the nation's total wealth, while the poorest households held only 1 percent.[2] This trend has had an unmistakable geographic element: as the wealthy continue to get wealthier and the poor poorer, the poorest communities are largely concentrated in the Rust Belt and southern states, while wealth and opportunity gravitate to major urban centers largely on the coasts.[3] Today, more than 50 million Americans live in

---

1 Ana Kent, Lowell Ricketts, and Ray Boshara, "What Wealth Inequality in America Looks Like: Key Facts & Figures," *Open Vault Blog* (blog), *Federal Reserve Bank of St. Louis*, August 14, 2019, https://www.stlouisfed.org/open-vault/2019/august/wealth-inequality-in-america-facts-figures.

2 Kent et al. "What Wealth Inequality in America Looks Like: Key Facts & Figures."

3 Raj Chetty et al., "The Fading American Dream: Trends in Absolute Income Mobility Since 1940" (working paper, National Bureau of Economic Research, Cambridge, MA, December 2016).

economically distressed communities.[4] Those communities tend to offer very little economic mobility for residents, all but guaranteeing deeper and more entrenched intergenerational poverty. Such is the picture of wealth inequality in America today.

Enter Opportunity Zones (OZ). Included in the Tax Cuts and Jobs Act of 2017 (TCJA)—and based on a previous bill that Sen. Tim Scott (R-SC) co-sponsored with colleagues on both sides of the aisle, including Sen. Cory Booker (D-NJ), the Opportunity Zones legislation sought to address growing economic inequality in low-income census tracts through federal tax incentives that encourage private investment in these communities. The Act recognized that barriers to accessing capital are a common contributor to economic inequality, since many areas in the nation have little to no market for new development and investment. The sponsors believed the flow of capital to coastal cities through private equity and venture capital, which largely avoided midwestern and southern states, was a major driver of this growing inequality. Champions of the legislation often cited the fact that in 2016, the year before the TCJA was passed, 75 percent of venture capital money went to startups in just three states: California, Massachusetts and New York. Surely, the thinking goes, talent must be more geographically distributed than that. Proponents of Opportunity Zones believed that the capital expected to follow the tax incentives could be the tool to rebalance this lopsidedness.

This theory, on its own, is compelling. We do agree with the general sentiment that traditional capital markets often irrationally overlook investable opportunities in both rural/non-major metro and urban low-income communities, perceiving them to be riskier than they actually are. However, we also believe—and, in fact, have observed first hand—that it does not automatically follow that a tax incentive such as Opportunity Zones will naturally result in a sudden wave of capital flowing into overlooked communities, and certainly not necessarily in ways that actually benefit low-income communities and the people who live there. More is required.

Specifically, what is required is a deep understanding of the assets and needs of low-income communities and the types of capital required to build upon the assets and meet the needs. If done right, Opportunity Zones can be a

---

4 Economic Innovation Group, "Over 50 Million Americans Live in Economically Distressed Communities," News release, (February 25, 2016).

powerful tool to foster mixed-income, truly integrated communities where wealth is shared and opportunity is abundant. If done wrong—that is, without further action and improvements to its current form—the Opportunity Zones legislation has potential to exacerbate the problems of inequality it was meant to remedy. Its success is dependent on a range of stakeholders, including policymakers, investors, and community residents themselves, helping to ensure that the process is transparent, that it receives proper buy-in from those who will be impacted, and that investments are ultimately consistent with what communities need.

HOW OPPORTUNITY ZONE INCENTIVES WORK

In its simplest form, the Tax Cut and Jobs Act created four new tax incentives for capital gains investors with liquid capital gains:

1. Investors may gain temporary deferral of existing capital gains that are reinvested into Opportunity Funds;

2. If investors hold their Opportunity Fund investments for five years, the basis of their original investment is increased by 10 percent (meaning they will only owe taxes on 90 percent of the rolled-over capital gains);

3. If investors hold for seven years, the basis increases by an additional 5 percent (meaning they will only owe taxes on 85 percent of the rolled-over capital gains). However, investors must recognize their original tax bill by December 31, 2026, at the latest, or until they sell their Opportunity Fund investments, if earlier; and

4. Investors may exclude new capital gains on Opportunity Fund investments held for at least 10 years from taxable income. In other words, after settling their original tax bill, patient investors in Opportunity Funds will not have capital gains taxes on their Opportunity Fund investments.

Opportunity Fund investments must be made in: (a) stock in a domestic corporation; (b) capital or profits interest in a domestic partnership; or (c) tangible property used in a trade of business of the Opportunity Fund that substantially improves the property. Opportunity Funds are prohibited from investing in federally defined "sin" businesses (e.g., racetrack or gambling facilities, liquor stores, massage parlors, etc.), but beyond those prohibitions, everything else is fair game.

It is important to understand that this incentive is not funded through any appropriations mechanism and is not a government "program." This is a *tax* incentive, delivered in the form of a "special treatment" of capital gains, to encourage private investors to invest private capital. The distinction is an important one, A "program" tends to carry structural guardrails, such as meaningful reporting, transparency, and accountability mechanisms. A tax incentive can be far less structured, as is the case with Opportunity Zones.

OPPORTUNITY FOR WHOM?

With this remarkably flexible new tool available, many people are asking how Opportunity Zones can be used to address problems in their community. We believe the answer lies in understanding the needs of low-income communities and the types of capital needed to address the roots of economic inequality. We also believe it's crucial to understand the nature of capital flows and how this incentive may change those flows to the benefit or detriment of the communities it is designed to serve.

It is a well-established principal that, holding all things constant, capital will flow to the highest-return, lowest-risk, lowest-friction environment. This means that capital seeks to maximize return while simultaneously reducing risk. The tension between risk taking and economic return leads to what is known as a "market-rate" return in which the capital markets, under ever-fluctuating conditions, agree that a given rate of return is acceptable for a given amount of risk. This market-rate return also is influenced by the friction involved in facilitating the investment. Investments that are simple to execute and monitor are considered low friction. Investments that are complex, time consuming, heavily regulated, and lacking transparency are high friction and typically require a higher rate of return to compensate investors for that friction.

The trouble is, the market has never been particularly good at valuing the risk/return profile of low-income communities because of an inherent bias, the roots of which lie largely in racism and discrimination. Our modern financial markets, designed in a historical and societal context, have systematically oppressed poor people—specifically, people of color—since the founding of this country. Today, looking at overall patterns of asset allocation in our economy, it is not difficult to spot the inherent prejudice of the capital markets: Of the $71.4 trillion in assets under management today, Black owned/managed funds account for only 1.1 percent. This essay is not a treatise on the history of oppressive capital markets, but that is the unavoidable cornerstone upon which this essay is founded. Without that knowledge and understanding, we cannot hope to address growing economic inequality using this new tool or any other. It is within this history and contemporary reality, therefore, that we analyze how Opportunity Zones can help address inequality and promote more equitable and inclusive mixed-income communities.

Our collective years of experience and a mountain of research tell us that thriving communities are mixed-income communities[5]—and that mixed-income communities require a variety of housing opportunities that not only serve households of varied incomes but also acknowledge and honor the historical and cultural norms within a given community. These exemplar communities offer adequate access to transit, employment, health care, and healthy foods. They possess high-quality schools that are accessible to their residents, and they tend to be more racially diverse than other communities.[6]

The financial tools needed to construct and maintain these communities include traditional debt tools, such as single-family mortgages, commercial real estate financing, small business loans, and equity investments. Equity, the scarcest of these tools, is ownership. It is the risk capital contributed by an owner, which is used to protect the lender and establish the means by which to distribute profits from a business or the appreciation of the asset. Equity typically is sourced from an individual's own savings, friends and family, or institutional players such as private equity funds. It is viewed as higher-risk/higher-return capital and thus more difficult to source. In low-income communities, the sources of equity we have outlined rarely, if ever, exist; businesses that start up in these communities tend to require lower-cost, more flexible, and patient capital.

Business owners in low-income communities are often low-income themselves, with little access to savings. Their friends and families also tend to be low-income with limited resources. Institutional players rarely invest capital in these places—whether due to prevailing biases and an undue perception of risk or to other reasons.

---

5   Raj Chetty, Nathaniel Hendren, and Lawrence F. Katz, "The Effects of Exposure to Better Neighborhoods on Children: New Evidence from the Moving to Opportunity Experiment," *American Economic Review* 106, no. 4 (2016): 855-902.

6   Ludwig et al., "Long-Term Neighborhood Effects on Low-Income Families: Evidence from Moving to Opportunity," (working paper, National Bureau of Economic Research, Cambridge, MA, February 2013).

Real estate projects in low-income areas, which typically have very limited budgets and are designed to build primarily affordable housing, often obtain equity from federal programs, such as the Low-Income Housing Tax Credit (LIHTC). These programs are dramatically oversubscribed and typically cap the amount of economic return available to investors, effectively pushing out market-rate capital. Furthermore, these tools often make financing mixed-income and mixed-use developments far more complicated. LIHTC income limits make it difficult to produce affordable units for middle-income households, so investor interest in mixed-income and mixed-use development diminishes.

Opportunity Zones would seem an ideal tool to remedy the challenges of real estate investing and to deliver the type of capital most needed for projects in low-income areas. The incentive provides a substantial tax break for investors; therefore, in theory, the investor should be willing to take a lower before-tax "market rate" of return. In addition, the investor is increasingly rewarded for being patient and keeping the capital invested. And there are few regulations to limit the types of investment allowed, which maximizes this tool's flexibility. Nonetheless, there are reasons for concern.

The Opportunity Zone incentive was not really designed for investment in real estate. The authors of the bill believed that the lack of equity capital in low-income communities was hindering the creation of new businesses and the growth of existing ones, and they thought the OZ market would consist largely of private equity and venture capital firms investing in new and growing businesses. If business owners could access the equity they need, they could grow, hire more people to work within the neighborhoods, and pay higher wages, which would indirectly reduce the economic disparity in a given census tract.

However, real estate has now become the dominant form of Opportunity Zone investments. According to Novogradac, as of December 2019, 74 percent of known Opportunity Funds were investing some portion of their funds into real estate and 69 percent of reporting funds were investing *exclusively* in real estate, while only 3.2 percent of reporting funds were investing exclusively in operating businesses. This is largely due to the way the incentive's regulations were issued, and also because real estate provides the lowest-friction environment for OZ investment. The incentive's rules require a certain percentage of the Opportunity Funds' assets be held in a specific geography, referred to as the Opportunity

Zone. But as businesses grow and hire people, they tend to open new facilities in other geographies as they follow their customers. By contrast, real estate does not move. Removing that friction alone is likely to keep tilting OZ investment toward real estate for the foreseeable future.

The focus on real estate may present both an opportunity and threat for the community development field. If harnessed correctly, it could bring untold amounts of desperately needed equity to our sector. If left unchecked, there is a significant chance the incentive could greatly exacerbate the problems of gentrification and displacement plaguing some communities. In addition, it's possible this new capital will simply follow the old channels flowing largely to costal urban centers, again leaving behind the Rust Belt and rural communities.

Some of these concerns seem already to be coming true. In March 2019, Zillow issued a report studying the increase in land value across Opportunity Zone census tracts, census tracts eligible but not selected for OZ designation, and non-eligible tracts. Sales price for Opportunity Zone properties increased by more than 20 percent year-over-year after the selection of the Opportunity Zones.[7] By comparison, properties in census tracts that were eligible but not selected rose by only 8.4 percent. While many factors could explain this rise and disparity, it's a powerful datapoint, and it suggests that investors are seeing the value in investing in low-income communities. However, this run-up in value appears to be happening only in large metro markets, including gentrifying neighborhoods in cities such as Oakland, Portland, and New York, which were on an upward trajectory to begin with and did not need tax-advantaged capital.

For low-income people, this type of rapid appreciation in real estate values is a mixed bag, at best. The value of their homes may be rising, creating new sources of equity (assuming they own their homes). In addition, multifamily affordable housing projects that already have land control may be able to access additional financing at more attractive rates because of the increased value of their collateral. However, projects that have not yet acquired land in an Opportunity Zone, and renters already living in these communities, are likely to experience significant additional burdens due to rising land values. The OZ incentive creates a new and powerful motivation for land owners in low-

---

7   Alexander Casey, "Sale Prices Surge in Neighborhoods with New Tax Break," *Zillow*, March 18, 2019, https://www.zillow.com/research/prices-surge-opportunity-zones-23393/.

income census tracts to maximize profits. The greater the profit maximization, the greater the equity invested in Opportunity Funds will appreciate, which will greatly enhance their rewards. The problem is that affordable housing and mixed-use developments typically offer lower overall capital appreciation, making them less compelling than they were before the incentive was created.

EARLY LESSONS AND POTENTIAL MODELS OF IMPACT

With these headwinds in mind, there is still hope in turning the incentive toward serving low-income communities' needs. A relatively small but committed group of fund managers across the country are providing a glimpse of Opportunity Zones' potential in distinctly different ways, delivering both a healthy economic return as well as real and quantifiable positive community impact. For example:

- Renaissance Equity Partners, LLC ("Renaissance") is raising a nationwide Opportunity Zone fund focused on supporting development in partnership with historically black colleges and universities (HBCUs). The fund seeks to partner with HBCUs as anchor institutions that drive significant economic activity in their respective markets. These institutions frequently possess excess land; they also generate demand for retail commercial offerings and housing on and around their campuses. However, the traditional capital markets and the development community frequently overlook or dismiss HBCUs, often because of racial biases. Renaissance sees a market opportunity in providing much-needed retail and housing amenities to the students and employees of HBCUs and also in partnering with these institutions to diversify their revenue streams. (Beyond its direct impact, Renaissance is one of the very few Opportunity Zone funds owned and managed by a person of color.)

- Enterprise Community Investment's OZ efforts center on mixed-use, mixed-income investment strategies in varying types of communities— from densely urban, gentrifying neighborhoods where affordable housing is increasingly scarce to smaller, lesser-known towns where more comprehensive redevelopment efforts are called for.

Based on Enterprise's experience so far, several realities have become clear in the early days of Opportunity Zones. First, we are indeed observing a place-based bias on the part of investors: Investors appear reticent to put their

OZ capital into non-urban cores and small cities proximate to larger metro markets, preferring instead to invest in larger metro regions such as Los Angeles, California. This is partly to be expected, but we believe there is still an irrational bias at play here. Smaller but dynamic towns like Greenville, South Carolina, represent a promising model of economic revitalization. These towns respond to the shifting preferences and geographic dynamics of the American landscape by offering the opportunity richness and clustering benefits of an urban environment while remaining more affordable to residents and businesses and within reach of people who historically have been disconnected from opportunity. According to researchers like Ross DeVol, midsized and even smaller cities ("micropolitans") can be a key to rural resurgence.[8] The investor bias toward major markets is especially unfortunate because Opportunity Zones offer, at least in theory, a unique chance to address the geographic inequality of opportunity that researcher Raj Chetty's profound work has laid painfully bare.

A second early takeaway is that the structure of Opportunity Zones limits the type of impact that is feasible. Deeply affordable housing, for example, is more difficult for OZ equity to produce, given the lower cash flow and inherent ceiling on potential capital appreciation in affordable housing. This limits the potential scalability of affordable housing developments that would serve lower-income residents, such as those earning below 60 percent of the Area Median Income (AMI). At the time of this writing, officials in the U.S. Treasury Department are considering how they might better structure the incentives to enable pairing of Opportunity Zones investments with Low-Income Housing Tax Credits. For the moment, however, Opportunity Zones are not an especially viable tool for creating deeply affordable housing, at least not without some measure of additional subsidy.

Within this constraint, however, also lies opportunity. Many people in the community development space increasingly lament the scarcity of "workforce" housing options for moderate-income households—those that earn too much to qualify for most subsidized low-income housing but too little to afford market-rate options (often found in the 80 to 100 percent range of AMI). This segment

---

8   Ross DeVol and Shelly J. Wisecarver, *Micropolitan Success Stories from the Heartland*, (Bentonville, AR: Walton Family Foundation, 2018), https://8ce82b94a8c4fdc3ea6d-b1d233e3bc3cb10858bea65ff05e18f2.ssl.cf2.rackcdn.com/d7/f9/00e59918410b83b3a3471533dd44/micropolitan-success-stories-report-print-updated-5.11.2018.pdf.

of the population might include teachers, government workers, firefighters, and artists—in short, those who contribute to the community but are getting squeezed out of neighborhoods by housing market pressures. Enterprise's OZ efforts thus far are demonstrating that mixed-income developments that integrate market-rate rents with workforce rents are economically feasible, as the cash flow from the market-rate rents serves to boost the project's overall return profile (particularly after factoring in the OZ tax benefit). In many cases, through this mixed-income strategy we are also able to work with developers to achieve more deeply affordable rents (namely, those targeted for households below 60 percent of AMI) for a project's non-market-rate units. Again, by sheer virtue of the numbers, this strategy allows for only so many additional affordable or workforce units to be built, which likely means it will be difficult to scale up in ways that produce a broad impact. However, we believe that there is unique value in this mixed-income approach.

CONCLUSIONS

As we have suggested, thriving communities are in fact mixed-income communities, places where diverse housing options meet the diversity of housing needs. A strategy centered around mixed-income housing developments not only serves to relieve housing pressures in a community, which tends to have positive spillover effects for everyone, but also fosters greater *integration* of households from different income bands, which we know is critical for inclusive growth and economic mobility for lower-income residents. That, of course, is the spirit behind Opportunity Zones.

Despite the glimpses of potential benefits represented in the examples we have featured, however, an untold number of Opportunity Zone funds currently being formed are decidedly *not* impact-oriented. And given the current lax regulatory framework, there is reason to be concerned that more will follow. While we believe that the fate of Opportunity Zones is neither inevitably good nor inevitably bad, we do think we are at an important juncture. It is still within our collective power to shape the tool as a force for good. To ensure that Opportunity Zones serve to narrow the wealth inequality gap rather than exacerbate it, all of us—policymakers, philanthropists, researchers, developers, investors, and residents themselves—have crucial roles to play.

Figure 1: A Special Note About Philanthropy

Philanthropy is well-positioned to play an important but precarious, role in the Opportunity Zone marketplace. Private philanthropy has deep knowledge and expertise in the community development finance sector, having funded the system since its inception. The Ford Foundation, The John D. and Catherine T. McArthur Foundation, the Rockefeller Foundation, the W.K. Kellogg Foundation, and many others have substantially contributed to some of the sector's most important and powerful innovations, including the Low-Income Housing Tax Credit and the New Markets Tax Credit; the Rental Assistance Demonstration and Housing Choice Voucher programs; and the Community Development Financial Institutions Fund, among others. That expertise is still relevant today.

It is philanthropy's obligation to empower the organizations already operating in the community development finance space and trust their judgment. These organizations know the capital needs of the communities they serve and what it will take to make Opportunity Zones address those needs. Few of our community development finance partners have substantial experience managing true equity products outside of federal tax credit programs, which are substantially different from OZs. These organizations need funding for training, technical expertise, fundraising, and the like. To begin filling this gap, The Kresge Foundation partnered with the Rockefeller Foundation, Calvert Impact Capital, Plante Moran, and Holland and Knight Foundations in creating an emerging Opportunity Fund Manager incubator.

Philanthropy's next obligation is to think local. There is very little federal oversight over this private tax incentive and virtually no guardrails preventing practices that could greatly harm the communities we serve. The legislation gave state governors the opportunity and obligation to designate Opportunity Zones on a relatively tight timeline, which created an impression of state or even local control over the incentive. However, many communities are now waking up to the fact that unless an Opportunity Fund voluntarily identifies itself, no state, mayor, city council, or resident will ever know what Opportunity Fund invested in its community, where it got its money, and what it invested in. Maybe that won't matter to a policymaker or resident, as there are other local controls that exist to ensure community benefit; but maybe it will. Looking to the work of the Rockefeller Foundation and the Annie E. Casey Foundation, we see examples of how foundations can help equip local government leaders to understand the incentive better and to create strategies that allow cities to play both offense and defense in the face of a changing landscape.

Philanthropy must remain vigilant about demanding transparency and accountability. It's impossible to know how OZ designation will affect a community over time without being able to identify the players and their incentives. Private market investment strategies, particularly those that lack transparency and accountability, have traditionally not been good for low-income communities. We need only look back to the recent financial crisis to see how the far more regulated and transparent derivatives market and sub-prime mortgage market decimated low-income communities, especially those of color, across the country. The crisis was preceded by many anecdotes of how loosening credit standards brought home ownership and wealth building to millions of Americans. as the Great Recession began, there were just as many stories of how the market destroyed generations of wealth and devastated communities. That is where we find ourselves today: evaluating by anecdote. For every Opportunity Zone cheerleader claiming this incentive will transform low-income communities for the better, there is a detractor claiming the opposite. To some extent, proponents of the current legislation have resisted requiring fund managers to publicly disclose their investors, amounts invested, fund investments, dispositions, and certain social outcome metrics, fearing this could dampen investor appetite and reduce the overall size of the market. That may be true. But philanthropy needs to ask itself: "Whom do we serve?" The answer should be obvious: A smaller, more transparent market that aligns with community needs is far better than a large, investor-friendly market with little transparency. Philanthropy must resist the seduction of phrases like "trillion-dollar market" and "investing at scale." Experience has taught us that while the amount of capital matters, the type of capital matters more. Without full transparency in the market, we face the very real risk of becoming a primary driver of many of the social harms we all seek to address. In the absence of full transparency, philanthropy should be extremely cautious about endorsing Opportunity Zones. And in the absence of proof, philanthropy should default to skepticism about whether this incentive, overall, will truly serve the needs of low-income communities.

IMPLICATIONS FOR ACTION

Implications for Policy

- Federal officials must address the shortcomings of the Opportunity Zones legislation, a law that was remarkably thin on details and guardrails. While there are many issues to address, perhaps none is more important than the need to improve transparency through more robust reporting requirements. Currently, investors are required to report very little on their Opportunity Zone investments to the Internal Revenue Service. This leaves lawmakers, researchers, and community representatives with inadequate information to judge the efficacy of the tax incentive.

- Local policymakers need to engage with community groups to understand the nature and scale of capital needed to support local priorities. Based on that feedback and understanding, policymakers should craft strategies that support local objectives, simultaneously keeping in mind the needs of fund managers and investors. They can use any number of policy levers at their disposal, such as fast-track zoning, permitting, and entitlement processes, for projects that support community priorities.

- When a community identifies threats to its priorities, local government can and should exercise greater scrutiny. For example, if an affordable housing development project in an Opportunity Zone that is receiving tax abatement changes hands, the municipality should require disclosure of OZ-motivated capital. The municipality also should require additional due diligence, including an affordability study and enhanced plan review, before approving any continuance of abatement or new entitlement. This approach can be expanded across the toolset of state and local government, which can fill much of the vacuum left by the federal government's lack of robust reporting requirements.

Implications for Research and Evaluation

- Researchers can evaluate the short- and long-term impact of the OZ incentive by comparing investments and outcomes in those places selected as Opportunity Zones with places that met the same criteria but were not chosen to participate.[9] Successful implementation of this recommendation will require more robust reporting requirements for investors so that researchers have the data needed for evaluation.

Implications for Development and Investment

- Investors must question the basis on which they have historically determined that certain communities, especially those that are home to low-income individuals and people of color, are higher-risk than they actually are. Senator Booker has referred to Opportunity Zones as "domestic emerging markets," suggesting that these long-overlooked communities are a new frontier of high-potential returns for investors who are brave enough to jettison old modes. We agree that investors who look at Opportunity Zones through a new lens may be rewarded with high-return, high-impact opportunities.

Implications for Residents and Community Members

- With Opportunity Zones, communities have new impetus to examine themselves not from a deficit perspective (here is what missing and what we need) but with an asset mindset (here is what we have and why you should invest in us). Communities should seize this opportunity to identify their assets and investable opportunities.

■ ■ ■

AARON SEYBERT *is a social investment officer at The Kresge Foundation where he supports the Social Investment Practice and the Detroit Program. Previously, he served as executive director at JPMorgan Chase Bank. He started his career in impact investing at Cinnaire (formerly the Great Lakes Capital Fund) addressing affordable housing, and previously worked with Legal Aid of Central*

---

9   The Opportunity Zone designation process generally allowed for no more than 25 percent of a state's low-income census tracts to be designated.

Michigan. Seybert earned a bachelor in business administration in corporate finance and accounting from Central Michigan University in Mt. Pleasant, Mich., and a juris doctorate from the Michigan State University College of Law.

■ ■ ■

LORI CHATMAN is a senior vice president of Enterprise Community Investment, Inc., and serves as president of the Enterprise Community Loan Fund, Inc. Lori is responsible for setting and implementing the strategy for Enterprise to raise and deploy capital through large-scale national, regional and local debt funds as well as tax advantaged equity through Qualified Opportunity Funds and New Markets Tax Credits. Chatman joined Enterprise in November 2004 with more than 15 years of community development experience. Prior to her current position, she was the senior vice president and chief credit officer of the Enterprise Community Loan Fund, Enterprise's U.S. Treasury-certified Community Development Financial Institution (CDFI). Before joining Enterprise, Chatman was the director of lending for the Calvert Social Investment Foundation (now Calvert Impact Capital), where she managed their portfolio of loans to CDFIs, community development corporations, community service organizations and international microfinance institutions. Chatman was also responsible for delivering a broad menu of portfolio and asset management services under contractual arrangements with a host of institutional investors, including administering several portfolios of loans funded by these investors.

■ ■ ■

In his role as Senior Director of Impact Investing at Enterprise, **ROBERT BACHMANN** provides leadership and support for various components of Enterprise's Creative Capital team including Enterprise's Opportunity Zone Funds and the Enterprise Community Impact Note, where he focuses on capital raising, fund operations and strategy, impact, and policy. In his previous role at Enterprise as Chief of Staff to the CEO, Bachmann served as key support and advisor to the CEO on a range of matters, including organizational strategy, board governance, speechwriting and external communications, fundraising, stakeholder engagement, operational issues, and other critical priorities to the organization. Prior to Enterprise, Bachmann worked at Citi Community Development in the bank's Community Reinvestment Act (CRA) division, and prior to that, he served both as an aide to the chairman of the Financial Crisis Inquiry Commission and as a special assistant on the Obama-Biden Transition Team in 2008, following his role on the Obama presidential campaign.

REBUILDING THE BOND MARKET FOR MIXED-INCOME HOUSING

Carol Galante, Carolina Reid, and Nathaniel Decker
Terner Center for Housing Innovation, University of California, Berkeley

While mixed-income housing is often discussed as a means of transforming areas of concentrated poverty, it can also advance housing opportunity and racial equity in higher-income and gentrifying neighborhoods. Some localities have attempted to expand access to affordable housing in these neighborhoods through inclusionary zoning, which requires developers to build affordable units as part of a market-rate project. However, these projects are often contested, and high rates of inclusionary units can make a development financially infeasible.

We believe that "80-20" deals—which use tax-exempt bonds to finance mixed-income housing—offer a promising means to generate and preserve low-cost income-restricted housing in opportunity neighborhoods. Due to their structure, 80-20 deals can be used to increase access to higher-income neighborhoods as well as preserve affordable housing in gentrifying neighborhoods. Moreover, they rely on an underutilized source of funding: Each year, states leave billions of dollars in bond authority on the table.

Tapping into this potential will require building the capacity of the affordable housing and community development industry to do market-rate rental development or to partner with market-rate developers, since 80-20 deals require large projects and experienced teams from both the private and public sectors. This is due largely to the high fixed costs of bond financing and the complex federal administrative and compliance regulations that come with bonds. Nonetheless, we believe that this is an opportune time to reconsider the potential of mixed-income, bond-financed deals. Expanding public and private sector capacity to arrange 80-20 deals would tap into an underutilized funding stream without reducing the resources for 100% affordable projects. Furthermore, as cities increasingly turn to inclusionary zoning and other policies to expand the supply of affordable housing, 80-20s may help make more projects financially feasible.

In this essay, we explain what 80-20s are and how these deals are structured, trace the reasons for the rise and fall in their popularity, provide examples of current 80-20 deals and programs, and suggest steps that private and public actors can take to make better use of this type of deal.

WHAT ARE 80-20s AND HOW DO THEY WORK?

"80-20" is a shorthand term for housing projects that combine market-rate units (usually 80 percent of total units) and affordable units (usually 20 percent of the units which are reserved for families at or below 50 percent of the Area Median Income) in a single deal funded through tax-exempt private activity bonds. These bonds—issued by a state Housing Finance Agency or similar allocating body—provide a subsidy for affordable housing because the interest paid to the bond investors is not taxed at the federal or (usually) state level, allowing investors to accept a lower rate on the bond. This lower interest rate translates into lower costs to finance the development; the savings are passed on to the project, thus facilitating the construction or acquisition of projects that are a mix of market-rate and affordable housing. In addition, the large size of 80-20 projects (which are rarely fewer than 100 units) gives these developments a catalytic effect on neighborhoods, increasing demand and land values for adjacent properties and property tax receipts.

80-20s are an effective means for state and local governments to provide low- and moderate-income families with access to opportunity neighborhoods. These deals work where there is adequate demand for the market-rate units; as a result, they work well in neighborhoods that tend to be higher-income and with stronger labor markets. 80-20s tap into this market demand by providing high-quality (often luxury) projects that are affordable to both the market-rate tenants and the low- and moderate-income tenants. The affordable units expand housing accessibility in neighborhoods that are otherwise often closed off to lower-income households, thereby disrupting entrenched patterns of income segregation. As long as the affordable units are identical to the market rate units and are scattered across the building, residents report no substantial frictions among tenants based on income.[1]

80-20s may also promote racial inclusion. Black and Latinx households, in particular, are more likely to be both low-income and renters. The neighborhoods that are best suited for 80-20 development have more stable and/or higher rents, which tend have a higher share of non-Latinx white residents. Thus the affordable units of 80-20s can be a means of providing minority renters access to whiter or more integrated neighborhoods. Local governments and nonprofits can further this goal by ensuring that the affordable units are marketed to a racially diverse group and that tenant selection and income verification practices do not disadvantage minority groups.

States do not have limitless ability to issue tax-exempt bonds for housing. The federal government allocates an annual "volume cap" to each state and restricts how the funds can be used.[2] In many states, the majority of these funds have gone to support first-time homebuyer and multifamily rental housing.[3] In 2018, states received $37.1 billion in new volume cap—a considerable sum in comparison to the $950 million allocated for the HOME Investment Partnerships Program (HOME), $3 billion for Community Development Block Grants (CDBG), and approximately $10 billion for Low-Income Housing Tax Credits (LIHTC) in 2018. Apartment buildings financed with volume cap must set aside at least 20% of their units for low-income families.

Perhaps because of these restrictions, a significant share of this bond authority is left on the table. While exact numbers are hard to come by, estimates suggest that at least $4.7 billion of volume cap went unused in 2018 because it was not allocated in time.[4]

---

1 Julie Satow, "Living in the Mix," *The New York Times*, August 29, 2014, https://www.nytimes.com/2014/08/31/realestate/affordable-housing-in-new-yorks-luxury-buildings.html.

2 For a more in-depth description of volume cap and multifamily volume cap deals in general, see: Justin Cooper, *Multifamily Rental Housing: Financing with Tax-Exempt Bonds* (Orrick Herrington & Sutcliffe LLP, 2010), https://www.orrick.com/Insights/2010/06/Multifamily-Rental-Housing-Financing-With-Tax-Exempt-Bonds.

3 Other uses include certain kinds of industrial development, nonprofit hospitals, and student loans.

4 Council of Development Finance Agencies, *CDFA Annual Volume Cap Report: An Analysis of 2018 Private Activity Bond & Volume Cap Trends* (Council of Development Finance Agencies, 2019), https://www.cdfa.net/cdfa/cdfaweb.nsf/ord/201910-2018VolumeCapReport.html/$file/CDFA%202018%20Volume%20Cap%20Report.pdf.

WHY HAVE 80-20 DEALS BECOME LESS COMMON SINCE THE 1970s AND EARLY 1980s?

In the 1970s and early 1980s, 80-20 deals were popular across the United States. The first state Housing Finance Agencies (HFAs) and local issuers were established in the 1960s, and by the mid-1970s most states had an HFA. In 1974 Congress authorized the issuance of tax-exempt bonds for privately owned apartment buildings. The exceptionally high interest rates of the 1970s and the early 1980s (e.g., 16.5 percent for a Freddie Mac 30-year fixed mortgage in 1981) caused demand for tax-exempt mortgage debt to spike, and state and local issuers responded by issuing large quantities of tax-exempt bonds.[5]

The Tax Reform Act of 1986, however, instituted an entirely new system of financing low-income rental housing by establishing LIHTC, setting limits to the amount of private activity bonds a state could issue and restricting the uses of tax-exempt bonds for housing finance. Annual multifamily bond issuance (bond issues to finance apartment complexes) fell from a peak of $21.8 billion ($51.77 billion today) in 1985 to just $2.84 billion ($6.40 billion today) in 1987.

Since then, issuers have slowly regained capacity and authority as new sources of federal funds have flowed in and their volume cap authority increased. 80-20 deals, however, remain relatively rare. This is likely because using bonds to finance housing can be complex. The most effective 80-20 programs involve state agencies with substantial balance sheets and staff capacity, which not all state (or local) issuers possess. Furthermore, from the perspective of LIHTC investors, market-rate units add additional risks because these units have uncertain demand relative to the constant and strong demand for affordable units. There are also tricky tax credit allocation issues for LIHTC investors if they are investing in projects where a substantial portion of the units are market rate.

EXAMPLES OF SUCCESSFUL 80-20 PROGRAMS

While the number of 80-20 deals has decreased overall since the late 1970s and early 1980s, evidence from a few states and localities suggests that they still can be successful, at least in certain markets.

---

[5] Trevor W. Nagel and Walter J. St. Onge, "Housing Bonds and Tax Reform: The Perils of a Partial Analysis of Low-Income Housing Programs," *Yale Law & Policy Review* 6, no. 2 (1988): 287–08.

New York

New York has the longest-running and highest-production 80-20 programs in the country and has demonstrated that 80-20s are a flexible, effective method of generating mixed-income housing. There are two major types of mixed-income bond financing programs in New York. Both programs are in high demand, primarily because of a large tax abatement provided by New York City. The first program is a traditional 80 percent market rate, 20 percent affordable housing program run by the New York State HFA, which is subsidized only by the bonds. From 2005 to 2013, this program produced over 12,000 units in New York City. The majority of these units are sited in stable, high-opportunity areas with high market rents. Over the past two decades, the HFA has adjusted this program to provide just enough subsidy to make 80-20s more attractive to developers than 100 percent market-rate deals.

The other mixed-income bond program is run by the local issuer, the New York City Housing Development Corporation (HDC). HDC uses mixed-income bond financing differently than the state, establishing programs that require a third income band for middle-income households (a disproportionately housing-cost burdened group in New York City). This program has found success in neighborhoods that, while not the hottest markets, are seeing increased investment. The additional income-restricted units require additional subsidies, which HDC provides in the form of subsidy mortgages funded from its corporate reserves.

San Antonio, Texas

While New York's program focuses on integrating affordable units into higher-market rent areas, in neighborhoods of San Antonio, Texas, the San Antonio Housing Trust, the local bond issuer, has established a pipeline of mixed-income bond deals with a focus on neighborhood revitalization. San Antonio structures its deals with multiple income tiers, including substantial market-rate portions, and seeks to site them in neighborhoods that market-rate developers may still be wary of approaching without subsidies. The 80-20 deals have served to "prove" their neighborhood markets, catalyzing nearby investments while locking in affordable units down to 30 percent of Area Median Income. San Antonio makes these deals work by bundling them with the LIHTC 4 percent credit, other federal subsidies (e.g., HOME), and a local property tax abatement.

Minnesota

Issuers in Minnesota have used mixed-income bond deals to further their policy goals of deconcentrating affordable housing development and supporting transit-oriented development. Recent projects in the Twin Cities have highlighted both the challenges of mixed-income deals and the measures that can be taken to address these challenges. When LIHTC investors made it clear they would not accept the risk that came from the market-rate portion of the projects, developers used creative financial structures to shield these investors.[6] Additional local subsidies also were required so the state and local governments used Tax Increment Financing (TIF) notes to cover this gap. TIF notes proved well-suited to these developments, as the market-rate component of the deals generated a large tax increment that could be used to support the affordable component.

As these examples illustrate, 80-20s have the potential to support a variety of policy objectives by boosting the financial viability of mixed-income projects and expanding access to affordable housing in opportunity neighborhoods. 80-20s tap into latent demand for the market-rate units; in effect, they work with the market to expand access to affordable housing rather than enforcing new siting patterns through a LIHTC Qualified Allocation Plan.

Although there has not been a systematic review of the location of 80-20 deals, anecdotal evidence suggests that these projects face less community opposition than 100 percent affordable deals because of their large market-rate component. 80-20 projects tend to have high-quality design and physical components, since potential tenants for the market-rate units are choosing between the 80-20 project and other amenity-rich market-rate properties. As a result, 80-20 projects may be more effective in overcoming NIMBY objections than other affordable projects and could work in concert with the Affirmatively Furthering Fair Housing rule (AFFH) and other policies that seek to expand the supply of housing in higher resourced neighborhoods. However, they are not a panacea for building in communities with restrictive or exclusionary zoning ordinances that limit larger scale multifamily rental developments.

---

6   One deal was divided into two components, one 100 percent affordable and the other 100 percent market rate, to provide two separate financings for a single project. Another deal was split into one 100 percent affordable building and another 100 percent market-rate building on the same property, with separate but linked financings. For more detail on the first project and other mixed-income projects in Minnesota, see: Mariia Zimmerman, "Twin Cities Mixed-Income Housing Case Studies," https://static1.squarespace.com/static/5021cc16e4b0c203353d08c5/t/568d2181c647ad1e518a2fac/1452089729125/MIH_final_Oct+2015+final+draft.pdf

Undoing longstanding patterns of residential segregation will ultimately require sustained attention to local land use controls and/or the use of fair share housing policies, such as Massachusetts' Chapter 40B,[7] which provide a "stick" for localities resistant to new affordable housing supply.

ALIGNING MARKET, SUBSIDY, AND POLICY

Mixed-income bond deals require capacity among a diverse set of government and market actors. These deals are complex, expensive to do at smaller scale, and often use multiple sources of equity and debt. Deals generally require some amount of subsidy beyond the tax-exempt debt, and these subsidies usually are provided by the state or local government or the issuer itself. Deals also often require the affordable deal partners to be comfortable with (or shielded from) the market-rate component of the deal and the market-rate deal partners to be comfortable with (or shielded from) the affordable component. The current affordable housing development ecosystem is set up to do 100 percent LIHTC projects, meaning that the incentives for mixed-income development driven by the market side is limited. This is a missed opportunity because 80-20s benefit from market mechanisms that help ensure the projects are high-quality and well-sited.

What needs to happen to rejuvenate the use of 80-20 deals? First, state and local issuers and policymakers play an essential role in supporting and driving demand for 80-20 programs. New York City and San Antonio's 80-20 programs have succeeded in large part because of local tax abatement programs that drive demand for bond financing and make the projects more financially feasible. But, as the case of Minnesota shows, local governments have a wide range of other policy levers that can promote 80-20 development, including Tax Increment Financing, inclusionary zoning, density bonuses, and local subsidies. State governments can provide additional subsidy through state housing tax credits, state housing trust funds, or directly through state HFAs. California's HFA, for example, has recently created the Mixed-Income Program a subsidy debt product specifically for bond-financed mixed-income housing. While many states already prioritize housing in their volume cap allocations, some do not,

---

7 Chapter 40B is a state statute that enables local zoning boards of appeal to approve affordable housing developments under flexible rules if at least 20-25 percent of the units have long-term affordability restrictions.

and some even discourage 80-20 developments, preferring only 100 percent affordable projects even as their volume cap allocations expire.

State and local policymakers also have a role to play in ensuring that 80-20s have appropriate affordability restrictions and in overseeing some management aspects of the affordable units. The affordability protections that come with the bonds themselves are minimal, providing no guarantee of below-market rents for the low-income tenants and relatively short periods of income restriction. It is the responsibility of the issuer to create and enforce a regulatory agreement that ensures that the affordable units' rents are set at appropriate levels and kept affordable for a substantial time period. Developers of 80-20 deals often have little or no experience marketing units to low-income tenants, selecting tenants, and certifying incomes. Issuers can direct developers to partner with organizations that have experience with these tasks.

Second, the federal government has a major role in promoting the development of mixed-income housing. The most significant recent action was the 2018 Consolidated Appropriations Act which—in addition to increasing LIHTC allocations—included provisions that allow for income averaging in LIHTC projects, making mixed-income in 9% percent LIHTC deals more feasible. A number of additional actions could also have substantial impacts. A slight change in the tax code that facilitates the "recycling" of tax-exempt bonds, for instance, could dramatically expand the amount of volume cap and LIHTC available for all tax-exempt bond-financed rental housing projects, without requiring an increase to the volume cap limits.[8]

The Federal Housing Administration (FHA) and Ginnie Mae serve an important role in 80-20 deal development in a number of ways, including by providing a construction-to-permanent loan product and through established risk-sharing programs with Fannie Mae, Freddie Mac, and many state HFAs that help to speed the origination of FHA multifamily loans. Additionally, FHA has recently piloted discounted insurance premiums to mixed-income projects. Housing affordability is central to FHA's mission, and the agency is willing to work in tertiary markets that many private lenders might avoid.

---

8 Allowing "recycled" bond proceeds to be used for all allowable uses of volume cap (presently they can only be used for housing) could allow states to allocate more of their volume cap to housing (and receive more 4 percent LIHTC) without diminishing tax-exempt bonds resources for non-multifamily uses. Legislation has already been introduced with this change, see Mark A. Willis and Luis Hernandez, "Proposed Legislation Expands Private Activity Bond Recycling," *The Stoop* (blog), *NYU Furman Center*, July 9, 2019, https://furmancenter.org/thestoop/entry/proposed-legislation-expands-private-activity-bond-recycling.

Fannie Mae and Freddie Mac currently play the broadest range of roles in multifamily bond deals and could take many different actions to support 80-20 developments nationwide. Currently Fannie and Freddie provide credit enhancement, buy the mortgages used in bond deals, buy the bonds themselves, and have recently re-entered the tax credit equity markets. Their market power, affordable housing goals, and diverse roles in the market provide them with many means of promoting 80-20 projects including new credit enhancement products, new mortgage product types, and new bond-buying or LIHTC-investment programs tailored to 80-20s.

Issuers have a range of options to promote the generation of 80-20 deals. All issuers can signal to the market that they are interested in 80-20s and have volume cap and associated LIHTC to support these deals. Many issuers, however, have limited ability to generate deals themselves. Almost all local and many state issuers are conduit issuers for multifamily deals, meaning that they are intermediaries but not lenders themselves. The most productive 80-20 programs are pooled issuances in which the issuer is the lender, allowing the issuer to establish the terms of its mortgage products. This structure requires the issuer to have a balance sheet, maintain staff capacity, and assume financial risk but allows them to compete in the market and build up assets that can be deployed as additional subsidy. For example, from 2003 to 2015 the New York City Housing Development Corporation provided $1.5 billion in subsidy loans to support over 80,000 units of affordable housing. Knowledge sharing between state and local issuers, particularly between pooled issuers and conduit issuers, could be a useful first step in building capacity.

Banks commonly provide credit enhancement and loans in bond deals and play an important role in 80-20 development. Regional banks, commercial and investment banks, and some non-bank financial institutions are all active in traditional multifamily bond deals, but many are unfamiliar with 80-20s. The Community Affairs Office of the Federal Reserve System, however, could play a role in raising the visibility and knowledge of this financing product, and regulators more generally could clarify that these deals would be eligible for Community Reinvestment Act credit. Improved capacity for underwriting these deals and structuring mortgage products could play a part in reinvigorating the 80-20 market.

CONCLUSIONS

80-20 deals are not a panacea and will not address all the gaps in affordable rental housing. Nor will they likely lead to dramatic changes in patterns of residential segregation that still characterize many U.S. cities. However, they do provide an opportunity to expand mixed-income housing by integrating more affordable units into market-rate deals. More research is needed to help clarify the barriers to expanding 80-20 practices, and more financial analysis is needed to identify the markets in which 80-20 deals work best and support the expansion of this tool. This could have multiple benefits, such as achieving affordability and inclusion in markets that clearly have market demand/opportunity, stemming displacement in gentrifying areas, working with local incentives to get more affordable homes built with much less per-unit subsidy, and maximizing the use of existing subsidies.

It is likely that many neighborhoods across the United States could support 80-20 developments. The right programs and products to generate these developments will look different from city to city, based on differences in the market and policy priorities. The impact of these programs could be substantial. A robust 80-20 pipeline should improve the siting of low-income units by tapping market forces to generate deals. It should increase the total volume of affordable housing generated by using currently unused tax-exempt bonds and associated tax credits. It may increase the total volume of all housing (both affordable and market-rate) generated in opportunity neighborhoods by better aligning local policies with financing programs. It should lead to measurable positive spillover effects in neighborhoods by proving markets and catalyzing additional investment. It should also limit displacement in rising markets. Mixed-income deals have been shown to provide all these benefits. Establishing a public and private sector financing ecosystem that promotes instead of stymies mixed-income development will help expand access to affordable housing and support the goals of income integration.

IMPLICATIONS FOR ACTION

Implications for Policy

- State and local policymakers can implement a range of programs and policies to drive demand for 80-20s including implementing regulations like inclusionary zoning and providing additional subsidies such as TIF financing. Governments can also provide oversight capacity on 80-20 deals, ensuring that the properties have appropriate affordability restrictions.

- State and local policymakers can pursue zoning reforms that prevent exclusionary (higher-income) communities from denying building permits for apartments and other denser forms of housing.
- State and local bond issuers can begin to advance 80-20 development by sharing knowledge with other issuers, showing the market they are eager to allocate private-activity bonds for this purpose and potentially becoming direct lenders themselves.
- The federal government can take steps to advance 80-20 development by enacting legislative changes that promote increased use of recycled bonds and creating financial products to support 80-20s from FHA and Ginnie Mae.
- Fannie Mae and Freddie Mac can establish new credit enhancement products, new mortgage product types, and new bond-buying or LIHTC-investment programs tailored to 80-20s.

Implications for Research and Action

- There is very little research on 80-20s in general. Studying who the low-income residents of these properties are and what their social and economic outcomes are relative to similar families would help clarify the public benefits of these projects and may help improve management practices.
- Financial analysis can determine market and policy conditions most conducive to 80-20 developments and assist state and local governments in crafting 80-20 programs suitable to local conditions and needs.

Implications for Development and Investment

- Both affordable and market-rate developers can become more familiar with 80-20 deals and consider this deal type when examining potential projects.
- Banks and other financial institutions can build capacity for underwriting and provide new mortgage products to support 80-20 deals.

Implications for Residents and Community Members

- Residents living in 80-20 properties can share their experiences of the benefits and challenges of living in these types of mixed-income communities.

Community members, advocates, and community organizing groups can be proactive in tackling the exclusionary politics that prevent approval of 80-20 buildings, especially in communities where more affordable housing is needed.

■ ■ ■

CAROL GALANTE is the I. Donald Terner Professor in Affordable Housing and Urban Planning at UC Berkeley and the founder and Faculty Director of the Terner Center for Housing Innovation and the Terner Housing Lab, a new accelerator program working with early- stage ventures on housing affordability. Galante previously served in the Obama Administration as Assistant Secretary for Housing/Federal Housing Commissioner at the U.S. Department of Housing and Urban Development and as Deputy Assistant Secretary for Multifamily Housing Programs. Prior to her appointment at HUD, she served for over ten years as President and CEO of BRIDGE Housing Corporation. She also serves on the Advisory Board of Factory OS, an innovative new company changing how we build. Galante holds a Master of City Planning from UC Berkeley and a Bachelor of Arts from Ohio Wesleyan.

■ ■ ■

CAROLINA REID is an Assistant Professor in the Department of City and Regional Planning and the Faculty Research Advisor at the Terner Center for Housing Innovation. Reid specializes in housing and community development, with a specific focus on place-based anti-poverty strategies including policies to expand access to affordable housing and homeownership for low-income and minority households, the Community Reinvestment Act, and neighborhood stabilization.

■ ■ ■

NATHANIEL DECKER is a doctoral candidate in the city and regional planning department at UC Berkeley. Prior to this he was a senior associate at Forsyth Street Advisors, an advisory and asset management firm based in New York focused on affordable housing, real estate, and municipal and impact investment. His recent research has examined topics such as the behaviors of small rental property owners, the impact of technology on the housing search, and the drivers of rent changes for units. Decker received his masters in urban planning from Cornell University in 2011 and his B.A. from Oberlin College in 2004.

The Role of Development Entities

These essays show how developers, property managers, and owner-operators have overcome challenges in building and sustaining inclusive, equitable mixed-income communities. In these examples from the field, local actors have addressed the competing interests of community members, residents, investors, and local government leaders in ways that aim to produce and sustain racially diverse, mixed-income communities.

In "Seven Strategies to Advance Equity, Inclusion, and Resiliency in Mixed-Income Communities," Cady Seabaugh and Vincent Bennett of McCormack Baron Salazar provide insight into their organization's strategy for ensuring their mixed-income development communities are designed and operated to promote inclusion, equity, and resiliency, a concept they illuminate as a key element to sustainability in the face of increasingly risky environmental contexts. McCormack Baron Salazar has a multi-decade national legacy in affordable housing, and combining a retrospective analysis of affordable housing development in the U.S with their own organization's learning the authors seek to share their core strategies in the hope of influencing policy and practice in the field, because as the authors assert, "When mixed-income developments are not designed equitably...and instead are created principally to provide tax breaks and other incentives to developers, inequities built into the design can increase divisions and exacerbate the prejudices of wealth."

In "What Works for Building and Sustaining Mixed-Income Communities: A Perspective from the Development Community," Vicki Davis, Daryl J. Carter, and Rosemarie Hepner describe five key strategies for building and sustaining mixed-income communities: Developing the right mix of affordable to market-rate units, overcoming financing barriers, creating and sustaining a community, building stakeholder support and working with local and state regulations.

In "A Call for Property Management Transformation to Meet the Challenges of Mixed-Income Communities," Frankie Blackburn and Bill Traynor present a guide for meaningful community building in mixed-income developments. They provide in-depth analysis of a case study from Pittsburgh, where developer and property-management investments in transforming the organizational culture at TREK Development led to positive outcomes for residents. Their essay touches on common challenges in mixed-income communities: conflict among community members, typical site management and operations issues, and property managements' efforts to reconcile the needs of all community members without being overly punitive or exclusionary. The authors propose intentional community-building practices as a way of strengthening community ties in order to build thriving mixed-income communities.

In "Achieving Durable Mixed-Income Communities through Affordable Housing Preservation: A Successful Model of Scattered-Site Housing Redevelopment in West Philadelphia," Michael Norton, Karen Black, and Jacob Rosch describe a model of scattered-site affordable housing development implemented by West Philadelphia Real Estate and Neighborhood Restorations (WPRE/NR) to create 1,100 affordable rental housing units in 760 single-family homes and duplexes using a mix of creative land acquisition, Low Income Housing Tax Credits, and private financing. The WPRE/NT model has effectively built in long-term affordability in some of West Philadelphia's most rapidly changing housing markets. The essay introduces the Displacement Risk Ratio (DRR) methodology, developed by Reinvestment Fund to analyze gentrification pressures. The authors compare changes in the DRR in West Philadelphia neighborhoods and the location and timing of WPRE-NR developments. In neighborhoods facing tremendous displacement pressure, WPRE/NR's development activities have created long-term affordable units for low and moderate income, predominantly black households. In West Philadelphia's more distressed areas, WPRE/NR investments have served as a stabilizing force and provided a much-needed boost to depressed housing values.

SEVEN STRATEGIES TO ADVANCE EQUITY, INCLUSION, AND RESILIENCY IN MIXED-INCOME COMMUNITIES

Cady Seabaugh and Vince Bennett
McCormack Baron Salazar

City living has become fashionable again. Across the United States, cities are welcoming new urban dwellers, primarily young professionals and retirees seeking easier and more environmentally friendly access to entertainment, recreation, and jobs. But as attention and resources flow back into urban areas and developers and the real estate market respond, existing populations—often low-income and poor—risk being ignored or displaced. To ensure that the new residential communities are affordable, sustainable, and designed for all, policymakers, planners, and developers must apply important lessons learned about building for equity, inclusion, and resiliency.

By themselves, neither the private nor the public sector has succeeded in creating sustainable, desirable, affordable housing and economically integrated neighborhoods. Together, however, the mixed-finance, mixed-income, public-private housing model now favored in federal policy encourages market forces to supply affordable housing options, increase absorption rates in large planned developments, decrease the concentration of poverty, and revitalize urban neighborhoods. When located close to job centers, transit stations, schools, grocery stores, or services, mixed-income housing provides more than just another housing product: it creates sustainable communities and activates smart growth principles by reducing travel and congestion.

The inclusion of "resiliency" as a broad concept in such developments, is gaining urgency in the face of increasing forceful weather and environmental events that are destroying older affordable housing units and dispersing already-vulnerable residents. Resiliency in this context applies to the quality of reconstruction, the social and emotional capacity of vulnerable residents, including children, and the financing mechanisms that force responsiveness and protect investment.

The approach taken by our company, McCormack Baron Salazar, prioritizes equity and resiliency in mixed-finance, mixed-income development. Our approach emerged from lessons that span the deep past of public housing strategy up through present-day weather events. In this essay, we briefly revisit the history before sharing lessons from McCormack Baron Salazar's (MBS) current approach, illustrated with examples of recent experiences.

THE HISTORY AND LANDSCAPE OF HOUSING DEVELOPMENT

Many traditional urban neighborhoods that had housing types suitable for an array of incomes and family sizes, disappeared as the result of discriminatory policies of the mid-20th century that created the suburban White middle class. People of color and immigrants were abandoned to increasingly unsafe housing situations in decaying city neighborhoods. One public policy response was to designate such tracts as blighted, and move residents to newly built public housing. But time has shown that those developments often were poorly designed, inadequately managed, and under-resourced, which only increased the racial and economic segregation, instability, and isolation (see box below).

In the early 1990s, as federal public housing programs struggled to shed their image as bleak, isolated, and crime-ridden, new approaches emerged that prioritized social and economic integration. The most distressed developments were targeted for demolition and replacement with a mixed-income approach implemented through the competitive HOPE VI program, also called the Urban Revitalization Demonstration program. However, concerns arose regarding accountability, inadequate standards and record-keeping, and the well-being of very-poor residents displaced by HOPE VI redevelopments.

From HOPE VI emerged the Choice Neighborhoods Initiative, a pilot public-private neighborhood turnaround program. It engages private developers and financial institutions in replacing obsolete, deteriorating publicly owned housing that isolates poor residents with modern, privately owned and managed mixed-income housing supported by coordinated private,

A History of Segregation, Instability, and Isolation in Public Housing

The consequences of inadequate financing and concentrated poverty are apparent in developments like the Pruitt Homes and Igoe apartments in St. Louis. First occupied in 1954, the Pruitt-Igoe development encompassed 33 high-rise buildings and nearly 3,000 housing units that were racially segregated by design and were intended to include two-thirds middle-income and one-third public housing units. Living conditions began to decline immediately. The St. Louis Housing Authority, saddled with construction debt, could not cover maintenance with the income it received in rent. 'White flight' following public housing desegregation in 1955 exacerbated the problems of inadequate revenue, and left increased poverty, crime, and isolation. In a futile and cruel effort to compensate for their financial bind, the housing authority continued raising rents until residents were paying up to half of their incomes to live there. Ultimately, in 1969, renters throughout St. Louis joined together in a nine-month rent strike calling for, among other things, rents that were tied to income. The strike ended in victory—an important milestone in the struggle for tenants' rights—but money was never made available for maintenance, and the quality of life at Pruitt-Igoe never improved. By 1976, Pruitt-Igoe was completely demolished.

The consequences of isolation and poor design can be seen in the history of developments like O'Fallon Place in St. Louis, where MBS is headquartered. O'Fallon Place is an old-style, crime-ridden, impoverished Section 8 development. The development's original design has played a major role in its deficiencies. The barracks-style layout has closed streets, allowing only one way in and one way out. It is disconnected from the surrounding street grid, creating a monolithic superblock with pickets of indefensible (i.e., crime-permissive) space. Emergency vehicles have difficulty managing its narrow streets. Inside, the units include small, poorly designed rooms, outdated appliance hook-ups, poor ventilation that fosters mold, and physical barriers for people with disabilities.

---

philanthropic, and local neighborhood investments. To be selected for the program, communities must bring together local leaders, residents, housing authorities, educators, police, business owners, and nonprofit organizations to improve education and job training, economic development, commercial development, and job creation. These tie-ins encourage coordination with other federal investments, such as: the Justice Department's Byrne Grants, which address crime, safety and reentry; the Department of Education's Promise Neighborhoods, which encourage school choice and school infrastructure; the Treasury Department's New Markets Tax Credits, which support economic development and job creation; and Transportation Department and Environmental Protection Agency programs for rehabilitating deteriorating infrastructure and public services.

The Choice Neighborhoods Initiative has proven to be among the most successful uses of federal Low-Income Housing Tax Credits (LIHTC) yet

Poorly Designed Mixed-Income Developments Exacerbate Inequity

Some housing complexes in Manhattan, Boston, Honolulu, and elsewhere have allowed mixed-income developments that require separate entrances for market rate and subsidized residents. Not only are the entrances separate, but the apartment and building amenities are unequal.

One such mixed-residential development is Lincoln Square in Manhattan. Its gleaming building entrance at 50 Riverside Boulevard provides exclusive welcome to its market rate residents with 24/7 doormen and a hand-blown glass chandelier in the lobby. Down the street is the building entrance accessible to subsidized renters, at 40 Riverside Boulevard. A feature story in the *New York Daily News* in January 2016 described amenities available to residents at 50 Riverside Boulevard: two gyms, a pool, a movie theater, a bowling alley, and exclusive access to the building's courtyard. Renters on the "poor" side have a bike storage closet, an unfinished laundry room, and a common space that faces the courtyard that they are not allowed to enter. Such "poor doors" in New York State have since been banned, although Lincoln Square was grandfathered in. (In Honolulu, opposition in late 2017 to "poor doors" in a proposed mixed-income high-rise was successful in opening all entrances to all residents. Only market rate residents, however, have access to the pool.)

Similarly, the stunning One Greenway complex in Boston is providing much needed mixed-income residential real estate in a space-starved city. The tower, with its entrance on Kneeland Street, offers a large array of amenities for market rate residents, including pet services. Less-affluent neighbors who enter the complex at 66 Hudson, however, are allowed to share a "landscaped urban retreat" called The Green and can enjoy their neighbor's dogs there, but are not allowed to keep pets in their subsidized units.

---

tested.[1] When mixed-income developments are *not* designed equitably, however, and instead are created principally to provide tax breaks and other incentives to developers, inequities built into the design can increase divisions and exacerbate the prejudices of wealth.

MCCORMACK BARON SALAZAR'S FOCUS: EQUITY, INCLUSION, AND RESILIENCY

Since 1971, MBS has focused on creating not just affordable housing but also equitable communities for all people from all incomes and backgrounds. Fifty

---

[1] In cities such as Memphis, New Orleans, and Pittsburgh, the Choice Neighborhoods Initiative has produced major community improvements, including: a 40 percent increase in employment of public housing residents and 30 percent decrease in crime in Memphis; a 53 percent employment rate of the public housing residents in mixed-income communities in New Orleans; and 60 percent of the middle and high school youth from Pittsburgh neighborhoods participating in enrichment programs that keep them on track for college and employment. McCormack Baron Salazar calculates that its Choice Neighborhoods projects have secured a 3:1 ratio of local and private investment for every U.S Department of Housing and Urban Development dollar spent.

years of experience and learning inform the firm's work in every aspect of real estate development and management. The most important lessons can be distilled into seven key elements of successful mixed-income development:

1. A diversity of financing sources
2. High standards and a uniform approach to design
3. Equally available market rate amenities and finishes
4. Community and resident involvement and leadership
5. Wrap-around services for lower-income residents
6. Management teams trained specifically for mixed-income populations
7. Attention to resiliency and sustainability

Each of these approaches addresses a different challenge posed by building a mixed-income community in an urban setting, and together they become an ever-evolving solution.

1. A Mix of Financing Sources

One of the biggest challenges facing urban housing development is the fact that, under current market conditions, the revenues generated from affordable rental are not sufficient to cover the costs of land and construction through private investment. In many cities, these costs are so high that even luxury market rate apartments cannot be covered solely by private sources.

Furthermore, during operations, the rents and operating subsidies paid on low-income apartments generally do not cover the costs of operating the development to a market rate standard. This results in dependence on and depletion of capital reserves and a corresponding deterioration of community conditions. As conditions worsen, rents are lowered to even less-sustainable levels. The archetypical example of this downward spiral is found in the mid-20th century public housing model, exemplified by Pruitt-Igoe.

Even if financially feasible, large amounts of private investment generally will not be made in neighborhoods that are perceived as low-income unless there is some reason to believe that conditions will change. The result is continued disinvestment in the neighborhood and further deterioration of its real estate and infrastructure.

Finally, mixed-finance structures create multiple points of accountability for the

Diversity In Financing Creates Stability

The Harmony Oaks Apartments, in New Orleans, offers an example of the financial stability gained through using a mix of financing sources to underwrite a mixed-income development. Harmony Oaks is a 460-unit, mixed-income HOPE VI community that was set to close in the fall of 2008. Rebuilding in New Orleans after Hurricane Katrina and during the Great Recession presented myriad financing challenges, including finding an investor, escalating construction costs, and building for a market that was not reestablished. Lenders would only underwrite $2 million in traditional debt toward a total development cost of $161 million. With boosts and incentives in the tax credit program, low-income housing tax credits resulted in $56.3 million in tax credit equity from Goldman Sachs, but the remaining $103 million came from government and philanthropic sources. And, once constructed, the rents from the 123 market rate units and 144 LIHTC units helped to offset the deficits in operating subsidy on the 193 public housing apartments.

The mixed-financing approach seems to have given Harmony Oaks and similar developments extra resilience over the long term. During the COVID-19 pandemic in 2020, for example, HUD subsidies could be quickly adjusted to account for the income lost by public housing residents. As a result, the public housing subsidies helped to somewhat bridge the lost rent from market rate and tax credit units. By the middle of April 2020, 98 percent of subsidized rent had been received at Harmony Oaks, compared to 79 percent of resident-paid rent.

Similarly, a public-private partnership enabled MBS to create Renaissance Square, an affordable housing community, in Puerto Rico in 2016. The partnership leveraged private funding to redevelop three existing public housing sites into vibrant, sustainable, mixed-income neighborhoods. HUD, Puerto Rico Department of Housing, and the Puerto Rico Public Housing Administration committed significant funding for the $35.5 million development. It also received Low-Income Housing Tax Credit equity, with Hunt Capital Partners as the syndicator and Citi Community Capital as the investor. Citi also provided a construction loan.

---

developer and owner, who have long-term obligations to private-sector lenders and investors, public-sector agencies, government programs, and community residents and stakeholders. This ensures that there are checks and balances throughout the life of the real estate investment for both financial performance and community goals.

2. High Standards and a Uniform Approach to Design

The quality of the design and construction of a mixed-income community is a critical component of the overall development strategy. If the physical development is done well, it will attract market rate renters, it will reflect the high expectations set by the community, and it will signal to the larger market that people are investing in the area. If the development is done poorly, it will have the opposite effect: market rate renters will go elsewhere, resulting in

Competitive Quality and Uniform Design

An example of this approach can be found in the Larimer/East Liberty Choice Neighborhood in Pittsburgh, PA. In the early 2010s, the East Liberty neighborhood was booming. Centrally located, with strong historical assets that were attractive to renovators and access public transit service, East Liberty attracted employers such as Google and technology start-ups, retailers like Target and Whole Foods, and market rate housing investors who built new, mid-rise buildings that were attractive to millennials working at the neighborhood start-ups. Directly adjacent to East Liberty, the Larimer neighborhood was disinvested, with several large Section 8 and public housing sites; smaller, poorly maintained single-family homes; and severely deteriorating infrastructure.

When HUD awarded the neighborhood a Choice Neighborhood Grant in 2013, the new plan worked to address current residents' fear of gentrification by including a mix of incomes in any new development and supporting current homeowners with assistance to maintain their properties. At the same time, the design of the new construction reflected the aesthetics of the East Liberty developments, linking the previously disparate neighborhoods through high-quality design and materials. The site design demarcates previously vague green space into parks and reconnects the street grid to provide safer, more direct access to transit stations. The new mixed-income community is attractive to new potential residents, makes returning residents proud, and elevates the value of the surrounding neighborhood by building upon existing strengths like green space and transit access.

---

lower market rate rents—which, in turn, will reduce the diversity of incomes in the community. Poor design and materials also signal to the community that the residents are less deserving, decreasing neighborhood pride and expectations. This can lead to community detachment. Finally, the broader market interprets low-quality design and materials as a sign of disinvestment and decline, leading to increased stigma on the community.

If the expectation is that the development has to compete for residents in the marketplace and therefore must reflect a competitive level of quality, it must be solidly built with strong architectural design; have great curb appeal; be attractively landscaped; and be well maintained, safe, and secure.

At the same time, a successful mixed-income development should be seamlessly integrated into the surrounding neighborhood. The goal is not to replace the existing community, but rather to build on its strengths and stabilize areas of weakness. The mixed-income development should be an extension of, and improvement to, the existing neighborhood. The density, height, and architectural style should reflect and build upon that of the surrounding community and integrate into the existing context. This integration includes

New housing in the Larimer/East Liberty neighborhood in Pittsburgh, PA

the style of the new buildings as well as the connections with streets, walkways, bike paths, community institutions, and parkland. These elements reinforce that the new community is neither a gentrifying effort (if the surrounding neighborhood is lower income) nor a lower-income enclave (if the surrounding neighborhood has higher levels of investment). Rather, the development should reflect the best values of mixed-income development combined with the values and strengths of the existing neighborhood.

3. Equally Available Market Rate Amenities and Finishes

One of the philosophical goals of a mixed-income community is that there is no perceived difference between neighbors. Any neighbor's apartment looks like another's; the only difference is what people pay in rent. This allows lower-income residents to live with pride and market rate residents to view the community as comparable to any other market rate complex.

Since everyone will have the same interior finishes, the finishes must be high-quality enough to appeal to and meet the expectation of residents from all targeted income levels but not so high that the development cannot be financed. Apartments should have architectural details, durable fixtures, and full appliance packages (including, whenever possible, in-unit washers, dryers, and dishwashers). Not only does this approach create equity among renters, but the savings to ongoing maintenance are significant. The higher-quality fixtures pay themselves off in lower long-term replacement costs, and providing a full large-appliance package prevents damage to doorways, floors, hallways, and stairwells from resident moves. Higher-quality counter tops and backsplashes look good to market renters and hold up well under constant use by families.

For income mixing to work, high-quality amenities in a mixed-income community must also be available to all residents, regardless of what they pay in rent. To be competitive in the market, apartment complexes are expected to offer community-level amenities such as fitness rooms, business centers, club houses and club rooms, playgrounds, bike repair and storage, pools, amenity decks and dog parks, and more. Not only do such amenities provide essential health and wellness opportunities for all residents, without access for lower-income residents the development simply replicates economic segregation on a micro-neighborhood level. When the amenities are maintained and managed to a high level, residents will not differentiate between neighbors; in fact, they will have opportunities to interact with neighbors around the shared amenities, which hopefully allows them to recognize a common set of values.

4. Community and Resident Involvement and Leadership

In any successful mixed-income effort, community stakeholders must be true partners in the process of designing, building, and sustaining racially diverse, mixed-income communities. These stakeholders include future residents, other residents in the immediate area, neighborhood institutions, schools, businesses, non-profits, churches, politicians, advocates and others. These stakeholders must be actively involved in every stage of development, from the earliest planning through implementation of the plan and during ongoing operations. Ultimately, community members must be invested in the development's success and believe that they will benefit by gaining a better place to live, a better job, a safer neighborhood, more customers, or more opportunities for themselves, their children, and their neighbors. Without participation and communication, however, the community can feel a sense of disengagement and disenfranchisement at any stage in the process.

It is important to note that creating this partnership may take time. The history of many urban neighborhoods is one of broken promises and development projects that have been done *to* communities rather than *in partnership with* communities. Residents and organizations may approach the community engagement process with a great deal of cynicism and distrust, or simply choose

Power of Resident Involvement

A small example of the power of resident involvement can be found in the names of our apartment communities. Many of our community names are not created in a vacuum by a distant marketing team but through workshops with community members and residents who want to leave the mark of their influence in the new development. During one of these workshops in Memphis, the residents of the community started listing all of the famous African-American musicians that got their start in the neighborhood. All of these "legends" came from this area. The ensuing name for the apartment complex, "Legends Park," resonated with the existing stakeholders while appealing to the broader market with no knowledge of the name's origins. The result is a strong connection for all residents to the community and its name.

The Club Room at East Meadows in San Antonio is open for use by all residents.

not to engage at all. A process in which the community is actively engaged, respectfully listened to, and in which promises are kept, can begin to shift that dynamic and help build trust over time.

The fact that a significant percentage of the housing units in mixed-income communities are affordable to people already living in the community is a critical aspect to building this trust. Rather than displacing people in the neighborhood, one of the key goals of mixed-income housing development is to provide opportunities for current residents to live in high-quality, market rate-standard housing.

A method for community engagement must be established early in the development process and be adequately funded and staffed to ensure active participation from a broad cross-section of the community. Key strategies include: being clear and up-front about the goals of the development and financial constraints; respecting the time of participants by keeping the process short and focused; ensuring that the process is open and accessible to all stakeholders in the community (including accommodating for language, age, disabilities, and written and technological literacy levels); varying the engagement types and times (e.g., with large public meetings, smaller focus groups, and/or neighborhood surveys); and, above all, listening to community members to understand their vision and then reflecting that vision in the plan. If community members see their vision realized, they will have a stronger sense of ownership over the development and will support the success of the investment.

MSB keeps the community involved beyond the planning period through regularly scheduled community meetings, newsletters, email blasts, and other events and communications as the project is constructed. These communication strategies keep people updated on progress, underscores that agreements made during planning are being adhered to during implementation, and keeps everyone invested in a successful outcome.

The process of community involvement also builds social networks among residents and helps them develop a sense of community and shared destiny. Leaders emerge, and leadership training occurs, as residents learn critical information about their community's strengths and needs, and actively engage in creating a plan that builds on strengths to address needs. This process builds a community's knowledge and skills and ultimately prepares them to assume responsibility for sustaining the community during operations, with a resident association and regular communication with stakeholders. Property management should view both groups as key advisors who have insight into the market and a strong sense of what is working and what needs improvement.

Public art at Legends Park reflects the area's role in fostering African-American musicians.

5. Wrap-Around Services for Lower-Income Residents

Providing an affordable apartment built to market rate standards helps to significantly stabilize lower-income families. But simply living in a mixed-income community does not transform their lives or push them up the economic ladder. For many low-income families, housing is just one of myriad barriers to success.

Human capital is the term used to refer to an individual's knowledge, skills, and abilities that contribute to economic and social growth. Experience suggests that healthy communities not only provide safe and affordable housing for residents, but also offer a wide range of family-strengthening programs and services that increase human capital. These services include high-quality childcare, healthcare, job training, education, and youth development, among others. We often partner with Urban Strategies, Inc. (USI), a national nonprofit with extensive experience in the design and implementation of human capital building, to develop a plan for providing wrap-around services to lower-income residents.

The human capital development approach is designed to place families on a path toward self-sufficiency and upward mobility. Our comprehensive supportive services program comprises all of the resources that help residents overcome barriers to success, including evidence-based intensive case management and connections to education, job training and placement, physical and mental health services, and enrichment activities for children and youth. These services and programs are provided through strong partnerships with high-quality local providers. The services are offered through a single point of entry (with case management or a liaison) to ensure seamless coordination between families and provider agencies and connection to a full continuum of services.

Providing human capital development and wrap-around services helps to bridge the financial gap between market rate residents and lower-income residents. It ensures that residents who can work have access to jobs, childcare options, and transportation. It helps children join after-school activities and youth find summer employment. It helps residents stay healthier and live longer, and it strengthens the community for all residents.

6. Training Management Teams Explicitly for Mixed-Income Populations

The expectations for property management in a mixed-income community should be the same as in a market rate community. That is to say, the property needs to be maintained to the same high levels as the construction and design. At the same time, property management teams share the same implicit bias as the rest of the population and cannot be assumed to understand how to manage to the needs of lower-income residents in their community. Sometimes the traditional goals of property management (e.g., maximize occupancy while reducing costs) conflict with the goals of a mixed-income complex (e.g., create a community in which all residents can thrive). Property managers also need to understand the complexities of a mixed-income development, recognizing that their "customers" are the residents and the property owners—and also the broader community stakeholders, investors, and government entities.

Property managers need to start with the same high-quality standards that went into the design and construction of the development. While strong design, high-quality finishes, and an involved community will reduce wear and tear on the property, managers must do their part by continually walking the site and inspecting units to ensure ongoing maintenance. Strong management works with residents to establish and maintain high standards for the community— and incorporates a feedback loop for when those expectations are not being

People-Centered Property Management Strategies

High-quality property management was on display by McCormack Baron's property management division during the Covid-19 pandemic. While many other property owners simply notified residents that they were not going to evict them for four months, McCormack Baron Management began working to help residents understand how the crisis had affected them—financially, mentally and physically. As challenges were identified, managers connected residents to resources and service providers. They logged and tracked issues and concerns across the portfolio to identify patterns and share solutions. The results demonstrated deepened understanding of the crisis and of the need for additional legislation, funding, and programming to address post-crisis realities.

met—and works to foster a sense of community for all residents through communications, events, and programs.

Strategies for managing mixed-income communities should acknowledge and address the unique challenges facing lower-income residents. While the goal is to manage to market rate standards, it must be acknowledged that the context within which these developments exist is very different from those of many market rate rental developments and therefore requires a different approach. The property management team must understand the immediate and long-term goals for the property, apart from maximizing returns, and they must see themselves as part of the public-private partnership. Property managers must be able to recognize and address the particular needs of low-income residents, including linking them with needed services and support, acting as a liaison with community institutions such as schools and hospitals, and working to approach each resident and their challenges without racial and economic bias or assumptions.

Because the mixed-income model has many partners investing in its success, the property management team must also serve as a connection to other partners. This includes addressing issues that may arise in the community by working with community partners, with neighboring businesses and institutions, with police and security services, with local elected officials and staff, and with residents of the development.

The goal is to create a true community that incorporates the elements found in any successful neighborhood: a sense of community, safety, stability, and opportunity. Success occurs when residents take ownership of the community and help ensure its long-term sustainability by actively helping to make sure the community is safe, the property and grounds look good, and neighbors are working together to create the kind of community they want.

7. Attention to Resiliency and Sustainability

The growing number of devastating weather events threatens the stability of financially vulnerable populations by destroying older public housing structures, in addition to other impacts. With few financial or emotional resources available to recreate their communities or rebuild their lives, residents disperse as best they can when a major environmental threat occurs. On several public housing sites demolished by extreme weather, MBS has had the opportunity to apply principles of equity and resiliency to the construction of new multi-unit, mixed-income housing. Post-disaster reconstruction has become an opportunity to use new housing designs, financial models, construction practices, and community-building techniques to strengthen the resilience and sustainability of the developments and their residents, in preparation for the storms that will inevitably follow.

We view resilience in structural, financial, and human terms, and we define it as the ability to recover quickly from or adjust to difficulties, adversity, or change. Specifically:

- Structural resilience refers to the components built into physical structures that make them better able to withstand disasters and recover rapidly. This type of resiliency is linked to sustainability, in the sense that structural elements put in place to address sustainable water and energy (e.g., low-flow toilets, reclaimed furnishing materials, LED lighting) help to manage normal operating costs *and* are less likely to fail if the structures that house them are safe from weather-related destruction.

- Financial resilience refers to having sufficient monetary resources for planning, building, management, and repair. A key dimension of financial resilience for mixed-income housing involves having a mixture of public and private investment. Mixed-income housing can even act as a kind of fail-safe protection for residents who fear that repairs will not be made in a timely manner after damaging storms. Simply put, private debt requires repayment, which comes from market rate rents that will only be paid if units are habitable.

Support Resiliency By Being Prepared

Two months after MBS opened Villas on the Strand and Cedars at Carver Park, in Galveston, Texas in late August 2017, Hurricane Harvey barreled up the coastline. A week before the storm hit, the general manager of the two new properties opened her emergency preparation guide and took action. She updated the resident lists, noting which residents would need help in case of evacuation. She created IDs for all staff and residents, in case access onto and around the island was restricted as it had been after Hurricane Ike. And she ordered supplies, including generators, 2-way radios, cases of water, flashlights, batteries, and disposable cameras.

Four days out, a letter was sent to all residents with preparation instructions and emergency phone numbers. Directional signs were posted in hallways to let residents know how to get out, because doors that might be affected by the storm would remain shut. The maintenance team installed shutters over lower-level doors and secured the electrical systems. Residents had the option of moving their cars to elevated off-site garages.

The properties' high-quality construction and well-prepared management gave residents peace of mind, and few chose to evacuate. Even with 30 inches of rain, residents emerged after the storm to find some scattered debris—but no flood damage.

- Human resilience refers to people's ability to bounce back quickly—to personally "weather the storm." Often, the greatest victims of disasters are those who lack resilience—physical, economic, and social—to protect themselves beforehand and to pick up the pieces afterward. Compared to those in higher income groups, people with lower incomes, people with disabilities, and seniors have more difficulty preparing for and evacuating storms, have fewer financial resources to apply toward recovery, and are less capable of negotiating disaster recovery bureaucracy. Beyond the external effects, the impact of trauma and dislocation on lower-income residents, including children, can be more acute. Structural resilience can contribute to human resilience, because it reduces the personal and social costs that occur when residents must flee their homes to escape extreme weather rather than being able to shelter in place. Intentional efforts to build social cohesion through housing equity and inclusion, amenities, and wrap-around services further creates the resilience residents need to move forward after a major disruption rather than continuing to suffer.

MBS's experiences suggest two overarching lessons about building resilience and sustainability into equitable, inclusive mixed-income housing developments.

First, take a long view and prepare for the inevitable. Just as resiliency requires effort and forethought, the devastating human impact of disasters often can be traced to shortsighted planning, failed infrastructure, poor preparation, and uneven responses. For that reason, the Renaissance Square development in Puerto Rico was conceptualized from the beginning as an eco-conscious property combining intelligent, energy-saving design with aesthetics and function. On an island with well-known energy challenges and serving a financially constrained population, Renaissance Square was designed with such features as photovoltaic panels, high-efficiency cooling systems, and environmentally friendly building materials that would reduce energy consumption and save money for tenants.

Importantly for Renaissance Square's physical resilience, the buildings were designed to withstand a direct hit by a Category 4 storm, including hurricane-rated windows, doors, and roofs, and reinforced structural components. The sites also are designed to manage stormwater run-off to reduce the impact of heavy rains. And, like all MBS developments in hurricane-prone locations, a management preparedness plan is in place to address communications, site preparation, and recovery. Renaissance Square's resilience was tested in September 2017 by Hurricanes Irma and Maria. Although the storms damaged or destroyed more than 250,000 homes in Puerto Rico, Renaissance Square—which was nearing completion—suffered no serious damage. The only project delays were the result of interruptions to the island's electrical service and deliveries.

Second, building social cohesion will increase human resilience after extreme weather events, even among economically vulnerable groups. Neighbor-to-neighbor supports are especially important in times of crisis. Thus, mixed-income communities where people are connected are more capable of withstanding external challenges.

CONCLUSION

Cities have a chance to move away from pockets of residential poverty and gentrified urban cores to become places of opportunity for all. New approaches to subsidized affordable housing are working to change the fortunes of poor and low-income residents by focusing on equity and inclusion in a mixed-income environment. This suite of successful strategies can catalyze a vast transformation to our nation's biggest urban trouble spots, including and especially in areas where violent weather events have the capacity to upend lives.

The need is great: More than one in four U.S. households spends 50 percent or more of income on rent.[2] There is a national shortage[3] of 7.4 million homes affordable to the lowest-income families. Deferred maintenance on 100-percent publicly owned housing was estimated by at $26 billion by the U.S Department of Housing and Urban Development (HUD) in its last official report (2010)[4] and was growing by $3.4 billion each year. For every three units added to the overall rental stock between 1995 and 2005, two units have been permanently removed from the inventory. Many of these units built since 2005 targeted the higher end of the market and were unaffordable to people with more modest incomes. The housing boom-and-bust of the years that followed did little to improve the situation.

Today, a look through project submissions to HUD shows that public-private public housing transformation projects in 48 cities await federal support. In limbo is $5.7 billion in housing infrastructure investment, with most funding coming from private sources. Based on estimates by the National Association of Homebuilders, these projects would produce 26,000 tax-paying good wage construction jobs and 23,000 privately maintained, modern, healthy, low-impact apartments and homes for families, seniors, and veterans. Equally important, formerly homeless veterans and others experiencing homelessness would be among those housed.

To get these kinds of results, programs like the Choice Neighborhoods concept must go to scale. Expanding efforts such as these, using the strategies detailed here, would be a strong and cost-effective step toward fulfilling the promise of urban America.

---

2   Joint Center for Housing Studies of Harvard University, Harvard Graduate School of Design, Harvard Kennedy School, *America's Rental Housing 2020*, (Cambridge, MA: Joint Center for Housing Studies of Harvard University, 2020), https://www.jchs.harvard.edu/sites/default/files/Harvard_JCHS_Americas_Rental_Housing_2020.pdf.

3   National Low Income Housing Coalition, The Gap A Shortage of Affordable Homes, (Washington, DC: National Low Income Housing Coalition, 2020), https://reports.nlihc.org/sites/default/files/gap/Gap-Report_2020.pdf

4   Abt Associates Inc., *Capital Needs in the Public Housing Program*, (Cambridge, MA: Abt Associates Inc., 2010), https://www.hud.gov/sites/documents/PH_CAPITAL_NEEDS.PDF.

IMPLICATIONS FOR ACTION

Implications for Policy

- Policymakers should consider extending and expanding HUD funding for the Choice Neighborhood program to meet the demand for mixed-income development throughout the nation.

Implications for Research and Evaluation

- Evaluators should consider the long-term effects of living within a mixed-income community for lower-income households, examining the impacts of supportive services provided to individuals and families. Measures should be tracked for relevant short-and long-term outcomes, such as employment, educational attainment, and health, among others. Incorporating a practice of consistent evaluation will ensure the property is well-serving residents in thriving in the community.

Implications for Development and Investment

- Developers should establish methods for community engagement and communication early in the development process, and staff and fund them adequately to ensure active participation from a broad cross-section of the community. The process should be open and accessible to all stakeholders in the community regardless of language, age, disabilities, and literacy level.
- Developers should listen to community members' vision for the community and use it to create a plan that builds on strengths to address needs and cultivates residents' social networks, leadership capacity, and human capital.
- Developers should build to market rate standards, meaning that all units include the same high-quality furnishings and are interchangeable, and all amenities are available to all tenants regardless of income, while also attending to the particular needs of lower-income households.
- Developers should ensure that current neighborhood residents can afford to live in new, high-quality mixed-income developments rather than displacing people who are already committed to the neighborhood.
- Developers should create a plan for providing wrap-around services to lower-income residents, preferably with a single point of entry, seamless coordination between families and providers, and connections to a full

continuum of services.

- Lenders and investors should consider more flexible requirements so that financing generates opportunities for higher-quality developments that include a mix of financing sources.

- Developers should use post-disaster reconstruction as an opportunity to apply new housing designs, financial models, construction practices, and community-building techniques to strengthen the resilience and sustainability of mixed-income developments and their residents.

Implications for Residents and Community Members

- Residents and community members should actively participate in every stage of project development, from planning through implementation and during ongoing operations.

- Residents and community members can share responsibilities for creating and adhering to high standards for a caring, supportive community.

■ ■ ■

CADY SEABAUGH *is a Vice President at McCormack Baron Salazar, overseeing special projects, new initiatives and strategic opportunities. She has played a key role in the firm's Choice Neighborhood efforts, developing strategies and approaches to transform disinvested public and assisted housing sites into holistic, stable and resilient communities for families and residents of all economic backgrounds.*

■ ■ ■

VINCENT R. BENNETT *is President of McCormack Baron Salazar, a national leader in the development of mixed-income communities. In the past 40 years, MBS has developed over 22,000 rental and for-sale homes in 47 cities with total development costs over $4 billion. The company is directed by its mission to transform places into communities where all people can thrive.*

WHAT WORKS FOR BUILDING AND SUSTAINING MIXED-INCOME COMMUNITIES: A PERSPECTIVE FROM THE DEVELOPMENT COMMUNITY

Vicki Davis
Urban Atlantic

Daryl Carter
Avanath Capital Management, LLC

Rosemarie Hepner
Urban Land Institute Terwilliger Center for Housing

Mixed-income housing has become an important tool for expanding housing supply in both high-opportunity and emerging neighborhoods. Housing that accommodates a range of incomes in one community can have enormous benefits for individuals and families, including social and economic mobility. For developers, building mixed-income communities is a worthy goal but one that raises obstacles as they seek to satisfy the different and sometimes competing needs of various stakeholders, including investors, local government leaders, and residents.

Investors expect developers to meet certain financial benchmarks to guarantee a return on funding. Local governments rely on developers to fulfill their planning goals and meet community needs, including the provision of more housing and retail options. Residents can demand that developers meet a vision they have for their neighborhood, but they are not always aligned around a unified vision. Furthermore, residents often push back on projects that include below market-rate housing. Consequently, proposals for mixed-income and affordable housing tend to spend an inordinate amount of time in the approval and permitting process, and sometimes projects are completely derailed by neighborhood opposition. These competing interests, compounded by other development and financing challenges, discourage some developers from pursuing mixed-income development.

Despite the obstacles, we urge more of our development colleagues to take up the mission of creating and sustaining mixed-income communities. The benefits are significant for residents and communities, for promoting the mission of purposeful developers, and for bringing development companies financial success. In this essay, we encourage developers, residents, and public actors to work together to create housing that meets the needs of individuals and families at all income levels. We suggest a way forward by sharing lessons from our decades in the development industry.

WHO WE ARE

The authors of this essay include two real estate professionals with extensive experience building affordable and mixed-income communities. Together, we have more than 50 years in the residential real estate field, and our development companies have built or preserved thousands of homes, primarily in medium- or high-density multifamily projects.

Vicki Davis is managing partner of Urban Atlantic Development, a company based on the East Coast that has its roots in building subsidized, affordable rental housing but which, over time, has focused largely on mixed-income and mixed-use new construction and redevelopment projects. Urban Atlantic focuses on creating investments that benefit people, serve local economies, and support a healthy environment. The development company first became involved in mixed-income housing in 1995 through the U.S. Department of Housing and Urban Development (HUD)'s now-defunct HOPE VI program, which redeveloped severely distressed public housing sites. Over the past 20 years, Urban Atlantic and its affiliates have developed, financed, and preserved more than 9,000 housing units, 700,000 square feet of commercial and retail space, and 700 acres of land in urban areas in 10 states, with over $2.4 billion in development projects plus $2 billion in third-party investment projects.

Daryl Carter is founder, chairman, and CEO of Avanath Capital Management, a Southern California-based investment firm managing real estate and real estate-related investments. Avanath's focus is on acquiring Low-Income Housing Tax Credit (LIHTC), Section 8, and other affordable properties with the goal of investing in them and maintaining them as affordable or mixed-income housing. Over the past two years, Avanath has acquired over $300 million in affordable apartment communities nationwide.

Vicki and Daryl also serve on the National Advisory Board of the Urban Land Institute (ULI)'s Terwilliger Center for Housing, and the third author of this essay, Rosemarie Hepner, serves on the Center's staff. Established in 2007 with a gift from longtime member and former ULI chairman J. Ronald Terwilliger, the Center integrates ULI's wide-ranging housing activities into a program of work with three objectives: to catalyze the production of housing, provide thought leadership on the housing industry, and inspire a broader commitment to housing. The Terwilliger Center for Housing seeks to advance best practices in residential development and public policy and to support ULI members and local communities in creating and sustaining a full spectrum of housing opportunities, particularly for lower- and moderate-income households.

WHY WE SUPPORT AND BUILD MIXED-INCOME COMMUNITIES

Our own upbringings provided the foundation for our commitment to creating mixed-income communities that support individual, family, and community well-being. When Daryl was growing up, he saw firsthand how important an economically diverse, predominately Black neighborhood was to families like his. Daryl's father worked at General Motors' Clark Street Assembly plant in Detroit, which was close to their home. Like many others who worked at the plant, he picked Daryl up from school on his walk home from work every day. The neighborhood had no crime or gang problems, and families from all different backgrounds—from autoworkers to doctors—lived side by side. But in the 1980s, when the plant moved 25 miles away to Warren, Michigan, the neighborhood changed—and not for the better. Many families moved away, and for those who stayed, the longer commute prevented fathers from being available after school.

Avanath's portfolio reflects Daryl's understanding of how important mixed-income communities are for the people who live in them, especially children. By bringing new sources of funding and new partners to communities, we dispel misconceptions about the risks of investing in underserved neighborhoods and places where people of color constitute the majority of the population. When building and rehabilitating housing, we seek to bring institutional capital to underserved areas to support families in those neighborhoods. And in more established, higher-income neighborhoods, our projects seek to expand access to those areas of opportunities for lower-income individuals and families.

Research supports this approach to equity and inclusion, demonstrating that opportunities for economic stability and upward mobility are greater when low-income families live in economically integrated neighborhoods.[1] Building mixed-income projects in higher-income markets close to good schools and connected to transportation, services, and amenities improves overall health and well-being and positively affects children's educational attainment.[2,3] Further, increasing affordable housing options in urban cores can reduce car dependency, as those households have better access to public transit.[4] This can alleviate traffic constraints, reduce costs for infrastructure repairs, and improve air quality.[5,6]

HOW WE BUILD AND SUSTAIN MIXED-INCOME COMMUNITIES: KEY STRATEGIES

Our companies' missions, along with the right partners, the right opportunities, and a lot of grit, have made it possible to provide targeted affordable housing in even the most expensive markets. We share here some strategies that have

---

1 Pamela M. Blumenthal and John R. McGinty, *Housing Policy Levers to Promote Economic Mobility*, (Washington, DC: Urban Institute, 2015), https://www.urban.org/sites/default/files/publication/71496/2000428-housing-policy-levers-to-promote-economic-mobility_0.pdf

2 Ingrid Gould Ellen and Keren Horn, *Housing and Educational Opportunity: Characteristics of Local Schools near Families with Federal Housing Assistance* (Washington, DC: Poverty & Race Research Action Council, 2018), https://files.eric.ed.gov/fulltext/ED593784.pdf.

3 Nabihah Maqbool, Janet Viveiros, and Mindy Ault, *The Impacts of Affordable Housing on Health: A Research Summary* (Washington, DC: National Housing Conference, 2015), https://www.nhc.org/wp-content/uploads/2017/03/The-Impacts-of-Affordable-Housing-on-Health-A-Research-Summary.pdf.

4 Susan Desantis, Thomas B. Cook, and Rolf Pendall, "Myths & Facts about Affordable & High Density Housing" (Sacramento, CA: California Department of Housing & Community Development, 2002), https://www.losgatosca.gov/DocumentCenter/View/2716/Myths--Facts-about-Afford--Hi-Density-Housing

5 Amanda Howell, Kristina M. Currans, Gregory Norton & Kelly J. Clifton, "Transportation impacts of affordable housing: Informing development review with travel behavior analysis," *Journal of Transport and Land Use* 11, no. 1 (2018): 103.

6 William Fulton, "A Low-Cost Solution to Traffic," Governing, February 2017, https://www.governing.com/columns/urban-notebook/gov-traffic-housing-sun-belt.html.

facilitated successful mixed-income housing in our properties, including developing the right mix of affordable to market-rate units, overcoming financing barriers, creating and sustaining a community, building stakeholder support, and working with local and state regulations. For each, we identify some useful tools as well as some pain points and areas for improvement.

Developing the Right Mix

The ratio of affordable to market-rate units is important, because market-rate rents often are needed to cross-subsidize the rents of the affordable units to make projects financially feasible. Finding the right mix also enables residents with diverse incomes—whether earning 15 percent of area median income (AMI) or affording million-dollar townhouses—to live side by side and benefit from new investment in the neighborhood. But the "right" ratio depends entirely on the market, which can vary from site to site. In harder-to-serve markets, the mix could tilt more toward units that lower-income households can afford. At some Avanath properties, half the units are affordable to households with incomes between 40 and 60 percent of AMI, and half are for households with incomes between 80 and 100 percent of AMI. However, in other markets where the AMI ranges are not as broad, the difference in rents charged do not vary widely.

Urban Atlantic's mixed-income projects tend to have an 80/20 split: 80 percent of the units are market rate, while 20 percent are affordable to lower-income households, typically with incomes at or below 60 percent of AMI. This mix of incomes has been effective in creating stable, integrated communities, particularly in markets where there is a strong and growing demand for market-rate housing. An example is Urban Atlantic's redevelopment of the former Walter Reed Army Medical Center in Washington, DC, carried

Figure 1: What Worked Here: The Parks at Walter Reed

Urban Atlantic can include low-income housing in new developments in a high-cost market like Washington, DC through financial and extensive programmatic support from the local government. For the Water Reed site, the Washington, DC government assisted the development through gap financing from the city's Housing Production Trust Fund, and assistance during the development process. Further, the city facilitated partnerships with public and nonprofit service providers, which enables the development to meet the needs of the lowest-income households. These services connect residents with job opportunities, medical assistance, healthy activities, and food options.

out in collaboration with the Hines real estate investment firm and Triden Development Group. The Parks at Walter Reed is a $1 billion, 66-acre mixed-income and mixed-use project that will create 2,100 new homes. The firm has committed to setting aside 20 percent (432 homes) to be affordable at different income targets; 139 are for households at or below 30 percent of AMI, 179 are for those with incomes at 50 percent of AMI, and 114 are for households with incomes up to 80 percent of AMI. Urban Atlantic offered this affordability structure as a part of the competition for the site, and the 20 percent commitment was then codified in its zoning. The affordable and market-rate units are scattered throughout the development to create a truly mixed-income community, with the exception of the extremely low-income tenants—those at or below 30 percent of AMI—many of whom are formerly homeless individuals. The 30 percent of AMI and below homes are clustered together because very low-income residents will receive support services.

Overcoming Financing Barriers

Finance plays a big role in building mixed-income communities, but the variety of debt and equity sources needed—and the related requirements and administration—make financing mixed-income projects particularly challenging. It is also challenging to finance mixed-income properties in communities that have faced decades of disinvestment. These neighborhoods are often communities of color. Indeed, race is frequently the unspoken reason for pushback from investors who refer to "neighborhood safety" or "residential turnover" as reasons to avoid investments in those communities. But when we build mixed-income projects in "tough" neighborhoods—places that are disconnected from jobs, where there are high crime rates, high vacancy rates, poor-quality schools, and few services and amenities—we are looking for opportunities to close the economic and opportunity gap that persists between Whites and people of color. We want our projects to be part of the solution in promoting racial equity and righting the wrongs from past development practices, and we know that several developers, investors, and banks have been investing in emerging communities for decades with tremendous success and less risk than may be perceived.

Key drivers of cost in the development of mixed-income communities include:
- *Land costs,* which vary significantly according to location and market type. In high-cost markets, land can account for up to 35 percent of total

development costs.[7] Sometimes, when affordable housing is mandated as part of a mixed-use development, the developer can acquire the land at a reduced cost. Often, however, developers of affordable or mixed-income projects compete for sites at a disadvantage with market-rate developers.

- *Labor and materials costs.* The cost of materials associated with building mixed-income communities is on par with the costs for market-rate buildings, because the quality and amenities offered must attract the market-rate residents. Labor costs are an increasingly important cost driver as the industry continues to face a shortage of construction laborers. Like land costs, the cost of labor is highly market-specific. In addition, the sources of project financing can affect labor costs. Requirements such as the Davis-Bacon Act, which established federal prevailing wage rules that guide most regulation of wages and benefits for people working on publicly funded projects—including housing projects funded with federal housing assistance—theoretically can increase labor costs in a mixed-income property above those in a market-rate property. An unintended consequence of these regulations has been a tendency for developers to produce income-segregated housing because it is easier to develop financially.

- *Costs associated with entitlement and permitting.* The process for entitling land and securing necessary approvals and permits can be lengthy. Most jurisdictions impose several requirements, with compliance reviewed and approved as part of a public process. When changes are needed to comply with zoning or subdivision guidelines, the process can become even more complex. The costs associated with entitlement and permitting have been identified as a key reason for rising housing costs.[8]

Because the costs are high, developers require multiple financing sources to make mixed-income communities "pencil out." Typical sources include LIHTCs for the affordable housing, and low-cost loans, grants, and other public and private money to cover the affordable and market-rate housing, along with any commercial components. Unfortunately, these financing sources do not

---

7   Robert Hickey and Lisa Sturtevant, *Public Land & Affordable Housing in the Washington, D.C., Region: Best Practices and Recommendations* (Washington, DC: Urban Land Institute and National Housing Conference, 2015), https://ulidigitalmarketing.blob.core.windows.net/ulidcnc/2019/03/ULI_PublicLandReport_Final020615.pdf.

8   "Housing Development Toolkit," The White House, accessed September 10, 2019. https://www.whitehouse.gov/sites/whitehouse.gov/files/images/Housing_Development_Toolkit%20f.2.pdf, (2016).

Figure 2: What Worked Here: Raising Capital

Low vacancy and turnover rates are readily available data points that can change minds, build support, and raise capital. Avanath uses these data to persuade institutional investors that our properties perform better than conventional multifamily buildings. For instance, delinquency rates for our Section 8 residents are lower than for other residents because most voucher holders wait 5 to 10 years to obtain their voucher and therefore are not inclined to risk losing it by not paying rent on time. We also refer our low-income residents to partnering banks, such as Wells Fargo, which will help them set up an account. By joining the formal banking system, residents reduce their credit risk and no longer have to pay check-cashing fees, which puts more money in their pockets.

mix well. In fact, 100 percent affordable deals are much easier to finance than mixed-income (and mixed-use) projects. For example, for a straightforward affordable housing project, Urban Atlantic may bring together equity from the LIHTC program along with land equity and gap financing from a local jurisdiction. In contrast, a mixed-income project marries conventional financing with affordable financing, for which the requirements and risk tolerances often do not align.

The ability to assemble the necessary financing for these types of projects depends on the structure of the project. To attract both affordable and market-rate lenders and investors, the risks and rewards must be legally separated from each other, even when the physical properties are in the same building. Developers must reconcile what happens if the affordable housing fails and goes into foreclosure and how the market-rate units will be affected—and vice versa. To separate the real estate collateral so that affordable and market-rate risks can be made independent of each other, developers of mixed-income projects end up having to "condominium-ize" the property—establishing different owners for the affordable and market-rate units. In Urban Atlantic's mixed-income properties, the units are operated and leased out of the same facility but financed separately. (Common areas have common use agreements.) The arrangement is tedious but allows investors with different profit and risk motivations to work together while keeping the business terms separate.

For Avanath's acquisition and rehabilitation projects, about 55 to 60 percent of the project costs are leveraged, while the rest is equity from Avanath's investment fund. The fund's sources include insurance companies, banks, foundations, and venture funds. Because these projects do not need LIHTC financing, they do not have to adhere to the same regulatory or other requirements associated with tax credit deals. Instead, Avanath must demonstrate the performance of its properties to build the institutional support critical for raising capital.

The challenge here is that some people do not embrace the value of investing in mixed-income housing and see only risks and no upside. In particular, private investors historically have hesitated to invest in communities of color, believing stereotypically that rents would not be paid on time and the performance of properties would not be strong. The subsequent lack of investment in many minority neighborhoods has reinforced racial and economic segregation. Avanath's experience, however, is that the risks associated with our mixed-income properties are significantly lower than those for other multifamily investments. Typical delinquency rates among multifamily residential properties are between 60 and 100 basis points, while Avanath's mixed-income properties post delinquency rates of about 35 basis points. In addition, vacancy and turnover rates are very low in our properties. For example, across five properties in Orlando, Florida, we currently have three vacancies, and in Naples, Florida, we have one vacancy in a 200-unit property, with a waiting list of more than 100 people. When we demonstrate the critical unmet need for housing at the rent levels we are providing—and the positive income flow associated with low vacancy and turnover rates—we build confidence in our properties and attract institutional investors to finance them.

Creating and Sustaining a Community

Because we are committed to having a positive impact on families and

Figure 3: A Note on Opportunity Zones

Opportunity Zones will play a pivotal role in both Avanath and Urban Atlantic's efforts to create mixed-income communities.

Urban Atlantic has deployed $100 million in Opportunity Zone developments in multiple locations and has over $1.5 billion of additional Opportunity Zone development opportunities in its pipeline. Examining development in these zones before and after the financing, Urban Atlantic has found that the Opportunity Zones drew more investors and helped leverage new debt and state funding resources, thereby increasing the feasibility and pace of investment.

Thirteen of Avanath's properties are in designated Opportunity Zones, five of which have redevelopment potential. These are all affordable or workforce communities with the potential to help reinvestment in areas where capital is needed.

communities through the projects we build and manage, after we secure financing for a property we strategize about how to establish and sustain the elements of an equitable, inclusive, high-opportunity community.

A hallmark of our community-building approach is for developers to take a very positive, customer service-oriented stance. We listen to residents' needs, and we have a line item in the property's operating budget so we can respond accordingly, usually by partnering with a local nonprofit to provide services to residents on site. In 2014, for example, after purchasing the Northpointe Apartments in Long Beach, California,—a property with high turnover rates and rent delinquencies, located in a high-crime neighborhood—Avanath held forums so that residents could share their concerns directly with developers, elected leaders, and public safety officials. We learned that Northpointe, which had 528 Section 8 units, and the neighboring Seaport Apartments, with 400 market-rate units, together were home to more than 2,000 children. So, after acquiring Northpointe, Avanath invested heavily in renovations and partnerships to provide recreational, mentoring, and other activities for children. A basketball court was installed on vacant space in the center of the property; a nonprofit organization affiliated with a local AME church agreed to provide a range of services to Northpointe's predominantly Latinx and Black families; and an after-school program now serves nearly 1,000 children living at the property. These programs and activities, which residents requested, have proven crucial for improving residents' safety and sense of community.

With encouragement from Long Beach's mayor, Avanath then purchased and renovated the Seaport Apartments, offering rents affordable at 80 to 100 percent of AMI. Owning nearly 1,000 units between the two properties enabled Avanath to make a significant impact on the surrounding neighborhood. Today, Seaport is 99 percent occupied, and there is a waiting list for apartments at Northpointe. The neighborhood also has been designated an Opportunity Zone, which should facilitate even more investment.

As the Northpointe example illustrates, another key strategy for building and sustaining community is to provide facilities and amenities that make mixed-income communities appealing and supportive to residents. At family-oriented developments, for example, Urban Atlantic builds a playground and a classroom at the community center. We then arrange the provision of services tailored to residents' needs, which we leverage through third-party grants, partnerships with service providers, and in-kind contributions. In very low-income communities, we build spaces, such as offices and community rooms, that enable local service providers (e.g., food programs) to come to us.

Avanath spends a lot of time considering which programs or amenities will enhance the community *and* reflect positively on our budgets. For an Austin, Texas, property, upgrading our fitness room and pool reduced turnover; for an age-restricted property in another location, we partnered with health organizations to offer an onsite clinic and health programs to keep residents healthy; and for properties with families, we provide after-school programs. Avanath has found that working closely with local housing authorities—in addition to soliciting resident input—helps us understand the community's needs. While some housing authorities are more robust and sophisticated than others, all are invaluable in helping us figure out which programs will be popular, how to implement them, and how they can be reimbursed through local subsidies or tax credits.

Sometimes these programs do not work out. One of our mentoring programs with NFL retirees found mixed success, but we continue to try different things. Sometimes we just need to provide space to a nonprofit service provider, and other times we make a more substantial contribution. There is no template or method for assigning a line item in our budget for these amenities, and while this individualized approach is time consuming and expensive, we have found it does save us money elsewhere in our budgets, whether it comes from resident tenancy or property upkeep.

One important but challenging element of creating and sustaining a mixed-income community is retail. The presence of retail is fundamental to attracting market-rate residents to the community, but it is often very difficult to attract retailers to lower-income, emerging submarkets. A 2011 Urban Atlantic project

Figure 4: What Worked Here: Northpointe and Seaport Apartments

When we build multifamily mixed-income projects, the "how" involves not only the bricks and concrete, but also the amenities and services that build community. For these apartments, after-school care was particularly successful. Offering activities such as dance, art, sports, or drama gives parents working long hours the peace of mind that their children are being entertained and properly cared for after school. There are many other upsides when we provide these services. These programs reduce resident turnover and maintenance requests, which helps Avanath's bottom line. When neighbors get to know one another, there is a better sense of community and respect for the space.

in Washington, D.C.'s Brentwood neighborhood underscored this challenge. Rhode Island Row is a 274-unit, mixed-income, mixed-use development with 70,000 square feet of ground-floor retail space adjacent to the Brentwood Metrorail station. The development involved a partnership between Urban Atlantic and A&R Development Corporation, along with the Washington Metropolitan Area Transit Authority (WMATA), which owned the land. Setting aside 20 percent of the units for very low-income households was critical to gaining community support for the project. At the time, however, the Brentwood neighborhood was an untested market, and the lack of potential customers posed too high a risk for many retailers. Furthermore, it was very important to the community and the developer that the retail be authentic and relevant to the households living at Rhode Island Row.

To address these concerns, developers set aside 55 units for households with incomes at 50 percent of AMI, and the retail effort targeted locally owned businesses. Urban Atlantic used a Department of Motor Vehicles (DMV) office as an anchor, and New Market Tax Credits equity supported the retail spaces. Seven years after the project was completed, the retail space at Rhode Island Row now is more than 85 percent leased, with a wide variety of food offerings, including a restaurant for after-church meals on Sundays, a drugstore, and the DMV office. More than 10 percent of the space goes to local retailers, at favorable rates.

Retail also is a challenge when building mixed-income communities in high-income, opportunity-rich neighborhoods. In these places, it can be easier financially to incorporate affordable housing into the development through cross-subsidies from the market-rate rents. However, it is more difficult to ensure that the retail businesses serve households in the affordable units as well as in the market-rate ones. One solution is to attract a grocery store to the development, to ensure that all residents have access to and can afford the food and other goods they need. Although Avanath does not build retail or mixed-use developments, we have found that lower-income residents rely more on technology for retail services than do higher-income residents. Therefore, we have looked for ways to use new technologies to bring food goods or services to residents of our properties. For example, we secured a reduced rate for online food delivery services such as Blue Apron, which increased residents' access to healthy food options. And, at an upcoming property near Seattle, Washington, The Lodge at Peasley Canyon, Avanath has installed Amazon cold storage lockers, which makes it easier for residents to order goods—including groceries—and have them delivered right to their homes.

Building Stakeholder Support

New or rehabilitated mixed-income residential projects can dramatically transform neighborhoods and attract new investments where they have long been absent. For such transformative projects to succeed, developers must have buy-in from many different stakeholders. But many proposed multifamily developments face neighborhood opposition over fears of increased traffic, over-burdened local infrastructure and schools, and loss of the neighborhood's character. Building support among residents is often a major challenge, as upper-income residents have concerns about bringing low-income people into their neighborhoods and lower-income residents of emerging neighborhoods worry about gentrification and displacement. All of these concerns can stall development projects. In fact, research suggests that properties serving low-income households face more intense opposition and prolonged delays than other properties.[9] It is common for developers to spend considerable time and money working to address neighborhood concerns through extensive community meetings and by making substantial physical changes to their proposed developments.

For this reason, proactive and transparent communication with community members is essential to the development process. While securing approval for Urban Atlantic's Walter Reed project, for example, the local redevelopment agency convened a community advisory commission, appointed by the mayor and including diverse community leaders and stakeholders, which met at least six times per year. This commission took an active role in receiving feedback and providing official recommendations. Urban Atlantic found this method tremendously helpful in creating open, continuous communication with the community.

It is important to include all community stakeholders in the decision-making process. This cannot be accomplished solely through community meetings, because residents who are working, providing child care, or physically incapacitated will not be able to attend. Surveys, neighborhood events,

---

9   Corianne Scally, "Who, Why, and How Communities Oppose Affordable Housing," *Shelterforce* (blog), April 23, 2014, https://shelterforce.org/2014/04/23/who_why_and_how_communities_oppose_affordable_housing/.

Figure 5: What Worked Here: Stakeholder Support

In Urban Atlantic's projects in Washington, DC, outreach to the local Advisory Neighborhood Commissions (ANCs) has been crucial because City Council members give considerable weight to their opinions about projects. Urban Atlantic uses several communication and outreach strategies to reach ANC members and other residents, including a detailed website through which people can provide feedback online and learn about in-person feedback opportunities.

For Avanath's projects, the local housing authority is an important partner. It guides the developer's outreach and works out the economic details for the programs and amenities incorporated into the properties.

---

online outreach, focus groups, websites, on-site physical message boards, and one-on-one outreach can supplement community meetings and should be made available at various times during the day and in multiple languages to accommodate non-English-speaking community members. Special attention should be given to the needs of residents with disabilities, senior citizens, and impaired residents because they often are most vulnerable to displacement.

A growing number of public policies and tools also exist to build stakeholder support and offset negative responses to plans for affordable and mixed-income housing development. Massachusetts and Connecticut both offer incentives for municipalities to build more affordable housing, for instance. Connecticut offers technical and financial assistance to municipalities to cover feasibility studies, infrastructure improvements, engineering costs, and other costs. Massachusetts even has financial incentives specifically for schools if the additional housing will bring more students into the public school system. When those approaches fail to quell opposition, state laws like Massachusetts's Comprehensive Permit Act (Chapter 40B) have been established to overturn a local zoning authority's rejection of a development that would include affordable units.

Working within Local and State Regulations

We cannot overstate how much impact regulations, particularly zoning, have on what gets built and where. Local communities specify the allowable types and densities of development and the requirements related to lot coverage, setbacks, and open space. The local zoning ordinance may also include specific site or design requirements to which projects must adhere. For these reasons, local zoning requirements are key drivers of the cost of developing housing. It has been estimated that local and state regulations account for up to 30 percent of the cost of developing multifamily housing.[10]

Local zoning requirements can assist developers of mixed-income housing developments by requiring that a specified proportion of new homes be affordable. On the other hand, local and state regulations can also create roadblocks for the development of mixed-income and mixed-use projects. In many municipalities, zoning regulations expressly *prohibit* the mixing of uses on a single parcel. To build a single-use project (i.e., all residential), there might be a relatively straightforward "by-right" development process. But to build a mixed-use project, a separate process exists that involves requesting rezoning, which often includes a mandate for public input. Going through the rezoning process adds time and, ultimately, cost to the project and sometimes makes it infeasible to build at all.

Parking requirements can be especially costly for multifamily housing construction. The costs associated with providing parking vary by market, but they can be as much as $50,000 per space underground and $25,000 per space above ground.[11] These costs, which add to the difficulty of delivering affordable housing, are often based on outdated zoning ordinances that do not take into account changes in public transit access, car ownership, or ride sharing patterns.[12] In many urban markets, actual parking use—especially near public transit stations that serve affordable households—is almost zero, and it may not need to be subsidized in addition to the direct housing subsidy. Some states and communities have acted to revise and lower parking requirements for developments located near public transit; California, for example, did so through state law. Several zones in Washington, DC, may also serve as templates for future urban development because they have no parking minimums, and parking is left to the discretion of the developer.

Aside from zoning and land use requirements, special regulations apply to affordable housing that receives public funds. As noted earlier, prevailing

---

10 Paul Emrath and Caitlin Walter, *Regulation: Over 30 Percent of the Cost of a Multifamily Development* (Washington, DC: National Association of Home Builders and National Multifamily Housing Council, 2018), http://www.nahbclassic.org/generic.aspx?genericContentID=262391.

11 Peter Albert, Tom Jones, Gabriel Metcalf, and Chad Thompson, "Reducing Housing Costs by Rethinking Parking Requirements," in *Housing Strategy for San Francisco*, (San Francisco, CA: SPUR, 2006).

12 Donald Shoup, "Cutting the Costs of Parking Requirements," *ACCESS*, Spring 2016, www.accessmagazine.org/spring-2016/cutting-the-cost-of-parking-requirements/.

Figure 6: What Worked Here: Regulatory Reform

Minnesota conducted an ideas competition in 2014 that focused on the need to lower the cost of affordable housing. The winning proposal, by the University of Minnesota's Center for Urban and Regional Affairs, identified several administrative and regulatory changes that would improve efficiency and lower costs. One involved an outdated building code provision mandating that affordable units have a separate dining room. This has now been modified so it no longer applies to smaller units, saving on space and costs. Similarly, the winning proposal also helped establish MinnDocs, a uniform set of loan documents to streamline approval processes, saving time and costs.

---

wage laws are one example. State prevailing wage laws can apply to an entire building, even if it includes market-rate units and commercial space. Research has indicated this can add anywhere from 10 to 25 percent to construction costs.[13,14] Projects that are 100 percent market rate, and therefore not reliant on public funding, are not subject to such requirements, which can make them less expensive to deliver.

In addition, these properties have compliance considerations that include paperwork to certify residents' incomes and administration of lotteries for the affordable units. Lotteries require developers to sift through thousands of applicants to fill just a handful of income-restricted units. The bureaucracy and administration that comes with providing affordable housing is sometimes too onerous for market-rate developers to take on, so they avoid these projects altogether.

IMPLICATIONS FOR ACTION

Developers who build residential and mixed-use projects are on the front line of building homes that support individual and family well-being and form the bedrock for thriving neighborhoods. In a society that faces persistent racial and economic segregation, we are striving to build inclusive, equitable communities that promote opportunity for all. In this essay we outlined what has worked for us, and we hope these strategies can be replicated by others pursuing mixed-

---

[13] Jeff Leieritz, "Prevailing Wage's Impact on Affordable Housing," *Associated Builders and Contractors Newsline*, February 17, 2016, https://www.abc.org/News-Media/Newsline/entryid/4976/prevailing-wage-s-impact-on-affordable-housing.

[14] Meyer Memorial Trust Cost Effectiveness Work Group, *The Cost of Affordable Housing Development in Oregon*, (Portland, OR: Meyer Memorial Trust, 2015), https://www.oregon.gov/lcd/UP/Documents/Cost_of_AffordableHousingDev_Oregon.pdf.

income housing and mixed-use developments. We have also identified parts of the process that are frustrating, outdated, overly cumbersome, and costly. Our final thoughts and recommendations follow. Each element mentioned can be improved upon with modernization, more research, targeted advocacy, and a stronger commitment by developers and other stakeholders who wish to see more inclusion and equity in our communities.

Implications for Policy

- Local governments should modernize local land use and zoning policies to prioritize policies that facilitate mixed-income housing and mixed-use development. Where outdated regulations exist, developers, advocates, and public leaders should pursue reform by replicating good policies that exist elsewhere.

- Local governments should streamline development review and approval processes to save time and costs. While it is important to ensure that public money for affordable housing is used responsibly and that below-market-rate housing is occupied by the families for which it is intended, making the process, technology, and systems more efficient would encourage more developers to build mixed-income projects.

- Policy makers should use local funding and density bonuses to provide the gap financing that makes mixed-income developments feasible.

- In places where good policies are producing success, leaders should take an active role in sharing information and insights with policy makers in other locations.

- Local governments and community leaders should enact protections for existing residents to ensure they can remain in neighborhoods that undergo dramatic changes.

Implications for Research and Evaluation

- All stakeholders should take a greater role in sharing research findings on the positive impacts from mixed-income communities.

- More research and evaluation is needed to cultivate support from investors and community members. This includes more evaluations of health, educational, and economic well-being outcomes associated with living in mixed-income communities and more research on the turnover rates, timeliness of rent payments, operational considerations, and financial performance of mixed-income properties.

Implications for Development and Investment

- To demonstrate the value of investing in emerging, low-income communities and to support necessary research on the impact of mixed-income community projects, developers should be transparent about their operations and make data available to investors and researchers.

- In places where good strategies are producing success, developers should take an active role in sharing information and insights with stakeholders in other locations.

- Developers and mixed-income property owners should look for simple, low-cost ways in which technology can be used to enhance resident life (e.g., by making retail options available or by enabling residents to communicate maintenance problems and other requests).

- The investment industry should modernize and simplify the capital stacks to encourage financing of mixed-income community development.

Implications for Residents and Community Members

- Residents and community members who live in mixed-income communities can share their stories and advocate to public policy makers about the many benefits of an integrated society.

- Community members should prioritize educating residents on what "affordable" housing really means and who it serves. Residents may be surprised by the types of jobs and incomes that struggle to afford housing in their communities.

- Residents and community members should better understand how the location of housing intersects with everyday concerns, like traffic, to societal benefits like educational attainment, and health and well-being. Once we learn the positive impact that comes from having attainable housing in close proximity to jobs, schools, and community amenities, as Daryl experienced growing up, we can appreciate the value of offering housing at different income levels.

■ ■ ■

VICKI DAVIS is responsible for managing the acquisition, planning, design, and implementation of all Urban Atlantic projects, and asset management of properties that the company owns and its Mid-City Community CDE investment portfolio. With over 30 years of experience in real estate development, she formerly served as Deputy Director of the Maryland Housing Fund at Maryland DHCD. Her experience also includes portfolio management for MNC Financial-South Charles Realty and multifamily development for Trammell Crow Residential. Ms. Davis holds a MBA in Finance from American University, an MS in Engineering & Construction Management from University of Texas, and a BS in Civil Engineering from the University of Maryland.

■ ■ ■

DARYL J. CARTER is the Founder, Chairman and CEO of Avanath Capital Management, LLC, a California-based investment firm that acquires, renovates, and operates apartment properties, with an emphasis on affordable and workforce communities. Mr. Carter directs the overall strategy and operations of the Company. Mr. Carter has 39 years of experience in the commercial real estate industry. Previously, he was an Executive Managing Director of Centerline Capital Group. Mr. Carter became part of the Centerline team when his company, Capri Capital Finance, was acquired by Centerline in 2005. Mr. Carter co-founded and served as Co-Chairman of the Capri Capital family of companies. Prior to Capri, Mr. Carter was Regional Vice President at Westinghouse Credit Corporation and a Second Vice President at Continental Bank. Mr. Carter holds a Master's in Architecture and a Master's in Business Administration, both from the Massachusetts Institute of Technology. He received a Bachelor of Science degree in Architecture from the University of Michigan.

■ ■ ■

ROSEMARIE HEPNER serves as Director of the ULI Terwilliger Center for Housing. For the Center, Ms. Hepner manages the housing awards program, supports the Housing Opportunity Conference, assists with research and publications, and collaborates with ULI's other departments and District Councils on projects. Before joining ULI in 2017, she worked for two international development nonprofits, most recently as the International Capital Markets Specialist at Habitat for Humanity International. In that role, Ms. Hepner supported the operations for the MicroBuild Fund (Habitat's housing microfinance fund), and managed the State of Housing Microfinance survey reports. Ms. Hepner holds a Master's in City and Regional Planning from The Catholic University of America's School of Architecture and Planning, where her research focused on low-income housing practices and design. Her thesis examined housing reconstruction in informal settlements post-disaster. Ms. Hepner also holds a B.A. from The George Washington University's Elliott School of International Affairs.

A CALL FOR PROPERTY MANAGEMENT TRANSFORMATION TO MEET THE CHALLENGES OF MIXED-INCOME COMMUNITIES

Frankie Blackburn and Bill Traynor
Trusted Space Partners

As long-time affordable housing developers and community builders, we believe in the ideal of mixed-income communities. We have experienced genuine success in our work within communities, as well as authentic moments of personal growth and fun in our personal lives by living side by side with diverse neighbors. We have observed people from very different backgrounds getting to know each other in new ways by exchanging small favors of value, and we have watched a site staff team hold small-group "design sessions" with diverse residents to solve a shared problem. The truth is, however, that these moments have been hard won and few and far between. This may be no wonder, given the huge human and financial resources committed to bricks-and-mortar development compared with the limited ingenuity and investment devoted to sorting out the complex human aspects of daily operations and community building in contexts where residents come from very different cultural and class backgrounds. There is no doubt that this is the hardest part of this work to figure out—but we must.

We assert that the principle difference between communities and neighborhoods that work and those that languish is that the former have a network—a group of people who make the choice to embrace differences and to cultivate and act on their interconnectedness. This group works to develop the personal capacity to form mutually beneficial relationships in order to tackle tough challenges, plan for an uncertain future, and cultivate quality of life.

This is particularly true in the context of public housing transformation work, where deeply subsidized housing communities are being replaced with mixed-income communities. The truth is that the public housing residents, the market-rate residents, the residents benefitting from other housing subsidies, the owner-manager agents, the service providers, and the surrounding neighbors are all in the same boat when it comes to the relative success of their community. If there is a new network of mutual respect, reciprocity, and shared decision-making, it will need to come from members of all of these groups; each will need to change how it operates relative to its boat-mates.

Efforts to forge networks among diverse members of a "transformed" community face these core challenges:

- Will long-time, publicly assisted residents who now live in a transformed community—but one where most biases against them still remain—trust a new invitation to reach out and connect across lines of difference?
- Will new residents of a different economic class, who may feel they are taking a risk to move into a mixed-income neighborhood, suspend judgment and fear long enough to lean into genuine "neighboring" relationships of mutual benefit?
- Will the owner-manager agents, property managers, asset managers, and maintenance staff step out of their compliance-centric professional roles and adopt human-centered practices and protocols that support genuine relationships across race, age, and income for collective place making?
- Will supportive service staff stop "helping" long enough to listen, and will they learn to trust that most, if not all, residents have the capacity and wherewithal to not only help themselves but help others and contribute to community life?

These are the shifts, we believe, that can begin to change an operating culture rooted in fear and isolation into one rooted in aspiration, connection, and reciprocity.

During the past decade, we have had the good fortune to work with several owner/manager groups who understand this challenge and share our quest to spark new, better ways for relating to one another as workers and as residents of affordable housing communities (whether mixed-income or 100 percent subsidized). One of those, TREK Development Group in Pittsburgh, took the bold and unusual step of asking each staff member to sign a covenant, pledging three core behaviors related to positive human interdependence. TREK now is in the process of asking residents who live in the planned communities to make the same commitment. This strategy, combined with other key steps, has positioned TREK as a trailblazer in developing a new approach for operating affordable and mixed-income housing communities. This paper examines TREK's initial journey in detail, in hopes of encouraging others to join or to share similar experiments, so we can learn from each other.

TREK DEVELOPMENT GROUP'S JOURNEY: AN ACTION LEARNING MODEL

Five years ago, the authors of this essay were approached by Bethany Friel, a senior staff member of TREK Development Group in Pittsburgh, Pennsylvania, to support their efforts to improve the quality of life for residents and staff in their real estate portfolio of 70 communities and their growing property management portfolio of nearly 500 units. As a regional developer, Trek's portfolio includes market-rate, mixed-income, and mixed-use developments in gentrifying urban settings; 100 percent deeply subsidized complexes in both rural and suburban neighborhoods; and public housing transformation initiatives in urban neighborhoods of entrenched poverty. The company, which began in 1991, is owned and led by its founder, Bill Gatti. TREK enjoys a reputation for thoughtful, creative design, especially in re-purposing older, pre-existing structures within the financial and regulatory constraints of affordable housing development. The vast majority of units are located in the greater Pittsburgh area and serve a very diverse resident population, with incomes at every income level.[1] Of TREK's 47 employees, 32 are dedicated to property management and two to resident services.

Our team included Trusted Space Partners (Frankie Blackburn, Bill Traynor, and Yerodin Avent) and the National Initiative of Mixed-Income Communities (Mark Joseph and Taryn Gress). Over the course of three years, we provided on-site technical assistance, facilitation support for several staff gatherings, and coaching by phone to individuals and small teams.

TREK Development Group would be the first to acknowledge that their learning journey is not complete, but we believe the positive indicators are significant enough to be informative. We see five major signs of internal

---

1 Trek Development Group, accessed January 23, 2020, http://trekdevelopment.com/

change that we view as critical to the creation, operation, and sustainability of thriving, mixed-income communities—signs that we hope can serve as guideposts for other like-minded companies and nonprofits. First, TREK's property management division is now viewed within the company as being as important as the real estate development side, if not more so. As CEO Bill Gatti states, "Even though it generates considerably less top line revenue, the opportunity cost and human cost of doing [property management] poorly are very high." Second, everyone in the company is clear about the common goal of creating connected and aspirational places, and they have a specific blueprint for which daily behaviors are needed to achieve this goal. Third, senior staff try to model their expectations for how communities should operate by actively working to implement the vision of a connected and aspirational environment inside the company. Fourth, TREK has a growing toolkit of intentional spaces and practices that site staff use to connect with residents and neighbors, along with inspiring and informative stories of success from four pilot sites. Fifth, specific changes have been made in the type of person recruited to serve as a site manager and in methods for supporting and holding these staff accountable.

It is important to note that these changes did not happen overnight but rather over a four-year period, with many steps forward and backward. The remainder of this essay identifies nine key decisions made by TREK Development Group and four innovations in internal operating characteristics that contributed to TREK's ability to successfully manage mixed-income housing.

NINE KEY DECISIONS

1. Bring Property Management In-House

When our team first met with TREK Development Group, company leaders were in the early years of building an internal property management division. Bill Gatti and senior partner, John Ginocchi explained that this decision arose out of a desire for greater control over the quality of housing they had worked so hard to produce and because of the extra challenges they faced in redeveloping older, deeply subsidized housing. Both partners believe that a direct relationship with site managers and their teams is essential to effectively support and hold them accountable for TREK's broad range of desired outcomes. We concur completely and cannot imagine an owner being able to spark a positive shift in the underlying operating culture of a housing complex without greater control of the human capital needed to do this work.

2. Approach Growth and Expansion Thoughtfully

TREK's goal was to manage 1,000 units, understanding that growth is necessary in order to sustain the work. However, TREK also believes in growing only as fast as the commitment to high-quality work and outcomes can be met. This operating principle is different from that of many other affordable housing organizations, which try to grow too quickly. The negative impact of growing too fast over a large geographic area is felt most keenly in the property management side of the affordable housing business, as site manager positions turn over fairly frequently and new people are trained and supervised largely by people who are rarely physically present.

3. Avoid the Resident Services Trap

Many resident service divisions of affordable housing companies end up feeling siloed, at odds with other divisions of their company and unempowered to demand and co-design a more productive way of creating thriving places to live and work. The landscape of resident services interventions deployed in the field also tends to be confusing, uninspired, and—despite rhetoric to the contrary—still largely deficit-based, with the default being some version of a "case management" approach. To their credit, TREK's leaders were looking for an alternative from the get-go. They purposefully went looking for the new talent needed to create a more holistic orientation toward residents and staff and found Bethany Friel. Friel has a master's degree and significant work experience in social work. Just as importantly she has a creative, entrepreneurial spirit with vision and imagination; humility to recognize her own need to listen, learn, and seek advice and wisdom from others; and the ability to be persistent while meeting others where they are in the moment. TREK's leaders gave Friel the resources, freedom, and partnership she needed to design, test, and integrate an approach that fit with the vision of connected communities.

4. Slow Down to Listen and Build Accurate Assessments

Bethany spent much of her first six months at TREK talking and listening to site staff (resident services coordinators and property managers) and participating in many internal meetings to plan new communities. She observed TREK's leaders out in the community as they addressed concerns about future development plans and filled in where needed to address resident challenges at existing sites. Friel emerged from this time with several observations about the gap between TREK's thoughtful approach and the day-to-day operations of existing communities:

- Property site managers controlled all of the decision-making power at their sites and routinely dismissed or ignored the value offered by resident service coordinators, even though these staff were often more educated and experienced in working with people.
- Site managers felt isolated from others in the company and often reinvented the wheel, acting from a place of self-protection rather than with a spirit of collaboration and shared mission.
- In general, property management staff approached "people problems," such as conflict between neighbors or a child's unruly behavior, as if there were a cookie-cutter solution. They didn't apply as much careful assessment to these problems that they applied to a broken furnace or other operational challenges.
- In some but not all cases, the site manager's underlying assumption was that residents of affordable housing should be grateful for good-quality housing.
- Negative energy was present everywhere and all the time; people on all sides of the table were not happy.

Based on these observations, Friel gave herself this mandate for moving forward: (1) Infuse the commitment to innovation and entrepreneurial spirit from TREK's development side into the management side; (2) build connections between and among site managers and service providers; (3) make meaningful, cost-effective investments in this work; and (4) infuse joy and hope into the picture at all times. In this way, her decision to slow down from the hectic pace of housing management, listen, and learn led to a more impactful strategy than if she had proceeded with pre-existing assumptions.

5. Require Senior-Level Commitment

During the early months, Friel was able to engage, inspire, support, and hold accountable TREK's principals, Bill Gatti and John Ginocchi, in staying true to the path of change they sought by bringing her in—even when the pressures of an on-going real estate development and management operation were overwhelming. Likewise, Gatti and Ginocchi took time to teach Friel about their core business, allowing her to ask many time-consuming questions and including her in conversations beyond her immediate scope. We cannot overemphasize the importance of having an internal catalytic team with a very strong sense of mutual respect and cross-sector learning to initiate, sustain, and spread the shifts in operating culture that are needed to create thriving, mixed-income communities.

6. Stay Focused on Internal Systems Change and Have Courage to Seek Help When Needed

Soon after joining TREK's staff, Friel read a paper about how the Triple Aim team, a partnership between Trusted Space Partners (TSP) and the National Initiative on Mixed-Income Communities (NIMC), had shifted the operating culture of a 900-unit affordable housing complex in Washington, DC. At her urging, TREK's senior partners decided to invest in bringing the Triple Aim team to Pittsburgh to meet, exchange best practices, and assess several of their current community challenges. Over the course of a year, including several site visits and regular phone check-ins, our Triple Aim team shared with TREK our framework, tools, and lessons about how to shift the operating culture and create new networks of shared connection and aspiration. (See a summary of Triple Aim on the next page.) The TREK team helped the Triple Aim team understand the context within which they were working, and together we selected two pilot sites to focus on for joint action learning.

7. Deploy Two Powerful Tools: CEO Participation and Network Night

We all needed to be present in the very beginning to co-execute strategies together. During the early phase of our Triple Aim partnership with TREK Development Group, it was critical that the two senior partners—often distracted with the intensity of their leadership positions but with persistent nudging by Friel—remained at the "action learning table" and committed to modeling new behaviors. It also was essential that TREK leaders got comfortable with having the Triple Aim team present as close-in partners, so that Triple Aim served not as a new "program" to be handed off but as a system intervention that required high-quality execution.

Network Night is a monthly gathering of property management staff and residents based on principles of inclusivity, freedom of choice, and fairness combined with several other new relationship-building practices. The interactions can quickly reverse toxicity between staff and residents and help to surface residents who have ideas and interest in working with staff to make

Figure 1: Summary of the Triple Aim Approach

Triple Aim is a framework jointly developed by Trusted Space Partners and the National Initiative on Mixed Income Communities in 2013 to help spark a deeper and more integrated approach to the daily operation of affordable housing, with a particular focus on the diversity and inclusion challenges of mixed-income complexes.

Core Belief: We are all human beings—residents, staff, neighbors, and partners—and we are all interdependent on each other for a high-quality life.

Underlying Philosophy: We believe that a systems approach to mixed-income communities is essential. Two fundamental shifts are needed: (1) **a goal shift** from separately defined goals for asset management, property management, and resident services to a unified "triple aim" that emphasizes the shared interests of all involved; and (2) **an operating shift** from narrowly focusing on maintaining compliance, collecting rent, and crisis management to creating an aspirational culture of human connection and co-investment among owners, staff, and residents. The diagram below illustrates how these two shifts lead to individual and community transformation in addition to increased operating efficiency.

COMMUNITY TRANSFORMATION
Physical, economic and social revitalization

Co-Investment Operating Culture

INDIVIDUAL TRANSFORMATION
Social and economic advancement of all residents

OPERATING EFFICIENCY
Increased property revenue and property reduced costs

Underlying Strategy: We promote three interwoven strategies: creation of intentional spaces, use of intentional practices, and formation of a new network (not an organization). Each strategy is designed to spark and support mindset shifts, mutual exchanges, and collaborative action.

- An **intentional space** is any gathering, small or large, that is carefully designed to support greater human connection and exchange among the people involved (e.g., "a monthly gathering of residents and staff that disrupts normal power divisions and supports new relationships and collaborative problem solving"). A property manager can also convert a rent recertification moment into an intentional "space" that achieves the compliance goal and invites the resident to become a part of an ongoing network of residents and staff, perhaps envisioning a specific contribution he/she/they might be able to make.
- **Intentional practices** are the devices, questions, and tactics used to make new connections in intentional spaces.
- **Networks** offer a more flexible form for on-going connection than the traditional model of a tenant organization or neighborhood association.

Figure 2: Network Building Has Personal and Community Impact

Theresa, a resident in one TREK site, ignored several notices inviting her to Network Night—until three smiling TREK staff members showed up at her door with packets of hot chocolate and popcorn to issue a personal invitation. The next week, she attended the gathering and was pleasantly surprised by how comfortable and meaningful it felt. When asked by a staff member to help set up for the next monthly gathering, she gladly said yes. Theresa began joining a small circle of staff and residents who met to plan each of the larger monthly gatherings. She now says these early steps of involvement, made with warm encouragement from her new staff and resident friends, helped her resolve a bad situation in her life, begin a new search for a job, and experience a new beginning after years of suffering from depression.

At an 82-unit complex just outside of Pittsburgh, Network Action Team members addressed concerns about residents not cleaning up after their dogs, trash and cigarettes not being put in approved containers, and bikes being left strewn around the property. The team of staff and residents had difficult but meaningful conversations about these concerns, which touched on issues of parenting, safety, sanitation, and aesthetics. They decided to implement a Beautiful Buildings Contest as a way to reach out to neighbors and start conversations related to safety and neighborhood pride. The contest was a tremendous success and led to a much larger group of residents feeling connected with the growing network and a greater sense of self-agency and shared ownership of the community.

improvements. Consistent practice of Network Nights in TREK's sites has led to the formation of a rotating Network Action Team of residents and staff who meet bi-weekly to conduct leadership development, mutual support, and action planning to strengthen the new neighborhood network. During a two-year period, the Trusted Space Partners team visited TREK's sites twice, participated in community gatherings, accompanied a Network Action Team in a peer visit to a community-building team in Cleveland, held regular strategy sessions with Friel and other TREK site staff, and provided resources and tips for managing expansion of the network.

8. Take Risks to Leverage Moments of Opportunity

After a year of learning and experimenting with Triple Aim, TREK Development Group applied to the local housing authority to become the planning coordinator and lead developer for a Choice Neighborhoods planning grant in Pittsburgh, using Triple Aim as its core approach. The Triple Aim team and TREK together designed a series of retreats and team-building steps to ensure that the housing authority was on board at the leadership level and onsite. Triple Aim team members visited Pittsburgh and the Choice neighborhood frequently to roll out and demonstrate a system of new intentional spaces and practices with residents and partners who initially were very skeptical. It soon became clear that additional staff support was needed, so TREK and Triple Aim created a new "Community Network Builder" position, which they filled with Montia Robinson-Dinkins, who is skilled at creating spaces to build relationships and who also had deep experience in the community where redevelopment was taking place.

Over the two-year planning process that followed, this "intervention team" designed and wove together the following intentional spaces and practices on a consistent basis:

- Creation of a compelling invitation to residents and staff;
- Proactive door knocking and street outreach with a fun and creative flare;
- Weekly drop-in spaces for questions and ideas to bubble up and relationships to form;
- Monthly Network Nights for relationship building, table talks about issues and ideas, and neighbor-to-neighbor exchanges;
- Naming and claiming of a new neighborhood network, with colorful branding and t-shirts;

Figure 3: Planning for a New Opportunity Mobilizes and Empower Residents

Evidence of a shift in operating culture emerged as residents of the Bedford Dwellings complex, a TREK site, began to help facilitate the planning process for a potential Choice Neighborhood project. Residents brainstormed events and programs that they wanted and were willing to lead, leading to the adoption of nine new resident-led initiatives, including a Sisters Circle, a Summer Fest, a clean hallway contest, a senior appreciation luncheon, an on-going "coffee shop hour," and the decision to take the coffee hour on the road to different parts of the large complex.

Perhaps the best evidence of new self-agency and aspirational behavior was when a core group of "resident stewards" politely asked the non-residents present in one of the many Choice Planning sessions to leave the room so they could reach consensus on a critical phasing question posed by the project managers. In another example, a resident who had attended meetings but never spoken took time to prepare and present to the full group on a range of relevant topics. And five community partners successfully used the Network Night framework to connect with Bedford residents, leading to more authentic exchanges and relationships.

When asked about his most transformative moment in pursuing the Triple Aim strategy, TREK CEO Bill Gatti says it was watching the resident steward team slowly take ownership of the Bedford Connect Network Nights: "Their excitement was palpable and inspiring. In many cases, their ability to deal with disappointment and feel empathy for others exceeds my own. *They* felt bad for *me* when we failed to win the Choice Neighborhood implementation grant."

- Follow-up relationship building with people who seemed excited by the new spaces and new ways of relating to each other;
- Formation of a core steward team to help with all of the strategies and to form ad hoc design teams to go deeper on specific issues as they arose; and
- Financial support for resident-led events and ideas as they surfaced.

Before these very intentional strategies were consistently and collaboratively used, the housing authority had only met monthly with the resident council, typically attended by just three or four residents. Since formation of the new partnership and adoption of the Triple Aim approach, 16 monthly "Bedford Connects" network nights have been held, with an average attendance of 25 to 35 residents. More than 200 residents, most of whom had never been to a resident gathering before, have attended at least one Bedford Connect night.

9. Walk the Talk Internally with Staff Synergy Sessions

While the Choice Planning team was taking a deep dive into implementing the Triple Aim approach in one neighborhood, TREK's senior staff team focused on how to more intentionally create an aspirational and connected environment among all TREK divisions and within staff teams. The most dramatic shift was represented by a decision to host regular all-staff Synergy Sessions, fashioned out of the same principles as the neighborhood Network Night gatherings: inclusion, freedom of choice, focus on gifts/assets, and small-group conversations on topics chosen by participants. These sessions led to new and better lines of communication and human exchange between senior staff and front-line management staff. A complete team of senior staff members—not just the director of property management—now had a collective and more accurate assessment of on-site challenges and successes. And on-site staff members witnessed key leaders caring about and modelling the practices they were being asked to adopt.

Senior staff followed the Synergy Sessions with a series of on-site listening sessions. These helped site staff understand that the senior staff, especially TREK's CEO, were very serious about creating a higher-quality environment than the typical affordable housing community offers. Moreover, a few on-site staff emerged who seemed ready to experiment with the Triple Aim approach, including property managers, maintenance workers, and service coordinators. Friel sought out these staff and recruited several of them to experiment with Network Night in their sites. The expansion of Network Night, which increased the number of pilot sites from two to four, reached a more diverse range of properties, generated many lessons, inspiring existing sites to stay the course, and increased the number of "choir members" inside the organization who were excited and committed to this new way of operating.

FOUR INNOVATIONS

Operating cultures do not change quickly or easily, especially in affordable housing and mixed-income environments where the property management and resident-services fields hang onto old traditions of service-driven practice and face incessant demands for financial, legal, and regulatory compliance. It's fair to say that these dynamics exacerbate rather than ameliorate years of built-up resentment and mistrust on the part of residents who are constantly being prodded to prove their eligibility, allow inspectors to walk through their homes, and participate in the next social services activity intended to fix their "brokenness."

TREK faced two big mid-course challenges: (1) several key internal leaders, both at the corporate and site level, didn't buy in to the Triple Aim approach but did not openly reveal their lack of support; and (2) the senior leaders and site staff who were committed to Triple Aim struggled to communicate to others the daily manifestation of the vision, especially as it applied to every single staff person, including janitors, accountants, and office assistants. Many staff understood the concept of building connections with residents and supporting resident-led initiatives but did not know how to put the concepts into practice in the middle of a routine maintenance call, while listening to a resident complain about another resident, or when trying to solve a nagging problem such as rodents, loitering, and dirty common spaces. A few site managers and maintenance workers actively resisted the approach, either by ignoring requests for experimentation or implementing a strategy half-heartedly. Even though these moments of active and passive resistance were challenging to TREK's Senior Team, the pain provided the extra kick needed to make some important innovations—reforms worthy of replication throughout the affordable and mixed-income housing industry.

Innovation One: A New Approach to Co-Leading a Housing Development Company

In virtually all of the housing companies with which we have experience, the real estate side of the business receives the greatest share of leadership time, attention, and recognition. This was true of TREK Development Group, too. CEO Gatti and Senior Vice President Ginocchi, are the two key leaders and visionaries of TREK and, until recently, were both primarily focused on building and advancing their real estate development pipeline in as thoughtful and meaningful way as possible.

When they made the decision in 2015 to bring property management in-house, at least for most of their portfolio, Gatti and Ginocchi assumed they needed a new third person whose primary experience was in housing management, particularly of affordable housing. A new partner was recruited and hired, and he went to work building the management division. In many respects, Bill and John viewed property management as a necessary ingredient but not one needing their close attention or shared ownership, and the new head of the property management team kept mostly to himself. Bill and John did not realize a big shift in approach was needed until Bethany Friel came on board and encountered serious resistance from site staff to basic calls for improved quality and attention to the Triple Aim strategy. The following changes, made over time, created the extra organizational emphasis and space needed to continue on the Triple Aim path:

- Friel was promoted to a newly created position, director of mission, culture, and people, and placed on equal footing with the director of property management.

- A new property management director was carefully recruited and hired. The importance of Triple Aim to the company was a significant component of this new director's recruitment, vetting, and on-boarding.

- Ginocchi, who has deep experience with housing management issues, was promoted from vice president of development to executive vice president. He now manages the company's operations and supervises both the director of property management and the director of mission, culture and people. This move signaled and embodied TREK's prioritization of high-quality housing management above all else.

- In his new role, Ginocchi asked Friel to temporarily assume the role of a regional property manager, so she could better understand the management business and better evaluate gaps in TREK's basic management operations.

- Two long-time site managers with considerable staff influence were replaced, along with a number of site-based maintenance workers. (As the operating culture began to shift, these staff expressed feeling uncomfortable with the changes and opted to leave. No one was fired).

- TREK hired a local human resources company with a commitment to high-quality performance that was in sync with the Triple Aim initiative to support hiring decisions, performance review practices, and other HR issues.

TREK's senior leaders now emphasize the importance of supporting all staff's personal development. For example, they formed a book club focused on personal agency; the first book, read by 10 staff members including company executives, was *Dare to Lead* by Brené Brown. "I am learning things about staff members that I would have never known otherwise, and I see [the book club] helping us recognize and address behaviors that are roadblocks to good leadership," one of TREK's senior leaders observed.

Innovation Two: Hospitality Covenant with Pledge and Core Practices

In response to the painful moments of passive and active resistance referred to earlier, our Triple Aim team went back to the drawing board to see how we could communicate expectations more clearly and with a greater sense of inspiration and urgency. We were most focused on TREK staff but also knew that residents must be involved in considering new ways of operating and behaving. We sought to create lots of new "two-way streets."

Bill Gatti often refers to his vision for TREK to provide a deeper level of hospitality in all moments, small and large, when developing and operating a housing community. When pressed, he tells of traveling in foreign countries where he and his family have been received with extraordinary hospitality and how that brings out the best in him and his family while visiting a new place. Gatti is not talking about hospitality as hotels often do but in its ancient form of reciprocal exchange between two strangers.[2] Our core team, including Gatti, took time away from the office environment to attempt to convert this concept of deep hospitality into three core values and a beginning set of five shared practices. We knew that if the idea of deep hospitality was to take root and grow inside the company and among residents, it had to rise above all other

---

2 Ancient Greece had two rules of hospitality: (1) Respect from host to guest. The host must be hospitable to the guest and provide him/her with food and drink and a bath, if required. It is not polite to ask questions until the guest has stated his/her needs. (2) Respect from guest to host. The guest must be courteous to the host and not be a burden.

Figure 4: Hospitality Covenant

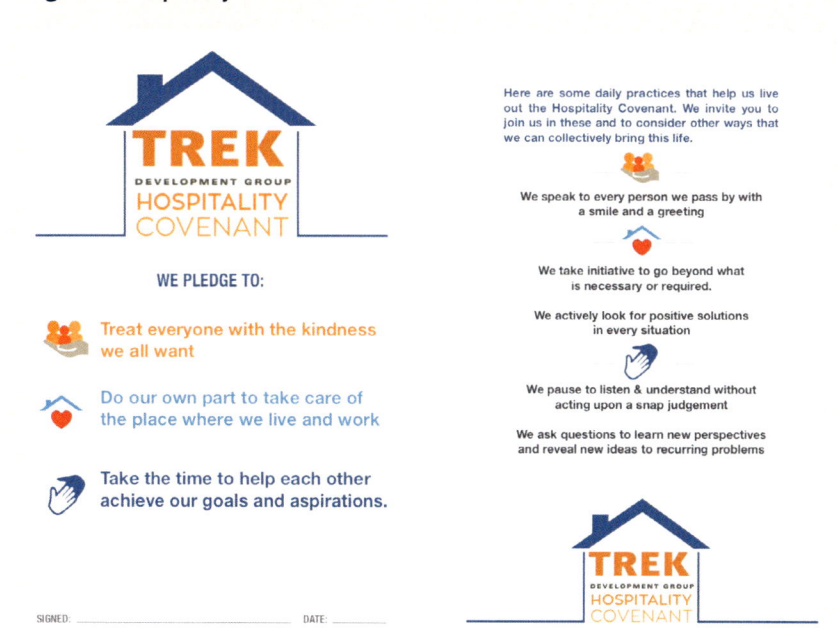

TREK DEVELOPMENT GROUP HOSPITALITY COVENANT

WE PLEDGE TO:

- Treat everyone with the kindness we all want
- Do our own part to take care of the place where we live and work
- Take the time to help each other achieve our goals and aspirations.

SIGNED: _____ DATE: _____

Here are some daily practices that help us live out the Hospitality Covenant. We invite you to join us in these and to consider other ways that we can collectively bring this life.

We speak to every person we pass by with a smile and a greeting

We take initiative to go beyond what is necessary or required.

We actively look for positive solutions in every situation

We pause to listen & understand without acting upon a snap judgement

We ask questions to learn new perspectives and reveal new ideas to recurring problems

TREK DEVELOPMENT GROUP HOSPITALITY COVENANT

---

core values and operating principles, and it had to be something that every person could keep in their mind at every moment of the day. (It is important to note that TREK had a set of well-articulated and communicated core values prior to the journey with Triple Aim.) The graphic above shows where we landed with this "Hospitality Covenant."

In truth, the easiest step was to come up with the concept for a hospitality covenant. Friel assumed leadership of the hardest part—securing wide buy-in and implementation among the 40+ members of TREK's workforce and then introducing the covenant to residents. Her initial steps included: (1) engaging the senior leadership team in bi-weekly accountability meetings to model the behavior change, (2) executing a creative roll-out of the covenant in a staff-wide Synergy Session, (3) producing posters and postcards with the covenant that are always displayed and available to staff and residents in every lobby of every TREK-owned building, (4) creating a staff recognition program to reward those who actively demonstrate use of the covenant and pledges, (5) forming internal design teams to reform basic operational tools to align with the covenant (e.g.,

Figure 5: What Does the Hospitality Covenant Look Like in Action?

"Treating people with kindness means we notice people, we value people, and we respect each other as humans first. It doesn't mean we put smiley faces in our emails or fake smiles on our faces. It means we acknowledge someone and recognize them as a person first.

Even in the hard conversations we have on a regular basis, we uphold someone's dignity by being clear and respectful while acknowledging the difficult pieces of the conversation. For example, I just had to tell a woman with a large family, who assumed she was moving into a redeveloped mixed-income community, that we did not have any more three-bedroom units. She was so angry and yelling and crying over the phone. I genuinely felt awful. I apologized and listened to her stress. I then explained to her the process, and I let her know what she should expect now. I acknowledged that it sucked.

We talked a few more times over a two-day period. I gave her my time, 20 minutes here and there. I wanted to preserve what little was left of the relationship because I wanted our next interaction, when her name came up on the waiting list, to go well and I wanted her to not mistrust us. Being kind and holding a boundary *can* happen at the same time. It's just really hard to do."

—Bethany Friel, Director of Mission, Culture, and People

---

rent collection policy and procedure, staff performance reviews, new staff training), and (6) introducing the covenant to residents during the annual rent certification.

Innovation Three: Integrated Site Teams with Shared Goals and Practices

While the Hospitality Covenant was being introduced to all staff, Friel and Triple Aim worked with one site staff team at the original pilot site, Dinwiddie, to develop three practical tools to support greater site staff integration, with the goal of making the operating culture one of shared connection and aspiration. This team included a property manager, a leasing assistant, a part-time resident services staff, a lead maintenance staff, and a janitor. The three tools are:

- A **site-based strategic planning framework**, which helps a team develop specific annual goals focused on the operating culture and integrated with project operations goals.
- An **all-staff meeting ritual** (to be held either weekly or every other week) for peer learning about specific day-to-day operations, so that everyone ends up knowing something about every role and can monitor progress toward shared goals.
- An **action planning format** that facilitates refinement of annual goals as learning and new situations occur during the year.

In the first year of experimentation, the Dinwiddie team selected the shared

Figure 6: Sample Team Goals

The integrated site team at Dinwiddie came up with these annual goals:

- Help residents connect across the "sections" of Dinwiddie, as well as with other contiguous buildings and homes in the immediate neighborhood.
- Work to make Dinwiddie a "family-friendly housing community" and make this known in the larger community.
- Increase the number of residents who are active and engaged as a part of our living community at Dinwiddie.
- Participate in learning about our community operating budget and use it as a critical tool for planning, setting expense control targets, and setting other community goals

goals summarized in the box above, in addition to expected targets for rent, retention, expenses, etc. They also followed a basic meeting ritual that involved check-ins on what is "new and good" in team members' lives; a "nugget of wisdom" to discuss; brief updates on management, maintenance, and community building activities; consideration of an "innovation moment" selected during the previous meeting; and meeting facilitation duties that are shared by all staff. During an interview with individual staff at Dinwiddie, a longtime maintenance staff member remarked, "I often joke about these weekly meetings, but I actually think they have helped us improve as a team and have improved our work."

Innovation Four: New Strategies for Recruiting and New Operating Norms for Property Managers

A common thread in all of the goals, steps, and conversations set forth in this essay is the pivotal role of the site property manager. TREK senior staff and the Triple Aim team acknowledged that it is hard to find and retain people who are both committed to and skilled at creating connected, aspirational housing communities. We have agreed that until this challenge is addressed, much of the innovation will not hold firm and produce lasting results, either for operating efficiency or people-related outcomes. We also recognize that our focus on the role of property managers is still a work in progress.

One experiment underway at TREK is to help some resident service coordinators transition to joint roles as service coordinators and site property managers. People in both positions need to exhibit strong commitment and capacity for building shared aspirations and connections with and among staff, residents, and partners. And both need to understand the importance of—and be willing to learn—the daily operations of collecting rent, repairing units, complying with regulations, and meeting budgets. TREK is banking on the hunch that it is easier to teach a resident service coordinator the property management side of the business than to convince or teach a more rigid, traditional property manager how to create the kinds of intentional spaces and practices needed to build inclusive community.

In the 82-unit property mentioned earlier, which is 100 percent deeply subsidized, former Service Coordinator Kara Rea, who now is a newly appointed site manager, has been onsite for more than two years and has actively implemented a community network-building strategy. She holds monthly Network Nights, formed weekly mutual support circles, and recruited and supported a team of residents to help steward the expansion of the new neighborhood network. When asked to reflect on this experiment, TREK's Ginocchi recalled attending a Network Night at which 20 residents discussed Kara's pending transition to the joint role of services coordinator/property manager. "I heard a lot of good comments and praise regarding Kara and her role, as well as their approval of her new position," John says. "There was some concern that her social service role may be diminished as she takes on management responsibility. But I am excited to see how hiring a social worker as a property manager unfolds. All indications are that this structure will be transformative and something hopefully that we can keep replicating."

Rea and Friel, along with the rest of TREK's leaders and partners, are committed to demonstrating that the intentional weaving together of the framework, tools, and innovations described in this essay will improve outcomes for both the company and the residents of its mixed-income communities. And that's exactly what seems to be happening. In a recent note from the field, Friel summed up how TREK's new property management approach, although sometimes hard to implement, is having some dramatic effects:

> Last week we were doing our first round of apartment inspections. We really took a holistic approach; we talked shop and checked in on [people]. We were nearing the end of the day and went into a middle-aged single woman's apartment. It was spotless. As Kara walked in, she asked about [the woman's pet]. The resident started to cry and said she was gone; I assumed she meant the pet had passed away and that was why she was crying. We looked over the apartment, and as Kara was

talking with the resident, who was still teary eyed, I noticed a note on her table. The note read something like, "You can keep all the furniture and whatever personal belongings you need—including clothing." It was dated for that day, and it was essentially a suicide note.

I probed a little to assess [the resident] quickly and then asked about the note. After dismissing the maintenance man, Kara and I stayed with her to learn more of what was happening. We thought she was having negative symptoms to her medications. After leaving a message with her doctor, we called the crisis line. During that call, we learned that she had taken 80 mg of a strong anti-depressant on top of other medications within a 24-hour period. We stayed with her until the ambulance came and she was admitted for treatment.

There is so much more to the story, and who knows what things will be like when she returns home. But I do know that by taking a more intentional approach to a regular task, we helped her live one more day.

IMPLICATIONS FOR ACTION

Implications for Policy

- Federal, state, and local housing agencies should more clearly define what constitutes high-quality site management and ensure the prioritization of development proposals that demonstrate genuine commitment to this higher-quality standard, including innovative practices to achieve a vision of co-investment with a broad range of residents, neighbors, and partners.

- Housing and community development advocacy organizations at all levels should (1) develop a specific platform that calls for and inspires an approach to property management, resident services, and resident associations that is built from a vision of shared interdependence and quality of life; and (2) communicate the equal importance of these reforms to increases in the affordable housing pipeline.

Implications for Research and Evaluation

- A well-funded, long-term research effort is needed to document the positive impact of the Triple Aim approach and other similar innovations on both the physical and financial sustainability of mixed-income communities over time.

- Research is needed about models for transforming traditional housing companies, which tend to be led by White, upper-class professionals, into diverse, inclusive organizations that reflect the communities served.

- HUD, local public housing authorities, and other housing agencies should evaluate current policies requiring the creation of hierarchal and exclusionary resident associations and tenant councils to determine the impact of this approach on the daily operating culture of housing complexes, whether mixed-income or deeply subsidized.

Implications for Development and Investment

- All sectors of the housing industry need to jointly invest in creating a new kind of intentional, well-branded career pipeline to attract and retain diverse young people with the commitment and compassion needed to serve as effective property managers and as future leaders of the industry.

- Special public-private venture capital is needed to encourage housing development organizations across the country to build internal property management capability and to phase out of third-party contracts, the vast majority of which do not produce high-quality, thriving communities.

- Private foundations should invest in supporting the leaders of nonprofit and profit-based housing organizations to more fully understand the White supremacist underpinnings of our current housing system (private and public) and to develop capacity for sharing positional power across lines of difference, both in their own organizations and in the community.

Implications for Residents and Community Members

- Many advocacy organizations representing residents and community members need to evaluate their own way of operating, both internally and externally, to ensure their efforts are leading to reforms that liberate everyone to bring their best selves to solving neighborhood challenges, rather than perpetuating old forms of domination and control.

■ ■ ■

Trusted Space Partners is a team of experienced community developers and designers who are supporting collaborative community change initiatives all over the United States. These initiatives are firmly grounded in the wisdom of people who live and work together in local communities.

The Partners, **FRANKIE BLACKBURN** *and* **BILL TRAYNOR**, *are long time practitioners who have worked at the grass roots level in community for a combined 60 years. Both Blackburn and Traynor have direct experience as organizers, developers, social designers and Executive Directors of powerful local organizations focused on building new networks of residents and institutions that cross traditional boundaries.*

ACHIEVING DURABLE MIXED-INCOME COMMUNITIES THROUGH AFFORDABLE HOUSING PRESERVATION: A SUCCESSFUL MODEL OF SCATTERED-SITE HOUSING REDEVELOPMENT IN WEST PHILADELPHIA

Michael H. Norton
Reinvestment Fund

Karen Black
May 8 Consulting

Jacob Rosch
Reinvestment Fund

A critical feature of thriving mixed-income communities is the availability of a range of housing options that a broad spectrum of individuals and families can afford. To sustain mixed-income communities, policymakers and mission-driven entities need an array of tools to create and preserve affordable housing options for low- and moderate-income residents. In many cities across the country, however, well-intentioned efforts to revitalize distressed neighborhoods are creating conditions in which improvements to the housing stock and local amenities have begun to drive housing values and rents to levels that long-term residents, particularly low- and moderate-income renters of color, cannot afford.

West Philadelphia is one such place. It includes numerous sub-neighborhoods, from historically middle-class African-American areas to enclaves of immigrants from Africa, the Caribbean, China, and South Asia, to clusters of college students and their professors. Sections of West Philadelphia have been some of the city's most racially and economically diverse for decades, while others remain racially isolated areas of concentrated, intergenerational poverty. The housing stock runs the gamut from modest rowhouses to Victorian mansions to large apartment buildings.

West Philadelphia has three universities and several large hospitals. In a city economy driven by "eds and meds," the presence of these institutions makes the area west of the Schuylkill River a major employment hub. The legacy of university-driven redevelopment efforts from Urban Renewal through today also underscores an explicit racial dimension to discussions of neighborhood change throughout West Philadelphia. The wholesale transformation of what was known as the Black Bottom neighborhood—an enclave of Black residents living near the University of Pennsylvania—in the 1960s into what is known today as University City—a wealthier White enclave—is a stark example of urban "revitalization" that displaced whole communities of color.

Many long-time residents of modest means in West Philadelphia are Black, while many of the more affluent newer residents typically are not, especially near the universities and hospitals. While the area has begun to change, both racially and economically, it remains predominantly African American. Eighty-five percent of the homeowners in West Philadelphia, writ large, are Black, despite making up only 74 percent of the community's population.

Today, long-time residents of West Philadelphia face multiple displacement pressures. On one hand, rapidly increasing real estate values extending from the growth of local universities and hospitals put pressure on residents in the gentrifying neighborhoods of West Philadelphia. On the other hand, blight and housing deterioration put pressure on residents living in the increasingly concentrated areas of distress. As low- and moderate-income residents of color are priced out of gentrifying areas, previously mixed-income communities are left more racially and economically homogenous than ever.

This essay describes a model of scattered-site affordable housing development implemented by West Philadelphia Real Estate and Neighborhood Restorations (WPRE/NR). From 1989 to 2015 WPRE/NR created 1,100 affordable rental housing units in 760 single-family homes and duplexes, mainly in high-poverty areas of West Philadelphia, using a mix of creative land acquisition, Low Income Housing Tax Credits (LIHTC), and private financing.[1]

WPRE/NR's scattered-site approach to redevelopment provides an instructive example for others weighing different strategies to create and sustain mixed-income communities. In some of West Philadelphia's most rapidly changing housing markets, WPRE/NR's activity has effectively established long-term (typically 30 years under the LIHTC program) affordability, increasing the likelihood these communities will remain places where a racially and economically diverse range of residents can afford to live and benefit from better housing quality and improved neighborhood amenities.

At the same time, practitioners and public officials must remain cognizant of the tension inherent in redevelopment activities that improve housing conditions for some low-income residents, but may also lead to higher property taxes or rents for other long-time residents. This case study highlights the viability of context-specific strategies, including a mix of public and private developers and a novel use of existing financial products, to address the increasingly acute shortage of affordable housing.

WEST PHILADELPHIA CONTEXT

West Philadelphia is home to roughly 238,000 residents. Nearly 73 percent are Black, well above the citywide population (41 percent). Across West Philadelphia, the share of the Black population varies from nearly 100 percent in block groups of neighborhoods such as Carrol Park and Haddington to less than 10 percent in some University City block groups. About 25,000 undergraduate students attend Drexel University and the University of Pennsylvania (Penn) each year, making up about 10 percent of the overall population in West Philadelphia. An additional 20,000 graduate students attend the universities, although an unknown number live outside of West Philadelphia.[2] The University of the Sciences is a much smaller institution not far from Penn, with about 1,200 students. Roughly one in 10 West Philadelphia residents is foreign born.

---

1   Reinvestment Fund, a local community development financial institution focused on investing in underserved areas, is one capital source for WPRE/NR development activity in West Philadelphia.

2   "Fast Facts," Drexel University, accessed January 21, 2020, https://drexel.edu/about/glance/fast-facts/.; "Facts," University of Pennsylvania, accessed January 21, 2020, https://home.www.upenn.edu/about/facts.

West Philadelphia also is an economically diverse area that encompasses many different types of neighborhoods. Map 1 presents an overview of West Philadelphia neighborhoods, the variation in block group-level poverty rates, and the location of traditional subsidized housing developments.

The neighborhoods surrounding Penn and Drexel universities and the Overbrook Farms neighborhood on the western border are home to West Philadelphia's most affluent households whose incomes are commensurate with those in some of the wealthiest neighborhoods in the city. The Wynnefield and Powelton Village neighborhoods are both long-standing middle-class neighborhoods, the former predominantly Black, the latter more racially diverse. Other West Philadelphia neighborhoods have struggled with deep and persistent poverty. In 2018, over a quarter of all families in West Philadelphia (26 percent) lived in poverty, compared with 20 percent citywide.[3] Areas with lower rents are becoming increasingly concentrated in a narrower geography between expanding areas of price appreciation, Fairmount Park, and the western edge of the city.

West Philadelphia is home to a number of long-term affordable housing developments, including public housing and other affordable housing options (see Map 1). However, several neighborhoods, particularly those surrounding the University of Pennsylvania and Drexel University, have been under increasing real estate pressure throughout much of the last 20 years. Some areas have completely transformed (racially and economically) and are largely unaffordable for low- to moderate-income residents.

The relationship between the universities and West Philadelphia residents is complicated. For well over 70 years, university investment activity and political clout (predominantly Penn's) has been an outsized force in West Philadelphia development. While the universities no longer undertake such extreme measures as they did with the wholesale elimination of the historic Black Bottom community, which took place via eminent domain in the 1960s, both Penn and Drexel continue to have a major impact on housing market activity and prices.

Two Penn initiatives have been particularly transformative: an employer-assisted down payment program that encouraged many employees and faculty

---

3   In West Philadelphia 33 percent of the Black population and 31 percent of the White population live in poverty. While family poverty stands at 20 percent citywide, approximately 25 percent of Philadelphians live in families at or below the poverty level making it one of the poorest big cities in America.

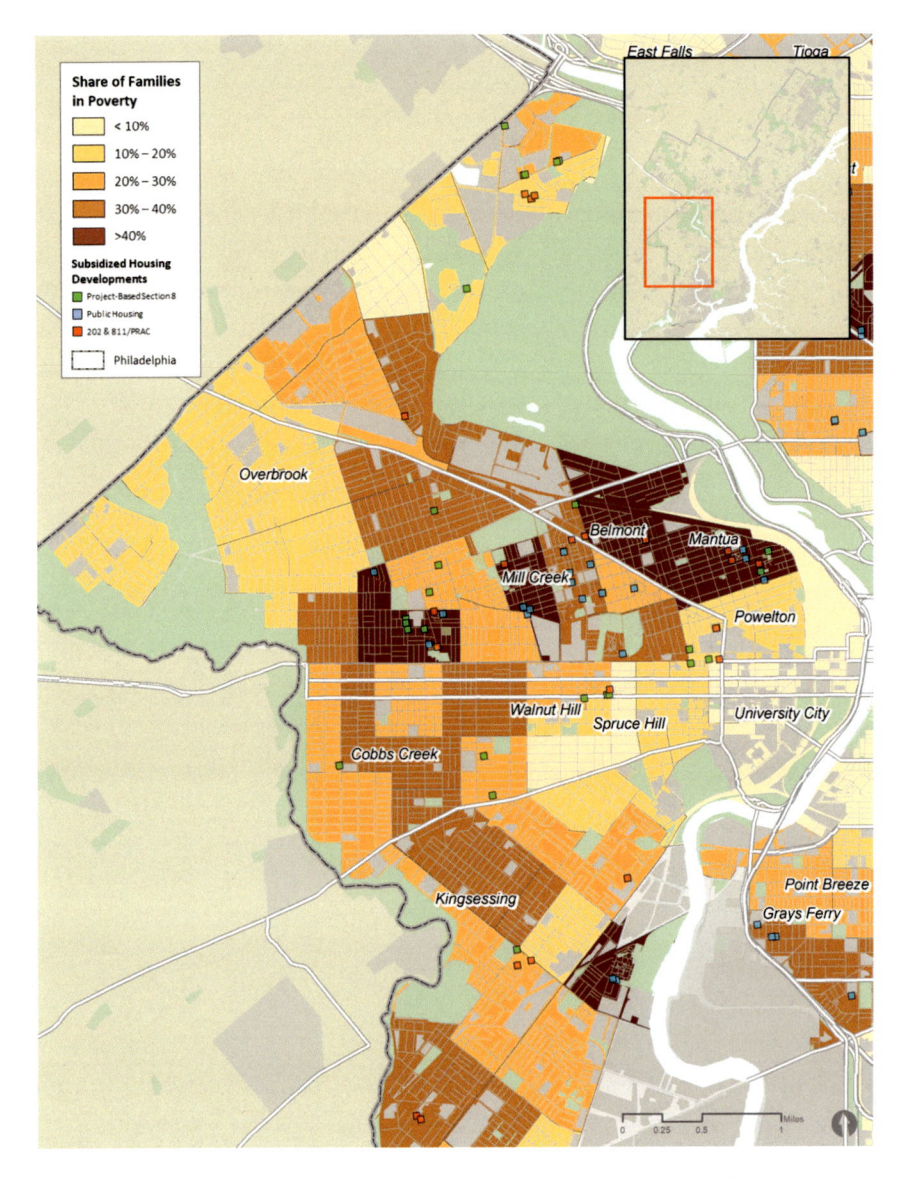

Source: American Communities Survey, Five-year Estimates, 2014-2018; U.S Department of Housing and Urban Development: Office of Policy Development and Research, Picture of Subsidized Households (2018). Note: 202 & 811/PRAC refer to supportive housing for elderly and disabled individuals.

Map 1: West Philadelphia Neighborhoods, Poverty Rates, and Subsidized Housing Developments

to purchase homes nearby, and the cooperative management and funding of a local elementary school in partnership with the School District of Philadelphia that has led to an influx of families with higher incomes seeking access to what is now one of the city's best-rated schools. There is some indication that this may have, in turn, led graduate students to seek housing in lower-cost areas farther to the west, moving Penn's impact much farther from campus.[4] Drexel, meanwhile, has transitioned from a predominantly commuter campus to a residential one with vastly expanded curricular offerings and enrollment; the school has built a number of new dorms and many more Drexel students are now seeking off-campus housing in West Philadelphia.

The universities are also major job engines: Between the main university and health system, Penn is the largest employer in the city, and Drexel has consistently been in the top 10 (Children's Hospital of Philadelphia, also located in University City, is the fifth largest employer). The growth of Penn and Drexel has made University City the second largest job center in the region (after Philadelphia's downtown) with expanding opportunities in education, health care, technical research, and support services for these industries increasingly locating in University City. This expansion has drawn increasing numbers of White and Asian individuals and families with higher incomes to University City; while many of these families live in areas surrounding Penn and Drexel, over time they have begun pushing farther out into adjacent neighborhoods, bringing higher incomes, higher home values, demand for higher-priced amenities, and a threat of displacement for long-term Black residents with more modest incomes.[5]

Although many of West Philadelphia's Black residents may view the universities with caution, in recent years both Penn and Drexel have endeavored to

---

[4] Judith Rodin, *The University and Urban Revival: Out of the Ivory Tower and Into the Streets* (Philadelphia, PA: University of Pennsylvania Press, 2015).; Harley F. Etienne, *Pushing Back the Gates: Neighborhood Perspectives on University-Driven Revitalization in West Philadelphia*, (Philadelphia, PA: Temple University Press, 2012).

[5] Kevin Gillen and Susan Wachter, "Neighborhood Value Updated: West Philadelphia Price Indexes," https://www.slideshare.net/PennUrbanResearch/neighborhood-value-updated-west-philadelphia-price-indexes, (2011).; Emily Dowdall, *Philadelphia's Changing Neighborhoods: Gentrification and Other Shifts Since 2000*. (Philadelphia, PA: Pew Charitable Trusts, 2016), https://www.pewtrusts.org/-/media/assets/2016/05/philadelphias_changing_neighborhoods.pdf; Seth Chizeck, "Gentrification and Changes in the Stock of Low-Cost Rental Housing in Philadelphia, 2000 to 2014," *Cascade Focus, Federal Reserve Bank of Philadelphia*, January 2017, https://www.philadelphiafed.org/-/media/community-development/publications/cascade-focus/gentrification-and-changes-in-the-stock-of-low-cost-rental-housing/cascade-focus_5.pdf?la=en.

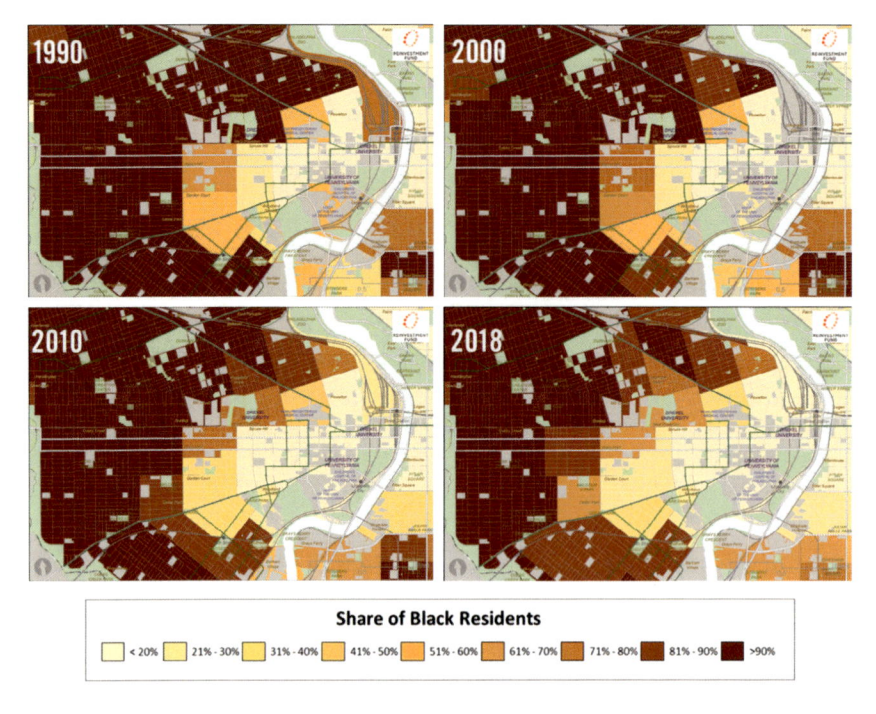

Note: Rates measure non-Hispanic Black residents as share of total population

Map 2: Black Populations In West Philadelphia Block Groups: 1990–2018

contribute to community development and improve access to opportunity. Examples include: participation in the West Philadelphia Skills Initiative, which trains local residents for jobs with the area's major employers; public health services provided through the hospital system; collaborative teaching and research on needs in local communities; and the West Philadelphia Promise Zone, for which Drexel is a leading supporter. Each university also has a center dedicated to community engagement.

Neighborhoods outside the orbit of University City have had a different set of challenges. Many middle-class Black neighborhoods were hard hit by the foreclosure crisis. Since 1990, the overall population in West Philadelphia has declined by more than 20,000 residents (from 258,336 in 1990 to 237,660 in 2014-18), contributing to pockets of vacancy and blight. While West Philadelphia's Black community has remained largely stable over the last two decades, the geography of the Black community has begun to shift as White and

Asian residents have moved into the neighborhoods farther out from Penn and Drexel. Map 2, shows changes in the Black population between 1990 and 2018.

GENESIS OF WEST PHILADELPHIA REAL ESTATE AND NEIGHBORHOOD RESTORATIONS

WPRE/NR was created by two private developers in 1989 to rehabilitate abandoned rowhouse shells into affordable housing, using Low Income Housing Tax Credits (LIHTC). Since 1989, WPRE/NR has produced more than 1,100 units of affordable rental housing in 760 single-family houses and duplexes, leading to direct investment of more than $200 million in West Philadelphia.

WPRE/NR homes are located in some of West Philadelphia's most economically distressed blocks as well as blocks that have been rapidly transformed through the displacement of long-term residents. All WPRE/NR residents are low-income, and most (over 70 percent) are Black.

Map 3 shows the location of WPRE/NR properties and contemporary Black populations and poverty rates across West Philadelphia. Many of the WPRE/NR properties developed after 2010 are currently located in areas that have both high rates of poverty and high concentrations of Black residents. A cluster of properties, mostly built before 2005, are located east of Cobbs Creek in a community that has undergone dramatic changes since WPRE/NR began working in the area (Maps 4 and 5). Today, this area has a lower poverty rate and fewer Black residents than other areas of West Philadelphia; but this was not the case at the turn of the 21st century when WPRE/NR was developing many of these units.

In 1984, WPRE/NR co-founder, Scott Mazo, was working in West Philadelphia as a painter and contractor when he bought his first abandoned shell, based on the observation that vacant rowhouse prices in the neighborhood were low and rents were stable enough to cover monthly mortgage payments. Using no public subsidy, he tore out everything down to the studs, rebuilt the unit, and then leased the house for an affordable rent that also turned a small profit.

Having met with some early success, Mazo partnered with co-founder Jim Levin in 1989. Together they purchased nine vacant properties on otherwise viable, well-maintained streets in West Philadelphia and applied to the

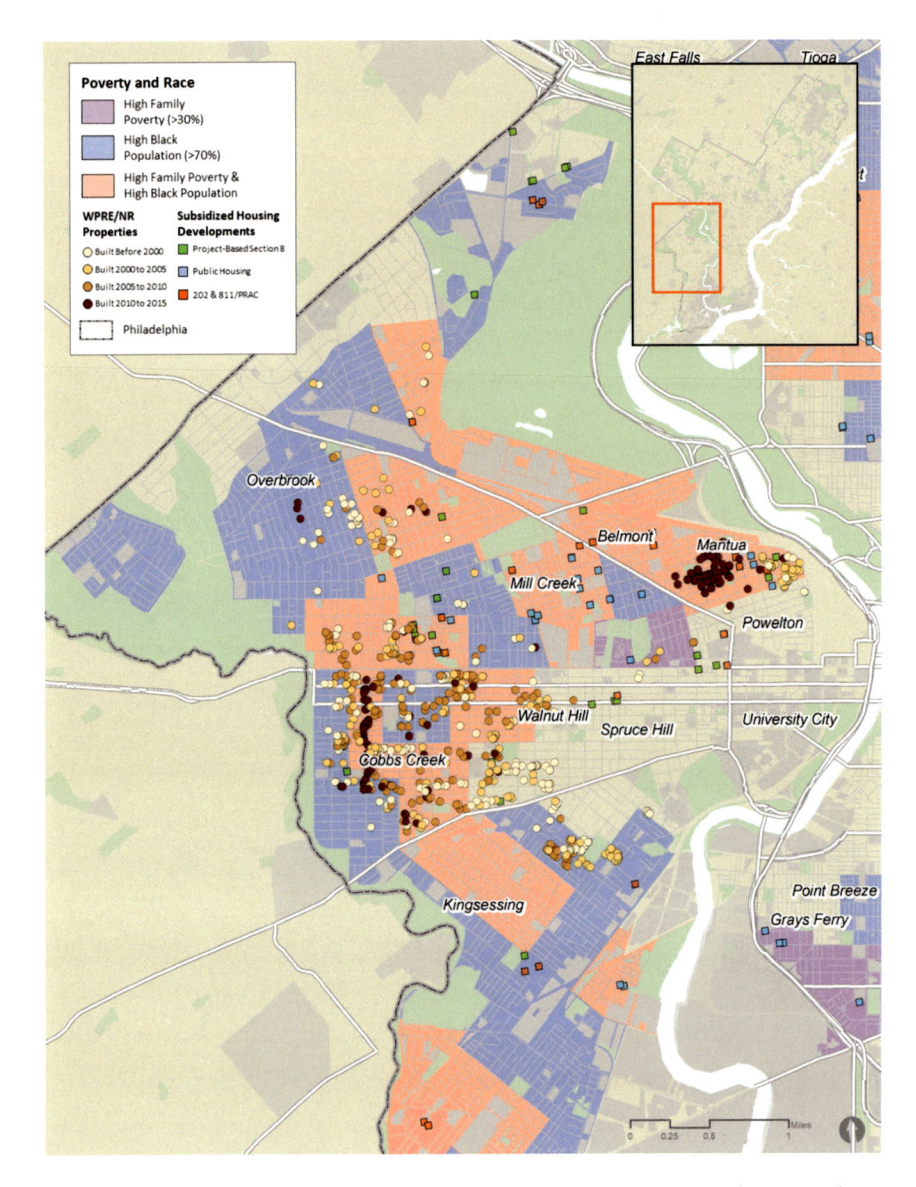

Source: American Communities Survey, Five-year Estimates, 2014-2018; U.S Department of Housing and Urban Development: Office of Policy Development and Research, Picture of Subsidized Households (2018). Note: 202 & 811/PRAC refer to supportive housing for elderly and disabled individuals.

Map 3: WPRE/NR Developments, By 2016 Poverty Rate and Black Population

Pennsylvania Housing Finance Agency (PHFA) for tax credits to finance their redevelopment. By focusing on vacant homes scattered on otherwise well occupied blocks, they believed their work could create new affordable homes while also helping to stabilize the surrounding community by removing the blighting influence of vacant homes.

A scattered-site LIHTC model was new to PHFA, and it initially rejected the idea. However, PHFA was eventually convinced there was enough demand for affordable single-family homes. Over the past three decades, PHFA has approved Neighborhood Restorations to develop 24 different scattered-site redevelopment projects with LIHTC funding.

A critical goal of WPRE/NR became the production of houses that are indistinguishable from those in the surrounding neighborhood—single-family rowhouses and duplexes whose exterior is in the same or better condition of those surrounding them.[6] Today, one would be hard pressed to distinguish WPRE/NR units from the surrounding community. By ensuring that homes blend in with the fabric of the local community, and by targeting renovations to vacant properties on otherwise occupied blocks, WPRE/NR's investments have helped stabilize the communities in which it invests.

When WPRE first began transforming vacant rowhouses into rental units in 1989, neighbors were nervous about the idea of White investors coming into their predominantly Black neighborhood, extracting rents and leaving. To help gain their trust, Mazo and Levin spent a lot of time on site speaking with neighbors, sharing their goals for their investment, and answering neighbors' questions. WPRE/NR leaders also earned neighbors' trust by hiring local neighborhood contractors and by moving their office and personal homes into the neighborhood. In some cases, their projects also included home repairs to adjacent existing homes to ensure all homeowners on the block benefited, and to protect WPRE/NR's investment.

---

6 The vast majority of WPRE/NR properties are renovated row homes, which are an iconic single-family housing stock that dominates the residential real estate landscape throughout the city. Rehabbing these homes while maintaining 'the row' was a fundamental way the WPRE/NR investments helped to maintain the character of individual streets throughout West Philadelphia.

WPRE/NR'S SCATTERED-SITE MODEL

Step 1: Acquire Property

WPRE/NR's scattered-site model relies on the availability of low-cost properties that can be acquired and renovated to create affordable housing. For the most part, these are rowhouse shells that have been abandoned for more than 10 years. Early on, WPRE/NR focused on acquiring individual properties on blocks that contained just a few vacant properties.

Abandoned homes are purchased with an acquisition line of credit from Reinvestment Fund, a local community development financial institution (CDFI) committed to building wealth in historically underserved areas. The acquisition line is paid off once the developer receives tax credits and closes on the construction loan. Over the years, WPRE/NR purchased these abandoned homes for a range of prices including $1 for city-owned properties, below-market-value bids at tax sales, and market value for privately owned listed properties.[7] The average cost paid for the scattered-site vacant housing units from 1989 to 2015 was $13,380 (adjusted for inflation to 2015 dollars).

The two biggest challenges in land acquisition have been (1) city failure to clear title to publicly owned properties, leaving WPRE/NR with substantial back taxes and liens that have taken years to correct; and (2) dramatically rising house prices in 2006-2007 and again in more recent years, which have endangered the viability of the model. Over time, owing to the growing development pressure in the area, opportunities to work on blocks that contain only a few vacant properties became rarer. In response, WPRE/NR began purchasing clusters of homes on blocks with higher vacancy rates, working to ensure that they could acquire a sufficient number of these properties to stabilize the block. WPRE/NR also has begun construction of new units on vacant sites when the rowhouses in an area are unaffordable.

Step 2: Create an Eligible LIHTC Project

With site control of multiple abandoned properties clustered in the same area and private financing secured, WPRE/NR applies to PHFA for LIHTC funding. To make a project LIHTC-eligible, another investor—typically a business that

---

7 Beginning in 1996, WPRE/NR obtained city-owned abandoned homes in West Philadelphia for $1 for use in the developments under the Rendell (former Philadelphia mayor) Administration.

wants to take advantage of tax credits—must be party to the deal. If WPRE/NR's project is selected by PHFA, the investor partner who receives the tax credits typically pays the present value of the LIHTC credits over a period of time. These funds are used by WPRE/NR for construction and development of the scattered site units.

WPRE/NR has applied for and received LIHTC support for 24 redevelopment projects since 1989. The smallest LIHTC award, in 1991, was used to redevelop 10 units—six single-family homes and two duplexes. Two of the largest projects, in 2004 and 2006, entailed the redevelopment of approximately 80 single-family homes each.

Step 3: Rehabilitate Abandoned Houses

Managing construction costs is critical for the viability of the model. Focusing on renovations rather than new construction helps keep costs low. Per unit, WPRE/NR's scattered site development costs were 24 percent lower than development costs for new-construction, multifamily LIHTC housing in Philadelphia.[8]

At capacity, WPRE/NR can complete about 60 homes per year or five homes per month. Houses are stripped down to their bare bones and re-built on the same footprint and with the same square footage. In each home, WPRE/NR provides new plumbing, wiring, roof, floors, studs and walls, using a general contractor to oversee the rehabilitation. General contractors that work with WPRE must provide documentation that they have 50 percent minority employees and at least 50 percent local resident employees. The City of Philadelphia tracks minority participation rates through its monthly workforce participation audits. In 2013, for example, the city notified WPRE/NR that for a project internally referred to as WPRE III, 68 of 121 total employees working on site (56 percent) were minority employees and 62 (51 percent) were local employees.[9]

Since 2008, WPRE/NR has used sustainable building practices to ensure each home receives LEED certification from the U.S. Green Building Council and

---

[8] Reinvestment Fund, *West Philadelphia Scattered Site Model: An Affordable Housing Impact Study*. (Reinvestment Fund, 2016), https://www.reinvestment.com/wp-content/uploads/2016/12/WPhila_Scattered-Site_2016.pdf.

[9] City of Philadelphia Office of Housing and Community Development, unpublished letter, February 5, 2013.

Energy Star certification from the U.S. Environmental Protection Agency. This ensures that all houses are energy efficient and utility costs are reduced to increase the home's affordability. It also helps keep homes warm, safe, and dry with the lowest possible indoor air pollutants.

Step 4: Provide High-Touch Property Management. Completed units are rented to qualified low-income tenants. Tenants sign a one- or two-year lease but stay an average of 3.9 years. The LIHTC program requires that tenants must have incomes at or below 60 percent of Area Median Income. In the first 10 years of operation, almost 90 percent of WPRE/NR tenants had Section 8/Housing Choice vouchers. In 2015, 40 percent of tenants used a Section 8 voucher, and the other 60 percent paid the affordable market rents set by the LIHTC program, without assistance.

WPRE/NR's property management company, Prime Property Management, leases and manages the organization's portfolio of units. Prime Property Management is responsible for fixing all systems within the house and the home's structure. The company has a full-time staff of 16 employees. Half of these employees perform maintenance on houses, while the other half provide administrative support. All but one of Prime Property Management's 16 employees are Black and live in Philadelphia. About 70 percent of these employees currently live in West Philadelphia neighborhoods, and all were neighborhood residents when hired.

Holding maintenance and operating costs low allows WPRE/NR to make a profit while keeping rents affordable. Since 2000, the average maintenance cost per unit has been $1,200 per year. Operating expenses, which include insurance, legal and professional fees, advertising, and taxes, average $3,380 per year or roughly $282 per month.

WPRE/NR also recognize the challenges confronted by many of their tenants. Since 2004, WPRE has given each tenant access to social services through the Public Health Management Corporation (PHMC), a local nonprofit health institute. These services include preventative health programs, job training and placement programs, childcare assistance services, substance abuse treatment, legal services, and mortgage counseling. WPRE/NR provides information to tenants about these services and pays PHMC's fees when a tenant chooses to participate in a program. In addition, since 2004, 10 percent of all rehabilitated homes have been accessible for persons with disabilities.

WPRE/NR INVESTMENTS AND MITIGATING RESIDENT DISPLACEMENT RISK

Reinvestment Fund developed the Displacement Risk Ratio (DRR) to understand whether households may be facing financial pressure to leave their homes and neighborhoods due to circumstances beyond their control (e.g., rapidly rising taxes/insurance, rent increases, or conversion of rental property into owner-occupied stock). WPRE/NR has modified the location and timing of its developments in response to changes in the DRR in West Philadelphia.

The DRR is calculated through the following steps:

- Set 2000 census median family incomes as a benchmark for each block group in Philadelphia.
- Inflate block group median family incomes each year using the Consumer Price Index (CPI).
- For each block group, calculate the ratio of the median home sale price to the inflated median income, using rolling two-year periods.
- Subtract the citywide ratio from each block group ratio to establish a citywide reference.

The calculation identifies places where households with an economic profile similar to that of previous area residents may no longer be able to afford to do so. This feature makes the DRR well-suited to examining the concurrence of resident displacement risk and WPRE/NR investments.

Map 4 presents changes in the DRR from 2000 to 2017 along with the location of WPRE investments, represented as blue dots, appearing in the years that each project came online. In Philadelphia, block groups with DRR scores that reach above 3.0 over time are generally considered no longer affordable to the typical household in the "start year" (2000).

Across these maps, the displacement pressure builds in block groups branching out from University City—north into Powelton Village and Mantua, and farther west and south along Baltimore Ave. The WPRE/NR investments are locking in long-term affordable units within and nearby increasingly hot housing markets, represented by the darkest areas on the maps. In these block groups, long-time residents or residents with incomes similar to the block group's 2000 residents are likely experiencing the greatest displacement

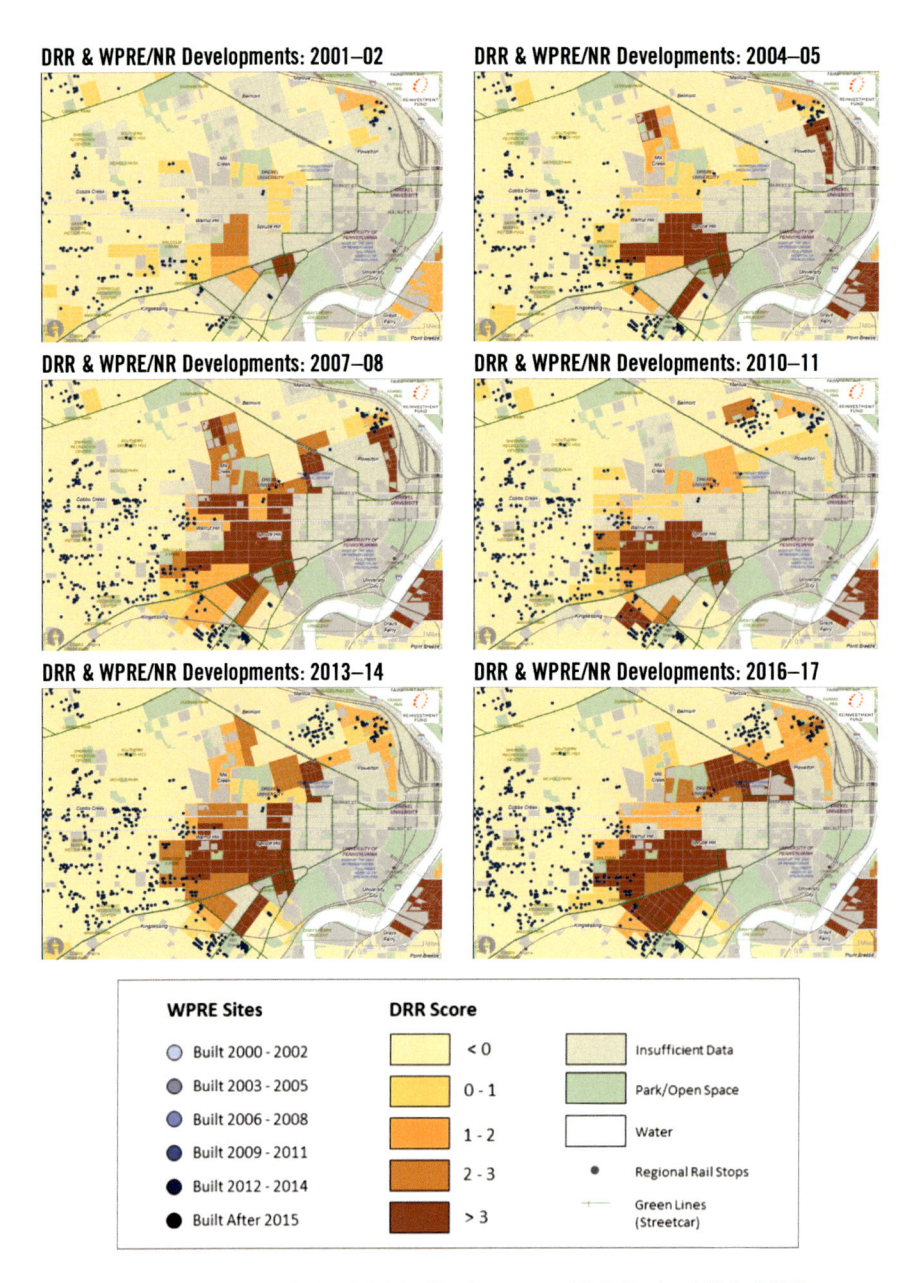

Map 4: Changes In West Philadelphia Displacement Risk Ratio: 2001–2017

pressure. These are areas that are undergoing substantial redevelopment activities led primarily by the University of Pennsylvania and Drexel University.

Other studies have documented ways in which LIHTC developments have positive impacts in low-income communities. By contributing to rising home prices in the predominantly Black and historically disinvested areas where WPRE/NR properties are located, WPRE/NR is both helping to stabilize housing values for long-term residents, but also potentially contributing to the rising displacement pressure facing residents. This adverse consequence is balanced by the creation of a stock of high-quality affordable housing in some of West Philadelphia's more rapidly appreciating housing markets, thus maintaining a racial and economic mix.[10]

Map 5 shows how the Black population in West Philadelphia has changed during this same period along with the location of WPRE investments. Comparing the change in the Black population over time, it is clear that many WPRE/NR properties are located in or directly adjacent to neighborhoods undergoing substantial demographic changes. As more low- and moderate-income residents of color have been priced out of these areas, the availability of WPRE/NR units allows some residents to stay in place, helping to maintain mixed-income and mixed-race communities.

DISCUSSION

To date, WPRE/NR has created over 1,100 housing units in an area that is home to nearly 86,000 households. The observed impact of these redevelopment activities highlights a critical tension for those working in community development space in cities across the country: Redevelopment activities that improve housing conditions in underserved markets may also drive price appreciation in the broader neighborhood. However, developments that contribute to rising property values in the surrounding community can be a boon to long-term residents if those residents are able to stay in the community.

In the western half of West Philadelphia, home values remain so low that the risks of displacement pressure stemming from WPRE/NR's activity (or that of

---

10 Reinvestment Fund. "Assessing Impact: Study Finds that NRLP and TRF Relationship Results in an Improved Community". https://www.reinvestment.com/wp-content/uploads/2005/12/NRLP_Assessing_Impact-Brief_2005.pdf; https://www.reinvestment.com/wp-content/uploads/2016/12/WPhila_ScatteredSite_2016.pdf (2016).

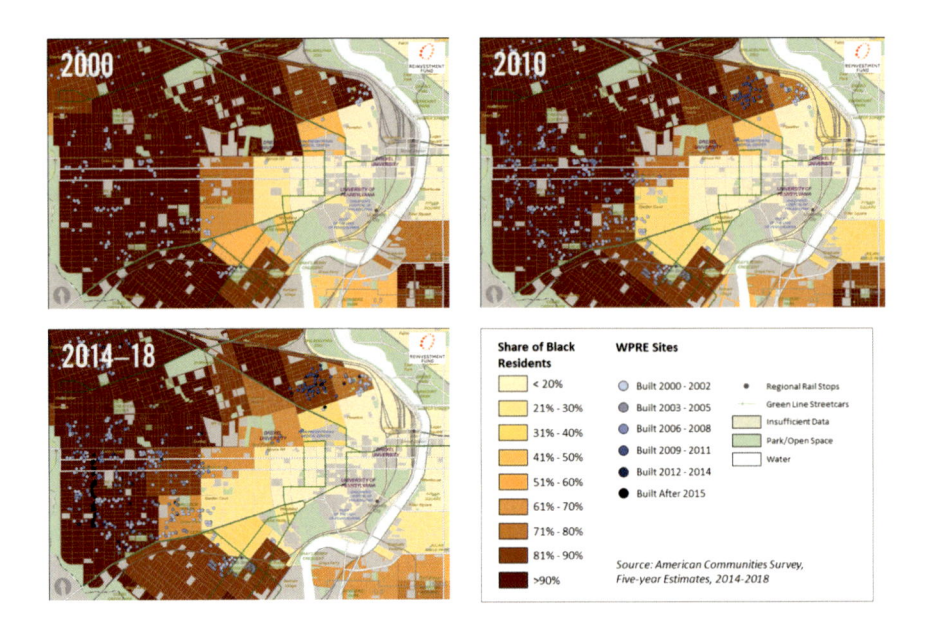

Map 5: Changes In West Philadelphia Black Population and WPRE/NR Sites, 2000–2018

the University of Pennsylvania or Drexel University) remain negligible. These areas of West Philadelphia continue to be home to Black populations that exceed 75 percent of all block group residents. However, in neighborhoods just outside University City, such as Powelton Village, West Powelton, Mantua, Cedar Park, and Walnut Hill, WPRE/NR's units are either on the leading edge, or directly within areas experiencing tremendous displacement pressure. These also are areas of West Philadelphia where the Black population is moving inversely with home price appreciation: As the displacement pressure has increased, the Black population has steadily declined. WPRE/NR's development activities create long-term affordable units for low- and moderate-income, predominantly Black households. These homes are located near some of the city's largest concentration of employment; their production is also proceeding within an environment of ongoing market-rate development that continues to push real estate values higher. This reality puts pressure on local residents who are not fortunate enough to secure these, or similar, housing situations. At the same time, in West Philadelphia's more distressed areas, WPRE/NR investments serve as a stabilizing force and provide a much-needed boost to depressed housing values.

CONCLUSIONS

WPRE/NR is unusual in its commitment to community, its long-term connection to place, and its determination to create a housing product that fits into the neighborhood fabric. This approach to development is something that Reinvestment Fund also seeks in developers of housing for lower-income people. The two entity's work in West Philadelphia over the past 30 years offer evidence that it is possible to leverage limited public subsidies to create high-quality affordable housing that generates a sustainable profit over the long term. Looking ahead, as WPRE/NR's initial properties in West Philadelphia approach the end of the 30-year LIHTC term, the affordability requirements attached to these units will begin to expire. At this time, the owners have expressed no interest in raising rents even where market rents have risen substantially.

WPRE/NR is extraordinarily proud of the contributions its efforts have made to creating and sustaining mixed-income neighborhoods of opportunity, and leaders expect the properties, at current rent levels, to provide a reliable income stream once their debt is retired. As the rental restrictions sunset for these properties, WPRE/NR's founders plan to research approaches used by other well-managed scattered-site projects financed by LIHTC so that their properties remain affordable.

Looking ahead, it is unclear whether there are enough other developers and enough LIHTC subsidy, or both, to support comparable efforts to redevelop West Philadelphia's aging and in some cases crumbling housing stock with high-quality, affordable housing options for individuals and families of modest means. It also is uncertain whether market-rate development will drive rents in the neighborhoods adjacent to University City to the point where lower-income residents, particularly Black residents, are concentrated in increasingly narrow portions of West Philadelphia in housing that is becoming obsolete and, in many instances, hazardous. What *is* clear from WPRE/NR's work, however, is that as communities exert their voice in decisions around development activities within their community, the model outlined can be held up as a positive force in the community, unlike developments that simply deliver a product.

IMPLICATIONS FOR ACTION

WPRE/NR's experience in West Philadelphia provides an instructive example of affordable housing development that preserve affordable housing units in rapidly appreciating markets while also stabilizing conditions and improving property values in distressed markets. The key learnings presented in this essay point to a range of potential implications for policymakers, researchers, developers, and local residents.

Implications for Policy

Policymakers who are interested in ways to protect long term residents in rapidly appreciating markets should consider promoting similar scattered-site models as one approach, among many, to preserve affordability in appreciating neighborhoods. Many cities, Philadelphia included, have implemented Longtime Owner Occupant Programs (LOOPs) that cap property tax increases for homeowners. Circuit breaker programs can also place caps on property tax increases for residents at certain income thresholds. The scattered-site model presented here is an economically viable and important complement to more traditional approaches to affordable housing in large multifamily developments and, increasingly, lower-density developments; moreover, the approach directly supports renters, whereas LOOPs and circuit breakers tend to support homeowners. This model also points to the multidimensional benefits of a scattered-site LIHTC model not often recognized by housing finance agencies responsible for allocating tax credits.

Implications for Research and Evaluation

Prior evaluation of the WPRE/NR model identified efficiencies related to development costs as well as boosts to property values of nearby properties compared to single-site LIHTC developments in West Philadelphia. Future research could examine the differential impact of the WPRE/NR model in other markets. In West Philadelphia, the presence of a large jobs hub anchored by multiple universities and hospitals has provided a floor for the housing market, on which WPRE/NR's investments could build. Could scattered-site investments like those provided by WPRE/NR also prove to be a stabilizing force in weaker and more isolated housing markets that lack anchors such as these? It would also be very important for future research to identify benchmarks for affordable housing development that could be considered 'enough' for different types of markets. That is, how much affordability should be built into gentrifying markets to ensure continuation of the historical makeup of residents in the community? And what is the right mix of affordable and market-rate housing development to stabilize and turn around more distressed areas?

Implications for Development and Investment

When WPRE/NR began, it was not considered a creditworthy borrower for traditional bank financing. So leaders turned to Reinvestment Fund, a local CDFI. Having a "high-touch" capital partner with access to patient capital, experience executing deals with a complicated capital stack that included layers of tax credits and other public subsidies, and on-the-ground knowledge of the markets went a long way toward getting the scattered-site model off the ground. WPRE/NR is now bankable with traditional lenders, yet it remains a capital partner of Reinvestment Fund due to the long-standing relationship developed over time, the CDFI's fine-grained understanding of the business model and the neighborhoods it serves, and Reinvestment Fund's confidence in WPRE/NR's ability to consistently generate returns to meet debt obligations. For other private developers looking for opportunities to create affordable housing in rapidly appreciating markets, it will be important to find a capital partner with similar financial flexibility, experience, and market local knowledge.

Implications for Residents and Community Members

In 2005, Reinvestment Fund conducted interviews and a small survey of roughly 50 WPRE/NR residents to better understand how occupancy in these properties was influencing their quality of life. Key findings suggested that virtually all study participants enjoyed higher-quality housing than in their previous residences; a majority considered their blocks more desirable than their previous living situations; and roughly half indicated their new residences allowed them to save more effectively and contributed to a heightened sense of personal responsibility.

An additional lesson to be taken from the WPRE/NR experience, especially as it relates to community members, is that well-managed subsidized housing can be an asset in a community. Exerting community voice to block all development in a neighborhood may well be counterproductive. WPRE/NR takes formerly abandoned and blighted properties and returns them to productive use; they are well maintained and tenanted with families who take pride in their homes and, by all reports, act as good neighbors. Owing to some combination of actual bad experiences and stereotypes about subsidized-housing tenants, neighbors may not welcome development and the new residents, and may also work to block the creation of high-quality affordable housing.

■ ■ ■

MICHAEL NORTON serves as Chief Policy Analyst at Reinvestment Fund. In this role he supports all research related to Reinvestment Fund's organizational goals and mission. Dr. Norton works closely with a range of partners, including small non-profit organizations, local and national philanthropies, private companies, colleges and universities, school districts, federal, state, and city governments and agencies. His work leverages nearly a decade of experience as researcher and project director to develop data driven solutions—solutions that meet the unique needs of Reinvestment Fund and our key stakeholders in the public and private sectors. Dr. Norton completed his doctoral studies in Sociology at Temple University, where his research examined the relationship between primary and secondary mortgage market activity and neighborhood change in the Philadelphia region at the turn of the 21st century. He also teaches in the John Glenn School for Public Affairs at The Ohio State University.

■ ■ ■

KAREN L. BLACK is the CEO of May 8 Consulting, Inc. a woman-owned social impact consulting firm. May 8's research and coalition building has supported the creation of many innovative state and local laws and policies that create affordable housing, reactivate problem properties and attract new investment. Black is also a lecturer at the University of Pennsylvania and a Senior Research Fellow at Drexel University's Lindy Institute for Urban Innovation.

■ ■ ■

JACOB L. ROSCH is a senior policy analyst with Reinvestment Fund. At Reinvestment Fund, Mr. Rosch leads projects to help philanthropic, government, and private investors design strategies to build healthy and thriving communities, support the expansion of high quality childcare, and improve the lives of residents and families in disadvantaged communities. His most recent projects have investigated the supply of infant and toddler care in Philadelphia area, the impact of scattered site housing projects, and the role of "middle market" neighborhoods in legacy cities.

6

WHAT IS NEEDED BEYOND MIXED-INCOME HOUSING?

Comprehensive Approaches to Mixed-Income Communities

These essays expand our understanding of design and planning strategies to help create inclusive, equitable mixed-income communities. They address core challenges and opportunities beyond the building of housing units, exploring how to use design strategies to enhance the health, wellbeing and social dynamics among the demographically diverse array of residents who live in these communities. Each essay offers practical ideas for how to design and advance inclusion and equity within mixed-income neighborhoods.

In "Ten Urban Design Strategies for Fostering Equity and Inclusion in Mixed-Income Neighborhoods," Emily Talen of the University of Chicago describes how the design of urban neighborhoods has been used in the past to demarcate differences in populations based on race, income, and other identities. Rather than feed into this historical trend, she recommends 10 design strategies that highlight the potential for mixed-income neighborhoods to support and sustain diverse populations. She argues that "residents of diverse neighborhoods…are being enlisted as active participants in a broader societal objective that seeks equity and inclusion in our neighborhoods—the opposite of what the American pattern of settlement has usually been about." Urban planners, developers, architects and others will benefit from incorporating her design strategies as they consider changes in the built environment.

In a polarized society mixed-income communities must address the critical challenge of exclusionary social dynamics. In their essay "Promising Practices to Promote Inclusive Social Dynamics in Mixed-Income Communities," Joni Hirsch and Mark Joseph advocate for more expansive engagement strategies that focus on a shift in operating culture and deeper levels of inclusion at both the individual and structural level. They spotlight several innovative models currently implemented in the U.S. and Canada. Ultimately the authors argue, "We must seek to change the underlying social and structural conditions that breed fear, isolation, and distrust in mixed-income communities. We must approach individual and community transformation in ways that firmly contextualize historical and structural conditions. And we must use intentional, conceptually driven practices to shift (or, more boldly, disrupt) existing operating cultures among all people and organizations that touch the mixed-income community."

In "Recognizing and Incentivizing Mixed-Income Communities Designed for Health," Sara Karerat and Lisa Creighton from the Center for Active Design explore strategies that have long-term implications for the health outcomes of individuals and communities. They describe innovations that provide the evidence-based guidance necessary for developers, building managers, and building owners to design housing that supports, rather than detracts from, resident health: the Fitwel® Certification System and the Healthy Housing Rewards™ financial incentive program. The authors argue that these certification systems should be incorporated into housing for people of all income levels. Karerat and Creighton's essay is especially timely given the global pandemic; as they write, "In the face of rising chronic disease rates and intensifying economic disparities—deeply aggravated in 2019-20 by the COVID-19 pandemic—this is a crucial time to prioritize health through health-promoting, mixed-income communities."

In "Mixed-Income Communities Need Mixed-Income Early Care and Education," Matthew Tinsley and Mary Ann Dewan from the Santa Clara County Office of Education in Northern California make the case for greater attention to the value of including early care and education as part of the design of and investment in mixed-income communities. They suggest that a focus on programs and services for children 0-5 years of age and their families may be an effective strategy to advance the goals of mixed-income community development projects, especially when complemented by school improvement efforts. They review the evidence for the impact of early care and education on low-income children and their mothers, as well as on middle-income children who receive care in mixed-income early care settings. They spotlight existing policies and practices that promote child care programs in mixed-income communities and provide specific examples of mixed-income developments that have set aside units designed specifically for family childcare home provider businesses.

TEN URBAN DESIGN STRATEGIES FOR FOSTERING EQUITY AND INCLUSION IN MIXED-INCOME NEIGHBORHOODS

Emily Talen
University of Chicago

Design for social diversity is challenging because it asks urban dwellers to use place as a connector rather than a divider. Residents of diverse neighborhoods—where diversity is based on income, race, or ethnicity—are being asked to reverse the usual association between place and difference, where attention to one has meant delimiting the other. They are being encouraged to have a heightened sense of place and, at the same time, have a more relaxed attitude about difference. They are being enlisted as active participants in a broader societal objective that seeks equity and inclusion in our neighborhoods—the opposite of what the American pattern of settlement has usually been about.

In highly diverse areas, there are special challenges to forming a unified vision of what the neighborhood should be and how it should grow. Social diversity is often fragile and sensitive to context. This makes public participation even more essential, since the ability to take control of neighborhood change may very well be the best strategy for sustaining diversity. Diverse neighborhoods already have to work through social mix on a daily basis. It seems that planners could, at a minimum, ensure that there is a process in place for dealing with conflicts over issues having to do with the design and use of space.

THE IMPORTANCE OF DESIGN

The design of a built environment affects the accessibility, interactions, movements, identity, mix, and security of people who live there. Design is especially important for mixed-income neighborhoods,[1] for several reasons:

Mixed-income neighborhoods face the added challenge of trying to accommodate residents with varied needs, tastes, and backgrounds. This diversity can accentuate the meaning and implications of physical design: boundaries can take on special significance, connectivity can clash with a heightened need for privacy, and visual coherence can conflict with diverse tastes and styles. The differences among residents may cause some to be suspicious of others, so design needs to be a positive aspect of neighborhood life—not an added stress point. And to the degree that mixed-income neighborhoods also are mixed-race neighborhoods, intentionality about design is needed to ensure neighborhood success.

Many physical transitions tend to occur in diverse neighborhoods, as different kinds of people do different kinds of things. For example, a single block may include single-family homes, apartments over stores, group homes (e.g., senior housing), and uses that vary from schools to car repair shops. The variation in activities is likely to require variation in building types and styles, as well as the type and quality of spaces and uses. Without some element of design coherence in which the built environment supports rather than degrades the public realm, and where diverse uses and building types are integrated way rather than chaotic, this variation can be a source of stress.

Because diverse, mixed-income neighborhoods often are subject to targeted policies such as rent control, tax relief, zoning changes, or regulations on new developments, design is needed to ensure that the policies are both positive for neighborhood residents and sensitive to design variation.

Design can help focus residents' attention on the public realm, which includes not only obvious spaces such as parks and playgrounds but also public land that weaves through every neighborhood, including sidewalks and crosswalks, bus stops, and plazas. In diverse places, high-quality public spaces can serve as the glue that holds a population together, helping residents think about their similarities and connections rather than their differences and conflicts.

The absence of attention to the design of public and private places can create a stressful, chaotic neighborhood. This is not about instilling extreme order and

---

1 Emily Talen and Sungduck Lee, *Design for Social Diversity*. (London: Routledge, 2018).

homogenization—it is about finding the right balance between design quality and random chaos.

Design affects the quality and means of social connection. For example, a neighborhood that is walkable and pedestrian-oriented tends to include public spaces that support casual or spontaneous interactions, and more social interaction might lead to a greater sense of community, social capital, and collective efficacy—effects that are especially important in mixed-income areas.

Design is not the sole means for balancing the complexities of mixed-income and mixed-race neighborhoods; it would be wrong to expect design to do too much. But in the United States, the strategy of leveraging design to promote social diversity, equity, and inclusion has been underplayed. This caution is no doubt driven by the fact that physical design has been cast as a cure-all throughout planning history. And yet, the failure to articulate the urban design needs and requirements of mixed-income neighborhoods seems like a missed opportunity. To address that gap, this essay highlights 10 specific design strategies, specific to diverse neighborhoods that can be used to foster equity and inclusion in mixed-income (and mixed-race) neighborhoods.

TEN URBAN DESIGN STRATEGIES FOR MIXED-INCOME NEIGHBORHOODS

The following design strategies can be calibrated for use in a variety of neighborhood settings and densities, including in some non-diverse contexts. However, the strategies take on special import—indeed, are imperative— in neighborhoods that are trying to achieve or sustain a diverse, mixed-income population.

1. Housing Type Mix

A mixture of housing types, sizes, and tenures, both single-family and multi-family, ensures that social mobility does not require geographic mobility by providing opportunities for residents to change their housing "in place." (A mix of housing ages is important, too, since older units often are more affordable than new ones.) The concept of housing mix steers us away from the idea that neighborhoods represent monocultural reflections of social standing and toward the idea that diverse neighborhoods need to provide multiple living options.

To support a mixture of housing types, diverse neighborhoods need zoning codes that focus less on buildings' uses than on how buildings fit together to form a coherent streetscape. This orientation, known as "form-based" coding, encapsulates an approach to zoning reform that, although it applies to many of the design strategies discussed below, directly affects the flexibility needed to mix housing types. Such codes go beyond simple floor area ratios (FARs) and unit sizes to regulate factors such as buildings' height, location on a lot, and parking. Focusing on how buildings can be regulated to provide coherency and a well-designed public realm reduces the focus on use singularity and encourages use diversity. Codes should allow a range of options for blocks to accommodate multiple housing types and for buildings to house multiple uses (e.g., residential, lodging, office or retail spaces).

2. Multi-Family Units in Single-Family Blocks

Form-based codes can help ensure that new housing is compatible with existing neighborhood character. Neighborhoods that have been only single-family should allow the addition of multi-family housing, but in a way that is compatible with and respects the character of the single-family housing neighborhood. Numerous examples of successfully integrated housing types exist, often with stately apartment buildings on corner intersections and single-family housing in between. Or, new multi-family housing can easily take on the basic typology of the preexisting single-family housing.

3. Courtyards, Closes, and Other Forgotten Housing Types

Mixed-income neighborhoods should make ample use of innovations in housing type, including multi-family arrangements that accommodate diverse housing needs, such as small housing units that provide options for low- to moderate-income households as well as additional rental income for existing property owners. Small units include accessory apartments, micro-units, or "granny flats." Courtyard housing and closes (i.e., short looped streets with housing around them) are especially appropriate for integrating smaller housing types into an existing neighborhood. (Housing-type integration was important to early 20th century planners, who were skilled at fitting in attached row houses amongst single-family housing.) And, if small-unit infill is encouraged in neighborhoods near public transit, parking will be less of an issue and existing residents might be less resistant.

4. Linkages between Different Housing Types

Transition spaces, the areas between different housing types, should be designed purposefully for active use and to form a visual link from one type to another. Vacant lots and other under-utilized spaces, or the juxtaposition of different housing types without transitions or a sense of context, can awkwardly accentuate the differences. The appropriate design strategy is to pay attention to the publicly owned land in such areas. For example, transitional open areas can be designed as pocket parks, and streets can be designed as connecting spaces. "Woonerfs"—streets intended to be shared by cars, bicycles, and people—are particularly useful design elements in neighborhoods with mixed housing types.

5. Fitting in Small Businesses

Diverse people need diverse businesses. The business diversity required likely is not in the form of "town centers" or mega-developments but locally owned small businesses which in a mixed-income, mixed-race community would, in turn, encourage business and service diversity. Small, independent businesses in diverse areas need to be protected and nurtured, and new small business growth encouraged. In design terms, this means encouraging building-type and architectural variety, which might require some degree of design control. The key is to find the right balance between design coherence and design variety by aligning building frontages, limiting blank walls, and ensuring building transparency (i.e., windows). Another strategy is to find places to fit in small businesses—for example, adjacent to alleys and near existing commercial buildings. Encouraging live/work units, artists' lofts, and light manufacturing in the underutilized land adjacent to major transportation corridors may help small businesses and entrepreneurs gain a foothold (or retain their presence) in a diverse community. Such places can function as low-rent business incubators. Urban design can play a role in fitting these varied uses together in a coherent way.

6. Neighborhood Identity Space

To counteract disparate residents' impulse to wall off and separate from each other, mixed-income neighborhoods need a strong, shared neighborhood identity. Public spaces, images, symbols, and landmarks provide a way to bind people together around a shared identity. Often, however, a diverse neighborhood has no centralized, accessible space. In this case, designers should ascertain the places where a diverse cross-section of the population crosses paths—perhaps at the geographic center of the neighborhood—and create a plaza or other public space there to foster neighborhood identity.

7. Streets as Social Seams

Strategies that use streets to enhance neighbors' social connections are based on the observations that: (a) the built environment can constrain or promote passive contact, (b) social interaction may ultimately be tied to the amount of passive contact that occurs, and (c) human interaction at the neighborhood scale is a pedestrian phenomenon. These observations suggest that streets are good social connectors, if designed for that purpose—and that it is useful to view a streetscape as a habitable space rather than as a conduit simply for moving cars.

Using streets as "social seams" can be as simple as delineating safe places to cross existing streets, calming traffic down on busy streets, or instituting better pedestrian pathways. If streets can be conceptualized as a form of public space, they can act as linkages between otherwise separated places. However, overly busy thoroughfares—streets with six lanes of traffic buzzing through the center of the community—can pose a problem in diverse places. In well-traveled areas, ample sidewalk width and street trees could be used to buffer pedestrians from cars and enhance the area's ability to function as collective space. To better define the public area, buildings could be encouraged to form a distinct, well-demarcated frontage that conveys a sense of the public realm. A "build-to" line can help create a better sense of enclosure on the street, thus helping the street maintain its function as an important connective space.

8. Natural Surveillance

In diverse, mixed-income neighborhoods, people need to feel safe and secure as they mix socially and economically and form connections with people of other social groups. The solution is not to support seclusion and withdrawal—that only breeds fear. Instead, design strategies must help counteract the tensions and fear.

One important principle is to enhance natural forms of surveillance, control, and responsibility for public spaces. It should take relatively little effort for people to keep an eye on things as part of their everyday routines. Design can help make it easy for people to focus their "eyes on the street"—to pay attention to and taking responsibility for the neighborhood's security—by ensuring that buildings front and face the public space. People should be able to look out of their windows directly onto the public realm; and public places like parks should not be fronted by garages, parking lots, or the sides of buildings.

9. Activated Dead Space

Another aspect of using design to increase security is to activate "dead" space—empty, unclaimed, or underutilized land for which no one seems to be taking responsibility and from which passersby have little security. Empty space is not simply someone's side yard or an industrial zone; it is space that fronts the public realm but has no connection to it and where decreased areas of activity undermine security.

Dead space often happens in commercial corridors, especially in the form of surface parking lots. Short of having 24-hour police patrols, the best way to increase security in these areas is to line them with active uses. As with all other urban design strategies, this is accomplished via a combination of regulation and incentive. Surface parking lots should be replaced with parking garages lined with commercial space, and traffic calming measures could be instituted to help a commercial street function as a public space rather than a traffic artery. The effect would be a greater sense that the area has public value, thus providing a better sense of security.

10. Softened Strong Edges

Diverse places tend to have strong edges, such as transportation and industrial corridors or large, impermeable districts of various kinds. Some edges provide legibility and identity. But others—a noisy highway, a barren industrial landscape, a metallic railyard—need to be buffered to protect residences from these harsh conditions. Design solutions include establishing a greenway or adding resilient building types (e.g., offices or light industrial buildings) for startup businesses.

SUSTAINING MIXED-INCOME NEIGHBORHOODS THROUGH THE PLANNING PROCESS

Using urban design strategies to sustain diverse, mixed-income neighborhoods in 21st century America will require an engaged public. Nothing in urban design truly succeeds without community buy-in. And the best way to get buy-in is to engage the public in a way that is truly meaningful— where input is not merely lip service but is considered essential. It will be impossible to leverage design for diversity without adequate attention to the public process. What would a planning process devoted to sustaining social diversity be like? I suggest a four-step approach to sustaining social diversity.

Step 1: Decide Which Neighborhoods Should be Targeted for a Neighborhood Planning Effort Directed at Sustaining Diversity

This requires stepping outside of usual procedures. Most often, neighborhoods are selected for planning work based on their level of distress or an opportunity to stimulate private investment. Taking a somewhat different approach, planners could identify neighborhoods with high levels of social diversity, defined either by income, race, ethnicity, or in relation to some other diversity criteria. Planners also could consider threats to existing diversity, the potential for instability (e.g., gentrification, displacement, disinvestment), and the likelihood of success (suggested by citizen interest and active, engaged local leadership). Depending on available resources, a number of diverse neighborhoods could be targeted for special planning effort and focus.

Step 2: Assemble a Neighborhood Planning Group Composed of Local Leaders Who Represent the Diversity of the Neighborhood

This group would be formally and strategically recruited, something that research has shown is critical for building citizen participation at the neighborhood level. The group would be enlisted to support the diversity-sustaining process being proposed. This is essential, given the reality that effective social organization and neighborhood diversity do not generally correlate. As Wilson and Taub, put it, "strong neighborhoods…work against the notion of intergroup harmony and integration."[2] One way to counteract that tendency is to develop a set of shared goals, around which diverse residents can unite. The citizen planning group would be the catalyst for formulating that shared set of objectives.

---

2   William Julius Wilson and Richard P. Taub, *There Goes the Neighborhood: Racial, Ethnic, and Class Tensions in Four Chicago Neighborhoods and Their Meaning for America.* (New York: Alfred A. Knopf, 2006), 181.

Step 3: Have the Citizen's Planning Group Look for Ways to Increase Public Awareness of Neighborhood Diversity

Researchers who study diverse neighborhoods have argued that the maintenance of diversity requires a statement of commitment to diversity and inclusiveness.[3] Efforts must be made to increase recognition and understanding of the kinds of diversity present, of which residents may have only a vague notion. The ideas to be communicated need to be simple, straightforward, and visually interesting; presented in a manner that is readily understood; and suitable for publication and exhibition throughout the neighborhood. The information should highlight racial, ethnic, income, age, and household diversity and include some explanation of how the level and type of diversity has changed over time. Graphical output of various kinds can be exhibited in well-traversed public places, including websites.

Step 4: Formulate and Implement a Neighborhood Plan

A neighborhood plan lays out the concept of a shared future in concrete terms and provides a framework for channeling individual ideas toward something tangible: collectively realized, positive outcomes for the diverse neighborhood. Collaborative planning efforts of this type, which often occur in the form of charrettes, are now recognized as indispensable.[4] The trick is to orient them to the specific needs, issues, and constraints of a diverse, mixed-income neighborhood.

Implementation of the neighborhood plan can focus on three things: (a) establishing a process for shared management of the built environment as an ongoing neighborhood-stabilizing strategy; (b) achieving regulatory reforms, including new types of codes that encourage a coherent yet flexible guide for the built environment; and (c) recommending public investments that will stimulate positive changes, giving the neighborhood the kinds of improvements it needs without undermining its diversity.

---

3 John McKnight and Peter Block, *The Abundant Community Awakening the Power of Families and Neighborhoods*. 1st ed. (San Francisco: Berrett-Koehler Publishers, 2010).

4 Bill Lennetz and Aarin Lutzenhiser, *The Charrette Handbook: The Essential Guide to Design-Based Public Involvement*, 2nd ed. (Chicago, Illinois; Washington, D.C: APA Planners Press, 2014).

IMPLICATIONS FOR ACTION

Implications for Policy

- Enact form-based zoning codes that focus less on use restrictions and more on ways to integrate a diverse set of uses and housing types within a neighborhood.
- Allow multi-family housing in neighborhoods that currently have only single-family homes.
- Use form-based codes to ensure that new housing is compatible with existing neighborhood character.

Implications for Development and Investment

- Innovate with housing type. Make more use of courtyards, closes (short looped streets), micro-units, accessory dwellings, and other creative methods of small-unit integration.

Implications for Research and Evaluation

- Assess where a city's most economically and racially diverse neighborhoods are located.
- Assess what a city's diverse neighborhoods need for long-term support: How well does their zoning, their public space, and their mix of housing types support the needs of a socially, racially and economically diverse population?

Implications for Residents and Community Members

- Organize to ensure that policy makers, developers, and civic leaders pay attention to publicly owned land. Collectivize to convert neglected public land into useable space, such as pocket parks.
- Push for zoning reforms that allow housing-type and land-use diversity.
- Be open to fitting in small businesses, live/work units, and non-polluting, low-impact light manufacturing on underutilized land.

■ ■ ■

EMILY TALEN is Professor of Urbanism at the University of Chicago, where she teaches urban design and directs the Urbanism Lab. She holds a Ph.D. in urban geography from the University of California,

Santa Barbara. She is a Fellow of the American Institute of Certified Planners, and the recipient of a Guggenheim Fellowship. Talen has written extensively on the topics of urban design and social equity. Her latest book is Neighborhood (Oxford University Press, 2018).

PROMISING PRACTICES TO PROMOTE INCLUSIVE SOCIAL DYNAMICS IN MIXED-INCOME COMMUNITIES[1]

Joni R. Hirsch
Fines and Fees Justice Center

Mark L. Joseph
National Initiative on Mixed-Income Communities, Case Western Reserve University

Mixed-income communities have the promise to provide an environment in which residents with a variety of social and economic backgrounds can thrive. Living in a socially and economically diverse community has clear benefits, however, significant social challenges also often arise. One primary lesson that has emerged from past mixed-income interventions (particularly where public housing sites have been redeveloped into new mixed-income communities) is that high-quality housing and supportive services alone are not enough to ensure that low-income families feel like they belong and can fully benefit from living in the revitalized communities.[2] Further, while conventional "community building" efforts aim to engage residents and provide spaces for interaction, research shows that promoting and sustaining meaningful relationships across divisions of race and class is particularly difficult,[3] and there

---

1   A version of this essay was previously released as a Mixed-Income Strategic Alliance research brief with support from the Robert Wood Johnson Foundation; Mixed-Income Strategic Alliance, *Promoting Inclusive Social Dynamics in Mixed-Income Communities: Promising Practices*, (Cleveland, OH: Case Western Reserve University, 2019).

2   Robert J. Chaskin and Mark L. Joseph, *Integrating the Inner City: The Promise and Perils of Mixed-Income Public Housing Transformation* (Chicago: University of Chicago Press, 2015).; Mark L. Joseph and Miyoung Yoon, "Mixed-Income Development," In *Wiley-Blackwell Encyclopedia of Urban and Regional Studies*, edited by Anthony M. Orum John Wiley & Sons Press, 2019.

3   Robert Chaskin and Mark Joseph, "Contested Space: Design Principles and Regulatory Regimes in Mixed-Income Communities Replacing Public Housing Complexes in Chicago," *Annals of the American*

often are limited opportunities for equitable participation in local deliberation and decision-making in socioeconomically diverse environments. Deeply held attitudes and behaviors—including perceptions of difference, othering, lack of trust, and bias—can reinforce the marginalization of low-income residents in a mixed-income setting. Today's political and social environment of race-baiting and exclusion further exacerbates and complicates the us-versus-them group segregation dynamics that often naturally emerge in mixed-income communities. Therefore, in addition to the financial, operational, economic, legal, political, and other consequential dynamics at play in mixed-income communities, "social dynamics" are especially critical to address proactively.

We identify three main categories that make up what we refer to as "social dynamics": perceptual dynamics, relational dynamics, and influence and power dynamics.[4] Perceptual dynamics concern individual identity, efficacy, and self-agency; aspirations for self and family; neighborhood frames; and perceptions of one's role in the broader community. Relational dynamics concern how individuals are connected to each other, which encompasses factors such as social capital, social support, social networks, and social cohesion. Influence and power dynamics concern how individuals can impact their surrounding environment through voice and local influence, participation, governance, collective efficacy, and informal social control.

While recognizing the complexity of cultivating inclusive dynamics across these three levels, we believe there are two main imperatives to ensure that all people in mixed-income communities feel like they belong, can thrive socially, and can influence life in their community:

- Promote an enhanced and sustained vision, clarity, and communication among all stakeholders about a shared commitment to inclusion in the mixed-income environment, with a keen anticipation of challenging social dynamics that may arise due to socioeconomic and racial diversity.

Academy of Political and Social Science 660 (2015): 136-154.; Khare, Amy T., Mark Joseph, and Robert Chaskin. "The Enduring Significance of Race in Mixed-income Developments." *Urban Affairs Review* 50 no. 4 (2014): 1-30. James Fraser, Deidre Oakley and Diane Levy, "Mixed-Messages on Mixed-Income," *Cityscape* 15, no. 2 (2013): 83-100.; Levy, Diane, Zach McDade, and Kassie Bertumen. 2013. Mixed-Income Living: Anticipated and Realized Benefits for Low-Income Households. *Cityscape* 15 (2013): 15-28.

4   Thus our definition of social dynamics is broader than more typical concepts of social cohesion, social relations or social inclusion. National Initiative on Mixed-Income Communities, *State of the Field Scan #1: Social Dynamics in Mixed Income Developments.* (Cleveland, OH: Case Western Reserve University, 2013).

- Implement intentional strategies to translate this shared vision into durable policies, practices, and routines that promote inclusivity.

Trusted Space Partners, a consulting group with deep experience in community building that we highlight later in this essay, advocates for an "operating culture shift," which refers to a significant change in the way that institutions, organizations, and individuals take or fail to take responsibility for cultivating inclusive mixed-income communities.[5] In Trusted Space Partners' view, to achieve mixed-income communities where all residents (and professionals) can thrive, existing community and institutional contexts that are so often (and increasingly) shaped by fear, division, and isolation must be replaced by an operating culture grounded in aspiration and connectedness. They assert that creating and sustaining inclusive mixed-income communities requires stakeholders (planners, developers, property managers, service providers, institutional representatives, funders, and resident leaders among many others) to navigate this endeavor with more holistic, proactive, and human-centered approaches than are characteristic of most past and existing efforts. This process demands intentional practices and spaces, dedicated capacity, and a deep commitment to shifting the way we think about, address, and encourage relationships among residents, community members, and professionals.

In this essay, we first briefly describe the existing individual, social, and structural exclusion that establishes the imperative to promote inclusive social dynamics in mixed-income communities. We then provide a brief overview of the shortcomings of conventional community-building efforts. Next, we highlight four promising models: trauma-informed community building; the Trusted Space Partners community network building model; the Kindred interracial, interclass parent engagement model in Washington D.C.; and the Regent Park inclusive governance model in Toronto, Canada. We share key insights drawn from those examples about how to cultivate more inclusive communities, and we conclude with implications for action.

---

5   Trusted Space Partners and the co-authors are part of a collaborative venture called Triple Aim Impact to provide technical assistance for community network building and other strategies in mixed-income communities.

EXISTING CONTEXT OF SOCIAL ISOLATION AND EXCLUSION

To cultivate inclusive social dynamics across race and class differences, those working to promote mixed-income communities must have a clear sense of the existing and often self-perpetuating conditions of isolation and exclusion. These conditions of exclusion can be categorized at the individual, social, and structural levels.[6]

The individual level includes physical, mental, emotional, and behavioral health challenges, and internalized racism. These conditions create barriers to meaningful participation in community life, generate negative neighborhood frames, and limit perceptions of aspiration, belonging, self-agency, and the ability to envision and effect personal change.

The social level includes disconnection, othering, interpersonal racism and discrimination, stigma, and negative perceptions of peers. These conditions limit social interaction, the formation of social networks, conflict resolution, shared learning, empathy, and compromise. Because of these conditions, a collective sense of community often does not naturally emerge, particularly across differences. Even in places with relatively high levels of neighboring (where individuals have established shared expectations and values that enable them to live well together), relationships most often emerge amongst people of similar housing tenures, incomes, and races. Research also shows that the more diverse a community is, the less frequent interaction occurs, even among individuals of the same social group.[7]

The structural level includes differential means and access to high-quality services, amenities, and educational opportunities; disparities in participation and voice in decision-making by race and class; economic exclusion and income disparities; and structural and institutional racism.

In our view, the most promising practices to promote inclusive social dynamics should address exclusionary conditions at all three levels.

---

6   This section draws on the research of Morgan Bulger, PhD, see, Morgan Bulger, "Toward a Theory of Social Inclusion: The Design and Practice of Social Inclusion in Mixed-Income Communities" (PhD diss., Case Western Reserve University, 2018), https://etd.ohiolink.edu/!etd.send_file?accession=-case1531151650737104&disposition=inline

7   Robert Putnam, "E Pluribus Unum: Diversity and Community in the Twenty-First Century," *Scandinavian Political Studies* 30 (2007): 137-74.

CONVENTIONAL COMMUNITY BUILDING IN MIXED-INCOME COMMUNITIES AND ITS SHORTFALLS

Many mixed-income efforts (particularly in planned mixed-income developments) have included explicit efforts to promote engagement and a sense of community among residents, in recognition of naturally existing divisions. Through social events and programs that are open to everyone in the community, these efforts generally intervene at the social level with a focus on providing opportunities for individuals to interact with one another. These strategies may include intentionally shaping the physical space to encourage social mixing through common areas and other designed features, activities on site, shared amenities and institutions, and place-making strategies. Creating attractive spaces and opportunities for residents to mix, while important, is limited; it fails to reflect the individual–level conditions (e.g., trauma, prevalent stigmatization) and broader structural conditions (e.g., structural racism) in which social divisions are embedded. These strategies also generally focus on resident-to-resident connection rather than genuine engagement or relationship-building with those in positions of local and institutional power.

Some efforts intentionally combine supportive services (sometimes referred to as "human capital" or "social services") with community-building efforts. Through case management and new programs and supports that focus on health, education, and economic self-sufficiency, this approach tends to incorporate both social-level and individual-level strategies to better address components of isolation and exclusion. These approaches recognize that promoting individual well-being creates a more level social playing field, though these approaches do not generally address the individual attitudes and perceptions of higher-income residents—who play a significant role in creating inclusive (or exclusive) social dynamics.

Most mixed-income community interventions also fail to incorporate a focus on structural-level inclusion, such as equitable participation, inclusive governance, and equitable informal social control (without which low-income residents' actions, voice, and access to space may be constrained and disproportionately monitored and sanctioned). Where tenant councils, or other structures for public-housing and other low-income residents, do exist these structures tend to be less influential than condo associations or structures for market-rate renters or home-owners.[8] In failing to interrogate the equity of formal and informal rules, regulations, governance structures, and norms, these approaches do not recognize the underlying culture and systems that perpetuate fear, isolation, and division.

HOW TO PROMOTE MORE INCLUSIVE SOCIAL DYNAMICS

The following questions may guide decision makers seeking more effective approaches to promote inclusive social dynamics in mixed-income communities.

Why? Theory of Change

- Is there a comprehensive strategy in place that addresses perceptual, relational, and influence/power challenges and opportunities? Does this comprehensive strategy employ a trauma-informed/healing-informed, asset-based (as opposed to needs-based) frame?
- Have stakeholders jointly named the existing underlying enduring historical conditions that perpetuate isolation and exclusion and their implications?
- Have community stakeholders articulated a commitment to self-reflection, transformation and an "operating culture" shift away from the status quo?

Who? Community Stewardship

- Are residents, community members, and other community and institutional stakeholders "stewarding" the process of cultivating an inclusive mixed-income community? Are there intentional efforts to identify and build the local capacity of community "stewards"?
- Is there a shared understanding that promoting inclusive social dynamics is not a task that can be assigned to a particular person or organization in an initiative, and that *everyone* has a role?
- Is there comfort with the need for local power-building and advocacy to promote the interests of marginalized residents?

---

8 Robert Chaskin, Amy Khare and Mark Joseph, "Participation, Deliberation, and Decisionmaking: The Dynamics of Inclusion and Exclusion in Mixed-Income Developments," *Urban Affairs Review* 48 no. 6 (2012): 863-906.

How? Strategic Implementation

- Is there organizational infrastructure that will incubate, support, sustain, and resource this process?

- Will intentional strategies to shift the operating culture be incorporated into all routines, practices, and activities?

PROMISING PRACTICES FOR CULTIVATING INCLUSIVE SOCIAL DYNAMICS IN MIXED-INCOME SETTINGS

Each of the models highlighted below is notable for its explicit approach to addressing individual, social, and structural barriers. Unlike programs and approaches that mainly encourage interaction amongst diverse community members, each of these examples is grounded in a theory that acknowledges the underlying exclusionary conditions and a need to radically shift existing mental models, operating culture, and practices.[9]

Trauma-Informed Community Building

Trauma-informed community building (TICB) is an approach to community-based work that prioritizes community healing and empowerment. This approach requires stakeholders to recognize individual and community-level trauma, which may have resulted from violence, racism, and historical harms and often cause distrust of new programs and leadership. TICB applies the trauma-informed lens from the social services field to community-building efforts to better acknowledge and address the deep challenges of individual, community, and structural contexts in high-poverty neighborhoods. In a community setting (unlike in more traditional social services), the focus should be placed on the experiences of and implications for all community members, including professionals. This method emphasizes long-term consistency, reliability, and transparency of resources and supported provided to community members, and is particularly attentive to how key actors position themselves to avoid reinforcing inequity.

TICB was developed by Emily Weinstein, formerly of BRIDGE Housing, and Jessica Wolin, of San Francisco State University in the course of their work

---

[9] It should be noted that each of these examples are relatively new, and all are still being piloted and modified on a relatively small scale of a single site or a few sites. There is still much to be learned about their implementation, results, sustainability, and scalability.

with the HOPE SF mixed-income public housing transformation initiative in San Francisco.[10] Today, the trauma-informed community building approach influences place-based initiatives around the country, but the model does not have a specific centralized home. In April 2018, the Urban Institute published a practical guide to inform practitioners, housing authorities, and other stakeholders on trauma-informed community building and engagement.[11]

The strategies and desired impacts of TICB are conceptualized at the individual, social, and structural level. At the individual level, trauma-informed strategies strive to provide repeated and consistent opportunities for individuals to engage with the opportunities for personal and community support, and offer reliable incentives and personal rewards. In order to increase trust, motivation, and self-efficacy, strategies aim to meet residents at their current state of readiness and to avoid overpromising or introducing unrealistic expectations.[12] The goal is to help residents envision change in their lives—despite their past experiences with people and systems failing them—and to increase their capacity to influence this change. One exemplary aspect of the TICB model is its efforts to proactively create space and incentives for community members to take on leadership roles. At the social level, engagement and regular peer-to-peer activities are rooted in personal sharing and mutual support to create shared positive experiences and trust between residents and staff and to cultivate community leadership. At the structural or "systems" level, TICB approaches aim to build organizational and institutional partnerships for long-term investment. Crucial pieces of this involve effectively positioning and equipping community members to communicate their vision for avoiding processes that reinforce trauma, and promoting healing-oriented approaches.

The model acknowledges that without these changes, systems will continue to fail individuals, reinforcing inequities and deepening mistrust of those in positions of power. The trauma-informed community-building lens has proved

---

10 Emily Weinstein, Jessica Wolin, and Sharon Rose, *Trauma-Informed Community Building. A Model for Strengthening Community in Trauma Affected Neighborhoods*, (San Francisco, CA: BRIDGE Housing, 2014), https://bridgehousing.com/PDFs/TICB.Paper5.14.pdf

11 Elsa Falkenburger, Olivia Arena and Jessica Wolin, *Trauma-Informed Community Building and Engagement*. (Washington, DC: Urban Institute, 2018). https://www.urban.org/research/publication/trauma-informed-community-building-and-engagement

12 HOPE SF Learning Center, *A Formative Evaluation of the TICB Model and its Implementation in Potrero Hill*. (San Francisco, CA: HOPE SF Learning Center, 2015), http://www.aecf.org/m/resourcedoc/hope-TraumaInformedCommunity_Building-2015.pdf

effective at expanding awareness and shifting narratives, although it is relatively early in its implementation phase and outcomes have not yet been measured well. For example, trauma-informed language may be incorporated in strategy documents, but implementation efforts thus far have lacked clear mechanisms to track and evaluate outcomes. Another key challenge is the task of institutionalizing and sustaining a TICB focus. For example, at the Potrero Hill public housing development in San Francisco where this approach originated, considerable staff turnover and the relocation/construction phases of the mixed-income transformation disrupted local activities. Finally, there is a danger that a trauma-informed focus will reinforce a deficit focus, without a strong associated focus on existing resilience and on the imperative of individual and collective healing.

Trusted Space Partners

The Trusted Space Partners model of community network-building[13] aims to create a new organizational and community operating culture rooted in connection and aspiration. This process works to shift energy and focus away from siloed institutional and community processes that can foster isolation, division, and fear. Rather than working primarily through resident organizations and associations, the Trusted Space model seeks to create a new, fresh, inclusive, flexible, and open community network with no gatekeeping and many ways to join and participate. Using creative, dynamic open space techniques and intentional practices to foster meaningful exchange, community network-building helps identify shared interests and build trusting relationships.

Trusted Space Partners was founded by Bill Traynor and Frankie Blackburn. Traynor honed his perspectives and approaches on community network-building during his time leading Lawrence CommunityWorks in Massachusetts, and Blackburn did so while leading Impact Silver Spring in Maryland. Today, members of the Trusted Space team train and coach city planning departments, public housing authorities, real estate developers, property owners, managers,

---

13 Frankie Blackburn and Bill Traynor, "A Call for Property Management Transformation To Meet the Challenges of Mixed-Income Communities," in *What Works to Promote Inclusive, Equitable Mixed-Income Communities*, eds. Amy T. Khare and Mark L. Joseph (2020).; Frankie Blackburn, *The Power of Intentional Networks in Mixed Income Housing*. (Graham, NC: Trusted Space Partners, 2015), http://www.trustedspacepartners.com/uploads/7/7/3/4/77349929/final_-_the_power_of_intentional_networks_in_mixed_income_housing.pdf

residents, and community partners and provide on-the-ground implementation and technical assistance in numerous cities across the United States.

Trusted Space's community network-building approaches are particularly intentional about weaving together individual-level, community-level, and systems-level transformations, through both a goal shift and an operating shift amongst stakeholders and community members. At the root of the Trusted Space theory is the belief that every individual, whether a decision-maker or not, has wisdom and value to contribute. When provided intentional spaces and opportunities to exchange, individuals can engage in relationships of trust and mutual benefit across lines of difference. The model calls for a goal shift, from distinct goals held by disparate stakeholders, residents, and neighbors in a community to a shared aspirational vision. As referenced earlier, the model also calls for an operating culture shift in the way that individuals and groups interact and operate (moving away from compliance-driven, risk-averse and fear-driven routines and practices). The Trusted Space team helps build networks and promote operating culture shifts in a number of settings and communities, including the affordable housing and mixed-income community space.

The notion of an operating culture shift has been generally compelling to partners in various community initiatives. Some elements of the strategy have been relatively easy for community members to launch and adopt, such as the monthly NeighborUp Night[14] gathering for residents, staff and community members, in which interaction is fast-paced and curated with numerous opportunities to derive actionable value from time spent with others that evening. The "party with a purpose" elements are the same every time: heavy recruitment for diverse attendance, a lively and energetic welcome, a visually festive and positively disruptive atmosphere that primes attendees for a different meeting experience, a "new and good" opening in a seated circle where all voices in the room are heard saying something positive within the first 15 minutes of the event, a "table talk" period where meeting attendees spontaneously select and host conversation topics for the evening, a "marketplace" in a standing circle when attendees exchange information and favors or make positive declarations about self-improvement, and finally a "bump and spark" opportunity to mix and mingle. NeighborUp Night is just

---

14 Frankie Blackburn, William Traynor and Yerodin Avent, "Practical Ideas for Addressing Micro-Segregation in Mixed Income Communities," July 6, 2018, *Shelterforce* (blog), https://shelterforce.org/2018/07/06/practical-ideas-for-addressing-micro-segregation-in-mixed-income-communities/

one "device" in Trusted Space Partners' community network-building regimen that also includes community pop-ups, steward-seeking, mutual support cohorts, and idea contests.

While the activities of community network-building have been relatively easy to launch, it has proven far harder to ground these activities within a broader, sustained shift in operating culture—one that meaningfully changes mindsets about the trajectory and possibilities for the community, blurs and bridges lines of difference, and elevates residents and other community members to a different position of influence in order to shape decision-making and achieve durable policy and systems change. A key ingredient to help sustain and deepen the work is the organizational infrastructure and staffing dedicated to orchestrating the overall process, integrating these processes into everyday work flow, and taking responsibility for persistence and sustainability from coordination across various partners involved in the effort.

Kindred

Kindred, founded by Laura Wilson Phelan in Washington, D.C., is an organization that builds structures and relationships for parents from diverse backgrounds to advance racially and economically just outcomes for children within their school communities. The core of the model involves carefully curated small dialogue groups in a school setting, which bring together diverse parents to build interracial, interclass relationships and create space for honest conversations and action-oriented projects about equity. Kindred aims to shift parents' attitudes and behaviors in a way that will change school behaviors, alter resource allocation, and improve student outcomes. There is an explicit focus on equity and coalition building, with a priority of creating a sustainable model by training cohorts of parents to lead ongoing dialogue groups and equity-driven actions. Kindred's model includes the intent to build a digital platform for parents so they can connect across schools on issues of equity. Ultimately, Phelan expects to create a critical mass of parents who, transformed by their interracial, interclass experiences, become lifelong advocates for social justice in their priorities and actions, including how they raise their children. Kindred currently is designed as a 3-year program at each school, funded in part by each school (sources vary depending on whether it is a charter school or public school) but mostly through foundations and individual philanthropy.

Kindred has invested in two external evaluations to assess whether the program's intended impact is being realized.[15] These evaluations[16][17] offer insight into the sustainability of the model and stages of Kindred's theory of change. The evaluators found that parents who participated in Kindred's program experienced a change in their beliefs, values and networks, especially related to building empathy, valuing diversity, increasing their efficacy, and diversifying their social capital networks. Further, parents who participated in Kindred accessed more informational and support resources, either through other parents or the schools. The October 2018 evaluation found there was no diminished effect on trust or sense of community in the school where parents, rather than Kindred staff, facilitated the dialogue groups; nor were discussions of the school's issues involving race, ethnicity, and equity.

This evaluation found promising indicators of a whole-school effect from Kindred's programs, including culture shift to make the school environments more equity-driven. For example, at one site parents took the initiative to draft and post an equity statement. They also changed PTA meetings so that every other one is conducted in Spanish with English translation while the other is the reverse, to enable a more welcoming, inclusive setting for families whose first language is Spanish. These changes were coupled with a noticeable shift in topics raised on the parent listserv and in PTA meetings to focus on creating equitable opportunity for families to access resources. Parents also gained comfort in naming race and disadvantage in different school experiences, and their activism increased. Taken together, the evaluations suggest that the Kindred model has effects at all three levels of social dynamics: individual, social, and structural.

Unlike the other examples highlighted here, the Kindred model operates in mixed-income schools rather than mixed-income housing communities, and thus the social dynamics are shaped by a different set of organizational and systemic realities and constraints. However, the sophisticated, intentional model

---

15 Megan Gallagher and Erica Greenberg, *Kindred Pilot Studies: Summary of Findings from Parent Surveys and Focus Groups*, (Washington DC: Urban Institute, 2017), https://kindredcommunities.org/wp-loads/2017/03/Kindred-Urban-Pilot-Study-2017.pdf

16 Community Science, *Evaluation of the Kindred Program Final Report*, (Gaithersburg, MD: Community Science, 2018).

17 Alysse Henkel, *Evaluation of the Kindred Parent Dialogue Groups at Six Schools: Programs at Amidon Bowen Elementary School, Bancroft Elementary School, EL Haynes Public Charter Elementary School, Garrison Elementary School, Miner Elementary School, and Washington Yu Ying Public Charter School in the 2018-2019 School Year*, (2020).

of cultivating mixed-income, cross-racial groups to promote individual mindset shifts, meaningful relations, and ultimately advocacy and policy change seems likely to apply in other settings such as mixed-income housing communities.

Regent Park

Regent Park, a mixed-income community in Toronto, Canada, has instituted an innovative governance model meant to increase tenant influence and power in decision-making and build leadership capacity. Regent Park is a revitalized Toronto Community Housing (THC) public housing site that began a mixed-income community transformation in 2009. The mixed-income design includes completely separate buildings for subsidized tenants and condo owners, which creates a fundamental level of segregation in the community. Anticipating that there would be an imbalance of influence and representation, and having experienced adverse social outcomes in previous mixed-income conversions, THC's plan to revitalize Regent Park prioritized social inclusion goals—building a cohesive, integrated community while also celebrating its diversity—through the creation of a Regent Park Social Development Plan.

Julio Rigores, the Manager at the Resident and Community Services Division at Toronto Community Housing, led the development of the current Regent Park governance model in collaboration with TCH tenants. The prior system of governance—the Regent Park Neighbourhood Initiative (RPNI)—had played a key role in promoting resident voices, including early advocacy for the community's revitalization. RPNI disbanded, however, in early 2014 due to leadership and financial issues, leaving tenants without a working governance structure. In accordance with the Regent Park Social Development Plan and in response to the Neighbourhood Integration Study conducted in partnership with the University of Toronto, THC set out to develop an innovative new system that would ensure THC residents influenced the governance of Regent Park. Anticipating a 70:30 ratio of market-rate to subsidized residents in the new mixed-income community, the new system (and, notably, the process used to design it) would build tenant capacity and representation so that residents could be more equal participants and decision-makers in important choices about funding streams and service provision.

The Regent Park governance structure consists of representational mechanisms on both the private condo side and the THC side, as well as a combined Regent Park Neighborhood Association (RPNA). At the building level, THC's representational system mirrors the existing condo boards, which have three directors per building. Thus, Regent Park instituted a three-person elected building committee for each building. THC building committee members make up a site-wide tenant council, which has a seven-member leadership team. Representatives from the condos and tenant council form the RPNA. Terms generally last three years; bi-annual elections are held to fill unexpected vacancies. Subcommittees within the RPNA focus on priority areas identified collectively (including safety, maintenance, gardens, employment, and programs and services). While THC provides financial support for collaborative projects and staffing for capacity-building efforts, RPNA is funded independently at the grassroots level, through connections with neighborhood agencies and in-kind contributions. All of RPNA's elected members are volunteers.

The governance model uses intentional structures and processes to build individual capacity, cultivate new relationships, and create and maintain inclusive decision-making and power sharing systems. These structures exist at the individual building level and the neighborhood level (through collaborations between TCH buildings and Regent Park condo boards). At the individual level, THC offers opportunities for leadership training and capacity building through workshops on civic engagement, marketing and communications, community organizing, advocacy, and similar topics. The workshops begin with training and capacity building for elected representatives. These processes also are meant to promote social cohesion and more meaningful integration in the new mixed-income community. For example, at building celebrations—local gatherings within individual buildings—residents come together to celebrate their community's diversity. Participation in committees and the neighborhood association provide other spaces to interact with neighbors on equal footing, promoting relationships and building trust.

Ultimately, the model aims to create an equitable governance structure for local decision-making that responds directly to local needs and desired outcomes. Some early signs of success and some clear challenges have emerged. There is a general culture of resident involvement in neighborhood activity, although it is worth noting that complicated social tensions do arise. In the RPNA, for example, some residents have felt that their neighbors do not fully understand their backgrounds or recognize the need for individuals to exercise their own voices rather than being advocated for by others. Sometimes, well-intentioned market-rate residents speak on behalf of TCH tenants, preventing them from speaking up for themselves. There also is general stereotyping and prejudice to combat on both sides. The current focal measures of success are participation and engagement in processes and events such as community surveys, building celebrations, Leadership Cafes, and elections. Both THC residents and market residents have shown strong interest in community participation, and all RPNA positions remain filled. One staff member noted that, regardless of income, residents are most likely to actively participate when three aspects come together: personal enjoyment, the social connection, and recognizing the benefit to the community.

IMPLICATIONS FOR ACTION

The approaches and experiences of the promising models we have described hold some implications for action by all stakeholder groups involved in mixed-income community interventions. These broad, cross-cutting recommendations are:

- Develop a shared vision and explicit commitment;
- Promote skills and build knowledge;
- Establish role clarity and accountability;
- Sharpen strategy and intentionality; and
- Facilitate assessment and learning.

In addition, we offer the following implications for stakeholders in specific roles.

Implications for Policy and Practice

- Elevate attention to the importance of inclusive social dynamics by incorporating it into project descriptions, proposals, reports, and other strategic documents.
- Provide trainings, workshops, and learning opportunities to create a platform of shared understanding and common language among staff and partners. Anticipate turnover and the need for to refresh current and new staff.
- Maintain ongoing discussions about historical and contemporary marginalization on the basis of race and class and its implications for current efforts; draw from a growing set of resources and tools on racial equity and inclusion.

- Revise job descriptions and staff roles to incorporate a focus on shifting the operating culture, and modify performance reviews to incorporate assessments of progress in attending to social dynamics, including racial equity and inclusion.
- Build out job pipelines that recruit candidates whose backgrounds include sensitivity to and skills in managing operating culture.
- Promote community "stewardship" and consider the identification, recruitment, training, and ongoing support of a growing cohort of community "stewards" who can embrace the responsibility of cultivating inclusive social dynamics within organizations and in the community.
- Design, activate, and curate spaces—meeting rooms, lounges, parks, gathering places—that can serve as intentional, safe spaces for comfortable informal and formal interaction across lines of difference.
- Co-develop a clear plan, structures, and processes for decision making and governance that promote voice and influence from an array of community members.
- Ensure that program guidelines, regulatory and compliance requirements, and other policies consider inclusive social dynamics and promote the development of specific strategies that facilitate positive change at individual, social, and structural levels.

Implications for Research and Evaluation

- Help advance the formulation of theories of change and evidence pathways (including the perceptual, relational, and influence/power pathways) about inclusive social dynamics as an element of mixed-income community interventions.
- Develop metrics and methods to track and document progress; institute regular check-ins on progress and opportunities for determining course correction.
- Build and disseminate evidence on strategies to promote inclusive social dynamics, including community network building, trauma-informed community building, inclusive spaces and venues, and inclusive governance mechanisms.
- Establish formal and informal partnerships with funders, policymakers, and practitioners that can support the learning, evaluation, and evidence-

building process. Engage as a learning partner in peer-to-peer organizational relationships for learning exchanges and mutual accountability.

Implications for Development and Investment

- Developers should elevate the focus on managing social dynamics alongside the commitment to physical revitalization and social services, with a requisite commitment of time and resources.

- Developers and their property management partners should make clear that success on financial bottom-line issues (e.g., reducing turnover, maintaining high occupancy, promoting safety and security, reducing vandalism and property damage, reducing littering) all are contingent on strong and inclusive social dynamics and a community where all residents respect each other and value the shared community norms and expectations.

- Funders should use requests for proposals, notices of funding availability, and other funding guidelines to promote consideration of inclusive social dynamics. Funders should ensure that program and policy staff stay focused on these issues throughout the intervention, not just during the selection process.

Implications for Residents and Community Members

Residents and community members should:

- Probe implementers to understand how residents are expected to benefit from living in the mixed-income community, and to understand how implementers define and see inclusive dynamics as connected to the community's positive outcomes.

- Contribute ideas, aspirations, and concerns to help shape the intervention's goals, definitions, visions, and commitments.

- Participate in trainings, workshops, and other learning opportunities about inclusive social dynamics and marginalization and their implications for the current project.

- Seek to understand and help shape the plan and structure for decision-making and governance so that it lifts up a wide range of community voices and reflects the everyday routines and practices needed to shift the operating culture.

CONCLUSIONS

Research and practice indicate that the path toward inclusive mixed-income communities leads through much more than social services and community engagement activities. If we really want to promote inclusive social dynamics across race and class, our efforts must help transform individual behaviors, attitudes, and actions. We must seek to change the underlying social and structural conditions that breed fear, isolation, and distrust in mixed-income communities. We must approach individual and community transformation in ways that firmly contextualize historical and structural conditions. And we must use intentional, conceptually driven practices to shift (or, more boldly, disrupt) existing operating cultures among all people and organizations that touch the mixed-income community. With asset-based and trauma-informed approaches, a shared and clear narrative, mechanisms to cultivate inclusive behavior, a willingness to shift influence and power, and intentionality and persistence, we will have a greater chance of creating mixed-income communities where everyone can truly thrive.

■ ■ ■

JONI HIRSCH *is a Policy and Program Associate at the Fines and Fees Justice Center where she delivers hands on technical assistance and support to jurisdictions working to reform their local use of criminal justice-related fines and fees. Previously, at the Center for the Study of Social Policy and National Initiative on Mixed-Income Communities, she managed a team of community builders who designed and implemented network-building strategies in public housing communities slated for mixed-income redevelopment. Prior to her work with NIMC, Hirsch's work centered on fair housing policy. Hirsch holds a BA from Amherst College and a Masters in City Planning from UC Berkeley.*

■ ■ ■

MARK JOSEPH, *Ph.D. is the Leona Bevis and Marguerite Haynam Associate Professor of Community Development at the Jack, Joseph and Morton Mandel School of Applied Social Sciences at Case Western Reserve University. His research focus is mixed-income development as a strategy for promoting urban equity and inclusion. He is the Founding Director of the National Initiative on Mixed-Income Communities, which conducts research and consulting projects in cities that have included Austin, Calgary, Chicago, Cleveland, Memphis, Minneapolis, Nashville, Pittsburgh, San Francisco, Seattle, Toronto, Tulsa, and Washington, D.C. He is the co-author of Integrating the Inner City: The Promise and Perils of Mixed-Income Public Housing Transformation. He received his undergraduate degree from Harvard University, a Ph.D. from the University of Chicago, was a Post-Doctoral Scholar at the University of Chicago and a Harlech Scholar at Oxford University.*

RECOGNIZING AND INCENTIVIZING MIXED-INCOME COMMUNITIES DESIGNED FOR HEALTH

Sara Karerat and Lisa Creighton
Center for Active Design

In the United States, low-income communities and communities of color have disproportionately high rates of chronic disease, such as heart disease, cancer, depression, and asthma.[1] The long-term implications of these disparities can be dire. Nationally, non-Hispanic Blacks have an average life expectancy of about 75 years—four years less than the average for non-Hispanic Whites—largely due to an increased prevalence of preventable chronic diseases.[2] The Latinx population is nearly 90 percent more likely to experience diabetes than the White population. And adults in families earning less than $35,000 per year are more than five times more likely to experience serious psychological distress than those with family incomes of $100,000 or more. Clearly, race and socioeconomic status play a key role in health outcomes.[3]

In order to truly address these health disparities, investment in high-quality, health-promoting housing is particularly important for communities facing the greatest health challenges. Housing is one of the leading social determinants of health, and simply increasing access to high-quality, affordable housing can

---

1   Thomas Bodenheimer, Ellen Chen, and Heather D. Bennett, "Confronting the growing burden of chronic disease: Can the U.S. health care workforce do the job?," *Health Affairs* 28, no. 1 (Jan-February 2009): 64-74.

2   National Institutes of Health, "NIH Establishes New Research Program to Address Health Disparities of Chronic Diseases," news release, August 24, 2016, https://www.nih.gov/news-events/news-releases/nih-establishes-new-research-program-address-health-disparities-chronic-diseases.

3   U.S Department of Health and Human Services, Centers for Disease Control and Prevention, National Center for Health Statistics. *Health, United States, 2016: With Chartbook on Long-term Trends in Health.* (Hyattsville, MD: Centers for Disease Control and Prevention, 2017).

positively impact health outcomes and reduce healthcare costs.[4] All people should have an opportunity to achieve an optimal quality of life, and the design and operations of housing can serve to bolster health.

At the Center for Active Design (CfAD), we strive to stimulate systemic change through financial incentives, certification programs, recognition, and advocacy that increase access to healthy environments. To that end, we work with organizations like Fannie Mae to spur widespread change and to use housing as a mechanism to tackle health disparities across the nation. In this essay, we address why seemingly minor shifts in housing design can have a profound impact on physical, mental, and social health (defined as the capacity to create and foster meaningful relationships with others). We first explore the role housing plays in health before examining the evolution of the healthy design movement. We then discuss how incentivizing health-promoting, mixed-income communities that are designed for health can enhance health outcomes.

HOUSING AS A SOCIAL DETERMINANT OF HEALTH

A growing understanding of how the place in which someone lives can influence health status has drawn attention to the social determinants of health. Defined by the U.S Health Resources and Services Administration as "conditions in the social environment in which people are born, live, learn, work, and play that affect a wide range of health functioning and quality-of-life outcomes and risks," social determinants encompass a breadth of environmental conditions such as housing, green space, air quality, local transit, and food access.[5]

Health disparities faced by low-income and minority populations are frequently related to negative conditions in residential communities, often caused by a lack of consistent investment within and across neighborhoods. In urban housing for low-income families, for example, environmental conditions such as mold, poor ventilation, and pests have been linked to poor health.[6] At a neighborhood

---

4   Lauren Taylor, "Housing and Health: An Overview of the Literature," *Health Affairs*, 2018.

5   Health Resources and Services Administration, *Health Equity Report 2017*, (Rockville, MD: Health Resources and Services Administration, 2018), https://www.hrsa.gov/sites/default/files/hrsa/health-equity/2017-HRSA-health-equity-report-PRINTER.pdf.

6   Gary Adamkiewicz et al., "Environmental Conditions in Low-Income Urban Housing: Clustering and Associations with Self-Reported Health," *American Journal of Public Health* 104, no. 9 (September 2014): 1650-1656.

level, safe street infrastructure, walkability, and access to affordable fruits and vegetables, parks, and public transportation are some of the ways the built environment is tied to health.[7] Many of these elements are not consistent across communities, with low-wealth areas and neighborhoods that are occupied by people of color experiencing the less-favorable conditions.[8] Improving these conditions is one step toward supporting healthy communities and promoting a country in which everyone has the opportunity to attain their highest level of health possible—a condition commonly referred to as health equity.

Studies suggest that moving from a low-income to middle-income community can have a powerful impact on health outcomes. An evaluation of benefits and disadvantages of living in one of Chicago's new mixed-income developments found that relocated public housing residents had less stress and more self-esteem after fewer than two years of living in the new environment.[9] These positive changes can be attributed to a variety of factors, ranging from increased stability and safety of the surroundings to increased access to neighborhood amenities.

The relationship between health and the design of our buildings, streets, and neighborhoods is not speculative. Over more than a century, our understanding of the connection between the built environment and health outcomes has continued to expand. In the 19th century, rapidly urbanized cities like New York faced a significant rise in communicable diseases such as tuberculosis, cholera, and yellow fever. At the time, these conditions were thought to be linked to individual moral failings, but the spread stopped after policy and infrastructure changes were implemented.[10] By reducing overcrowding, improving sanitation, and implementing housing policies to increase access to fresh water, light, and air, cities finally were able to control and reverse the

---

7 Mary Northridge, Elliot D. Sclar, and Padmini Biswas, "Sorting Out the Connections Between the Built Environment and Health: A Conceptual Framework for Navigating Pathways and Planning Healthy Cities," *Journal of Urban Health* 8, no. 4 (December 2003): 556-568.

8 Penny Gordon-Larsen et al., "Inequality in the Built Environment Underlies Key Health Disparities in Physical Activity and Obesity," *Pediatrics* 117, no. 2 (February 2006): 417-424.; Nicole I. Larson, Mary T. Story, and Melissa C. Nelson, "Neighborhood Environments: Disparities in Access to Healthy Foods in the U.S.," *American Journal of Preventive Medicine* 36, no. 1 (January 2009): 74-81.

9 Joseph, Mark L. and Robert Chaskin, "Living in a Mixed-Income Development: Resident Perceptions of the Benefits and Disadvantages of Two Developments in Chicago," *Urban Studies* 47, no. 11 (March 2010): 1–20.

10 James Krieger and Donna L. Higgins, "Housing and Health: Time Again for Public Health Action," *Public Health Matters* 92, no.5 (May 2002): 758-768.

spread of disease. These learnings reemerged and regained traction when the COVID-19 pandemic began in 2019.

Just as design strategies such as increasing access to light, improving indoor ventilation, and installing comprehensive sewer systems help to control infectious diseases in cities, tactical changes to the built environment have the potential to decrease the prevalence of chronic disease and promote health equity. Chronic health conditions have taken center stage as leading contributors to death and disability in the United States, with rates of type 2 diabetes, obesity, asthma, coronary heart disease, and hypertension rising to epidemic proportions. Thanks to an ever-growing body of research, the connection between the design of the built environment and physical, social, and mental health outcomes has never been clearer. In residential settings, a range of design decisions—from the inclusion of green space to the development of safe bike lanes—as well as operations decisions, such as setting mixed-income requirements and implementing an Indoor Air Quality policy, have the power to positively influence individual and community health.[11]

EVOLUTION OF THE HEALTHY DESIGN MOVEMENT

Two developments, the meteoric rise of sustainable or green development practices and the popularization of active design practices, have driven the success of the healthy building movement.

Sustainability and Green Development

The environmental sustainability movement began to impact development practices in earnest in the late 1990s and early 2000s. Since then, green or sustainable building has become a commonly accepted best practice. This rapid expansion over the past two decades shows how social impact measures and incentives can incite a movement and truly transform the market.

The sustainability movement deepened engagement with stakeholders in the real estate industry who are responsible for designing and managing the built environment. Instead of simply considering financial gain, leading companies began to focus on the triple bottom line of *people*, *planet*, and *profits*. The

---

11 James F. Sallis et al., "Co-benefits of Designing Communities for Active Living: An Exploration of Literature," International Journal of Behavioral Nutrition and Physical Activity 12, no.1 (February 2015): 30.

notion of the triple bottom line was popularized by green building certification systems, whose standards focus on minimizing environmental impacts through reduced energy and water use and on diminishing environmental disturbances at the building site. Despite not explicitly addressing health promotion, green standards have been shown to improve indoor environmental quality, which is associated with diminished asthma rates and enhanced mental health.[12] Green building certification systems include the Building Research Establishment Environmental Assessment Method, commonly referred to as BREEAM, launched in 1990; Leadership in Energy and Environmental Design (LEED),[13] originally launched as a pilot program in 1998; BOMA BEST; Energy Star; and Enterprise Green Communities, among others.

Building on the work of the green building community, the healthy building movement has resulted in new health-specific certification systems in response to growing demand. Fitwel®, described later, is a building certification system focused directly on promoting health and well-being. These certification systems are strengthening awareness around the importance of improving residential environments and increasing access to healthy housing, as the demand for healthy development continues to rapidly expand.

Active Design

Between 2010 and 2020, demand for health-promoting spaces—both indoors and outdoors—grew significantly, gaining momentum after the city of New York released its *Active Design Guidelines* in 2010.[14] Active design is an evidence-based approach to development that uses urban planning and architecture solutions to support healthy communities. The term "active design" was coined by the New York City interagency collaboration that produced the *Guidelines*. The *Guidelines* were developed in response to the growing realization that physical activity has largely been designed out of our daily lives. In most parts of the country, transportation to activities of daily

---

12 Joseph G. Allen et al., "Green Buildings and Health," *Current Environmental Health Reports* 2, no. 3 (July 2015): 250-258.

13 Today, BREEAM has certified more than 2.2 million buildings across 77 countries and LEED has reached more than 92,000 buildings in 165 countries.

14 New York City Departments of Design and Construction, Health and Mental Hygiene, Transportation, and City Planning, *Active Design Guidelines: Promoting Physical Activity and Health in Design*, (New York, NY: New York City Departments of Design and Construction, Health and Mental Hygiene, Transportation, and City Planning, 2010).

living—including commuting to and from sedentary office jobs and schools—often occurs by car, not by walking. Leisure time has become increasingly sedentary with each new generation, as "play time" has been replaced with "screen time." This reality has had shocking physical, mental, and social health effects, with an estimated 250,000 deaths per year in the United States being attributed to physical inactivity alone.[15] As one part of his commitment to addressing physical inactivity within New York City, former Mayor Michael Bloomberg signed an executive order requiring that active design be incorporated within all city-funded buildings and street construction projects.

The benefits of "activity-friendly environments" go much deeper than simply increasing physical activity, however. Active design also positively influences physical health, mental health, social health, safety, environmental sustainability, and economic well-being. A study led by James Sallis, a leading researcher of the built environment and health, found that features such as park proximity, mixed land use, trees and greenery, street connectivity, and building design were especially likely to offer multiple co-benefits.[16]

Healthy Building

Using the sustainability framework as a model, the "healthy building movement" emerged with a framework of design and operations strategies aimed specifically at meeting the holistic health needs of people living in neighborhoods, especially in mixed-income communities, and educating the real estate industry on how it influences community well-being. This movement holds that mixed-income housing that is designed to support residents' health can benefit tenants and building owners alike. Specifically, health-promoting housing has been shown to increase tenant retention, resulting in lower costs for building owners.[17] Reduced turnover results in cost savings for building owners, while increased housing stability can strengthen neighborhood social

---

15 Frank W. Booth et al., "Waging War on Modern Chronic Diseases: Primary Prevention through Exercise Biology," *Journal of Applied Physiology* 88, no.2 (February 2000): 774-787.

16 James F. Sallis et al., "Co-benefits of Designing Communities"

17 Terry Lassar et al., *Building for Wellness: The Business Case*, (Washington, D.C: Urban Land Institute, 2014), https://uli.org/wp-content/uploads/ULI-Documents/Building-for-Wellness-The-Business-Case.pdf.

ties and positively influence mental health, provide the housing is in good condition.[18,19]

Consumer interest in health-promoting home environments is growing, and the demand currently outstrips the supply. A market report published by Dodge Data and Analytics (formerly McGraw Hill Construction) found that 71 percent of homeowners cited proximity to walking paths, sidewalks, and trails to be very or somewhat important in their decision of where to live;[20] however, the average walk score of U.S. cities with populations over 200,000 is only 47 out of 100.[21] In addition, a survey distributed by the Harvard Joint Center for Housing Studies found that nearly one in four homeowners was concerned about the impact their home has on their health or the well-being of other occupants.[22] By boosting the supply of housing designed with health in mind, the healthy building movement aims to meet this growing demand and increase access to health-promoting environments for all people, regardless of income level.

INCENTIVIZING MIXED-INCOME COMMUNITIES DESIGNED FOR HEALTH

Since its founding in 2012, the Center for Active Design (CfAD) has focused on developing practical, implementable design strategies that promote health and create equitable access to public and private spaces. This mission has expanded to explore how design and development practice can affect the civic health of communities by inspiring greater trust, participation, and stewardship.[23]

---

18 Linsey Isaacs and Derek Mearns, "Keeping Turnover Costs Low," *Multifamily Executive*, February 11, 2013.

19 Catherine E. Ross, John R. Reynolds, and Karlyn J. Geis, "The Contingent Meaning of Neighborhood Stability for Residents' Psychological Well-Being," American Sociological Review 65, no. 4 (August 2000): 581-597.

20 McGraw Hill Construction, *The Drive Toward Healthier Buildings: The Market Drivers and Impact of Building Design and Construction on Occupant Health, Well-Being and Productivity*, (Hamilton, NJ: McGraw Hill Construction, 2014).

21 Mariela Alfonzo, "Making the Economic Case for More Walkability," *UrbanLand*, May 8, 2015.

22 Mariel Wolfson and Elizabeth La Jeunesse, "Challenges and Opportunities in Creating Healthy Homes: Helping Consumers Make Informed Decisions," (working paper, Harvard Joint Center for Housing Studies, Harvard University, Cambridge, MA, March 2016).

23 See CfAD's publication, Center for Active Design, *Assembly: Civic Design Guidelines*. (New York, NY: Center for Active Design, 2018).

Our strategy for incentivizing inclusive, equitable mixed-income communities that are designed for health has two core components: (1) working with actors across the real estate industry to implement the Fitwel® Certification System as a framework for optimizing health within commercial and residential buildings and sites; and (2) partnership with Fannie Mae to advance the Healthy Housing Rewards™ (HHR) financial incentive program. The two strands of work complement each other because certification systems like Fitwel® provide the evidence-based foundation and guidance necessary for developers, building managers, and building owners to design housing that supports rather than detracts from resident health. However, certification systems tend primarily to reach market rate properties, as the desirable features can be used to garner rental premiums. In order to equitably impact health disparities, health-promoting strategies like those within Fitwel® should be incorporated into housing for people of all income levels—a goal that Healthy Housing Rewards is designed to achieve.

The Fitwel® Certification System

Fitwel® was developed in 2011 by the Centers for Disease Control and Prevention (CDC) and the General Services Administration (GSA) as a means of embedding active design principles into standard practice. We have found, however, that by translating public health research into concrete, implementable strategies, Fitwel® has successfully engaged property owners, facility managers, architects, and others in the quest to improve holistic population health.

Fitwel® is rooted in a strong evidence base, supported by more than 3,000 research studies, and based on input from experts in public health, design, and development.[24] After thorough pilot testing, Fitwel® was launched for public use in March 2017 by CfAD, which serves as the licensed operator of the certification program. Fitwel® was initially created for workplaces but was subsequently modified for application to residential settings, because populations around the world spend a majority of their time in and around their homes. In November 2017, CfAD released the Fitwel® scorecard for multifamily residential buildings, which was developed in partnership with the Centers for Disease Control and Prevention.

Fitwel® for multifamily residential use encompasses more than 70 evidence-

---

24 "About Fitwel: Who We Are," Center for Active Design, 2019, https://www.fitwel.org/about.

based design and operational strategies divided across 12 sections that promote health through enhancing the built environment. Each section focuses on different aspects of the residential environment, including neighborhood siting as well as exterior and interior spaces. Each strategy addresses one or more of Fitwel®'s seven health impact categories:

1. Physical activity;
2. Occupant safety;
3. Morbidity;
4. Social equity for vulnerable populations;
5. Feelings of well-being;
6. Community health; and
7. Healthy food options.

Through these categories of impact, Fitwel® promotes physical, mental, and social well-being, treating health as an interconnected system.

Fitwel® was designed to offer users a straightforward and educational experience. In support of this goal, Fitwel® is accessed and administered through a web portal that provides comprehensive information on implementing each of the strategies, sample evidence behind the strategies, and documentation required for certification. The Fitwel® portal also allows teams to complete an initial assessment of their project to better understand existing strengths and opportunities to further the building's impact. Each opportunity is paired with information on how the strategy connects to health, clarifying the specific benefit. For example, project teams will learn that by providing a sufficient number of dedicated lactation rooms or stations in their workplace, they can increase productivity while also decreasing health claims and absenteeism rates. This information allows project teams to better understand how each enhancement can maximize the health of occupants.

The Fitwel® portal also enables users to track a range of data points and evaluate the impact their projects are having on the seven Fitwel® Health Impact Categories. For example, project teams can see the impact that improved indoor air quality has on morbidity and absenteeism and the importance of access to daylight for instilling feelings of well-being among occupants. Through the benchmarking and certification process, companies can use the Fitwel® portal to demonstrate to other vested parties, such as tenants, employees, residents, and investors, how they are working to address some of today's most pressing health concerns.

Since launching publicly in 2017, awareness of Fitwel® and the importance of health-promoting buildings has expanded. As of February 2020, more than 1,000 projects were registered, more than 400 of which were certified or pending certification. Through these efforts, over 830,000 individuals across more than 40 countries have been positively affected.

The Healthy Housing Rewards™ Incentive Program

Healthy Housing Rewards™ (HHR), a program designed by Fannie Mae in partnership with CfAD, aims to incentivize affordable housing developers to invest in designing with the health of their residents in mind, an approach that can help to promote and sustain mixed-income communities. Through the HHR program, developers of affordable housing properties that meet or exceed the minimum certification standards of Fitwel® are eligible for below-market-rate loan pricing from Fannie Mae.

The framework behind Healthy Housing Rewards™ grew out of a multi-year effort that included establishing an industry-wide standard for healthy housing. With support from The Kresge Foundation and the Robert Wood Johnson Foundation, CfAD used its core knowledge and expertise in health-promoting design and leveraged the expertise of its network of partners to define healthy housing. This effort involved delineating relevant health categories that would be impacted; conducting an in-depth analysis of peer-reviewed publications and case studies that link design and operations strategies to health impacts; reviewing related verification and certification programs; and consulting with experts in the public health, real estate development, and finance communities.

The model on which HHR was based, Fannie Mae's multifamily green finance program, began in 2012 with $58 million in loans to multifamily property owners and reached $27.6 billion in new financing by 2017. That same year, Fannie Mae launched HHR to provide financial incentives for borrowers who incorporate health-promoting design and operations features in their newly constructed or rehabilitated multifamily affordable rental properties. Borrowers must meet or exceed Fitwel® for multifamily residential certification standards in order to qualify for HHR incentives. (The box on the next page offers an example of HHR in action.)

Using Healthy Design to Redevelop Amani Place

Like many cities across the United States, Atlanta, Georgia, is in the midst of an affordable housing crisis driven by a mix of significant population shifts, economic growth, and rapidly changing communities. According to the Harvard Joint Center for Housing Studies, 31 percent of households in the Atlanta Metropolitan Area were cost-burdened in 2017.*

The former Edgewood Court development, now known as Amani Place, is located 10 minutes east of downtown Atlanta in Kirkwood-Edgewood, an area that has experienced a rapid influx of investment in recent years leading to new condos, apartments, restaurants, and retail establishments. The area experienced a 9.5 percent rent spike in 2016, and the median sale price for a home in Edgewood tripled between 2015 and 2020. While the neighborhood is becoming more economically affluent, the need to maintain a mix of affordability has become even more important.

Two developers, Jonathan Rose Companies and Columbia Residential, teamed up to turn Edgewood Court into Amani Place, a garden-style development. The original development, built in the 1950s, contained 204 U.S Department of Housing and Urban Development Section 8 units that needed maintenance and modernization. Both developers were experienced in green building certifications, and when they acquired the property in December 2017, they saw an overlap between their efforts to promote sustainability and Fitwel®'s focus on health promotion. Using the Healthy Housing Rewards™ program for financing, they redeveloped the property into 222 units, all designated for households at or below 60 percent of area median income.

Amani Place has several amenities designed to promote physical, mental, and social health, including:

- A pedestrian network and safe street infrastructure throughout the development;
- Indoor air quality and integrated pest management policies that feature environmentally friendly products and contribute to improved indoor air quality;
- An outdoor fitness circuit with permanent fitness equipment and compelling signage encouraging residents to engage in regular physical activity;
- A communal kitchen with space for residents to attend cooking classes and healthy eating demonstrations;
- A central community center with space for residents to socialize and participate in on-site health and wellness programs; and
- A community garden where residents can access fresh produce and social interaction.

The redevelopment process was guided by feedback from residents, who shared their major pain points during a series of community meetings. One of the most common complaints was fear of crime within the development and surrounding area. Fear of crime is associated with negative physical and mental health outcomes. In response, the community center was strategically placed in an area known as a hotspot for criminal activity, signaling to residents that the property management was stepping up to increase safety. And, in response to air quality concerns, the renovation replaced all flooring, windows, and appliances; sealed buildings; installed new HVAC; and replaced all duct work. The financing for this project included funding for a full-time resident services coordinator to help ensure that residents have an on-site contact to share feedback with, even after the redevelopment is completed.

* Harvard Joint Center for Housing Studies tabulations of U.S Census Bureau, (2006-2018) American Community Survey 1-Year Estimates using the Missouri Data Center, https://www.jchs.harvard.edu/many-renters-are-burdened-housing-costs.

Incentive programs like HHR are important because mixed-income housing developments are not well-subsidized and capital stacks are often difficult to put together, which limits their feasibility in the very communities that experience the most severe income segregation. Fortunately, other entities are following Fannie Mae's leadership on this approach. Massachusetts Housing Partnership launched its Healthy Housing Financing program, modeled on Fannie Mae's incentive, in 2019, and CfAD is in discussions with other financial institutions about creating similar financial incentive programs for affordable housing.

CONCLUSIONS

Building on the success of the sustainability movement, the Fitwel® certification system and Healthy Housing Rewards™ program have introduced incentives for designing and building health-promoting affordable housing. If HHR grows similarly to the program on which it was based, CfAD's partnership with Fannie Mae has potential to have a major impact on multifamily affordable housing across the United States.

However, there is more work to be done, and in the face of rising chronic disease rates and intensifying economic disparities—deeply aggravated in 2019-20 by the COVID-19 pandemic—this is a crucial time to prioritize health by designing and creating health-promoting, mixed-income communities. Just as the sustainability movement transformed real estate development over the past few decades, the industry is now on the brink of a full-fledged market transformation oriented toward promoting human health. In 2018, Fitwel® alone saw an 80% increase in certifications when compared with the previous year.[25]

Without financial intervention, the mixed-income and affordable housing sector is at risk of being left behind. Through the continued dissemination and expansion of incentive-based programs, CfAD is committed to bringing healthier environments to all populations. By advancing a systematic approach to revolutionize how multifamily affordable housing is designed, constructed, and located, we can decrease the health disparities plaguing our nation and continue to work toward a healthier future for us all.

---

25 Center for Active Design, "Fitwel® Announces an 80% Increase in Certifications in One Year, Showing a Surging Trend in Building for Health," news release, February 14, 2019, https://www.businesswire.com/news/home/20190214005098/en/Fitwel%C2%AE-Announces-80-increase-Certifications-Year-Showing.

IMPLICATIONS FOR ACTION

The following implications for action can operationalize our ambition for healthier, more equitable communities.

Implications for Policy

- State housing finance agencies (HFAs) should incorporate credits for implementation of individual health-promoting design and operations strategies and/or application of holistic health-promoting certification systems into their affordable housing Qualified Action Plans (QAP). Many states, including California, Georgia, and Illinois, have already started integrating health-promoting strategies into their QAPs. However, a more coordinated approach is needed across the state HFAs.

- Given the connection between health and housing, Medicaid should allow expansion of reimbursement policies to cover housing-related costs. Access to affordable housing is one of the leading social determinants of health, and without a high-quality, safe place to live, it becomes difficult to pursue economic opportunity and achieve an optimum quality of life.

Implications for Research and Evaluation

- Multi-sector stakeholders, including academic research partners, should identify metrics that clearly demonstrate how the implementation of health-promoting strategies within mixed-income communities positively impacts health and financial returns. Investors need to understand how health-promoting mixed-income communities affect their bottom line and which metrics they should be tracking to determine impact. For example, is tenant turnover diminished in these developments or are maintenance costs reduced due to an increased sense of ownership from residents?

- Academic research partners should work with vested parties to gather baseline information about residents' health behaviors and perceptions before they move in and then throughout their time living in a health-promoting mixed-income development. This will improve understanding of hypothesized connections that are not yet fully supported by research. Knowledge of the health impact of mixed-income communities is growing, and there is an opportunity to expand our understanding further through strategic evaluation.

Implications for Development and Investment

- The healthcare sector—including hospitals and health insurers—has an opportunity to invest in mixed-income community development as a way to further its mission. At its core, the healthcare sector is focused on improving patients' health while maintaining profitability. Investing in strategic community development has the power to bring those two motivations together, and several leaders have already seen a return on their investment by doing so. UnitedHealthcare, Bon Secours Mercy Health, and CommonSpirit Health have all integrated community development into their broader strategy, realizing that in order to truly impact the health of all patients, they must influence social, environmental, and economic conditions.[26]

- Financial institutions should continue to explore collaborative efforts, such as that between the Center for Active Design and Fannie Mae, to develop innovative incentives to motivate developers, private investors, and state financing organizations to prioritize mixed-income development.

Implications for Residents and Community Members

- Community members should advocate for involvement throughout the development process. To amplify their voices, community members should join forces with community-based organizations that can ensure their health-related needs are incorporated into development plans.

■ ■ ■

SARA KARERAT *is a Senior Associate at the Center for Active Design (CfAD), where she supports the organization's initiatives that pair public health research with design strategies to improve the health of communities both domestically and internationally. Previously, Ms. Karerat worked as a communications associate with the Partnership for a Healthier America, where she developed strategic campaigns to motivate healthy behavior change among target populations. Ms. Karerat holds a Master of Public Health from Columbia University and a Bachelor of Arts from Hamilton College, where she majored in Public Policy.*

---

26 Center for Active Design, Healthcare: A Cure for Housing, (New York, NY: Center for Active Design, 2019).

LISA CREIGHTON is the Vice President of Strategy and Development at the Center for Active Design, where she helps guide the strategic growth and direction of the organization and its signature Fitwel Certification System. Her past experience includes over a decade of making progress toward improving community health within the municipal, education, and private sectors. Prior to entering the field of public health, Creighton worked in investment banking where she specialized in global mergers and acquisitions in the life science and healthcare sectors. Creighton holds a Master of Public Health and Master of Business Administration from Johns Hopkins University and a Bachelor of Arts from New York University.

MIXED-INCOME COMMUNITIES NEED MIXED-INCOME EARLY CARE AND EDUCATION

Matthew R. Tinsley and Mary Ann Dewan
Santa Clara County Office of Education

Mixed-income communities, defined as those intentionally created to support and sustain families with a variety of income and educational levels living and working together, represent a public policy approach to reducing the negative outcomes associated with concentrated poverty. Mixed-income communities have improved housing quality, reduced crime, bolstered associated improvements in quality of life for returning residents, and produced physical and economic revitalization. However, the more human-centered goals of enhancing social cohesion and increasing the economic success of lower-income residents are harder to achieve. Instead, many mixed-income developments have "tended to reproduce marginalization and stigmatization by race and class rather than generate more inclusive environments of social connection." Based on these findings, Mark Joseph has concluded that: (1) Improved housing conditions do not change educational or labor-market opportunities, (2) physical integration is not sufficient to build social ties across racial and income groups, (3) social mixing can lead to negative outcomes for racially or otherwise marginalized residents, (4) the market orientation of mixed-income projects may be a barrier to their social goals, and (5) programmatic and operational choices by project developers reduce the ability of low-income residents to return to these communities.[1]

These conclusions suggest it is time to put much more emphasis on increasing social cohesion among residents of mixed-income projects if this approach is to reduce the negative outcomes associated with concentrated poverty. This

---

[1] Mark L. Joseph, "Promoting Poverty Deconcentration and Racial Desegregation through Mixed-Income Development". In *Toward Solving Segregation: A Policy Agenda for Housing and Urban Neighborhoods* eds, Molly Metzger and Henry Webber, eds (Oxford: Oxford University Press, 2018).

essay explores schools and early childhood care and education as mechanisms for doing so. As professional educators and educational system leaders, we wholeheartedly support the consideration of schools as key drivers of student success and community vitality in neighborhood initiatives. And we suggest that a focus on early care and education (ECE)—programs and services for children 0-5 years of age and their families—may be more direct and effective than focusing on schools alone to advance the goals of mixed-income community development, especially when complemented by school improvement efforts.

THE KEY ROLE OF SCHOOLS IN MIXED-INCOME COMMUNITIES

Citing growing interest in schools as a factor in sustaining mixed-income communities, Joseph and Feldman [2] explored whether and how schools that serve the residents of a mixed-income community could serve as levers of physical, economic, *and* human-centered improvements. Schools have several ways to contribute to outcomes in mixed-income communities: by improving the academic and social-emotional development of low-income children, and their subsequent life outcomes; by providing a community amenity that attracts higher-income families and prevents out-migration of existing residents; by facilitating the interaction between families of differing socio-economic backgrounds for "meaningful and sustained contact," potentially facilitating the enhanced social cohesion required to break the social isolation of low-income families from the rest of society; by fostering a sense of shared interest through developing a school community with a common identity; and by acting as an institutional resource and public investment in the community.[3] A demonstration of this theory in action is the Purpose Built Community (PBC) projects, modeled on the East Lake neighborhood of Atlanta, which seeks to create an educational pipeline in each community. Each of the 16 PBC projects includes a neighborhood school, either newly constructed or significantly refurbished, and often operating under a charter that increases school autonomy and local influence.[4]

---

2   Mark L. Joseph and Jessica Feldman, "Creating and Sustaining Successful Mixed-Income Communities: Conceptualizing the Role of Schools," *Education and Urban Society* 41, no. 6 (March 2009): 623-652.

3   Joseph and Feldman, "Creating and Sustaining"

4   Education Pipeline," Purpose Built Communities. https://purposebuiltcommunities.org/our-approach/education-pipeline/

However, although there is "theoretical promise" for these effects, barriers also exist: High-performing schools may have the unintended consequence of increasing local housing prices; class differences might generate internal disparities of influence and resource allocation; and there is not enough research on these proposed mechanisms to support their real-world effectiveness.[5]

THE ROLE OF EARLY CARE AND EDUCATION IN MIXED-INCOME COMMUNITIES

Public education and other fields of public policy are increasingly looking "upstream" to early childhood for solutions to racial-ethnic achievement gaps and other concerns that have proven so resistant to school improvement efforts. This more holistic approach to education also acknowledges the fact that children's brain development and learning are most rapid, and most sensitive to interventions, before they turn five years old. In mixed-income communities, the provision of high-quality ECE programs has the potential to improve the economic success of low-income residents and residents of color in three ways supported by research: by improving the academic and other life outcomes for children who are enrolled in the programs, by improving immediate economic prospects for their parents (and, consequently, families), and by improving the community's social cohesion.

Effects on Children's Outcomes

Extensive research has been conducted on the effects of high-quality ECE programs on children's academic, social-emotional, and life-course outcomes. Within this literature, evidence suggests that the impacts are greater for children from lower-income families[6] and for Black children.[7] Perhaps the most impactful of these studies is the work of Professor James Heckman, a Nobel laureate in economics, on the HighScope Perry Preschool Program.[7] This program served 123 low-income Black children who were assessed to

---

5 Joseph and Feldman, "Creating and Sustaining"

6 Elliot M. Tucker-Drob, "Preschools Reduce Early Academic Achievement Gaps: A Longitudinal Twin Approach," *Psychol Sci* 23 no. 3. March 2012: 310–319. https://www.ncbi.nlm.nih.gov/pmc/articles/PMC3543777/#R14.

7 Daphna Bassok, "Do Black and Hispanic Children Benefit More From Preschool? Understanding Differences in Preschool Effects Across Racial Groups." *Child Development* 81 no. 6 (November/December 2010): 1828-1845.

be at high risk of school failure. Researchers randomly assigned 58 children to a program group that received a high-quality preschool program at ages 3 and 4 and 65 to another group that received no preschool program. Children who participated in the program were subsequently followed into their early 40s.[8] Participation in the program resulted in increased school achievement and higher rates of employment, increased annual earnings and home and car ownership, and lower arrest and conviction rates and drug use. Subsequent return on investment analysis has suggested that each dollar invested in the program generated a return of seven to twelve dollars back to society through lower costs and higher tax receipts.[9] While economic analyses of Perry Preschool and similar programs[10] have had a tremendous impact on the public policy conversation around ECE, they have also been criticized as being based on small sample sizes and dated studies that began in the 1960s and 1970s and so do not adequately capture the current landscape.[11]

In 2017, the RAND Corporation published an analysis of research findings on early childhood (prenatal to age 5) interventions that comprehensively answered the question of whether ECE interventions have beneficial outcomes for children.[12] The study identified 115 program evaluations that met criteria for scientific rigor, encompassing a variety of program designs (e.g., preschool and formal playgroups, home visiting programs, parent education, cash transfers or in-kind benefits). Almost all of these programs were targeted to low-income families and most lasted less than one year (home visiting programs typically lasted longer). Of the 115 programs, 102 demonstrated a positive impact on at least one measured outcome, and positive impacts were found on 30 percent of outcomes across all interventions—a rate six times higher than expected by chance. Nineteen of the 25 studies that included benefit-cost

---

[8] Lawrence J. Schweinhart et al. "The High/Scope Perry Preschool Study through age 40: Summary, Conclusions, and Frequently Asked Questions". http://nieer.org/wp-content/uploads/2014/09/specialsummary_rev2011_02_2.pdf, (2005).

[9] James J. Heckman et al., "A New Cost-Benefit and Rate of Return Analysis for the Perry Preschool Program: A Summary." IZA Policy Paper Number 17, University of Bonn, Bonn, Germany, July 2010.

[10] Gabriella Conti, James J. Heckman, and Rodrigo Pinto, "The Effects of Two Influential Early Childhood Interventions on Health and Healthy Behaviors." National Bureau of Economic Research Working Paper 21454, August 2015. http://www.nber.org/papers/w21454

[11] Heckman, "A New Cost-Benefit"

[12] Jill S. Cannon et al. *Investing Early: Taking Stock of Outcomes and Economic Returns from Early Childhood Programs* (Santa Monica, CA: RAND Corporation, 2017), https://www.rand.org/pubs/research_reports/RR1993.html

analyses found positive returns, ranging from $2-$4 for each dollar invested, with increased earnings by the participating child later in life often being the largest benefit of the intervention.

Effects on Mothers and Families

In addition to the lifetime benefits that accrue to children enrolled in high-quality ECE programs, their mothers also experience an immediate benefit. A recent study found that maternal workforce participation in areas without access to child care ("child care deserts") is 3 percent lower than in areas with easier access to care, and the difference is even greater (4.7 percent) in Census tracts where family incomes fall below the national median.[13] No such effect was found on labor force participation rates among men. This study also found that Hispanic/Latinx families are disproportionately more likely to live in child care deserts, an important finding given that a rapidly growing proportion of the nation's children, ages 0-5, live in Hispanic/Latinx families. While these results do not support the conclusion that a lack of access to child care causes decreased work force participation, a recent review of the literature concluded that "reduced out-of-pocket costs for ECE and increased availability of public ECE…has positive impacts on mothers' labor force participation and work hours," and the accompanying economic analysis found that a 10 percent decrease in the price of child care would lead to a 0.5-2.5 percent increase in maternal employment.[14] Indeed, the cost-benefit analyses of high-quality ECE programs cited earlier have determined that a significant proportion of the return on investment generated by these programs is driven by increased earnings of the enrolled child's family when mothers who have access to high-quality child care return to work more quickly, work longer hours, or participate in education and training opportunities.

Effects on Community Cohesion

Access to high-quality ECE may increase social cohesion in a community by providing a shared core amenity that currently is lacking in many communities, including those where middle-income families live. In a 2015 Washington Post

---

13 Rasheed Malik and Katie Hamm, *Mapping America's Child Care Deserts*. (Washington, DC: Center for American Progress, 2017) https://www.americanprogress.org/issues/early-childhood/reports/2017/08/30/437988/mapping-americas-child-care-deserts/

14 Taryn W. Morrissey, "Child Care and Parent Labor Force Participation: A Review of the Research Literature," *Review of Economics of the Household* 15 no.1 (March 2017): 1–24.

poll,[15] 53 percent of all respondents, 54 percent of working mothers, and 56 percent of parents in families earning less than $50,000 per year, agreed it was "somewhat" or "very" difficult to find high-quality, affordable child care. Similarly, 63 percent of respondents to a 2016 poll by National Public Radio, the Robert Wood Johnson Foundation, and the Harvard T.H. Chan School of Public Health[16] stated that they had "just a few" or "only one" "realistic" option for child care. While this number was higher (79 percent) for families who report their household finances as "not strong," even among financially "strong" families" 63 percent reported limited child care options.

These responses are consistent with a 2017 finding that, in the 22 states studied, approximately half of residents live in "child care deserts."[17] In this study, a child care desert was operationalized as a Census tract with at least 50 children under the age of five and either no licensed or registered child care provider or a greater than 3:1 ratio of children under the age of five to the cumulative child care capacity.[18] Across the 22 states included in this analysis, between 24 and 62 percent of residents lived in "child care deserts," with the highest rate in our home state of California. Recently, we performed a similar analysis for Santa Clara County, California, as part of the development of the county-wide Early Learning Master Plan.[19] In Santa Clara County, one of the wealthiest regions in the country, 28 percent of children ages 0-5 live in Zip Codes that meet the criteria for a "child care desert"—and more than one third of these Zip Codes are in affluent cities.

Evidence suggests that middle-income families will enroll in ECE programs alongside low-income families. Examining enrollment in universal preschool programs in Oklahoma and Georgia, Cascio and Whitmore Schanzenbach[20]

---

15 Danielle Paquette and Peyton M. Craighill, "The Surprising Number of Parents Scaling Back at Work to Care for Kids." *Washington Post.* August 6, 2015. https://www.washingtonpost.com/page/2010-2019/WashingtonPost/2015/08/07/National-Politics/Polling/release_405.xml?tid=a_mcntx

16 Danielle Paquette and Peyton M. Craighill, "The Surprising Number of Parents Scaling Back at Work to Care for Kids." *Washington Post.* August 6, 2015. https://www.washingtonpost.com/page/2010-2019/WashingtonPost/2015/08/07/National-Politics/Polling/release_405.xml?tid=a_mcntx

17 Malik and Hamm, *Mapping America's Child Care Deserts*

18 Malik and Hamm, *Mapping America's Child Care Deserts*

19 Jennifer Anthony et al., *Santa Clara County Early Learning Master Plan,* 2017 https://www.sccoe.org/elmp2017/2017%20ELMP/ELMP%20-%20Full%20Plan.pdf

20 Elizabeth U. Cascio and Diane Whitmore Schanzenbach. "The Impacts of Expanding Access to High-Quality Preschool Education." *Brookings Papers on Economic Activity* (Fall 2013). https://www.

find that "four or five out of every 10 public preschool enrollees whose mothers have at least some college education would otherwise have been enrolled in private preschools." Their analysis suggests that this take-up is, at least in part, due to a reduction in childcare expenses as middle-income families move from private, fee-paying, to publicly subsidized preschool—although it should be noted that this reduction is relatively small ($450-500 in child care expenses for the nine-month academic year). Taken together, these findings suggest that middle-income families need access to ECE and will enroll their children in programs alongside low-income children if those programs are available. As a result, providing access could be a core amenity for low-income families <u>and</u> the middle-income families with children that Joseph and Feldman[21] suggest are so important to the success of a mixed-income community.

Effects on Middle-Income Children

While much of the evidence for the beneficial impacts of quality ECE has focused on low-income children and families, there is evidence that middle-income children benefit from these programs as well. A recent Century Foundation report[22] cites research[23] on the universal pre-kindergarten programs in Tulsa and Boston showing that middle-income children who attended these programs show increased learning outcomes compared with middle-income peers who did not attend. The same report also presents results from a longer-term outcomes study suggesting that participating in a high-quality ECE program leads to a 5 percent increase in lifetime earnings for children in families with incomes over 180 percent of the federal poverty level, compared with a 10 percent increase for children from families below this threshold. Most intriguingly, this report also presents data suggesting that "classrooms with a mix of lower- and higher-income children showed greater positive effects…than classrooms with similar average socioeconomic status (SES) but less income diversity. That means that it is a benefit to both middle- and low-income children to attend programs in which children of different economic

---

brookings.edu/bpea-articles/the-impacts-of-expanding-access-to-high-quality-preschool-education/

21 Mark L. Joseph, "Promoting Poverty Deconcentration"

22 Halley Potter and Julie Kashen. *Together From the Start: Expanding Early Childhood Investments for Middle-Class and Low-Income Families.* New York, NY: The Century Foundation, 2015

23 Jeanne L. Reid. "Socioeconomic Diversity and Early Learning: The Missing Link in Policy for High-Quality Preschools." In *The Future of School Integration: Socioeconomic Diversity as an Education Reform Strategy*, ed. Richard D. Kahlenberg. (New York, NY: The Century Foundation, 2012), 67-125.

backgrounds learn side by side."[24] Hence, creating mixed-income ECE programs not only provides middle-income families with access to preschool and child care but may also result in better outcomes for their children than attending more homogenous programs. Further analysis of this result indicates that this "effect appears to operate through direct peer interactions, not instructional quality or other aspects of quality in preschool classrooms"—suggesting that it is the children's experience of diversity among their classmates that drives these improved outcomes.[25]

OPERATIONALIZING A FOCUS ON EARLY CARE AND EDUCATION IN MIXED-INCOME COMMUNITIES

Several existing practices and policies can support efforts to provide child care programs in mixed-income communities. These include:

Including Child Care Programs among A Development's Resident Services

The National Initiative on Mixed-Income Communities (NIMC)'s State of the Field Scan #2 found[26] that approximately one-third of the mixed-income developments surveyed offer childcare and preschool among their resident services, with approximately half of those offering services on-site. The majority of projects that do provide child care services contract with local agencies, rather than operating as direct service providers. Unfortunately, child care services are the lowest rated by recipients when asked whether the services meet their needs. This may be because the most common household structure among respondents in the study was a single parent with children (60 percent of households) suggesting a very high demand for child care that may be difficult to meet. Interestingly, many of the Purpose Built Community projects (PBCs) that include schools as a center piece of their design also include ECE opportunities.[27]

---

24 Halley Potter and Julie Kashen. *Together From the Start*

25 Halley Potter and Julie Kashen. *Together From the Start*

26 National Initiative on Mixed-Income Communities and The American City Coalition. *State of the Field Scan #2 Resident Services in Mixed-Income Developments Phase 1: Survey Findings and Analysis.* (Cleveland, OH: National Initiative on Mixed-Income Communities, 2015), https://case.edu/socialwork/nimc/sites/case.edu.nimc/files/2018-10/NIMC_State-of-the-Field-Scan-2_Resident-Services-in-Mixed-Income-Developments.pdf

27 "Education Pipeline," Purpose Built Communities. https://purposebuiltcommunities.org/our-approach/education-pipeline/

Operating Mixed-Income Programs That Enroll "over-income" Children alongside Publicly Subsidized Students

Many ECE providers already do this to some extent. For example, Head Start allows up to 10 percent enrollment of "children who would benefit" but who are not eligible by virtue of family income, and up to 35 percent enrollment of children from families with incomes between 100 and 130 percent of the federal poverty level, provided that all interested children below the poverty level are being served.[28] Many providers who focus on low-income families also enroll fee-paying families to diversify their income stream and to fully utilize their classroom capacity, while providers who predominantly enroll higher-income children will often reserve a small number of "scholarship" slots for children from lower-income families. For example, some school districts[29] in Santa Clara County offer fee-based and subsidized preschool spaces in the same classrooms. ECE providers are so well-versed in the financial and compliance complexities of enrolling and serving children funded through a variety of different means in their classrooms that the term "braided funding" has been coined to describe the practice.[30]

Including Licensable Space for ECE Programs in New Buildings Constructed or Redesigned in Mixed-Income Communities

The lack of affordable, appropriate physical space is a significant barrier to expansion for many ECE providers. For example, a survey of ECE providers in Santa Clara County in 2013 found[31] that "rent/lease/purchase issues" and "finding a suitable property" were listed as the two most common problems in opening a new facility. One approach for developers of mixed-income communities is to build the shell of a preschool center with classrooms, restrooms, laundry and food handing spaces, and administrative offices that can be finished by the program provider. A key to this approach is to work

---

28 "Sec. 645 Participation in Head Start Programs." Head Start Policy and Regulations. https://eclkc.ohs.acf.hhs.gov/policy/head-start-act/sec-645-participation-head-start-programs

29 "Preschool and Early Learning," Campbell Union School District, https://www.campbellusd.org/preschool

30 Margie Wallen and Angela Hubbard. *Blending and Braiding Early Childhood Program Funding Streams Tools* (Chicago, IL: Ounce of Prevention Fund, 2013) https://www.buildinitiative.org/Portals/0/Uploads/Documents/resource-center/community-systems-development/3E%202%20Blended-Funding-Toolkit.pdf

31 Local Early Education Planning Council of Santa Clara County. *Community Needs Assessment Issue Brief Early Learning Facilities—Friend or Foe?* (Santa Clara, CA: Local Early Education Planning Council of Santa Clara County, 2013). https://www.sccoe.org/depts/students/lpc/Documents/2013-Assessment/Facilities-Issue-Brief.pdf

with the ECE provider early in design development to ensure that licensing issues, such as meeting minimums for unencumbered floor space, access to secured outside play areas, and restroom design are understood and addressed. Several examples of this approach exist, including the HOPE SF mixed-income transformation initiative that will redevelop four public housing sites in San Francisco; it includes a commitment "to improving access to high-quality early care and education,"[32] beginning with a Head Start preschool in the Hunters View redevelopment.[33]

Building with the Needs of Family Child Care Home Providers (FCCH) in Mind

FCCH providers offer child care in their own homes and, in California, may be licensed or unlicensed depending on the number of children they care for and whether or not they are paid using public subsidies. Approximately one third of children ages 0-4 who are cared for by a non-relative are in FCCH care.[34] Many families prefer the smaller, more intimate, care that an FCCH arrangement can provide or choose them for cultural, convenience, or cost reasons. FCCH also provides a career option for (typically) women that allows them to work from home with comparatively low barriers to entry or education requirements. While licensing requirements for FCCH settings typically are less involved than those for centers, which serve more children, they can create barriers to operating these programs. One mixed-income development in Santa Clara County, Depot Commons in Morgan Hill, includes three buildings with 12 co-housing units and a fourth building that consists of a second-story, two-bedroom unit for an FCCH with an additional 1,175 square feet of first floor space dedicated solely to the family child care business, which is licensed to serve 12 children[35] and has been in operation since the complex was constructed. Another example approach is the 12 "in-home child care" units serving 75 children across five sites owned by King County Housing Authority (KCHA). These units are designed to meet the state's child care licensing

---

32 "Child Care," HOPE SF. http://www.hope-sf.org/childcare.php

33 "Hunters View". HOPE SF. http://www.hope-sf.org/hunters.php

34 Kristin Anderson Moore et al. *Child Care: Indicators of Child and Youth Well-Being*. (Bethesda, MD: Child Trends Data Bank, 2016). https://www.childtrends.org/wp-content/uploads/2016/05/21_Child_Care-1.pdf

35 Jan Stokley. *Linking Child Care Development and Housing Development: Tools for Child Care Providers and Advocates*. (Oakland, CA: National Economic Development & Law Center, 2002). http://www.buildingchildcare.net/uploads/pdfs/NEDLC-Linking-Hsg-CC.pdf

requirements, and KCHA has contracted with local organizations to provide culturally relevant professional development and technical assistance to help child care providers meet licensing requirements and quality standards.[36]

CONCLUSIONS

Mixed-income communities need mixed-income early care and education options. Mixed-income communities are intentionally designed to improve outcomes for low-income families by providing them with surroundings and services that increase their likelihood of economic success and decrease their social isolation from higher-income families and communities. Including mixed-income ECE in these communities harnesses the demonstrated power of early childhood interventions to address both goals. Experience and expertise with ECE programs are emerging in the mixed-income development community; this, coupled with the demand for ECE among low- and middle-income households, suggests that ECE providers would find the opportunity to partner in mixed-income communities very attractive. Access to ECE should be considered as much of a public good as schools, roads, and parks and should be included in the design of every community.

IMPLICATIONS FOR ACTION

Implications for Policy

- Include early care and education as a priority in city general plans to support a focus on ECE needs in long-range community planning documents and development reviews.
- Include ECE facilities as a community benefit in development agreements, and create template language that can be included in development agreements for mixed-income projects.

Implications for Research and Evaluation

- Conduct research on the effects of mixed-income ECE within mixed-income developments to determine the relative socio-economic and racial heterogeneity of students in those programs, compared with publicly subsidized and fee-paying ECE programs in surrounding areas.

---

36 Ted Dezember, personal communication, February 20, 2020.

- Conduct research on program outcomes (e.g., school readiness) for ECE program graduates from mixed-income ECE programs within mixed-income developments, compared with publicly subsidized and fee-paying ECE programs in surrounding areas.
- Compare social integration and cohesion in mixed-income developments that include mixed-income ECE programs with those that do not.

Implications for Development and Investment

- Facilitate connections among property developers, public agencies, financing authorities, and the local ECE community so that local networks of expertise are established before opportunities become available and project planning begins.
- Make technical assistance available to developers interested in including ECE facilities in their development plans, to support the design of licensable facilities.

Implications for Residents and Community Members

- Raise awareness of the need for ECE in low-income communities and communities of color, and highlight access to ECE as a tool for improving educational and economic opportunities in the short and long term to support self-advocacy by residents.
- Publicize the inclusion of ECE facilities in the mixed-income project design as early as possible to encourage community support for the project.
- Highlight the benefits of racially and socio-economically diverse classrooms for young children's academic and social-emotional development.

■ ■ ■

Dr. MATTHEW TINSLEY is the Director, Strong Start at the Santa Clara County Office of Education. Dr. Tinsley's role is to manage the Strong Start Initiative, a coalition of community leaders, early education providers, nonprofit organizations, elected officials, members of the business community, and other key stakeholders who are committed to expanding access to high quality early learning opportunities for all children age 0 to 8 in Santa Clara County. He is also a member of the inaugural cohort of the Robert Wood Johnson Foundation's Culture of Health Leaders Program, a leadership development program addressing barriers to health equity and improving the social determinants of health.

MARY ANN DEWAN, Ph.D. is the Santa Clara County Superintendent of Schools. Dr. Dewan is recognized for her expertise and experience in early learning, data driven decision-making, special education, education reform, change leadership, and her commitment to serve the community. She is passionate about diversity, inclusion, equity, and social justice. Her leadership is driven by a commitment to ensuring all youth have quality educational opportunities. Dr. Dewan is an experienced educator having served in a variety of leadership roles including Deputy Superintendent, Chief Schools Officer, Assistant Superintendent, Executive Director, Director of Special Education, principal, and teacher. She has served in education for over 30 years. She is a member of the Santa Clara County Women's Equality 2020 Commission and brings the voice of education to various committees and boards on which she serves. She holds a Ph.D. in educational leadership.

7

THE PATH FORWARD FOR GREATER URBAN EQUITY AND INCLUSION

The Path Forward for Greater Urban Equity and Inclusion

These two essays provide closing reflections on this compilation of essays and chart a course forward for the next generation of place-based efforts to foster greater diversity and opportunity across the urban landscape.

In "The Person-Role-System Framework as a Key to Promoting Racial Equity," JaNay Queen Nazaire tackles the question of how systems and societal structures can realistically be disrupted and transformed to shift from perpetuating racial equity to advancing antiracist policy and practice. She argues that systems change begins with mindset and behavior shifts at the level of individual decision-makers and draws from essays in the volume that discuss narrative shifts as core to the change process. She introduces the person-role-system framework as a tool for recognizing "the dynamic interplay between the mental viewpoints of people as individuals, their responsibilities in their personal and professional roles, and the overall impact of their actions on a system." Her exhortation seems particular timely in the current moment of national upheaval against enduring systemic racism as she calls for "reckoning with history, shifting beliefs, building relationships and reshaping cultural and institutional values to center humanity, share power, and work under the belief that our fates are shared." Nazaire concludes her essay with four questions for readers to ponder, including: "Are you taking the right everyday actions to promote more equitable outcomes, when you have the opportunity? Are you taking those actions effectively? Are there actions you take that may be driven more by Whiteness and singular power as the norm rather than humanity, shared power and collective accountability?"

In "Taking Stock: What *May* Work and Implications for the Future of the Mixed-Income Approach" Rachel Bratt has bravely embraced her role as the author of the final essay in the volume and stepped up to the herculean task of reviewing and reflecting on the entire essay collection. She carefully organizes her review around the questions about mixed-income communities posed in the framing essay by co-editors Amy Khare and Mark Joseph that opened the volume, including equitable sharing of revitalization benefits, social outcomes, promising innovations, threats to inclusion and equity, and actionable implications for stakeholders. Drawing from literally each of the essays, she provides a comprehensive roadmap of the key topics, policies, and strategies explored by volume essays. While cataloging the numerous emerging innovations and approaches detailed in the essays, she expresses disappointment in how little definitive evidence there is about the social benefits of mixed-income strategies for low-income households, hence her essay title: what may work. She calls for a more robust research agenda to advance the evidence base and conveys her hope that this disruptive societal moment might "yield momentum to assess how mixed-income housing could contribute to more racially just housing patterns."

THE PERSON-ROLE-SYSTEM FRAMEWORK AS A KEY TO PROMOTING RACIAL EQUITY

JaNay Queen Nazaire
Living Cities

It is a painful reality that inequality is entrenched across the country. The gap between the wealthy and everyone else continues to widen, and people from Wall Street to Main Street are tuned in to economic inequality's regnant existence. It is so commonplace that the topic shows up in mainstream media platforms from CNBC to Rolling Stone Magazine. What is finally becoming more explicit is the persistent inequality that exists for Black and Latinx people across every indicator of well-being, be it housing, employment, health, education, criminal justice involvement, or net worth. While this essay is focused on the Black and Latinx experience, grave disparities and enduring marginalization for Indigenous people are also critical to acknowledge and address.

The founding ethos of America has always been in stark juxtaposition with the inequality and inequity that define this country's realities. Analyzing the impacts of policy and legislation such as the Electoral College, Plessy v. Ferguson, redlining, GI Bill, and Highway Act, we can articulate how the American government has played a role in creating inequality. With just these few examples of critical decision points in the nation's timeline, we can show that Black and Latinx people were consistently and disproportionately marginalized by policy or excluded from securing the purported benefits. To understand how inequality persists, especially for Black, Latinx, and Indigenous people, we must interrogate our culture and systems to get to the root causes and fix them. Given all that we know and all we are learning, we must ask ourselves: If we had the power for a fresh start, what is the America we imagine for ourselves and how might we create it?

This volume has focused on mixed-income communities as one platform for a fresh approach to societal change. The essays in the volume are replete with information about where we are making progress and where we are falling short and with ideas about how to advance more effective policy and practice. But how will these ideas be advanced and sustained? For this fresh start to promote equitable and inclusive communities in which all are welcomed to thrive, I believe a paradigm shift is required. We need a new and different way to shape the cultural and institutional values that effectuate a society driven by belief in our collective shared fate and, as Khare and Joseph state in their opening essay, "strengthened by a sense of mutual prosperity."[1] Reckoning with the dissonance of our country's sordid past, we must acknowledge the harm and work intentionally to undo the impact of its legacy by interrogating why we believe what we believe and how history has informed these beliefs.[2] This essay explores what is required for us to shift away from the beliefs, behaviors, and systems that result in inequality and offers ways to reassess and reshape the values and principles that weave throughout the fabric of our institutions and communities.

THE PERSON-ROLE-SYSTEM FRAMEWORK

In contemplating *how* to generate a fresh start and *what* we might do within our relative spheres of influence to change systems and promote well-being for all, we can deploy the "Person-Role-System" framework, which recognizes the dynamic interplay between the mental viewpoints of people as individuals, their responsibilities in their personal and professional roles, and the overall impact of their actions on a system.[3] As human beings, each of us has a mental model—a set of beliefs and experiences that shape our worldview and drive our behavior. We take this mental model into every social and professional sphere we enter. In those settings, we have roles that we play and we have agency and power we can use. Our choices and behaviors, combined with the choices and

---

1   Amy T. Khare and Mark L. Joseph, "Prioritizing Inclusion and Equity in the Next Generation of Mixed-Income Communities," in *What Works to Promote Inclusive, Equitable Mixed-Income Communities*, eds., Mark L. Joseph and Amy T. Khare (San Francisco: Federal Reserve Bank of San Francisco, 2020).

2   Ibram Kendi, *Stamped from the Beginning: A History of Racist Ideas in America* (Bold Type Books: 2016).

3   Annie E. Casey Foundation, "*Person Role System Briefing Note*," 2013, https://www.aecf.org/m/blogdoc/PersonRoleSystemFramework-2013.pdf.

behaviors of others, generate the outcomes produced by the system. Thus, to effectuate change we must first start with ourselves and other individuals.

At the personal level, as human beings living, working, and playing in our various communities, we must actively work to understand history and interrogate our beliefs and biases, asking ourselves, "What do I believe and why do I believe it?" We must take inventory of the various roles we play– in our families, communities, workplaces, social circles, religious groups, extracurricular activities—and assess how we show up, what we represent, what ideas we perpetuate, where we are silent, when we are complicit, and whether we hold others accountable for what they say and how they behave, especially when it is not in service of more opportunity and better outcomes for us all.

Next, we must contemplate how our personal traits, proclivities, and experiences influence our behavior and choices in the roles we occupy. We must ask, "How do my personal beliefs and values impact the ways in which I exercise leadership and power? How is this impacting other people? On what things do we get to 'make the call'? What is our boundary of formal authority, and how do we use it to maintain or disrupt status quo in systems? How do we use it to transform systems to ensure better outcomes for those impacted?"

Too many of us, too often, are unaware, have a limited understanding of, or are afraid of our power. But we all have both formal and informal power. Formal power is what we are authorized to do within the scope of our social or professional role—for example as a director, coordinator, worker, resident, or parent. Informal power is the influence we have through our relationships beyond the formal authority that comes with a designated role.

Becoming aware of the power we have and what we can do with it is the first necessary step. Practicing how to use that power to create more equitable outcomes is the second step. Our institutions and communities are great places to begin our practice because they make up the systems in which we exist, which leads to the third step: We must stop distancing ourselves, in our concept of the change process, from "the system." It is not separate from us or beyond our control. In fact, people make up the systems we occupy and are responsible for the outputs produced by the system. We are its operators, playing the role of facilitator to ensure the system functions and perpetuates itself. But if we adopt a new mindset based in antiracist values and prioritizing human well-being, we can leverage our formal and informal power to transform institutions and systems and produce better outcomes for all. Leveraging the power we have in our roles to make choices that are in service of more equitable outcomes for people will ultimately enable us to recreate systems we need to thrive collectively. But this will not occur without reckoning with history, shifting beliefs, building relationships, and reshaping cultural and institutional values to center humanity, share power, and work under the belief that our fates are shared.

PERSON

The person-role-system framework is an invitation for us to adopt new mental models as part of a paradigm shift in the way we operate. Our mental models are shaped by the "core beliefs and values embedded in our culture(s) and institution(s) that make up our 'worldview'"[4] and direct our decisions, choices, and behaviors, which happen for ourselves, our communities, our institutions, and our systems. With America's fraught history, we must recognize how the worldview of our founding fathers is deeply embedded in what each of us chooses to believe and how we choose to behave in our multiple spheres of influence. We can no longer blame flawed policymaking, failed implementation, and limited resources without also calling into account our "conscious and unconscious thoughts and deeply held assumptions that affect how we make sense of the world."[5] Interrogating our beliefs begins by reckoning with our history.

Understanding History, Reimagining the Future

Before colonization in the Americas, there were no racialized social categories. Race was constructed to support colonization, domination, and power. To create the America as we know it today, immigrants had to give up their culture, language, and values to "become White" and earn the related privileges,[6] including access to a capital market founded in human bondage, stolen land, and genocide but peddled as available to everyone as long as one

---

4 Andrew Grant-Thomas, Curtis Ogden, and Cynthia Silva Parker, *Using Systems Thinking to Address Structural Racism*, Interaction Institute for Social Change, 2014, http://interactioninstitute.org/wp-content/uploads/2014/12/Facing-Race-Handout-actual.pdf.

5 Grant-Thomas, Ogden, Silva Parker, *Using Systems Thinkin*

6 "Home," The People's Institute for Survival and Beyond, accessed September 15, 2020, https://www.pisab.org/.

bought into the central tenet of individual responsibility and, explicitly or implicitly, supported White supremacy. The New York Times' 1619 project[7] highlights how the founding fathers, including Thomas Jefferson, worked hard to cloak their intentional decisions to hoard and wield power on behalf of a White ruling class by lifting up race-neutral language about liberty and freedom for all. Black and Indigenous people, however, were positioned as inferior—and this belief system was built into the foundation of this nation, ensuring the intergenerational transfer of beliefs and behaviors that would result in the inequality we continue to experience in communities, institutions, and systems.

Khare and Joseph's essay opens this volume with an acknowledgment of the harm done, and they call for a recommitment to bridging the gap between intent and impact.[8] The call is for every person from every background to be willing to come together and help advance the intent of mixed-income communities designed to realize the promise of America. In their purest form, mixed-income communities would look like diverse dinner tables, robust learning environments, caring neighbors, access to healthy foods, diverse opportunities for recreation, healthy climates, and, ultimately, better outcomes for all people. The manifestation of each person's commitment to the collective "we" would represent an "inescapable network of mutuality, tied in a single garment of destiny,"[9] in which the Kiswahili principle *ubuntu*—I am, because you are—reigns.

Interrogating Assumptions

Reshaping our cultural and institutional values begins with reimagining our communities being strengthened by a belief in mutuality. For example, in his contribution to this volume Michaeljit Sandhu invites each of us to check our assumptions about how positive outcomes will happen in mixed-income housing communities. For many, the notion of a well-ordered mixed-income housing community assumes that social order will be forged mostly at the behest of "law-abiding" and "rule-following" middle-income families and the

---

7 Nicole Hannah-Jones, "Episode 5: The Land of Our Fathers, Part 2," *The New York Times* (The New York Times, October 12, 2019), https://www.nytimes.com/2019/10/11/podcasts/1619-slavery-farm-loan-discrimination.html.

8 Khare and Joseph, "Prioritizing Inclusion and Equity"

9 Martin Luther King, "Letters from a Birmingham Jail," Letter from a Birmingham Jail [King, Jr.], 1963, https://www.africa.upenn.edu/Articles_Gen/Letter_Birmingham.html.

dutiful acceptance of the lower-income families, who need lessons in character and behavior.[10] The prevailing mindset assumes that the residents paying market rates are "expected to form bridging and bonding relationships" with residents who pay subsidized rates. It does not necessarily assume mutual exchange or benefit; rather, a paternalistic approach whereby market-rate paying residents are to bestow their value upon the low-income residents, lift them up, broaden their scope, and introduce them to economic opportunities. This mindset inherently assumes that a person who qualifies as a middle-income resident has a superior set of beliefs, principles and values that drive their behavior, and that the opposite is true for a person who has a lower income.

Allowing these assumptions to persist in mixed-income housing development is problematic, because people of color often are overrepresented in the lower-income category of residents. These assumptions reinforce the belief that people of color's perceived failings are inherent rather than caused by generations of systemic racism. We know that the wealth of many White Americans is rooted in human bondage, stolen land, genocide, and structural exclusion. We can identify numerous moments throughout history in which government and business leaders established rules, regulations, legislation, and processes that enabled wealth generation for some groups of people and categorically denied or disrupted wealth generation for other groups of people—for example the destruction of Black Wall Street in Tulsa, the GI Bill, redlining, the Highway Act, and, most recently, the CARES Act. When we fail to shift the lens and interrogate our assumptions about the role and expectations of market-rate residents, we miss the opportunity to understand how and why better outcomes are not being achieved in these communities. Market-rate renters often see mixed-income housing opportunities purely as an opportunity to advance their own well-being, without attention to the communal goal of advancing opportunity and well-being for all people in a community.

As people who have a role to play in designing and developing mixed-income housing communities, we can change the narrative and the practice if each of us grapples with the history of housing, understands how it has influenced our beliefs, and determines how we might change our minds and behaviors to be in service of stronger and healthier communities. It begins with each one of us.

---

10 Michaeljit Sandhu, "Reassessing Market-Rate Residents' Role in Mixed-Income Developments," in *What Works to Promote Inclusive, Equitable Mixed-Income Communities*, eds. Mark L. Joseph and Amy T. Khare (San Francisco: Federal Reserve Bank of San Francisco, 2020).

We must interrogate what we fundamentally believe about people and about differences in outcomes according to race and class, and we must examine how those beliefs materialize and drive the choices we make in our various spheres of influence.

ROLE AND SYSTEM

Once we understand that our beliefs drive our behaviors in the roles we play within systems, the next question becomes, "Are we using these roles to produce outcomes that truly benefit all?" It is imperative that enough of us step more intentionally and consistently into our positional power to create the America to which we aspire. In his essay on state community development policy in California, Ben Metcalf illustrates how individual leaders used their role authority within the institution of government to impact the mixed-income housing system. California Governors Jerry Brown and Gavin Newsom both "pushed to use state power in new and creative ways to help the state address racial and economic inequities while also facilitating economic gains."[11]

Undoing and Remaking Dysfunctional Systems

Metcalf's essay illustrates what is possible when someone has personal will and role authority coupled with the tools of government to create more inclusion and equity. His essay offers two particularly important takeaways. First, these leaders and their teams used data to understand the realities, patterns, and disparities of the current housing landscape in order to shift their mindset about a policy approach and inform their decision making. One key pattern was that the Low-Income Housing Tax Credit (LIHTC)—universally seen as the federal government's most successful affordable housing policy—while useful to spur affordable housing development did not generate substantial profit, so there was a tendency to develop affordable housing in poorer areas. Building in poorer neighborhoods was cheaper, and developers could generate a bit more revenue given the lower development costs. But the lack of neighborhood resources—including grocery stores, businesses, restaurants, and high-quality schools—defeated much of the purpose of providing affordable housing for the families who most needed to benefit.

---

11 Ben Metcalf, "California For All: How State Action Can Foster Inclusive Mixed-Income Communities," in *What Works to Promote Inclusive, Equitable Mixed-Income Communities*, eds., Mark L. Joseph and Amy T. Khare (San Francisco: Federal Reserve Bank of San Francisco, 2020).

Metcalf's second key takeaway is that having the data allowed Governor Newsom and his team to adjust the state's LIHTC provisions and call for developers to change their behavior and be held accountable for their role in creating economic opportunity for residents. By requiring developers to develop affordable housing in more resourced neighborhoods, government leaders used their power to disrupt what on the surface was a race- and class-neutral policy and practice but actually had a disproportionate impact on families of color with lower incomes.

This California case study highlights how it is imperative to remember that if we can create these systems, policies, and practices, then we can also undo and recreate them so that they better serve all people. This notion is not farfetched. Just as the country's founding fathers and subsequent leaders created systems of business and government to benefit wealth and well-being for White, Protestant, land-owning men and their families, so leaders must now use the mechanisms in government and business to benefit all actors—with special attention to people of color, who have been marginalized for generations.

Disrupting Root Causes of Inequity

Aaron Seybert, Lori Chatman, and Rob Bachmann provide an example of the need for vigilance about policy intentions versus impact in their discussion of the Opportunity Zone tax incentive. This incentive was meant to help increase funding to new and growing businesses, especially those owned by entrepreneurs of color in economically strained areas. Investors saw these investments as too risky, however, and instead invested in less-risky real estate projects. With the purchased real estate concentrated in or near blighted areas, investors catalyze economic growth and are the primary beneficiaries of the return, while the intended beneficiaries may contend with gentrification and displacement.[12] Seybert, Chatman, and Bachmann remind us that "the market has never been particularly good at valuing the risk/return profile of low-income communities because of an inherent bias, the roots of which lie largely in racism and discrimination."[13] This reality is accepted because of our

---

12 Samantha Jacoby, *Potential Flaws of Opportunity Zones Loom, as Do Risks of Large-Scale Tax Avoidance*, Center on Budget and Policy Priorities, April 25, 2019, https://www.cbpp.org/research/federal-tax/potential-flaws-of-opportunity-zones-loom-as-do-risks-of-large-scale-tax.

13 Aaron Seybert, Lori Chatman, Rob Bachman, "Opportunity for Whom? A Call for Course Correction Given the Location and Targets of Early Opportunity Zone Investments," in *What Works to Promote Inclusive, Equitable Mixed-Income Communities*, eds., Mark L. Joseph and Amy T. Khare (San Francisco:

mental models about people of color and people who are poor; it is embedded in our culture, institutions, and systems, it dates back to our founding, and it is reinforced by dangerous narratives that ignore centuries of systemic discrimination. Wealthy investors are making a *choice* to avoid the perceived risk of investing in an economy that could give preference to entrepreneurs of color. These investors are actually leaving money on the table through investments they are not making because of their bias against investing in communities of color. Yet investors and the general population fail to recognize the amount of resources that went into de-risking and subsidizing the White population to enable them to be considered "safe" investments. Of course, the seminal example of Black underinvestment is the failed promise of "40 acres and mule" due to Reconstruction, which codified White land ownership and tipped the economic scales for generations. The practice was updated for the modern economy with banks' redlining practices, which codified disinvestment in Black communities in favor of White communities.

Another seminal example of racially discriminatory decisionmaking by individuals within a system involves the U.S. Department of Agriculture (USDA). The USDA can give loans to support struggling farmers, yet for years Black farmers were discriminated against and were unable to access these de-risking loans. The loan system the USDA set up was administered through local county committees that were completely White-controlled. They gave preference to White farmers, and when Black farmers complained to the USDA their complaints were ignored. Unfortunately, it took a class action lawsuit in the late 1990s for the USDA to admit this discrimination. Even with one of the largest civil rights settlements in U.S. history,[14] the wealth Black farmers lost has never been recovered. Here is another example of people with decision-making authority largely granting loans to Whites and denying loans to Blacks. The irony is that, in many cases, the difference between a Black farmer's land and a White farmer's land is merely where the fence begins and ends. It begs the questions, "What do the loan officers believe about Black farmers and why do they believe it? What is the root of these beliefs? What must happen to disrupt and shift those mental models, to shift how the loan officers play their roles, to shift how the entire system works?"

Federal Reserve Bank of San Francisco, 2020).

14 Hannah-Jones, "Episode 5"

A similar story can be told about mortgage lending and how Black families with the same credit-risk rating as White families are charged higher interest rates. There has been a recent focus on the racism inherent in property appraisals, with Black families' homes being valued less than their White counterparts' even when all things remain equal. Consider also that Black homeowners pay more than their fair share in property taxes, given that they receive fewer services in their communities and less value for their homes when compared to similar White communities.[15] With trends like these, we must identify the root cause to disrupt its pattern of destruction. Otherwise, we will continue to experience the compounding impacts of centuries of inequality.

Coronavirus' Disparate Impact: A Case in Point

More recently, the COVID-19 pandemic has forced people who have long been in denial to acknowledge the biases people hold and the inequities in our communities, institutions, and systems that have a disparate impact. It quickly became plain, for instance, that:

- Black and Latinx people are over-represented in low-wage jobs[16] in industries vulnerable to significant lay-offs[17] and in frontline jobs deemed "essential," in every state. These essential jobs, such as stocking grocery stores and warehouses and working in restaurants, as delivery persons, and in hospitals, often are the lowest paid, offer the least sick leave and health benefits,[18] and require some of the greatest health risks because of an inability to socially distance.

---

15 Theresa Wiltz, *Black Homeowners Pay More Than 'Fair Share' in Property Taxes, Black Homeowners Pay More Than 'Fair Share' in Property Taxes*, The Pew Charitable Trusts (Pew Charitable Trusts, June 25, 2020), https://www.pewtrusts.org/en/research-and-analysis/blogs/stateline/2020/06/25/black-homeowners-pay-more-than-fair-share-in-property-taxes.

16 Connor Maxwell, Danyelle Solomon, and Abril Castro, *Systematic Inequality and Economic Opportunity*, Center for American Progress, August 7, 2019, https://www.americanprogress.org/issues/race/reports/2019/08/07/472910/systematic-inequality-economic-opportunity/.

17 Connor Maxwell and Danyelle Solomon, *The Economic Fallout of the Coronavirus for People of Color*, Center for American Progress, May 8, 2020, https://www.americanprogress.org/issues/race/news/2020/04/14/483125/economic-fallout-coronavirus-people-color/.

18 Richard E. Besser, "As Coronavirus Spreads, the Bill for Our Public Health Failures Is Due," The Washington Post (WP Company, March 6, 2020), https://www.washingtonpost.com/opinions/as-coronavirus-spreads-the-bill-for-our-public-health-failures-is-due/2020/03/05/9da09ed6-5f10-11ea-b29b-9db-42f7803a7_story.html.

- The Black-White wealth gap[19]—with White families having an average of 10 times the net wealth of Black families—makes it far more difficult for Black families to weather the severe financial downturn associated with the pandemic. A history of practices, from redlining in the 1930s and lack of access to the GI Bill after World War II to predatory lending practices in the first decade of this century, has kept most people of color from accumulating any meaningful amount of wealth through homeownership—one of the prime ways in which White families have built and passed on wealth.

- Blacks in the U.S. are at significantly higher risk for serious complications or death from COVID-19 due to racial health disparities in pre-existing conditions, such as asthma and lung disease.[20] Land use policies over the years have sited landfills, hazardous waste sites, and other industrial facilities in neighborhoods that are highly segregated due to discriminatory laws, practices, and disinvestment. The stay-in-place orders that have been active in all 50 states mean that millions of Black and Latinx families are unable to leave these same neighborhoods, which also often lack green spaces to exercise or grocery stores with fresh food or cleaning supplies.

- Black, Indigenous, Latinx, and other people of color have less access to COVID-19 benefits because policymakers failed to account for or address existing racial disparities. For example, long-standing racial disparities in loan approval rates meant that many small-business owners of color did not have the pre-existing relationships with financial institutions needed[21] to expedite their applications for the federal Paycheck Protection Program. A recent Brookings report indicates that, while there will be widespread economic pain as a result of the pandemic, Black-owned businesses are

---

19 Kriston McIntosh et al., *Examining the Black-White Wealth Gap*, Brookings (Brookings, February 27, 2020), https://www.brookings.edu/blog/up-front/2020/02/27/examining-the-black-white-wealth-gap/.

20 Dionna Cheatham and Iris Marechal, *Respiratory Health Disparities in the United States and Their Economic Repercussions*, (Washington Center for Equitable Growth, July 12, 2018), https://equitablegrowth.org/respiratory-health-disparities-in-the-united-states-and-their-economic-repercussions/.

21 Emily Flitter, "Black-Owned Businesses Could Face Hurdles in Federal Aid Program," *The New York Times* (The New York Times, April 10, 2020), https://www.nytimes.com/2020/04/10/business/minority-business-coronavirus-loans.html.

likely to bear the heaviest burden.[22] Up to 90 percent of businesses owned by people of color have been or likely will be unable to get a loan.[23]

These outcomes result from a set of interrelated systems that have failed people of color, including but not limited to health care, housing, civic infrastructure, food, clean water, transportation, and workforce. The simultaneous failure of all these systems to respond adequately and equitably speaks to deeper fault lines in our society that we must address at their core.

Gaining Equity Will Require Losing Privilege

If we have any hope for a productive and vibrant society in which everyone thrives, the paradigm must shift and our beliefs and behaviors must change to enable more equitable decisions in the roles we play. Obviously, this is a tall order. To make these shifts, people in positions of power at all levels will have to grapple with changes that feel like loss. People who have long been in power must relinquish it and step aside because it has largely benefitted them and their social sphere. The national call by community organizers and advocates of equity to center people of color and marginalized groups will require decentering Whiteness. Unfortunately, Whiteness in America is too often synonymous with privilege, access, power, and status quo. (It is telling that when the People's Institute for Survival and Beyond's workshop on undoing racism poses the question, "What do you like about being White," the common theme among all participants who identify as White is their ability to move through the world relatively unharmed and uninterrupted.)

More recently, in a COVID-19 world, this shift has involved White and wealthy people losing the ability to feign ignorance about the disparate impact suffered by diverse groups in America. Black people have experienced the worst death rates, Black and Latinx people have lost more jobs, Asian Americans have experienced more hate crimes.

Using mixed-income housing as the frame of reference for her essay, Tiffany

---

22 Andre M. Perry and David Harshbarger, *Coronavirus Economic Relief Cannot Neglect Black-Owned Business*, Brookings (Brookings, June 17, 2020), https://www.brookings.edu/blog/the-avenue/2020/04/08/coronavirus-economic-relief-cannot-neglect-black-owned-business/.

23 Marcus Baram, "'That Was It-Silence': As Bailout Funds Evaporate, Minority-Owned Businesses Say They've Been Shut Out," Fast Company (Fast Company, April 30, 2020), https://www.fastcompany.com/90498767/that-was-it-silence-as-bailout-funds-evaporate-minority-owned-businesses-say-theyve-been-shut-out.

Manuel describes how biased beliefs drive behaviors and produce inequitable outcomes for people of color and poor people. Because people simply do not know or understand history, "when the thorny issues of racial and economic segregation come up in the media, arise in community meetings, or require public comment in other community forums"[24] they are not adequately addressed and fall short of supporting beneficial policy solutions. Manuel courageously waves the red flag, warning that when we create and implement policies we must simultaneously change and reframe the narrative to influence public perception, change public discourse, and build public desire for greater inclusion and interdependence. We can begin this process when we begin reckoning with history and interrogating the root cause of our persistent problems.

In their essay in this volume, Aly Andrews and Sydney VanKuren offer a way to disrupt the misinformation that prevents mixed-income housing communities from realizing their potential. The "empathetic planning" approach they advocate could allow all relevant stakeholders in a mixed-income housing project to reduce biases, eliminate tensions, reflect on what *can* work, and consider the positive outcomes that *can* be created from shared visioning and collective contributions.[25] This essay underscores the fact that our current paradigm defaults to separating out "other" people and to resisting diversity and inclusion as a first choice. Powell and Menendian (2016) define othering as "a term that not only encompasses the many expressions of prejudice on the basis of group identities, but…argue[s] that it provides a clarifying frame that reveals a set of common processes and conditions that propagate group-based inequality and marginality."[26] Othering exists by design, and we are conditioned to go along with what we know,[27] using shortcuts to make simple

---

24 Tiffany Manuel, "How Do Fish See Water? Building Public Will to Advance Inclusive Communities," in *What Works to Promote Inclusive, Equitable Mixed-Income Communities*, eds., Mark L. Joseph and Amy T. Khare (San Francisco: Federal Reserve Bank of San Francisco, 2020).

25 Aly Andrews and Sydney VanKuren, "Addressing Resistance to Mixed-Income Communities through Empathetic Planning Techniques" in *What Works to Promote Inclusive, Equitable Mixed-Income Communities*, eds., Mark L. Joseph and Amy T. Khare (San Francisco: Federal Reserve Bank of San Francisco, 2020).

26 john a powell and Stephen Menendian, "The Problem of Othering: Towards Inclusiveness and Belonging," Othering and Belonging, August 29, 2018, http://www.otheringandbelonging.org/the-problem-of-othering/.

27 Ronald Abadian Heifetz, Alexander Grashow, and Martin Linsky, *The Practice of Adaptive Leadership: Tools and Tactics for Changing Your Organization and the World* (Boston, MA: Harvard Business Press, 2009).

decisions[28] and choosing what is comforting.[29] Although we are hard-wired to adapt, survive, and ultimately thrive in changing environments, we resist that which feels unfamiliar to us and takes us out of our comfort zone. Our conditioning forces us to resist other ways, which presents a great challenge to shifting a paradigm and creating new mental models. Drawing from the insights in Douglas Farr's *Sustainable Nation*, Andrews and VanKuren characterize this trait as "loss aversion," noting that "most people prefer to avoid a loss rather than acquire an equal gain, and value the magnitude of the loss as twice the value of the gain."[30] This reasoning leads us to an additional question: What will be lost if we adopt new mental models and shift the current paradigm so that we have better outcomes for more people? Determining the answer to this question is both a process and an important outcome in and of itself and will requires a racial equity analysis to imagine a new and better future for all. It *is the work* we must do as individuals and in our roles as influential members of communities and systems.

A Moment of Pain and Promise

As we look to the future and imagine the inclusive, equitable communities we want, we must remember that we have a choice in *how* we show up and *what* we do to contribute or prevent better outcomes for all people. Sandhu calls us to account with a reminder that we "should see the decision not to strive for a more inclusive and engaged community as a choice, rather than an inevitable product of self-interest or social norms."[31] The danger in choosing self-interest is that it reinforces the notion of individualism and maintains the pretense that each of us can be healthy, successful, and whole on our own—as if all we each need to do is pull ourselves up by our bootstraps and we will, regardless of the systemic barriers stacked against some of us, realize the American dream. This problematic mindset is based on our nation's racist history, 400 years in the making, and is at the root of the harm and trauma plaguing us all.

There is pain and promise in this moment. We must move away from individualism and independence and toward community and interdependence,

---

28 Daniel Kahneman, in *Thinking, Fast and Slow* (New York: Farrar, Straus and Giroux, 2013), p. 98.

29 Beverly Daniel Tatum, *Why Do All the Black Kids Sit Together in the Cafeteria* (Basic Books, 1999).

30 Andrews and VanKuren, "Addressing Resistance"

31 Michaeljit Sandhu, "Reassessing Market-Rate Residents'"

recognizing we are all indeed a part of an "inescapable network of mutuality, tied in a single garment of destiny."[32] And so I leave you with these four questions to consider:

- What do you believe about the potential to truly achieve full equity for African Americans and Latinx? And, why do you believe that? What are you currently doing to expand your thinking?

- Are you taking the right everyday actions to promote more equitable outcomes, when you have the opportunity? Are you taking those actions effectively? Are there actions you take that may be driven more by norms of Whiteness and singular power rather than humanity, shared power, and collective accountability?

- Thomas Paine said, "We have the power to begin the world over again." As you restart your own personal world, post-pandemic and post-summer of racial reckoning, how are you using your personal power to "begin all over again" in your roles within your systems?

- How are you using and interpreting the data and information available to you? Do you have the data and information that you need to be effective as an antiracist in your role in your system? Are you including diverse perspectives for interpretation? What is the basis of your analysis? By what standards are you analyzing your personal and organizational results?

Your answers will be a step toward beginning again—toward taking on the work and pain of individual and systems disruption—so that we may realize the promise of an American dream we all can embrace.

■ ■ ■

As Chief Strategy Officer at Living Cities, **JANAY QUEEN NAZAIRE**, *Ph.D. convenes and leverages public, private, and philanthropic stakeholders in American cities, identifies and tests innovative approaches to deploy millions in public and private capital for investing in people of color, and harnesses and facilitates the power and resources of 19 multibillion-dollar foundations and financial institutions working collectively towards systems change. Throughout her career, Dr. Nazaire has worked across sectors, at every level of government, domestically, and internationally to provide innovative, creative, and solution-focused leadership and strategy to address social and economic challenges for children, adults, families, and communities.*

---

32 Martin Luther King, "Letters from a Birmingham Jail"

WHAT *MAY* WORK ABOUT THE MIXED-INCOME APPROACH: REFLECTIONS AND IMPLICATIONS FOR THE FUTURE

Rachel G. Bratt
Tufts University

Amy Khare and Mark Joseph have a clear mission: to see many more inclusive and equitable mixed-income communities that welcome diverse racial and income groups. As they note in the introduction to this volume, their hope and belief is that mixed-income communities can contribute to an "inclusive, equitable America, where neighborhoods are places where differences are affirmed and valued, not ignored or scorned. [They] envision a nation where your ZIP Code is not the strongest predictor of your life chances..." While they acknowledge the criticisms of the mixed-income approach, the editors believe these communities would provide a path to greater mobility and an escape from poverty.

Khare and Joseph's ambitious goals for the mixed-income approach notwithstanding, producing and maintaining housing that is affordable to lower-income households, within a market economy, is a daunting task in itself. With developers needing to rely on a host of public subsidies and private funding sources, as well as having to secure municipal and community approval, any affordable housing initiative is likely to take years to complete. Thus, a key tension surrounding the mixed-income agenda is how to balance the desire to "just get affordable housing built" with the broader set of social objectives that Khare and Joseph articulate.[1] This conflict was, for example, at the center of the debate in New York City concerning several inclusionary housing buildings having separate entrances for the low-income and market-

---

1   The essays by Metcalf, and Seabaugh and Bennett touch on this issue.

rate tenants, with no access to the amenities in the building for the former group.[2]

In commissioning the dozens of essays contained in *What Works to Promote Inclusive, Equitable Mixed-Income Communities*, the editors were interested in answering five overriding questions, which are presented in their opening essay:

- How can the benefits of mixed-income community revitalization be shared more equitably?
- How can mixed-income communities be leveraged to produce a broader range of positive—indeed, transformative—individual, household, community, and societal outcomes?
- What are the most promising innovations to be expanded in the next generation of mixed-income community efforts?
- What are the greatest threats to efforts to promote more inclusion and equity through mixed-income communities, and what steps should be taken to counter them?
- What are the practical, actionable implications of current experiences and findings for policymakers, developers, investors, residents and community members, researchers, and other important stakeholders?

Beyond these central questions, Khare and Joseph articulate at least three closely related concerns. First, they are interested in highlighting "strategies to promote *racial* equity and inclusion as well as mixing across income and class." This suggests a further component of the first question: To what extent are mixed-income developments serving a diverse racial population?

Khare and Joseph also believe that, in addition to the fairness argument, the case for greater inclusion and equity should be based on powerful economic

---

2 Schwartz and Tsenkova briefly discuss "poor doors" in New York City, which were banned in 2015. Developers have found a new way of creating physical separation between market-rate and subsidized residents, by building separate structures on the same site, each housing lower or higher income populations. (Justin Moyer, "NYC Bans 'poor doors'—Separate Entrances for Low-Income Tenants," *Washington Post*, June 30, 2015. https://www.washingtonpost.com/news/morning-mix/wp/2015/06/30/nyc-bans-poor-doors-separate-entrances-for-low-income-tenants/ and Shelby Welinder, "Opinion: City Has Gone from Allowing 'Poor Doors' to Permitting 'Poor Buildings,'" *City Limits*, Nov. 4, 2019, https://citylimits.org/2019/11/04/opinion-city-has-gone-from-allowing-poor-doors-to-permitting-poor-buildings/). See also Joseph, 2019a. This harkens back to early public housing developments, such as Pruitt-Igoe in St. Louis, which provided housing for White and Black tenants in two separate buildings. The Gurstein essay discusses a "portfolio" model in which income mixing is achieved through different buildings housing different income levels.

and social values. Thus, inclusive mixed-income communities have the potential to "emphasize the value of people of color and the value of people who are economically constrained" and can result in "greater opportunity for marginalized people actually generat(ing) increased opportunities for all people." This leads to an expansion of the second question: Is there evidence that mixed-income communities also generate increased and sustained opportunities for all?

The editors also assert that the focus of the volume will be on three major place-based approaches to promoting mixed-income communities: (1) mixed-income developments in high-poverty neighborhoods, such as public and assisted housing transformations; (2) inclusionary housing and zoning strategies; and (3) affordable housing preservation and other mechanisms to prevent displacement in gentrifying areas. Taking these three strategies into account, Khare and Joseph are also implicitly elaborating on the third question: To what extent does each of the three place-based strategies promote the central goals for mixed-income housing and under what conditions is each most effective at generating inclusive and equitable outcomes?

Framing a large number of essays around these central questions and trying to ensure that they are, indeed, addressed and molded into a coherent whole is a challenging task. This concluding essay discusses the extent to which the editors' central questions have been answered, while also articulating several areas that warrant further examination. Before launching into this effort, however, a few broad observations about the overall contributions and limitations of the volume are warranted.

What Works to Promote Inclusive, Equitable Mixed-Income Communities advances our understanding of mixed-income communities in several important ways. First, it underscores the values underlying the mixed-income housing concept and the commitment of advocates to develop initiatives that meet its many goals. Second, it emphasizes the importance of communication among key stakeholders and of resident involvement in any discussion about mixed-income communities. Third, it offers a number of concrete examples of innovative and promising strategies, from many locales across the country, that involve a mixed-income approach. And fourth, departing from the usual line-up of authors in a book such as this—scholars and policy analysts—this volume includes the voices of many diverse stakeholders, such as developers, housing finance agencies, nonprofit organizations, and residents.

Yet, a significant limitation of the book is that it offers only sparse information about outcomes of specific mixed-income developments and it does not, therefore, manage to provide clear guidance about whether various strategies achieve those ends. Many of the examples presented describe only limited anecdotal information, or the initiatives are still in the planning stage, thereby precluding evaluation and the kind of documentation needed to guide policy. Thus, the overriding question of "what works" should be more accurately framed as "what may work" or "what can be tried" to produce the sought-after larger social and economic goals of the mixed-income strategy. Nevertheless, an overriding contribution of the book is that within its breadth and richness many seemingly promising strategies are offered, along with suggestions for additional research that could more fully answer what, exactly, does or does not work concerning the mixed-income approach.

In summarizing a number of the findings in this volume, sorted according to the key questions posed, three caveats are important. First, several of the examples could be placed in more than one of the categories of the editors' questions. It was a subjective exercise to decide where a given author's observations fit best. Second, although an attempt was made to mention each of the essays in the volume, some essays were omitted or cited without elaboration. Sometimes the project being described did not, in this writer's view, contribute to a fuller understanding of the mixed-income approach (although the material presented may be interesting and insightful in other ways). In a few other cases, assertions were made about the importance of some feature of a mixed-income housing development but with little or no supporting evidence or explanations about the variations in, for example, market conditions, that could help guide key decisions. Also, a few essays were completed after this concluding essay was written. Third, while an attempt was made to cite the findings of each essay that best responds to the editors' questions, I take full responsibility for any errors of omission or misinterpretation, and extend apologies to the authors for any such oversights.

1. How can the benefits of mixed-income community revitalization be shared more equitably? To what extent are mixed-income developments serving a diverse racial population?

Before turning to the answers suggested by the essays, it is first important to discuss what the volume tells us about the simpler and more straightforward question of whether mixed-income housing (compared to other types of affordable housing) provides positive outcomes for lower-income residents. This is an essential precursor to understanding how various strategies may promote the desired results and whether they can be "shared more equitably."

Indeed, at the core of the mixed-income housing strategy is a series of beliefs and assumptions about how these developments can contribute to positive social and economic outcomes for lower-income residents, beyond the provision of decent, affordable housing.[3] However, the actual benefits of this approach have been hard to quantify and far from conclusive.[4] For example, a U.S Department of Housing and Urban Development summary of several studies on mixed-income housing concluded that "low-income residents who formerly lived in public housing have realized little or no economic or educational benefit from living in a new mixed-income setting"; in particular, "the evidence of sustained educational gains for children who have moved into a mixed-income community is also slight."[5] At the same time, the summary

---

3 U.S. Department of Housing and Urban Development, *HOPE VI Program Authority and Funding History*, (Washington, DC: U.S Department of Housing and Urban Development, 2007). https://portal.hud.gov/hudportal/documents/huddoc?id=DOC_9838.pdf; Mark L. Joseph, Robert J. Chaskin and Henry S. Webber. "The Theoretical Basis for Addressing Poverty through Mixed-Income Development." *Urban Affairs Review*, 42, no.3 (2007): 369-409.

4 See, for example, Paul C. Brophy and Rhonda N. Smith. "Mixed-Income Housing: Factors for Success," *Cityscape* 3 no. 2 (1997): 3–31; Robert R. Chaskin and Mark L. Joseph. *Integrating the Inner City: The Promise and Perils of Mixed-Income Public Housing Transformation*. (Chicago, IL: University of Chicago Press, 2015).; Aaron Gornstein and Ann Verrilli. *Mixed-Income Housing in the Suburbs: Lessons from Massachusetts*. (Boston: Citizens' Housing and Planning Association, 2006). https://www.chapa.org/sites/default/files/sssssssss.pdf; Erin M. Graves, "Mixed Outcome Developments." *Journal of the American Planning Association* 77 no. 2 (2011):143-153; Mark L. Joseph, "Promoting Poverty Deconcentration and Racial Desegregation through Mixed-Income Development," In *Facing Segregation: Housing Policy Solutions for A Stronger Society*, eds. Molly W. Metzler and Henry S. Webber (New York, NY: Oxford University Press, 2018); Mark L. Joseph, "Separate but Equal Redux: The New York City Poor Door Issue," In *The Dream Revisited: Contemporary Debates about Housing, Segregation, and Opportunity*, eds. Ingrid Gould Ellen and Justin P. Steil (New York: Columbia University Press, 2019).; Diane K. Levy, Zach McDade, and Kassie Bertumen, "Mixed-Income Living: Anticipated and Realized Benefits for Low-Income Households," *Cityscape* 15, no. 2 (2013) 15-28.; Sandra M. Moore and Susan K. Glassman. *The Neighborhood and Its School in Community Revitalization: Tools for Developers of Mixed-Income Housing Communities*, (St. Louis, MO: Urban Strategies, Inc., 2007).; National Initiative on Mixed-Income Communities, *State of the Field Scan #1: Social Dynamics in Mixed-Income Developments*, (Cleveland, Ohio: Case Western Reserve University, 2013).; William Ryan, Allan Sloan, Mania Seferi, and Elaine Werby, *All in Together: An Evaluation of Mixed-Income Multi-Family Housing* (Boston, Housing Finance Authority, 1974).; Alex Schwartz and Kian Tajbakhsh, "Mixed-Income Housing: Unanswered Questions." *Cityscape* 3 no. 2 (1997):71-92; Laura Tach, Rolf Pendall and Alexandra Derian, *Income Mixing Across Scales: Rationale, Trends, Policies, Practice and Research for More Inclusive Neighborhoods and Metropolitan Areas*. (Washington, DC: The Urban Institute, 2014), http://www.urban.org/sites/default/files/publication/22226/412998-Income-Mixing-across-Scales-Rationale-Trends-Policies-Practice-and-Research-for-More-Inclusive-Neighborhoods-and-Metropolitan-Areas.PDF.

5 As cited in U.S. Department of Housing and Urban Development, "Confronting Concentrated Poverty with a Mixed-Income Strategy," *Evidence Matters*, Spring 2013, https://www.huduser.gov/portal/periodicals/em/spring13/highlight1.html.

also noted that "the mixed-income housing strategy is successful in providing a safe environment with good quality, affordable housing in lower-poverty neighborhoods near desired resources, amenities, and services. In this sense, the strategy provides a stable platform from which low-income families may be able to improve their life chances."[6]

As noted earlier, the essays in this book provide very limited information on this issue. In the one essay that responds to this question,[7] Sandhu notes: "There is little evidence that market-rate residents form strong connections with their neighbors or provide them with job contacts. Although there is stronger support for successful social control at mixed-income sites, it is not clear that market-rate residents are directly responsible for the documented decreases in crime and increased feelings of subjective safety." Thus, "the role of market rate residents is mixed" or, I would add, inconclusive.

Sandhu's conclusion is far less positive than what proponents might hope for. While nearly all the residents he spoke with, regardless of income, "expressed enthusiasm for their mixed-income sites, [since] they provided safe, stable, affordable housing…the hope that a well-designed, well-maintained home can solve for a range of social and structural problems, from joblessness to racial prejudice to health disparities, may be too utopian. Perhaps, for mixed-income developments, providing affordable housing in a relatively desegregated setting should be seen as a strong enough start."

This perspective notwithstanding, what do the essays say about the first set of questions? The editors define equity to mean that people receive a fairer "share of resources, opportunities, social supports and power, given their differential needs and circumstances." For an initiative to be equitable it must address "structural disparities that exist between people of different backgrounds." Applying this definition to mixed-income housing, one approach may be to give preference for occupancy to extremely low-income households and to people of varying racial backgrounds (within the guidelines of the Fair Housing Act). Another strategy would be to provide opportunities for these households to

---

6   U.S. Department of Housing and Urban Development, "Confronting Concentrated Poverty"

7   In another essay, Adams, et al. provide a wonderful description of how a group of teens living in a mixed-income development in Minneapolis formed a baking business, with apparently good results. However, the skills to launch the initiative were the result of the human development program offered at the development, rather than an outcome of the mixed-income model itself. The essay does not explain whether funding for the program was related to the mixed-income model.

live in low-poverty areas with good schools and other locational advantages. In both these scenarios, sufficient resident supports should be available to enhance the personal and economic security of residents in the various mixed-income communities. The following examines each strategy in turn.

Giving Occupancy Preference to Extremely Low-Income Households and Racial Minorities to Live in Mixed-Income Developments.[8] A few essays in the volume present data pertaining to this point. Bostic, et al. cite a 2013 analysis of over 12,000 LIHTC properties which found that 93 percent of the units were occupied by households earning 60 percent or less of AMI. Schwartz and Tsenkova describe New York City's rich array of mixed-income strategies including at least one that specifically targets extremely low- and low-income people, including the formerly homeless. And Grady and Boos note that state housing finance agencies can provide incentives for LIHTC developments to include extremely low-income households: In Ohio, in 2018, 41 percent of the units funded with competitive LIHTCs had income limits below the statutory maximum (i.e., 60 percent of AMI).

Siting Mixed-Income Developments in Low Poverty/High-Opportunity Areas. There is ongoing controversy about where mixed-income developments should be located. Goetz, et al.[9] reject the policy approach of siting mixed-income housing in high-opportunity areas. In a thoughtful reprise of a decades-old controversy, they argue that by investing in programs that help people move out of areas of concentrated poverty, those areas are left behind. While they are agnostic on the issue of mixed-income housing, they support greater investment and acknowledgment of the overall worth and dignity of poorer communities. Indeed, several articles discuss the siting of mixed-income housing in what appear to be lower-opportunity urban neighborhoods.

For example, Galante, et al. note that San Antonio's 80-20 developments aim to promote neighborhood revitalization where market-rate development needs coaxing. Kneebone, et al. describe the Small Sites Program in San Francisco, which focuses on areas that are gentrifying. The program provides loans to nonprofit organizations to buy buildings that are at risk of being sold to private

---

8   The federal Consolidated Appropriations Act of 2018 permitted a new minimum set-aside for LIHTC properties. As Grady and Boos state: the "average income test" allows "LIHTC units to serve households with incomes between 20 percent and 80 percent of AMI, provided the weighted average of income restrictions on LIHTC units does not exceed 60 percent of AMI."

9   Editors' Note: For the purposes of this essay et al. is used for any essay with 3 or more authors.

investors, thereby creating permanently affordable units. Norton, et al., discuss how West Philadelphia Real Estate and Neighborhood Restorations's efforts have created 1,100 affordable rental housing units in 760 single-family homes and duplexes, mainly in high-poverty areas of West Philadelphia, using a mix of creative land acquisition, LIHTCs, and private financing. The focus is on acquiring low-cost abandoned structures in weak market areas that have the potential for revitalization and gentrification. Similarly, Holley, et al., present a case study of the Weinland Park mixed-income, mixed-race neighborhood in Columbus, Ohio that includes a redeveloped scattered-site Section 8 project. The Holley et al. and Norton, et al. examples are both noteworthy in that they are adjacent to major universities, suggesting that the investment in these areas is supported by a major local institution.

The argument for investment in poorer (or perhaps transitioning) urban neighborhoods notwithstanding, siting mixed-income housing in high-opportunity areas is a frequently described mixed-income strategy in the volume. For example:

- Chicago's Regional Housing Initiative, described by Snyderman and Riley, is a financing strategy that aims to increase the range of affordable rental housing near jobs, good schools, and transit, especially in low-poverty suburban neighborhoods. Rental housing developments are selected and subsidies are provided to (typically) 25 percent of the units in any one building.

- Galante, et al., note that in New York City the majority of so-called 80-20 developments are in high-opportunity areas.

- In Ohio, the state housing finance agency has created incentives for affordable housing development in economically strong neighborhoods. Consequently, in 2018, Grady and Boos report that 40 percent of competitive LIHTC awards were situated in high- or very high-opportunity census tracts.

- The National Housing Trust's High Opportunity Partner Engagement initiative focuses on the need for units in high-opportunity, low-poverty areas to be made available to voucher holders through acquiring existing buildings with high property values. Kye, et al. note that this is believed to be more financially feasible than new construction and less likely to encounter community opposition.

- A social impact real estate fund is being created to provide voucher recipients mobility counseling, which will encourage them to move to service-enriched mixed-income housing in high opportunity areas with high performing schools. The fund will acquire multifamily properties that will have market rents with set-asides for the lower income households. Buder notes that a "pay for success approach would provide a small monetary reward for each year that a low-income child is housed in a high opportunity neighborhood."

- Bostic, et al. argue that in more affluent areas there should be more, rather than fewer, subsidized units in mixed-income developments. However, in Minnesota, the focus is on deconcentrating affordable housing development, according to Galante, et al.

- Research in California and litigation in Texas has resulted in a greater share of affordable housing being developed in wealthier communities. Metcalf observes that communities have been pushed to adopt mixed-income housing strategies, thereby creating opportunities for lower-income families in areas that would otherwise be unaffordable.

Availability of Appropriate Support Services. Several essays articulate the importance of services, such as case management, social activities, and other neighborhood/school-focused programs being available on-site or within the community.[10] According to Seabaugh and Bennett, safe and affordable housing is the starting point, but an array of human capital programs and services are needed to promote economic mobility. Working with local housing authorities or private management, residents can help determine and shape needed services and supports. Tinsley and Dewan suggest that developers of mixed-income communities should focus on providing early care and education programs for the young children living there. However, data demonstrating the comparative efficacy of various types of services, in terms of enhancing income, employment opportunities, or school performance, are not presented.

Some service programs may result in secondary positive outcomes. For example, Tinsley and Dewan argue that children from both lower- and higher-income households who are enrolled in the same early care and education program will experience concrete benefits from learning side by side. This may also benefit parents, who gain an opportunity for purposeful and meaningful interactions

---

10 See essays by Kneebone, et al.; Davis, et al.; Kye, et al.; Buder; Adams, et al.; and Van Dyke and Kissman.

through their child's program. In addition, although the proposals outlined by Boyd and Oakley are still on the "drawing board," these authors suggest that mixed-income communities can provide a good context for helping young Black fathers to attain parenting skills, enhance their job prospects, and develop a sense of empowerment. In addition to these positive outcomes, the essay suggests that these would, in turn, result in benefits for the mixed-income communities.

2. How can mixed-income communities be leveraged to produce a broader range of positive—indeed, transformative—individual, household, community, and societal outcomes? Is there evidence that mixed-income communities also generate increased and sustained opportunities for all?

As noted above, the essays present only minimal evidence about whether mixed-income communities provide greater opportunities for marginalized people, let alone produce benefits for others, as posed by these questions. At a general level, several authors note that racial/economic segregation has broad negative impacts and that the elimination of these patterns is beneficial. Once again, the paper by Sandhu most closely responds to the questions raised here. Yet, somewhat ironically, he points out that although mixed-income development may be justified in terms of the presumed benefits to the lower income residents, the benefits seem to tilt in favor of (not in addition to) the more affluent households. Beyond this observation, the essays in the volume offer some interesting strategies, but data about outcomes is sparse at best. As discussed below, a few essays focus on spillover neighborhood effects of mixed-income housing.

Spillover Neighborhood Effects. A campaign by Housing Illinois,[11] described by essay author Tiffany Manuel, highlights the critical role that people who typically reside in affordable housing play in a given community. A "social returns report" created for a mixed-income development in Arlington, VA, also noted by Manuel, showed the benefits accruing to the surrounding neighborhood; researchers were able to "quantify returns from residents who made strong use of the surrounding transit system, took advantage of after-school programs, and returned to school at the local community college."

Bostic, et al. note that mixed-income LIHTC developments—those containing at least five market-rate units—have a greater effect on surrounding home prices

---

11 "We Need the People Who Need Affordable Housing"

than more "conventional" LIHTC properties that have four or fewer market-rate apartments. However, as Bostic et al. further observe, when LIHTCs with almost only subsidized units are located in low-income areas, they have greater positive impacts on property values. Does this argue against mixed-income housing, period, or that such housing should be located in lower-income areas? The latter conclusion would seemingly support the position of those who believe that continued investment in high poverty areas is particularly important and would be counter to the idea of locating developments in high-opportunity areas, as described in the prior section. Yet, Bostic et al. also find that in stronger markets, mixed-income developments have greater spillovers than those with only subsidized units. A key conclusion is that LIHTC developments with only subsidized units have positive impacts in all market areas.

3. What are the most promising innovations to be expanded in the next generation of mixed-income community efforts? To what extent does each of the three place-based strategies promote the central goals for mixed-income housing, considering the local context?

An assessment of the "most promising" innovations—including a comparative analysis of the three place-based strategies—must await more research, because the essays do not provide sufficient information on outcomes of the various efforts. However, several of my earlier responses highlighted innovative programs that warrant further study, and I cite additional interesting strategies from the essays here.

Counseling and Supportive Services Focused on the Housing Search. Snyderman and Riley describe Chicago's Regional Housing Initiative (RHI), which has developed a single, regional referral waitlist that includes its own buildings as well as units from participating public housing authorities. RHI staff give prospective tenants basic information on educational and support services to help them select their preferred locations and prepare for the move. Modeled after the Chicago program, Kneebone, et al. describe how the Baltimore Regional Housing Partnership offers a comprehensive counseling and housing search program to assist recipients of Housing Choice Vouchers to locate in higher-income neighborhoods.

Resident Involvement in Development and Management; Staff Commitment. Communication and participation mechanisms that encourage tenant and community resident involvement as a development is being planned can contribute to the development's success. Seabaugh and Bennet further observe that participation should be built into management procedures, and development and management staff must understand this will take a great deal of time and a different level of engagement with residents. There must be a commitment to a shared decision-making model, transparency about goals and constraints, and adequate funding. Moreover, staff must be committed to delivering top-quality service and trained to work in a mixed-income environment.[12]

Hirsch and Joseph delve into the social dynamics of mixed-income communities and suggest that there are a number of promising strategies to promote greater inclusiveness. Each depends on an explicit focus on inclusive social dynamics and requires significant involvement and commitment on the part of owners, management staff, and residents.

Central to Pittsburgh's TREK Development Group's management approach is its "Hospitality Covenant," according to Blackburn and Traynor. The covenant articulates the importance of kindness, personal responsibility, and assisting others to attain their personal goals and reframes the role of housing management to focus not just on "maintaining compliance, collecting rent, and crisis management" but also on creating an "aspirational culture of human connection and co-investment among owners, staff, and residents."

Van Dyke and Kissman explain the Seattle Housing Authority's commitment to community building, which involves the development of organizational infrastructure. Examples include having a staff member at each HOPE VI development who is dedicated to building community and establishing homeowners associations that intentionally and proactively educate owners about the community's mix of incomes and its implications for a cohesive neighborhood. These efforts have yielded distinct benefits and a shared mission, even when faced with difficult issues.

Community Land Trusts. CLTs, an innovative approach that incorporates significant roles for residents in the operation of a development, are fostering

---

12 McCormick, Joseph, and Chaskin note that lower-income households in a mixed-income development perceived "differential treatment by property management," which contributed to the "relocated public housing residents' sense of alienation and disrepute." This was in addition to feelings of being marginalized or treated poorly by their higher-income neighbors (p. 297). It is possible that with a carefully planned and executed resident management team, or advisory group, this problem could be alleviated. See Naomi J. McCormick, Mark L. Joseph, and Robert J. Chaskin, "The New Stigma of Relocated Public Housing Residents: Challenges to Social Identity in Mixed-Income Developments," *City & Community* 11 no. 3 (2012): 285-308.

the creation and preservation of mixed-income communities in a variety of market areas, including recovering, revitalizing, gentrifying, and high-opportunity areas. Thaden and Pickett present several innovative models.

4. What are the greatest threats to efforts to promote more inclusion and equity through mixed-income communities, and what steps should be taken to counter them?

As noted at the outset of this essay, just producing high-quality affordable housing is a challenging task. But developing the types of mixed-income communities discussed in this volume is even more difficult, due to their explicit focus on promoting community, equity, inclusion, social mix, and resident involvement. To achieve these goals, mixed-income housing developers may encounter both the expected challenges, as well as additional ones. Both types of threats and obstacles are described below.

Insufficient Attention to the Array of Community Opinions, Variations in Community Perceptions, and Biases; Lack of Attention to Communication and Messaging Strategies. Holley, et al., describe how a survey of residents in a mixed-income development in Columbus, OH produced a nuanced picture of diversity while also underscoring the complexity of building a mixed-income/mixed race community. Even among the same broad racial, income, and age groups, respondents expressed wide variations in experiences and perspectives. Meanwhile, Talen notes that residents of a socially diverse neighborhood can play a central role in a neighborhood planning process that focuses, in part, on increasing public awareness of that diversity.

Rodriguez and Rashid suggest that community organizations can incorporate a Black feminist approach—"oppositional knowledge"—to build inclusive mixed-income housing. This approach involves "using knowledge of places as a tool for resistance and resilience in the postindustrial city."

Two essays focus on strategies to deal with peoples' general resistance to change, such as proposals to develop mixed-income housing. First, Andrews and VanKuren explain that an empathetic planner must understand the biases, or heuristics, that prompt people to make decisions that may not be based on a full examination or understanding of the issue but, instead, stem from perceptions and experiences. Second, Manuel observes that "deep-seated narratives," particularly related to racial and economic segregation, may reduce support for affordable housing and inclusive communities. They may, however, be countered by evidence presented by scholars. It is important to both understand the public's view, while also underscoring that racial and economic segregation affects everyone, is connected to a whole range of related issues, and that it may be solvable through policies and investments such as mixed-race and mixed-income development.

Insufficient Subsidies to Cover Development and Basic Management, and Complexity of Financing Arrangements.[13] Davis, et al., articulate an important truth about the LIHTC program: the subsidy is essential but not sufficient to develop affordable and/or mixed-income housing. Therefore, much of the complexity of putting together affordable housing deals is due to the need to secure a number of distinct funding sources and subsidies. Developers of mixed-income housing also have to pay attention to the financial feasibility and marketability of the non-affordable units.

Bostic, et al. state that mixed-income housing using LIHTCs is "unlikely to be achievable (or economically feasible) in most of the communities where such developments are likely to be located." Indeed, across the country, (only) 24 percent of LIHTC developments have subsidized and market-rate units; in Chicago, the percentage is about double, although the proportion of market rate units is low.[14]

The large mixed-income developer, McCormack Baron Salazar, advocates a mixed-finance approach that combines public subsidies with private financing. As described by Seabaugh and Bennett, this provides accountability to the various stakeholders and also helps to protect the income stream during economic downturns. For example, during the COVID-19 pandemic, in developments with both HUD and LIHTC subsidies, the former stream of financial support helped to offset unpaid rent by market-rate and LIHTC tenants.

---

13 While the importance of subsidies in affordable housing development is widely acknowledged, there is a debate about whether housing subsidies contribute to mixed-income housing tracts. Kneebone, et al. found that "Census tracts that contain subsidized households tend to be more racially and ethnically diverse." However, Luther, et al. observe that, relative to their MSAs, "mixed-income tracts" lack subsidized affordable rental housing.

14 In view of the overall scarcity and demand for housing affordable to low-income households, Bostic, et al. do not support income mixing in LIHTC developments unless there is an economic necessity for including the market-rate units to achieve the maximum number of affordable units. They advocate including low-income units in market-rate developments, rather than units geared to high-income households being included in low-income developments.

Reliance on Anti-Exclusionary Zoning Programs without Additional Subsidies, Incentives, and Sanctions. Policies such as Massachusetts's 40B program, which promotes affordable units through a state override of local zoning, do not ensure positive outcomes. Even if developers have some leverage over local zoning laws, which enables them to build housing with a set-aside for affordable housing, there is no guarantee that the program will be utilized and that affordable housing targets will be achieved.[15] This counters a point in the essay by Kneebone, et al. that the Massachusetts program "ensures that all of its cities meet their fair share of affordable housing production by streamlining the approvals process for projects that include units targeted to lower-income households." Davis, et al., also mention the 40B program.

California has been a leader in mandating that each local government meet the housing needs of all community residents. As described by Metcalf, the state reviews local zoning plans and regulations to ensure that opportunities exist for private developers to build both market-rate and affordable housing. A new streamlining program allows new, affordable housing to be built in communities that are not keeping pace with their state-mandated affordable housing goals; as of April 2019, only 11 of 540 cities were in compliance. Among other sanctions, a new requirement precludes the ability of cities to refuse a mixed-income or affordable housing project. Another California effort involves promoting mixed-income communities in racially/ethnically concentrated areas.

Kneebone, et al., discuss Minneapolis's elimination of single-family zoning as a way to discourage exclusivity. However, it is too soon to know the results of that initiative.

Gentrification and Displacement of Lower-Income Households in Mixed-Income Communities. The threat of displacement may be mitigated by safeguarding against predatory landlord activities (e.g., improper evictions), rent regulation, subsidized housing, legal aid for tenants, just-cause eviction ordinances, right of first refusal laws, condo conversion controls, community

---

15 Compliance with the state-mandated goal—that each city and town should have no less than 10 percent of its year-round housing stock earmarked as affordable housing—has been limited. Although progress is being made, most municipalities have not attained the goal. Bratt and Vladeck found that only 40 municipalities out of 351 (11.4 percent) had passed the 10 percent threshold; see Rachel G. Bratt and Abigail Vladeck. "Addressing Restrictive Zoning for Affordable Housing: Experiences in Four States." *Housing Policy Debate*, 24 no. 3 (2014):594-636.

land trusts, residential preference for jobs created through redevelopment, housing trust funds, land banks and dedicated revenue for affordable housing from taxes, fees, or general funds. Cassola describes innovative efforts in Seattle and Portland, OR that are using such strategies. Also, Thaden and Pickett's essay on community land trusts, mentioned earlier, underscores their importance as a hedge against gentrification and displacement. Meanwhile, Norton, et al. note that a scattered site development approach can develop and preserve affordable housing in rapidly appreciating markets while also stabilizing conditions and improving property values in distressed markets.

5. What are the practical, actionable implications of current experiences and findings for policymakers, developers, investors, residents and community members, researchers, and other important stakeholders?

Many of the most thoughtful suggestions for new programs or procedures that are discussed in the various essays have already been noted above; only a few additional suggestions are presented here. In addition, in view of the breadth of this question, the caveat stated at the outset warrants repeating: this essay may have inadvertently overlooked some interesting, insightful proposals that are presented in the 38 essays in this volume.

Siting and Design. Siting near schools is likely desirable for mixed-income developments, according to Kye, et al. Design is also an important component of socially diverse neighborhoods; Talen notes that several design strategies can minimize stresses and promote and support residents' quality of life. Design strategies also can reinforce existing neighborhood characteristics, attract market-rate tenants, and promote resiliency and sustainability, according to Seabaugh and Bennett. In addition, Talen discusses how a mix of various housing types, carefully designed open/public spaces, a commitment to include small businesses, and form-based coding can all work together to form coherent and appealing streetscapes.

Karerat and Creighton note that the Center for Active Design, based in New York City, promotes programs that incorporate good housing design elements to support resident health. One such program, operated in partnership with Fannie Mae, may serve as an incentive to mixed-income and other affordable housing developers. Buildings that meet a minimum standard, based on the Fitwel certification process, are eligible for below-market loan pricing from Fannie Mae.

Developers of mixed-income developments should consider the advice of Seabaugh and Bennett, who strongly advocate that all apartments have the same level of high-quality finishes and access to amenities. This approach both reinforces goals of equity and has proven to be cost-effective in terms of long-term maintenance costs.

Tenant Selection and Marketing. As Sandhu points out, the selection of higher-income households applying to move into mixed-income developments should be made carefully, with market-rate tenants recruited based on their desire to be part of a social venture, not simply (perhaps) getting an apartment at (what may be) a somewhat below-market rental price. Market-rate residents should be better educated about what it means to live in a mixed-income community and better supported in their decision to do so. In fact, if the development has an explicit focus on promoting inclusive social dynamics, as outlined by Hirsch and Joseph, this could have a significant appeal for progressive, race-conscious prospective tenants.

Communities that have successfully embraced a mixed-income model should make a point of highlighting this unique and desirable characteristic for marketing purposes. The importance of promoting public awareness of socially diverse neighborhoods is underscored by Talen; similarly, Van Dyke and Kissman note that at least one of Seattle's HOPE VI developments explicitly calls itself a multicultural community and uses the label for marketing purposes.

Regulations and Special Agreements. The future of the Affirmatively Furthering Fair Housing rule is uncertain, but in its 2015 form it has the potential to play an important role in developing mixed-income communities. According to O'Regan and Zimmerman, although "mixed-income goals are not explicitly incorporated into the AFFH rule," it emphasizes that housing must be viewed more broadly in order to create "truly integrated living patterns" and "areas of opportunity." Tenant composition of a mixed-income complex is not, in itself, the major focus; rather, it is "whether and how those communities are linked to high-quality jobs, public education, public safety, transit, etc. …There is also an explicit aspiration in AFFH for social inclusion—not just presence—of all members of a community," the authors state.

Finally, Boyd and Oakley describe how community benefit agreements between mixed-income communities and developers could provide quality-of-life improvements for residents, including physical spaces to accommodate activities such as service delivery, career advancement, education, and recreation). Rosado adds that, with good community input, these agreements can support mixed-income housing development and provide a hedge against displacement for low-income residents in gentrifying areas.

Research Questions to Move the Mixed-Income Agenda Forward

This volume is filled with fine essays, reflecting the care and thoughtfulness of the editors in commissioning and compiling the work. Yet, I am sobered by how much we still do not know about the mixed-income strategy. Khare and Joseph conclude the Editors' Introduction by saying: "While mixed-income interventions have evolved considerably over the past 30 years, we have yet to realize the potential of these place-based interventions to play a much greater part in helping to address racism, classism, and other forms of societal isolation and marginalization." The question is why. At least three responses seem plausible: (1) the mixed-income model, in and of itself, is not able to meet the hoped-for social goals; or (2) the optimum mixed-income model has not yet been developed; or (3) research to date has not been sufficiently in-depth and comprehensive to assess the full contributions and benefits of the mixed-income model. We must develop a clear and far-reaching research strategy to put the question to rest, one way or the other. The first three questions, below, address this key issue, followed by two additional research questions.

1. Is the income mixing in a given housing development the key factor in determining success (i.e., attaining the desired social goals while assuring the development's viability) or are other attributes of the development more important? And to what extent is the level of income mixing important in producing positive outcomes? Several of the essays in the volume discuss programs or services connected to a particular mixed-income development. While beneficial effects may be reported, it is not possible to know whether they are the result of the income mixing in the development or whether they are more attributable to the various programs that are being offered. As noted earlier, this is, perhaps, the central question about mixed-income housing that begs for an expansive research effort.[16] A matched longitudinal study is needed that would track resident outcomes (e.g., educational attainment,

---

16 See also Diane K. Levy, Zach McDade, and Kassie Dumlao, *Effects From Living in Mixed-Income Communities for Low-Income Families*. (Washington DC: Urban Institute, 2010), https://www.urban.org/sites/default/files/publication/27116/412292-Effects-from-Living-in-Mixed-Income-Communities-for-Low-Income-Families.PDF

school experiences of children, changes in employment and household income, personal feelings of safety and security) in mixed-income developments, compared with completely affordable developments that have similar characteristics in terms of age, design, management, level of social services, market context, location, etc. It is important to hold constant, as much as possible, all variables except (a) whether there is income mixing and (b) the extent of income mixing (e.g., varying percentages of low-income, extremely low-income, and market-rate residents). Ideally, there would be some degree of randomized assignment of residents to the two different housing interventions or some means of controlling for underlying differences among residents.

Indeed, there is a question about how much income mixing is needed to make a difference (if, indeed, differences exist), as discussed by the Davis et al. and Kneebone et al. essays. Schwartz and Tsenkova explore the interplay between market context and the level of income mixing and note that: "Mixed-income housing typically requires less subsidy in more affluent neighborhoods that command relatively high rents," since those higher rents can "cross-subsidize" units occupied by low- and moderate-income households. Nevertheless, "with sufficient government subsidy mixed-income housing also is viable in low-income neighborhoods." But we still do not know *if* the level of mixing is an important contributor to any observed positive outcomes for lower-income households and, if it is, how to determine optimum ratios. This would be an important component of the overall research effort.

2. If income mixing is a key determinant of positive outcomes, what are the mechanisms through which the outcomes are achieved? Another key aspect of the research design addressing the first question would involve a close examination of resident experiences. Not only would various outcomes be tracked, in-depth interviews would provide a deeper understanding of the causes behind the observed changes (if any). As Kneebone, et al., have asked: "Are mixed-income neighborhoods good for poor children because they provide meaningful exposure to people from different backgrounds? Or because they provide access to resources and institutional capacity not present in poor neighborhoods? Or because they increase collective efficacy and political mobilization for neighborhood investments?"

In addition, if lower-income residents reported an increase in income it would be important to know whether this was the result of a better job opportunity that followed contact with a higher-income neighbor or whether the housing stability and lower rent allowed the individual to move up in their job. Another route to a positive outcome could be that the resident was able to pursue an educational program (either provided on-site or elsewhere) that made her/him/them more competitive in the job market. It is likely that the better job would be directly attributable to the mixed-income model only if it resulted from a contact with another resident. The dynamics behind the various outcomes also may be due to living in affordable housing, period, whether or not the development has a mix of incomes, or to the availability of a good social service or educational program that could, perhaps, be accessed independently of the mixed-income development in which the resident lives.

In addition to understanding the potential positive outcomes for lower-income residents, we are still confronted with the question of *whether* and *how* inclusive, equitable mixed-income communities improve overall living conditions and/or advance the quality of life for all residents, regardless of income. And, too, how can we assess whether the income mixing translates into reduced management costs or ease of renting units? In short, understanding what and how changes occur due to the mixed-income nature of the development is essential for developing model programs.

3. Is income mixing more important at the building or neighborhood level?

Bostic, et al. concluded their essay by observing that "LIHTC developments can be important components of broader strategies to promote mixed-income neighborhoods." Indeed, there is an open question about the relative importance of building-level versus neighborhood mixing in producing positive outcomes for lower-income residents. Are there observable differences in outcomes for lower-income residents of a mixed-income building if it is located in a low-poverty, high-opportunity neighborhood versus a high-poverty, low-opportunity neighborhood? Using the same two neighborhood scenarios, what if the building only has residents with low-income residents, and none with higher incomes? Of course, research to answer these questions should include a number of sub-categories, such as the extent of income mixing among a range of income groups (e.g., extremely low-income, low-income, households between 80-120 percent of AMI, and those above 120 percent) and specific characteristics of the low-opportunity and high-opportunity neighborhoods (taking into account factors such as school quality, crime rates, housing vacancy rates, access to public transportation and neighborhood amenities, etc.).

Clearly, a research effort with the breadth and complexity described in these first three questions is a major undertaking. The challenges are compounded by the relative scarcity of mixed-income neighborhoods across the country: Kneebone, et al., note that "just one-tenth of major-metro neighborhoods contained a significant share of poor, middle-class, and higher-income households living in close proximity." And Luther, et al. observe that it is "incredibly difficult" for neighborhoods in large metropolitan areas to attain "strong urban densities and balanced income mixes."

4. What have large-scale mixed-income housing initiatives revealed about how to achieve income mixing? Responding to general perceptions that federally subsidized housing programs have been stigmatizing, due to the concentrations of very low-income households and the distinctive design of early public housing developments, several federal efforts—notably the HOPE VI program and the Choice Neighborhoods Initiative—have explicitly promoted a mixed-income approach. The results, however, appear very limited. Out of a total of 260 HOPE VI developments, the majority did not have a mix of incomes: 69 percent provided housing for tenants at public-housing or affordable-income levels, only 47 percent included any mixed-income units at all, and just one quarter of the developments included residents with a broad range of incomes (public, affordable, and market-rate).[17] Of the first five sites where the Choice Neighborhoods Initiative was implemented, only two included both subsidized and unsubsidized units within the buildings. One grantee did not include any higher-income units at all, instead focusing exclusively on units targeted to very low- and low-income households; all the units in the two other sites involved some type of subsidy.[18]

The findings to date suggest that further study is needed to more fully understand the reasons why these two programs—both of which had an explicit mixed-income objective—were not able to provide more such developments. Of course, the rationale for maintaining a preference for federally funded mixed-income housing should be based on the answers to the

---

17 Taryn Gress, Seungjong Cho, and Mark Joseph, *HOPE VI Data Compilation and Analysis*. (Cleveland: OH: National Initiative on Mixed-Income Communities, 2016), https://www.huduser.gov/portal/sites/default/files/pdf/HOPE-VI-Data-Compilation-and-Analysis.pdf

18 Rolf Pendall et al., *Choice Neighborhoods: Baseline Conditions and Early Progress* (Washington, DC: Urban Institute and MDRC, 2015), https://www.huduser.gov/portal/sites/default/files/pdf/Baseline-Conditions-Early-Progress.pdf

several research questions posed above.

5. What strategies to cover the costs of social service programs are most promising? Does the mixed-income model provide any concrete advantages, making it easier for owners to cover these costs?

Since the idea of mixed-income housing emerged in the 1960s, scholars and practitioners have agreed that the mixed-income approach is not sufficient to promote its broader set of objectives, which involve providing social and economic opportunities for lower income residents; other types of assistance are essential for the presumed benefits of the mixed-income approach to be realized.[19] In fact, interest in housing and neighborhood-based services programs arose far before the concept of mixed-income housing gained traction.[20] HUD has acknowledged that housing assistance alone is not sufficient to enable households to become self-sufficient and that a broad mission of the agency is "to employ housing as a platform to improve families' quality of life."[21]

As previously noted, several of the essays in this volume discuss the importance of having resident services connected to the housing development. This, then, points to the importance of resident services coordinators. Whether a housing development is focused on mixing incomes or not, and whether the goal is to bring resident services directly into the building or to partner with other local agencies, a coordinator typically is viewed as essential. Van Dyke and Kissman

---

19 Elsewhere I have outlined other components (in addition to support services) that are essential for a successful mixed-income (or, truly, any) housing development to be financially viable and of high quality. These include: a design and style that fits in with the existing neighborhood; building materials and construction decisions that promote cost-effective and trouble-free long-term management; use of energy-efficient materials; adequate levels of subsidies to support development, management, and affordable rental levels; professional and respectful management with repairs and other maintenance needs promptly addressed; mechanisms for resident involvement; and locations that promote mobility and access to good schools (Bratt, 2018).

20 Between 1889 and the 1920s, hundreds of neighborhood-based initiatives, known as settlement houses, were created in poor areas of cities across the country and offered an array of programs aimed at providing opportunities and services to low-income populations, including art, education, job training and programs specifically geared to children. While the likely importance of these initiatives was part of the discussions in the early days of federally funded low-income housing programs, starting in the 1930s, the combined efforts of the "housers" and social welfare professionals did not result in a coherent housing/social services model. As Newman and Schnare have noted: "Collectively, the efforts of the housing and welfare systems to elevate housing assistance to a vehicle for social advancement cannot be viewed as a success... [T]he issue was raised and wrestled with, but... ultimately it was overshadowed by the press of other demands..." (Sandra J. Newman and Ann B. Schnare, *Beyond Bricks and Mortar: Reexamining the Purpose and Effects of Housing Assistance* (Report No. 92-3), Washington, DC: Urban Institute Press, 1992).

21 U.S. Department of Housing and Urban Development. 2020. *Pathways to Opportunity: HUD's Self-Sufficiency Programs*, (Washington, DC: U.S. Department of Housing and Urban Development, 2020), "https://www.huduser.gov/portal/pdredge/pdr_edge_featd_article_112315.html

also emphasize the importance of each mixed-income development having a staff member dedicated to community building, who may also provide help with social service referrals.

But the question of how to fund such positions and the services themselves can be daunting. When possible, organizations cover resident services costs out of the building's cash flow,[22] by expanding day-to-day management operations, by assessing potential projects to ensure that the operating budgets include stable sources to fund resident services, or by providing fewer services more intensely.[23]

In their essay, Karerat and Creighton discuss an innovative partnership arrangement with Fannie Mae, the Healthy Housing Rewards Incentive Program, that provides financial benefits to affordable housing developers. This could, perhaps, help to fund resident services and community-building efforts. Additional sources of funding may come from leasing part of the building at reduced rentals to key service providers, such as day care centers, in exchange for service provision at low or no cost to residents. Leasing space to other public, private, or nonprofit entities also can produce an income stream that offsets the costs of services. Philanthropic donations and public grants may further help to cover the costs of the desired programs.[24] In addition to noting several of the above possible revenue sources, Davis, et al. note that programs can be supported by partnering with local social service providers. They also suggest that services can help the development's financial bottom line by decreasing resident turnover. Buder discusses research which shows that the short-term costs of providing services are covered by long-term savings to governments at all levels.

It is possible that the mixed-income model may have some unique advantages over other housing strategies for funding resident services programs. Some

---

[22] Indeed, a survey of representatives of 60 mixed-income developments found that most services are covered from operating funds. See, National Initiative on Mixed-Income Communities, *State of the Field Scan #2: Resident Services in Mixed-Income Developments Phase 1: Survey Findings and Analysis*. (Cleveland, OH: National Initiative on Mixed-Income Communities, 2015).

[23] Rachel G. Bratt, Larry A. Rosenthal and Robert J. Wiener, "Organizational Adaptations of Nonprofit Housing Organizations in the U.S.: Insights from the Boston and San Francisco Bay Areas." In *Affordable Housing Governance and Finance: Innovations, Partnerships and Comparative Perspectives*, eds. Gerard van Bortel, Vincent Gruis, Ben Pluijmers, and Joost Nieuwenhuijzen (Taylor & Francis, 2019).

[24] Rachel G. Bratt, "Viewing Housing Holistically: The Resident-Focused Component of the Housing-Plus Agenda." *Journal of the American Planning Association* 74 no. 1 (2008):100-110.

of the market-rate rentals could be used to cover the costs, or buildings with higher-income clientele may be able to attract higher rental rates from businesses that are interested in locating in the building. When the National Initiative on Mixed-Income Housing explored variations in tenants' income levels, resident services staffing, and budgets in 60 mixed-income developments they found some promising results: "The most diverse developments, with residents from across the income spectrum, reported relatively high median budgets and a relatively high respondent rating of service strength and impact. Developments with a 'bimodal' mix of higher-income residents along with the lowest income residents reported the largest resident services budgets."[25] Nevertheless, the researchers were not able to tease out the relative importance of the mixed-income model per se.

Finally, although there is a clear sense that funding, physical space, and coordination are necessary components of resident services in mixed-income developments, research still needs to explore which types of programs are most essential for given populations. While most housing developments have some kind of outcome tracking system, the measures typically capture participants' participation in programs rather than outcomes such as employment, education, health, or wellness.[26] Without additional explorations and comparisons between mixed-income and completely low-income developments, both with comparable service components, it is not feasible to assess the extent to which the mixed-income model may have some unique advantages in supporting resident-focused services.

Concluding Note

Despite the lack of definitive evidence about the social benefits of mixed-income housing for lower-income residents presented in this volume, there is continued interest and support for this approach. This may be due, at least in part, to the fact that the alternatives seem less appealing. As Alan Mallach has observed, "While the advantages of integration are uncertain, the disadvantages of residualization and poverty concentration, which are the inevitable by-product of the absence of spatial integration in a market-oriented polity, are

---

25 National Initiative on Mixed-Income Communities, "State of the Field Scan #2"

26 National Initiative on Mixed-Income Communities, "State of the Field Scan #2"

compelling."[27]

Of course, it may not even be fair to judge the mixed-income approach by the standard of whether it provides specific social and economic outcomes for lower-income households. Perhaps, as Sandhu suggests, it is enough for people to live in homes that feel safe, affordable, and are an improvement over their prior housing. And, too, it is possible that the metrics we have been using to assess outcomes have been too short-sighted about the possible benefits of income and racial mixing for young children emerging years into the future, in yet-to-be-established ways, and not just in terms of their school performance or in the job opportunities or incomes of their parents.

If we were not living in the midst of the COVID-19 pandemic, the thoughts above would have been the essence of this concluding section. Indeed, this book was conceived and the articles were (mostly) written long before the world knew anything about a disease that now dominates our lives. Work on this essay began before any real concerns about the virus took hold in the United States and was completed in fall 2020, when an opening economy in many locales was accompanied by major surges in illnesses and with many school systems offering only virtual teaching at least through the beginning months of the academic year. With households across the country struggling to pay rent and mortgage payments, with government resources being stretched beyond any previously known limits to cover emergency relief to businesses, unemployed workers, and low- and middle-income taxpayers, and with continuing dysfunction at the federal level about what type of stimulus program should be enacted, the overriding recommendation of this essay—to launch some significant research efforts—may seem highly unlikely in the near future.

Yet, at the same time, the current period also may offer opportunities for increased engagement with the issues discussed in this volume. As local and state governments struggle to meet the housing (and other) needs of their constituents, foundations, private developers, and universities may choose to form partnerships around a robust research agenda that could include serious explorations into the mixed-income housing approach. Studying how mixed-income housing can not only meet housing needs but also provide opportunities to alleviate one of the most pernicious outcomes of institutional racism—segregated neighborhoods—may provide a concrete, proactive response to

---

[27] Cited in U.S. Department of Housing and Urban Development, "Confronting Concentrated Poverty"

the resurgence of the Black Lives Matter movement. Might this result in some momentum to assess how mixed-income housing could contribute to more racially just housing patterns? Beyond the mixed-income housing agenda, housing advocates must continue to underscore that all housing that is affordable to lower-income households is to be cherished and supported as much as possible. As the health and economic crises continue to unfold, we will need all the creativity, nimbleness, thoughtful responses, and existing housing resources to address what could turn into the biggest housing crisis of all time.

■ ■ ■

RACHEL G. BRATT, *Professor Emerita, Tufts University, has focused on a range of current and historical U.S. federal and state housing policies and programs, and the role of nonprofit housing organizations in producing affordable housing. She is the author or co-editor of three books, and has written or co-authored dozens of academic and popular articles and book chapters. In her role as a Visiting Scholar at the Federal Reserve Bank of Boston, in 2020 she completed a series of papers concerning HUD/FHA guidelines concerning mortgagors in end-stage default and foreclosure.*